Intellectual Property Law and Practice of the United Arab Emirates

Intellectual Property Law and Practice of the United Arab Emirates

Peter W. Hansen

Oxford University Press, Inc., publishes works that further Oxford University's objective of excellence in research, scholarship, and education.

Oxford   New York
Auckland   Cape Town   Dar es Salaam   Hong Kong   Karachi   Kuala Lumpur   Madrid   Melbourne
Mexico City   Nairobi   New Delhi   Shanghai   Taipei   Toronto

With offices in
Argentina   Austria   Brazil   Chile   Czech Republic   France   Greece   Guatemala   Hungary   Italy
Japan   Poland   Portugal   Singapore   South Korea   Switzerland   Thailand   Turkey   Ukraine
Vietnam

Copyright © 2009 by Oxford University Press, Inc.

Published by Oxford University Press, Inc.
198 Madison Avenue, New York, New York 10016

Oxford is a registered trademark of Oxford University Press
Oxford University Press is a registered trademark of Oxford University Press, Inc.

Library of Congress Cataloging-in-Publication Data
Hansen, Peter W.
  Intellectual property law and practice of the United Arab Emirates / Peter W. Hansen.
    p. cm.
  Includes bibliographical references and index.
  Summary: "This desk-book presents the intellectual property laws and practice in the United Arab Emirates with practice commentary and English translations of the laws in question. It covers patents, designs and know how; trademarks and copyrights"—Provided by publisher.
    ISBN 978-0-19-537016-4 ((pbk.) : alk. paper)
  1. Intellectual property—United Arab Emirates. I. Title.
  KMV1155.H36 2009
  346.535704'8—dc22   2009014875

1 2 3 4 5 6 7 8 9

Printed in the United States of America on acid-free paper

Note to Readers

This publication is designed to provide accurate and authoritative information in regard to the subject matter covered. It is based upon sources believed to be accurate and reliable and is intended to be current as of the time it was written. It is sold with the understanding that the publisher is not engaged in rendering legal, accounting, or other professional services. If legal advice or other expert assistance is required, the services of a competent professional person should be sought. Also, to confirm that the information has not been affected or changed by recent developments, traditional legal research techniques should be used, including checking primary sources where appropriate.

*(Based on the Declaration of Principles jointly adopted by a Committee of the
American Bar Association and a Committee of Publishers and Associations.)*

You may order this or any other Oxford University Press publication by
visiting the Oxford University Press website at www.oup.com

For my wife Hala

Contents

About the Author

Peter Hansen is a partner in the Dubai-based intellectual property firm, Cedar White Bradley. Educated and trained in Australia, he was formerly a partner of a major Australia law firm and has worked in intellectual property in the UAE since 2003. He studied Arabic in Jordan, Syria, Egypt and Yemen.

Preface

This book was conceived from a wish to have easy access to the key intellectual property laws and regulations of the United Arab Emirates (UAE). The substance of this book therefore consists of the laws and regulations in Arabic as published, and my English translations of them. To add some commentary seemed like a good idea if only to provoke a greater level of discussion about questions of interpretation and application of the law.

The Scope of This Book

There is a lot that this book does not do. The IP laws and regulations collected here, in Arabic and in translation, are only a selection of those that have been issued, but they are the most important for any IP practitioner. The selection of laws and regulations does not include any of the related areas of practice. For example, there is now a consumer protection law in the UAE. It is neither included in the texts nor discussed in the commentary. Other related subject areas not covered at all or in any detail include business associations and companies, printed matter and publishing, domain names, signage, geographical indications, circuit layouts, advertising, defamation, the penal justice system, computer related crimes, the customs system (beyond specific IP provisions), the arrangements between the Gulf Cooperation Council countries, commercial laws, and court practices and procedures. Each of these areas and its intersection with intellectual property subject matter is a potential area of study in itself.

In preparing the commentary for this book I have not undertaken a comprehensive study of issued court decisions and have referred to only a few of these decisions. The UAE is a civil law jurisdiction and so prior court decisions are not binding precedents. They may be a useful guide, but in my view their proper use requires a systematic study and analysis to identify what principles have been consistently adopted and the factual contexts in which those principles have been applied. The tendency to extract "rules" from prior decisions and to assume that when and how to apply the rule can be discerned from the rule itself is, in my view, one requiring further examination.

The reporting of cases with key facts deleted compounds the problems in using past court decisions. Until such a comprehensive study is undertaken, any commentary on the IP laws of the UAE will surely be incomplete.

This book also does not comment on all the subject areas that are dealt with in the laws and regulations. When there are comments, the comments do not necessarily seek to canvass all the issues that might relate to that subject. This is not a general IP handbook. The subjects and issues chosen for comment are those that have occurred to me as interesting or relevant based on my experience practicing in the UAE. No doubt others will see more and better than I have.

Another line of study that this book only begins to pursue is the tracing of the origins of the laws and regulations that are presently in place. In many cases, the meaning of the current provisions only becomes clear when one sees them against the provisions that they replaced, the international obligations with which they were seeking to comply, or the law from which they were inspired or adapted. In some parts of the commentary, I have made comparisons between the provisions of the laws and international conventions, but this has not been done systematically or with the depth that it deserves.

Not Official

There is nothing official about this book. The UAE authorities have not been involved in its preparation and have not endorsed the result. The translations are not official. This book would no doubt have benefited from the input of the UAE government agencies dealing with intellectual property matters. Understandably, government officials are busy people and do not always have the time to answer what may seem to be obscure questions from lawyers. There is also an understandable hesitancy on the part of government officials to give any kind of information unless one is armed with an order from the ruler or other high authority.

The Common Law/Civil Law Interface

Once there was perhaps a clear divide between the common law systems and the civil law systems. Features of a civil law system can certainly be detected in the laws of the UAE. But those features have traveled an indirect route, very often via the laws of Egypt. They have also been subjected to much alteration by the forces of international conventions and norms. The common law influences might be traced through British colonialism in Egypt and the role of the Empire in India and the Gulf, including the lands that eventually became the UAE, in the nineteenth and early twentieth centuries. The English law system is now winning the day in special jurisdictions like the Dubai International Financial Centre. It is probably fair to say that a large proportion of the lawyers working in the UAE (I am one of them) come from common law countries.

Despite the growing prevalence of the common law mentality in the UAE, some care and respect still needs to be shown by practitioners and others for those aspects of UAE laws that cannot be entirely re-packaged under the rubrics of the common law vocabulary. In this book, for example, I have decided to refer to the author's rights instead of copyright. The word "copyright" carries with it, in my view, a substantial amount of historical and cultural baggage that is not part of the UAE's author's rights law or its history.

It might be said that only civil law trained lawyers have the legal competence to comment on the laws of the UAE. There is probably a lot about that view that is right. On the other hand, there is a lot to be gained from seeing the laws from another perspective—one that many working in the legal field in the UAE and in other countries will share. One consequence of globalization is that national laws are often asked to satisfy the needs of various international communities. The UAE is more globalized than most nation states. Whether one sees with common law or civil law eyes, it would be fair to say that a successful law is one that is clear, complete, and reasonable enough for the individuals and businesses that live under it to comply with it, to rely on it in their dealings with others, and to prosper as a result.

Translating Arabic

Translation is an art, not a science. Some say that "all translation is explanation." Almost every step in making a translation is a matter of judgment in which there is often a vast space for different opinions. Different translators are guided by different principles. As a lawyer and not a professional translator, I have tried as much as possible to stay close to the Arabic word and phrase structure and to capture all of what is written, even if it has meant adopting a less than elegant prose style, whilst trying not to fall into "literal" or word by word translation. I have not tried to remove the "feeling" that the text is a translation from another language. For example, Arabic uses "and" where English might use a full stop. I have sometimes preserved structural features like this instead of trying to present the text as if it was originally written in English. Legal texts are not, in any case, meant to be "beautiful" but are rather intended to be certain and as clear as possible and to identify specific concepts, elements and criteria whose relationships with each other are unambiguous. It would be a happy result if these translations led to some level of debate about how certain legal texts should be understood and expressed in English.

As a matter of style, there is a tendency in Arabic to try not to use the same word repeatedly, or more than once in the same sentence. I was trained to use one word for one meaning and if I wanted to express that same meaning I should use that word again (however inelegant that may be), and not use an apparent synonym. The use of a different word would be taken as importing a different meaning. One of the puzzles for a translator of legal texts in Arabic is to try to determine when a different word signals a different meaning and when a different word is being used for the same meaning and merely to satisfy a stylistic requirement.

No doubt there will be controversial points in the way I have translated some expressions and there will very likely be different points of view about the meaning of certain phrases and articles. My hope is that the translations in this book represent a better alternative to what is presently available to practitioners.

Transliterations Used

There are many different systems for transliterating Arabic characters into Latin characters. I have not followed any of them. The transliterations that appear in this book are my impressions of how best to render the sounds of Arabic in Latin characters for the purposes of indicating to Arabic speakers what is the Arabic word or expression used and to give non-Arabic speakers a handle on an Arabic word so that it can be seen as different from other words with similar meanings.

Spellings, Dates, etc.

The spelling of English words used in this book follows conventions used in the United States of America and is not necessarily a reflection of spelling commonly in use in the UAE. For example, "trade mark" is spelled "trademark" throughout. "Colour" is spelled "color" and "licence" (the noun) is spelled "license." United States date conventions are also used so that, for example, 2/3/1998 is 3 February 1998.

Acknowledgments and Thanks

This book would not have been possible without the assistance and patience of my wife who has not only endured our life being "on hold" whilst I worked on this book, but has also contributed significantly to it in doing research, typing Arabic texts, and always being willing to engage with her husband in arcane discussions about the meaning of Arabic words and expressions. For her contribution, constant encouragement, and support I am deeply grateful.

My partner at Cedar White Bradley, Halim Shehadeh, has generously read drafts of various chapters, pointed out many of my errors, and tolerated me working irregular hours in the office to be able to translate and write. Thanks also to Jane Gilchrist and David Moore, who read and provided insightful comments on drafts, and to Matt Gallaway at OUP, who has been a constant source of encouragement from the beginning. The errors and omissions that remain are mine alone.

Peter W. Hansen, February 2009
E-mail: peparethos@xsmail.com

Brief Introduction to the Economic and Legal Context

The purpose of this brief introduction is to highlight some of the context in which the intellectual property laws of the UAE are required to operate and be effective in their various tasks. Therefore, the extent of the discussion of each of the subjects touched upon is limited to this purpose.

A Federation of Emirates

The word "emirate" is derived from the Arabic word "amir" meaning "prince" but also "chief," "leader," or "master." There are seven emirates because ultimately seven different rulers or ruling families were recognized after the withdrawal of the British from the Gulf in the late 1960s. Up until the 1850s, the coast of what is now the UAE was known as the "Pirate Coast" because of the prevalence of raids on shipping through the Gulf. After the local sheikhs signed a maritime truce with the United Kingdom, it became known as the "Trucial States" until the withdrawal of the British and the federation of the sheikhdoms or emirates in 1971, which gave birth to the United Arab Emirates as a nation. The emirates that make up the federation today are: Abu Dhabi, Dubai, Sharjah, Ajman, Umm Al Quwain, Fujeirah, and Ras Al Khaimah.

Economic Development

Although Abu Dhabi is the capital of the UAE, until recently it was Dubai that became the most well known of the emirates internationally. Dubai took an early lead in seeking to develop trade and investment and is today more like a modern metropolis than any of the other emirates, including Abu Dhabi. However, it was Abu Dhabi, the geographically largest of the emirates, that was gifted with substantial quantities of fossil fuels. With large reserves of oil revenues, Abu Dhabi has begun investing heavily in the development of the emirate to make it a center of culture and tourism, with plans for numerous museums, sporting events, and luxury hotels, such as the Louvre Abu Dhabi (to be completed in 2012), the Guggenheim Abu Dhabi (to be completed between 2011 and 2012), the Paris-Sorbonne University Abu Dhabi, New York University Abu Dhabi (opening in 2010) and Ferrari World, which will host the Formula 1 Grand Prix in 2009. It is not difficult to see a degree of economic rivalry between the emirates of Abu Dhabi and Dubai.

The commercial activity responsible for the rise of Dubai has in significant part been fostered by the extensive use of economic free zones, such as the Jebel Ali Free Zone, the Dubai Airport Free Zone, and the Dragon Mart (to name only three of many). Indeed, both inside and outside the free zones, there are extensive areas of warehouses where traders store, produce, assemble, and repackage products, the majority of which probably come from China, for distribution principally in the Middle East and Africa. The emirate of Sharjah has also sought to encourage industry and trade with the creation of industrial areas containing warehouses and light industry. Other emirates, also not blessed with significant quantities of fossil fuels, have developed ports and free zones to generate revenue.

Dubai has also sought to foster service and knowledge industries. Early examples of this were the Dubai Media City, Dubai Internet City, and Knowledge Village. The Dubai International Financial Centre (DIFC), established in 2004, aims to be a tax-free center of excellence in international banking and finance with its own stock exchange (now known as the NASDAQ Dubai) and laws in key areas including arbitration, corporations, contracts, employment, data protection, and intellectual property. As it continues to self-legislate, the DIFC is increasingly taking on the appearance of a state within a state. Various other free zones focus on technology (e.g., Dubai Silicon Oasis and Techno Park) and health care (e.g., Dubai Healthcare City).

An extraordinary wave of change and development has rolled across much of the UAE in the last fifty years or so to produce an increasingly diverse business environment covering all kinds of industrial sectors and service industries. The legal apparatus necessary for the efficient operation and sustainable growth of these industries has struggled to develop at the same rate. The continuing challenge for the leaders of this aspiring country is to develop laws and regulations that have a clarity of purpose and that are adapted to the economic conditions that they are seeking to foster. Intellectual property laws and procedures are part of that apparatus. Their ultimate objective must be the confidence and trust of those to whom they apply.

Demographics

One feature of the UAE makes it very different from other countries. A substantial majority of its inhabitants are not UAE nationals or citizens. The total population is probably between 4.5 and 5 million. Less than one million or twenty percent are UAE nationals. This means that the material conditions for living, everything from housing to utilities and transport infrastructure, are based on a population consisting in large part of people who belong to other countries and who, in certain circumstances, may go home permanently. The UAE has increasingly become highly dependent on maintaining a high percentage of foreign nationals as residents on its lands. Whatever long-term implications this may have for the future of the UAE, the immediate impact is the creation of a delicate balance between policies that encourage the inflow of foreign nationals and at the same time regulate, control, and profit from them. The threat of imbalance has recently become apparent with the international economic downturn and the fall in confidence in the financial and real estate markets in the region. The cancellation of residency visas and the departure of foreign nationals must be disconcerting indications of the need for policy adjustments.

The Legal Framework

Federation established a federal judicial system with the supreme federal court at its head and lower courts of first instance and appeal. The emirates of Abu Dhabi, Sharjah, Ajman, Umm Al Quwain, and Fujairah opted to incorporate their judicial systems into the federal system, whereas the emirates of Dubai and Ras Al Khaimah maintained their own systems. Dubai now has its own first instance, appeal and cassation courts. Dubai also maintains its own police force and prosecution, whereas police and prosecution in the other emirates are part of the federal system.

The civil law system, rather than common law system lies at the foundation of the UAE's laws and legal institutions. The laws of Egypt, which are based on French civil law, are the source or inspiration for many of the legal concepts and provisions in the laws of the UAE. The presence of the British in the Gulf during the first part of the last century also had its effects. More recently globalization has pulled the legal system of the UAE in different directions. The UAE's membership of the Gulf Cooperation Council is yet another line of political and economic force that will affect the future direction of the country. The laws and judicial system of the DIFC represent a major departure from the existing system, with laws written in English only and, in some cases, based on English law.

The judicial system has adopted many civil law features. Litigation is conducted by way of exchange of memoranda. The pleadings often make no clear distinction between fact and law. When matters of fact are disputed, or there are technical matters in issue, an expert may be appointed to make a report to the court. Oral argument and evidence are rare and there is no "trial" at the end of the proceedings. Prior judgments of the court are not binding. There is no procedure for discovery of documents. There are no specific courts or judges for IP matters.

Most judges are from other Arab countries, but that is rapidly changing as more Emiratis develop the necessary expertise.[1] The independence of the courts is guaranteed by the UAE Constitution.[2]

The Intellectual Property Laws

The importance of intellectual property to the leaders of the UAE was expressed in the issuing of a suite of IP laws in the early 1990s. At that time, the responsibility for patents and designs, trademarks, and author's rights fell across three different Ministries. The different styles and drafting of the IP laws can perhaps be traced back to this tripartite origin. There are many points at which a greater degree of cross-pollination between the responsible Ministries would have benefited the IP laws that resulted. Only recently has IP been brought under the single overview of the Ministry of Economy.

Perhaps in the early 1990s the UAE simply needed to have some IP laws and at that time the business environment in which those laws were to operate was still developing. It would have been difficult to foresee fully the role that the IP laws of the country would be required to play. The laws of other countries, such as Egypt, were looked to for guidance on what the UAE's IP regime should deal with and how it should do so. When the UAE joined the WTO and needed to bring its laws into compliance with the TRIPs Agreement, the focus was probably more on how to make the laws satisfy international obligations than any other objectives closer to home. Some of the changes to the laws that were made by the tranche of new laws and amending legislation at the beginning of this century appear to have been rushed and driven by the need to meet a deadline. This history has resulted in the IP laws of the UAE having a hybridized character. What is yet to be done is the difficult task of making a legal framework for the creation, use, and exploitation of intellectual property in the UAE that is tailored to its economic objectives and that will take it prosperously into the future. That task is difficult because it will need to be done with an understanding of what, in practical terms, the

---

1. There are 45 UAE national judges in the Dubai Courts as against 116 foreign national judges (EMIRATES TODAY, Arabic edition, February 5, 2009, at 2.)
2. Justice Moustafa Gamal Aldeen, at the end of his 10-year tenure at the Federal Supreme Court, has been quoted as saying: "In all of my 10 years here, I did not receive even one phone call where someone tried to persuade my decision one way or the other. No one has ever questioned me for judging a specific case. The independence of judges here is exemplary." (*A Judge's Verdict on Abu Dhabi*, THE NATIONAL, December 25, 2008, online edition).

various stakeholders need from the law. Those charged with drafting the UAE's IP laws of the future might start the process in the field, speaking to and getting a better understanding of the needs of businesses, investors, inventors, and designers of everything from software to clothing.

Of course, laws and regulations only go part of the way. Ultimately, implementation is what governments are judged by. In the UAE, overcoming the gulf that lies between the law and practice is the real challenge. Making laws that are written in a way that can guide the practice on the ground is the first step. Fostering a sense of ownership of the laws by those who are responsible for their implementation is the next. This is a matter of leadership and direction from within the responsible Ministry as to how the law is to be understood and what it means in practice. There is little doubt that when the Ministry makes a statement on an issue, those applying the law in the various administrative bodies are listening. Developing that leadership role will very likely require internal change and courage to speak out and bear the responsibility for taking a position. The IP laws of the UAE work in practice very often because of the good intentions and intelligence of those in minor official roles who want to make the system work for the benefit of their country.

Of course, the role and position of the relevant Ministries is a matter ultimately determined by the leaders of the nation. If there is to be a change toward service-driven government and away from government as a means of revenue generation,[3] that must come from the top. Similarly, basic information about the government's activities (such as filing, grant, and registration statistics) will only become more accessible if "open government" is embraced at high levels.

The Role of the Professions

The legal profession in the UAE is very young. With a few exceptions, only lawyers who are UAE nationals have rights of audience before the courts. The majority of the lawyers in the country are foreigners, filling positions such as in-house counsel or working in local law firms or legal consultancies. There are also firms of IP registration agents who often have no legal qualifications. Many of them have accounting backgrounds. Perhaps because of these various facts, the professions appear not to participate in any kind of disinterested activism for reform of laws or procedures. There is no professional body regulating the persons that deal with IP matters. Presently, it is the Ministry's responsibility to register and de-register IP agents. There is consequently no voice for the profession of IP agents and advisers and there is no think-tank

---

3. The fees for the UAE government's IP services are amongst the highest in the world.

for the generation of ideas and intellectual leadership. Sometimes the participants in a particular field have a vested interest in maintaining the status quo and actively discourage change or improvement. Without government leadership to create the conditions for relevant stakeholders including the professions to engage in development and reform, the confidence and respect that will come from better laws, regulations, and practices may remain elusive.

List of Laws and Regulations

Patent and Designs Laws and Regulations

Law/regulation	Issue date	Publication details (number and date of gazette)
Federal law no. 44 of 1992 in relation to the regulation and protection of industrial property for patents, industrial drawings and designs	October 12, 1992	No. 243, October 12, 1992, page 187.
Cabinet decision no. 11 of 1993— Implementing regulations for federal law no. 44 of 1992 in relation to regulation and protection of industrial property for patents, industrial drawings and designs	May 12, 1993	No. 251, May 29, 1993, page 33.
Ministerial decision no. 404 of 2000 [in relation to pharmaceutical products and patents]	April 30, 2000	No. 353, September 20, 2000.
Federal law no. 17 of 2002 in relation to the regulation and protection of industrial property for patents, industrial drawings and designs	November 19, 2002	No. 390, November 30, 2002, page 70.
Federal law no. 31 of 2006 amending federal law no. 17 of 2002 in relation to the regulation and protection of industrial property for patents, industrial drawings and designs	October 1, 2006	No. 455, October 12, 2006, page 11.

Trademark Laws and Regulations

Law/regulation	Issue date	Publication details (number and date of gazette)
Federal law no. 4 of 1979 in relation to the prevention of fraud and deception in commercial dealings	March 19, 1979	No. 67, March 31, 1979, page 29.
Ministerial decision no. 26 of 1984 concerning the implementing regulations for law no. 4 of 1979 in relation to the prevention of fraud and deception in commercial dealings	June 14, 1984	No. 141, July 31, 1984, page 67.
Ministerial decision no. 8 of 1988 amending some of the provisions of ministerial decision no. 26 of 1984 concerning the implementing regulations for law no. 4 of 1979 in relation to the prevention of fraud and deception in commercial dealings	January 17, 1988	No. 185, February 29, 1988, page 72.
Federal law no. 37 of 1992 in relation to trademarks	28 September 1992	No. 243, 12 October 1992, page 7.
Cabinet decision no. 15 of 1992 in relation to the fees for the procedures undertaken pursuant to the provisions of federal law no. 37 of 1992 in relation to trademarks	December 24, 1992	No. 247, January 31, 1993, page 24.
Ministerial decision no. 6 of 1993 concerning the implementing regulations for federal law no. 37 of 1992 in relation to trademarks	February 2, 1993	No. 248, February 28, 1993, page 57.
Cabinet decision no. 18 of 1993 in relation to the fees for procedures undertaken pursuant to the provisions of federal law no. 37 of 1992 in relation to trademarks	December 19, 1993	No. 260, December 30, 1993, page 25.
Ministerial decision no. 11 of 1995 amending ministerial decision no. 6 of 1993		Mentioned in ministerial decision no. 68 of 2001, amending ministerial decision no. 6 of 1993. Appears not to be published in the gazette.

Law/regulation	Issue date	Publication details (number and date of gazette)
Ministerial decision no. 5 of 1996 in relation to the payment of fees required to complete trademark registration		Mentioned in ministerial decision no. 67 of 1998. Appears not to be published in the gazette.
Ministerial decision no. 21 of 1997 in relation to the amendment of some provisions in ministerial decision no. 6 of 1993		Mentioned in ministerial decision no. 80 of 2005. Appears not to be published in the gazette.
Ministerial decision no. 67 of 1998 in relation to payment of fees for trademark registration	July 8, 1998	No. 326, November 10, 1998, page 189.
Ministerial decision no. 104 of 1998	October 14, 1998	No. 326, November 10, 1998, page 191.
Ministerial decision no. 106 of 1999 [concerning the refund of registration fees]	October 31, 1999	No. 341, November 10, 1999, page 131.
Federal law no. 19 of 2000 amending some of the provisions of federal law no. 37 of 1992 in relation to trademarks	September 16, 2000	No. 353, September 30, 2000 page 65.
Cabinet decision no. 18 of 2000 in relation to the fees for publication of trademarks in the journal of the Ministry of Economy and Commerce	December 18, 2000	No. 356, December 26, 2000, page 14.
Ministerial decision no. 25 of 2001 in relation to trademark publication fees in the journal issued by the Ministry	February 17, 2001	No. 359, February 28, 2001, page 169.
Ministerial decision no. 66 of 2001	May 2, 2001	No. 352, May 10, 2001, page 31.
Ministerial decision 67 of 2001 in relation to the collection of fees for publication of trademarks	May 2, 2001	No. 352, May 10, 2001, page 33.
Ministerial decision no. 68 of 2001 amending some of the provisions of ministerial decision no. 6 of 1993 with the implementing regulations for the law of trademarks	May 2, 2001	No. 352, May 10, 2001, page 36.
Ministerial decision no. 12 of 2002 in relation to payment of registration fees	February 3, 2002	No. 379, April 30, 2002, page 103.

Law/regulation	Issue date	Publication details (number and date of gazette)
Federal law no. 8 of 2002 amending some provisions of federal law no. 37 of 1992 in relation to trademarks	July 24, 2002	No. 384, July 31, 2002, page 11.
Ministerial decision no. 126 of 2003 amending ministerial decision no. 26 of 1984 concerning the implementing regulations for law no. 4 of 1979 in relation to the prevention of fraud and deception in commercial dealings	July 12, 2003	No. 400, July 30, 2003, page 139.
Ministerial decision no. 30 of 2004	October 13, 2004	No. 421, October 13, 2004, page 11.
Ministerial decision no. 80 of 2005 in relation to the registration of trademark registration agents	March 9, 2005	No. 427, April 10, 2005, page 178.
Federal law no. 24 of 2006 in relation to consumer protection	August 13, 2006	No. 453, August 26, 2006, page 23.
Cabinet decision no. 12 of 2007 in relation to the implementing regulations for federal law no. 24 of 2006 in relation to consumer protection	March 29, 2007	No. 464, April 30, 2007, page 40.
Federal decree no. 52 of 2007 in relation to the unified trademark law (system) for the Arabian Gulf Cooperation Council Countries	June 20, 2007	No. 466, June 28, 2007, page 87.
Ministerial decision no. 418 of 2007 in relation to use of trademark "Organic."	October 29, 2007	No. 473, November 15, 2007, page 139.

Author's Rights Laws and Regulations

Law/regulation	Issue date	Publication details (number and date of gazette)
Federal law no. 15 of 1980 in relation to printed matter and publishing	November 16, 1980	No. 85, November 30, 1980, page 5.
Federal law no. 40 of 1992 in relation to protection of intellectual works and the author's rights	September 28, 1992	No. 243, October 12, 1992, page 75.
Ministerial decision no. 411 of 1993 in relation to monitoring works protected pursuant to the provisions of federal law no. 40 of 1992 in relation to protection of intellectual works and the author's rights	September 1, 1993	No. 256, September 30, 1993, page 125.
Ministerial decision no. 412 of 1993 in relation to the deposit system for protection works and disposals that may occur	September 1, 1993	No. 256, September 30, 1993, page 132.
Federal law no. 7 of 2002 in relation to the rights of the author and neighboring rights	July 1, 2002	No. 383, July 14, 2002, page 11.
Ministerial decision no. 131 of 2004 in relation to the registration of works	March 22, 2004	No. 411, April 14, 2004, page 173.
Ministerial decision no. 132 of 2004 in relation to the register of imported and distributed works	March 22, 2004	No. 411, April 14, 2004, page 178.
Ministerial decision no. 133 of 2004 in relation to collecting societies for authors' rights and neighboring rights	March 22, 2004	No. 411, April 14, 2004, page 185.
Ministerial decision no. 134 of 2004 in relation to the compulsory licensing for copying and translating of works	March 22, 2004	No. 411, April 14, 2004, page 188.
Ministerial decision no. 288 of 2004 in relation to the fees connected with author's rights and neighboring rights	July 26, 2004	No. 417, August 11, 2004, page 206.
Federal law no. 32 of 2006 amending federal law no. 7 of 2002 in relation to authors' rights and neighboring rights	October 1, 2006	No. 455, October 11, 2006, page 13.

Decrees Concerning Intellectual Property

Decree	Issue date	Publication details (number and date of gazette)	Key dates
Federal decree no. 21 of 1975 in relation to the United Arab Emirates' accession to the World Intellectual Property Organization	April 26, 1975	No. 27, May 15, 1975, page 497.	Accession: June 24, 1974 Entry into force: September 24, 1974.
Federal decree no. 20 of 1996 in relation to the United Arab Emirates' accession to the Paris Convention for the protection of industrial property	March 31, 1996	No. 291, March 31, 1996, page 60.	Accession: June 19, 1996 Entry into force: September 19, 1996.
Federal decree no. 84 of 1998 in relation to the United Arab Emirates' accession to the Patent Cooperation Treaty	August 18, 1998	No. 323, September 30, 1998, page 25.	Accession: December 10, 1998 Entry into force: March 10, 1999.
Federal decree no. 10 of 2004 in relation to the United Arab Emirates accession to the agreements relating to the author's rights and neighboring rights (Berne, WIPO Copyright Treaty, Rome Convention)	February 19, 2004	No. 408, February 29, 2004, page 85.	Accession: April 14, 2004 Entry into force: July 14, 2004.
WIPO Copyright Treaty	As previous	As previous	Accession: April 14, 2004 Entry into force: July 14, 2004.
Rome Convention	As previous	As previous	Accession: October 14, 2004 Entry into force: January 14, 2005.
Federal decree no. 10 of 2005 in relation to the United Arab Emirates accession to the WIPO Performances and Phonograms Treaty (1996)	January 2005	No. 425, February 2005, page 52.	Accession: March 2005 Entry into force: June 2005.

List of Abbreviations

ARL 2002   Federal law no. 7 of 2002 in relation to the rights of the author and neighboring rights

Berne Convention   Berne Convention for the protection of literary and artistic works as revised and amended up to September 28, 1979

FDL 1979   Federal law no. 4 of 1979 in relation to the prevention of fraud and deception in commercial dealings

GCC TML   Federal decree no. 52 of 2007 in relation to the unified trademark law (system) for the Arabian Gulf Cooperation Council Countries

EGIP   Law no. 82 of 2002 issuing the law for the protection of intellectual property rights

Paris Convention   Paris Convention for the protection of industrial property as revised and amended up to September 28, 1979

PDL 2002   Federal law no. 17 of 2002 in relation to the regulation and protection of industrial property for patents, industrial drawings and designs

PDL 1992   Federal law no. 44 of 1992 in relation to the regulation and protection of industrial property for patents, industrial drawings and designs

PDR 1993   Cabinet decision no. 11 of 1993—Implementing regulations for federal law no. 44 of 1992 in relation to regulation and protection of industrial property for patents, industrial drawings and designs

Rome Convention   International convention for the protection of performers, producers of phonograms and broadcasting organizations, October 26, 1961

TML 1992   Federal law no. 37 of 1992 in relation to trademarks

TML 1992A	Federal law no. 37 of 1992 in relation to trademarks as amended by federal law no. 19 of 2000 and federal law no. 8 of 2002
TMR 1993	Ministerial decision no. 6 of 1993 concerning the implementing regulations for federal law no. 37 of 1992 in relation to trademarks
TRIPs Agreement	Agreement on trade-related aspects of intellectual property rights
UCL	Federal decree no. 85 of 2007 in relation to the Unified Customs system (law) for the states of the Cooperation Council of the Arabian Gulf States
WCT	WIPO Copyright Treaty, December 20, 1996
WIPO	World Intellectual Property Organization
WPPT	WIPO Performances and Phonograms Treaty, December 20, 1996
WTO	World Trade Organization

CHAPTER

1

Patents, Designs, and Know-How

1.1 Patents

Introduction

History of the UAE's Patent Law

In October 1992, the UAE issued its first law dealing with the protection of inventions and industrial drawings and designs.[1] Ten years later, the PDL 1992 was repealed and replaced by federal law no. 17 of 2002.[2] The PDL 2002 has been the subject of only one amending law that charged the references to the Minister and the Ministry (discussed below).[3]

The 1993 regulations were not expressly repealed, but to the extent that any of the regulations are inconsistent with the PDL 2002, they have been repealed.[4] The Ministry continues to refer to the PDR 1993 in its documents and so presumably it deems them still to be in force.[5] Without the PDR 1993 there would be no regulations and no guidance as to how some significant areas of the law should be dealt with. Article 72 of the PDL 2002 directs the Cabinet to issue implementing regulations upon the suggestion of the Minister. Nevertheless, the lack of any new regulations to the PDL 2002 has not stopped the Ministry from continuing to administer the law or from receiving patent and design applications and granting patents and designs.

Looking to the future, the Dubai International Financial Center (DIFC) has released for comment a draft patent law that is to apply within the jurisdiction of the DIFC. There may also be a push within the Ministry to issue a new patent and designs law.[6]

International Conventions

The first international intellectual property law convention to which the UAE became a party was the Paris Convention. It acceded to it on June 19, 1996 and it entered into force on September 19, 1996.[7] In relation to patents, it imposes a number of obligations on contracting parties including in

---

1. Federal law no. 44 of 1992 ("PDL 1992").
2. Federal law no. 17 of 2002 ("PDL 2002"). The language of article 73 of the PDL 2002 is clear in its intent to repeal the PDL 1992 rather than add to or amend it.
3. Federal law no. 31 of 2006 amending Federal law no. 17 of 2002 in relation to the regulation and protection of industrial property for patents, industrial drawings and designs.
4. Cabinet decision no. 11 of 1993 ("PDR 1993"). The repealing provision of the PDL 2002 is article 73.
5. A copy of the PDR 1993 was available on the Ministry of Economy's Web site at the time of writing.
6. The subject received some brief television coverage in late January 2009.
7. Paris Convention, as revised at Stockholm in 1967, and later amended. The dates are from WIPO.

relation to reciprocal treatment,[8] the right to claim priority from earlier filed patent applications,[9] the availability of divisional applications, the independence of patents for the same invention across countries,[10] the right of the inventor to be named,[11] compulsory licenses,[12] patented devices forming part of means of transport,[13] the importation of products manufactured by a process protected in the importing country,[14] and the temporary protection of inventions.[15]

In 1998, the UAE acceded to the Patent Cooperation Treaty (PCT).[16] The PCT establishes a system for the filing of a single application seeking patents in any of a number of designated member countries. A number of provisions in the PDL 2002 reflect the UAE's PCT membership.

The UAE became a member of the World Trade Organization in 1996 and in doing so committed to bring its intellectual property laws in line with the TRIPs Agreement. The deadline to comply was January 1, 2000. The PDL 2002 was intended to be TRIPs compliant.[17] The UAE is not presently a party to the Patent Law Treaty established in 2000.

Government Authorities Dealing with Patents

Both the PDL 1992 and the PDL 2002 named the Minister of Finance and Industry as being responsible for their implementation and administration. "The Department" was defined in both laws as the Department of Industrial Property.[18] In 2006 all references in the PDL 2002 to the Ministry of Finance and Industry and the Minister of Finance and Industrial were replaced by the Ministry of Economy and the Minister of Economy respectively.[19]

Patent applications are filed with the Department of Industrial Property at the Ministry's offices. The principal emirates for these purposes are Abu Dhabi, Dubai, and Sharjah. The Ministry is continuing to develop its online services. Its website can be found at http://www.economy.ae.

---

8. Paris, articles 2 and 3.
9. Paris, article 4.
10. Paris, article 4bis.
11. Paris, article 4ter.
12. Paris, article 5.
13. Paris, article 5ter.
14. Paris, article 5quater.
15. Paris, article 11.
16. Accession was on December 10, 1998 and it entered into force on March 10, 1999. (WIPO)
17. WTO, Council for Trade-Related Aspects of Intellectual Property Rights, Legislation Review, United Arab Emirates, report of meeting June 18–22, 2001, Introductory Statement.
18. The name of the Department is often translated in official documents as "Administration of Industrial Property."
19. Federal law no. 31 of 2006 amending Federal law no. 17 of 2002 in relation to the regulation and protection of industrial property for patents, industrial drawings, and designs.

Patent Statistics

The international patent applications (PCT) database maintained by WIPO contains the bibliographic data for more than 1.5 million PCT applications filed since 1978. The UAE is a designated country for close to one million of the applications. This means little until one sees it against the data for the number of applications that entered the UAE national phase. That data is not available in the WIPO database. The UAE patent office would have such information because it is receiving the national phase applications. That data does not appear to be reaching the WIPO database. Searching on WIPO's Patentscope database for international applications in which one of the applicants has a UAE residency reveals 161 PCT applications. Searching for PCT applicants with UAE nationality reveals 73 applications. Twenty-six PCT applications claim priority from a UAE application.[20] From the available data, it appears that Mr. Moosa Eisa Al Amri has filed ten PCT applications, the largest number filed by anyone resident in the UAE. The General Headquarters for the Armed Forces of the United Arab Emirates has filed six PCT applications.[21]

Another source of UAE patent filing information is the UAE OFFICIAL GAZETTE (to 2008) and the INDUSTRIAL PROPERTY JOURNAL (from 2008). The first group of patent applications accepted and published in the UAE was in the OFFICIAL GAZETTE of July 14, 2002, no. 383. It must have been a moment of national pride that the first accepted and published patent application in the list of nine patent applications published on that day was filed by an Emirati national, Mr. Mousa Eisa Al Amri, filed on April 20, 2002. He had to wait less than three months for the acceptance and publication of his patent application. The other eight applications published were filed during 1994.

Since the first acceptance and publication of patent applications in 2002, the UAE Patent Office has continued to publish for opposition purposes patent applications on a regular basis as follows:

Year	Number of Accepted Patent Applications Published	Official Gazette Numbers
2002	9	383
2003	11	396, 404
2004	15	412, 420, 423
2005	8	437
2006	49	459
2007	58	463, 464, 467, 469
Total number of patents published to 2007	150	

20. As at January 16, 2009.
21. See also WORLD PATENT REPORT—A STATISTICAL OVERVIEW 2008, for other statistics.

In March 2008, the Ministry issued the first INDUSTRIAL PROPERTY JOURNAL. The patent applications published in 2008 are as follows:

Number and date of JOURNAL	Number of accepted patent applications published
No. 1, March 2008	1
No. 2, April 2008	nil
No. 3, May 2008	nil
No. 4, June 2008	nil
No. 5, July 2008	2
No. 6, August 2008	3
Total number of patents published in 2008	6

Patent filing statistics available from the Ministry are as follows:[22]

Year	Number of patent applications filed
2001	352
2002	404
2003	442
2004	528
2005	627
Total patent filings from 2001 to 2005	2353

During the same period, only 43 patent applications were published for opposition purposes.

Patent Searching

It is not possible to carry out any kind of search for patents at the UAE Patent Office. Only once a patent application has been accepted and published in the INDUSTRIAL PROPERTY JOURNAL is it possible to know that an application for it was filed in the UAE. Because national phase entry information is not being received by WIPO from the UAE, it is not possible to see from the PCT database which PCT applications have entered the UAE national phase.

---

22. These numbers are from a document prepared by the Ministry of Economy titled "World Intellectual Property Day" dated April 22, 2007. Thanks to the Brand Owners' Protection Group for giving me a copy (*see* http://www.gulfbpg.com).

GCC Patents

The member states of the Cooperation Council of the Arab States of the Gulf are: Bahrain, Kuwait, Oman, Qatar, Saudi Arabia, and the United Arab Emirates. Its Supreme Council approved the GCC Patent Regulations in 1992 and the GCC Patent Office started receiving applications in 1998. Patents granted by the GCC Patent Office cover all the countries of the GCC and so are enforceable in each of the countries including the UAE. In November 2008, the GCC Patent Office reported that it had received nine thousand patent applications, five hundred of which were from countries of the Council, and that it had granted five hundred patents.[23] The gazettes of the GCC Patent Office are available on its Web site at http://www.gccpo.org. They are published in Arabic only. However, other information concerning procedures is available on the Web site in English.

What Is an Invention?

The PDL 2002 introduced into the law for the first time a definition of an invention:

> An idea arrived at by an inventor and that gives a new technical solution applicable to a specific problem in the domain of technology.[24]

This definition contains the key concepts of patents including that an invention must have an inventor, the invention must be new, it must have some applicability, and it must take our technological knowledge forward by solving a problem previously unsolved or not solved as well. These concepts are discussed below.

Novelty

Only inventions that are new may be the subject of a patent.[25] The PDL 2002 is silent on the issue of how and when novelty is to be assessed. However, the PDR 1993 sets out what matters must be determined in examination of a patent application. One of the matters to be determined is whether the invention is new.

> That the invention is new, that is, it has not been anticipated by the prior industrial art. Prior industrial art in this context means any disclosure that has been

---

23. AL WATAN, November 15, 2008.
24. PDL 2002, article 1.
25. PDL 2002, article 4.

made to the public in any place or at any time by written or oral description, by use, or any other means of knowing the invention, before the date of the filing of the application or the priority date requested or the commencement of temporary protection on the condition that the application was filed within 6 months of the date of commencement.[26]

Clearly, the requirement is for absolute novelty. The relevant prior art includes any public disclosure made anywhere prior to the relevant date. An earlier filed patent application would not, until it was open for public inspection, constitute part of the prior art against which novelty is to be assessed. This leaves open the possibility of double patenting—two patent applications for the same invention, each having been filed before the other was made public. In terms of novelty, both applicants are entitled to a patent. The PDL 2002 deals with the issue of double patenting by giving the person who files before others, or has an earlier priority date, the right to the patent for the invention.[27]

A possible consequence of these provisions is as follows. Assume that patentee A is granted a UAE patent for an invention. Patentee B discovered the same invention before patentee A's patent was disclosed and obtained patents for it outside the UAE. Each of the patentee's patents was validly granted because as at the priority date for each none had been disclosed. Each patentee has valid rights in the countries in which each has obtained a patent. Patentee B will not be able to import into the UAE products made embodying the invention without infringing patentee A's UAE patent. The moral of the story is that despite international novelty requirements, patent rights are national, and although filing first is an important milestone in seeking to protect an invention, so is the disclosure of the invention in order to prevent others from claiming novelty for the same invention. The timing of disclosure is a key part of patenting strategy.

The "first to file" right is supported by the right to seek cancellation of a patent, wholly or partially.[28] The cancellation provision mentions two possible cases of cancellation (in the context of setting out the notice requirements for them): (a) the patent was granted without satisfying the requirements for its grant, and (b) it was granted without taking into consideration "the priority of prior applications pursuant to article 11" of the PDL 2002 (concerning priority rights).[29]

---

26. PDR 1993, article 20.11.
27. PDL 2002, article 7.2.
28. PDL 2002, article 34[A] and [C].
29. PDL 2002, article 34[B],1 and 2.

Obviousness

The PDL 2002 does not address the issue of obviousness. Instead, it is dealt with in the PDR 1993 in the list of matters that are to be determined in examination. The invention must contain "creative activity"—a literal translation of "nashaatt ibtikaari"—"not obvious to the ordinary man skilled in the art to achieve intuitively based on the prior industrial art relating to the patent application."[30] "Creative activity" is probably to be understood as expressing the same concept as "inventive step."[31] In any case, its meaning is given by the rest of the provision—it must not be obvious, based on the prior art, to an ordinary person skilled in the art.

Industrial Applicability

Industrial applicability is a requirement for the grant of a patent: "any new invention . . . which is . . . capable of industrial exploitation."[32] It also gives a definition of "industrial application," presumably referring to the requirement for it to be capable of "industrial exploitation."[33] An invention is industrially applicable if it is possible to apply it or use it in any kind of industry (in its widest sense) including in agriculture, hunting, handicrafts, and services.[34] This requirement is repeated in the PDR 1993.[35]

Article 4 of the PDL 2002 refers to inventions "founded on a scientific basis and capable of industrial exploitation."[36] The expression "founded on a scientific basis" is possibly there to make it clear that "inventions" based on other forms of "knowledge," such as witchcraft or magic, are not patentable. It also introduces the idea that the invention must be able to withstand scientific scrutiny and its alleged benefits are able to be verified. In any case, it is not referred to as one of the matters to be determined in examination.

---

30. PDR 1993, article 20.12. It appears in the translation in this book as "inventive step."
31. The IPEG uses a literal translation of "inventive step"—"khattwa ibda'aee." An expression that could be translated literally as "inventive step" is used in the PDL 2002 in article 7— "khattwa ibtikariya"—when discussing the rights of persons who merely participate in implementation of the invention.
32. PDL 2002, article 4[1].
33. PDL 2002, article 4[1] uses the word "istighlal" and article 4[2] uses the word "tattbeeq."
34. PDL 2002, article 4[2].
35. PDR 1993, 20.13.
36. PDL 2002, article 4[1].

Sufficiency

The concept of sufficiency is an expression of the implied bargain that is struck between the inventor and the public that is at the foundation of the patent system. The inventor makes public the invention for the benefit of the public (the growth and development of knowledge and research) for which the inventor receives from the state a temporary monopoly. However, the inventor's side of the bargain is only fulfilled if the invention is sufficiently disclosed in the patent application to enable others to perform it.

In the PDL 2002, the principle of sufficiency is expressed by limiting the scope of protection granted by a patent to what is in the application seeking the grant of the patent.[37] That is to say, if it is not disclosed, it is not protected and no monopoly is given. The PDR 1993 requires that examination determine whether the inventive elements for which protection is requested are specifically stated in the application. They must be explained in the description and the engineering drawings. No other guidance is given as to what would constitute sufficient disclosure, to whom it must be sufficient, the degree of sufficiency, and so on.[38] However, it could be argued that the concepts appearing in the TRIPs Agreement provisions are to be imported into the UAE provisions. The TRIPs Agreement mentions that the level of disclosure required is to be such that the invention could be carried out by a person skilled in the art.[39] Indicating the best mode of carrying out the invention known to the inventor appears to be optional but it is included in the regulations.[40]

Patent or Utility Certificate?

Very many of the provisions in the PDL 2002 refer and apply to both patents and utility certificates. A utility certificate is defined as:

> The deed of protection that is granted by the Department in the name of the State for an invention that results from innovative activity that is insufficient for the grant of a patent.[41]

The invention for which a utility certificate is granted must nevertheless be novel and capable of industrial application.[42] The extent to which the

---

37. PDL 2002, article 16.
38. PDR 1993, article 20.14.
39. *See* article 6.1.c of the PDR 1993.
40. TRIPs Agreement, article 29.1 and article 6.1.e of the PDR 1993.
41. PDL 2002, article 1.
42. PDL 2002, article 5[1] mentions both novelty and industrial applicability.

invention may contain an insufficiency of innovative activity is not stated. The implication from the language used is that the insufficiency may be total provided that it is not so lacking in inventiveness that is not novel.

The fact that the invention lacks the degree of innovative activity required for the grant of a patent has consequence for the rights of the owner of the utility certificate. The right to prevent others from engaging in the acts that it is the right of the patentee to do is not expressed to extend to the owners of utility certificates, only to patentees.[43] The holder of either a patent or a utility certificate for a new method or application of a known industrial method or means receives only the right to use the method and practice any of the acts that are given to patentees in relation to products obtained directly from the method.[44] There are several points to note in this provision. First, an application for a patent for a new application of a known industrial method would face the challenge of obviousness. But that challenge has been removed for utility certificates—they may lack an inventive step and be obvious. The provision therefore must be aimed principally at utility certificates. Secondly, a "new application of a known method" is probably the substance of the concept of an "insufficient amount of innovative activity" for the grant of a patent. If the new application of the known method is obvious to someone skilled in the art, then it will lack the innovation required for the grant of a patent. Thirdly, the right to use the method and practice the acts of manufacture, use, sale, etc. is not expressed to be an exclusive right. It is not supported by a right of prevention. It is therefore a non-exclusive right. In other words, there appears to be no possibility of infringing a utility certificate and no entitlement to any remedy.

In other countries, similar forms of protection are known as utility models (Egypt). Australia had a system of petty patents that was recently replaced with the "innovation patent."

The term of the utility certificate is only ten years as opposed to twenty years for a patent.[45]

Patentable Subject Matter

The TRIPs Agreement requires that patents be "available for any inventions, whether products or processes, in all fields of technology, provided that they are new, involve an inventive step and are capable of industrial application."[46]

---

43. The rights of prevention are set out in the second and third paragraphs of article 15.1.a of the PDL 2002.
44. PDL 2002, article 15.1.b.
45. PDL 2002, article 14[1.].
46. The TRIPs Agreement, article 27.1.

However, it also permits members to exclude from patentability certain inventions.

Plants and Animals

Plant and animal research, biological methods for their reproduction, as well as plant and animal varieties, are not patentable, but microbiological methods and their products are.[47] The TRIPs Agreement permits the exclusion of biological processes for the production of plants and animals but not non-biological and microbiological processes. The PDL 2002 provision is probably compliant. However, plant varieties must also be protectable either by patents or a *sui generis* system.[48] Neither of these are available in the UAE.

Presumably the term "animals" in the PDL 2002 provision includes human beings and therefore the patenting of processes for the cloning of human beings and human gene sequencing is not possible.

Methods for the Treatment of Human Beings and Animals

Diagnostic, therapeutic, and surgical methods necessary for the treatment of human beings and animals are excluded from patentability.[49] This exclusion is consistent with article 27.3(a) of the TRIPs Agreement.

Principles, Discoveries, Theories, etc.

Principles, discoveries, and scientific theories, as well as mathematical methods, are not patentable.[50] This exclusion follows the well-established general principle in patent law that discoveries and principles in themselves are not patentable for lack of industrial applicability.[51] The useful employment of a principle or discovery may well constitute a patentable invention.

Business Methods

Plans or rules or methods followed for carrying on a commercial business are not patentable.[52] The exclusion groups such methods together with performing purely mental activities or games. The TRIPs Agreement does not expressly permit business methods to be excluded from what is patentable

---

47. PDL 2002, article 6.1.a.
48. The TRIPs agreement, article 27.3(b).
49. PDL 2002, article 6.1.b.
50. PDL 2002, article 6.1.c.
51. The exclusion is also consistent with the TRIPs Agreement which requires that patents be available for inventions capable of industrial application.
52. PDL 2002, article 6.1.d.

subject matter. If a business method satisfies all the criteria for being an invention and being patentable, it is difficult to see how the exclusion in the PDL 2002 can be justified. As a matter of principle, if a business method is truly a new technical solution to a specific technical problem, it should be entitled to protection.

Computer Programs

Computer programs are not in the list of matter excluded from patentability and therefore must, in principle, be patentable in the UAE. Their exclusion is not permitted by the TRIPs Agreement.

Inventions Contravening Public Order or Morals

Inventions whose *publication* or *exploitation* would lead to a contravention of public order or morals may not be patented in the UAE.[53] The exclusion permitted by the TRIPs Agreement relates to commercial *exploitation* that would contravene public order or morals. Not permitting a patent to be granted for inventions whose publication alone might contravene public order or morals is not expressly authorized by the TRIPs Agreement.[54] The TRIPs Agreement also requires that the exclusion not be made simply because the exploitation of the invention is prohibited by national law. For example, the emirate of Sharjah was recently reported to have banned the riding of bicycles in the streets because of the danger they represent to motorists. Following the TRIPs Agreement, such a ban would not be sufficient to justify not granting patents for bicycle inventions, even though the riding of bicycles might be contrary to the law.

Denying patents to inventions whose publication or exploitation would lead to a contravention of public order or morals introduces considerations of Islamic law. Shari'a is the source of the laws of the UAE, according to the Constitution.[55] In practice, it regulates matters concerning the family, but also deems certain subjects to be immoral. Potentially, inventions relating to the production or consumption of alcohol or pork would contravene the morality of the state (notwithstanding that both are widely available in most emirates of the UAE). The earning of interest from debts (usury) is held to be contrary to Islam and therefore inventions relating to certain financial matters may be contrary to morality.

---

53. PDL 2002, article 6.1.e.
54. TRIPs Agreement, article 27.2.
55. UAE Constitution, article 7.

National Defense

Inventions relating to national defense were, under the PDL 1992, not patentable.[56] The provision does not appear in the PDL 2002. However, there are now specific procedures for such inventions.[57]

Chemical Inventions Relating to Medical Drugs and Pharmaceutical Compounds

Chemical inventions relating to nutrition, medical drugs, and pharmaceutical compounds were excluded from being patentable under the PDL 1992 in certain circumstances.[58] The UAE availed itself of article 65.4 of the TRIPs Agreement, which permits a five-year delay in extending patent protection to areas of technology not protectable at that time. Hence the PDL 2002 expressly provided that such chemical inventions were protectable in the UAE from January 1, 2005.[59] Prior to this date, the Department was required to continue to receive applications for such patents and record them. If the applicant had a patent issued for the invention in a WTO member country and had been licensed to market the invention in that country, then the applicant would enjoy the right to market exclusively the invention in the UAE for five years after being licensed to do so by local authorities. The five-year protection period would end when either the application is granted or rejected.[60]

Inventors

The inventor, *prima facie*, has the right to what he or she invents. If two or more persons participate in the creation of an invention, they share the right to the invention. Persons who merely assist in the implementation of the invention without participating in any inventive step are not deemed to be inventors.[61] These principles of ownership are altered if the inventors are employees or have been commissioned (see the discussion below).

The inventor has the right to be named in the patent as the inventor. The inventor can declare not to be named, but such a declaration must be in writing.[62]

---

56. PDL 1992, article 6.4.
57. PDL 2002, article 6.2.
58. PDL 1992, article 6.2.
59. PDL 2002, article 70.
60. PDL 2002, article 71.
61. PDL 2002, article 7.1.
62. PDL 2002, article 10[1]. *See also* Paris Convention, article 4ter.

Employee Inventors

The creation of an invention during the carrying out of an employment contract results in the employer having the right to the invention, unless there is an agreement to the contrary.[63]

This is if the employee's role is an inventive one. If the employee's contract of employment does not include inventive activities as part of the employee's role, and the employee creates an invention related to his or her employment using the resources of the employer, the employer has the option to own the invention and may exercise that option within four months of the employee reporting the creation of the invention or otherwise becoming aware of it (if the employee fails to report it).[64] The employee is under an obligation to report the invention in writing.[65] The employee has a right to fair compensation, which can be determined by the court if compensation cannot be agreed.[66] The right to the invention passes to the employee if the employer does not exercise the option.

These provisions do not deal with the protection of the invention. Four months is a long time to wait to determine the ownership of the invention and therefore to determine who may seek to protect it. In the meantime, there is no obligation on either party not to disclose the invention and thereby destroy its novelty. How the provisions could work effectively in practice is open to question.

If an employment contract seeks to deny any of these rights to the employee (the right to additional compensation, the right to the invention if it is not taken up by the employer, the right to fair compensation if the employer exercises the right to the invention), it is deemed void.[67]

Each of these provisions apply to *inventions*, whether or not the subject of a patent filed later, or indeed whether the invention is patentable at all. The definition of an invention is very broad: "an idea arrived at by an inventor and that gives a new technical solution applicable to a specific problem in the domain of technology."[68] The broad drafting of the employee inventor provisions in the PDL 2002 may have effects beyond what was intended. Perhaps the provisions were intended to relate to patentable inventions only, but there is no evidence of that in the language of the provisions.

---

63. PDL 2002, article 9.1.
64. PDL 2002, article 9.3.
65. PDL 2002, article 9.4.
66. PDL 2002, article 9.5.
67. PDL 2002, article 9.6.
68. PDL 2002, article 1.

Contracted or Commissioned Inventors

The creation of an invention during the carrying out of a "commission contract" results in the commissioner having the right to the invention, unless there is an agreement to the contrary.[69]

The inventor is entitled to additional compensation if an amount is not specified in the contract and if the invention has an economic value above what the parties expected at the time of contracting. The amount of the additional compensation is to be specified by the court (presumably if the parties cannot agree).[70]

Joint Patentees

The right to an invention can be shared by virtue of the invention being created by more than one inventor[71] or as a result of assignment or other transmission of the right. Joint inventors could become joint patentees. As joint patentees, it appears they are to be treated as "tenants in common." This might be inferred from the fact that they are able to assign their right to the invention or patent independently of the other inventor/patentee and to exploit the rights given to patentees independently.[72] However, they may only license the exploitation of the invention jointly and not independently.

Patent Application

Although the inventor *prima facie* has the right to the invention, the PDL 2002 does not expressly give a right to file an application to obtain a patent or utility certificate. It simply says that the filing of applications and related matters are to be specified in the implementing regulations.[73] The application is to be made using Form 5 to the regulations.[74] The forms used by the Ministry change over time and the latest version needs to be obtained before use.

---

69. PDL 2002, article 9.1.
70. This is an interpretation of the articles 9.1 and 9.2 of the PDL 2002.
71. PDL 2002, article 7.
72. PDL 2002, article 20.
73. PDL 2002, article 10[2].
74. PDR 1993, article 5. The form as it was issued in 1993 is an annexure to the regulations.

The regulations list the following as having to be attached to the application:

1. The description (specification).[75]
2. The drawings.[76]
3. An abstract for the invention not exceeding two hundred words.[77]
4. An extract from the commercial register legalized up to the UAE Embassy.[78]
5. The document evidencing the entitlement of the applicant to the invention if the applicant is not the inventor, legalized up to the UAE Embassy.[79]
6. The power of attorney given to the agent filing the application, legalized up to the UAE Embassy.[80]
7. A certified copy of any priority application.[81] The regulations require the priority application to be legalized up to the UAE Embassy but a certified copy is sufficient.

Any document not in Arabic must be accompanied by an Arabic translation and if not in English, by an Arabic and English translation.[82] The letter from the Israeli Boycott Office mentioned in the regulations is no longer required.[83]

The description, drawings, and abstract must be filed with the application. All the other documents may be filed within ninety days if an undertaking to do so is given using Form 6. This period cannot be extended. If it is only the priority document that cannot be filed within the ninety days, only the priority claim is lost.[84] If the application is a PCT national phase entry, it is not necessary to file any kind of copy of the PCT application.

For those preparing the application, the drawings, etc., the regulations specify various formal requirements that need to be complied with, such as the paper margins and what can be included in the drawings.[85]

---

75. PDR 1993, article 6.1.
76. PDR 1993, article 6.2.
77. PDR 1993, article 6.3.
78. PDR 1993, article 6.4.
79. PDR 1993, article 6.5.
80. PDR 1993, article 6.7.
81. PDR 1993, article 6.8.
82. PDR 1993, article 6[C].
83. PDR 1993, article 6.10.
84. PDR 1993, article 6[E].
85. PDR 1993, articles 7 to 13.

One Invention Only

Each application for a patent must relate to one invention only, or a group of interrelated inventions formed around a single innovative concept.[86] A patent cannot be declared invalid if it is discovered that the requirement for the interrelatedness of the inventions was not met.[87] In some jurisdictions, divisional applications can be filed as a way of overcoming a lack of unity problem. However, divisional applications are not available in the UAE and any claims for inventions that do not meet the interrelatedness requirement would have to be deleted if identified in examination.

Divisional Applications

To provide for the filing of divisional applications is an obligation under the Paris Convention.[88] However, there are no provisions for divisional applications in the law or regulations. One of the circumstances in which an applicant might wish to file one or more divisional applications is if the examination of the application reveals that the application contains more than one invention. Instead of giving the applicant the right to divide the application, the PDL 2002 permits the patent application to relate to a group of interrelated inventions based on one innovative concept.[89] Failure to meet this requirement is not a ground for the invalidity of the patent.[90]

PCT Applications

The PDL 2002 provides that the Department may receive PCT applications and that the procedures for them are to be set out in the regulations.[91] No regulations have yet been issued, but as a matter of practice, applications are being received and the Department's forms and systems cater for them. If a patent application is a PCT national phase entry, it is not necessary to file a copy of the PCT application, but a copy of the PCT publication notice is required or an undertaking to file it at a later time.

---

86. PDL 2002, article 4 [3]. The UK Patents Act 1977 contains a similar provision: "the claims or claims . . . shall relate to one invention or to a group of inventions which are so linked as to form a single inventive concept" (section 14 (5) (d)).

87. PDL 2002, article 4 [4]. Compare the UK Patents Act 1977, article 26.

88. Paris Convention, Article 4, G.

89. PDL 2002, article 4.[3].

90. PDL 2002, article 4.[4].

91. PDL 2002, articles 37 and 38.

Priority Claims

A claim for priority can be made from the first filed patent application for the invention within twelve months of its filing date.[92] The method of calculation of the period is not set out in the law or regulations but the Paris Convention gives some guidance. The twelve (calendar) months are to be calculated from the day after the day on which the first application was filed.[93] If the first application was filed on January 1, 2008, the deadline for subsequent applications claiming priority would be January 2, 2009. If January 2, 2009 is an official holiday or the Patent Office is not open, the deadline is to be extended to the next working day.[94]

The law and regulations do not state whether the priority claim must be made at the time of filing the application or whether it can be made later. Certainly, the application must state the date and number of the priority application and the name of country in which it was filed,[95] but whether it must contain this information at the time of filing is not addressed. One of the matters for examination is whether the priority request is consistent with the provisions of any agreement between the UAE and the country in which the priority application was filed.[96] The timing of the making of the priority claim is not addressed.

The regulations make it clear that a copy of the priority application is one of the documents to be attached to the application.[97] However, the applicant or the applicant's agent may give an undertaking to file it within ninety days of filing the application.[98] The instructions given by the Patent Office for the preparation and filing of patent applications state that the priority document must be a certified copy.

The priority document must be translated to Arabic if it is in English and must be translated to English and Arabic if it is in a language other than English.

There are no provisions in the PDL 2002 or regulations relating to claiming multiple priorities. The Paris Convention provides that:

> No country of the Union may refuse a priority or a patent application on the ground that the applicant claims multiple priorities, even if they originate in

---

92. PDL 2002, article 11.2. The right to claim priority is enshrined in the Paris Convention, Article 4, A (1).
93. Paris Convention, Article 4, C (2).
94. Paris Convention, Article 4, C.(3).
95. PDL 2002, article 11.1.
96. PDR 1993, article 20.15.
97. PDR 1993, article [A.]8.
98. This is consistent with the Paris Convention: Article 4.D.(3). See the section above on filing a patent application.

different countries, or on the ground that an application claiming one or more priorities contains one or more elements that were not included in the application or applications whose priority is claimed, provided that, in both cases, there is unity of invention within the meaning of the law of the country.[99]

As matter of practice, multiple priority claims are permitted.[100]

Examination of Patent Applications

The Department's obligations under the law are to examine the patent application and to notify the applicant of the rejection of the application. It also has the right to request (presumably from the applicant) what it considers necessary in order to grant the patent.[101]

The examination procedure as described by the regulations separates the process into formal and substantive examination. Objections made as to form have ninety days from the delivery of the official notice in which to be resolved. Failure to resolve the issues results in the application being deemed not to have been filed.[102]

Substantive examination will only occur after the estimated examination fees have been paid within ninety days of delivery of the official notice. If the fees are not paid within the period, the application is deemed not to have been filed.[103]

The regulations list 15 matters that are to be determined in the examination process (no distinction is made between those that are formal and those that are substantive—items 1 to 4 in the list appear to be formal and the remainder substantive).[104] In summary, the matters for substantive examination are: that the invention is patentable subject matter,[105] that it does not relate to national defense,[106] that it does not contravene public morals,[107] that it has not been taken from another person,[108] that it is novel,[109] that it

---

99. Paris Convention, article 4 F.
100. For example, see design application nos. 15/2005 and 198/2005 (both published in INDUSTRIAL PROPERTY JOURNAL no. 6).
101. PDL 2002, article 12.
102. PDR 1993, article 92.
103. PDR 1993, article 93.
104. PDR 1993, article 20.
105. PDR 1993, articles 20.5, 20.6 and 20.7.
106. PDR 1993, article 20.8.
107. PDR 1993, article 20.9.
108. PDR 1993, article 20.10.
109. PDR 1993, article 20.11.

contains an inventive step,[110] that it is capable of industrial application,[111] that it is sufficiently disclosed,[112] and that the priority claim is in order.[113]

The examination of UAE patent applications has been outsourced to the Austrian Patent Office.[114] However, the Department may be seeking to establish its own examination capability in the UAE.

Appealing Examination Decisions

If a patent application is rejected, the applicant has sixty days from the date of notification of the rejection to file an appeal with the committee.[115]

Publication

Patent applications are published by the Patent Office upon acceptance for opposition purposes.[116] There are no provisions in the PDL 2002 for making patent applications available for public inspection prior to acceptance. There is a right to view patents in the presence of a responsible employee at the Department, but this appears to relate only to granted patents and as a matter of practice is not done.[117]

The PDL 2002 provides that granted patent applications are to be published in the "Journal," which is defined as a periodical publication issued by the Department.[118] The PDR 1993 provides that the decisions to grant patents are to be published in the OFFICIAL GAZETTE, in which the Ministries publish all new laws, regulations and decrees.[119] The publications of granted patents between 2002 and 2007 occurred in the OFFICIAL GAZETTE. The abstracts for the patents published were not part of those publications. They made available only basic information about the patent granted. The Paris Convention obliges each member of the Union to publish an official periodical journal with "the name of the proprietors of patents granted, with a brief designation of the inventions patented."[120] In March 2008, the Department issued the

---

110. PDR 1993, article 20.12.
111. PDR 1993, article 20.13.
112. PDR 1993, article 20.14.
113. PDR 1993, article 20.15.
114. PDR 1993, article 22 permits the Department to seek the assistance of others including foreign bodies outside the UAE.
115. PDL 2002, articles 7.3 and 12 [2].
116. PDL 2002, article 13 [1].
117. PDR 1993, article 91.
118. PDL 2002, articles 13 and 1.
119. PDR 1993, 24.2.
120. Paris Convention, article 12 (2)(a).

first edition of the INDUSTRIAL PROPERTY JOURNAL, which was followed by five others during 2008. The numbers of patents and designs published in 2008 are set out in the sections on patents and design statistics respectively.

Opposition

The right to oppose the grant of a patent application is first expressed in article 7.3 of the PDL 2002. Article 13 expresses the right again but together with the period of opposition and the forum: within sixty days of publication of the application and before the committee.[121] The regulations repeat the right, the period, and the forum.[122]

There are no provisions for obtaining an extension of the period in which to oppose or for filing a late notice of opposition.

It seems that there is a standing requirement in order to oppose. The opponent must have an "interest," an expression capable of broad interpretation.[123] It is nevertheless an important consideration in deciding who the proper opponent should be (for example, amongst a group of companies, or as between the licensee and the licensor of a competing invention). The purpose of the requirement may only be to deter frivolous oppositions. The procedures for patent oppositions follow those for cases coming before the committee.

There are no provisions in the law or regulations setting out or limiting the possible grounds of opposition. Presumably any and all of the requirements for grant can be raised as grounds of opposition. There is nothing that limits the opponent to these or indeed to grounds from within the patent law and regulations.

It appears that none of the patents published in the UAE between 2002 and 2007 were opposed, so the issues and procedures for oppositions may well yet be untested.

The Patent Term

The term of a patent is twenty years from the filing date in the UAE. The term for a utility certificate is ten years.[124]

---

121. PDL 2002, article 13.
122. PDR 1993, article 24.2.
123. The Arabic word here is "masslaha": PDL 2002, article 13. There are many similar expressions in Arabic and many of them are used in legal contexts.
124. PDL 2002, article 14.[1].

Under the PDL 1992, the patent term was 15 years with the possibility of renewal in special circumstances for a five-year period. This was inconsistent with the TRIPs Agreement.[125]

No patents were granted during the period in which the PDL 1992 was in force, or before the UAE's obligations under the TRIPs Agreement began The PDL 2002 provisions therefore have the effect of giving all patents a twenty-year term.

Patent Annuities

Annuities are the annual fees that are required to be paid to maintain a patent or utility certificate. The second annuity falls due in the year following the year of filing and it is due at the beginning of that year and each subsequent year for the term of the patent or utility certificate. It is a requirement of the Paris Convention that a grace period of not less than six months be given for the payment of annuities.[126] Consistent with this, the PDL 2002 provides for an initial three-month grace period, and then a further three months subject to payment of a fee.[127]

The regulations on this issue are presumably null and void because they are inconsistent with these provisions. Article 28 provided for the payment of annuities in the last three months of the year in which they were due, with a 30-day extension period.[128]

Annuities must be paid whether the patent or utility certificate has been granted or not.[129] They can also be paid in advance for all or some of the term.[130]

Rights of the Patentee

The principal right of the patentee is to exploit the invention the subject of the patent.[131] Although not expressly stated, it can be inferred that the right of exploitation is an exclusive one from the fact that it is accompanied by a right of prevention.

---

125. TRIPs Agreement, article 33.
126. Paris Convention, Article 5bis.1.
127. PDL 2002, article 14.[2].
128. PDR 1993, article 28.2.
129. PDL 2002, article 14.[5].
130. PDL 2002, article 14.[3].
131. PDL 2002, article 15.1.

In relation to a product patent, the right of exploitation includes the right to:

a. manufacture the product
b. use the product
c. offer the product for sale
d. sell the product
e. import the product for any of the above purposes

In the case of a process or method patent, the right of exploitation includes the right to:

a. use the process or method
b. use the product that is obtained directly by means of the process or method
c. offer for sale the product that is obtained directly by means of the process or method
d. sell the product that is obtained directly by means of the process or method
e. import for any of these purposes the product that is obtained directly by means of the process or method

The patentee also has the right to prevent others from doing any of the above acts during the term of the patent.[132] The rights of prevention do not extend to acts done for non-commercial or non-industrial purposes and do not limit what can be done with a product after it has been sold.[133]

Assignment

Both patent applications and granted patents can be assigned.[134] The assignment must be in writing and must be executed by both parties before a responsible employee at the Department or before a notary public in the UAE.[135] This is a highly impractical requirement since most patent applications filed in the UAE are filed by non-residents. This provision is not followed as a matter of practice and therefore raises the question of whether most patent assignments filed in the UAE are, strictly speaking, null and void for failure to comply with the law.

---

132. The rights of prevention are expressly provided for in the TRIPs Agreement: article 28.1.
133. PDL 2002, article 15.2.
134. PDL 2002, article 18[1]; PDR 1993, articles 29 and 30.
135. PDL 2002, article 18[2]. This provision was also in the PDL 1992, article 18.

Assignments must be recorded in the register.[136] Both assignments of applications and of granted patents are subject to Departmental vetting procedures and may be rejected on a wide range of grounds.[137]

Licenses

The provisions in the PDL 2002 regulating the granting of licenses for patents and utility certificates tend to favor the licensee and thereby place the onus on licensors to make express all limitations on the licensee's rights. The provisions also give to the Department rights to vet, approve, and record all licenses. Failure to comply with the provisions results in the license not being effective.

The Right to License

The owner may license the use or exploitation of "the right the subject of the protection."[138] The law gives to the owner a cluster of rights (as discussed above). Despite the use of the expression "the right the subject of the protection," the licensor should be able to break up the rights and license them separately giving, for example, the right to produce the product (in the case of a product patent) to one person and the rights to offer it for sale and sell it to another. Such "restrictions" would nevertheless need to be approved by the Department (discussed below).

If the patentee does not expressly specify in the license the particular "domains" and "means" of use and exploitation, then the licensee is deemed to have a right to use and exploit the invention in all domains and by all means.[139] This provision probably does not mean that if the license does not specify the specific rights being licensed, then the license is for all the rights arising from the patent protection. More likely it is saying that, for example, if the right to sell is being granted, the licensee may sell by any means, unless the agreement limits the means of selling, for example, through supermarkets. Similarly, if the invention can be used in a number of different fields, such as aerospace as well as civil aviation, the right granted is not limited to one or

---

136. PDL 2002, article 18[3].
137. PDR 1993, articles 30, 50, 51, 42 and 43. The drafting and internal referencing of these articles is complex. The Departmental vetting procedures and rejection grounds are in articles 42 and 43, but they were drafted referring only to know-how contracts. Article 50 seeks to replace certain terms of these articles so that they apply to licenses. Article 51 then seeks to replace all references to licenses (which are only there by replacement) with references to assignments, assignors, and assignees.
138. PDL 2002, article 54.
139. PDL 2002, article 57[1].

the other unless specified. If something specific is intended, it should be expressed to avoid being given a broad interpretation.

Duration of Licenses

The license term may not exceed the term of the protection given by the law.[140] This appears to mean that if the patent protection for an invention expires on January 1, 2010, the license may not specify a term beyond that date. It is unclear whether the patentee may include in the license provisions for the protection of invention-related know-how beyond the expiry of the patent, relying on the know-how provisions in the PDL 2002. Assuming that the patent license may not contain a license of the related know-how beyond the patent expiry (that is, assuming the most restrictive interpretation of the provision), the patentee will need to enter into a separate know-how license at the time of granting the patent license to try to maintain some level of protection beyond the patent expiry. Of course, the related know-how will need to be kept confidential during the term of the patent, notwithstanding that the invention itself had been published. Whether there is invention-related know-how, or whether such know-how is developed during the term of the patent license, is a question of fact in each case.

If no term is expressly stated in the license, the term of the license is deemed to be the entire term of the patent.[141]

In Writing and Signed by the Parties

The license must be in writing and signed by the parties[142] and therefore oral licenses are not recognized (a potentially important issue in infringement proceedings). The provision suggests that the license may be simply signed by the parties, but given the need for recordal of the license (discussed below), the recordal requirements should also be complied with. The license should therefore be signed before a notary and translated into Arabic.[143] Although not mentioned in the regulations, it may need legalization if executed outside the UAE.

---

140. PDL 2002, article 54.
141. Interpreting article 57 of the PDL 2002.
142. PDL 2002, article 54.
143. PDR 1993, article 50, which applies article 41 to licences.

Non-Exclusivity

All patent licenses are non-exclusive unless they are expressed to be otherwise. Equally, the grant of a license does not exclude the patentee from exploiting the invention unless such an exclusion is expressly stated.[144]

Geographical Limitations

The license is deemed to be a license for "all the lands of the State" unless expressly stated to be otherwise.[145] For example, if it is intended that the production of a patented product be done at a particular factory located at a particular address, then that needs to be expressed in the license, otherwise the licensee will be able to produce the product at any location in the UAE.

The Licensee's Right to Prevent Infringement

The licensee has the right to prevent infringement or threat or damage to the subject of the protection. However, the licensee may only instigate legal and judicial procedures and demand compensation after the licensee has informed the patentee by registered letter and the patentee does not undertake the "necessary procedures" within thirty days of the notice.[146]

This provision places a great weight on the patentee. What are the "necessary measures" that the patentee must take? For example, if the patentee sends the infringer a letter of demand, is that sufficient to stop the licensee's right to commence proceedings from arising? It probably means that the patentee must commence legal proceedings or the licensee will be entitled to do so. The thirty-day period then is the time in which the patentee has to consider the report of infringement, investigate the facts, take advice, demand that the infringement cease, and negotiate a settlement if possible.

The patentee has good reason to pursue the matter promptly because the licensee has the right to sue the patentee for damage resulting from the neglect or delay of the patentee.

There are many practical and legal issues that the law does not address, such as whether the patentee must be made a party to the proceedings, the defense of any counterclaim for invalidity, the consequences if the patent were found invalid, the costs of the proceedings, and the entitlement to damages.

---

144. PDL 2002, article 56.
145. PDL 2002, article 57[1].
146. PDL 2002, article 57[2].

Recordal of Licenses

Patent and utility certificate *licenses* must be recorded with the Department of Industrial Property at the Ministry.[147] Once recorded, the license must be published in the JOURNAL. Until it is published, it is deemed to have "no effect on others."[148] This concept is used in various places throughout the intellectual property laws of the UAE and potentially has different meanings in different contexts. Here we are dealing with a license contract, usually between two parties only. Who are the others on whom it might have an effect after it is published (and no effect before)? One interpretation is that the contract is not effective as between the parties themselves until after it has been vetted by the Department and approved, recorded and published (and the fees paid). On this view, "no effect on others" is a way of enforcing the monitoring and recordal of licenses (at the cost of making a significant intrusion into the freedom to conduct business).

Vetting of Licenses by the Department

All license contracts, assignments, amendments, and renewals are to be submitted to the Department for inspection of their terms and contents.[149]

The Department may request the parties to amend the contract if it contains "an offence against the use of any industrial property right or damage to the commercial competition related to the subject" of the contract. This is from the PDL 2002. The PDR 1993 provides for different vetting criteria: the Department may require the parties to amend the terms of the contract "so as to realise the interests of the parties within the framework of the law and the economic interests of the State."[150] If there is a conflict between the law and the regulations, then the law takes precedence over the regulations.[151]

The process of vetting licenses appears to be part of the recordal process. If the license is not in order, in the view of the Department, then it will not record the license. The grounds on which a recordal application can be rejected add another layer of compliance and criteria for vetting licenses. The provisions relating to the rejection of applications to record know-how licenses are said to apply to license contracts.[152] The following appear to be the relevant criteria for *rejecting* an application to record a license

---

147. PDL 2002, article 55.
148. PDL 2002, article 55 and PDR 1993, article 50.
149. PDL 2002, article 59[1].
150. PDR 1993, article 42.
151. PDL 2002, article 73.
152. PDR 1993, article 50.

(making the various adjustments to the provisions directed by article 50 of the PDR 1993):

a. that the term of the license and its renewal is longer than the term of protection;
b. that the license grants to the licensee rights that are not granted by the deed of protection;
c. that the license contains restrictions on trade or research or production or pricing;
d. that the license requires the return of documents containing the license [sic];
e. that the price paid for the license is not proportionate;
f. that the license contains other purchase obligations.[153]

The license recordal and vetting provisions have the potential to be extremely bureaucratic and a disincentive to business. Firstly, the parties must sign the license before a notary. That very often means that both parties must be in one place to go before the notary together. Once the notarized copy of the license is filed with the Department for recordal, the Department may request amendments. The parties may not be happy with what the Department wants and will have to negotiate a compromise or appeal to the committee against the decision.[154] If amendments are ultimately agreed, the parties may need to go back to the notary to execute a new version of the license. Whilst all this is happening, the license has not come into effect despite what the parties might have agreed, and their commercial plans are on hold. The degree to which the provisions are not consistent with commercial realities probably results in them being ignored more often than complied with.

Mortgages

Patents may be mortgaged as security for debts. However, the mortgage cannot be used as evidence "against others" until it has been recorded and published in the JOURNAL.[155] Mortgages are not expressly stated to be subject to Departmental vetting (as are assignments). However, if they are considered to be "ownership transfer agreements" then the vetting procedures and various grounds for rejection of a recordal application will apply.[156]

---

153. PDR 1993, article 43. This is a summary only. See the article for details.
154. PDR 1993, article 43 referring to and applying article 23.
155. PDL 2002, articles 21 and 22; PDR 1993, articles 31 and 33.
156. PDR 1993, article 51 referring to and applying articles 42 and 43.

Lender Attachments

Lenders may attach patents and have them sold at auction. The procedures for such attachments are set out in the Civil Procedures law. The lender must declare the attachment to the Department, as well as the price realized for the patent at auction. Until the attachment and realized price have been published in the JOURNAL, they are "not to have an effect on others."[157] How an auction result could not be effective until published is not clear.

Corrections and Amendments

The PDL 2002 does not contain any provisions for the amendment of patent applications. The PDR 1993 provides that the applicant may request a correction of written or calculation errors in the application or description. Amendments can also be made to the information in the application, including the description and the drawings. However, it seems that for this kind of alteration reasons need to be given and the amendment must not result in an "essential change" to what was filed.[158] There are no provisions in the law or regulations for the amendment or corrections of granted patents.

Improvements

Improvements, changes, or additions to an invention that have occurred after it was filed (or protected) may be the subject of an application for additional protection. It seems that the application for additional protection does not ordinarily result in an independent patent because the applicant may seek to transform the application into an independent patent before grant.

As at what date is the additional protection application to be assessed? The relevant provision reads: "The application for additional protection is subject to the same conditions that the original protection application was subject to." It remains unclear whether improvements must be novel, for example, as at the date of the original application or the date of the application for additional protection.[159] Article 38 of the PDR 1993 says that the regulations relating to filing, examination, and determination of applications apply to patents addition.

---

157. PDL 2002, article 23.
158. PDR 1993, article 21.
159. *See* article 36 of the PDL 2002.

Compulsory Licenses

There are extensive provisions in the PDL 2002 concerning compulsory licenses of patents and utility certificates.[160] The comments here do not seek to summarize the detail of those provisions but instead give a sketch of their main features.

A compulsory license may be granted in two different circumstances:

1. if the patentee has not exploited the invention sufficiently.[161]
2. if a patentee cannot exploit the patented invention without prejudice to patent rights previously granted.[162]

The "Insufficient Exploitation" Basis

To have a compulsory license granted on the basis of insufficient exploitation of the patent, the eight criteria set out in article 24 of the PDL 2002 must be satisfied, including that the applicant for the license must have made efforts to obtain a license from the patentee on reasonable terms. The threat of an application for this type of compulsory license could be used as leverage by a possible licensee in negotiations with the patentee for a license. Those negotiations may, in some cases, arise as a result of a patentee's allegation of infringement. The compulsory license therefore has a possible role in litigation.

The public policy purpose of the compulsory license is to encourage the inward flow of technology, or at least remove obstacles to it. The provisions are also designed to prevent foreign patentees from using the patent law to maintain the UAE as an import market only for their patented products. Although importation is one of the rights of the patentee, the fact that the patentee is importing the patented product is not sufficient to fend off an application for a compulsory license.[163] The patentee must do more than that with the patented rights in the UAE.

How is such a license obtained? Article 24 of the PDL 2002 says that the request for such a license is to be made in accordance with the procedures in article 30. But article 30 does not contain any application procedures. They are in article 28, which provides that an application for a compulsory license may be filed with the competent court. The Minister is also empowered to grant compulsory licenses, but only if the invention is important to the

---

160. PDL 2002, articles 24 to 32.
161. PDL 2002, article 24.
162. PDL 2002, article 30.
163. PDL 2002, article 24.2.

public interest.[164] In this case, the requirements that three years has passed since the granting of the patent and the applicant has attempted to negotiate a license on reasonable terms do not apply. The Minister's decision can be appealed.[165]

The "Prejudice to Prior Rights" Basis

If an invention serves different industrial purposes from a prior patented invention, or the later invention represents an obvious technical advancement of it, and despite these differences the second patentee cannot exploit the invention without prejudice to the rights of the earlier patentee, the second patentee may be granted a compulsory license to the extent necessary to exploit the invention.[166] The only other condition for the license is that it not be unconditional.[167] The relevant provision goes on to weaken the patentee's rights further. If the later invention serves the same industrial purpose, a compulsory license may be granted to the later patentee (being in effect a permission to infringe), provided that the earlier patentee is given a license for the later patent if he requests.[168]

There is some opportunity here for sophisticated patent infringers to construct the circumstances in which they could obtain a compulsory license of technology that would otherwise be unavailable to them. There may be cases where a careful study of the prior art, including the prior granted patent (that the infringer wants to exploit), will enable the writing of a patent application for "an obvious technical advancement" of the prior patented technology. The granting of that patent (assuming it must and does satisfy all other requirements) will then trigger the opportunity to obtain a compulsory license and exploit the technology of the prior patent.

What is unclear in the provisions is who may grant such a compulsory license. The provisions are written in the passive voice and no granting authority is mentioned. There are two possibilities: the court and the Minister. It appears that it is the court that has the general jurisdiction in relation to compulsory licenses. The Minister's jurisdiction appears to be limited to cases in which the invention is important to the public interest.[169]

---

164. PDL 2002, article 29.1.
165. PDL 2002, article 29.2.
166. PDL 2002, article 30.1.
167. PDL 2002, article 30.1 referring to article 24.1(c).
168. PDL 2002, article 30.2.
169. PDL 2002, article 29.1.

Cancellation of a Patent or Utility Certificate

The provisions in the PDL 2002 relating to the cancellation of a patent are very limited. The substantive points are:

(a) a person may apply to the court requesting cancellation of a patent or utility certificate;[170]

(b) the cancellation may be of part of the patent or certificate only;[171]

(c) any cancellation is effective from the date of grant (not filing).[172]

There are no substantive provisions relating to the grounds of cancellation, although there is mention of possible grounds in a provision specifying who must be notified of the cancellation proceedings. The patentee, the Department, and any person with a right relating to the patent must be notified if the cancellation is on the grounds that it was granted without satisfying the required conditions, or it was granted without taking into account relevant priority claims.[173]

Arguably, an application for the cancellation of a patent may be made on any reasonable grounds. Most of those are likely to be grounds that it needed to satisfy in order to be granted.

Misappropriating an Invention

If a person suffers damage as a result of the essential elements of that person's invention having been taken and put into an application for protection, that person may request the transfer of the application or granted patent or utility certificate to himself.[174] This provision stands alone without any apparatus for implementation. It is therefore not possible to say whether the request referred to may be made to the Ministry or the grievances committee or the court. It would be surprising if the Ministry would entertain such a serious application, requiring as it would the production of evidence of misappropriation and analysis of the invention the subject of the claim. It should be kept in mind by the parties to patent litigation. Its terms are broad and have the potential for defensive use.

---

170. PDL 2002, article 34 [A].
171. PDL 2002, article 34 [C].
172. PDL 2002, article 35.
173. PDL 2002, article 34 [B].
174. PDL 2002, article 8.

Criminal Offenses and Patent Infringement

The PDL 2002 does not contain a convenient list of elements that are to be satisfied to establish patent infringement (such as section 60 of the UK Patents Act 1977). Indeed, there is no section in the law on the subject of infringement *per se*. The structure of the protection granted by the law first gives rights to the patentee[175] and then criminalizes the infringement of those rights, as well as other acts.[176] The patentee's right to take civil action is expressed through provisions dealing with precautionary measures and orders for confiscation (discussed below).

The criminalized acts are as follows:

a. filing a false or forge document to obtain a patent, utility certificate, know-how or industrial drawing or design registration;
b. declaring information that is false to obtain a patent, utility certificate, know-how or industrial drawing or design registration;
c. copying an invention or method of manufacture or element of know-how;
d. intentionally infringing any right protected by this law.

Each of these is discussed below.

Fraud in Obtaining a Patent, etc., and Declaring False Information

The crime of filing documents that are forged (item a above) or the declaring of information that is false in order to obtain a patent or utility certificate (item b above) is not stated to require the intention of the defendant, as it does for the infringement of rights. The application of these provisions is potentially very broad, applying to agents as well as principals, and whether or not the documents were prepared by the person filing them or the information was generated by the person declaring it. That the falsity might have been created by an error seems to be irrelevant.

Copying an Invention, etc.

The concept of "copying" (item c above) does not fit well with that of an "invention," which one usually practices, uses, or exploits. The same applies to methods of manufacture. Copying an element of know-how might mean copying a document containing know-how that one has been given access

---

175. PDL 2002, article 15.
176. PDL 2002, article 62.

to on terms and doing so without the owner's permission. Perhaps a broad interpretation can be given to the provision, understanding "copying" to mean any embodiment of the invention in the form of a product or the use of a method or of know-how to produce a product. But characterized this way, the offense becomes the same as the next—infringing rights protected by the law. The difference between the two offenses would then only be that the infringement of rights must be intentional. A narrower interpretation needs to be found to prevent the copying offense subsuming the infringement offense.

Intentionally Infringing a Protected Right

Article 15 of the PDL 2002 sets out the rights of the patentee. In summary, those rights are the right to exploit the invention the subject of the patent and the right to prevent others from performing unauthorized acts of exploitation. The infringing acts (item d above) that are offenses under article 62 of the PDL 2002 are therefore:

(1) In relation to a product patent:
    a. to manufacture the product
    b. to use the product
    c. to offer the product for sale
    d. to sell the product
    e. to import the product for any of the above purposes
(2) In the case of a process or method patent:
    a. to use the process or method
    b. to use the product that is obtained directly by means of the process or method
    c. to offer for sale the product that is obtained directly by means of the process or method
    d. to sell the product that is obtained directly by means of the process or method
    e. to import for any of these purposes the product that is obtained directly by means of the process or method

The rights of registered design owners are set out in 51 of the PDL 2002. Those rights are rights of prevention only:

a. the right to prevent others from using the industrial drawing or design in the production of any product; and
b. the right to prevent others from importing any product related to the industrial drawing or design, or possessing it with the purpose of using it or offering it for sale or selling it.

It is difficult to see how, conceptually, a right of prevention could be infringed. One must therefore interpret that the rights of prevention were intended also to be exclusive positive rights in order for unauthorized acts in relation to industrial drawings and designs to be criminalized.

But there are other rights that are, in one way or another, protected by the PDL 2002. These include:

a. the inventor's right to the invention[177]
b. the inventor's right to be named as the inventor in the patent[178]
c. the patentee's right to fair compensation for the grant of a compulsory license[179]
d. the know-how owner's rights[180]
e. the licensee's rights[181]

It is not known whether the drafters of the law intended each of these protected rights to fall under the criminal provisions.

To establish an offense, the court must find that the infringement of the right was intentional. This should probably be interpreted to mean that the act was done knowing that it was an infringement of a right, and not to mean that the act itself was done intentionally (as opposed to accidently). On this view, ignorance of the wrongdoing, in infringements of industrial property rights, would be an adequate defense. For example, an importer who brings into the UAE patent infringing products but did not know they were infringing would not have committed an offense and would bear no criminal liability. Nevertheless, the importer has infringed the patentee's rights under article 15 of the PDL 2002 for which the patentee may commence an action for precautionary measures and seeking final remedies (see the discussion below).

If an offense is proved, the defendant may be liable to imprisonment and a fine of not less than 5000 dirhams (approximately US$1360) and not more than 100,000 dirhams (approximately US$27,200), or either one of them.

Precautionary Measures

A right holder, or a transferee of a right under the law, may seek from the court a precautionary attachment order against "an invention or industrial drawing or design or a business or part of it that is using or exploiting any

---

177. PDL 2002, article 7.
178. PDL 2002, article 10.
179. PDL 2002, article 24 (f).
180. PDL 2002, article 39.
181. PDL 2002, article 57.

kind of industrial property referred to." The application may be made if an infringement occurs or in the event of an unlawful act contravening the law or contracts or licenses granted pursuant to it.[182] Such applications are made *ex parte* to the urgent matters judge.

Who Can Apply for Precautionary Measures?

It appears to be clear that precautionary measures are available to licensees of rights as well as the rights holder. This is an interpretation of the reference to the transferee of some or all rights. It is confirmed by the availability of precautionary measures for infringements of the terms of contracts and licenses. However, reading article 57 [2], the licensee's right to commence infringement proceedings is limited to cases in which the rights holder fails to do so (see the discussion in the section on licenses).

What Events Make Precautionary Measures Available?

The reference to an act of infringement in article 60 of the PDL 2002 should probably be read as an infringement of the patentee's rights. "Unlawful events contravening the law" is probably a reference to infringement of the other miscellaneous rights given by the law (some of which are listed above in the section on infringement). There are various other obligations under the law but it is difficult to see how precautionary measures would be relevant to their "contravention." More interesting perhaps is that precautionary measures are available for contraventions of contracts and licenses. For example, if a licensee has contracted to make one thousand items of a patented product and makes twelve hundred, the extra two hundred items are in contravention of the license and the licensor may seek to attach them. The reference to contracts may be a reference to know-how contracts but know-how is not mentioned in the list of items that the order can be made against (see below). If the contract or license has not been recorded as required, it may not be able to be relied upon in any proceedings.

Against What May the Order Be Made?

A precautionary attachment order may be made against:

a. an invention
b. an industrial drawing or design
c. a business or the part of it using or exploiting the industrial property referred to

---

182. PDL 2002, article 60.

An infringement of the patent for a product, for example, would be the making of an unlicensed product that embodies the patented invention. This must be what is intended by the language of article 60, despite the absence of any mention of products or objects. The availability of orders to attach a business or part of it gives the court wider powers to cause the cessation of business activity and preserve the status quo as well as evidence, particularly in cases of the unlawful use of know-how. The power is consistent with the right of the court to order the confiscation of instruments and tools used in counterfeiting.[183]

Applications for a Deed of Protection

"What applies to the Deed of Protection in this regard also applies to applications for a Deed of Protection." This is the last sentence of article 60 of the PDL 2002. It suggests that a patent or design registration need not yet have been granted in order for the court to order a precautionary attachment. It is difficult to imagine that the court would grant an attachment order based on an application for a patent (even if, in some circumstances—such as where the patent has been granted in many other countries—it might be reasonable to do so). An English translation made available by the Ministry of Finance and Industry omits the sentence entirely.

Conditions for Granting and Maintaining a Precautionary Attachment Order

The applicant for a precautionary attachment order must deposit a security as assessed by the court before the order is issued and must file the substantive case for final relief within eight days of the issue of the order of the court.[184] (See the corresponding section in the trademarks chapter concerning some of the procedural issues).

Other Court Orders

The initial consideration in relation to the provisions of article 63 is whether the powers it gives to the court are in relation to criminal matters only or to both criminal and civil matters. On the one hand, it follows directly after the article concerning penalties and speaks of judgments of innocence,

---

183. PDL 2002, article 63 [1].
184. PDL 2002, article 61.

not something relevant to civil matters. On the other hand, there are no pro-visions in the PDL 2002 dealing with the orders that the court may make in civil cases (other than the precautionary measures provisions) and it speaks of the confiscation of attached items (which may be but is not necessarily a reference to precautionary attachment orders). It may well be a mix of the two, giving the judge the discretion to order what is suitable to the nature of the case before the court.

Injunctions

The most obvious omission from the list of what the court can order is an injunction—an order that the defendant cease doing the infringing acts. The court may order confiscation of attached or to-be-attached items and their destruction. It may also order the removal of "the effects of an action convening the law."[185] What circumstances this language was intended to address is open to interpretation. It is tempting to try to read into it an author-ity for the court to order a stop to contravening or infringing activity, but the words used do not support such an interpretation. Injunctive orders are vital tools in the fight against intellectual property infringements. Without them, infringers are able to continue infringing despite an attachment order. If an infringer buys new equipment or new stock of the infringing product the day after an attachment has been put on existing equipment and stock, the right holder must make another attachment application and begin the process again.[186] In trademark cases, the courts have made injunctive orders despite the absence of an express right to do so in the trademark law (see the section on injunctions in the trademarks chapter).

Also within the court's powers are orders for the confiscating of instru-ments and tools used in the "counterfeiting" ("tazweer" in Arabic). It is not clear that an infringement of a patent is always an act of counterfeiting, despite the language used. The intention was probably to refer to instruments and tools used in acts of contravention or infringement (consistent with the other language of the provisions).

These orders may be made in the case of a judgment of innocence. This is an important provision because without it the court could not make relevant orders in cases of infringement which do not satisfy all the elements of a criminal offence.

---

185. PDL 2002, article 63.
186. I have seen a defendant continue to deal in infringing products at the same time as an attachment was being placed on the known infringing products.

The Right to Claim Damages

A significant omission from the PDL 2002 is any entitlement of the right holder to sue for damages for infringement. The plaintiff must resort to other laws, such as the commercial transactions law, for a right to seek compensation.[187]

Defenses to Infringement

Although the PDL 2002 gives rights to patentees to prevent certain acts from being done without a license, those acts can be done without a license if they are for non-commercial or non-industrial purposes.[188] The rights granted by a patent do not apply to acts done for scientific research purposes.[189] These "defenses" are not expressed to be available in relation to infringements of utility certificates or industrial drawings or designs.[190]

Good faith acts done by a person in the UAE prior to the filing date or priority date of a patent or utility certificate, and that subsequently constitute an infringement, may give rise to a personal non-transferable right to continue to do those acts.[191] For example, if products were produced prior to the filing date of a patent and at that time it was not an infringement to produce them, but subsequently it became an infringement to offer them for sale, the defendant may be able to rely on this provision to fend off the patentee's attempt to stop their sale. Those prior acts may also be relevant to the novelty of the invention and could be raised in a challenge to the validity of the patent.

Customs

There are no provisions in the PDL 2002 and the PDR 1993 that deal with Customs or border control (unlike the ARL 2002). This is despite rights holders having rights to prevent importation of infringing products under the PDL 2002. There are presently no published procedures for the seizure of patent or registered design infringing products by Customs. Rights holders must seek an order from the court under the precautionary measures provisions if they wish to seize products at the ports. However, precautionary measures applications take time to prepare and orders take time to serve

---

187. Federal law no. 5 of 1985 in relation to civil transactions, article 282.
188. PDL 2002, article 15.2.
189. PDL 2002, article 19.1.
190. In relation to industrial drawings and designs, the deeming provisions of article 53 to do not extend to articles 15 and 19.
191. PDL 2002, article 17. In relation to designs, *see* article 52.

and be acted upon. They may not be the best mechanism for dealing with the impending arrival of a container of infringing products and ensuring it is not released from Customs' control.[192]

The Committee

The PDL 2002 provides for the formation of a committee whose role is to determine grievances filed by those concerned with decisions issued in relation to the application of the law and regulations.[193]

The committee is to be made up of:

a. a judge
b. two experts in the field of industrial property rights who are not employees of the department
c. a secretary[194]

Unlike the committee formed under article 13 of the TML 1992A (which has two members from the Ministry), this committee appears to be more independent of the Ministry whose decision is under review. The decisions of the committee can be appealed to the competent court within thirty days of being notified of it.[195]

The PDR 1993 contains extensive provisions regulating the procedures of the committee, including provisions relating to the form of petitions and replies, the secretary's role, hearings, experts, suspension of proceedings, and how decisions are to be made and served.[196]

1.2 Industrial Drawings and Designs

Introduction

Sources of the UAE's Industrial Drawings and Designs Law

The UAE's industrial drawings and design law is part of the PDL 2002. However, identifying precisely what the law of designs is within the PDL 2002 is no easy task. First, some of the PDL 2002 provisions have general

---

192. *See also* the discussion on Customs in the trademarks chapter.
193. PDL 2002, article 66.2.
194. PDL 2002, article 66.1.
195. PDL 2002, article 67.
196. PDR 1993, articles 68 to 87.

application, not specifically mentioning industrial drawings and designs. Secondly, there are some provisions that deal specifically with designs. Thirdly, there are some provisions that, although written for patents, are deemed by other provisions to apply to designs. And lastly, the same three scenarios are repeated in the PDR 1993 (that is, there are general provisions, specific provisions, and deeming provisions). In some cases, the PDR 1993 provisions add important elements to provisions to the PDL 2002 and in other cases they cut across or repeat provisions in the PDL 2002. The result is a complex web requiring careful negotiation. The commentary in this section is therefore somewhat like a map of the relevant provisions, showing how they are related, and in many cases referring the reader back to the commentary in the patent section.

The Dubai International Financial Center (DIFC) has published a draft patent law to apply within the jurisdictions of the DIFC that contains provisions dealing with industrial drawings. There may also be moves within the Ministry to issue a new patent and designs law.[197]

International Conventions

The UAE has a number of obligations under international intellectual property conventions in relation to designs. Under the Paris Convention, it has obligations in relation to reciprocal treatment,[198] the right to claim priority from an earlier filed design application,[199] payments for the maintenance of rights,[200] the obligation to provide protection for designs[201] and the temporary protection for inventions.[202]

The Berne Convention allows the countries of the Union to determine the extent of the application of their laws to works of applied art and industrial designs and models and the conditions under which that protection is granted.[203]

The UAE became a member of the World Trade Organization in 1996 and in doing so committed to bring its intellectual property laws in line with the TRIPs Agreement. The deadline to comply was January 1, 2000. The PDL 2002 was intended to be TRIPs compliant.[204] It is an obligation for members to provide for the protection of designs.[205]

---

197. The subject received some brief television coverage in late January 2009.
198. Paris, articles 2 and 3.
199. Paris, article 4.
200. Paris, article 5bis.
201. Paris, article 5quinquies.
202. Paris, article 11.
203. Berne Convention, article 2.7.
204. WTO, Council for Trade-Related Aspects of Intellectual Property Rights, Legislation Review, United Arab Emirates, report of meeting June 18–22, 2001, Introductory Statement.
205. TRIPs Agreement, article 25.

Government Authorities Dealing with Designs

The government authority dealing with industrial designs is the same as that dealing with patents: the Ministry of Economy. See the comments in the patents section above.

Designs Statistics

The first publication of a design application in the UAE was application no. 10/1998. It was filed on February 26, 1998 and published in the OFFICIAL GAZETTE no. 478 of March 31, 2008, along with sixty other design applications filed between 1998 and 2000. This same group of design applications was published again in the INDUSTRIAL PROPERTY JOURNAL no. 1 for March 2008.[206] The PDL 2002 provides that the granting of an industrial drawing or design is to be published in the JOURNAL (rather than the OFFICIAL GAZETTE) and that it should be published with the drawing or design.[207] The information published in the OFFICIAL GAZETTE included the application number and the filing date, nothing more. This may be the reason for the double publication.

In neither publication is the expiry date of these designs mentioned. If they were registered under the PDL 2002 with a ten-year term of protection from the filing date, then application no. 10/1998 had already expired at the time that it was published (as had three others published at the same time: 16/1998, 18/1998 and 19/1998). However, under the PDL 1992, designs were to be registered for five years from the filing date with the possibility of two further five-year periods. It is not apparent from the publications which protection term was applied (but see the section below on term of protection).

The following is a summary of the numbers of design applications published as accepted and as lapsed:

INDUSTRIAL PROPERTY JOURNAL number and date	Number designs published as accepted	Number of designs published as lapsed
No. 1, March 2008	60	326
No. 2, April 2008	57	182
No. 3, May 2008	82	132
No. 4, June 2008	153	153
No. 5, July 2008	85	50
No. 6, August 2008	101	55
Totals	538	898

---

206. The Journals are not being printed with a precise date.
207. PDL 2002, article 48.

Design application filing statistics available from the Ministry are as follows:[208]

Year	Number of design applications filed
2001	115
2002	125
2003	215
2004	304
2005	387
Total design applications filed from 2001 to 2005	1146

What Is an Industrial Drawing or Design?

The PDL 1992 contained a definition of "industrial design" only. In the PDL 2002 the definition was divided into two: one for industrial drawings and one for industrial designs.[209]

> Industrial drawing: Any creative composition of lines or colours that has a special appearance and that can be used for an industrial or handicraft product.
> Industrial design: Any creative bodily form that has a special appearance and that can be used for an industrial or handicraft product.

The principal difference between the old and the new law was the introduction of the word "creative," which was absent from the old law. Both industrial drawings and designs must now be "creative." Both industrial drawings and designs must have a special appearance and must be able to be used for industrial or handicraft purposes.[210]

"Creative or New"

The "creative" requirement in the definitions of industrial drawings and designs appears to be in conflict with article 47 of the PDL 2002, which says that an industrial drawing or design must be "creative *or* new."[211]

---

208. These numbers are from a document prepared by the Ministry of Economy titled "World Intellectual Property Day" dated April 22, 2007. Thanks to the Brand Owners' Protection Group for giving me a copy (*see* http://www.gulfbpg.com).
209. The TRIPs Agreement does not mention industrial drawings, only designs.
210. PDL 2002, article 1.
211. The language that is in the TRIPs Agreement, article 25, is "New or original."

The directions in the regulations require the examination process to determine whether the industrial drawing or design is "new or creative" and a definition is given of what this means:

> For an industrial drawing or design to be new or creative, it must not have been disclosed to the public at any time or place by any means of publication or use or any other means of knowing the industrial drawing or design, prior to filing the application or the priority date claimed. . . .[212]

This paragraph suggests that the "new or creative" means nothing over and above the absence of prior use or publication. It does not appear to add a requirement for a level of creativity or other effort. This is consistent with the TRIPs Agreement:

> Members may provide that designs are not new or original if they do not significantly differ from known designs or combinations of known design features.[213]

There is no mention of the need to take into account technical or functional considerations. The TRIPs Agreement makes this optional: "Members may provide that such protection shall not extend to designs dictated essentially by technical or functional considerations."[214]

The PDR 1993 provision quoted above expresses a very high level of novelty for designs, not permitting any disclosure to the public at any time or place by any means prior to the priority date. It does not mention whether designs are specific to products and whether the disclosure of a design in relation to one kind of product might destroy its novelty in relation to another kind of product. For example, it may not be novel to apply the shape of a space rocket to a pencil, but it might never have been applied to an electric shaver. Does its disclosure as a pencil make it not novel in relation to electric shavers? Indeed, the design may have been first disclosed as a space rocket. Would that have destroyed its novelty in relation to pencils and electric shavers?

Article 51 [B] of the PDL 2002 adds another level to the analysis:

> The acts referred to [i.e., acts of infringement] cannot be made lawful simply by a difference in the domain for which the industrial drawing or design is legally protected or it being related to a product that is different from the industrial drawing or design contained in the Deed of Protection.

---

212. PDR 1993, article 48.4.
213. TRIPs Agreement, article 25.
214. TRIPs Agreement, article 25.

This provision suggests that designs, although registered for a particular product, are protected in relation to all possible products. Such broad protection could only be justified, and indeed work as a practical matter, if the level of novelty required is absolute in the sense that the design must not have been published anywhere before the priority date in relation to any kind of product. The space rocket design, once used as a space rocket, will not be novel and not be protectable in relation to pencils and electric shavers once it has been disclosed (although its application to those specific products is "novel").

Use as an Industrial or Handicraft Product

The requirement for the drawing or design to be able to be used for an industrial or handicraft product appears in the definitions of industrial drawings and designs and is repeated in article 47 of the PDL 2002 and article 48.4 of the PDR 1993. Requiring that a design be able to be used for a product is understandable because the definition of a design requires it to have a bodily or three-dimensional character. However, in relation to drawings, the requirement has the potential to limit the kind of drawings that can be protected either to drawings of products (in which case they are no different from designs) or to drawings of ornamentation or decoration that can be used on products. Such drawings of ornamentation or decoration could be depicted without depicting the product itself and could therefore be applied to *any* industrial or handicraft product. It is difficult to imagine a drawing that could not be used for or on a product. The "use" requirement is relation to industrial drawings appears not to have any real content.

Not Contravening Public Order or Morals

The requirement for designs not to contravene public order or morals in article 47 of the PDL 2002 is a reflection of the same obligation in relation to patents in article 6.1.e. The general issue is discussed in the patents section and the trademarks chapter.

Creators

The PDL 2002 provisions concerning industrial drawings and designs do not mention the "type" of person who is the creator of the drawing or the design. No inventiveness is required so it is probably not appropriate to call the creator an inventor. That person could be called an author, as in an author of an applied work under the UAE's author's rights law (ARL 2002). To try to avoid leaning in one direction or another, in this commentary I use, to the extent that a term is needed, the word "creator" for the person who makes an industrial drawing or design.

Employee Creators and Contractors

Article 53 of the PDL 2002 applies article 9 concerning inventions made by employees to industrial drawings and designs. Article 9 is discussed in the patents section above. Presumably references to "the inventor" are to be replaced with references to the creator, "the invention" with references to industrial drawings and designs, and so on to the extent necessary.

Ownership and the First to File Principle

Article 53 of the PDL 2002 applies article 7 to industrial drawings and designs. The creator of an industrial drawing or design has the right to it (if he or she is not an employee or commissioned).[215] The creator is also the author for the purposes of the author's rights law and will have the rights granted to authors pursuant to the ARL 2002.

The person who files an application for an industrial drawing or design, or who has the earlier priority date, has the right to registration, but this is subject to an employer or commissioner not having a right to it, the drawing or design not having been misappropriated within the terms of article 8 of the PDL 2002, and the other conditions for obtaining registration being satisfied.[216] The owner of the right in the industrial drawing or design must be the applicant for registration.[217] There are potentially complex issues underlying these provisions. For example, two substantially similar industrial designs may be created by two different creators and each will have independent author's rights in them. The first to file will be entitled to the design registration, but the other will be entitled to reproduce the design pursuant to the author's rights law. Those reproductions may well be an infringement of the design registration even though made pursuant to a legitimate right. See the discussion below on the design copyright overlap issue.

---

215. PDL 2002, article 7.1
216. PDL 2002, article 7.2.
217. PDR 1993, article 48.2.

Joint Owners

Article 53 of the PDL 2002 applies paragraph 2 of article 7.1, concerning shared creation, and article 20, concerning joint ownership, to industrial drawings and designs. These subjects are discussed in the patents section above.

Filing a Design Application

There is no express statement in the PDL 2002 of the right to file an application for an industrial drawing or design. This is perhaps because there is no protection for industrial drawings and designs unless they are registered[218] and therefore it is not so much a right to obtain a registration as a necessity if one wants protection for it (but see the discussion below on the design copyright overlap issue).

The PDR 1993 sets out in some detail the formal requirements for industrial drawing and design applications.[219] Some of these requirements no longer apply (such as the letter from the Israeli Boycott Office). It is prudent to check on current procedures at the Ministry before taking any steps. The key documents for the filing of a UAE design application are: a power of attorney, an assignment from the creator of the design to the applicant, and a commercial extract for the applicant. Each of these must be notarized and legalized up to the UAE Embassy.

Priority Claims

Article 46 of the PDL applies article 11 concerning priority claims to industrial drawings and designs. Priority claims are discussed in the patents section above. The key difference is that the priority period for industrial drawings and designs is 6 months, not 12 months as it is for patents.[220] The examination of priority claims is mentioned in article 48.5 of the PDR 1993.

Examination of Design Applications

Article 48 of the PDR sets out the matters that are to be determined in the examination of an industrial drawing or design application. The requirements

---

218. PDL 2002, article 44.
219. PDR 1993, articles 45, 46, and 47.
220. PDL 2002, article 46.2.

incorporate the formal matters referred to in articles 45, 46, and 47 of the PDR 1993, as well as the procedures for the rectification of defects and substantive examination in articles 92 and 93 of the PDR 1993. The right to reject an application for registration is found in article 23 of the PDR 1993 and is applicable by virtue of article 49. The Department must issue a reasoned decision.

Appealing Examination Decisions

The right to appeal decisions to reject patent and utility certificate applications is found in article 12 [2] of the PDL 2002. However, there is nothing that brings such decisions in relation to industrial drawings and designs under this provision. Article 49 of the PDR 1993, however, applies article 23 to industrial drawings and designs. The applicant has sixty days from being notified of the decision to appeal to the committee. Decisions of the committee may be appealed to the competent court within thirty days of notice of the decision.[221]

Publication

The provision in article 13 of the PDL 2002 relating to publication does not seem to apply to industrial drawings and designs. By virtue only of article 49 of the PDR 1993 applying article 24 to industrial drawings and designs, the decision to grant an application is to be published in the OFFICIAL GAZETTE (now in the JOURNAL).

Opposition

The right to oppose an application for the registration of an industrial drawing or design is found in article 7.3 of the PDL 2002 and applies to industrial drawings and designs by virtue of article 53. The right is repeated in article 48 [2] of the PDL 2002. The provision in article 13 of the PDL 2002 granting a sixty-day opposition period does not apply to industrial drawings and designs. The sixty-day opposition period is given in article 48 [2] of the PDL 2002 and repeated by virtue of the article 49 of the PDR 1993 applying article 24 to industrial drawings and designs.

---

221. PDL 2002, article 67.

Neither the law nor the regulations addresses the question of grounds of opposition. However, they are likely to be any of the issues that could have been raised in the process of examination. No oppositions to the design applications published in 2008 have been reported.

The Term of Protection

The term of protection for industrial drawings and designs is ten years from the filing date in the UAE.[222]

Under the PDL 1992, the term of protection was five years with the possibility of renewal for two further five-year periods.[223] For an industrial design application that was filed under the PDL 1992, it was necessary to pay the annuities and renew the application to keep it on foot, despite the fact that the application had not matured to registration at the time when the first renewal was due. The first published application (no. 10/1998) had not reached its first renewal date at the time of the introduction of the PDL 2002, and so it would make sense for it to be treated as having a ten-year term under the PDL 2002.

Annuities

The provisions of article 14 of the PDL 2002 concerning annuities apply to industrial drawings and designs. Article 49 of the PDR 1993 applies article 28 concerning the same subject to industrial drawings and designs. These articles are discussed above in the patents section.

Rights Granted by Registration

The rights of registered design owners are set out in article 51 of the PDL 2002. Those rights are rights of prevention only:

a. the right to prevent others from using the industrial drawing or design in the production of any product; and
b. the right to prevent others from importing any product related to the industrial drawing or design, or possessing it with the purpose of using it or offering it for sale or selling it.

---

222. PDL 2002, article 49.
223. PDL 1992, article 48.

Assignment

Article 18 of the PDL 2002 concerning assignments applies to industrial drawings and designs by virtue of article 53. Article 49 of the PDR 1993 applies article 29 and 30 on the same subject to industrial drawings and designs. These assignment provisions are discussed in the patents section.

Licenses

The provisions in the PDL 2002 concerning licenses are drafted in a general way so that they apply to all forms of protection provided by the PDL 2002. The relevant articles (articles 54 to 59) are discussed above in the patents section.

Mortgages

Article 49 of the PDR 1993 applies article 31.1 to industrial drawings and designs. This appears to be an internal referencing error and should have been a reference to article 31 (because there is no article 31.1 in the PDR 1993.) In short, mortgages of industrial drawings and designs are required to be registered and published.

It appears that the provisions in articles 21 and 22 of the PDL 2002 concerning mortgages do not apply to industrial drawings and designs.

Amending a Design Application

Article 49 of the PDR 1993 applies article 21 to industrial drawings and designs. This article is discussed in the patents section.

Divisional Applications

As with patents, there are no provisions permitting divisional applications, but unlike with patents, there is no treaty obligation to provide for divisional applications. Perhaps article 45 of the PDL 2002 is linked to the absence of provisions for divisional applications—it permits a single application to contain up to 20 industrial drawings or designs if they are connected as to manufacture or use.

Compulsory Licenses

Article 53 of the PDL 2002 applies articles 24 to 32 concerning compulsory licenses to industrial drawings and designs. Article 49 of the PDR 1993 applies articles 34 and 35 on the same subject to industrial drawings and designs. These provisions are discussed in the patents section. One key point of difference between patents and designs in relation to the compulsory licenses is that what is permitted by the Paris Convention is different. Article 5B of the Paris Convention reads:

> The protection of industrial designs shall not, under any circumstance, be subject to any forfeiture, either by reason of failure to work or by reason of the importation of articles corresponding to those which are protected.

One interpretation of this provision would preclude the granting of compulsory licenses (being a kind of forfeiture) on the basis of insufficient exploitation (failure to work).

Cancellation

Article 53 of the PDL 2002 applies article 33 to 35 concerning surrenders of rights and cancellations to industrial drawings and designs. Article 49 of the PDR 1993 applies articles 36 and 37 on the same subject to industrial drawings and designs. These provisions are discussed in the patents section.

Precautionary Measures

Precautionary measures are available in relation to the rights obtained by the registration of an industrial design or drawing because the provisions are drafted generally to give the right to seek such measures to the "owner of the deed of protection."[224] "Deed of protection" is defined to include documents evidencing protection granted to industrial drawings and designs.[225] The precautionary measures provisions are discussed in the section on patents.

Criminal Offenses in Relation to Designs

It is a criminal offense to infringe intentionally any right protected by the law.[226] As we have seen above, the registered design owner is given only rights

---

224. PDL 2002, articles 60 and 61.
225. PDL 2002, article 1.
226. PDL 2002, article 62.

to prevent certain acts. Strictly speaking, the right to prevent certain acts cannot be infringed. To create a criminal offense, one needs to interpret article 51 liberally so as to read into it the exclusive right to do the acts that the owner has the right to prevent.

Design Infringement

See the discussion in the patent section on court orders and damages.

Defenses to Infringement

See the discussion on this subject in the patent section above.

Overlap between Author's Rights and Designs

The first article of the section of the PDL 2002 dealing with designs addresses the subject of the potential overlap between the moral and artistic rights of the author or creator in an industrial drawing or design and the effect of the provisions in the PDL 2002 relating to them. It provides that none of the provisions in the PDL 2002 are to contravene the "moral and artistic rights" connected with industrial drawings and designs, whether the source of those rights is the UAE law or international conventions to which the UAE is a party.[227]

The reference in this provision to "moral and artistic rights" is surely a reference to the rights given to authors under laws and conventions giving authors rights in their works (such as the ARL 2002). That the provisions of this law, the PDL 2002, are "not to contravene" those rights probably means that those rights are not affected by whatever is done or not done under the PDL 2002. For example, the registration of a drawing or design, or the failure to do so, should have no impact on the rights that the author or creator has under the ARL 2002 or relevant international conventions. The result must be then that an author who registers a product design under the PDL 2002 will have the rights that result from registration as well as the author's rights in the drawings for the design and in any three-dimensional models made. The design registration rights will expire after ten years but the author's financial rights will continue in the drawings for fifty years after the death of the author. To the extent that there are "applied works of art," the rights in them will expire twenty-five years after the year of first publication.[228]

---

227. PDL 2002, article 43.
228. ARL 2002, article 20.

There are potentially many other differences including what acts constitute infringement, and how the rights can be challenged, assigned, licensed, and so on.

However, the provision preserving the moral and artistic rights is immediately followed by:

> Industrial drawings and designs do not enjoy the protection established by this law unless registered in the special register at the Department.[229]

This provision appears to deny any rights in industrial drawings and designs unless they are registered, in which case the rights are those given by registration. It is tempting to try to reconcile this provision with article 43 discussed above by placing the emphasis on the word "industrial." The challenge is to distinguish industrial rights from moral and artistic rights. For example, author's rights would in principle subsist in a sculpture of a race horse. The same design could be registered as an industrial design (for example, as a children's toy). Applying article 44 of the PDL 2002, one might say that there are no industrial rights in the design until registered as an *industrial* design. The difficulty is that the author is entitled, under the ARL 2002, to license the reproduction of the design. Is there a point at which it becomes an industrial design as opposed to an artistic one, and therefore a point at which the author must register the design as an industrial design? The law and regulations do not give us an answer to this question, with the result that it is unclear how articles 43 and 44 are to work and what creators of designs must do to protect certain of their creations.

We have seen other legislators try to drive a wedge between these two groups of concepts: what is artistic on the one hand and what is industrial on the other. The idea that a work is artistic if it is not reproduced many times, say less than fifty, but is an industrial work and loses copyright protection if it is industrially applied more than fifty times, has been tried in other countries. The use of an arbitrary number like fifty on the one hand gives some practical guidance to creators, but on the other hand is not adapted to accommodate the many circumstances in which designs are made and applied, whether industrially or artistically.

1.3 Know-How

Provisions relating to the protection of know-how appeared in the PDL 1992, with supporting regulations in the PDR 1993. The PDL 2002 contains

---

229. PDL 2002, article 44.

substantially the same provisions as those that were in the PDL 1992. Presumably the PDR 1993 provisions are still in force because they do not appear to contradict any of the know-how provisions in the PDL 2002.

What Is Know-How?

Know-how must be of a technical nature and result from the practice of a profession or trade. It must also be capable of practical application.[230] This definition makes it clear that the PDL 2002 is not introducing a general code for the protection of confidential information. The obligations and protections relating to know-how will not apply to personal confidential information or indeed information relating to business transactions (not being of a technical nature). Know-how is just what the name suggests— knowledge of how to do something (not knowledge of facts or information in itself).

Exclusivity

Know-how is not necessarily exclusive and the protections of the law are not directed at the granting or guaranteeing exclusivity (in the way that trademark law is, for example). Another person may develop the very same know-how independently and be entitled to use and deal with it as its owner.[231] The fact that more than one person legitimately holds the same know-how does not affect the rights of any of them to protect that know-how against others.

What Is Protected?

Only unlawful use, disclosure, and publication of know-how are prohibited by the PDL 2002.[232] Any of these acts done without the permission of the owner are deemed to be unlawful, but only if the person knew of their confidential nature or cannot deny that he or she knew (meaning presumably that in all the circumstances he or she should have known).[233]

---

230. PDL 2002, article 1.
231. PDL 2002, article 40.
232. PDL 2002, article 39.
233. PDL 2002, article 42.

Conditions for Protection

The owner of know-how can only benefit from the protection provisions of the law if the know-how has not been published or put at the disposal of the public and a range of measures have been implemented to preserve the confidentiality of the information.[234] Those measures are extensively listed in article 39 of the PDR 1993 and include requirements as to how documents are managed, how employees acquire the know-how, what employment contracts should contain, how visits to the place of work are managed as well as confidentiality provisions for agreements with contractors, assignees of the know-how and anyone who enters into negotiations concerning the transfer of the know-how.

Know-How Contracts

Contracts relating to know-how are extensively regulated. Any such contract must be in writing. It must contain the specific elements of the know-how and the purpose of its use and conditions for its transfer. Failing these requirements, the contract will be void.[235]

Know-how contracts (whether assignments or licenses) must be recorded with the Department of Industrial Property at the Ministry.[236] The Department has the right to check the contact and to require the parties to amend the terms of the contract "so as to realise the interests of the parties within the framework of the law and the economic interests of the State."[237] If the parties do not comply, the Department may refuse to record the contract in the know-how contracts register. The requirement to submit the contract for checking by the Department also applies to amendments and renewals of the contract.

There are many grounds on which the Department may reject an application to record a know-how contract, including:

a. that the contract relates to matters that a patent or utility certificate may not be granted for;
b. that the term of the contract is longer than the term for patent protection;
c. if the know-how is available locally;

---

234. PDL 2002, article 39.
235. PDL 2002, article 41.
236. PDR 1993, article 41.1.
237. PDR 1993, article 42.

d. that the contract contains restrictions on trade or research or production or pricing;

e. that the contract requires the return of the know-how documents;

f. that the price paid for the know-how is not proportionate to what is received; and

g. that the contract contains other purchase obligations.[238]

It is not clear from the specific provisions relating to know-how contracts what the consequences are of failing to record a know-how contract, or not being able to record a know-how contract because the Department has rejected the application for its recordal. It is clear that the applicant has a right of appeal to committee against the Department's decision within sixty days.[239] One would only appeal the rejection if recording the contract was obligatory or there was some benefit to the parties in doing so. The implication is the contract would be void or illegal in some sense because the parties to it had not satisfied the requirement for recordal.

Article 65 of the PDL 2002 requires the employees of the Department not to disclose the secrets of their work or make public data or information they obtained in the course of their work, or to use it for their or others' benefit. The submission of a know-how contract to the Department should not therefore be an act prejudicial to the confidentiality of the know-how.

1.4 Patent and Trademark Registration Agents

Introduction

Article 68 of the PDL 2002 says that the implementing regulations shall regulate the profession of registration agents. Presumably these are agents for the obtaining of patents and the registration of industrial drawings and designs, and not other kinds of industrial property such as trademarks. Trademark agents are now regulated by a 2005 Ministerial decision.[240] Indeed, as a matter of practice, there are two separate sets of procedures for becoming a registration agent under the PDL 2002 and a trademark registration agent. Not all trademark agents are registered as patent agents (and vice versa).

---

238. PDR 1993, article 43. This is a summary only. See the article for details.
239. PDR 1993, articles 43 and 23.
240. Ministerial decision no. 80 of 2005 in relation to trademark registration agents.

As directed by article 66 of the PDL 1992 (and the corresponding provision of the PDL 2002, article 68), the PDR 1993 contains provisions relating to the regulation of registration agents. The following is a summary of those provisions:

1. To be a registration agent it is necessary to be registered.[241]
2. Applicants for and owners of industrial property may not authorize any to act before the Department unless they are a registered agent.[242]
3. To become a registered agent, one must be: an Emirati, a national of an Arab state or a specialist company with a registered office in the UAE, of sound mind, of good reputation, and hold a university degree.[243]
4. A registration committee is to examine applications and decide on them. There is a right of appeal from rejections.[244]
5. Registration is for one year and is renewable.[245]
6. The agent must state his or her name and registration number in all correspondence and papers issued by him or her.[246]
7. The agent must perform his or her work according to the principles of the profession and the provisions of the law and regulations.[247]

The regulations relating to trademark agents generally follow the same lines as those for registration agents under the PDR 1993.[248]

The provisions summarized above mention the "principles of the profession." There is no professional body for patent agents in the UAE and no other organization that brings agents together as a group. In some other countries, there are such professional bodies. Their role is to set standards of practice and conduct, and often they are involved in educating and admitting new members to the profession and disciplining those who bring the profession into disrepute. The notable omission from the UAE regulations is any requirement for knowledge of patents or designs for Emirati and Arab nationals. Companies specializing in industrial property presumably will have people with relevant knowledge but it is not expressed as a requirement. Equally, there are no requirements for continuing education. Without a patent profession body with some powers to guide, regulate, and discipline, it is difficult to see how standards of education, ethics, and service for the "profession" will be developed and maintained.

---

241. PDR 1993, article 57.
242. PDR 1993, article 62.
243. PDR 1993, article 58.
244. PDR 1993, article 60.
245. PDR 1993, article 60.
246. PDR 1993, article 63.
247. PDR 1993, article 63.
248. For details, see ministerial decision no. 80 of 2005.

Complaints Against Agents

Importantly, both the PDR 1993 and the 2005 trademark agent regulations refer to the possibility of filing complaints against agents. In relation to trademark agents, a complaint can be filed and the Ministry may undertake an investigation as to the offense imputed to the agent.[249] Where an agent has been found to have failed to "comply with his duties," he or she may be warned, suspended from practicing for a period, or have his or her registration as an agent cancelled. Separately, the agent may bear civil and criminal liability.[250]

Under the PDR 1993, there is also a complaints procedure and the registration committee may undertake an investigation of an agent "if a contravention of the provisions of the law or these regulations or the principles of the profession has been attributed to him."[251] If the accusations are proved it seems that the committee must cancel the agent's registration and the agent may appeal to the grievances committee.[252]

Many questions remain unanswered as to what the principles of the profession are, what the duties of an agent are and indeed how an agent can contravene the law or regulations when it is very difficult to find any provisions that deal with principles and duties (mostly they deal with the formal requirements for becoming an agent). There is a need for greater clarity as to what the duties of an agent are to the state and to the client and what constitutes a breach of ethical and professional duties. A code of ethics for registration agents would address such matters. The following are some suggestions as to what a code of ethics might deal with.

Conflicts of Interest

Legal conflicts of interest are a continuing source of consternation for owners of intellectual property and their agents. There are diverse views on what constitutes a conflict of interest and how it should be handled. It should be the role of the profession, led by a professional body, to lay down the principles, educate members, and enforce compliance with the rules. The following points might be considered in any future discussion about conflicts of interest.

---

249. Ministerial decision no. 80 of 2005, article 16.
250. Ministerial decision no. 80 of 2005, article 15.
251. PDR 1993, article 64 [1].
252. PDR 1993, article 64 [2] and [3].

What Is a Conflict of Interest?

A conflict of interest arises:

(a) if an agent is acting for a client and is asked to act for another client whose interests in the specific matter in question conflict or are likely to conflict with those of the first client;

(b) if the agent holds confidential information obtained from one client and could only act in the best interests of another client by sharing that information and thereby breaching the agent's duty of confidence to the first client;

(c) if the agent is the address for service for a granted or pending patent, or trademark or design application or registration and the agent is asked to take some action adverse or potentially adverse to those specific rights.

What Is Not a Conflict of Interest?

A legal conflict of interest should be distinguished from a commercial conflict. To act for two clients who compete is not a legal conflict of interest. Of course, there may be a real possibility of a legal conflict arising. One or more of the clients may not be comfortable with common representation and may decide to change representation.

If the UAE agent is being instructed by a lawyer or agent and not directly by the ultimate client, perhaps other considerations arise (in some cases the agent may not know who the ultimate client is), but the general principles still should still apply.

When a matter is urgent, or it would harm the client's interests not to act, it may be necessary or unavoidable for the agent to continue to act temporarily. In such cases, temporary "Chinese walls" may assist in reducing any damage to the clients as a result of the conflict that has arisen.

How Should a Conflict Be Handled?

This will depend on the facts of each case. The result must be the removal of the conflict of interest, so whatever solution is considered, the agent must be able to say that, when the tests for what is a conflict are applied, there is no longer a conflict of interest. In some cases, the result may be that the agent cannot act for either client in relation to the specific matter. In other cases, the agent may simply not accept the new instructions to act. Of course, if the new instruction comes from a relationship client (a client who shares its confidential business information with the agent and for whom the agent is the agent of choice for all intellectual property work), that client may be unhappy with the rejection of the instruction and may want to know how a conflict is possible. Because a greater amount of confidential information is given to agents by relationship clients, the risk of a conflict is also greater. The scope of possible legal conflicts begins to come closer to the realm of commercial conflicts.

Systems for Conflict Checking

Conflicts can only be identified if agents have maintained proper and searchable client and matter records. It would be the role of a patent profession body to set standards for such matters.

Money Held on Trust

A further area that requires consideration by the profession and its clients is that of trust money. The agents very commonly bill clients in advance of payment of certain fees and as a consequence they hold that money on behalf of the client until such time as the fees must be paid. In some cases, that money may sit with the agent for more than a year. Presently there is no accountability in relation to money held on trust for clients. Agents are free to use that money as they wish and for any purpose until it must be disbursed and they may delay disbursing the money for its intended purpose where there is an opportunity for delay. It is likely that most agents do not account for it separately in their bookkeeping. That the money is money held in trust and that there is an ethical obligation over and above the basic obligation to use it eventually for its intended purpose are not widely adopted concepts.

Competition in the Profession

A well-known barrier to competition among agents in the UAE is the requirement to pay government fees in order to make a change of agent. To change the address for service for a trademark registration, the government fees are 750 dirhams (about US$205)—a 500 dirham publication fee and a 250 dirham service fee. In a system that does not have multiclass applications for trademarks, the fees can be considerable. The amount of procedure and paperwork required for such a simple matter is also a great hindrance and adds further costs. Pending applications are more easily transferred to another agent by filing a letter and a power of attorney. No fees are required.

The result is that portfolios are often not moved due to the costs and are left with the agent that filed them, even though the owner would like to consolidate the management of the portfolio with another agent. The owner will often not change the official records and simply instruct the new agent with any new work. More than one agent will hold a power of attorney to act for the client. There is a risk in some cases that one or more of the agents will be unclear as to the extent of their responsibilities.

Professional Duties

The discussion about the professional duties of intellectual property agents would benefit greatly from the input of a professional body or from judges, as has happened in other jurisdictions. A good example of the courts taking the lead in the discussion of professional duties is the judgment of Jacob J in the *Halifax case*,[253] which dealt with the negligence of a trademark attorney firm. Although the case is about trademarks, the principles apply more generally. The following are some "duties" mentioned in that judgment that might be discussed by any future UAE professional body.

1. Duty to provide comprehensive advice

    Where a trademark agent undertakes to pursue a trademark application for a client, then his duties to that client extend to advising in relation to all legal pitfalls reasonably connected with that application. . . . He is under a duty to keep his client informed of the legal problems which may arise.[254]

2. Duty to warn of commercial consequences

    His duty extends to warning his client to consider any commercial problems which may arise as a result of the legal problems which he, as a trademark agent, should reasonably discern.[255]

3. Duty to obtain complete instructions

    His duty also extends to informing his client of any matter in relation to which he needs instructions on the facts to give proper advice.[256]

    If he fails to ask the client a question which he, as a trademark agent, ought to see was important, it is not open to him to say later, 'the client never told me.'[257]

---

253. Halifax Building Society v. Urquhart Dykes and Lord, RPC 55 (1997) (Jacob J).
254. *Halifax case*, at 67.
255. *Id.*
256. *Id.*
257. *Id.*

4. Duty to know your client

> A trademark agent's job in making or pursuing an application normally involves finding out just what his clients do.[258]

In practical terms, these duties might entail the following:

1. making a full and thorough assessment of all the issues in any case;
2. asking questions about anything you don't know and that might be relevant;
3. raising all the issues with the client;
4. recording your instructions (the facts) in your advice;
5. thinking strategically: planning the matter from beginning to end at the outset;
6. not gambling on certain things happening (hope is not a strategy);
7. assuming that the circumstances and the facts may change over time and making the necessary follow up.

Errors

Possibly for cultural reasons, there is a tendency in the region to cover up rather than disclose errors that occur. The missing of deadlines and the unintended lapsing of applications is a surprisingly common problem. Agents do not always have the right systems in place to ensure things get done on time and sometimes other matters take priority such as religious holidays or practices. Unfortunately, the covering up makes the problem greater because the "cover" introduces an element of deception or fraud which may not have otherwise been there. Cases of the alteration of official documents, including changing of dates, are more common than they should be.

Such problems persist partly because of a lack of clear regulations and standards of conduct for the profession. When what is right and wrong is made as clear as possible, it is more likely the right thing will be done. One of the areas for the attention of the Ministry or a professional body is the standard of honesty that is required, particularly in the face of errors or negligence, which is when agents should be required to act in the utmost good faith and fully and frankly disclose the matter at hand. Non-disclosure has made it impossible for clients to seek any form of recompense for damage or loss they may have suffered as a result. Clients seeking recompense for damage and loss suffered as result of an agent's error or negligence must look

---

258. *Halifax case*, at 76.

to the civil law for relief. It provides a general right to be compensated for losses resulting from another person's actions.[259]

Liens over Documents

It is not uncommon for agents to decline to release certificates of registration, for example, until such time as their fees are paid. There is no legal foundation for this in the regulations relating to registration agents. It may have a contractual basis in those cases in which such a right is specified in the agent's terms of engagement. There is also the much less respectable practice in the region of agents demanding a release from all liability in relation to their negligence or other acts, and using client documents in their possession (such as certificates of registration or legalized supporting documents that are difficult and costly to replace) as leverage to obtain the release. Any profession that condones such practices diminishes the public's confidence and trust in it.

Indemnity Insurance

Unlike in many other jurisdictions, there is no requirement in the UAE for registration agents working in intellectual property matters to carry any form of indemnity insurance.

---

259. Federal Law no. 5 of 1985 in relation to civil transactions, article 282.

CHAPTER

2

Trademarks

Introduction

History of the UAE's Trademark Law

The UAE legislated to protect consumers and promote transparency and honesty in trade as early as 1979 with federal law no. 4 in relation to the prevention of fraud and deception in commercial dealings (the FDL 1979).[1] The regulations to the law followed in 1984.[2] The FDL 1979 is still relevant today to some of the practices and procedures in the UAE despite the later introduction of trademark and consumer laws.

In September 1992, the UAE issued its first federal trademark law (the TML 1992).[3] That law in its amended form continues today to be the trademark law of the UAE. In February 1993, the Ministry of Economy and Commerce issued the regulations to the trademark law (the TMR 1993).[4]

The TML 1992 was first amended in 2000.[5] A reference to the trademark journal was added, replacing all references to the OFFICIAL GAZETTE.

---

1. Federal law no. 4 of 1979 in relation to the prevention of fraud and deception in commercial dealings.
2. Ministerial decision no. 26 of 1984 with the implementing regulations to law no. 4 of 1979 in relation to the prevention of fraud and deception in commercial dealings.
3. Federal law no. 37 of 1992 in relation to trademarks.
4. Ministerial decision no. 6 of 1993 with the implementing regulations for federal law no. 37 of 1992 in relation to trademarks.
5. Federal law no. 19 of 2000 amending some provisions of Federal law no. 37 of 1992 in relation to trademarks.

Following these amendments, trademarks ceased to be advertised for opposition purposes in the OFFICIAL GAZETTE and the first issue of the TRADEMARK JOURNAL appeared on May 22, 2001. It continues today to be the journal in which trademarks are advertised for opposition purposes.

The TML 1992 was then amended in 2002.[6] Although the amending law filled 11 pages of the OFFICIAL GAZETTE, many of the amendments were minor, altering only a few words of certain articles. The most substantive changes were principally in relation to the famous marks provisions.

The 1993 trademark regulations were not replaced and are today the current regulations. Numerous ministerial decisions have been published in relation to trademarks matters (see the list of laws and regulations). Most of them relate to official fees.

In 2007, a unified trademark law for the Gulf Cooperation Council (GCC) countries was decreed in the UAE (the GCC TML) but has not yet come into force (see Appendices A10 and B14). There are presently no clear indications of if and when the GCC TML will become the trademark law of the UAE.

The Dubai International Financial Centre (the DIFC) issued a draft trademark law in 2009 which, when implemented, will apply within the jurisdiction of the DIFC. The DIFC has the authority to issue its own laws in commercial matters. Only to the extent recognized by the DIFC trademark law will the UAE federal trademark law apply within the DIFC.[7]

International Conventions

The first international intellectual property law convention to which the UAE became a party was the Paris Convention. The UAE acceded to it on June 19, 1996 and it entered into force on September 19, 1996.[8] In relation to trademarks, the Paris Convention imposes a number of obligations on contracting parties including in relation to reciprocal treatment,[9] the right to claim priority from an earlier filed trademark application,[10] non-use of marks and cancellation,[11] the independence of trademark rights,[12] well-known

---

6. Federal law no. 8 of 2002 amending some provisions of Federal law no. 37 of 1992 in relation to trademarks.
7. For example, the draft law recognizes UAE registered trademarks. See the website http://www.difc.ae.
8. Paris Convention, as revised at Stockholm in 1967, and later amended. The dates are from WIPO.
9. Paris Convention, articles 2 and 3.
10. Paris Convention, article 4.
11. Paris Convention, article 5(C).
12. Paris Convention, article 6.

marks,[13] the use and registration of official symbols,[14] the assignment of trademarks,[15] service marks,[16] collective marks,[17] border protection,[18] unfair competition,[19] and temporary protection.[20]

The UAE became a member of the World Trade Organization in 1996 and in doing so committed to bring its intellectual property laws in line with the TRIPs Agreement. The deadline to comply was January 1, 2000. The 2002 amendments to the TML 1992 were intended to make the law TRIPs compliant.[21]

The UAE is not a party to the Madrid Agreement or the Madrid Protocol, unlike Bahrain, one of the other Gulf Cooperation Council (GCC) countries. If there is to be a unified trademark law for the GCC countries, it is difficult to see how it could function with only some countries of the GCC being part of the Madrid system.

Government Authorities Dealing with Trademarks

The TML 1992 named the Minister of Economy and Commerce as being responsible for its administration. Currently, the relevant minister is known as the Minister of Economy and it is the Ministry of Economy that is responsible for matters under the TML 1992A.

The Ministry of Economy has offices in each emirate, with a head office in Abu Dhabi. Probably the majority of trademark applications and other official documents are filed in the Dubai branch of the trademark office because most of the trademark agents are located in Dubai.[22] The Registrar of Trademarks is located in the Abu Dhabi office, as are the official files for trademark matters. Trademark opposition hearings are held in the Abu Dhabi office.

In relation to trademark enforcement, there are a number of other government agencies involved including police forces, economic development departments, municipalities, the prosecution, and customs authorities.

---

13. Paris Convention, article 6bis.
14. Paris Convention, article 6ter.
15. Paris Convention, article 6quater.
16. Paris Convention, article 6sexies.
17. Paris Convention, article 7bis.
18. Paris Convention, articles 9 and 10.
19. Paris Convention, article 10bis.
20. Paris Convention, article 11.
21. WTO, Council for Trade-Related Aspects of Intellectual Property Rights, Legislation Review, United Arab Emirates, report of meeting June 18–22, 2001, Introductory Statement.
22. Trademark agents registered in a particular emirate are required to file at the trademark office in that emirate, unless there is a good reason to file at the office in another emirate (such as the systems not functioning).

UAE Trademark Statistics

The first trademark filed under the TML 1992 was advertised in OFFICIAL GAZETTE no. 248 on February 7, 1993, together with 21 other accepted trademark applications. More than one hundred thousand trademark applications have been filed since that time (generating more than fifty million dirhams in filing fees alone).

Trademark filing and registration statistics available from the Ministry are as follows:[23]

Year	Trademark applications filed	Trademarks registered
2001	5563	2966
2002	5399	5525
2003	7113	8724
2004	8122	5448
2005	10281	6804

What Is a Trademark?

A trademark is anything that takes a distinctive form.[24] An indicative list of the kinds of things that may be trademarks is given:

names, words, signatures, letters, numbers, drawings, symbols, titles, impressions, stamps, images, inscriptions, advertisements, packaging or any other mark or combination of marks.

From this list, drawings, symbols, impressions, inscriptions, and images are given definitions.[25] "Mark" is not defined. There is no mention of marks having to be able to be graphically represented. The GCC TML requires trademarks to be signs capable of being visually perceived, but then separately permits marks that have the character of a sound or a smell to be trademarks.[26] There is a difference between being capable of graphic representation and being visually perceptible. A sound is not visually perceptible but it may be graphically represented by a musical score.

---

23. These numbers are from a document prepared by the Ministry of Economy titled "World Intellectual Property Day" dated April 22, 2007. Thanks to the Brand Owners' Protection Group for giving me a copy (*see* http://www.gulfbpg.com).
24. TML 1992A, article 2.
25. TML 1992A, article 1. These definitions do not appear in the GCC TML.
26. GCC TML, article 2.

The requirement for a trademark to have a "distinctive form" seems at first uncontroversial. Trademarks should be distinctive. However, introducing a requirement for distinctiveness into the definition of a trademark has the potential to cause mischief. Marks that do not take a distinctive form will fall entirely outside of the scope of the trademark law. This has two implications. First, marks that do not have a distinctive form but become distinctive through use may be excluded from the application of the law. Secondly, some enforcement provisions may not apply in certain cases. For example, the offense of using trademarks that are not capable of registration is limited to "trademarks," marks that take a distinctive form. Geographic names do not generally have a distinctive form and therefore are not trademarks under article 38.1 that are prohibited from use even though they are prohibited from registration under article 3.6. The same would apply to some marks that deceive the public, some famous marks, and so on (see the other provisions of article 3).

Images

The Arabic word from the indicative list of marks above translated as "images" is "suwar." It could also be translated as pictures or photographs. Images are defined as follows:

> Images of a person whether of the owner of the project or of another.[27]

This definition confirms that images of persons may be registered as trademarks. One could speculate that it was intended to address any perception that the Islamic tradition of not representing human beings is not to prevent the representation of human beings in trademarks in the UAE, in contrast to other countries such as Saudi Arabia where images of human beings are difficult to register as trademarks. The fact that this definition does not appear in the GCC TML may indicate an accommodation of Saudi Arabia and an allowance for the countries of the GCC to interpret the definition in accordance with their local practices and traditions.

Color Marks

There is no mention of color or color marks in the definition of a trademark. Marks that consist of a single color should not be able to be registered because they do not meet the basic requirement to be trademarks, namely, that they

---

27. TML 1992A, article 1.

take a distinctive form. However, a single color mark has been advertised as accepted in the UAE. The application was for a particular tone of the color orange (Pantone 021C).[28] Presumably it was accepted because it was shown in fact to be distinctive in the UAE, rather than because it has any inherent distinctiveness. The practice of the Ministry in the UAE is sometimes ahead of the law makers.

Sounds

The last sentence of the definition of a trademark provides that a sound may be considered to be part of a trademark if it accompanies the trademark. It seems that the drafters of the TML 1992 did not think that sounds could stand alone as trademarks but could be parts of trademarks. It is difficult to imagine what they had in mind. Perhaps it was musical jingles that accompany television advertisements for products and services that are the target of this provision. In any case, the trademark office procedures are not evidently adapted to accept applications for marks that partially consist of sound. The GCC TML provides that marks with the character of a sound may be trademarks.[29]

Smells

Smells are not mentioned in the indicative list of marks in the TML 1992A. They could nevertheless potentially be trademarks, although it is difficult to see how they would satisfy the requirement for distinctive form. The GCC TML provides that marks with the character of a smell may be trademarks.[30]

Used or Intended to Be Used

In order to be a trademark, a mark must be "used or intended to be used" to distinguish goods or products or services."[31] This concept is repeated in the provision dealing with the entitlement to register a trademark:

> *Any person who wishes to use a trademark to distinguish a good or products or services may apply to register it pursuant to the provisions of this law.*[32]

---

28. UAE trademark application no. 81124 appeared in the trademark journal on April 11, 2007, no. 68.
29. GCC TML, article 2.
30. GCC TML, article 2.
31. TML 1992A, article 2.
32. TML 1992A, article 7.

Incorporating a reference to purpose in the definition of a trademark has several consequences. A mark that is not used or intended to be used is not a trademark for the purposes of the law. For example, if a person seeks to register a trademark merely to sell it to someone else, it is not a trademark within the definition. A mark that is used or intended to be used but not for the purpose of distinguishing products or services may also not be a trademark. For example, a person may use an expression on a product, or adopt a special product feature, but the purpose may be to describe the product or to give it an additional technical feature.

If an intention to use the mark *as a trademark* is a criterion to be satisfied to obtain and maintain a valid trademark registration, then trademarks cannot be dealt with like any other piece of property. In the context of corporate groups, for example, consideration needs to be given to which entity in the group satisfies the requirement and therefore which entity should be the applicant. In circumstances where there is a parent company and two subsidiaries, the parent may make a decision to use a mark as a trademark but it will not use the mark itself. It will license its use to one of the subsidiaries. Should the parent or the subsidiary apply for registration? The parent is, in a properly managed licensing relationship, the owner and user of the mark because the subsidiary is using the mark under its control—control over the nature and quality of the products the mark is applied to. The mark serves to distinguish the parent's products despite the fact that the subsidiary may be making the products and applying the mark to them. The exercise of the relevant level of control preserves the true purpose of a trademark: to indicate the origin of the products or services. For the same reasons, there are risks in trademark ownership structures that separate ownership of marks from the entity that is controlling the nature and quality of the products (such as the use of trademark holding companies). A trademark becomes distinctive of its licensee or user, rather than its registered owner, if the right level of control over its use is not maintained by the registered owner.

To Indicate the Products of the Owner

The mark used or intended to be used may also be for the purpose of indicating that "the goods or products are those of the owner of the mark because they were manufactured or selected or traded in by the owner."[33] The manufacturing of a product, in most cases, determines the nature and quality of the product and so the mark placed on the products by the manufacturer could properly function as a badge of origin. The person who selected products or who traded in them has a much less close relationship with the

---

33. TML 1992A, article 2.

products, but arguably when a trader decides to sell this particular product, with its particular character and quality, under his or her brand, the trader is making that product his or her "own," such that his or her mark may function as a badge of origin. This scenario is to be distinguished from that of reselling or retailing the branded products of others, which is a service and may not result in any relevant connection with the nature and quality of the products.

Three-Dimensional Trademarks

Three-dimensional trademarks are not specifically mentioned in the indicative list of trademarks. However, several kinds of marks that have a three-dimensional character are mentioned: impressions, inscriptions, and packaging.

Impressions ("Damghat") and Inscriptions ("Nuquush")

Impressions are defined as being marks that are "dug in." The term used may also be translated as "stamp" or "imprint." They are contrasted with inscriptions that are marks that are "raised up" or "in relief."[34] Whether one sees an impression or inscription as raised up or dug in may be a matter of perspective. Inscriptions are mentioned in the indicative list of marks in the GCC TML but no definition of them is given. There is no reference to impressions.[35]

Packaging or Containers ("'Ubuwat")

The Arabic expression here is derived from the verb "to fill" or "to pack." Packaging is probably the closest translation but it may also be translated as containers. The implication is that the packaging is something separate and distinct from the product itself. The reference to packaging is the closest that the TML 1992A comes to acknowledging that trademarks can be three-dimensional. The GCC TML addresses the issue directly and includes packaging in its indicative list of marks (but uses the expression, "taghleef," in the sense of covering or wrapping) as well as shapes (presumably the shapes of products).

---

34. TML 1992A, article 1.
35. GCC TML, articles 2.

The Practice in Relation to Three-Dimensional Trademarks

A review of the applications that are published in the TRADEMARK JOURNAL leaves little doubt that the trademark office is accepting marks for registration that are three-dimensional in nature. However, the trademark office systems have not yet been adapted to process trademark application for marks that have three-dimensional characteristics. At present, the image of the mark in the application for registration must be no larger than 5 × 5 cms and only one such image may be used. In many cases, the distinctive features cannot be discerned in such a small image. It may be necessary to see the mark from different perspectives. It is particularly difficult to put more than one perspective of a mark in a 5 × 5 cms space. This has led applicants and their agents to try to use the space provided in the application for a written description of the mark to reveal the aspects that are not obvious in the image of the mark or to specify the distinctive feature.

The precise role of the written description in the interpretation of the registration and the scope of the rights that are granted to the applicant has not yet been the subject of discussion. For example, in the case of application no. 86833 (the details of which are shown below), two drill bits are shown in the image of the mark. It is unclear whether the mark consists of two drill bits or whether the image depicts two separate marks in the one application (it is not stated that they are a series of marks). The correct characterization of what registration has been granted for is critical in determining non-use, cancellation, and enforcement issues.

The following are some examples of three-dimensional marks that have been advertised for opposition in the UAE:

Appln. no.	Applicant	Journal	Mark published	Description as published
86833	Sandvik International	No. 70, 16 June 2007, p. 705.	An image of two drill bits	"The shape of two spiral drills, black in color, with a grey collar around the centre of each."
88363	Yves Saint Laurent	No. 72, 9 August 2007, p. 649.	A circular glass jar with a hexagonal cap.	"The mark consists of a distinctive three dimensional shape for a bottle and of a silver, white, black and light yellow mark."

Appln. no.	Applicant	Journal	Mark published	Description as published
69924	Honda Motor Co.	No. 49, 6 September, 2005, page 864.	An outline black and white drawing of a stand alone pull-start engine	"The mark consists of the three dimensional shape of an engine composed of a body and a fan with a circular cover which is part of the body of the engine. Above is a fuel tank with an opening on top. Connected to the side is a carburetor and exhaust."
69925	Honda Motor Co.	No. 49, 6 September, 2005, page 865.	An outline black and white drawing of a stand alone engine with the pull-start section in red	"The mark consists of the three dimensional shape of an engine in red and white, composed of a body and a fan with a red circular cover which is part of the body of the engine. Above is a fuel tank with an opening on top. Connected to the side is a carburetor and exhaust."
69926	Honda Motor Co.	No. 49, 6 September, 2005, page 866.	A color photo of a stand alone engine with a white petrol tank, a red pull-start section and black carburetor.	"The mark consists of a colored three dimensional image of an engine composed of a silver body and a fan with a red circular cover which is part of the body of the engine. Above is a white fuel tank with an opening on top. Connected to the side is a black carburetor and exhaust."

Who May Register a Trademark?

Both legal and natural persons may register trademarks. The applicant may be either a UAE national, or a foreign national that:

(a) carries on business or provides services in the UAE; or
(b) carries on business or provides services in a State that deals recipro-cally with the UAE.

Public legal persons (such as government entities that have a legal identity) may also register trademarks.[36]

Although expressed in the present tense, these requirements are probably not intended to be read as preventing persons who are not yet carrying on business from obtaining trademark registration. The present tense in the Arabic text also carries with it a future tense meaning.

Joint Ownership

There are no provisions in the law or regulations relating to ownership of a trademark by one or more persons jointly. There is nothing in principle that would prevent the registration of trademarks in more than one person's name. The Ministry does accept applications in the name of more than one applicant. In such cases, it would not be unreasonable for the Ministry to require an endorsement that the mark will be used together by the owners and not separately, but that is not currently a requirement.

Residency of the Applicant

The TMR 1993 says that the owner may file an application if he has residency in the UAE.[37] Otherwise, he must file the application through a lawyer's office. As a matter of practice, UAE companies may file their own trademark applications without using a trademark agent (as foreign applicants must). However, if the applicant is incorporated in a free zone, the Ministry tends to decline receiving their applications unless they are filed by a trademark agent.

---

36. Summarizing article 6 of the TML 1992A.
37. TMR 1993, article 3.

Under the GCC TML

Article 6 of the GCC TML is substantially the same as article 6 of the TML 1992A quoted above but for the extension of the concept of a "national" to nationals of any of the countries of the GCC. The reciprocal treatment requirement is now also extended to countries dealing reciprocally with the GCC countries. Absent from the GCC TML is the reference discussed above to "the person who wishes to use a trademark to distinguish" found in article 7 of the TML 1992A. There is only a reference to "a concerned person."[38] This may be because the concept of "using or intending to use to distinguish" is in the definition of a trademark in the GCC TML.[39]

Filing a Trademark Application

Single Class Applications Only

The UAE remains one of the countries that requires a separate trademark application for each international class of goods or services claimed.[40] If the examiner of the application raises an issue as to the proper classification of goods or services claimed in one application, it is not possible to transfer them to a co-pending application for the appropriate class (as one might be able to do with a multi-class application). However, and perhaps remarkably, the UAE practice allows substantial additions and alterations to the specification of goods and services during examination. Unfortunately, the GCC TML preserves the single class system.

The Application Form

An application for registration of a trademark is made using the form issued from time to time by the Ministry. The form of the application was not issued with the regulations to the law, although the regulations do state what is to be included in the application.[41]

---

38. GCC TML, article 9.
39. GCC TML, article 2.
40. TML 1992A, article 8; TMR 1993, article 4.
41. TMR 1993, article 5. The list in this article is now no longer entirely indicative of what must be in the application.

The File

It is necessary for the applicant (or the applicant's agent) to provide the physical file that will be used for the case at the trademark office. The file usually has a representation of the mark on the cover as well as other basic information, and must contain the following:

(a) the application form in Arabic;

(b) a copy of the agent's notarized and legalized power of attorney, or if the power of attorney is not yet available, an undertaking from the agent to file it within sixty days;[42]

(c) ten prints of the mark on 5 × 5cms pieces of white paper, placed in a envelope and attached to the cover of the file;

(d) a CD Rom with an electronic copy of the application form;

(e) a copy of the agent's trade license and trademark agent certificate.

The regulations contain a list of required application attachments.[43] The certificate of registration in the commercial register mentioned in the list is no longer required.

Filing the Application

Applications can be filed at the Ministry's offices in any of the emirates. The office receiving most applications is probably the Dubai office. Until October 2008, the Dubai trademark office was located in the Ministry of Economy building near the Dubai International Airport. It has now moved to new offices at the World Trade Centre roundabout on Sheikh Zayed Road. There is now a ticket queuing system in place of the more personal system in the old office (where computer systems too frequently crashed and the e-Dirham card machine for paying fees would often malfunction). There are many reasons why it may not be possible to file an application or other document on the day of intending to do so.[44] If the systems are down on the day of a priority deadline, for example, the office will usually backdate the application when filed the next day. In an age of web-based trademark office access, by which applications can be filed at any time of the day or night, the UAE system may be difficult to understand.

---

42. The sixty-day period may be extended by a further thirty days.

43. TMR 1993, article 7.

44. It is generally not possible to file applications and documents after 2 pm. Often it is not possible for an agent to file more than 25 or so applications in one day.

Classification of Goods and Services

A list of classes of goods and services in relation to which trademarks may be registered was published as "Attachment 1" to the TMR 1993.[45] The list is based on the Nice Classification of Goods and Services but Nice class 33 (for alcoholic beverages) was omitted and Nice class 34 was renumbered as class 33. The consequence of this is that the services classes began with class 34 and not 35 as in Nice and there were only 41 classes instead of 42. The word "beers" was also deleted from class heading for class 32.

The UAE does not follow the class system that was published as Attachment 1 to the TMR 1993 but instead presently follows the 9th edition of the Nice Classification of Goods and Services, with the exception that applications claiming Nice class 33 or "beers" in class 32 will not be accepted for filing. The classification divides goods and services into 45 classes, 34 classes for goods and 11 classes for services (classes 35 to 45). See also the discussion concerning marks that contravene public morals or public order.

When the UAE trademark office moved to the 8th edition of Nice, marks in class 42 were not reclassified, with the consequence that there are some marks on the register in class 42 covering hotels and restaurant services (for example) and others in class 43 covering the same services. Searches for marks in relation to old class 42 services need to be done in class 42 and the new 8th edition class. Generally speaking, the trademark office tends to use the Nice classification as a rule book rather than as a guide. A product or service may be objected to if it is not expressly listed in the Nice classification guide.

Convention Priority

Article 4 of the Paris Convention requires member states to give a right to claim priority from an earlier filed application. The TML 1992A does not contain any provision giving a right to claim priority on an earlier filed application as required by the Paris Convention. Curiously, the law was amended in 2002 to include a requirement that the certificate of registration contain information as to any priority claim.[46] The regulations provide that if priority is claimed, a copy of the "certificate of registration" is to be attached to the UAE application.[47] It seems to have been an oversight that the right to

---

45. TMR 1993, article 4.
46. TML 1992A, article 16.
47. TMR 1993, article 7.4.

claim priority has not been included in the law. One will not therefore find any mention of the priority period in the TML 1992A. As a party to the Paris Convention, the UAE is bound to follow the minimum standards that it sets. It requires that a priority period of six months from the filing of the first application be given for trademarks.

As a matter of practice, priority claims are made and accepted by the Ministry. The priority period is six months. Contrary to what is required by the regulations, the certificate of registration of the priority application does not need to be attached to the UAE application. The details of the priority claim should be given in the application form. If they are omitted, it should be possible to amend the application, at least prior to the application being examined. The applicant has three months from the application filing date to file a certified copy of the priority document, together with a translation under the letterhead and stamp of a licensed UAE translator.

Associated Marks

The TMR 1993 provides for the recording of associated marks in the register.[48] There is, however, no mention of them in the law itself. The concept of associated marks exists (or existed, as the case may be) in the laws of many countries (for example, Australia had associated marks) and is still used in some countries in the region (Qatar, for example). In broad terms, association of marks is to prevent marks that are the same or similar, and registered in relation to the same or similar goods and services, from being owned by different owners. Association of marks entails that the marks must be assigned together and not separately. For example, a registration for POREX in class 5 and a registration for POREX and logo in class 5 would very likely have to be associated as a condition of registration in countries where an association system is in use. Association might also be a requirement where the mark is to be registered in two related classes of goods (such as classes 3 and 5). In the UAE, where association of marks has not been implemented, it is possible to achieve by assignment what cannot be achieved through the registration process, namely, the ownership of similar marks for similar products or services by unrelated persons.

---

48. TMR 1993, article 22 [A].

Series Marks

An application for registration may be filed for a series of trademarks.[49] Two or more trademarks qualify as a series if they are identical in their essential elements and their differences are limited to matters not affecting their essential identity. Differences in color or the use of representations of the products are given as examples of non-essential differences. For example, if a seller of soap uses a lion logo as a trademark, but sometimes the lion logo is blue or green or purple, the different colored lion logos are a series of marks that could be sought to be registered in one application. Similarly, if the lion logo appears with an image of the soap and the image differs across the different kinds of soap offered, then those marks might constitute a series.

The decision to apply for a series of marks requires careful consideration. By presenting the marks in question as a series, one is in effect saying that the differences between them are not essential to the identity of the mark. It is a small step then to say that the differences are not distinctive elements of the marks. If one is seeking broader protection by filing the marks in series, the opposite may in fact be the result. The series identifies for potential infringers those features of the marks that the owner is not claiming any right to. In effect, series applications can be an admission against interest.

One area where perhaps series marks might assist trademark owners is in relation to the protection of "characters." Take for example an image of a wizard used to sell cleaning detergent. Sometimes the wizard is standing, sometimes running, sitting, or sleeping. Those different images of the same character might constitute a series of trademarks. Their differences do not affect the essential identity of the mark or character. One wants to convey the message to others that it does not matter whether this wizard is sitting or standing, etc. Perhaps here a series of marks broadens the protection obtained. One would hope that a court would find that a sitting version of the wizard would infringe the registered standing version.

Marks That May Not Be Registered

Article 3 of the TML 1992A deals with marks that may not be registered. It groups together marks against which there is a strict prohibition (such as the symbols of the Red Crescent) with marks about which a great degree of judgment must be exercised to determine whether they are prohibited or not.

---

49. TML 1992A, article 9. The provision is repeated in article 6 of the TMR 1993.

This second category includes: marks devoid of distinctveness, geographical names, the names of persons, deceptive marks, value diminishing marks and translations of famous or registered marks.[50] I will discuss these separately in other sections.

Marks That Contravene Public Morals or Public Order

It is not possible in the UAE to register trademarks with respect to goods or services that are considered to be contrary to certain Islamic values.[51] For example, the trademark office will reject applications covering pork products, alcoholic beverages, night clubs, discotheques, casinos, gambling, gaming, and escort services. Although most supermarkets in the emirate of Dubai have pork product sections, and although alcoholic beverages and the other problematic goods and services are widely available and consumed in Dubai and other emirates, they are not tolerated in the more conservative emirates. Consequently, at the trademark office level, the procedure has been to follow the line of the more conservative emirates.

Trademarks themselves may also be contrary to the principles of Islam as it is interpreted. For example, the trademark office may require that marks containing problematic words be amended to remove or replace the offending words (such as "BAR," "DRUG," "DEVIL," or "SEXY"). A literal and strict approach is taken to these issues. That the mark is a parody or joke or uses the problematic word for a positive purpose will not usually be taken into account.

The GCC TML contains substantially the same provision.[52] The implementation of the GCC TML law will raise the question of whether each country will be permitted to follow its own practices, or whether they will seek to harmonize their various practices. This is likely to raise difficult issues. For example, in Saudi Arabia it is not possible to register trademarks that depict a person or that show the outline of a woman's body. Islam is practiced throughout the GCC with different degrees of conservatism. Harmonization between the GCC countries may mean that the more conservative practices are taken as the minimum standard.

A further question is whether "public morals or public order" includes the general law itself, reading the provision as preventing the registration of trademarks whose use would be contrary to law. This would potentially open the provision to broader use. For example, in opposition proceedings it might

---

50. TML 1992A, paragraphs 1, 6, 7, 9, 11 and 14 of article 3.
51. Islam is the official religion of the UAE. See the UAE Constitution, article 7.
52. GCC TML, article 3.2.

be possible to argue that the use of a mark that is the subject of the application would result in the commission of a criminal offense under article 37 or 38 of the TML 1992A. Whether or not this would extend already available grounds of opposition is a matter for debate.

Official Symbols

More or less all symbols used by governments and international organizations, as well as imitations of them, may not be registered without authorization. It is common in the UAE for local businesses to want to use the colors of the UAE national flag in their trademarks. In some case, depending on how the colors are used, the mark is accepted, and doubtless there are cases where it is not. The word "Emirates" itself is arguably a symbol of the State. It is found as part of many registered marks and, in the case of Emirates Airlines, it is registered without disclaimers.

Symbols of the Red Crescent and Red Cross

The provision against the registration of these marks includes "any other similar symbols" and imitations of them. In addition to the symbols of the Red Cross and Red Crescent, there is also the Red Crystal which the ICRC adopted in 2006. Iran's Loin with Sun symbol is also a protected symbol with the same status as the others, as is Israel's Magen David Adom symbol (a red star of David). It is unclear whether the scope of this provision would include the symbols of organizations such as "Medecins san frontier," for example? Would "Lawyers Without Borders" (and various other copies of the concept) be an imitation of it? Such organizations might be deemed to be international organizations under paragraph 3 of article 3.

Purely Religious Symbols

It is not easy to say that a symbol is *purely* religious. For example, the hilal or crescent moon is a symbol of Islam, as is the color green, but it is difficult to say that they are purely religious symbols, both having uses in other contexts. The name "Jesus" is an important religious name but it is not purely religious. Many people have the name "Jesus." Perhaps the word "Allah" is purely religious. But in Arabic it simply means "the god." Perhaps closer to being purely religious is the name of the holy book of Islam, the Quran, and images of the Ka'ba or Al Aqsa Mosque (for example).

Honorific Titles

Representations containing honorific titles may be registered if the applicant can prove a legal entitlement to them.[53] Such titles may include "King," "HRH," "Sir," "Duke," and "Prince." In the UAE, the word "Sheikh" is used honorifically, although in Arabic it means a person of age and wisdom. There are many honorifics in other languages. For example, "ji" is an honorific in Hindi (Mahatma Gandhi was called "Gandhi-ji"). Educational qualifications also result in honorific titles such as "Doctor" or Ph.D. This is expressly recognized in the corresponding provision of the GCC TML.[54]

Marks Owned by Forbidden Persons

The UAE is one of the countries in the Middle East that maintains a level of boycott against Israel.[55] The boycott is managed by the Israeli Boycott Office. From the UAE, it is not possible to call phone numbers in Israel and Internet addresses ending in .il are blocked. Israeli nationals, persons as well as companies, are not able to file trademark applications in the UAE. The Ministry must cancel a trademark registration if the Israeli Boycott Office decides that the mark is the same or similar to an Israeli mark or symbol or emblem, or is owned by a person with whom it is prohibited to deal.[56]

Using Unregistrable Marks Is a Criminal Offense

The article 3 provisions discussed above are not only designed to keep certain marks from the register, but have a broader role in preventing certain marks from being used. It is a criminal offense to use a mark that is not capable of

---

53. TML 1992A, article 3.8.
54. Article 3.8.
55. The follow text comes from a 2003 document in the library of the Office of the United States Trade Representative: "While the UAE no longer enforces the secondary and tertiary aspects of the boycott, occasional government contracts continue to contain pro forma provisions requiring a contractual obligation to 'observe all regulations and instructions enforced from time to time by the League of Arab States regarding the boycott of Israel especially those related to blacklisted companies, ships, and persons.' Indeed, in a recent case, involving a delayed high-profile contract between an American firm and a local government agency, UAE government authorities instructed the Abu Dhabi Emirate, in writing, to exempt the U.S. firm from the provisions of the boycott clause."
56. TML 1992A, article 24; TMR 1993, article 24.

registration because it does not comply with the article 3 requirements expressed in paragraphs 2 to 14.[57] The content of these provisions is discussed above so need not be repeated here. However, there is a question of interpretation to be considered. How does one determine whether a mark is not capable of registration? If an application for registration has been filed and rejected because of one or more of the grounds in the relevant paragraphs of article 3 (such as that the mark is deceptive, contrary to public morals, a translation of a famous or registered mark, or a misleading geographical name), there is then good reason to believe that the mark is not capable of registration. In that case, its continued use in the UAE is likely to be an offense.

If the application to register a mark is rejected on the basis of either article 3.1 (the mark is not sufficiently distinctive) or article 10 (the mark is similar to a prior mark), it will not be an offense under article 38 to continue to use the mark in the UAE. Of course, it may be that it is an offense under other provisions (such as article 37) to use a mark that is similar to another.

Distinctiveness

In the discussion above concerning the definition of a trademark, we have seen that the definition incorporates a distinctiveness requirement: a trademark must take a distinctive form. The concept of "distinctive form" suggests that the mark must have some level of inherent distinctiveness and that even if the mark were one hundred percent distinctive as a matter of fact, if it was not also to some degree inherently distinctive it would not be a trademark and would not be entitled to registration. The general trend in trademark law is to make questions of distinctiveness purely questions of fact as to whether the mark distinguishes or is capable of doing so.[58] That may indeed be the Ministry practice in the UAE despite the language of the law.

The main distinctiveness requirement is set out in article 3:

> Marks that are devoid of any distinctive attribute or character or that consist of representations that are no more than customary names given to the goods and products and services or conventional drawings or ordinary images of the goods and products.[59]

This provision sets a very low level of distinctiveness for a mark to satisfy in order to be able to be registered. Put simply, the level of distinctiveness

---

57. TML 1992A, article 38.1.
58. For example, in Australia: see the *Trade Marks Act 1995*; *see also British Sugar v James Robertson* [1996] RPC 281, Jacob J.
59. TML 1992A, article 3.1.

must be more than none. Only marks devoid of any distinctive attribute or character are to be refused registration. This is consistent with the marks that are published in the TRADEMARK JOURNAL. Although the circumstances in which a mark is accepted for registration are not always apparent, including the extent to which evidence of use and fame may have been important in the final decision, the required level of distinctiveness appears to be very low. For example, the word EMIRATES is registered by Emirates Airlines. Although it is arguably entirely inherently non-distinctive, the mark is internationally well known for airline services.

In addition to prohibiting the registration of marks devoid of distinctiveness, the language of article 3 also prohibits the registration of trademarks that contain, as an element, a non-distinctive mark (reading the first line together with paragraph 1). This is probably a drafting lacunae because it is very clear from the practice in the UAE that the presence of a distinctive element (however minor) in an otherwise non-distinctive trademark (and vice versa) is sufficient to make it acceptable for registration.

The article 3.1 distinctiveness requirement also prevents the registration of marks that consist of representations that are not more than customary names for the products or services or conventional drawings or images of them. Such marks may be accepted for registration, but only if they are rendered in a distinctive manner and possibly with a disclaimer on the customary name or conventional image such as "registration grants no right to the [separate] exclusive use of x."

Conflicting Similar Marks

Prior to 2002, the law provided that similar marks may not be registered in the UAE in the *same class of goods services or services* [despite the possible lack of any similarity between the respective goods or services of interest).[60] Although the drafting of the provision was altered in 2002 to remove the concept of "the same class," the trademark office examination practice appears to follow the principle as it was in the law before it was amended. Indeed, in relation to opposition hearings, the trademark office recently issued notices to opponents that they should provide a copy of their UAE application mark *in the same class* as the mark that is being opposed or otherwise the opposition would be considered vexatious and unjustified.

Article 10 of the TML 1992A now reads (in relevant part):

a trademark that is identical or similar to a previously registered mark may not be registered for the same products or services, or for products or services that

---

60. TML 1992A, article 10.

are not the same, if the use of the mark for which registration is sought would give rise to the impression of a connection between it and the products or services of the owner of the registered mark or would lead to the possibility of damage to his interests.

The amended form of article 10 solves a number of problems. The Nice Agreement classes are generally seen as administrative tools only. The fact that two particular goods or services have been classified in the same class was not intended to mean that they will be relevantly similar for determining whether two marks are likely to conflict. For example, products for washing clothes may have no relevant connection with cosmetics, but both are in class 3; industrial oils are in class 4 but they have no relevant relationship with candles, also in that class; pharmaceutical products are not closely related to pesticides, but both are in class 5; Christmas trees are not similar to sporting products in class 28; advertising may have no connection with business management in class 35; and so on. Perhaps article 10 was originally drafted to avoid the need for difficult judgments to be made as to whether goods or services are similar or closely related.

A further problem with the old article 10 arose from the fact that goods or services in different classes may be relevantly similar, such as certain goods in classes 3 and 5, goods in classes 18, 25, and 28, services in classes 35 and 36, and goods and services in the classes for food products and restaurant services, and so on (something known and recognized in other jurisdictions in law and practice). Despite the 2002 amendments, it is common today for confusingly similar marks to be accepted for registration in the name of different owners in respect of similar or closely related goods or services falling in different classes.

The 2002 amendments to the TML 1992 introduced the concept of products and services that are not the same or similar, thus breaking away entirely from the "same class (or different class)" concept. However, there is an issue of translation and interpretation here to be considered. The key words are underlined and the words to be discussed are in square brackets:

> a trademark that is identical or similar to a previously registered mark may not be registered for the <u>same products or services, or for products or services that are [not the same/ not similar]</u>,[61] if . . .

The expression "the same products or services" appears in the Arabic text as "thaat al muntajaat aw khadamat." There would not be much debate about translating that as "the same goods or services." However, goods that are "ghair mumaathila" could be goods that are "not the same" or that are "not

---

61. The Sharjah Chamber of Commerce translation uses "not similar."

similar" (as indicated in the translation above). In Arabic, "mumaathila" is used variously to mean the same or similar. Indeed, in the second paragraph of article 10, "mumaathila" is clearly used to mean "similar." The issue is a critical one because the meaning and consequences will be very different.

Take an example to see the consequences of interpreting "ghair mumaathila" to mean "not similar." A has registered mark X for clothing and wants to oppose the registration of similar mark Y from being registered for the retailing of clothing, relying on article 10. If "mumaathila" means "similar," A would need to argue that the clothing is not similar to the retailing of clothing and that the use of the later mark would give an impression of a connection with his clothing business and that would damage his interests. In order to establish that an impression of a connection would arise, surely part of the argument would be that there is a similarity between clothing and the retailing of clothing (which is what A had first to deny). The paradoxical consequences are clear. Interpreting "ghair mumaathila" to mean "not the same" avoids these consequences and entails that in the opposition, A would only need to establish that the impression of a connection would arise, it being clear that clothing and the retailing of clothing are not the same.

Assuming "not the same" is the correct understanding of "ghair mumaathila," in examination of an application, an examiner ought to decide whether the goods (or services) are the same as those in the prior application or registration, and if they are not the same, ought then to consider whether an impression of a connection might arise from the use of the mark under examination.

How does one establish that the use of a similar mark would give rise to an impression of a connection between the mark and the products or services of the owner of the earlier mark (notwithstanding that the goods or services of interest are not the same as any of those covered by the prior mark)? Many of the arguments relate to the similarity of goods or services. For example, an impression of a connection might arise if consumers are likely to believe that the two kinds of goods are made by the same kind of business. A maker of soap might also make shampoos. A restaurant may also have its own range of products that it sells over the counter. One might also look at the materials from which the goods are made. Many diverse product types might be thought to come from the same source if, for example, they are all made from the same basic material. A similarity of purpose of the products might also give an impression of connection. There are many different kinds of transport— their common purpose might be enough to give an impression of connection if offered under the same or similar marks. The methods of offering the products might be relevant.

The rules for the comparison of marks is a subject that requires some comment, if only to indicate the diverse views on the subject. Trademark office practice is that identical marks may not be concurrently registered by different persons unless a letter of consent is provided, but where the later mark is, for example, a word that is the same or virtually the same as a word contained in a combination word and device mark, the trademark office may ask the applicant to add a device to the later mark. This suggests that aural similarity is irrelevant to the comparison (because the different devices are not pronounced). In cases in which a later combination mark is virtually identical to an earlier combination mark, the trademark office may ask the applicant of the later mark to disclaim rights in the identical elements. The view that disclaimers are relevant to comparisons of marks is one no longer widely adopted, although the related concept of discounting the value of non-distinctive elements continues to be widely accepted. In contrast to this approach, lawyers and trademark agents trained in western jurisdictions tend to employ the broader concept of confusing similarity in their advice and dealings with the trademark office. That concept is probably closer to what is provided for in the TML 1992A. Other trademark agents take their lead from the trademark office practice. The UAE courts have made comments on the comparison of marks, some of which may require reconciling. A thorough study of the cases is yet to be done.

Searching the Register

One of the main purposes of keeping a trademark register is to provide the public with information about what rights exist and who owns them. It is in the interest of the public, the government, and brand owners to have trans- parency in the market as to the origin of products and services and relative certainty that those appearing to be similar are from the same source. Consumer confusion and trademark disputes between businesses are ineffi- cient and adversely affect confidence. The trademark register performs an important role in achieving these objectives. There is presently no online access to the UAE trademark register and so it is inaccessible to the public. The law provides that anyone can obtain a certified extract of what is contained in the register upon payment of the fee.[62] However, finding what one wants an extract of is another matter. For example, it is not possible to perform owner searches at the trademark office.[63] The reason for this may be that all trademark owner names are recorded in Arabic transliteration only. The transliteration used is the one prepared by the agent at the time of filing. Latin character names can very often be transliterated into Arabic in many

---

62. TML 1992A, article 5[B].
63. This comment is based on experience in the Dubai trademark office. One agent has reported sometimes being able to do owner searches in the Abu Dhabi trademark office.

different ways. For some owners at least, their names are likely to be recorded in the trademark office system with different transliterations. Without an owner search facility, trademark owners are unable to verify or check their own records against official records. This makes the identification of errors and other discrepancies difficult.[64]

The most common kind of searches that businesses want to conduct are trademark availability searches, the purpose of which is to determine the level of risk involved in introducing a new brand in the UAE. A single search for a word mark in one class constitutes a search for the purposes of calculating the fees. There is no searching across classes. Each search in related classes is a separate search and would require a separate search application and a separate search fee. The assumption behind the system appears to be that if the same or similar mark is not registered in the class of interest, then the mark is available for use and registration. But clearly that is not what the law provides (the relevant tests are discussed above). There is nothing in principle from preventing the use of a mark for a medicated product in class 5 from infringing the rights of the owner of the same mark for the non-medicated version of that product in class 3. The same could be said of goods in classes 25 and 28, or 18 and 25, or 14 and 25, and so on. In other countries, trademark offices have developed groupings of classes of goods and services so that when the goods or services of interest in one class are searched, the associated classes can be automatically searched.

This limited view of what is required from a search extends into the trademark office itself, where examiners will only cite marks in the same class against the application being examined. If there is no relevant mark in the same class then the mark (all other conditions being satisfied) may be registered. Many trademark agents also follow this view in performing and advising on trademark searches. If this is the approach taken at the trademark office, then the agent is justified to some extent because the search done reflects what the examiner will do in examining the application. But it does not necessarily identify the issues and risks that a brand owner should be aware of when introducing a new brand. Unless related classes in which similar goods or services might be found are searched, all potentially relevant marks will not be identified. Consideration needs to be given to the classes to be searched in view of the goods or services of interest. Of course, the more classes searched, the higher the government fees.

Official search methods are also quite basic. The search can only be done by a staff member at the trademark office. The searcher will, if requested,

---

64. Bahrain, for example, now receives applications in English and Arabic.

search up to five terms that are related to the mark. If the mark is JOCASTA'S SWORD, one might ask for searches of the following:

JOCA in Latin characters (to see all the marks containing these letters)
ASTA in Latin characters (this would find e.g., JACASTA)
JOCAST in Arabic characters (to try to identify relevant transliterations)
SWOR in Latin characters (assuming the first part of the mark is more important)
SWOR in Arabic characters

If the results from those searches are not too great in number, the searcher will print the lists of marks found. The marks appear in the list without images.

By most standards, the above search strategy is inadequate. It would not find JOKAST, for example, or other phonetic equivalents. There are also a number of Arabic transliterations it would not find. Of course there are other possible strategies (perhaps not searching SWORD at all if it is not distinctive), but clearly five search terms performed by an employee mechanically is generally not adequate due diligence when introducing a new brand.

Searches of logos or devices are also not possible unless one searches for a relevant word and it happens that that word appears in the description of the mark. For example, if the principle feature of the logo is a triangle, one could search that word and hope that it does not produce too many results. The results will not show the images of the mark so it will be impossible to identity what marks are relevant to consider. In order to see the images of the marks found in the search, it is necessary to purchase certified copies of each of them at a rate of about US$26 each. Alternatively, one can search the past journals for the marks that have been published, but that could be a long and tedious process unless they are available in indexed and electronically searchable form.

Well-Known Marks

The obligations to protect well-known marks begin in the Paris Convention, article 6*bis* (1), which reads as follows:

> The countries of the Union undertake, ex officio if their legislation so permits, or at the request of an interested party, to refuse or to cancel the registration, and to prohibit the use, of a trademark which constitutes a reproduction, an imitation, or a translation, liable to create confusion, of a mark considered by the competent authority of the country of registration or use to be well known in that country as being already the mark of a person entitled to the benefits of

this Convention and used for identical or similar goods. These provisions shall also apply when the essential part of the mark constitutes a reproduction of any such well–known mark or an imitation liable to create confusion therewith.

This article does not mention services. Article 16.2 of the TRIPs Agreement remedies this: "Article 6*bis* of the Paris Convention (1967) shall apply, *mutatis mutandis*, to services."

The TRIPs Agreement also develops the idea of what is considered to be well known: "In determining whether a trademark is well known, Members shall take account of the knowledge of the trademark in the relevant sector of the public, including knowledge in the Member concerned which has been obtained as a result of the promotion of the trademark."[65]

Perhaps the most important step forward in the protection of well-known marks was the extension of the Paris Convention obligation to goods and services that are not similar to those for which the well-known mark is registered:

Article 6bis of the Paris Convention (1967) shall apply, mutatis mutandis, to goods or services which are not similar to those in respect of which a trademark is registered, provided that use of that trademark in relation to those goods or services would indicate a connection between those goods or services and the owner of the registered trademark and provided that the interests of the owner of the registered trademark are likely to be damaged by such use.[66]

The UAE sought to make its trademark law consistent with these obligations in its 2002 amendments to the TML 1992. Relevant amendments were made to articles 3, 4, 10, and 41. The article 3 prohibition against the registration of famous marks[67] reads:

14. Marks that are considered to be not more than translations of a famous mark or another previously registered mark if the registration of the mark would cause confusion amongst consumers in relation to the products that are distinguished by the mark or similar products.

The other relevant provision is article 4.1:

A trademark that has an international reputation exceeding the borders of the country from which it originates to other countries may not be registered except

---

65. TRIPs Agreement, article 16.2.
66. TRIPs Agreement, article 16.3.
67. I use the expression "famous marks" because the Arabic expression in this article is "'alamaat mashhoura." Whether this is the correct expression to capture the idea of well-known marks is a matter for discussion (another expression might be "ma'aroufa jayedan").

based on an application made by the original owner or based on an official authority from the owner.

Article 4.1 appears to prohibit only the registration of marks that are *the same* as marks that have an international reputation. Article 3.14 extends the prohibition on registration to *translations* of famous marks. However, the Paris Convention obligation is to refuse to register any trademark that constitutes a reproduction, imitation, or translation liable to create confusion, as well as marks the essential part of which is a reproduction or confusing imitation of a well-known mark. As it stands, it appears that there is no provision in the TML 1992A to prevent the registration of imitations of well-known or famous marks or marks whose essential part consists of a well-known or famous mark or a confusing imitation.

The Paris Convention obligation is also to prohibit the *use* of well-known marks. The translations of well-known marks referred to in article 3.14 are prohibited from use by the application of article 38.1. The result is that although translations of famous marks may be prohibited from use by article 38.1, unauthorized reproductions and imitations of well-known marks (as well as marks whose essential part is a well know mark or a confusing imitation) are not expressly prohibited from use by the TML 1992A.

The criminal provisions in article 37 do not mention famous or well-known marks (and indeed it is unclear whether they were intended to protect registered marks only or whether they extend to marks used but not registered in the UAE and marks that are not used and not registered in the UAE but well known in the UAE by virtue of the spread of their reputation). However, the 2002 amendment made to article 41 concerning precautionary measures provides that "owners of famous marks are not required to file a certificate evidencing registration of the mark."[68] If precautionary measures are available for unregistered famous marks, the implication must be that the owner of the famous mark has a right to protect the mark in the UAE despite the absence of a trademark registration. On what is that right based? The article 17 right to prevent others using the same or similar marks is limited to registered marks. Perhaps the criminal provisions in article 37.3 are open to an interpretation that makes use of unregistered well-known marks an offense. Another possibility is that the Paris Convention obligation is to be read into the TML 1992A by virtue of the UAE being a party to the Convention. On this view, a plaintiff would need only to refer to the Convention to support the application for precautionary measures against unauthorized use in the UAE of a famous mark or a confusing imitation of it.

The Paris Convention obligations include an obligation to cancel the registration of marks that constitute a reproduction, imitation, or translation

---

68. TML 1992A, article [C].

of a well-known mark, or whose essential part is a well-known mark or confusing imitation. Marks that are registered without a right may be cancelled by third parties.[69] "Without a right" ties the cancellation right back to the grounds for rejecting an application for registration. As we have seen above, although famous marks and translations of them may not be registered, imitations and marks whose essential part is a famous mark or a confusing imitation may be registered (if the famous mark is not already registered in the UAE in the relevant class). The cancellation right under the TML 1992A is therefore limited to reproductions and translations of famous marks.

The TRIPs Agreement extended the Paris Convention obligations to goods and services that are not similar to those for which the well-known mark is "registered." It is article 4.3 of the TML 1992A that expresses this concept and the conditions for its application.

> 3. A mark that has a reputation may not be registered to distinguish goods or services not similar or not identical to those distinguished by the mark, if:
>> a. the use of the mark would indicate a connection between the goods and services required to be distinguished by it and the goods and services of the owner of the original mark; or
>> b. the use of the mark would lead to the possibility of damage to the owner of the original mark.

This is, however, a prohibition against *registration* only. The right to *cancel* trademark registrations of well-known marks by persons not the owner for goods or services *unrelated* to those the mark is used to distinguish must be based on articles 20 [B] and 21, which in turn come back to article 4.3 (because of the reliance of these provisions on the grounds for rejecting an application for registration). The right to prevent the *use* of well-known marks by persons not the owner for goods or services *unrelated* to those the mark is used to distinguish is more difficult to find. One might try to read the TRIPs Agreement and Paris Convention obligations into the law so that article 37 would extend to protect well-known marks from unauthorized use in relation to unrelated goods or services, despite it not being adapted for that purpose.

Another possible interpretation of article 3.14 of the TML 1992A should also be mentioned. As well as translations of famous marks, the article prohibits the registration of "another previously registered mark if. . . ." The provision does not say where the other mark must be previously registered. On one interpretation, the previous registration could be in any country. Read this way, the provision would be a powerful tool against the misappropriation of foreign trademarks, whether well known or not, by means of

---

69. TML 1992A, articles 20 [B] and 21.

registration in the UAE. By the application of article 38.1, the *use* in the UAE of marks that are previously registered in another country is prohibited if the use would cause confusion in relation to the products that are distinguished by the mark or similar products. The other view is that such an interpretation cannot be justified by the language of the provision, which should be read as referring to marks previously registered in the UAE (despite the provision then merely repeating article 10 of the TML 1992A). Greater clarity on what marks are prohibited from *use* in the UAE would be helpful in the fight against counterfeits and trademark piracy.

Examination of Trademark Applications

The regulations require the section at the Ministry to examine trademark applications.[70] Before making a decision in relation to the application, the Ministry may seek further information from the applicant or impose conditions, restrictions, and amendments for acceptance of the application.[71] The purpose of the Ministry's conditions for acceptance may be to "particularize" or "clarify" the mark to prevent it being confused with another prior mark, or for any other reason. Confusion is presumed if the goods or services are identical. This presumption was added to the end of article 11 of the TML 1992A in 2002.[72]

The trademark office issues three kinds of examination reports: preliminary technical examination reports, conditional acceptances, and rejections. Each is a standard form which in some cases requires the examiner merely to tick a box. Reasons for requests are not always apparent.

Preliminary Technical Examination Report

This kind of report raises one or more of four possible issues:

(a) The examiner may request a copy of the certificate of registration for the mark in the applicant's home country or in a Paris Convention country. This request may be made when the examiner has some concern about the absolute registrability of the mark, such as if it contains the name of a geographical place in another country, or if the examiner is concerned about the applicant's entitlement to the mark.

---

70. TMR 1993, article 10.
71. TMR 1993, article 11; TML 1992A, article 11.
72. TML 1992A, article 11. The language is from article 16.1 of the TRIPs Agreement.

(b) The examiner may request a translation or clarification of the source of the mark. Once this information is provided, the examiner may raise a substantive objection to registration and issue a rejection or acceptance of the mark subject to conditions.

(c) The examiner may request that certain goods or services be removed from the specification because they contravene public morals. A reference to gaming services or casinos, for example, will attract such an objection (see the discussion above on this subject).

(d) The examiner may request that a distinctive element be added to the mark to distinguish it from a prior mark (usually identified in the report by application number only). The addition of an element to a mark will almost certainly change the scope of the rights obtained by registration from what was claimed at the filing date (contrary to the basic principle that the rights granted are those claimed upon filing). If any amendment to a mark is substantial enough to remove its similarity to another prior mark, the amendment will probably not be consistent with the principle in the law that the amendment "not affect the essential identity of the mark."[73] Of course, if the owner of the prior mark is vigilant, the owner will find the advertisement of the later mark and may oppose it on the grounds of similarity. Rarely will the examiner request that the similar element be removed from the mark.

The applicant is given one hundred days from the date of being notified of the report to deal with the matters raised. If the applicant files a response to the report within the one hundred-day period, the application will not be deemed to have lapsed. The Ministry may then either accept the application or issue a second report which will be either a conditional acceptance, a rejection, or a further technical report.

Conditional Acceptance

This kind of report refers to article 11 of the TML 1992A, which permits the Ministry to impose the restrictions and amendments it considers necessary to prevent confusion or for other reasons. Usually this report asks the applicant to accept a disclaimer as a condition of being granted acceptance for registration. A typical disclaimer would be: "No right to the exclusive use

---

73. TML 1992A, article 18. This provision relates only to registered marks, not marks the subject of an application. This distinction is reflected in the practice at the Ministry that more or less any amendment can be made, however substantial it may be, after filing but prior to acceptance of the application.

of [xxx] separate from the mark is granted." The disclaimed word or device might be a geographical name, a non-distinctive word or device, or a word the same as or similar to a word or device that appears in a prior mark. It seems that in some cases the Ministry uses such disclaimers to overcome what would otherwise be an objection based on a prior application or registration. Of course, disclaimers do not appear on the goods or services, only the register, so they are of little help to consumers in distinguishing similarly branded products.

The report states that the applicant has the right to appeal the decision to the trademarks committee by paying the 250 dirham fee (about US$68) within thirty days of the date of being informed of the conditional acceptance. It is not possible to file arguments in response to the report. The only way of dealing with a conditional acceptance report is to appeal or to accept the condition. If an applicant does not file an appeal or does not accept the condition for acceptance, the application is supposed to be deemed to be abandoned.[74] However, as a matter of practice, applications that receive a conditional acceptance report are not being abandoned. They can be accepted (but not appealed) during an indefinite time frame, provided that the penalty fees are paid. The penalty fee is ten percent per month of the fee that is due not exceeding the total amount of the fee initially due in one year. For example, if the applicant decides to accept the condition and pay the publication fee two years after the expiry of the thirty-day period, the 500 dirham publication fee must be paid together with a 1000 dirham penalty for the two-year delay. Such delays may unfairly leave later applicants in a state of uncertainty awaiting the outcome of the earlier application.

Rejection

Rejection notices (or "reasoned decisions for rejection") are based on one or more of three reasons as specified in the standard form. The first reason is that the mark is identical or similar to another mark such that its *use* would give rise to an impression of a connection with the goods or services of the owner of the prior mark or would lead to the possibility of damage to the owner's interests. This reason is based on the second part of article 10 of the TML 1992A.

The second possible reason is that the mark is identical or similar to another mark that has an earlier priority date, unless the owner can prove his right to the mark in an opposition to the advertised mark. This reason may be based on the first part of article 10 of the TML 1992A.

---

74. TML 1992A, article 12.

The third possible reason may be any other reason arising from the application (such as any of the other reasons mentioned in article 3 of the TML 1992A).

The rejection notice specifies that the applicant has the right to appeal the rejection to the trademarks committee by paying the 250 dirham fee (about US$68) within thirty days of the date of being informed of the rejection or otherwise the application will be considered to be abandoned. It is not possible to file arguments in response to the report. The only way of dealing with a rejection is to appeal within a non-extendible thirty-day period. If the applicant does not file an appeal, the application is deemed to be abandoned.[75]

Advertisement and Opposition to Registration of a Trademark

Advertisement

The Ministry must advertise any mark that it accepts for registration in the TRADEMARK JOURNAL and the applicant must publish it in two daily newspapers issued in the UAE in Arabic—all of which is to be done at the expense of the applicant.[76] The processes for these advertisements are remarkably complex. The following describes the procedures using the publication portal.[77]

(a) Advertisement in the journal: once the notice of acceptance is received (by e-mail, at least for agents), the "publication" fees must be paid within sixty days. The agent logs onto the publication portal, enters the application information (all in Arabic), representation of the mark, endorsements, etc., saves the draft publication, and prints two copies. The agent must then take the acceptance notice and the two prints of the draft publication notice to the trademark office and pay the 500 dirham publication fee per application by e-Dirham card. The trademark office takes a copy of the draft publication and stamps the other and gives it back to the agent, together with a receipt for payment of the fees. The agent then logs back onto the portal, finds the saved draft publication notice, enters the receipt number and date, and hits "send."

---

75. TML 1992A, article 12.
76. TML 1992A, article 14 [A]; TMR 1993, article 16.
77. For much of 2008, the publication portal was unavailable. During this period, agents were filing copies of the newspaper advertisements instead of the draft journal advertisements prepared for the portal, and these were being published in the journal.

The application details as uploaded will be published in the TRADEMARK JOURNAL. Throughout this process no one at the trademark office is checking the details of what is published against what was filed. Because the details as filed do not determine what is published, there is an opportunity for discrepancies to occur, by mistake or otherwise, that can only be identified by obtaining a copy of the application as originally filed, and in those cases in which endorsements are imposed or amendments are made during examination, by reviewing the entire official file. This can be done officially only by the agent for the application or a person holding a power of attorney from the applicant. Any person can request true copies of documents on the file at a cost of 100 dirhams per document.

(b) Advertisement in two daily newspapers: the same information in Arabic that was prepared for the advertisement in the TRADEMARK JOURNAL must be prepared in an 8-cms-wide column format, as if it were an advertisement by the Ministry of Economy, for publication in UAE Arabic newspapers such as AL BAYAN, AL FAJR, AL AKHBAR AL ARAB, AL WAHDA and AL KHALEEJ. Some of the newspapers have common ownership and offer the publication in two newspapers for 700 dirhams, provided that the length of the advertisement is no longer than 10 cms. If the specification of goods or services is long, more space will be required and additional publication fees will have to be paid. Once the advertisements appear, they must be identified and cut out for use in the process for payment of the registration fees (discussed below).

Opposition

Within thirty days of the date of the *last* advertisement, any concerned person may file a written opposition with the Ministry to the registration of the mark advertised.[78] This provision puts potential opponents in the difficult position of having to identify the application advertised in both the journal and the two daily newspapers and to calculate the opposition deadline from the date of the last of them. It is the date of the journal which is often taken as the relevant date for the purposes of calculating the deadline (for example, by the providers of international watching services), but that practice is not strictly correct. It is within the provisions of the law for the opponent to file the opposition within thirty days from the date of the last publication or at any earlier time and whether based on the advertisement in the official journal or one of the newspapers.

---

78. TML 1992A, article 14 [B]; TMR 1993, article 17.

The provisions allow for the filing of the notice of opposition by registered post or by e-mail. The opposition fees would have to be paid at the trademark office in any case, so it would make sense to file the opposition at the same time. Registered post and e-mail are therefore not generally used. The usual practice is for the opposition notice to be filed at the trademark office and the fees to be paid at the same time using the e-Dirham card—currently the only method of paying the fees.

A copy of the opponent's agent's power of attorney will also need to be filed, or if the power is not yet available, the agent can file an undertaking to file it within sixty days.

The Ministry must notify the applicant within 15 days of receiving the opposition, providing the applicant with a copy of the notice of opposition.[79] If the applicant does not file a written reply (commonly referred to as a counterstatement) within thirty days of official notice of the opposition, the applicant is deemed to have abandoned the application.[80] There is no requirement that the applicant serve a copy of the reply on the opponent (in addition to filing it with the Ministry). The opponent is left in the dark as to whether a reply was filed and must use informal methods to obtain a copy of it from the file at the Ministry in Abu Dhabi.

Content of the Notice of Opposition and Reply

There are no provisions that specify on what grounds an application for registration of a trademark may be opposed and no requirements as to the form or substance of the notice of opposition or reply. Perhaps as a consequence of this, there are different practices. It is common to see standard form opposition notices that do not disclose any aspect of the source of the dispute or the facts on which the opponent relies, citing instead the provisions of the law to which the registration of the mark would be contrary. Such notices do little to facilitate dispute resolution. Other notices seek to plead all the relevant facts and legal grounds for the opposition following the principle that the other party is entitled to know the case against it and that full disclosure is more likely to resolve the matter quickly. Indeed, in view of the way that the evidence procedures work (discussed below), the parties may not know anything of the case to be answered until the morning of the hearing.

---

79. TML 1992A [B]; TMR 1993, article 17.
80. TML 1992A [C]; TMR 1993, article 18.

Grounds of Opposition

The principle that appears to be followed is that any matter that the application for registration needs to satisfy in order to be accepted may be raised as a ground of opposition, although this is not something found in the law or regulations.

The following is a list of possible grounds of oppositions (in summary form only):

(1) Article 2: The trademark the subject of the application is not a mark within the meaning of article 2.

(2) Article 2: The trademark the subject of the application does not take a distinctive form as required by article 2.

(3) Article 2: The trademark the subject of the application is not used or intended to be used to distinguish goods or services as required by article 2.

(4) Article 3: The trademark the subject of the application is devoid of any distinctive attribute or character contrary to article 3.1.

(5) Article 3: The trademark the subject of the application consists of customary names given to the goods or services contrary to article 3.1.

(6) Article 3: The trademark the subject of the application consists of conventional drawings or ordinary images of the goods contrary to article 3.1.

(7) Article 3: The trademark the subject of the application contravenes public morals or public order contrary to article 3.2.

(8) Article 3: The trademark the subject of the application consists of or contains a public emblem contrary to article 3.3.

(9) Article 3: The trademark the subject of the application consists of or contains a symbol, or an imitation, of the Red Crescent or similar symbols contrary to article 3.4.

(10) Article 3: The trademark the subject of the application consists of or contains a symbol the same as or similar to a symbol of a purely religious nature contrary to article 3.5.

(11) Article 3: The trademark the subject of the application consists of or contains a geographic name the use of which would cause confusion as to the source of the goods or services contrary to article 3.6.

(12) Article 3: The trademark the subject of the application consists of or contains an unauthorized reference to another person contrary to article 3.7.

(13) Article 3: The trademark the subject of the application consists of or contains an unjustified honorific title contrary to article 3.8.

(14) Article 3: The trademark the subject of the application consists of or contains a mark whose nature is to deceive the public contrary to article 3.9.

(15) Article 3: The trademark the subject of the application consists of or contains a false statement as to the products or services contrary to article 3.9.

(16) Article 3: The trademark the subject of the application consists of or contains an illusory, copied, or false commercial name contrary to article 3.9.

(17) Article 3: The trademark the subject of the application consists of or contains a mark owned by a person with whom it is forbidden to deal contrary to article 3.10.

(18) Article 3: The trademark the subject of the application consists of or contains a mark whose registration for some products or services would reduce the value of other products or services distinguished by the mark contrary to article 3.11.

(19) Article 3: The trademark the subject of the application consists of or contains words such as "patent" or "copyright" contrary to article 3.12.

(20) Article 3: The trademark the subject of the application consists of or contains an image of local or foreign currency contrary to article 3.13.

(21) Article 3: The trademark the subject of the application consists of or contains not more than a translation of a famous or previously registered mark contrary to article 3.14.

(22) Article 4: The trademark the subject of the application is a mark with an international reputation and the applicant is not the owner or authorized by the owner contrary to article 4.1.

(23) Article 4: The trademark the subject of the application is a mark with a reputation and its use by the applicant for unrelated goods or services would indicate a connection with the original owner contrary to article 4.3.

(24) Article 6: The applicant for registration is not a person satisfying the requirements of article 6 concerning who may register a trademark.

(25) Article 7: The applicant does not wish to use the mark the subject of the application to distinguish goods or services contrary to article 7.

(26) Article 8: The application for registration claims products or services falling in more than one international class contrary to article 8.

(27) Article 9: The marks the subject of the application do not constitute a series of marks contrary to article 9.

(28) Article 10: The trademark the subject of the application consists of or contains a mark that is the same or similar to a previously registered mark contrary to article 10.

(29) Article 26: The application is an attempt to re-register a previously cancelled mark within the three-year period contrary to article 26.

First Use as a Ground of Opposition

On many occasions the UAE courts have recognized that the first use of a mark, or the first filing of an application for trademark registration, whichever is earlier, is the test for settling competing ownership claims.[81] In opposition proceedings, the trademark office will also look at who has priority of use in the UAE when there is use that precedes the priority date of the earliest trademark application. However, the TML 1992A does not contain any provision that supports this practice, assuming that one sees it as concerning the question of ownership of a mark. Prior use might be raised under provisions relating to use that is deceptive or confusing (see grounds of opposition (14), (16), and (23) above, for example). The question of ownership is mentioned only in relation to famous marks (see article 4.1 of the TML 1992A). It seems that the idea of ownership of a mark resulting from first use, that is earlier than any relevant priority date, is one borrowed from general trademark principles.

Evidence in Support of the Opposition

There are no provisions in the law or regulations that deal with the form, content, filing, or service of evidence in opposition matters. In practice, each party may hold all of its evidence and file it at the hearing. Each party may not know anything of the case of the other party—the facts or legal argument on which it will rely—until the submissions are put before the hearing officer.

The responses that come from the hearing officer to the tendering of certain kinds of evidence are a guide to what the evidence requirements might be but these do vary to some extent from case to case. The following considerations might be taken into account when preparing evidence in opposition matters:

(a) The evidence must generally be in Arabic. For example, a copy of a Saudi Arabian trademark registration certificate will be in Arabic and can be tendered as a simple copy. A simple copy of a U.S. trademark registration may be tendered but together with a translation from a licensed UAE translator. An annual company report in English would be very expensive and time consuming to translate. Only the pages to be relied upon might be translated into Arabic by a UAE licensed translator or a translator in another country and then legalized up to the UAE Embassy. If the report is in German, for example, a UAE translator may not be able to provide a sworn translation unless a

---

81. See the discussion on unregistered trademarks below.

translation into English has been made and legalized up to the UAE Embassy. Based on this, the UAE translator should be able to provide an Arabic translation of the English translation of the original German. These issues can be surprisingly arcane and complex and result in significant additional costs for the preparation of evidence.

(b) Original documents are preferred. For example, advertisements in the media, posters, flyers, brochures, letterheads, and business cards should all be originals and not copies.

(c) Summaries of information will often be rejected. For example, schedules of trademark portfolios are problematic because they are secondary information prepared by an interested party. The certificates of relevant trademark registrations should be tendered instead. Certificates of trademark registrations from countries in the GCC are often persuasive (depending on the issues), as are U.S. and European Community trademark registrations (if one is trying to prove prior registration or fame of a mark).

(d) Judgments issued in similar cases. These may be received when tendered. If they are in Arabic (such as a decision from the Board of Grievances in Saudi Arabia), a simple copy may be accepted. If they are in another language, they will need to be accompanied by an Arabic translation legalized up to the UAE Embassy if not made by a licensed UAE translator.

(e) Trade licenses, company incorporation certificates, etc. These are often relied upon as indicators of first use or adoption of a name or mark. They may be tendered as simply copies in Arabic and if not, with Arabic translations legalized up to the UAE Embassy or made by a UAE translator. The UAE translator may not give a sworn translation unless the document being translated has been legalized up to the UAE Embassy.

(f) Newspaper and other press reports. These may be tendered as copies in Arabic or with Arabic translations. Such reports may contain publicly available sales information or market share percentages for the products or brands in dispute.

(g) It is not possible to make a sworn written statement in the UAE because such a statement would have to be made before a notary public and a notary public will not witness a statement unless he or she can independently verify the truth of what is being stated (if such independent verification was available, the witness would probably not be making the statement). If oral testimony is required, it will be necessary to make it in another country and have it legalized up to the UAE Embassy. However, there is a tendency not to trust evidence based on personal testimony. It is preferable to tender the primary evidence such as annual reports, advertising material, and promotional material as original documents rather than put it all under an affidavit or declaration made under oath.

(h) Sales figures, advertising expenditure, and profits. For these, independent reports are the best evidence, such as an auditor's report or a report commissioned from one of the court appointed experts.

(i) A sample of the product showing the mark as used, together with the receipt of purchase in the UAE, may be tendered and will very likely make an impression.

The following is a translation of the part of a hearing notice setting out the requirements for the hearing:

> Before the hearing the following documents and procedures must be satisfied:
> 1. It is necessary to bring samples of use of the mark in the markets.
> 2. It is necessary to bring the notice of publication to assess the period of opposition.
> 3. The tendering of a licence or licences of the companies or establishments.
> 4. It is necessary to bring copies of certificates of registration in the state or outside.
> 5. An image of a sample of use from within the state.
> 6. Consideration as to the possibility of settlement between the parties or of amending the mark.
> 7. Legal translations of all documents proposed to be tendered.
> 8. The opponent must tender an application in the same class as that which has been opposed or otherwise the opposition will be considered vexatious and unjustified.

This last requirement is not always mentioned. Indeed, the list of requirements in hearing notices seems to vary.

The Hearing of the Opposition

Before deciding on the opposition, the Ministry must hear the submissions of the parties if a request to be heard is made.[82] As a matter of practice, some time after the applicant's reply has been filed (the delay will depend on the workload at the trademark office) the hearing officer will issue a notice of the date and time of the hearing. All hearings are conducted at the trademark office in Abu Dhabi. Before the hearing, each party that wishes to be heard must pay the hearing fees and bring the receipts of payment to the hearing—it is one of the first matters that the hearing officer will check. A failure to

---

82. TML 1992A, article 15 [A]; TMR 1993, article 19.

have paid the hearing fees or to bring the evidence of payment may result in a summary decision in favor of the other party.

The hearing officer will also want to check that the persons appearing before him have a suitable power of attorney, notarized and legalized. The hearing is conducted in Arabic. The hearing officers are often Egyptian and will speak in a somewhat formal version of their Egyptian dialect. The representatives of the parties will usually sit across the desk of the hearing officer. The opponent proceeds first and the applicant replies. They will dictate their submissions to the hearing officer as he types them into what is in effect a statement that merges together legal arguments and facts. The items of evidence are tendered whilst making the submissions. The representatives will sign their respective statements when complete. The hearing officer will use the statements as a basis for making a decision.

The process is a fairly informal one and each party will probably make interjections and comments as the other is making submissions. The hearing officer may also ask questions of the parties and will generally try to keep the order and not permit undignified conduct.[83]

Confidentiality Obligations in Opposition Proceedings

There are no provisions in the TML 1992A or the TMR 1993 dealing with the issue of confidentiality in opposition proceedings. For the parties to agree on terms of confidentiality for certain material used in such proceedings is also rare. But because there is no stated obligation to serve evidence used in support of an opposition or in defense of an opposed application on the other party, it is possible to keep evidence out of the hands of the other side until the hearing. At the hearing, the confidential evidence can be tendered and a request can be made that it not be shared with the other party. Normally the other party will ask for a copy of what is submitted. How the evidence will be dealt with is a matter for the hearing officer to decide.

Once the evidence is in the hands of the hearing officer, he or she is under an obligation not to disclose the information or to use it for his or her own benefit or the benefit of others. This obligation arises from article 65 of the

---

83. The informality can be very helpful to the parties, allowing flexibility and a full airing of the issues. However, it can also be prejudicial. In one case, a representative of a party for the next hearing in the queue was waiting outside the hearing officer's room. Seeing this, the hearing officer very kindly invited the waiting representative to sit in his office with the parties for the current hearing while they were making their submissions. The waiting representative heard the details of the case and decided he had information that would assist one of the parties and began to interject, offering general and unsubstantiated remarks. The hearing officer permitted this to continue until the other party raised strong objections and insisted that he leave the room because this was a hearing in which he had no business.

PDL 2002, which now applies to employees in the department of industrial property at the Ministry of Economy.[84] However, the files at the Abu Dhabi trademark office are often accessible to anyone appearing to have a plausible purpose.[85]

Reform of the Opposition Procedures

The opposition procedures are one area of the administration of trademark matters that are arguably ripe for reform. The current procedures lack procedural fairness, are not designed to bring out the real issues in the matter, and cause the parties to incur avoidable costs. In any future reform of the procedures, the following issues might be addressed:

    a. the calculation of the deadline for opposing,
    b. the content of the notice of opposition and the use of "pro-forma" notices,
    c. the service of the reply to the opposition on the other party,
    d. the obligations to serve the other party with copies of the evidence before the hearing,
    e. the rules of evidence in oppositions,
    f. the rules of procedure for opposition hearings.

It is unclear at this point whether GCC TML will have a positive effect on opposition procedures because most of what is relevant is more likely to be in the regulations to the law which have not yet been published.

The Opposition Decision

The Ministry is to issue a decision rejecting or accepting the mark for registration, and in the event of acceptance, it may impose restrictions or conditions of the kind that are able to be imposed during the process of examination (see the discussion above).[86] However, unlike examination, in which there

---

84. Previously the Ministry of Finance and Industry was responsible for patent matters. However, the PDL 2002 was amended by Federal law no. 31 of 2006 to bring the patent law and its administration under the authority of the Ministry of Economy, which is responsible for trademark matters.
85. On occasions when I have followed up on a matter in Abu Dhabi, I have been invited to search through many files unrelated to my matter and without supervision. The current level of security does not prevent possible tampering with the files and the documents in them.
86. TML 1992A, article 15 [B].

might be an opportunity to debate the issues with the examiner, the hearing officer's decision is final and the only way forward is to appeal it.

Appeals from Opposition Decisions

Opposition decisions may be appealed by either party to the trademark committee within 15 days of the date of being informed by the Ministry of the decision in the matter.[87] There are no stated restrictions on what kinds of decisions can be appealed and on what grounds. Presumably even decisions to accept the application but with restrictions or conditions can be appealed and this can be done on any grounds. The formation and procedures of the trademark committee are discussed below.

The decision of the trademark committee can be appealed to the court within thirty days of being informed of the decision.[88] If an opponent is raising an appeal to the court against the acceptance of the opposed mark, the registration procedures for the mark are to continue unless the court orders otherwise. This may be of real significance to the opponent if an infringement allegation or action is expected upon obtaining registration of the mark. The opponent in such a case may apply to the court to suspend the registration procedures pending the resolution of the matter.

Other Kinds of Oppositions

There is no opportunity to oppose the renewal of trademark registrations, although renewals are to be advertised.[89] However, applications to amend marks must be advertised when accepted and may be opposed in the same way as applications for registration.[90]

Opposition may also be filed by the licensor or licensee of a trademark to the other party's application to cancel the recordal of the license.[91]

Publication of Opposition Decisions

The decisions issued by the Ministry in trademark opposition cases are not made public by any means of publication. They are issued to the parties only.

---

87. TML 1992A, article 15 [C].
88. TML 1992A, article 15 [C].
89. TML 1992A, article 19 [B]; TMR 1993, article 32.
90. TML 1992A, article 18.
91. TML 1992A, article 33 [B]; TMR 1993, article 47.

The result of this is that the opposition practice of the Ministry as a whole is very difficult to discern and giving advice on how the Ministry might decide a particular matter based on past practice will inevitably be limited by the cases that have come to the particular adviser's attention. Although past cases are not binding or determinative of future cases, they are nevertheless instructive for the business community and trademark professionals. Greater transparency through publication of opposition decisions is also likely to improve confidence in the Ministry's functions.

Registration and Renewal

Effective Date of Registration and Expiry

Once a mark is registered, the registration is effective from the date of the filing of the application for registration.[92] The registration expires ten years later and may be renewed for successive periods of ten years.[93]

Registration Procedure

Once the opposition period has expired and no oppositions have been filed, the applicant must pay the registration fees within sixty days of the end of the opposition period.[94] To do this, the agent must attend the trademark office with cut-outs of the two newspaper advertisements pasted onto a form with the name and date of the newspaper where the advertisements appeared typed on it. Then the 5000 dirham (US$1360) registration fee can be paid.

The Registration Certificate

The owner of the mark is to be given a certificate of registration (in Arabic only), the contents of which is described in the law.[95] The certificate usually issues about four months after payment of the registration fees. Before the Ministry's procedures required the filing of electronic copies of trademark applications, errors in certificates of registration were very common. This has

---

92. TML 1992A, article 16.
93. TML 1992A, article 19 [A].
94. Late payment incurs a penalty of ten percent per month not exceeding the amount of the fee that is due—5000 dirhams in this case.
95. TML 1992A, article 16; TMR 1993, article 24.

now been significantly reduced, with errors occurring only when some form of human intervention is required such as in the resizing of images of the mark or amending specifications. Certificates can be returned to the Ministry for correction.

Renewal

An application for renewal may be filed in the last year of protection.[96] If the owner fails to renew the registration in this period, there is a grace period of three months during which the registration may be renewed after it has expired. The Ministry is required to notify the owner of the expiry and possible renewal in the month following the end of the period of protection.[97]

The official application fee for renewal is 500 dirhams (about US$135) if renewal is applied for in the last year of protection. If renewal is applied for during the three month grace period, then the fee is 1000 dirhams (about US$270). There are also the costs of publication in the journal (500 dirhams, about US$136) and in two newspapers (about 700 dirhams, about US$190) in addition to the renewal fee itself (5000 dirhams, about US$1360). If the application is still pending at the time that renewal is due, the renewal fees must be paid to keep the application on foot.

Appeals from Ministry Decisions

The Ministry is empowered to make a number of decisions in matters under the TML 1992A. However, there is no general right for interested parties to seek to challenge the Ministry's decisions or have them reviewed. The law provides for rights of appeal in specific cases only. In relation to applications for registration of a trademark, the Ministry may reject an application or suspend it until satisfaction of a condition or restriction Such decisions may be appealed to the trademark committee within thirty days of being informed of the decision.[98] Decisions of the trademark committee may in turn be appealed to the court within sixty days of being informed of the decision.[99]

The Ministry's decision to renew (or not renew) a registration is not subject to appeal or review by another authority. This is perhaps because there is

---

96. TML 1992A, article 19 [A].
97. TML 1992A, article 19 [D].
98. TML 1992A, article 12 [A].
99. TML 1992A, article 12 [B].

no examination of renewal applications.[100] If a renewal is permitted but the renewal procedures were not followed (for example, the renewal application was filed out of time), the Ministry's decision to renew should be reviewable by a court or other authority.

There is no right of appeal or review of Ministry decisions in relation to applications to record assignments or licenses despite the fact that significant consequences may flow from non-recordal.[101]

Appeals from decisions in opposition matters were discussed above in the section on oppositions.

The Trademark Committee

Where there is a right to appeal a decision of the Ministry, the appeal is generally to the trademark committee.[102] The committee is required to have the following members: the undersecretary to the Ministry (heading the committee), two members from the Ministry nominated by the Minister, a board member from the Federation of Chambers and Industry, and a member from the board of each of the chambers of commerce and industry in the UAE.[103] There is no requirement that any of the members of the committee have any expertise in legal or trademark matters.

The committee is required to meet at least once a month.[104] However, decisions from matters appealed to the committee are taking between one and two years to issue. It is understood that the committee has delegated its role to the registrar of trademarks and that the process has become one of internal review of examiners' decisions by the registrar. The delays are due to the workload of the registrar.

Incontestability of Ownership

Article 17 of the TML 1992A grants to trademark owners a higher level of protection of their rights in certain circumstances. The registered owner is

---

100. TML 1992A, article 19 [B].
101. *See* articles 29 and 31 of the TML 1992A.
102. The notable exception is appeals from Ministry decisions to cancel registration of marks. These are made directly to the competent civil court: article 20 [B], TML 1992A.
103. TML 1992A, article 13.
104. TML 1992A, article 13, third paragraph.

deemed to be the exclusive owner of a mark when the following conditions have been satisfied:

a. the owner has used the mark continuously for no less than five years from the date of registration, and
b. no decision has issued in which it is decided that the registered owner is not the owner of the mark.

Presumably the use must be in the UAE and the decision of non-ownership must have issued in the UAE, although this is not expressed. The five-year period of use referred to must be "from the date of registration." The registration date and the filing date in the UAE are not necessarily the same. The Dubai Court of Cassation is reported to have decided that the five-year period commences from the date of filing and not the date of registration.[105] On this view, presumably any five-year period of use after the filing date will generate the protection of article 17 and that the period of use need not commence on the filing date itself. In order to determine whether a trademark registration has the protection of article 17, the party seeking to challenge the registration will need to investigate the facts relating to the prior use of the mark. Only once the start of a period of continuous use has been identified will it be possible to assess whether a challenge to the ownership of the mark is still within the five-year time limit.

The protection obtained from five years of continuous use is that no dispute may be raised against the ownership of the mark. Article 17 does not prevent challenges to the registration of the mark that are based on other grounds.

There is no definition in the law of "continuous use" or other provision that might clarify its meaning in this context. It was not uncommon in the UAE for commercial agents to register their principal's mark whilst using it under license from the principal. Would that kind of "use" prevent the principal from later challenging the agent's claim to ownership and registration of the principal's mark? Following general principles, the agent's use of the mark under license is not the agent's use but the principal's use, provided that the principal has exercised control of the nature and quality of the goods or services of the agent. The agent should therefore not be able to use article 17 as a shield against a challenge by the owner because the agent's use has

---

105. Richard Price and Essam Al Tamimi, United Arab Emirates Court of Cassation Judgments 1998–2003, Brill, 2005, page 357, case no. 384/2000. It seems from the facts of this case that the mark was in use as at the filing date so no question arose as to what "from the date of registration" would mean if the use commences *after* that date.

been for the purpose of indicating a connection between the products and the principal, not between the products and himself.[106]

Cancellation for Non-Use

Only the court may make an order for the cancellation of a trademark from the register on the basis of non-use.[107] The Ministry therefore does not accept applications for removal for non-use.

Onus of Proof

Although the law does not expressly state on whom the onus of proving non-use falls, there is nothing to suggest that the usual position of the plaintiff bearing the onus is altered. The difficulty of "proving the negative" in non-use cases is well known in other jurisdictions and some countries have implemented laws that require the applicant for removal to raise only a case to be answered (having made reasonable inquiries as to whether the mark the subject of the removal application is in use or has been used in the relevant period). There is no such structure under the UAE law and there is no guidance as to what would constitute adequate evidence to prove that a mark had *not* been used in the relevant period. It is likely that the court would appoint an expert to look at the question. The expert would receive submissions and evidence from the parties and prepare a report for the court. This way of determining matters of fact would likely remove to a considerable extent the importance and weight of the onus of proof but does not relieve the applicant for removal of the factual inquiries needed to ensure at the outset that the application has at least apparent merit. That a court application is required appears to discourage non-use applications and consequently they are rarer than they should be. The result is that unused marks accumulate on the register until the renewal fees are not paid.

Used for Five Consecutive Years

Before the 2002 amendments, the TML 1992 required it to be proved that "the mark has not been *seriously* used for five consecutive years." The word

---

106. *See also* the discussion in relation to cancellation for non-use. The Paris Convention also contains provisions dealing with the registration of trademarks by agents: article 6septies.
107. TML 1992A, article 22.

"seriously" was removed by the 2002 amendments. It is unclear whether the removal of the word was intended to alter the nature of the use of the mark that might be relied upon to defend a registration from an attack for non-use, or whether it was simply thought that the word was superfluous. Article 7 of the TML 1992A suggests that the use required by the law is use that is for the purpose of distinguishing goods or services. Arguably, this introduces the ideas of substantiality and seriousness. "Use" that is merely for the purpose of maintaining a trademark registration, such as the publishing of advertisements for the mark every few years, may not be substantial or serious. Whether the products or services are available in the UAE may also be relevant. If UAE consumers have experienced the advertising and responded to it (by making orders or bookings, for example), and even if the products or services are ultimately delivered or enjoyed outside the UAE, there is a good argument that the mark has been used in the UAE. Cases involving the use of marks in internet advertising raise such issues. The GCC TML re-introduces the "serious use" concept that was removed from the UAE law in 2002 with the words "used in a serious manner."[108]

There is also the question of when the five-year non-use period begins and ends. May the five-year non-use period begin on the day of filing or must it not commence until the day of registration? It is commonly assumed that the applicant has five years from the filing date in which to commence use of the mark but there is no express provision in the law that supports this view.[109] Does the non-use period end the day of the filing of the court application? If so, the removal applicant must be sure not to disclose its intentions to seek to remove the mark to the owner of the registration before filing the removal application because that would give the owner an opportunity to orchestrate some use of the mark and break the five consecutive years of non-use. If this is how the five-year period is to be calculated, then any demands or negotiations should only be made only after the court application has been filed. The provisions appear not to be designed to encourage the parties to resolve issues prior to resorting to the court.

The form of the use of a mark sometimes arises in non-use proceedings. The Paris Convention provides for some flexibility on this issue:

> Use of a trademark by the proprietor in a form differing in elements which do not alter the distinctive character of the mark in the form in which it was registered in one of the countries of the Union shall not entail invalidation of the registration and shall not diminish the protection granted to the mark.[110]

---

108. GCC TML, article 25.
109. The TRIPs Agreement mentions a minimum non-use period of three years, after which a registration may be vulnerable to cancellation: article 19.1.
110. Paris Convention, article 5.C (2).

From the point of view of general principles, any use of the registered mark in a form that does not substantially affect the identity of the mark should be relevant use in the context of non-use (and other) proceedings.

Use by a Licensee

Use of the mark by another that is authorized by the owner is deemed to be use of it for the purposes of defeating a non-use application.[111] Under general principles, not all authorized use of a trademark constitutes trademark use. This is recognized in the TRIPs Agreement:

> When subject to the control of its owner, use of a trademark by another person shall be recognized as use of the trademark for the purpose of maintaining the registration.[112]

Trademark use arises in cases in which the use by the third party is not only authorized by the owner, but the owner also exercises the relevant level of control over the nature and quality of the goods or services such that the mark retains its essential function: to indicate the registered owner as the origin of the goods or services (its badge of origin function). It would be reasonable to assume that the UAE law has not adopted a lesser standard in this respect than that required by the general principles. A similar deeming provision was not included in the GCC TML.

Reasons for Non-Use

If the owner of the mark can prove that the reason for the non-use of the mark during the five-consecutive-year period was due to a reason beyond his control, registration for the mark may be maintained. Import restrictions and the imposition of other government conditions that prevent use are deemed to be adequate reasons for this purpose. The GCC TML requires a "justification" for the non-use, which may represent a less stringent test.[113]

---

111. TML 1992A, article 22 [B].
112. TRIPs Agreement, article 19.2.
113. GCC TML, article 25.

Cancellation of Trademark Registrations

Cancellation by the Owner

The owner of a registered mark may apply for its cancellation in respect of all or some of the goods or services for which it is registered.[114] The application is to be filed with the section at the Ministry.[115] If there is a license recorded against the registration, the registration may not be cancelled unless the licensee has consented in writing or the licensee has waived this right in the license agreement.[116]

Cancellation by the Ministry

The Ministry has the right to cancel a trademark registration that has been registered without a right.[117] This provision was added by the 2002 amendments to the law. Although it is not expressly stated that the Ministry may be moved to cancel a registration upon application by a third party, the Ministry has accepted such applications.[118] The Ministry may make a decision in the matter without consulting the registered owner and if the decision is to remove the registration, the concerned persons will be notified by the Ministry and will have an opportunity to be heard. It seems that either party may appeal the Ministry's decision to the court.

The grounds for removal that might be raised are presumably all of those that were required to be satisfied in order to obtain registration (see the section on oppositions above). Matters that have arisen after registration was obtained appear, based on the language of the provision, to be excluded. If the use of the mark has become misleading after it was registered, for example, one could not seek its removal under this provision.

In the case of a cancellation under article 21 (a court ordered cancellation), the application of article 17 (concerning incontestability of ownership) is expressly preserved. Perhaps no inference can be drawn from the fact that a similar non-prejudice provision is absent from article 20 [B] and that article 17 of the TML 1992A places a limit on the Ministry's right to cancel a registration if the request for cancellation is based on reasons relating to the

---

114. TML 1992A, article 20 [A.1].
115. TMR 1993, article 34.
116. TML 1992A, article 20 [A.2].
117. TML 1992A, article 20 [B].
118. The Zimmerli case, for example.

ownership of the mark and the requirement for a five-year period of continuous use has been satisfied.

The GCC TML does not contain a provision corresponding to article 20 [B] of the TML 1992A.

Court-Ordered Cancellation

Any person may request an order cancelling a trademark that has been unlawfully registered. Although it is not expressly stated, this provision must be referring to an application made to the court. The Ministry must cancel the registration when a final decision is filed with it in executable form.[119] As in the case of cancellation decided by the Ministry, it appears that the grounds must relate to matters that were to be satisfied at the time of registration and not matters arising after. The applicant must show that the mark was registered without a right to be registered (following the language of the provision). The applicant for cancellation must rely on those matters that might have been raised in the process of obtaining registration—in effect, the grounds of opposition.

Article 17 is expressed not to be prejudiced by the right to seek cancellation. This would therefore exclude applications for cancellation in circumstances where the mark has been continuously used for the required five-year period and no decision has issued deciding that the owner does not own the mark.

Cancellation Ordered by the Israeli Boycott Office

The Israeli Boycott Office has the power to order the Ministry to cancel the registration of a trademark in certain circumstances.[120] This provision is absent from the GCC TML.

Publication of Cancellation

Cancellation of trademark registrations must be published in the journal and in two daily newspapers at the expense of the applicant for cancellation.[121] The information to be published is set out in the regulations.[122]

---

119. TML 1992A, article 21.
120. TML 1992A, article 24.
121. TML 1992A, article 25.
122. TMR 1993, article 36.

Re-Registration of Cancelled Marks

Any person who seeks to remove a trademark from the register in order to obtain registration of it faces the obstacle presented by article 26 of the law: a mark may not be re-registered in the name of another person for three years from the date of cancellation.

This provision has surely been drafted more expansively than was intended. Clearly in a case where removal of the registration was ordered because another person is the real owner of the mark, that person should be able to obtain registration as soon as possible after removal. This provision, read literally, appears to prevent the court from making an order that the real owner be permitted to obtain registration. It does not prevent the court ordering that the unlawful registration be transferred to the real owner rather than cancelled.

It should also be possible for a successful applicant for removal for non-use to obtain registration upon removal of the unused mark. The purpose of the three-year non-registration period is to avoid consumer confusion as to the origin of the goods or services indicated by the mark when the mark is re-registered. But if the mark has not been used for five consecutive years, there is little chance of that. This is a good reason to read down the provision to apply only to cancellation of registered marks other than on the basis of non-use. But that would not ameliorate the prejudicial consequences the provision might have on brand owners seeking to recover their marks from illegitimate users and owners.

A number of matters are left unresolved by this provision. For example, if the real owner of a mark is successful in obtaining the cancellation of a registration in the name of an illegitimate person, and three years must pass until the real owner can obtain registration for the mark, what action can the real owner take against the cancelled owner for *using* the mark if the real owner does not have the benefit of a registration? What action can the real owner take against other infringers in the three-year period of non-registration? Presumably, the real owner will have a pending application for registration of the mark that will be suspended for three years. It must pass through the opposition period. The infringer may oppose it and in doing so succeed in delaying the real owner's registration for many more years. The damage to the real owner's market and to consumers could be considerable, especially in terms of lost opportunity (for which compensation is generally not available in the UAE).

The problems with this provision have, it seems, been identified by the drafters of the GCC TML, which contains the same provision but with additional wording, allowing the court to specify a re-registration waiting period of less than three years. In appropriate circumstances the court might order the period to be as little as one day in cases in which the real owner's mark is pending. But this does not address the other obstacles that could potentially be put in the real owner's way in obtaining registration. Another way of dealing with this issue would be to give the court broad powers to rectify the register so that real owners may be substituted for illegitimate ones expeditiously. The court and the Ministry both have the power to amend the register but it appears to be limited (amendment is discussed below).

Reasons for Cancellation Arising after Registration

A mark may have obtained registration legitimately but due to facts arising after registration, its use or registration becomes contrary to the provisions of the law. Marks may be misused and may become generic, for example, or may become misleading in the hands of the registered owner as a result of improper licensing or assignment. There are presently no provisions in the law directed at cancellation in such circumstances. The court and the Ministry may have a broad power to amend the register but it is not clear that it was intended to be used for such purposes.

Power to Amend the Register

The law gives to the competent civil court as well as the Ministry the power to amend the register.[123] On one reading of this provision, it is merely an administrative provision not intended to add another level to the more specific powers given to cancel registrations. On another reading, the provision gives the court and the Ministry broad powers to entertain all kinds of applications for changes to the register, including changes that alter substantive rights. It allows the following amendments:

a. the addition of information to the register that has been omitted; and
b. the removal or amendment of information that has been entered unlawfully or is inconsistent with the truth.

The right to amend information that is inconsistent with the truth has the potential to open trademark registrations to review on a wide range of grounds.

---

123. TML 1992A, article 23.

Assignments and Mortgages

Freedom to Assign, Mortgage, and Attach

The TRIPs Agreement requires member countries to permit assignments of trademarks with and without the goodwill of business in which they are used:

> Members may determine conditions on the licensing and assignment of trademarks, it being understood that the compulsory licensing of trademarks shall not be permitted and that the owner of a registered trademark shall have the right to assign the trademark with or without the transfer of the business to which the trademark belongs.[124]

This requirement is reflected in the first of the TML 1992A provisions dealing with assignments:

> The ownership of a trademark may be transferred or mortgaged or attached with or without the business or investment project that uses the trademark to distinguish its products or services.[125]

Historically, assignments of trademarks without the business in which they have been used were considered to have public policy implications because the severance of the link between the mark and the business producing the branded goods. The subsequent use of the same mark as a badge of origin for another business carried with it the risk that the consumer would be misled into believing falsely that the goods of the assignee were of the same nature and quality those of the assignor.

The TRIPs Agreement philosophy is now widespread with the result that the policing of assignments that lead to misleading conduct is left to competitor brand owners or consumers who are affected by any adverse consequences of the assignment. However, an unfettered freedom to assign needs to be accompanied by a mechanism for the rectification of the register for those cases in which the assignment has consequences that are contrary to the public policy of the law. The Paris Convention recognizes that assignments may be contrary to public policy:

> The foregoing provision does not impose upon the countries of the Union any obligation to regard as valid the assignment of any mark the use of which by the assignee would, in fact, be of such a nature as to mislead the public, particularly

---

124. TRIPs Agreement, article 21.
125. TML 1992A, article 27.

as regards the origin, nature, or essential qualities, of the goods to which the mark is applied.[126]

It is not certain that the cancellation provisions in the TML 1992A are adequate for the purpose of regulating assignments that may have adverse consequences on consumers (see the discussion on this subject above).

Sales of Business

The TML 1992A contains two provisions that address sales of business.

[A.] The transfer of the ownership of a business or investment project may include the trademark registered in the name of the transferor of the ownership that has a close connection with the business or investment project unless it has been agreed otherwise.
[B.] If the ownership of a business or investment project is transferred without the mark, the transferor of the ownership may continue to use the mark for the products or services for which the mark has been registered unless it has been agreed otherwise.[127]

The first provision permits the transfer of a business to include the trademark that is used in close connection with it. This provision seems merely to restate the provision that permits assignments with and without the business.[128] The parties may agree otherwise, meaning that they can agree not to include the mark in the sale, in which case, the owner may continue to use the mark for the goods or services for which the mark has been registered. It is unclear whether these provisions add anything to what is already expressed or implied by article 27. The permission for the owner of the mark to continue to use it after the sale of the business in which it was used does not address the consequences of the owner, as a result of the sale, losing something that made the products unique and therefore the subsequent use of mark by the owner misleading.[129]

---

126. TRIPs Agreement, article 6.
127. TML 1992A, article 28.
128. TML 1992A, article 27.
129. For example, where a bottled water producer sells the land and the spring from which the water for the product has been obtained, the use by the owner of the same mark in relation to water from another source might be misleading.

Unregistered Trademarks

Article 27 mentions only "trademarks," not registered trademarks or applications for them (consistent with the language of the TRIPs Agreement provision). Article 28 refers twice to registered marks. Transfers of ownership must be recorded in the register of marks (discussed below). The relevant provisions in the regulations use neutral language. On balance, one could probably interpret the law and regulations as allowing the assignment of both trademark registrations and applications. As a matter of practice, the assignments of applications can be recorded following the procedure described below.

A person who has used a mark in the UAE (but has not registered or applied to register it) has the right to obtain registration of it if that person is the first to use in the UAE (and subject to provisions protecting famous marks).[130] Whether such a right stands independently of the business in relation to which the mark is used and can be assigned separately from the business is an open question.

Necessity of Recordal

Transfers of ownership and mortgages of trademarks that are not recorded with the Ministry are "not effective against others."[131] Whether recorded or not, a transfer of ownership of a trademark registration is a conveyance of title between two parties and if validly executed should be able to be relied upon by either party as against the other (for example, where one of them denies the transfer of ownership). It is difficult to see how a valid assignment could not be effective as between the parties prior to being recorded with the Ministry. Some have interpreted the provision to mean that the assignee cannot enforce the rights obtained by the assignment against third parties until the assignment has been recorded and the assignee is the registered owner. That may be the only way to make sense of the provision even though it reduces its meaning to a statement of what should be apparent: only a registered owner can enforce the rights granted by registration.

If an unrecorded assignment or mortgage has no effect on third parties, a third party could validly take an assignment or mortgage of a trademark that had already been assigned or mortgaged but not recorded and do so even with notice of the earlier assignment or mortgage, obtaining a valid transfer

---

130. *See* for example, Dubai Court of Cassation cases no. 598 of 2003 and no. 136 of 2006.
131. TML 1992A, article 29. The word "al ghair" ("the other") is singular but has the sense of a general plural, as I have translated it. *See also* TMR 1993, article 37. The obligation to record mortgages is in article 42 of the TMR 1993.

of rights because the earlier transfer was not yet effective against others. The first transferee is exposed to a further assignment prior to recordal and should therefore be applying for the recordal of the transfer (as unjust as that may be) as soon as possible. If the second transferee filed an application to record before the first transferee filed a recordal application, there is a good argument that the second transfer should defeat the first transfer because it was not effective against others until recorded.

The GCC TML contains substantially the same requirement to record assignments, mortgages, and attachments and deems them not effective against others until recorded.[132]

Procedures for Recordal

Although the law and regulations do not distinguish between assignments of trademark registrations and of trademark applications, the procedures for recording each are different.

Assignments of trademark applications can be recorded by the assignee filing a letter requesting the recordal, supported by a legalized assignment document evidencing the assignment and a legalized power of attorney from the assignee to the trademark agent. In this case, the assignment does not need to be published, as it does for the assignment of a registration.

In the case of assignments of registrations, the assignee is to file an application for recordal using the required form,[133] supporting it with proof of the transfer of ownership, which is, according to current practice, a legalized assignment document.[134] The assignee must then publish the assignment in the journal and two daily newspapers at its cost.[135] The procedure is similar to that required for applications for trademark registration (described above).

There are penalties for late filing of applications to record assignments of registrations. If the recordal application is filed within three months of the date that the assignment document was notarized, then the application fee per registration is 250 dirhams (about US$68) and the publication fee is 500 dirhams (about US$136). In the next three-month period the application fee is increased to 500 dirhams and in the next three months after that it is increased to 750 dirhams (about US$204), which is the maximum application fee, whatever the delay in filing.

132. GCC TML, article 28.3. The TML 1992A does not include a requirement for the recordal of attachments. The provision in the GCC TML includes attachments.
133. TMR 1993, article 37.
134. The regulations do not mention that the assignment must be legalized: TMR 1993A, article 38.
135. TMR 1993, article 41.

Agreements to Assign

There are no provisions in the trademark law or regulations dealing with agreements to assign trademark-related rights.

Licensing Trademarks

The licensing of trademarks in the UAE is extensively regulated compared to some other jurisdictions. The requirements for legalized contracts and the recordal of licenses impose substantial burdens on the freedom to conduct business. The result appears to be that the legal requirements are widely ignored. Because businesses in the UAE have historically been licensees, the provisions lean to some extent in their favor (see, for example, the granting of a right to oppose the cancellation of license recordals).

The Requirement for Writing and Legalization

Trademark licenses must be made pursuant to a written and legalized contract.[136] They therefore cannot be oral, implied, or partly oral and partly written. The requirement for legalization means that the contract must be witnessed by a notary public. Major business transactions are conducted throughout the world without the need for notarization. Why trademark licenses require such overview is unclear. If the contract is made in the UAE, it must be made before a UAE notary. UAE notaries do not simply witness the signing of the document but also review it for compliance with the law. The notary can (and often will) refuse to notarize documents unless certain changes are made to matters of substance and form. The contracting parties should consider executing the license contract in a jurisdiction where notaries act merely as witnesses. Licenses executed outside the UAE must be legalized up to the UAE embassy in that country and then stamped by the Ministry of Foreign Affairs in the UAE. If the license is not in Arabic, it will have to be translated either by a UAE licensed translator or a foreign translator and legalized up to the UAE Embassy before it can be used for official purposes in the UAE.

---

136. TML 1992A, article 30.

Registered Marks Only

Trademark licenses can only be granted in relation to registered trademarks. This appears to be the implication of the provisions relating to licenses. For example, the goods or services the subject of the license may be some or all of those that are registered.[137] The term of the license must not exceed the registration term (see below). In principle, there should be no reason why an unregistered but used mark or a mark the subject of an application could not be licensed, provided that the licensor has some identifiable right in the mark. Such licenses would not fit within the current regulatory framework for the licensing of trademarks and may therefore not be recognized.

The Term of Licenses

The term of a trademark license must not exceed the term of registration.[138] This is potentially a highly inconvenient limitation. Very often, the license will deal with many marks, possibly the same mark in different classes or a cluster of similar marks, each of which will be the subject of separate trademark registrations and which may have been filed on different dates. The expiry dates for each will therefore be different. This provision would require either that separate license contracts be entered into for each or that the license contract expire with respect to different marks on different dates. The complexity is then doubled by the arrangements that need to be made for renewal of the registrations and the remaking of the license contracts after renewal. If sub-licenses have been granted, the same considerations and obligations would apply. The requirement for recordal of licenses adds another level of bureaucracy (see below).

Unjustified Restrictions in Licenses

Trademark licenses may not contain restrictions on the licensee that do not result from the rights granted by trademark registration or that are not necessary for the preservation of those rights.[139] There are numerous possible terms that are often included in trademark license contracts that are not directly related to the registered rights or the preservation of them, especially if the trademark license is part of a larger transaction document. Such terms could relate to anything from how notices must be delivered to procedures

---

137. TML 1922A, article 30 [A].
138. TML 1992A, article 30 [B].
139. TML 1992A, article 34.

for dispute resolution to restrictions on export of branded products. The level of uncertainty in how this provision is to be understood makes drafting and advising on trademark licenses very difficult.

Permitted Terms in Trademark Licenses

The permitted terms in Trademark Licenses are:

1. The license may be granted for some or all of the goods or services covered by the trademark registration.[140]
2. The license may limit the geographical area (in the UAE) in which the goods or services are marketed.[141] The implication of this provision is that other geographical limitations such as those on the place of production or the places where the products are to be sold may not be permitted. The scope of the concept of "marketing" is unclear.
3. The license may specify the term of the license.[142] This provision requires that article 31 be taken into account (which contains the obligation to record licenses). However, it is article 30 [B] that deals with the duration of licenses (they must not exceed the registration term). The reference to article 31 in article 34.2 appears to be an error. The issue of the limitations of license terms is discussed above.
4. The owner may impose conditions that permit the monitoring of the quality of the products to which the license applies.[143] These provisions are the heart of any licensing agreement and are the basis upon which the owner of the licensed mark can ensure that the mark remains distinctive of the owner's goods or services and not become distinctive of the licensee. Managing this risk is the key to the licensing of brands. What terms and conditions are required in any particular case will depend on the specific facts. The principle is that the owner must exercise control over the nature and quality of the goods or services to the extent that it is as if the goods or services are being produced or delivered by the owner. The level of control required will vary from case to case. The license contract gives the owner the *means* to exercise such control—it is not in itself an act in the exercise of control. Licensors who license their brands under the appropriate terms and conditions but who do not exercise the relevant level of control put their brands

---

140. TML 1992A, article 30 [A].
141. TML 1992A, article 34.1. The Arabic word used here is "tasweeq," commonly translated as "marketing."
142. TML 1992A, article 34.2.
143. TML 1992A, article 34.3. The omission of any reference to services in this provision may simply be an error.

at risk. There is no reason to believe that the principles that should be applied in the UAE are any different.

5. The owner may impose obligations that are directed at stopping the licensee from doing acts that would adversely affect the value of the products or services that bear the mark.[144] This provision seems to permit terms relating to how the products or services are offered or sold after they have been produced. For example, the licensor may require that food products not be offered in any supermarket that offers pork products because that might reduce the value of the products in the eyes of Muslims.

Exclusive or Non-Exclusive?

If the license contract does not specify whether the owner of the mark may or may not use the mark that is licensed, the license will be deemed to be non-exclusive as against the owner, who will be able to use the licensed mark concurrently with the licensee.[145] That presumably means that the owner may grant licenses to others. It seems therefore that all licenses are non-exclusive unless expressed to be otherwise.

Trademark Licenses Must Be Recorded

The license contract must be recorded with the Ministry and published.[146] The publishing requirements are set out in the regulations and include publication in the journal and two daily newspapers.[147]

Until recorded with the Ministry, licenses are not effective against others.[148] The meaning of this expression was discussed above in the context of assignments. The issues it raises for licenses are slightly different. A license is usually a contract between two parties and the contract is effective only as between them and no one else. It is unclear who "the others" would be other than the two parties to the contract. If it is referring to them, it means that the signing of a contract by the parties has no effect until it has been recorded with the Ministry. If this is indeed the meaning of the provision, it represents a serious incursion into the freedom to contract and do business. The parties will remain in an uncertain state as to whether they have in fact entered into

---

144. TML 1992A, article 34.4.
145. TML 1992A, article 30 [A].
146. TML 1992A, article 31.
147. TMR 1993, article 45.
148. TML 1992A, article 31.

a contract until they have passed through the recordal process. It also means that the effective date of all trademark licenses should be the date on which the Ministry records it.

Just as the parties appear not to enter into an effective license simply by signing a contract, they also do not necessarily terminate it by agreement. The law contains procedures for the cancellation of license recordals and the right to oppose an application for cancellation. The implication is that the right to use the mark only ultimately terminates upon cancelation of the license recordal. The cancellation procedures are discussed below.

Cancellation of License Recordals

The licensor or the licensee may seek the cancellation of the recordal of a trademark license. Evidence of expiry or termination of the license must support the application for cancellation.[149] The Ministry must inform the other party to the license and that party has the right to oppose the cancellation.[150]

Upon receiving notice of the cancellation application, the other party has thirty days to oppose the cancellation.[151] Either party may request a hearing. There is no process set down for the filing and service of evidence and submissions. Either party may appeal the decision to the trademark committee within 15 days of notice of the decision. The trademark committee's decision may be appealed to the court within thirty days of notice. The cancellation decision must ultimately be published.[152]

Agency Laws

The commercial agency laws of the UAE may be relevant to consider when dealing with trademark licensing issues. However, a discussion of them here is beyond the scope of this book.

Monitoring Marks

Marks that are commonly known as "certification marks" are dealt with in two articles in the law under the title of marks indicating that a product or

---

149. TML 1992A, article 33 [A]; TMR 1993, article 46.
150. TML 1992A, article 33 [B].
151. *See* article 47 of the TMR 1993.
152. TMR 1993, articles 49, 50 and 51.

service has been monitored (or checked) and examined.[153] It seems that only "legal persons" may apply to register such a mark and that they must be "responsible" for monitoring or examination of products or services as to any of their characteristics. The language of the article in the law refers to applying for a *license* for registration but the regulations refer to applications for registration only.[154] The reference to a license may be connected with the fact that Ministerial approval is required for the registration of such marks.[155] For an example of what appears to be a monitoring mark, see ministerial decision no. 418 of 2007 in relation to the use of the "Organic" trademark (appendices A13 and B17).

Criminal Action Against Infringement

The following is an interpretation of the specific offenses under article 37 of the TML 1992A relating to counterfeiting and imitation of trademarks.

Article 37.1 Offenses

The provision reads as follows:

> 1. Anyone who has counterfeited a lawfully registered trade mark or has imitated it in a manner that will lead to the deception of the public, whether in relation to goods and services that the original mark distinguishes, or those that are similar to them, and anyone who has used a counterfeited or imitated trade mark with knowledge of that.

This article makes a distinction between three different acts: counterfeiting, imitating, and using.

1. Counterfeiting a Registered Trademark

The concept of counterfeiting is not defined in the law. The Arabic verb that is used is "zawwara," the same verb that is used in relation to the counterfeiting of money, for example (just as in English). The sense it carries is of an exact copy. The copying is stated to be of the registered trademark, not of the product as a whole (following the language of the provision).

---

153. TML 1992A, articles 35 and 36.
154. Compare article 35 [A] of the TML 1992A with article 52 of the TMR 1993.
155. TML 1992A, article 35 [B].

There appears to be no requirement for the defendant to know that the mark is registered (but knowledge of the counterfeiting or imitation is required for the use offenses—see below). Perhaps the defendant's knowledge of wrongdoing is to be presumed in cases in which a mark has been counterfeited or imitated because the level of similarity is so high that the likelihood that the defendant did not know he or she was engaging in an unlawful act is extremely low.

This offense, as well as that of imitating a registered trademark, does not appear to require the *use* of the mark. It is an offense relating to the act of making the counterfeit trademark. The defendant need not have used the mark in the sense of offered the product for sale.

This offense concerns only trademarks that are registered pursuant to the UAE law (and not unregistered marks or marks registered in other countries).

2. Imitating a Registered Trademark

The Arabic verb translated here as "imitating" is "qallada" meaning to copy. When paired with "zawwara" ("counterfeited"), it suggests a sense that the copy of the mark need not be exact but must be nearly so. The level of copying must be such that it will lead to the deception of the public.

The 2002 amending law added the following words to the article: "whether in relation to goods or services that the original mark distinguishes or those that are similar." These words seem to qualify both the act of counterfeiting and of imitating marks and to introduce the concept that those acts must be done in relation to products or services. It seems that it is not enough simply to reproduce a mark but it must be done in relation to relevant goods or services. That may mean that the counterfeited or imitated mark must, in relation to goods, for example, be applied to them to complete the offense.

It is curious that the amendment was not added to the article so that it applies also to the offense of using a counterfeited or imitated mark. One hypothesis is that the amendment to the paragraph was put in the wrong place. It may have made more sense to put it at the end of the paragraph so that it reads:

> 1. Anyone who has counterfeited a lawfully registered trade mark or has imitated it in a manner that will lead to the deception of the public, and anyone who has used a counterfeited or imitated trade mark with knowledge of that, whether in relation to goods and services that the original mark distinguishes, or those that are similar to them.

On the interpretation suggested here, the counterfeiting and imitation offenses are directed at the producers of products bearing counterfeited and imitated marks, not the users or sellers of them. The products bearing the counterfeited or imitated trademark must be the same as or similar to those for which the mark being counterfeited or imitated is registered in the UAE.

3. Using a Counterfeited or Imitated Trademark

Use of a trademark carries with it the idea that the mark is being dealt with in such a way as to perform its trademark function—to distinguish goods and services. Such use normally begins with the offer to sell the products bearing the mark. But it is not clear that this is the intention here, particularly given that offenses relating to offering products for sale are dealt with separately in article 37. Perhaps "using" here has another meaning such as applying the counterfeited or imitated mark to packaging or advertising, thus connecting its meaning more with the pre-trademark use offenses of counterfeiting and imitating a trademark. As discussed above in relation to the imitation of a mark offense, this offense does not appear to require that the use be in relation to the goods or services for which the mark is registered or those that are similar (based on the position of the relevant words in the article).

Article 37.2 Offenses

The provision reads:

> 2. Anyone who has, in bad faith, put on his products a registered trade mark owned by another or used that mark without a right.

Two acts are identified by this provision: putting a trademark on products and using a trademark.

4. Putting Another's Registered Trademark on Products

This offense seems to cover the same territory as the article 37.1 offenses (as interpreted above) but with three differences: (a) the provision mentions only the registered mark and not a counterfeit or imitation of it; (b) it does not mention the goods and services for which the mark is registered; and (c) it introduces the concept of bad faith (whereas only knowledge is mentioned in article 37.1). Perhaps the provision is directed at the act of applying registered marks to any goods or services when it is done with the intention to deceive. But the question remains whether it adds anything to the use offense in article 37.1.

5. Using Another's Registered Trademark Without a Right

Like the other offense in this provision, it is broadly drafted without a reference to the goods or services. It also requires bad faith. The question here is whether "use" should be interpreted to mean something similar to the concept of "putting" that appears in the provision or whether it means trademark use in the sense of offering a product for sale, marketing it, etc.

Article 37.3 Offenses

The provision reads as follows:

> 3. Anyone who has sold, or offered for sale or circulation, or possessed with the intention of selling, products bearing a counterfeited or imitated trademark or a mark placed on them knowing that he has no right to do so, as well as anyone who has provided or offered to provide services under a counterfeited or imitated trademark or has used it knowing that he has no right to do so.

In relation to products, three acts are penalized in this provision: selling, offering for sale or circulation, and possession with intention to sell. In relation to services, the penalized acts are: providing a service and offering to provide a service. Use of a counterfeited or imitated mark knowingly without a right is also added.

6. Selling or Offering for Sale or Circulation Products Bearing a Counterfeited or Imitated Trademark or Another Person's Mark

This offense requires the defendant to have sold or offered for sale or circulation products bearing a counterfeited or imitated trademark. There is no requirement that: (a) the trademark in question be registered in the UAE, and (b) that the registered products and the products to which counterfeited or imitated marks are applied be the same or similar. One argument is that the amendment that was made to article 37.1, adding a reference to goods and services that the mark originally distinguishes, was intended as a kind of definition of counterfeited and imitated marks, so that wherever those expressions are used, the reference to goods and services is to be understood. The same argument might be made in relation to the registration issue— article 37.1 requires the counterfeit or imitation to be of a registered mark. If this is indeed how article 37.3 is to be understood, it limits it scope considerably.

In cases of the act of counterfeiting or imitation of marks discussed above, there is a good argument that the knowledge can be presumed. But when the offense is based on an act of selling or possession with the intention of sale, knowledge cannot be inferred from the act in the same way. Many of the cases that have come before the UAE courts have raised this issue and judges have inferred from specific circumstances that the defendant knew that the products carried a counterfeit or imitated mark. For example, selling from the back of a truck or in irregular circumstances may be indicative of relevant knowledge. The defendant may also have admitted knowledge by referring to the products as being of "second quality" or some other expression in use in the market at that time.

7. Possessing, with the Intention of Sale, Products Bearing a Counterfeited or Imitated Trademark or Another Person's Mark

Possession with intention of sale is a more difficult offense to prove because the intention to sell is something to be inferred from the circumstances. Evidence of the acceptance of payment would certainly be a strong indicator of the intention. The presence of the product on a shop shelf is less strong, being open to the assertion that it is for display only and not for sale (however implausible that may be). The issues discussed above in relation to the offense of selling and offering for sale also apply to this offense.

8. Providing or Offering to Provide Services under a Counterfeited or Imitated Trademark

Here also there is the requirement for the defendant's knowledge of the fact that the mark is counterfeited or imitated or that the mark belongs to someone else and he has no right to use it. In the case of services being offered under such marks, establishing the required state of knowledge might be done by a demand letter. The defendant's continued use would then complete the crime.

9. Using a Trademark Without a Right Knowingly

The language here is very broad, distinguishing providing or offering to provide services from use of a mark knowingly without a right. Precisely what conduct it seeks to encompass beyond what is expressed in the previous offense is not clear.

The GCC TML Offenses

Article 39 in the GCC TML corresponds to article 37 in the TML 1992A. The provisions that correspond to article 37 of the TML 1992A have been divided into two parts. It seems that the intention is for the first group of offenses to deal with the *production* of counterfeit or imitation products (perhaps corresponding to the offenses in articles 37.1 and 37.2 of the TML 1992A) and for the second group to deal with *trading* in such products (corresponding to article 37.3 of the TML 1992A). The former are given harsher penalties than the latter. The GCC TML provisions appear to be modeled on the TML 1992A provisions.

The Law for the Prevention of Fraud and Deception in Commercial Dealings

The broad objectives of the FDL 1979 are reflected in its first two articles, which penalize a wide range of acts in commercial dealings that are deceptive, as well as acts of falsifying or corrupting products or dealing with such products. The focus is on food and drugs and raw produce. The language of the provisions perhaps reflects the UAE preoccupations thirty years ago. The law is not expressly an anti-counterfeiting law but can have application to brand counterfeiting. The law does not use the word used in the TML 1992A for counterfeiting ("zawwara") and does not mention trademarks. Despite this, some trademark infringements would very likely fall within the offenses described in the FDL 1979. The following are some examples:

1. Where a counterfeit branded product is sold and the buyer believes it is genuine—this may be an offense under article 1.4, which penalizes deception in relation to the origin or source of the product.
2. Where a counterfeit branded product is sold, the buyer believes it is genuine and the counterfeit does not have the same specifications or characteristics as the genuine product—this may be an offense under articles 1.1 and 1.3, which penalize deception in relation to product specifications and characteristics.
3. Where a trader shows a buyer a genuine product but delivers a counterfeit, this may be an offense under article 1.2.
4. Offering for sale a counterfeit branded product is offering for sale a false product and so would also fall within the language of article 2.2.
5. The importation of falsified products is not permitted by article 4.

Both the Ministry of Economy and Commerce and the courts have a role to play in relation to the FDL 1979. The Minister may order re-export of false or corrupted products to their origin or their destruction if not re-exported in good time.[156] It is the employees of the Ministry who are to act as judicial officers for the proving of violations under the law and may enter shops and other places (without a warrant) and may take samples.[157] There is no mention of the Ministry as having the power to impose the penalties under the law. It may have been contemplated by the drafter of the law that all cases where punishment is required would be transferred to the prosecutor. Clearly, the punishment of imprisonment in articles 1, 2, 3, 8 and 11, and expulsion of non-nationals from the country under article 10, could only be ordered by the court. Nevertheless, fines and other penalties such as shop

---

156. FDL 1979, article 4.
157. FDL 1979, article 6 and 7.

closures and trade license cancellations[158] are being imposed by authorities such as the Dubai Department for Economic Development.[159]

Enforcement with the Dubai Police

The "Economic Crimes Section" of the Dubai Police, located in the general headquarters, receives complaints in relation to the infringement of intellectual property rights. The section specializes in handling cases involving the counterfeiting of currency and has had many years of experience in product counterfeit cases.

Not all cases of product counterfeits are suitable to take to the Dubai Police. Significant Police resources go into the setup of a case and the execution of a raid and so "minor" cases (such as a sighting of a few counterfeit products in a shop) may be best taken to other authorities. This means that a good deal of brand-owner managed and funded investigation work needs to go into the case before taking it to the Police. If the investigation reveals a trader offering for sale a significant quantity of counterfeit products, then the case may be suitable for the Police.

To initiate a case with the section, a complaint must be filed. This is usually done by an agent on behalf of a brand owner. The complaint must be supported by the agent's power of attorney and copies of the relevant and current UAE trademark registrations. It is likely that the officers receiving the complaint will want to see a sample of the counterfeit product being offered, as well as a sample of the genuine product to compare it against. The officers will consider the case from a number of angles, including whether the information put before them is credible, how the prosecutor will view it when they go to request the warrant, what issues might arise at the Criminal Laboratory (which has to analyze the products and then produce for the court an expert's report) and what practical issues might arise in the execution of the raid given the location of the trader and of any known warehouse for the products. There are no fees to be paid for filing the complaint or for any other of the Police procedures.

Once the complaint is accepted, the Police do not simply carry out a raid on the trader on their own initiative (as is sometimes assumed) unless there are special circumstances and they are confident of the commission of a crime and the availability of the necessary evidence. The most important part of the

---

158. FDL 1979, article 10.
159. The trade license authorities, such as the Dubai Department for Economic Development, were given certain powers in relation to the proving of offenses by the 2003 amendments to the regulations: see article 2 of ministerial decision no. 126 of 2003 amending ministerial decision no. 26 of 1984 concerning the implementing regulations for law no. 4 of 1979 in relation to the prevention of fraud and deception in commercial dealings.

case is the setup and execution of the raid, which must be coordinated with the Police. The brand owner's investigator, who has identified the trader and obtained the information and sample, must offer to buy a quantity of products and negotiate the terms. The trader will normally want a deposit (perhaps as much as fifty percent of the purchase price) or may demand full payment at the time of placing the order. The Police prefer to see money change hands at the delivery in order to provide better evidence of the commission of the crime (of selling counterfeit products). Demanding full payment in advance is one of the ways in which traders have often tried to protect themselves against being raided. However, there are ways around the problem (that cannot be discussed here for obvious reasons). The cash that is to be handed over to the trader at the raid is usually photocopied first, so it can be compared with the cash found in the possession of the persons arrested at the delivery.

Once the deal is set up, the time and place of the delivery must be agreed with the trader. It cannot be assumed that the Police will be available at the arranged time. They have other cases and often urgent matters arise that may cause them to drop planned cases at the last minute. They have limited resources and if a sufficient number of officers are not available, the delivery will have to be rescheduled. It was previously the case that all raids had to be arranged for the morning before the break time, which is at about one or two pm when there is a change of shift. Of course, this became known in the market and traders began insisting on delivery in the afternoon only. Presently, the Police are more flexible and in principle a raid can be done at anytime.

The delivery can be carried out anywhere: in front of the shop, at the warehouse, at a shipping company's premises, on the side of the street or in a car park.[160] But there are practical considerations. The Police, the delivery truck, and the investigator/buyer all need to have easy access. Some of the Dubai markets are extremely busy and crowded and can be difficult to access quickly because of traffic or the maze of alleys to be navigated. Consequently, deliveries are very often late and the Police may understandably become impatient. Too much communication between the delivery truck and the buyer can raise suspicion. If the delivery is in front of the trader's shop, the dynamics of the raid may be different.

Once the goods have arrived and the buyer has checked them, the remainder of the purchase price will be handed over to the person sent by the trader to deliver the goods. That person may be an employee of the trader or may simply be a hired hand for the job. In any case, that person will be arrested and the truck with the products will be taken back to

---

160. Raids have been carried out right beside Police headquarters, such is the level of fearlessness of the traders.

Police headquarters. The Police will question the delivery person about where he obtained the products so that the warehouse can be found (if not known already). At this point it is critical that the delivery person does not tip off the shop or the warehouse about the raid, so the use of mobile phones must be controlled. There have been cases where one or more of the delivery persons have run away, possibly for fear of going to jail or because they were working illegally or because they wanted to inform the boss of what had happened.

The Police will usually then proceed to the shop, enter it, search it, and remove any products that are covered by the complaint (but not other counterfeits that they may find). They will also arrest the person who did the deal with the buyer—if that person happens to be there. They may also arrest the manager of the shop. If the manager is not there, they will usually call him or her to come to the shop or to the headquarters. The Police will interrogate those at the shop about the location of the rest of the products or the warehouse and will use techniques to extract the information without applying any physical force. They will generally not study or take copies of any documents in the shop (there is usually no time for reading) but will look for sets of keys to the warehouse, which are critical in the event that the warehouse is eventually found. The brand owner or the agent is responsible for organizing transport for the products from the delivery and the shop to the Police headquarters, where the products will be counted, sorted into types, repackaged, and made ready for storage.

The raid may have been set up so that all available stock was brought to the delivery. If not, the search for the warehouse will be the next step. Sometimes the investigator has already obtained this information—it can be very difficult to get and a lot of time and money can be invested in finding warehouses with no results. There is no real control over the warehousing of products and the locations used by a particular trader do not need to be recorded with any authority. The difficulties are compounded by the fact that traders often share warehouses or sublet spaces, warehouses are often not signboarded or are incorrectly signboarded and sometimes products are stored on personal premises such as apartments, for which the Police will need further authority to enter. Warehouses in free zones raise further difficulties. The warehouse districts in Dubai and Sharjah are vast, and searching for a specific warehouse (even with a lot of clues) can be like looking for a needle in a haystack.

Sometimes those arrested make the grave mistake of giving false information about the location of the warehouse and send the Police on a "goose chase," usually changing the story or having a loss of memory as they go along. There is no substitute for having the location of the warehouse to avoid such problems. But once the Police arrive at the warehouse there is no guarantee that they will get in. They usually will not enter by force—they must be let in; hence the importance of getting the keys during the raid. It is very frustrating to find the warehouse, knowing it is full of counterfeit products, and see the Police leave the site because the keys were not found and the manager is refusing to bring them to the Police. The Police are under pressure to wrap up the case and they always have other cases to attend to.

Once inside the warehouse, it must be inspected. It may be very hot if it is summer (there is never any ventilation or air conditioning), it may be dark with no lighting or electricity, and it will certainly be dirty and dusty.[161] It is prudent to come prepared for these conditions. Sometimes the counterfeit products will be obvious (in some cases the entire warehouse will be full of the products that are the subject of the complaint) but often there will be thousands of boxes or sewn bags to be opened and inspected. The Police do not have the manpower to do this work so it is usually done by the agent of the brand owner (who generally accompanies the Police through the entire process to support them according to their instructions) It may be necessary to organize labor and trucks with some urgency, to load and transport the products to Police headquarters.

Back at Police headquarters the file for the case must be prepared. The seized products must be counted and described so that the information can be included in the Police case report. The complainant must make a statement to one of the officers in the interrogation unit, which will go in the file. The complainant will be an individual and not the brand owner on whose behalf the complaint was filed. It is often an employee of the agent. It is that person's personal details that will go into the file and that will be available to the accused, including some form of personal ID, personal address, and phone number. This clearly exposes the complainant to the risk of some kind of revenge for the action taken and is difficult to justify. It is in fact that person's case. This has a number of other consequences. Inquiries about the case at the court or the prosecution must be made by that person. It is also that person that the court or the prosecution will call to give yet another statement to support the case. In the ordinary course, that may be fine, but if the complainant is an employee and leaves the employment of the agent it can cause a major headache.

The passports of those arrested and accused are taken and held until the end of the case. However, it is common for an accused to substitute his passport for that of another person (such as his wife) so that he can continue to travel and do business. The accused will be called by the prosecution to give a statement when the prosecution is preparing the case for transfer to the court.

---

161. Other dangers inside warehouses include (based on experience: poorly constructed platforms or storage areas and access ramps, exposed electrical wiring, broken glass and other objects that might injure, broken sanitation and the presence of rat poison or traps. With rents so high in the UAE, finding laborers living inside warehouses is not uncommon.

Samples of each of the product types seized must be taken and the Police will transfer these to the Criminal Laboratory (also located inside Police headquarters). The remainder of the seized products must be transported to storage by the brand owner's agent. The agent will usually have the trucks on standby to be ready to attend the headquarters (or warehouse), collect the seized goods, and transport them to the storage location. The storage company must be independent of the parties (for example, the brand owner may not use its own storage facilities) and remains under an obligation not to release the goods until ordered by the Police or prosecution to do so after a final judgment. The storage costs in cases in which large quantities are seized can be crippling. Very small quantities can sometimes be stored by the Police (the prosecution has a seized goods section and limited space for storage). The agent must give an undertaking to be responsibility for all storage costs.

The entire Police operation is usually completed in a day, even if sometimes a very long one. The arrested persons may spend the night in the Police cells (if there is room) pending delivery of passports, for example. Once the Police case file is complete, the goods have been sent to storage and the arrested persons are released, the file is transferred to a local Police station, usually the station of the area in which the raid was conducted (or crime was committed). It is that station's responsibility to transfer the file to the prosecution. When making inquiries about the case, the station case number and name are useful pieces of information (such as Muraqqabat Station, case no. 123/2008). Sometimes the station is very expeditious in getting the file to the prosecution. In other cases, there have been many months delay (for reasons usually related to workload).

Meanwhile, the Criminal Laboratory is preparing its expert's report on whether the product is genuine or not. The Lab makes its analysis by comparing the seized product and the genuine equivalent product (and not what is contained in the certificate of trademark registration). If there is no genuine equivalent product (for example, the brand owner only makes sports cars and the seized product is a jacket with the brand owner's logo), the Lab cannot confirm in its report to the court that the product is a counterfeit. The reason for this perhaps goes back to the fact that the case is classified by the prosecution and the court as one of "fraud in commercial dealings" (which is not about registered trademark rights and the comparison of marks). In view of the language of article 37 of the TML 1992A, a case under the trademark law would only require the Lab to determine whether a registered trademark, and not a product as a whole, had been counterfeited. In cases in which there is no corresponding genuine product, the brand owner must provide a letter explaining that it does not make products of the kind seized but that still leaves the Lab report inconclusive. A letter from the brand owner confirming that the product is not genuine is of no assistance to the Lab. Similar problems can occur if the genuine products are very expensive (such as a watch that retails for US$10,000) and the brand owner is not in a position to provide a genuine product for every case. Generally, the Dubai Criminal Laboratory is highly professional in its work, handles a large number of cases of all kinds with limited resources, and does its very best in the circumstances. The Lab is also receptive to product training and visits to explain issues in the case.

Once the file reaches the prosecutor, he or she begins his or her own investigation of the case and will very likely call the complainant and the charged persons to make statements in relation to the case. The statements must be made in Arabic. For non-Arabic speakers, the prosecution will provide a translator. Of the complainant, the prosecutor may ask any of a wide range of questions including how the accused became known to the complainant; the history of the interaction with the accused; the details of the deals done; the things that the accused had said to the complainant about the products and whether he or she said the products were not genuine; the details of the raid/delivery/seizure; the nature, place of manufacture origin, and price of the genuine products; and the price of the counterfeit products. The witness should have a good deal of detail at hand when making the statement. This means that the case should have been well prepared in the very early stages if the prosecutor is to be assisted at this stage. The complainant is usually not the person who actually had the contact with the accused. That person is usually the investigator, but an investigator would be of no value after a single case if his or her identity had to be revealed as the complainant. Some prosecutors have rightly insisted on getting the first-hand information from the investigator, but of course the entire system works on keeping the investigator's identity hidden. Mostly the prosecutors will accept the evidence from the agent who instructed the investigator, especially if the investigator is an employee of the agent.

Some of the prosecutor's questions may be directed toward determining whether the accused was "set up" (as is often alleged in defense). This is sometimes referred to as entrapment. The scenario that prosecutors are concerned about is one in which the investigator asks the trader if he has products branded X and the trader says "No I don't have any in stock, but I can get them for you." The investigator then makes an order and the trader is caught selling the counterfeit product. The trader will then tell the prosecutor that he has never sold counterfeits and he only did it because he was asked by the investigator. The way to ensure there is an answer to this is to seek to catch only those traders who say they have stock of the product. This may exclude as possible targets those who sell on an order basis only. An alternative might be to make several buys of the product before the raid in order to show a pattern of selling the counterfeit products.

One of the concerns that brand owners sometimes express is that the present system does not catch the persons who are really benefiting from and driving the sale of counterfeit products in Dubai. Those arrested in Police cases are either the driver of the delivery truck (but he is often released), the person managing the warehouse (but the case against this person might be weak if he has not been involved in doing the deal), or the person at the shop who did the deal (who is often just an employee and not the manager). It is not as common as it should be that the owner of the business is accused. In many cases, an Emirati national will own 51 percent or more of the business. That person may or may not be directly involved in the running of the business and may or may not have knowledge of the trading in counterfeits. But the question as to whether that person had knowledge of the trading in counterfeits is usually not asked. If local owners had liability for the actions of the businesses from which they make a living, they would be required to exercise some control over them and ensure that their activities are legal. On one view, it is this distance between ownership and control is at the root of the counterfeiting problem. The current system catches employees doing what their boss tells them to, more than it does the managers or owners of the business. Sometimes the local owners will try to intervene to rescue the manager from prosecution, but unless their interests are severely affected, the gesture may only be a token attempt. It is, in the end, the manager's or employee's problem.

Once the prosecutor has completed his own investigation, he will initiate the case in Dubai Courts of First Instance and it will be given a court case number. The defendants will often appoint their own lawyers who will file memoranda in their defense (assuming they plead not guilty). Defense arguments are many and varied and include "the defendant had no knowledge that the products were counterfeit" through to "the Police action was illegal." There are generally no oral submissions by the prosecutor or the defense and there is no final hearing in which arguments are presented. After the Lab report has been filed and it appears that no more memoranda from the parties are necessary, the judge will issue a decision of guilt or innocence.

The penalties issued by the Dubai courts in criminal cases against sellers of counterfeiters have been the source of some discussion. The TML 1992A provides for a fine of not less than 5000 dirhams and/or imprisonment as the punishment for counterfeiting cases.[162] The trend appears to be for the Court of First Instance to order a fine of 10,000 dirhams (about US$2720) as a matter of course and on appeal for the court to reduce the amount to 5000 dirhams (about US$1360). Over the last five years it seems that penalties have gone down over time, not up.[163] One might speculate that this has

---

162. TML 1992A, article 37.
163. In one of the first cases I handled in Dubai in 2003/4, the defendant spent a month in prison. Prison sentences for trading in counterfeits in Dubai are now rare.

something to do with the court workload (which has increased during this time). If penalties from the Dubai courts are higher than can be obtained elsewhere (such as at the Dubai Department of Economic Development), then more complainants may choose to pursue criminal cases, thus increasing the workload of the police, the prosecution and the court. The provisions of the trademark law are quite adequate with no limit on the monetary penalty that can be imposed. At present, the traders in counterfeits remain undeterred by the penalties, which they probably see as a minor tax on business.[164]

GCC TML changes the penalties structure by giving an upper limit to monetary fines of 1,000,000 Saudi riyals (about US$257,000) or the local equivalent, but does not impose any minimum fines, which means in principle that fines lower than 5000 dirhams (about US$1360) could be ordered (being the minimum fine under article 37 of the TML 1992A).

The other penalties usually include an order for the destruction of the seized goods and the publication of the judgment at the expense of the defendant. There have been cases in which the judge does not order the destruction of the goods but rather the destruction of the trademarks. This idea is found in article 43 of the TML 1992A:

> The court may also order the destruction of the unlawful marks or order when necessary the destruction of the products. . . .[165]

In cases in which the destruction of the marks is ordered, practical issues arise about how the whole process will be managed. The products are in a warehouse that is paid for by the brand owner but under the control of the prosecution. To access them for removal of the branding is the first challenge. Then there are the questions about what exactly the branding is, how the branding is to be removed, and by whom and with what result. Does it matter if the products are destroyed in the process? The products can then be handed back to the defendant, who is free to rebrand them (possibly in the same way) and sell or otherwise deal with them. The rebranding issue also arises when it is not possible to destroy the products, possibly because the Dubai Municipality will not allow it due to environmental or other concerns.

The destruction process itself can be more tortuous and time consuming than all the preceding steps. Coordination is required between the

---

164. Penalties should represent a deterrent: see TRIPs Agreement, article 61 concerning criminal penalties: "Remedies available shall include imprisonment and/or monetary fines sufficient to provide a deterrent. . . ."
165. Discussed further in the commentary below on article 43 of the TML 1992A.

prosecution, the Municipality (that controls the rubbish dumps), the Police, the storage company, and the agent for brand owner. The Municipality is trying to reduce the quantity of waste it has to deal with. In counterfeit product cases, very often will try to find an alternative to running the products over with a bulldozer and burying them in the sand. Ultimately, the destruction process adds significantly to time spent and costs incurred by the brand owner.

Brand owners often want to publicize a successful case in order to deter others from trading in counterfeit products. Any press release should be submitted to the Police for vetting before release. Of course, until the defendant has been convicted, he is presumed innocent and all pre-conviction commentary on the case should be consistent with that. Naming the defendant, or the defendant's business, before he is convicted is likely to be problematic. The best way to manage publicizing a case may be to engage the services of a public relations company that deals with such issues day-to-day and knows the current practices and issues.

Criminal Enforcement in Other Emirates

The police and the prosecution in other emirates such as Abu Dhabi, Ajman, and Umm Al Quwain[166] will accept complaints in relation to persons trading in counterfeit products. It is best to approach them to discuss the issues and plan the case once the target has been identified.

Administrative Enforcement

Dubai Department of Economic Development

The principal function of the Dubai Department of Economic Development is the licensing of businesses to operate in the emirate of Dubai. However, its broader function is to promote economic development in Dubai and as part of this it has a Commercial Protection Section (CPS), that works within its Compliance Division, whose role is to enforce compliance with the law and "reduce the negative effect of commercial fraud, trademark infringement

---

166. The Ajman Police have been active in counterfeiting cases for many years. The Umm Al Quwain Police did their first counterfeiting case a few years ago against a car windscreen maker.

and counterfeiting."[167] The CPS will receive complaints in relation to a range of commercial fraud and trademark violations and has a team of inspectors who act on such complaints.

The procedures for taking action against one or more traders offering products that infringe a trademark registered in the UAE are presently as follows:

The complaint: A complaint in Arabic must be prepared and filed with the CPS. The complaint can cover an unlimited number of traders but inspection fees are charged on a per trader basis (see the schedule below). The complaint can also include more than one brand, in cases where the trader complained of is offering more than one of the brands of the complainant, but this will increase the complaint filing fees (see the schedule below). A separate complaint must be filed by each of the brand owners whose brands are being infringed in those cases in which brand owners are working together against traders selling goods that infringe their rights.

The complaint should contain details of the name and location of the trader complained of. A detailed location description is important to assist the inspectors to find the trader's shop. There is no single functional address system in Dubai, so often the best location descriptions may be something like: "behind the Abu Baqr mosque in front of the tailor shop." Drawing a map can also be useful for the inspectors.

Trademark registration certificates: The complaint must be supported by copies of the UAE trademark registration certificates for the concerned marks. The copies do not need to be certified copies from the Ministry of Economy. However, if the registration has expired and the renewal certificate has not yet issued, the CPS may not act because it does not know whether the renewal will be permitted by the Ministry, despite evidence of the payment of the renewal fees.

Power of attorney: If the complaint is being filed by an agent, a simple copy of the agent's legalized power of attorney should be attached to the complaint.

Product samples: The complaint should be accompanied by a sample of the product purchased from the trader complained of, as well as a sample of the genuine product. In some cases, for example where large or expensive products are involved, this can raise practical problems that are best discussed with the CPS before filing the complaint.

Product comparisons: In some cases, especially those in which the trader is selling both genuine and counterfeit products, the inspectors may need some assistance in distinguishing the two when they visit the shop. They may ask

---

167. "Commercial protection section's guide and chart of fines," Dubai Department of Economic Development.

for a list of points of similarity and difference or may need the agent to explain the comparison points to them.

The fees to be paid are calculated as follows:

Fee for filing a complaint against the infringement of one registered trademark (this is not refundable if the complaint is rejected by the review committee)	2000 dirhams (about US$544)
Fee for each additional registered trademark covered by the complaint	2000 dirhams (about US$544)
Fee for the first five shops or locations covered by the complaint	500 dirhams (about US$136)
Fee for the 6th to the 10th shop or location covered by the complaint	1,500 dirhams (about US$408)
Fee for the 11th to the 15th shop or location covered by the complaint	2,500 dirhams (about US$680)
Fee for the 16th to the 20th shop or location covered by the complaint	3,000 dirhams (about US$816)
Fee for more than 21 shops or locations covered by the complaint	5,000 dirhams (about US$1360)

The fee structure is best suited to cases in which a single brand owner has a single mark and has identified a number of retail shops selling counterfeits. The costs increase significantly when the brand owner has several brands that are being infringed by the shops identified. If the shops are selling counterfeits of the brands of several different brand owners, each brand owner will have to file separate complaints at the same time. There is a special fee schedule for federations of brand owners but this does not assist brand owners that are simply working together—they must belong to a recognized federation and the power of attorney must be from that federation (and not the individual brand owners).

When the complaint is presented to the CPS, it will be given an initial review to ensure that there are no obvious deficiencies before it is passed to a review committee for approval. One of the key issues for the review committee to decide is if the case is one on which they should take action. Based on experience, the cases that are most likely to be accepted are those in which the infringing product is identical or nearly identical to the genuine product. The particular infringing product should also be one that is specifically stated in the trademark registration certificate (general descriptions such as "electronic goods" can encounter difficulties). The cases that are most likely to be rejected by the committee are those in which, although the product or its packaging is a "rip-off" of the genuine product, the consumer is likely to know that it is not a genuine product. Complaints are handled on a case-by-case basis and it is therefore difficult to generalize about what kinds of cases will be accepted. There are no published guidelines.

It may take several days or longer for the complaint to be approved by the review committee. The agent will have to follow up to see if the complaint has been accepted. Once accepted, the fees must be paid, which means the agent must bring the fees in cash to the Economic Department (there is no electronic form of payment and checks are not acceptable). The complaint then goes to the inspectors, who visit the trader against whom the complaint was made. Generally, neither the agent nor any other person is permitted to attend the trader's shop with the inspectors. Indeed, the day and time of the inspectors' visit is often not disclosed to the complainant.

The agent must then follow up with the CPS to find out the results of the visit to the trader's shop. The inspectors are empowered to enter and search the shop and may seize products and documents showing the source of the products. They will prepare for their file a report of their visit to the trader. Although the CPS will not give copies of the inspectors' report to the complainant, they will communicate the basic information such as from which shops products were seized, the number of products seized, and the brands used on the products. If there is any doubt about whether any of the products seized are counterfeit, they will sometimes give the agent a sample and ask the brand owner to confirm that it is not genuine.

After the inspectors' visit to the trader's shop, the CPS will require the manager to attend a meeting with the head of the CPS to explain why he is offering counterfeit or imitation products for sale and to prove where he got them from. The CPS will also check its own records to see whether the trader has any prior offenses. Often the trader will say that he was not aware that the products were counterfeit or imitations. The CPS will make a determination of the appropriate penalty taking into account the seriousness of the violation (for example, whether the products might be a danger to human health), whether the trader imported the products or bought them locally, and whether he has had other offenses.

The penalties that the CPS can impose are based on the law for the prevention of fraud and deception in commercial dealings and not the trademark law (under which only the court may order penalties). The following are the monetary penalties that the CPS may impose in commercial fraud cases as published by the CPS:

Violation	First Offense	Second Offense	Third Offense
Importing and selling counterfeit goods	5000 dirhams	15,000 dirhams	20,000 dirhams
Marketing counterfeit goods	500 dirhams	5000 dirhams	10,000 dirhams
Selling goods that have been attached by the DDED	5000 dirhams	15,000 dirhams	20,000 dirhams

Violation	First Offense	Second Offense	Third Offense
Refusing to sign the sample form, attachment order, or confiscation papers	1000 dirhams	2000 dirhams	3000 dirhams
Manufacturing, offering for sale, or selling packaging materials to be used for counterfeit products	5000 dirhams	15,000 dirhams	20,000 dirhams
Putting misleading information on products or the shop or the packaging	10,000 dirhams	20,000 dirhams	30,000 dirhams

The CPS also has the power to order the temporary closure of the shop (which it says it will do upon the second offense) and the cancellation of the trade license (which it says it will do upon the third offense).[168] These penalties are found in article 10 of the FDL 1979 and may be imposed for violations of articles 2 or 3 of the law. In serious cases, the CPS may transfer the case to the public prosecution.

Storage of the seized products is handled by the CPS, for which it does not charge fees. The CPS also looks after the destruction of the products (in cooperation with the Municipality). The CPS will provide a copy of the Municipality destruction report if requested.

Enforcement in the Emirate of Sharjah

The Sharjah Economic Development Department (SEDD) is similar in its roles to the Dubai Development for Economic Development and has also had a role in monitoring the markets and removing counterfeit goods from them. The Sharjah Municipality also has a similar remit in relation to counterfeit products. Whether one authority or the other has capability or is active at any particular time is a matter of internal resources and structuring. Five years ago the SEDD was very active and the Municipality was not. In recent times, it has been the Municipality that has shown real commitment to the cause and handled some significant cases. The circumstances on the ground at the time that enforcement action is required should be assessed for suitability to the case in terms of availability of staff and other resources, required procedures, fees to be paid, powers to enter warehouses and storage facilities, destruction of the seized goods, and overall transparency.

---

168. *See* page 5 of "Commercial protection section's guide and chart of fines," Dubai Department of Economic Development.

Civil Actions Concerning Trademarks

Trademark Infringement?

Strictly speaking, there is no cause of action that one might call "trademark infringement" in the UAE. There is, however, a right to claim compensation for damage resulting from the commission of any one of the criminal acts in articles 37 and 38 of the TML 1992A. A case for compensation must be raised in a competent civil court and may seek from the person responsible for the damage "compensation commensurate with the damage suffered."[169] The language of the provision is clear in limiting the compensation that can be claimed to damage that has been suffered and so claims for loss of opportunity and expected benefits or profits should not be entertained.[170]

Perhaps because of the manner in which the right to compensation is tied in the law to the criminal offenses, it is common practice to start a criminal case first and once a prosecution of the accused persons has been commenced, a civil claim for damages is then filed. Adding a civil claim to a criminal case is a way of the complainant having some involvement in a case that would otherwise be entirely in the hands of the prosecutor, of putting additional pressure on the defendant, whether for substantive or strategic reasons, and of potentially being compensated. The civil case will usually be suspended pending the outcome of the criminal case and in the event that the offenses are not proved and there is a verdict of innocence, the prospects of success for the civil case become poor. If the civil case proceeds, the plaintiff would request the judge to appoint an expert to make an assessment of damages. The expert would take evidence, make inquiries and hear the parties, as he sees fit, and produce a report for the court. The report may be challenged and either party may request that another expert be appointed.

A civil case may be commenced in circumstances unrelated to a criminal prosecution. If the plaintiff has made an application for precautionary measures, then a civil case must be commenced within eight days, otherwise the seized items will be released (discussed below). A civil case for compensation under article 40 could be raised entirely independently of either a criminal case or an application for precautionary measures, but the plaintiff in such a case will face the burden of proving all the necessary elements—the

---

169. TML 1992A, article 40.
170. The provision appears to be consistent with article 45.1 of the TRIPs Agreement: "The judicial authorities shall have the authority to order the infringer to pay the right holder damages adequate to compensate for the injury the right holder has suffered because of an infringement of that person's intellectual property right by an infringer who knowingly, or with reasonable grounds to know, engaged in infringing activity."

commission of a criminal offense under article 37 or 38, damage suffered, and that the commission of the offenses caused the damage. The evidence to be relied upon must be gathered before the commencement of the case because of the high likelihood that any relevant evidence will be destroyed once notice is given. There are no obligations for traders to keep or disclose books of account[171] and there is no discovery process. If a trademark owner wants to commence a stand-alone civil case (not preceded by a criminal case or a case for precautionary measures), it may be prudent to commission a court-approved expert to carry out an undercover investigation of the infringement and prepare a report of the facts required for the case before commencing proceedings.

Availability of Injunctions

It is often asked whether a trademark owner has a right to an injunction in the UAE. What the court may order is set out in article 43 of the TML 1992A and there is nothing in the list of possible orders that resembles an injunction. However, the 2002 amendments added to article 17 the following paragraph:

> The owner of a registered mark is to enjoy the right to prevent others from using the same or a similar mark to distinguish products or services that are the same or similar or related to the products and services for which the mark is registered to the extent that it leads to the causing of confusion amongst consumers.

Article 44 of the TRIPs Agreement provides that "The judicial authorities shall have the authority to order a party to desist from an infringement. . . ." It is an open question as to whether the new article 17 paragraph satisfies the TRIPs Agreement requirement because giving an owner of a registered trademark a right is not entirely the same as giving "judicial authorities" the authority to order that a party desist from infringement. A question that arises from the introduction of the new paragraph in article 17 is whether the trademark owner's right to prevent others from using the same or a similar mark, etc., extends to preventing the commission of criminal offenses under articles 37 and 38, bearing in mind that those articles are expressed in very different language and concepts, and may cover a set of circumstances not coextensive with those covered by the second paragraph of article 17. The question is important because an injunction may not be available in some

---

171. *See also* Essam Al Tamimi, The Practical Guide to Litigation and Arbitration in the United Arab Emirates (2003).

civil cases that are based on a criminal prosecution to the extent that the criminal offenses cannot be characterized as falling within the scope of the second paragraph of article 17. Article 17 is also not linked to the right to seek damages, which is limited to acts stated in articles 37 and 38. One would not therefore commence a civil case on the basis of article 17 alone if a claim for damages under the TML 1992A is to be made. As a matter of practice, the UAE courts have granted "stop" orders as part of the relief granted to successful plaintiffs in appropriate circumstances.

What the Court May Order

The following is a commentary on article 43 of the TML 1992A, the provision of the law that sets out what the court may order in cases brought under the trademark law. The list of possible orders does not appear to be exhaustive and the court may derive the power to make other orders from other legislation. These orders can be made in cases where the verdict is one of innocence.

1. Confiscation Orders

The court may order the confiscation of things that have been attached or that are yet to be attached. Confiscation here means the permanent seizure of things that were temporarily seized (or attached), perhaps by the Police or perhaps as a result of a precautionary measures order. Sometimes the court's orders in a case will not mention destruction because it is understood that if they are permanently confiscated that is equivalent to or will entail destruction.

The provision permits the court to subtract the value of the items confiscated from the fines or compensation. This is in effect compensating the defendant infringer for the loss of the confiscated items, which appears to be inconsistent with the TRIPs Agreement obligations:

> In order to create an effective deterrent to infringement, the judicial authorities shall have the authority to order that goods that they have found to be infringing be, without compensation of any sort, disposed of outside the channels of commerce in such a manner as to avoid any harm caused to the right holder, or, unless this would be contrary to existing constitutional requirements, destroyed.[172]

---

172. TRIPs Agreement, article 46.

The TRIPs Agreement provision suggests that no adjustment should be made to fines or compensation to account for the confiscation of the items but that the items may, for example, be given away to a charity or to needy people, which would presumably be disposals outside of the channels of commerce. The items may also be destroyed.

2. Destruction Orders

The court may order the destruction of unlawful marks or, when necessary, the destruction of the products and packaging bearing the marks.

The relevant TRIPs Agreement provision reads:

> In regard to counterfeit trademark goods, the simple removal of the trademark unlawfully affixed shall not be sufficient, other than in exceptional cases, to permit release of the goods into the channels of commerce.[173]

"Counterfeit trademark goods" are defined in the TRIPs Agreement to mean:

> any goods, including packaging, bearing without authorization a trademark which is identical to the trademark validly registered in respect of such goods, or which cannot be distinguished in its essential aspects from such a trademark, and which thereby infringes the rights of the owner of the trademark in question under the law of the country of importation.[174]

According to the TRIPs Agreement requirements for counterfeit products, orders for the removal of the unlawful marks from the products should be the exception, not the rule. That is probably consistent with the practice of judges in the Dubai courts who usually order destruction of counterfeit products.

The court may also order the destruction of machines and tools that were used *specifically* for the counterfeiting operation. The TRIPs Agreement provision employs the concept of "predominant use" which is probably broader than the language in article 43:

> The judicial authorities shall also have the authority to order that materials and implements the predominant use of which has been in the creation of the infringing goods be, without compensation of any sort, disposed of outside the channels of commerce in such a manner as to minimize the risks of further infringements.[175]

---

173. TRIPs Agreement, article 46.
174. TRIPs Agreement, footnote to article 51.
175. TRIPs Agreement, article 46.

3. Publication Orders

The court may order the publication of the judgment in the journal and in any one of the Arabic newspapers issued in the UAE at the expense of the defendant.

Precautionary Measures

It is possible to approach the judge of urgent matters on an *ex parte* basis for the precautionary measures set out in article 41 of the TML 1992A. This can be done before raising a "main case." The petition to the court must be supported by a certificate of trademark registration in the UAE, unless the infringed mark is a famous one. Article 41 does not set out in what circumstances such an application may be made but orders that can be made are limited to matters relating to the commission of any crime stated in the TML 1992A. The inference is therefore that the applicant must allege offenses under article 37 or 38 to establish a basis for the petition and may not rely on the right in article 17 to prevent others from using a similar mark (which is not a criminal provision).

The court may order the gathering of information relating to the crime (making of lists and descriptions of products and machines, locations of shops, packaging, etc.) and the attachment[176] of those things that are the subject of the crime.[177] The TRIPs Agreement obligations are expressed in different terms. Judicial authorities shall have the authority to order measures to prevent infringement of an intellectual property right.[178] An attachment does not prevent infringement—it merely seizes the goods that are specifically described in the plaintiff's application and must include their exact location and quantity. Although the specific goods may have been identified and attached by the court bailiff, the attachee may continue to advertise the products, take orders, import more stock and use the infringing branding. What the TRIPs Agreement obligation contemplates is something similar to an interlocutory injunction, which is aimed at the infringer's conduct as a whole, and not simply specific assets. It might be thought that the precautionary measures provisions in the TML 1992A are similar to Anton Piller orders, which permit searching and seizure. However, attachments appear to have originally been part of the apparatus for creditors obtaining security for debts, and therefore their form and execution is handled with a level of

---

176. Al Tamimi, *supra* note 171, at 73: "An attachment is a seizure of assets ordered by the court at the claimant's request, prior to judgment in order to preserve those assets during the trial."
177. Summarizing article 41.1 of the TML 1992A.
178. TRIPs Agreement, article 50.1.

specificity that is not often suitable for intellectual property cases. This is illustrated by a case in Dubai, in which the bailiff arrived at the warehouse and identified the products that were revealed by the investigation and referred to in the precautionary measures application. However, after the investigation, further stock had arrived and there were many more infringing products available to seize than anticipated. Quantities of infringing packaging were unexpectedly also found in the warehouse. Neither the new stock nor the packaging was referred to in the orders and so the bailiff would not attach them. The infringer had removed them from the warehouse within hours and well before a new precautionary measures application could be prepared and filed.

The attachment order may only be issued after the applicant has filed financial security. This is something that needs to be handled carefully because it may come under attack later. Even if the urgent matters judge does not ask for the security or fully deal with the issue, the applicant must ensure that the judge makes an estimation of the security required and that the applicant files the financial security in executable form (and not simply an undertaking to compensate). There are obvious practical difficulties here because until the attachment has been made and the quantity of products and machines to be seized is known, it is very difficult to estimate the damage that might be caused to the attachee by the attachment. Attachments of counterfeit products have been lifted because the applicant filed (and the judge accepted) an undertaking as security and the court did not give the applicant an opportunity to remedy the inadequacy of the security when challenged.[179]

Once the urgent matters judge has issued the order, the applicant must then coordinate with the court bailiff to go to the location of the products to be attached. The timing of the visit can be very important in order to catch the attachee with the products and other evidence of the crime. Properly briefing the bailiff is a key step.

Before the 2002 amendments to the TML 1992, article 41 gave the applicant eight days from the issue of the attachment order in which to file a civil case (or to have a criminal case commenced). That provision was removed by the 2002 amendments. Presumably one must now look to the civil procedures law for the timeframe in which a main case must be filed in order to maintain the attachment. Article 255.2 of that law reads as follows:

> In the case where an urgent matters judge issues an attachment order, the attachor must—within 8 days at the most from the date of making the attachment—raise

---

179. *See* Dubai Court, case no. 147 of 2005.

before a competent court a case to prove that the attachment is well founded, or otherwise the attachment will be void.[180]

The old article 41 permitted a criminal or a civil case to be raised within eight days. If it is correct that article 255.2 of the civil procedures law is now the relevant provision, then only the filing of a civil case can maintain an attachment.

The deletion of the timeframe in article 41 of the TML 1992 has had the effect of rendering article 42 concerning the attachee's right to compensation uncertain because the timeframes indicated in it rely on the timeframe in article 41 (which is no longer there). Notwithstanding this, what is intended by the provision is as follows:

1. If the applicant does not file a main case within eight days, the attachee may file a case for compensation within ninety days of the date that was the applicant's deadline to file the main case.
2. If the applicant files a main case, within ninety days of the issue of a final decision in the case raised against him the attachee may file a case for compensation.

Precautionary measures applications are perhaps not used as much as they could be. In cases where the infringement is of a kind that the Police or other authorities are hesitant to take on, such as the infringement of a trademark registration for the shape of a product or get-up, or in case in which services rather than goods are involved, a civil case may be the only option. Evidence secured by a court bailiff in implementing a precautionary measures order could put the main case on a solid footing and deliver to the infringer a serious first blow. The costs involved in a civil case are probably higher than in most criminal or administrative cases and they are likely to take longer to complete.

Other Considerations

There are a number of features of litigation in the UAE that should be taken into account when deciding on the legal strategy that is appropriate to deal with a particular trademark problem. Generally speaking, costs orders do not work as a disincentive to litigation. Parties will fight on without any real fear

---

180. Federal law no. 11of 1992 issuing the civil procedures law, article 255.2 (author's translation). The maximum period permitted by the TRIPs Agreement is 20 working days or 31 calendar days, whichever is longer (article 50.6).

of costs. The lack of any discovery process removes any fear that information (or the truth) will have to be revealed in the proceedings. Parties may withhold relevant facts and are therefore not discouraged to litigate despite being, in fact, culpable. It is also rare for the litigants, or persons with relevant evidence, to face examination in the court. There are no trials as such in the UAE. The final assessment of the case is based on what the lawyers have written in the submissions and any expert's report. Many cases in other jurisdictions settle when the parties meet in court—a less likely scenario in the UAE. Lawyers in the UAE often work on a fixed-fee basis for taking a case and charge the same amount whether the case settles or proceeds. That again means that once the lawyer is appointed, the litigant has no real reason to settle because the cost will be the same (unlike in time-charging arrangements). Success fees for lawyers are also common. This encourages lawyers to proceed to win rather than settle. Uncertainty in the law can dissuade litigation but it can also have the opposite effect, with each party seeing in the law what it wants. A lack of availability and use of precedents encourages unpredictable interpretations of the law. Entering into civil litigation with the intention of settling is probably taking a greater gamble than it might be in other jurisdictions. Settlement may be more likely under the threat of a criminal conviction.

Appeals from first instances decisions are a matter of course. Perhaps this is because the appeal courts will reconsider a wide range of matters of fact and law and the parties will often hold back relevant evidence to file before the court of appeal, rather than filing it before the court of first instance and thereby giving the other side a greater opportunity to respond to it. Tactics of this kind are common and widely accepted.

Customs

There are no provisions in the TML 1992A concerning border measures or the control of the importation or exportation of infringing products by Customs (unlike the ARL 2002). The act of importing or exporting goods bearing an infringing trademark is not one of the criminal offenses under the TML 1992A.

International Obligations

The obligation under the TRIPs Agreement is to "adopt procedures" rather than implement laws and regulations that give right holders the opportunity to prevent the release from customs of counterfeit products. Those procedures do not need to apply to goods in transit.[181] Compared to other areas of the TRIPs Agreement, the border measures provisions are relatively weak. The Paris Convention obligation is very general in nature. Article 9 (1) of the Convention provides: "All goods unlawfully bearing a trademark or trade name shall be seized on importation into those countries of the Union where such mark or trade name is entitled to legal protection."

GCC Customs Law

The Unified Customs Law of the GCC States (UCL) is in force in the UAE.[182] The law is principally concerned with the procedures for the movement of goods into, between, and out of the states of the Gulf Cooperation Council (Saudi Arabia, Kuwait, Bahrain, Qatar, the United Arab Emirates, and Oman) and the management of Customs duties. It does not contain, for example, a section on procedures for intellectual property infringement. The rights and obligations of the Customs authorities must be interpreted from various provisions throughout the law. The following is one such interpretation.

"Prohibited goods" are defined in the UCL as "any goods that the state has prohibited from being imported or exported pursuant to the provision of this law or any other law." The TML 1992A does not prohibit the importation or exportation of goods infringing the rights of registered trademark owners. The FDL 1979 does prohibit the importation of falsified or corrupted products, but its language leaves it open to a wide range of interpretations.[183] The definition of "prohibited goods" is critical in order to bring trademark infringing products within the scope of the other prohibitions and procedures in the UCL. One could argue that under the TML 1992A the possession of counterfeit goods with the intention to sell is a crime and that importing is a species of possession. The difficulty is with the intention to sell. Goods can be imported for re-export or transit. There may be no intention to sell.

Article 24 of the UCL prohibits the entry, exit, and transiting of prohibited or contravening goods but it does not assist in bringing trademark infringing goods within the definition of what are prohibited goods.[184] Smuggling is

---

181. TRIPs Agreement, article 51.
182. Federal Decree no. 85 of 2007 in relation to the Unified Customs system (law) for the states of the Cooperation Council of the Arabian Gulf States. The unified law came into force on January 1, 2002.
183. FDL 1979, article 4.
184. In one recent case, the Dubai courts treated article 24 of the UCL as banning the transiting of goods violating the law (being goods that would infringe a registered trademark in the UAE if offered for sale) and did not strictly follow the definition of "prohibited goods" in the UCL. See Dubai First Instance Court case no. 325 of 2004 and subsequent appeal cases.

subject to penalties.[185] A wide range of acts may constitute smuggling including "transporting or possessing prohibited or restricted goods."[186] But if prohibited goods are those that cannot be imported or exported, and exporting and importing of trademark infringing goods is not contrary to the law, then importing or exporting trademark infringing goods is not a species of smuggling.

Free Zones and Duty-Free Shops

The UCL contains specific provisions in relation to free zones and duty-free shops.[187] Article 80 bans the entry into free zones and duty-free shops of "goods infringing the system relating to the protection of commercial, industrial, literary, and artistic property in respect of which a resolution has been issued by the competent authorities." The language adopted is curious and the role of the competent authorities is unclear. The intention appears to be to prohibit goods that infringe intellectual property rights from entering free zones and duty-free shops.

Transiting Goods

The transiting of counterfeit goods is a much-discussed subject. Neither the TRIPs Agreement nor the Paris Convention deals with it.[188] However, the Dubai Courts have upheld a Dubai Customs seizure of transiting counterfeit goods on the basis of article 24 of the UCL and the Dubai Customs law (notwithstanding the interpretation issues discussed above).[189]

Many Authorities

The UAE constitution provides that the individual emirates are to have authority in relation to all matters not exclusively given to the jurisdiction

---

185. UCL, article 145.
186. UCL, article 143.
187. UCL, Chapter IV.
188. TRIPs Agreement, article 51, footnote 13; Paris Convention, article 9 (4).
189. Dubai law no. 4 of 1998, article 7, paragraph 1, article 114.5 and article 4 of the schedule attached to the law. *See* Dubai First Instance Court case no. 325 of 2004 and subsequent appeal cases.

of the federation.[190] Border control and Customs are not areas of federal jurisdiction.[191] "Member emirates exercise sovereignty over their territorial lands and waters in relation to all matters for which the federation is not given jurisdiction by this constitution."[192] Consequently, there are seven Customs authorities in the UAE, one for each emirate. In the emirate of Dubai, Customs falls under the Dubai Ports, Customs and Free Zones Corporation (as does DP World, the now famous port operator, and JAFZA, the Jebel Ali Free Zone Authority). Dubai Ports, Customs and Free Zones Corporation is a Dubai government entity and Dubai Customs is a Dubai government department.[193]

Dubai Customs Intellectual Property Rights (IPR) Unit

In 2005, an IPR Unit was created at Dubai Customs and the head of the CPS at the Dubai Department for Economic Development become the head of the new unit. In October 2006, Dubai Customs issued a policy concerning the recordal of trademarks with Customs and the fees for recordals and filing complaints.[194] Prior to the setting up of the IPR Unit, complaints were filed by brand owners (and containers were seized and destructions ordered) without the need either for the relevant trademarks to be recorded with Customs or for fees to be paid. The system then had more the character of a government service provided for the common good.

Under the current Dubai Customs policy, complaints may only be filed if the relevant trademark is recorded with Dubai Customs. Simply having a validly registered trademark in the UAE is no longer sufficient to be entitled to any form of border protection. Fees are to be paid for filing a complaint (2000 dirhams—about US$545), together with a security deposit (5000 dirhams—about US$1360) in the case where the seizure is not initiated by Customs. If the complaint proves to be incorrect and no infringing goods are found in the shipment, the brand owner "will be responsible for all expenses and fees resulting from the stopping of the shipment the subject of the complaint and the required fees for stopping or delaying the means of transport

---

190. UAE Constitution, article 116.
191. UAE Constitution, articles 120 and 121.
192. UAE Constitution, article 3.
193. *See* http://www.dubai.ae. On the FAQ page about Dubai Customs, the question is asked and answered: "Is Dubai Customs private, government or semi-government? Dubai Customs is a Dubai government department." (December 2008.) *See also* the Moody Investor Services report, "Demystifying Dubai Inc," October 2008, on the blurring of government boundaries.
194. Dubai Customs, policy DCP 11. *See* appendices A22 and B28.

carrying the goods, and the fees for storage, offloading, handling and trans-portation, or any expense or fees resulting from his complaint."[195] The owner of the shipment will be responsible for these fees and expenses when the complaint is correct.[196]

In those cases in which Dubai Customs reports the temporary suspension of a suspicious shipment to the brand owner or its agent, the brand owner will have only a few days to file a complaint. Usually a sample from the suspended shipment will be given to the brand owner in order for the brand owner to determine whether the products are genuine or not, but not always.[197] Once a seizure has been made, Dubai Customs will provide the complainant with details of the seizure. It is not possible for the brand owner to inspect the shipment itself. Under article 57 of the TRIPs Agreement, there is no obligation for the authorities to permit inspection or give information (but they must have the authority to do so, if they wish).

Before Dubai Customs will make a determination as to whether the goods should be confiscated and destroyed, it may want an expert's report to be prepared to confirm the infringement. This is particularly likely where there is a protesting consignee. Such reports are prepared by private "laboratories" and usually cost several thousand dollars. If the report is favorable and Dubai Customs accepts the merits of the case, it will issue a destruction order with a time frame for challenging it. If the consignee wants to challenge the order, it must file a case in court against the complainant, joining Dubai Customs (the Dubai Ports, Customs and Free Zones Corporation). If Dubai Customs proposes to release the goods, the complainant must seek and obtain an order from a court to stop the release.

Sharjah Customs

Customs in the emirate of Sharjah initiated a trademark recordal system in 2007 on the model of the Dubai Customs system (requiring the payment of a separate set of fees to Sharjah Customs). None of the customs authorities in the other emirates have yet set up similar systems. Dubai Customs claims that its system was the first in the Middle East.

---

195. Dubai Customs Policy DCP 11, article 6.
196. Dubai Customs Policy DCP 11, article 9.
197. In one recent case, only photographs were given to the brand owner. Without a sample, the brand owner was unable to confirm that the products were counterfeit and therefore could not file a complaint. The products were released.

Dubai Customs Statistics

The number of UAE registered trademarks recorded by Dubai Customs to September 2008 is as follows:[198]

2006 (starting in November)	2007	2008 (to September)
9	336	218

The UAE does not have a multiclass trademark registration system and so a single mark registered for goods in three classes will have three registration certificates and will require three Customs recordals. These numbers represent recordals rather than the trademarks recorded (which is likely to be less).

The number of trademark complaints filed with Dubai Customs to September 2008 is as follows:

2006 (starting in November)	2007	2008 (to September)
7	72	64

Dubai Customs is also conducting regular brand owner training sessions to raise awareness amongst customs inspectors and others of the brands that are protected in the UAE, and of the indicators of suspicious products. Since 2006 Dubai Customs has held six such training sessions during which eighty brand owner presentations were given.

UAE as the Provenance of Counterfeits

Despite the efforts of Dubai Customs and the other UAE customs authorities, the UAE continues to have a significant profile in statistics for counterfeit products. The following numbers are taken from the European Commission's "Report on Community Customs Activities on Counterfeit and Piracy— Results at the European Border 2007":[199]

Percentages of seized products in 2007 with the UAE as the provenance

Cosmetics, personal care products	2.27 percent
Clothing	1.77 percent
Electrical equipment	2.40 percent
CDs, DVDs, cassettes	2.65 percent
Cigarettes	7.30 percent
Medicines	14.70 percent

---

198. These statistics are taken from a booklet issued by the IPR Unit at Dubai Customs titled "Who are we?."

199. *See* page 20 of the report.

It is unlikely that the UAE is the country of production for many of these products. Rather, it is more likely that they are being imported into free zones in some form, perhaps unbranded in some cases, and then exported to the European markets where some are being seized at the borders. The purpose in many cases may be to hide the real origin of the products. The UAE is 4th place in the list of provenance countries for counterfeit goods being seized at the European borders (China leads the table by far with over 50 percent of the total).

Dragon Mart

The Dragon Mart in Dubai is a free zone established for Chinese traders to exhibit and sell their goods. It has become well known for counterfeit products. It has recently come under the jurisdiction of Dubai Customs and complaints can now be filed in relation to traders in the Dragon Mart offering counterfeit products. The details of the procedures are yet to be settled in practice.

Trademark Agents

The regulations in relation to trademark agents are discussed in the section on registration agents in the patents chapter.

CHAPTER

3

Author's Rights and Neighboring Rights

Introduction

History of the UAE's Author's Rights Law

The UAE Constitution gives the Federation exclusive jurisdiction to legislate in relation to the protection of "literary, artistic and industrial property and the rights of authors—printed matter and publishing. . . ."[1]

---

1. UAE Constitution, article 121.

Although the UAE issued its first author's rights law in 1992, the 1980 law in relation to printed matter and publishing extensively regulated the matter in which author's rights might have subsisted. The main areas dealt with by the 1980 publishing law are the licensing and regulation of various forms of media, including printing presses, newspaper publishers, and cinemas, and of publications and films, their circulation, import, and export. It also sets out a number of prohibitions against the publication of certain material, including criticism of the head of state and the rulers of the emirates, as well as insults against Islam, the system of government, unjust imputations of blame against Arabs, or misrepresentation of Arabic culture or heritage.[2] It establishes the Film Censorship Committee and empowers it to remove parts of films containing unacceptable content. Several provisions relate more directly to intellectual property. Its definition section includes a definition of a "work," just as the ARL 2002 does. Publishers of newspapers and periodicals are not permitted to reproduce literary works without the consent of the author. Authors and sources must be mentioned. Misleading expressions, pictures, or images are not permitted to appear in advertisements.[3]

From 1992 to 2002 the protection of author's rights was enshrined in the ARL 1992 and managed under two regulations, ministerial decisions nos. 411 and 412 of 1993. The first of these regulations laid down the system of obtaining approval for the publication, exhibition, or circulation of intellectual works (which was in addition to the regulatory regime under the printed matter and publishing law). This approval was necessary to seek registration of a work under the system established by the other ministerial decision, no. 412. Article 34 of the ARL 1992 permitted but did not oblige owners of intellectual works to register their works with the Ministry.

In 2002, the ARL 2002 was issued and came into force. The changes made to the law were intended to comply with the UAE's international obligations (as discussed in the next section). It appears that the new Egyptian intellectual property law of 2002 (referred to in this commentary as the EGIP) had a significant effect on the drafters of the ARL 2002 because a significant part of the language used is identical or very similar (see the footnotes throughout the translation of the ARL 2002 in Appendix A14). It appears that parts of the ARL 1992 and of the EGIP were pieced together. Readers can judge for themselves whether such a "mosaic" approach to drafting is the best way to produce a functional law for the regulation of the rights of authors and neighboring rights.

In 2004, four new regulations issued from the Ministry concerning the registration of works (decision no. 131 of 2004), the register of imported

---

2. Federal law no. 15 of 1980 in relation to printed matter and publishing, articles 70, 71, and 77.
3. Federal law no. 15 of 1980 in relation to printed matter and publishing, articles 1, 46 and 82.

and distributed works (decision no. 132 of 2004), the collective management of rights (decision no. 133 of 2004), and compulsory licensing (decision no. 134 of 2004). The last three of these are new areas of regulation. The first covers the same ground as the regulations issued under decision no. 412 of 1993 (the registration of works) although the previous decision was not expressly cancelled. The extent to which the 1993 regulations are still relevant is discussed at a number of points in this commentary. In 2005, decision no. 288 was issued to set down the fees for certain steps, such as the granting of collective management licenses and the issue of certificates of disposal of works.

The Dubai International Financial Center (DIFC) has recently released for comment a draft copyright law that is to apply within the jurisdiction of the DIFC.

International Conventions

The UAE's international obligations to legislate for the protection of copyright works arose as a result of its entry into the WTO rather than from its accession to Berne and other conventions. Under article 9 of the TRIPs Agreement, parties are obliged to comply with articles 1 to 21 of the Berne Convention. The UAE's deadline to comply with the TRIPs Agreement was January 1, 2000. At that time, the UAE was yet to accede to any of the copyright conventions. In any case, the UAE's intention was to make its laws comply with its obligations under TRIPs and the Berne Convention.[4] It was in 2004 that the UAE acceded to the Berne Convention, the WIPO Copyright Treaty, and the Rome Convention. In 2005 it acceded to the WIPO Performances and Phonograms Treaty.[5]

Government Authorities Dealing with Author's Rights

The ARL 1992 and the ARL 2002 named the Minister of Information and Culture as the responsible minister for the administration of the law. Also under this Minister's jurisdiction is the law in relation to printed matter

---

4. In response to a question put by the United States in the WTO Council for Trade-Related Aspects of Intellectual Property Rights, the UAE replied, speaking about the proposed amendments to the 1992 law: "The draft amendment will provide more detailed measures to enforce copyrights as referred to in the TRIPs Agreement. The obligations arising from article 9 of the TRIPs Agreement (Berne Convention articles 1–21, except article 6bis) will be met through the extension of the scope of terms of various categories and subjects of copyright as well as the nature of protection." Legislative review, report of meeting June 18–22, 2001.
5. See the list of laws for the accession and other dates.

and publishing. In 2006, responsibility for the ARL 2002 and its administration was moved to the Minister of Economy, who as a result of similar changes to the PDL 2002 now has responsibility for all intellectual property laws in the UAE. The Ministry of Information and Culture continues to handle matters to do with censorship and the printed matter and publishing law. The head office of the Ministry of Economy is located in Abu Dhabi.

Authors

An author is "a person who creates a work".[6]

Natural and Legal Persons

The ARL 2002 employs both the concept of a natural person as well as that of a legal person.[7] A legal person is a person created by the law, such as a company.[8]

An author is referred to in the ARL 2002 simply as "a person" without further qualification as to whether a natural or legal person.[9] From the point of view of everyday experience and common sense, authors are always natural persons—only natural persons can be creative. However, the ARL 2002 gives some special attributes to legal persons. A legal person has, according to the law, the ability to direct the creation of a collective work.[10] In what circumstances this might be possible is difficult to imagine. Legal persons usually have no ability to "direct" other than as a result of the decisions and actions of natural persons, who are themselves potential authors of the directed works. The producer of a sound recording can be a legal person if it "records" the performer.[11] A producer of an audio-visual work can be a legal person if it provided the necessary conditions to produce the work and

---

6. ARL 2002, article 1, the definition of "author."
7. For example, both concepts appear side by side in article 26 of the ARL 2002.
8. "Legal person" here is a translation of the Arabic expression "shakhss 'atibaari." It is commonly translated as "artificial or judicial person" (as in Faruqi's *Law Dictionary*, p.200). The breadth of the concept at any particular time is a matter of the current state of the laws that create such artificial persons. In article 39 of the ARL 2002, there is a reference to commercial and professional firms or establishments, as if they were not natural or legal persons for the purposes of the ARL 2002. If that it is so, it would potentially limit the application of articles such as article 26 of the ARL 2002 dealing with authorship of collective works.
9. ARL 2002, article 1.
10. ARL 2002, article 26.
11. ARL 2002, article 1, the definition of a "producer of sound recordings."

takes responsibility for its production.[12] Less problematically perhaps, a crime may be committed in the name of, or on account of, a legal person[13] and a publisher that is a legal person may be deemed to be the author of a work.[14]

The provisions that deem legal persons to be authors generally seek to make complex authorship circumstances more simple, particularly when teams of people are involved in production of the work. In terms of proving authorship and ownership of rights, however, it is possible that the deeming provisions only serve to move the problem they seek to solve to other issues such as whether the legal person in fact "directed" the work (in the case of collective works). On one view, these provisions require the proving of a fact for which there cannot ever be any evidence. It is a "category mistake" to speak of legal persons directing works. Of course, laws in other countries have dealt with the same issues and it may be that there are conceptually more tidy ways of addressing the problems that these provisions seek to solve.

"Named" Authors

The person who puts his name on a work is deemed to be author unless proven otherwise. This is part of the definition of the author in article 1 of the ARL 2002. It appears to be a summary of what is set out in article 15.1 of the Berne Convention, which reads (in relevant part):

> In order that the author of a literary or artistic work protected by this Convention shall, in the absence of proof to the contrary, be regarded as such, and consequently be entitled to institute infringement proceedings in the countries of the Union, it shall be sufficient for his name to appear on the work in the usual manner.

The context in which this idea is expressed is the enforcement of rights and the entitlement to institute infringement proceedings. This context has not been carried over into the ARL 2002. Nevertheless, the "named" author provision in the definition of "author" in the ARL 2002 should probably be seen as creating a presumption of authorship for the purposes of instituting legal proceedings. If the plaintiff's name is on the work, no further proof of authorship need be evidenced unless the defendant can bring evidence to rebut the presumption.

---

12. ARL 2002, article 1, the definition of a "producer of audio-visual works."
13. ARL 2002, article 39.
14. ARL 2002, article 1, definition of "author."

The presumption also extends to persons to whom the work is attributed upon publication.[15]

Anonymous and Pseudonymous Authors

The Berne Convention refers to two kinds of pseudonymous works. The first kind is where the pseudonym adopted by the author leaves no doubt as to the author's identity.[16] In this case, the author is to be treated in the same way as a "named" author discussed above. The known author is presumed to be the author despite publishing under a pseudonym.

The second kind of pseudonymous work is where the identity of the author is unknown, in which case the publisher is to act as the representative of the author and is entitled to protect and enforce the author's rights. Once the author becomes known, the arrangement ends. Anonymous works are treated in the same way.[17]

These provisions appear to have flowed into the ARL 2002 in the following form:

> The author of a work is also considered to be the one who publishes a work without a name or under a pseudonym or in any other way, on the condition that there is no doubt in knowing the true identity of the author. If there is such a doubt, the publisher or producer of the work, whether or not a natural or legal person, is deemed to be the representative of the author in exercising his rights until the real identity of the author is known.[18]

There appears to be a lack of correspondence between the Berne Convention provisions and the ARL 2002 provisions. The ARL 2002 deems the publisher to be the author when there is no doubt as to who the author is, which leads to the question: if the author of the anonymous or pseudonymous work is known without doubt, why would the publisher need to be deemed to be the author? A possible explanation of this anomaly is that the "one who publishes" is not a reference to a third-party publisher but to the author, so that the meaning of the provision is that the author of a published anonymous or pseudonymous work is the author, if his identity is known without doubt. This may seem tautological but it does make sense of the provision (and perhaps reveals that its drafting could be improved). The problem arises from taking the Berne provision relating to the first kind of pseudonymous work

---

15. ARL 2002, article 1.
16. Berne Convention, article 15.1.
17. Berne Convention, article 15.3.
18. ARL 2002, article 1.

(mentioned above) out of its original context.[19] The same kind of problem was discussed in relation to "named" authors.

The second scenario is clear. Where there is a doubt as to who is the author of an anonymous or pseudonymous work, and until the author is known, the publisher acts as the author's representative.

Intestate Authors

Prior to October 12, 2006, the Ministry of Information and Culture exercised the financial and moral rights of authors who died without an heir or testator. Since this date, the responsibility has fallen on the Ministry of Economy.[20] No criteria are given in the ARL 2002 for identifying over which works the Ministry has jurisdiction in this respect. The range of possible works is vast. Potentially all works might be entitled to protection in the UAE (although the number of authors that die intestate must be limited). If all works that are entitled to protection in the UAE were registered with the Ministry, it might then be able to take control of the works of intestate authors. Consistent with Berne Convention obligations, there is no obligation under the ARL 2002 to register works in the UAE. However, there is a reasonable argument that ministerial decision no. 132 of 2004 in relation to the register of imported and distributed works seeks to create a system of registration of all imported (or foreign) works dealt with in the UAE (see the discussion on this subject in the section on registration of works below).

The Ministry's entitlement to the intestate author's financial rights entails that it may deal with them or exploit them as if it was the author or the author's successor. It may assign them or license them or claim the royalties from licenses already on foot. Article 42 then constitutes a form of statutory assignment.

In relation to the intestate author's moral rights, the Ministry has an obligation to protect the moral rights granted by the law, even after the expiry of the financial rights. What practical measures the Ministry could take to identify and protect such rights is unclear.

In the case of a joint author who dies intestate, the author's rights pass to the other joint author or authors.[21]

---

19. The last sentence of article 15.1 of the Berne Convention. The article does not mention the one who publishes or the publisher.
20. ARL 2002, article 42. October 12, 2006 is the effective date of federal law no. 32 of 2006 that amended the ARL 2002.
21. ARL 2002, article 25.

Joint Authors

The ARL 2002 defines a joint work as follows:

> A work in whose creation a number of persons participated, whether or not it is possible to separate each person's share, and which is not classified as a collective work.[22]

This definition foreshadows two possible scenarios: a joint work where the individual contributions can be identified and a joint work where they cannot.

> If a number of persons participated in the creation of a work and it is not possible to separate the contribution of each of them, all of the participants are considered to be authors of the work equally, unless otherwise agreed in writing.[23]

This kind of joint work, where contributions cannot be separated, might be called a "merged joint work."

Despite what the definition of a joint work suggests, the article dealing with joint works does not discuss the case in which the individual contributions can be distinguished. Instead, and as if it were conceptually the same, it discusses the case of authors contributing different kinds of art. This kind of joint work might be called an "assembled joint work." In this case, each of the contributors may exploit their individual contributions alone as long as it does not damage the exploitation of the joint work. What is missing from the article is any consideration of the case in which the individual contributions are distinguishable and are of the same kind of art (for example, a film made in three parts, each part identifiable and contributed by a different film-makers, or a painting composed of panels contributed by different artists).

The authors of merged joint works are authors "equally" and they may not exercise their rights individually. Presumably they are something akin to "joint tenants" who may not assign their rights without the consent of the other "tenants." They may alter their legal status in relation to each other by written agreement *prior* to creating the work. The drafting of the article suggests that they can alter the "equality" between them, allocating to each different and unequal shares in the work, at any time. They may also agree not to be joint authors at all and have some other relationship instead. It would be prudent to clarify the nature of the relationship in the agreement for any collaborative artistic ventures.

---

22. ARL 2002, article 1.
23. ARL 2002, article 25.

In relation to authors of assembled joint works, they may exercise their rights to exploit their contributions to the work independently of the other authors provided that the exploitation does not damage the others' ability to exploit the work. They are akin to "tenants in common." They are joint authors in relation to the work that combines their respective works but remain sole authors of their individual contributions.

Authors of Collective Works

The concept of a collective work, as it is expressed in the ARL 2002, is used to put the ownership of a work that is authored by a group of authors in the hands of a single natural or legal person. The criteria for a collective work are:

a. the work is created by a group of authors;

b. the group of authors created the work under the direction of a natural or legal person (the "director");

c. the director of the work is responsible for publication of the work in his name and under his supervision;

d. the contributions of the authors are incorporated into the work for the purpose intended by the director; and

e. the contributions of the authors to the work are not able to be separated or distinguished.[24]

Article 26 of the ARL appears to introduce a further criterion: that the natural or legal person directing the work is to have directed the creation or creativity of it.[25] If the criteria for the existence of a collective work are satisfied, the director alone may exercise the financial and moral rights in relation to it.

That a collective work is one created by a group of authors limits it application. Presumably, a group means more than one author. Collective works cannot be produced by a director and an author if that is the correct understanding of "group." It is unclear whether the director of the work may be one of the group of authors. It may be a question of fact only.

The director of the work may be a natural or legal person. The idea of legal persons as directors is problematic and has been discussed above. Legal persons, such as companies, usually act through their employees or representatives. A company as an entity could not, except through the efforts of a human being, direct the creation or creativity of a work. The representative

---

24. ARL 2002, article 1, definition of "collective work."

25. The Arabic text here is: "wajha bil ibtikaar al mussanaf al jamaa'i."

of the legal person who is directing the work is, in the first instance, likely to be the owner of the rights in the collective work rather than the legal person itself. A separate set of arrangements will need to be made to transfer the director's rights in the collective work to the legal person. Arguably, in the context of moving ownership of works from individual authors to companies, the concept of a collective work merely shifts the problem to the level of the relationship between the director of the work and the company.

The nature of the direction exerted is also important. It must be direction of the creation or creativity of the work. This suggests that more is required than providing the conditions to do the work and giving a general instruction to create the work. The direction it seems must be such that it affects what is creative or distinctive about the work. In this sense, the direction need not be in relation to every detail but should be over those matters that are part of the creative effort (for example, in creating an architectural drawing it may not matter that the director had no role in measuring the site for the building and setting up the drawing software).

The director's effort must also be such that it results in the incorporation in the work of the authors' contributions "for the general purpose intended" by the director. If the result is not what the director intended it may not be a collective work. Such a work may instead be a joint work of the contributing authors. This might be one of the arguments that a group of authors could raise in an attempt to defeat a claim of ownership of the work by the person alleging to have directed the work.

The director of the work must also perform other roles if the work is to be a collective work. The director is to be responsible for the publication of the work, which he or she is to supervise and do in his or her name. The director is in effect the author of the work and may alone exercise the financial and moral rights in the work (unless there is an agreement to the contrary).[26] The contributing authors have no right to have the work attributed to them and are not required to be compensated for the exploitation of the work.

Another limiting criterion is the requirement for the contributions of the authors to be inseparable or indistinguishable. Many works produced by groups of authors preserve the contributions of each, especially works produced in office environments. Reports, advice and analyses are often prepared by several authors, each contributing a section or part.

What is difficult about the collective work concept as it is used in the ARL 2002 is that it is unclear precisely which creative contexts it was intended to address.[27] With its many criteria for use, it is certainly not a solution for all

---

26. ARL 2002, article 26.
27. M. F. Makeen, *Authorship/Ownership of Copyright Works under Egyptian Authors' Rights Law*, 38 INT'L. REV. INTELL. PROP. & COMP. L. 572 at 581 says that the concept of a collective work was developed in France to cover the making of dictionaries.

collective creation circumstances and will only apply to them in a very patchy manner. So much in the application of the provisions will depend on establishing somewhat elusive matters of fact, such as that direction was exercised by the director and that the director's intention was realized as a result of that direction. It might also be difficult, in some contexts, to prove who the contributing authors were and that their contributions to the work cannot be distinguished or separated.

Employees as Authors

The ARL 2002 does not contain any provisions deeming the works of employees to be owned by the employer (as is found in many other, particularly common law, jurisdictions). The potential application of the collective work provisions to employees is clear. Whether that was how the drafters intended to deal with employee authors is not known. Nevertheless, there are also limits to the utility of the concept of a collective work in the employment context. The most apparent limitation is that not all employees work in groups. The collective work concept probably has no application to the work of a single employee. The provisions also do not assist in cases in which an employee, or a group of employees, works in a creative way without direction or supervision.

If employees are not producing collective works then their works are either joint works (with other employees) or works in which they individually hold the financial and moral rights. The employer who wants to be sure to own the financial rights in such works must establish a set of arrangements within the business to achieve this, taking into account the requirements in the law for assignments and the limitations on disposal of future intellectual production. Indeed, the employer might be faced with a decision to make as to which style of ownership regime is suitable for the employer's particular business—one structured around the production of collective works by employees or one that avoids the concept of a collective work and focuses instead on employee agreements to assign financial rights and to execute assignments when required. In any case, the options given by the ARL 2002 are difficult to see as business-friendly. Anecdotal evidence suggests that most businesses in the UAE ignore the issue, in some cases to their detriment.

Commissioned Authors

The ARL 2002 does not address directly the position of an author who is commissioned to produce a creative work. Based on the conceptual scheme of the ARL 2002, the position of a commissioned author is substantially the same as an author working alone (unless the circumstances are such that the joint or collective work provisions are invoked). However, expectations may be different. The commissioner of the work may believe incorrectly that because the author has been commissioned to produce the work, all rights in the final work will vest in the commissioner and not the author. Subject to any agreement that would alter the usual position (such as an agreement to assign the rights in the work), the author is the holder of all rights. A reasonable inference is that the commissioner receives an implied license[28] to use the work for the purpose for which it was commissioned but not beyond that. If it is the intention of the parties for the outcome to be otherwise, an appropriate agreement should be put in place.

To Which Authors Does the Law Apply?

There are no specific provisions in the ARL 2002 or the regulations to it that directly address this question. The subject of the works of "foreigners" arises in article 44 of the ARL 2002. It reads as follows:

> In the domain of conflict of laws, the provisions of this law apply to the works and performances and sound recordings and broadcast programs of foreigners, on the condition that there is reciprocal treatment, and without prejudice to the provisions of international agreements in force in the State.

The protection of the Berne Convention, to which the UAE became a party after it enacted the ARL 2002, applies to authors who are nationals of one of the countries of the Union (among others).[29] Members of the Union may not discriminate between nationals and foreign nationals of Union countries:

> Authors shall enjoy, in respect of works for which they are protected under this Convention, in countries of the Union other than the country of origin, the rights which their respective laws do now or may hereafter grant to their nationals, as well as the rights specially granted by this Convention.[30]

The concept of no less favorable treatment for foreigners found in the TRIPs Agreement encompasses this idea:

> Each Member shall accord to the nationals of other Members treatment no less favourable than that it accords its own nationals with regard to the protection of intellectual property.[31]

---

28. See the discussion below on licenses. The relevant provisions of the law do not obviously contemplate implied licenses.
29. Berne Convention, article 3.1.
30. Berne Convention, article 5.1.
31. TRIPs Agreement, article 3.

The UAE Constitution confirms that foreigners in the UAE enjoy the rights and freedoms as determined in the international agreements to which the UAE is a party.[32]

Foreign national authors should therefore enjoy in the UAE the same rights as UAE nationals. However, article 44 of the ARL 2002 focuses on the works rather than the nationals. It states that the law applies to the works, performances, sound recordings and broadcast programs of foreigners. In so far as a foreign national author seeks to enforce or deal with a work in the UAE, the UAE law will apply. For example, if the UAE law grants a broader set of rights to the author than the author's own country, the author may enjoy those broader rights in the UAE (because UAE nationals enjoy them) but not in the author's own country. One exception to this is the duration of rights. If the duration of the author's rights in the country of origin[33] is fifty years after the death of the author (such as the UAE), and the rights holder seeks to enforce the rights in the work in a country where the duration is seventy years after the death of the author, then the rights will be deemed to have expired when they expired in country of origin.[34] It is therefore potentially a disadvantage to publish first in a country with a shorter rights duration.

The UAE may also have obligations to protect works of authors whose nations are not parties to the Berne Convention and with whom the UAE does not necessarily enjoy the "reciprocal treatment" referred to in article 44 of the ARL 2002. Authors who are nationals of countries that are not members of the Union are protected by the Convention if their works were first published in one of the Union countries.[35] Furthermore, such authors, not being Union country nationals, but residing habitually in one of the countries of the Union, are deemed to be nationals of that country.[36]

---

32. UAE Constitution, article 40.
33. "Country of origin" is term defined in article 5.4 of the Berne Convention. In essence, the country of origin is the country of first publication. There is no use of this concept in the ARL 2002 or its regulations.
34. Berne Convention, article 7.8: "In any case, the term shall be governed by the legislation of the country where the protection in claimed; however, unless the legislation of that country otherwise provides, the term shall not exceed the term fixed in the country of origin of the work."
35. Berne Convention, article 3.1.
36. Berne Convention, article 3.2.

Basic Character of a Work

Like the concept of the author, the concept of "the work" is at the heart of the UAE's author's rights law. In the ARL 2002, the definition of a work is the first of the specific definitions. It reads as follows:

> Work: Any creative work in the field of literature, or the arts, or the sciences, of whatever kind or manner of expression, or whatever its importance or its purpose.[37]

The Word for "Work"

The Arabic word used for the defined term "work" is "mussannaf." This is the word that is used throughout the ARL 2002.[38] The Arabic word for "work" used in the expression "any creative work" is "ta'leef," a close synonym for "mussannaf."[39]

"Mussannaf" is derived from the verb "ssannafa" which has two related meanings: (a) to classify, systematize or arrange, and (b) to compile or compose. It is the second of these meanings that appears to have been drawn upon in adopting the word "mussannaf," meaning something compiled or composed. It was perhaps adopted because it is more neutral than other words as to what is required to produce a "mussannaf" (such as any particular level of creativity or innovation) and as to what the result of the compiling or composition must be.

"Creative" Work

The works that are the subject of the ARL 2002 are works that are "creative." The word "creative" is a translation of the Arabic word "mubtakar." A literal translation of this word would render it as "created."[40] However, in English almost anything can be created—it is a word closely synonymous with "made." The Arabic word "mubtakar" imparts a stronger sense of creativity having been employed to produce the work. The English word that probably

---

37. ARL 2002, article 1.
38. It is also the word used in the ARL 1992 and in the EGIP. Indeed, to trace its history would reach back at least to Egypt's 1954 author's rights law.
39. The ARL 1992 used the word "'amal" here in its definition of "mussannaf." Whether the change to "ta'leef" in the ARL 2002 has any significance is not apparent.
40. A translation issued by the Ministry of Information and Culture (ISBN 9948-8500-4-1) uses the word "created."

best captures that idea is the word "creative" and hence it is the word used in the translations in this book.

The ARL 2002 gives a definition of "creativity".[41] The Arabic word is "ibti-kaar, which has the same root as "mubtakar," or "creative." It can perhaps give some guidance as to what is intended by the requirement that a work be "creative." The definition of "creativity" reads:

> The innovative characteristic that gives to the work originality and distinctiveness.[42]

The Arabic word for "innovative" here, "ibda'ee," could also be translated as "inventive," "creative," "original," "imaginative" or "artistic." Creativity is the characteristic that gives to the work "originality" and "distinctiveness."

Originality

The Arabic word used here is "Assaala," which comes from the same root as the word "assal," meaning origin or source, and is commonly used to refer to a genuine or original item as opposed to a copy. We can probably infer that the requirement of originality is at least a requirement that the work not be copied from another work. In that sense, it is a "new" work.

Distinctiveness

Distinctiveness or "tamayyuz" imparts the idea of difference from other works—it is what makes something distinguishable from other things. Something that is merely a copy cannot be distinguished from the original and is not distinctive. A creative work therefore is a work that has one or more characteristics that enables it to be distinguished from other works.

The use of the concept of distinctiveness here was probably not intended to carry with it the meanings it has in a trademark law context, which requires levels of difference that permit consumers to distinguish one product from another.

---

41. The word "creativity" is used only three times in the ARL 2002, once for the definition in article 1, and once in each of articles 3 and 26. The definition of "creativity" in the EGIP is substantially the same as the definition in the ARL 2002 except that the concept of distinctiveness has been added to the UAE provision.
42. ARL 2002, article 1.

The Level of Creativity Required

From the definition of creativity discussed above, it seems that the work need only not be a copy, and have sufficient differences from other works to be able to be distinguished from them. Another perspective on this question can be gained by looking at the provision dealing with "collections" of works that are not protected by the law. Such collections enjoy the protection of the law if the collection or arrangement is distinguished by creativity or if the efforts that have gone into collection are distinguished by creativity. The concept of "creative efforts" (or literally, "efforts by means of, or using, creativity") refers us back to the author and what the author must do: make efforts that use the author's creativity (rather than any other faculty). This may be a slight development of the meaning but it does have implications. Not any efforts will produce a "work" that is protected by the law. For example, if an artist knocks over a tin of paint by accident and the spill produces a pattern on the canvas that happened to be there, is the result a protected work? It was created by a person, the artist, and the result is something original (it is not a copy) and distinctive (it is not similar to other works), so it meets the criteria discussed above. But no creative effort went into it—it was created by accident. The work would not be a work under the ARL 2002. This line of thought could be further supported by the definition of an author: "The person who creates a work."[43] Here the word for "create" ("ibtakara") carries with it the idea of intention and does not mean simply "cause." On this view, it has a meaning closer to the verb "to craft," suggesting more strongly the employment of creativity. The author, it could be said, is the person who crafted the work.[44]

The Field of Literature, or the Arts or the Sciences

The Berne Convention states that "The expression 'literary and artistic works' shall include every production in the literary, scientific, and artistic domain, whatever may be the mode or form of its expression."[45] The ARL 2002 has adopted most of this language for its definition for a work.[46] What significance do the words "in the field of literature, or the arts, or the sciences" have in determining the scope of the definition of a work?

---

43. ARL 2002, article 1.
44. Silke Von Lewinski, International Copyright Law and Policy, (2008) ¶ 3.32: "the level of creativity or individuality required for protection in author's rights countries is higher than that in copyright countries. Consequently, fewer works are protected."
45. Berne Convention, article 1.
46. The definition in the ARL 1992 was simply: "Any creative literary, scientific or artistic work."

Is a shopping list a work in the field of literature or the arts? Let's assume it is creative in the required sense—the author has made a sophisticated and artistic list with drawings and notes about where to find the items in the supermarket. It is not a poem or a novel or other literary form, and will not be published as such. It was not created by a poet or a novelist or other person trained in literature or the arts. What makes it literary or artistic is that it creatively uses the tools of literature and the arts—words, sentences, and drawings. These arguably are sufficient to bring our shopping list into the field of literature and the arts and the realm of protected works. This example also illustrates that a work need not bear any particular form in the field of literature or the arts or the sciences and the author need not be qualified in one of those fields. A work need not be of any particular "kind or manner of expression," and mostly relevantly for our shopping list, need not have any "importance" or "particular purpose."[47]

The Requirement of Expression

The definition of a work speaks of the manner of its expression. Must all works be expressed? Expression is also mentioned in article 3 of the ARL 2002. Thoughts, procedures, methods of operation, mathematical concepts, principles, and mere facts will only enjoy the protection of the law if a creative form of expression is applied to them.

The Arabic word used in both articles is "ta'beer," commonly translated as "expression." Like the word "expression," the meaning of "ta'beer" reaches back to more basic ideas of "going out of, or over" or "crossing over." To express oneself is to bring what is inside to the outside. Words from the same root as "ta'beer" mean "sentence" and "word," "idiom," and "interpretation." The "ta'beer" or expression is not necessarily of something that is tangible or visible, although it must surely be perceptible. Consistent with that is that oral expressions such as speeches and audio works may be works.[48] Unexpressed ideas or works are not protected works because they have not "crossed over" from the mind of the author to the outside world in a perceptible form of some kind—they have not taken on a form of expression. It is the creative manner of expression that is "applied" to thoughts, procedures, etc., that is the subject of the author's rights.

---

47. Each of the expressions in quotes is from the definition of a work: ARL 2002, article 1.
48. ARL 2002, article 2.

Financial and Moral Rights of Authors

Financial Rights of Authors

"Financial rights" is not a defined term and there is no article in the ARL 2002 that explains what they are. They are first mentioned in the definition of "public domain"—works enter the public domain when the period of protection for the financial rights expires. This suggests that the financial rights are those that expire and that are protected prior to expiry. Article 5.4 of the ARL 2002 (concerning moral rights) mentions the "financial rights of exploitation." The author's right to license exploitation of the work is presumably a financial right. As detailed by article 7 of the ARL 2002, the right to license exploitation of the work includes the following rights:

a. To license reproduction of the work
b. To license electronic downloading of the work
c. To license electronic storage of the work
d. To license the acting of the work by any means
e. To license the broadcast or re-broadcast the work
f. To license the public performance of the work
g. To license the transmission of the work
h. To license the translation of the work
i. To license the alteration of the work
j. To license the amendment of the work
k. To license the rental of the work
l. To license the lending of the work
m. To license any kind of publishing of the work
n. To license to give any kind of access to the work including by means of computer or communication networks

The right to exploit a work is expressed as the right exclusively to license certain acts rather than as the right exclusively to do and authorize others to do certain acts. Perhaps this originates from article 9.1 of the Berne Convention: "Authors of literary and artistic works protected by this Convention shall have the exclusive right of authorizing the reproduction of these works, in any manner or form." Article 147 of the EGIP contains the same idea, but there it is accompanied by the right to prevent exploitation as well as to license it.

If an author can license forms of exploitation, it must be implied that the author has the right to do those same acts himself. Although the drafting of the provision is not entirely consistent with this view, it is reasonable to infer that the financial rights of the author are the rights to exploit and to license the exploitation of the work in any way, including by doing and licensing any of the acts referred to in the list above.

The practical significance of this interpretation becomes clear in the discussions below on assignment and infringement of rights.

Moral Rights of Authors

The Berne Convention protects two moral rights of the author, the right of paternity and the right of integrity:

> Independently of the author's economic rights, and even after the transfer of the said rights, the author shall have the right to claim authorship of the work and to object to any distortion, mutilation or other modification of, or other derogatory action in relation to, the said work, which would be prejudicial to his honor or reputation.[49]

These rights are expressed in the ARL 2002 in articles 5.2 and 5.3. In addition to these, the author enjoys two other rights: the right to publish or not and the right to withdraw the work from circulation. Neither of these arises from international convention obligations. It is possible that both were carried over from the EGIP. The first moral right granted in the EGIP is the right to publish or not, just as it is in the ARL 2002 (although expressed as a right to *decide* to publish for the first time).[50] The EGIP also contains a right to withdraw the work from circulation if serious reasons justifying it arise. Under the ARL 2002, it is a right that must be exercised through the court and the applicant for the order to withdraw must pay fair compensation to the holder of the financial rights prior to the execution of the withdrawal order.[51]

Can Moral Rights Be Waived?

The moral rights in the ARL 2002 are expressed to be not limited by time and not able to be alienated. The Arabic expression that I have translated as "alienated" is "tanaazul" which is commonly used to mean transfer or assign, but also to give up or let go of a right. There is no obligation for Berne member countries to make moral rights unable to be assigned or waived. In countries adopting an author's rights system, it is common to make moral rights unable to be assigned or waived, whereas common law countries tend to follow the

---

49. Berne Convention, article 6bis 1. The reference to honor and reputation was introduced to accommodate common law countries. *See* Von Lewinski, *supra* note 44, ¶ 5.104.
50. EGIP, article 143.1 and ARL 2002, article 5.1.
51. ARL 2002, article 5.4. Compare EGIP, article 144.

opposite approach.[52] To limit the author's ability to assign moral rights is consistent with the nature of the right. They are personal and for the author's personal protection. It would not make sense for them to be held by someone other than the author. However, not permitting the author to waive or give up (as opposed to transfer) his or her moral rights could be highly inconvenient in the use, management, and exploitation of the financial rights in works. In any case, that appears to be the position taken under the ARL 2002.

Treatment of Different Kinds of Works

Works of Architecture and Engineering Drawings

"Works of architecture" are mentioned in the ARL 2002 as one of the kinds of protected works. The expression is accompanied by "engineering drawings and plans."[53] "Works of architecture" in this context is probably a reference to architectural drawings, sketches, and plans, rather than the three-dimensional objects that result from architectural drawings, etc. Those objects are also protected works but referred to under the expression "three-dimensional works relating to . . . architectural designs."[54] In any case, architectural works, whether in two-dimensional or three-dimensional form, are intended to be protected by the law.

In contrast to architectural works, there is no reference in the indicative list of protected works to "three-dimensional works relating to . . . engineering designs," despite the reference to engineering drawings and plans.[55] One of the questions that sometimes arises in practice is whether ownership of engineering drawings can be the basis for alleging infringement in relation to three-dimensional products that reproduce the engineering drawings. Although the drawings are works in the field of the arts or sciences, there is a reasonable argument that the objects industrially mass produced from them are not.[56]

---

52. *See* Von Lewinski, *supra* note 44, ¶ 5.97.
53. ARL 2002, article 2.7.
54. ARL 2002, article 2.11.
55. This is consistent with the list in the Berne Convention: article 2 1.
56. See the section in the patents chapter on the author's rights and designs overlap.

Ownership of Rights in Buildings

"Three-dimensional works relating to . . . architectural designs" could encompass a wide range of designed three-dimensional objects including buildings of all kinds, special purpose structures (industrial or technological), the physical layouts of cities and suburbs, golf courses, and land reclamations in the sea. It would include the preliminary models for these as well as their ultimate real world embodiment.

Who is the author of a three-dimensional work relating to architectural designs? The rights in the architect's drawings for the three-dimensional work lie with the author of those drawings—the architect. But the building itself is made by someone else—the builder or construction company. It would not be possible to build the building from the architect's plans without the permission of the architect because reproducing the drawings in a three-dimensional form would be an unauthorized reproduction of the architect's work, albeit in a different dimension, and would constitute an infringement of the author's rights.[57] When a builder builds a building in accordance with the architect's drawings, and produces a three-dimensional architectural work, the builder is not exercising the kind of creativity that the author's rights law is concerned with. The builder is not an author in this context. It is the architect who is the author of the building (and the drawings), and not any of the other parties involved in the construction of the building according to the drawings. Of course, if the building is constructed without drawings, or according to the builder's whim or creativity, then the author's rights in the building may belong to the builder.

The ownership of author's rights in a building can be spread across several authors. The designer or architect of the physical structure of the building may be different from the interior designer and again different from the landscape architect, each potentially holding author's rights in different aspects of the one project. Correctly identifying the relevant owners is critical when it comes to determining the duration of the author's rights, identifying the parties to deal with for licenses and assignments and those whose moral rights must be respected.

The owner (or client) of an architectural project may feel that he or she owns "everything" because, in the end, the owner is the one financing the realization of the project. The project owner may have even had the initial idea of the building—its identifying and main functional features. But usually little exists in terms of author's rights material until the architects get involved. It is the architects who are generating the intellectual and creative content

---

57. Article 29 of the ARL 2002 expressly refers to the infringement of drawings and designs by the construction of the three-dimensional object that they depict. The article is discussed below.

of the project, and most importantly, they are realizing that content in the initial material form—drawings, plans and three-dimensional models. It is in those material forms that the author's rights subsist.

The owner of the project who commissioned the production of the architectural drawings may be able to argue that a license from the author of the drawings should be implied so the building contemplated by the drawings can be built. The construction of the building is a purpose that was likely to have been clear to the architects when they were commissioned and they should not be able to prevent the project reaching fruition, despite the fact of their ownership of the rights in the drawings. Ideally, the project owner would ensure that ownership of the author's rights vests in him or her at the outset, and that relevant moral rights are waived (if possible), so that the project owner has total freedom in terms of what is constructed from the drawings and how they might be altered.

Naming of Buildings

Whatever the fate of the author's rights in the architectural drawings and the three-dimensional object that is produced from them, the architect maintains his or her moral rights (unless waived). One of those rights is the right of attribution—the right to have the work attributed to him or herself.[58] When a "signature" building or other important architectural work is created, the owner of the project may want to be associated with the work and attribute it to himself or herself. But the naming of buildings after the name of the project owner has the potential to be inconsistent with the author's moral right to have the building attributed to him or her. There is also a trend toward endorsing buildings and architectural projects which also has the potential to conflict with the architect's moral right of attribution (such as The Tiger Woods Dubai, the Michael Schumacher World Champion Tower, Dubai, the Boris Becker Business Tower, etc.). The issue of attribution is something best dealt with at the outset of the project.

Seizure and Destruction of Buildings

Article 29 of the ARL 2002 provides that buildings that infringe an author's rights in the underlying two-dimensional designs or plans may not be seized, confiscated, or ordered to be destroyed or changed, if the purpose is to preserve the rights of the author. Instead, the author is entitled to fair compensation.

---

58. ARL 2002, article 5.2.

One of the key questions arising from article 29 is simple enough: what is a building? It is an important question because it determines when an object may *not* be the subject of a seizure order and *not* be destroyed?

The Arabic word in the text of article 29 for buildings is "mabaani" (the plural for "mabna"). This word is derived from the root "bana" meaning to build. The word "mabna" could refer to anything that is built. The ordinary use of the word in Arabic perhaps suggests that it refers to constructions that humans (or animals) inhabit in some way, temporarily or permanently. A construction that processes something and that humans could not enter would probably not be called a "mabna" in Arabic (but rather a "massna'" or factory). Certainly, interpretations of the ordinary usage of these words are at best rough guides only.

Could a water treatment plant that infringed another's rights in the two-dimensional drawings of such a plant be ordered to be seized and destroyed? Is it a building for these purposes? If we adopt the interpretation of the word "mabna" discussed above, it is probably not a building. Article 29 would therefore not apply and a seizure and destruction order could in principle be obtained. The same could be argued to apply to a two-story concrete mixing system, a complex system of pipes for petroleum refining, a golf course, and a creatively designed land reclamation in the sea.

Merchandizing Architectural Works

By the same logic that three-dimensional works might infringe two-dimensional works, two-dimensional reproductions of three-dimensional architectural works might infringe the architect's rights in the work. Since the two-dimensional drawings and the three-dimensional building that resulted from them are both works in which author's rights might subsist, the infringement may be of both works. Taking photographs of the iconic Burj Al Arab in Dubai and reproducing it on T-shirts, for example, is in the first instance, an infringement of author's rights in the building. Reproducing such building designs in the form of tourist souvenirs, key rings, illuminated home decorations, and so on also requires authorization.

Making a single copy of an architectural work located in a public place for personal use and non-profit and non-professional purposes is permitted.[59] It is also permitted to exhibit an architectural work in a broadcast program if the work is located in a public place. It seems that the program may be for commercial purposes and no compensation need be paid to the holder of the rights in the architectural work. This may save the many programs that have been made about Dubai and the UAE that feature images of the Burj Al Arab.

---

59. ARL 2002, article 22.1. See the discussion on permitted acts.

The Burj Dubai, hailed to be tallest building in the world, will no doubt be a popular focus for future programs.

Works of Art

Works of Fine Art

The ARL 2002 gives some guidance as to what works of fine art are: "works of drawing by means of lines or colours, sculpture, printing on stone, on fabric, on wood and on metals, or any similar works in the field of the fine arts."[60] The ARL 1992 did not contain this definition and did not use the expression "works of fine art," but did identify "works of drawing, painting, architecture, sculpture, decorative art, etching, plans, sketches and three-dimensional works" as protected works.[61]

Works of fine art receive no special treatment in relation to the duration of their protection and so the duration will be the life of the author plus fifty years (unlike works of applied art).

Works of fine art may be shown in broadcast programs without infringing the rights in them if they are works that are located permanently in a public place.[62] Filming to broadcast a temporary exhibition of sculpture would not fall under this exception and therefore would require the permission of the owners of the rights in the sculptures. Despite the permission, the moral rights of the authors must be respected.

Making a single copy of a work of fine art for personal use for non-profit and non-professional purposes is not permitted unless it is located in a public place and the author has consented.[63] It is therefore an infringement of the author's rights to go to a *private* gallery and take a photograph of a sculpture for personal purposes. Whether a public gallery or museum is a public place is open to debate.

Works of Applied Art

The expression "works of applied art" appeared in the ARL 1992 as one of the kinds of works to which the protection of the law extended, whether they were "works of handicraft or works produced by industrial processes."[64]

In English, the term "applied art" is used in contrast to the term "fine art" to identify art that is intended to be applied to functional or everyday objects.

60. ARL 2002, article 2.8.
61. ARL 1992, article 2(i) (using the words of a WIPO translation).
62. ARL 2002, article 22.7.
63. ARL 2002, article 22.1.
64. ARL 1992, article 2. The words here are from a WIPO translation.

Works that result from a wide range of arts or crafts might be called works of applied art, including works of pottery and ceramics, woodwork, carving, sewing, weaving, embroidery, stained glass, glass blowing, jewelry and other metal work, and cabinet or furniture making. Many of these have a "handmade" character to them but that need not be an essential characteristic (as the definition in the ARL 1992 suggests). Many industrially applied designs could be called works of applied art such as designs of motor vehicles, home appliances, tools, and equipment.

At an international level, the protection of works of applied art has been a matter of contention. The consequence of this is that under the Berne Convention, member countries may determine the extent and condition of protection for works of applied art.[65] This entails that members may protect works of applied art by means of copyright law or designs law or both. The issue of the overlap between the UAE's author's rights law and the designs law is discussed in the designs section of the patents chapter.

Works of applied art continued to be one of the kinds of protected works under the ARL 2002 but the term is not explained as it was in the ARL 1992.[66] The financial rights of authors of works of applied art expire 25 years from the first Gregorian year after the year of first publication of the work.[67] The Berne Convention leaves it to members of the Union to determine the period of protection for works of applied art in so far as they are protected as artistic works, but the protection period is to be not less than 25 years.[68]

Works of applied art may be shown in broadcast programs without infringing the rights in them if they are works that are located permanently in a public place.[69] Filming for broadcasting a temporary exhibition of the latest model of a sports car, for example, would not fall within this permission and therefore would require the permission of the owners of the rights in the sports car designs. The moral rights of the author must also be respected.

Making a single copy of a work of applied art for personal use for non-profit and non-professional purposes is, as we saw with works of fine art, not permitted unless it is located in a public place and the author has consented.[70] It would be an infringement of the rights of the author to take a photograph for personal purposes of one of the sports cars at a temporary exhibition.

---

65. The Berne Convention, article 2.7.
66. ARL 2002, article 2.10.
67. ARL 2002, article 20.5.
68. The Berne Convention, article 7.4.
69. ARL 2002, article 22.7.
70. ARL 2002, article 22.1.

Works of Plastic Art

The expression "works of plastic art"[71] appears in neither the ARL 1992 nor the Berne Convention. It does, however, appear in the EGIP together with "works of applied art," just as it does in the ARL 2002.[72] This category of works is mentioned only once in the ARL 2002: along with works of fine art and applied art, works of plastic art may be shown in broadcast programs without infringing the rights in them if they are works that are located permanently in a public place.[73]

The term "plastic art" is a translation of the Arabic expression "al fan al tashkeeli." It is probably unrelated to the English expression "plastic art" meaning art that is made from flexible or malleable materials. In Arabic, and in some Arabic countries, it can refer to all kinds of fine arts, particularly painting. Curiously, the description of fine art in the ARL 2002 does not specifically mention painting. It is possible that the term was intended to cover painting, but that does not explain why it was grouped together with works of applied art. It is also possible that the expression refers principally to the art of Arabic calligraphy which is described in a way that brings it close to the meaning of the adjective "tashkeeli," the art of varying or molding the forms of Arabic letters to produce a work of abstract art (that does not depict persons). One would probably need to look into the drafting of the EGIP to seek answers to these questions.

Like works of fine art, works of plastic art enjoy protection for the life of the author plus fifty years. However, works of plastic art are not excluded from the "personal use" permission in the ARL 2002 (like works of fine art and applied art),[74] which means that a single copy may be made for the copier's personal use for non-profit and non-professional purposes. The rationale for this is not apparent.

Audio, Visual, and Audio-Visual Works

"Audio, visual and audio-visual works" are identified as kinds of works that are protected by the law,[75] but none of them is expressly defined. Audio-visual works are referred to in the definitions of a "producer of audio-visual works" and a "public performance,"[76] and in the provisions concerning

---

71. ARL 2002, article 2.10.
72. EGIP, article 140.11.
73. ARL 2002, article 22.7.
74. ARL 2002, article 22.1.
75. ARL 2002, article 2.6.
76. ARL 2002, article 1.

renting works,[77] the financial rights of performers[78] and joint ownership of such works.[79] Each of the terms "audio work," "visual work" and "audio-visual work" is probably to be understood in its ordinary meaning, without limits or qualifications: An audio work is a fixation or recording of any kind of sound or sounds (but see the discussion below), a visual work is a fixation or recording of an image or images (there is nothing to indicate that a single image may not be a visual work) and an audio-visual work is a fixation or recording of both sound and images (whether fixed in a single medium or made from a combination of each). There is no requirement as to the nature or the media used or the manner of production of the sound or images. A "film" with sound and images in any medium would be an audio-visual work.[80] A film without sound, such as a silent film or a soundless film in an art installation, would be a visual work. Potentially a simple photograph could also be a visual work—celluloid films are no more than a series of these.[81]

In relation to audio works, the ARL 2002 contains a definition of sound recordings, presumably incorporated as part of the apparatus for the granting of neighboring rights to producers of sound recordings. That definition is limited to fixations of specific performances. There is no reason to infer that the meaning of audio works should be limited to fixations of specific performances in the way that sound recordings are. The concept of an audio work belongs to the domain of author's rights and the concept of sound recording belongs to the domain of neighboring rights. Audio works may be fixations of sounds of any nature, performed or otherwise.

Producers of Audio-Visual Works

The term "producer of audio-visual works" is a defined term in the ARL 2002, but curiously it is not used in the text of the law as such. It reads: "the natural or legal person who provides the necessary conditions to produce an audio-visual work, and who takes on the responsibility of its production."[82] The producer is not one of the joint authors of audio-visual works.[83] The role of the producer is as follows:

> 4. The producer, during the agreed period for the exploitation of the audio-visual, audio or visual work, is to be the representative of the authors of the

---

77. ARL 2002, article 8.
78. ARL 2002, article 17.
79. ARL 2002, article 27.
80. There is no definition of "film" in the ARL 2002.
81. There is no definition of photographs in the ARL 2002.
82. ARL 2002, article 1—the definition of "producer of audio-visual works."
83. ARL 2002, article 27.1.

work and their successors, in agreeing to the exploitation of the work, without prejudice to the rights of the authors of the literary works, or extracted or adapted musical works, unless otherwise agreed in writing.

The producer is deemed to be the publisher of this work and has the rights of the publisher for it and for its reproductions, within the limits of the purposes of financial exploitation.[84]

The producer, although not one of the authors of the audio-visual work, is to be the representative of the authors in exploiting the work, and at the same time, is deemed to be the publisher and to have the rights of the publisher. There are no provisions in the ARL 2002 that give specific rights to publishers, although the right of publication is one of the author's financial rights.

It is not clear that the role of representative of the authors and that of publisher is consistent. A representative is usually someone acting as an agent and has a duty to account to the principals. In any case the role of representative is subject to any agreement in writing to the contrary. Having the right to publish appears to be exclusive and results in the denial of a publishing right to the authors of the audio-visual work. It appears to be the intention of the ARL 2002 to vest the right of publication in audio-visual works in the producer and to deny that right to the authors. For having provided the conditions for the production of the work, this is the producer's reward—the grant of an author's right without being an author. In effect, the role of representative of the authors is entirely subjugated by the producer's right of publication.

Joint Authors in Audio, Visual, and Audio-Visual Works

The following persons are deemed to be joint authors of an audio, visual, or audio-visual work:

(a) the author of the scenario of the work;
(b) the person who adapted an existing literary work to an audio-visual use;
(c) the author of the dialogue for the work;
(d) the composer of music that is made especially for the work;
(e) the director, if he exercised effective control over the production of the work; and
(f) the author of the prior work from which the new work is derived.[85]

---

84. ARL 2002, article 27.
85. ARL 2002, article 27.1.

It is unclear here whether "joint author" is being given a meaning intended to be consistent with the article 25 definition dealing with joint authors in general or whether a new meaning is being introduced. The production of a film, with the need for contributions of different kinds of art, would fall within the concept of an "assembled joint work" discussed above. The contributing authors of assembled joint works have the right to exploit their contribution separately without prejudice to the exploitation of the joint work, which resembles the right of the individual literary and musical authors of an audio-visual work to exploit independently their contributions.[86]

One question is whether the joint authors in the audio, visual or audio-visual works are like joint authors of any other kind of joint work—they may only exploit the joint work jointly. The question may be irrelevant, at least as far as audio-visual works are concerned. If the producer has the right of publication to the exclusion of the authors, then what remains of the joint authors' rights of exploitation must be very limited. Publication is defined as making a work available to the public.[87] On this analysis, being a joint author of an audio-visual work gives moral rights but no financial rights of exploitation of any value because of the grant of the publication right to the producer. If the authors are to have any rights in the final product, they must negotiate for them and cannot take them for granted. Their respective rights in their individual contributions remain intact without prejudice to the producer's rights in the work.

The role of the director is also reduced to that of a joint author despite exercising effective control over the production of the work. Such control would normally cause the work to be a collective work and the director to be its author and holder of the financial and moral rights.[88] It seems that the intentions of the drafters was to make audio, visual, and audio-visual works an exception to the normal application of the concept of a collective work and to deem them to be joint works despite possibly satisfying the criteria for collective works with the director as author.

Because the definition of sound recordings includes the process of fixing sounds with pictures to produce audio-visual works, it is possible that one of the authors of an audio-visual work will in some cases also be a producer of a sound recording and be the holder of the neighboring rights given to producers of sound recordings under article 18. This is in addition to the rights given to authors of audio-visual works. It is not clear whether this was an intended consequence.

---

86. Compare: ARL 2002, articles 25 and 27.2.
87. ARL 2002, article 1, definitions.
88. ARL 2002, article 26.

Renting Audio-Visual Works

The right to license the rental of a work is one of the author's financial rights.[89] The provision dealing with audio-visual works reads: "there is no right to rent audio-visual works unless the rental is for the ordinary exploitation of the work."[90] This provision is probably not a limit on the author's right to license the rental of an audio-visual work. Instead it appears to address the licensed right to rent and puts a limit on what kind of renting the licensee may engage in. The rental must be for "the ordinary exploitation" of the work. What is "ordinary exploitation"? If the provision concerns the purposes for which the licensee of the rental right may rent, it is probably intended to prevent the licensee from renting the work for purposes that would infringe the author's rights, such as the broadcasting of the work. "Ordinary exploitation,"[91] although perhaps an odd expression in this context, probably means renting for the purpose of home entertainment or other non-infringing uses.

Collections of Works

The Berne Convention requires the protection of collections:

> Collections of literary or artistic works such as encyclopaedias and anthologies which, by reason of the selection and arrangement of their contents, constitute intellectual creations shall be protected as such, without prejudice to the copyright in each of the works forming part of such collections.[92]

Under the ARL 2002, collections of literary and artistic works and of folkloric expressions are deemed to be derivative works.[93] Derivative works are mentioned as one of the kinds of works that are protected by the law.[94]

As is clear from the Berne Convention article above, a collection is an intellectual creation because of the selection and arrangement of its contents. The implication is that the contents themselves need not be protected or protectable. The article does refer to "literary or artistic works" (as does the

---

89. ARL 2002, article 7. If the above analysis concerning audio-visual works is right, the rental right will lie with the producer because it is a form of publication, the right to which is given to the producer.
90. ARL 2002, article 8.
91. The Arabic word used here is "istighlaal" rather than "istikhdaan" or "istima'aal" (the words for "use").
92. Berne Convention, article 2.5.
93. ARL 2002, article 1, definition of "derivative work."
94. ARL 2002, article 2.

ARL 2002 provision) but that does not necessarily imply that they must be works for which protection is currently available (as opposed to works whose period of protection has expired, for example). This idea is made clear in the ARL 2002 because it expressly grants protection to collections of works to which protection is denied:

> However, collections of what is referred to in paragraphs 1, 2 and 3 of this article enjoy the protection of the law if the collecting or arrangement of them or any efforts that have gone into them are distinguished by creativity.[95]

The works that are denied protection ("referred to in paragraphs 1, 2 and 3") are (in summary) official documents of various kinds, reports and information about events and current affairs that are purely informational, and works that have ended up in the public domain. A trade directory consisting of many small and "uncreative" advertisements for trades persons is a collection of literary works. The individual works (the advertisements) contributed by the trades persons are very rudimentary and probably not protectable as literary works. Yet the overall result required the application of creativity and ingenuity. According to the taxonomy of the ARL 2002, it is a derivative work based on unprotected works and protectable as such.

For those wishing to make collections of works, the first assessment that must be made is whether the underlying works are presently or were previously protected. If they are not protected and were not previously protected, there should be no need to consider financial or moral rights. If they were protected works, then moral rights may need to be respected. If they are presently protected works, the financial rights will prevent the making of a collection without the author's consent.

The fact that a newspaper, for example, is permitted by the law to reproduce certain protected works does not mean that they can then be published in a collection without the author's permission. This is expressly provided for in article 23 of the ARL 2002.

Computer Programs and Databases

> Computer programs are protected as literary works within the meaning of Article 2 of the Berne Convention. Such protection applies to computer programs, whatever may be the mode or form of their expression.[96]

---

95. ARL 2002, article 3, last paragraph.
96. WIPO Copyright Treaty, article 4.

Source Code and Object Code

The ARL 2002 mentions "computer programs and their applications" in its list of protected works.[97] The TRIPs Agreement refers to source and object codes.

> Computer programs, whether in source or object code, shall be protected as literary works under the Berne Convention (1971).[98]

What is the distinction between a computer program and its applications, source and object code? When a computer programmer writes a program, he or she is writing a source code in a programming language (such as "Visual Basic"). The source code cannot be read by a computer unless it is converted (or compiled) into a executable or machine-readable program—that is the object code. When a consumer purchases computer software off the shelf, it is a copy of the executable object code that is being obtained. The source code is not directly available in the object code but can be discovered through a process called decompiling. The reference in the ARL 2002 to "computer programs and their applications" is presumably a reference to the source code and the object code. Both are, in principle, to be protected as literary works.

Back-Ups, Replacements, and Adaptations

Authors of computer programs enjoy the financial and moral rights granted by articles 5 and 7 of the ARL 2002. Assuming that a computer program meets the criteria for protection, it cannot, for example, be reproduced without the permission of the rights holder. There are a number of exceptions to this. The relevant provision reads:

> Making a single copy of a computer program or its applications or a database with the knowledge of the lawful possessor, who has the right to adapt it but only within the limits of the licensed purpose, or for the purpose of back-up, or as a replacement for when the original copy is lost or destroyed or unusable, on the condition that the substitute or adapted copy is destroyed as soon as the copier no longer has the right to possess the original copy, even if the copy is carried or stored on a computer.[99]

---

97. ARL 2002, article 2.2.
98. TRIPs Agreement, article 10.1.
99. ARL 2002, article 22.2. A translation issued by the Ministry of Information and Culture reads: "Making a sole copy of a computer programme with the acknowledgement of its legitimate acquisitor who has a unit to derive its application or databases from, provided that such act occurs in the limits of the licensed purpose or the purpose to retain or substitute at

The provision appears to be an adaptation of the corresponding EGIP provision in article 171. It reads:

> Making a single copy of a computer program with the knowledge of the lawful possessor of it for the purpose of back-up or replacement when the original copy is lost or destroyed or useable, or adaptation of the program even if this adaptation exceeds the extent necessary for the use of the program, as long as it is within the licensed purpose. The original or adapted copy must be destroyed upon the termination of the basis for the possession. The implementing regulations for the law are to specify the circumstances and conditions of adaptation of programs.

The provision from the EGIP makes a clear distinction between copying a program for back-up or replacement purposes, on the one hand, and adapting the program, on the other hand. Making a single back-up or replacement copy must be done with the knowledge of the "lawful possessor." This is presumably the licensee, but it would be the licensee that is doing the copying. Perhaps the intention was to say that the copy is only lawful if it was made by the licensee. The same ambiguity is in the UAE provision. The EGIP seems to treat adaptation of a program as quite a different matter, indicating that special regulations may be required for it. What factual situation the term "adaptation" was intended to refer to is unclear. "Iqtibaas" in Arabic usually means adaptation of a literary work, but also means quoting, citing, extracting, selecting or borrowing. To adapt a computer program, one must presumably have access to the source code and this would not normally be available to end users of applications. It may be a reference to the decompilation or reverse compiling of programs, which does not necessarily involve the copying of the source code but rather the transfer of the code to another language, something like the making of a translation. In any case, the adaptation must be within the scope of the licensed purpose (but perhaps not necessarily within the scope of the license). Unlike the EGIP provision, the UAE article was drafted to include applications and databases. A right to adapt the licensed copy of a database may be an essential part of being able to use it effectively.

The EGIP provision requires the destruction of the original or the adapted copy of the program but the UAE provision requires the substitute or adapted copy to be destroyed when the right to possess the original expires. In either case, the terms of the license may contain different obligations or indeed a permission to keep and use the original.

---

the time of losing the original, been damaged or became invalid to use. The reserve or derived copy must be destroyed even if it was stored in a computer as soon as the right of acquisition of the original copy is no more valid."

Rental of Computer Programs

The rental right in relation to computer programs is limited. "There is no right to rent computer programs unless the program itself is the subject of the rental." This is a reflection of article 7 of the WCT, which permits the rental right not to apply where the computer program is "not the essential object of the rental." It is useful to see this provision in the light of the TRIPs Agreement article:

> In respect of at least computer programs and cinematographic works, a Member shall provide authors and their successors in title the right to authorize or to prohibit the commercial rental to the public of originals or copies of their copyright works. A Member shall be excepted from this obligation in respect of cinematographic works unless such rental has led to widespread copying of such works which is materially impairing the exclusive right of reproduction conferred in that Member on authors and their successors in title. In respect of computer programs, this obligation does not apply to rentals where the program itself is not the essential object of the rental.[100]

Perhaps a better way to understand the ARL 2002 provision is to see it as denying holders of rights in computer programs the right to *prevent* the rental of their computer programs unless the program itself is the subject of the rental. For example, the holder of the rights in a computer program that is legitimately installed in a television set for its ordinary functioning could not prevent the rental of the television on the basis of those rights or indeed demand royalties from the rental, because the television is the subject of the rental, not the program. Seen this way, the provision could have been drafted as one of the permitted acts in article 22 of the ARL 2002.

Criminal Offenses

The permissions in relation to the copying of computer programs are important to understand because the consequences of certain acts may be criminal. Article 38 of the ARL 2002 makes it an offense punishable by imprisonment and a fine to *download* or *store* any copy of a computer program or its applications or databases without permission.[101] To the crimes of downloading and storing is added the crime of unauthorized *use* of a computer program or an application or a database. The downloading offense is directly related to the author's rights, it being a form of reproduction. Storage of an unauthorized computer program is an offense even if it does not involve

---

100. TRIPs Agreement, article 11.
101. ARL 2002, article 38.3.

any reproduction. Such an offense appears to be aimed at those who buy copied software rather than those who do the copying. Authorization of the *use* of a computer program is not one of the rights of the author, unless one sees use as a form of exploitation. It is also directed at end users (who of course may be the copiers). When seen from the point of view of the absence of similar protection for other types of literary and artistic works, it is indeed a substantial extension of rights for a very specific class of works. The extension of such a right to other kinds of works is unlikely to be as politically acceptable. Imagine if it were a crime to read or keep a pirated book or look at an unauthorized reproduction of a piece of art.

As literary works, computer programs fall within the provision given by article 37 of the ARL 2002, which makes various unauthorized acts criminal and liable to punishment by imprisonment or fine. The punishments are to be multiplied by the number of works involved in the crime.

Technical protection systems also receive specific treatment. It is an offense to disable or impair any technical protection or electronic information intended to protect or regulate rights, just as it is to manufacture or import devices for manipulating protection systems.[102] These provisions are aimed at code breakers and hackers of various kinds.

Assignments

It was felt necessary by the drafters of the law to include an article about assignments of rights in computer programs and databases.[103] The article provides that transfers of financial rights in computer programs and databases are subject to the license that appears on the program or database. A transfer of financial rights does not normally relieve the assignor of obligations owed to licensees unless the licensees consent to the transfer to the assignee of the obligations owed to them. This provision may be saying that the assignor is relieved of its obligations to the licensee and that the assignee is now bound to the licensees and is under the obligations to the licensees that are stated in the user license. Despite the transfer, the "purchaser or user of the program is obliged to comply with the conditions stated in the license." The licensee user has no contract with the assignee. The assignor, with whom the user has a contract, may cease to exist. This provision appears to bind the licensee to the assignee of the financial rights. In effect, article 12 appears to be a kind of statutory novation.

---

102. ARL 2002, article 38.1 and 38.2. *See also* WPPT, articles 18 and 19; WCT, articles 11 and 12.
103. ARL 2002, article 12.

Databases

The ARL 2002 provisions dealing with computer programs also extend to databases, as if they were more or less the same.[104] However, as mere collections of information they may not always be intellectual creations. The relevant TRIPs provision reads as follows:

> Compilations of data or other material, whether in machine readable or other form, which by reason of the selection or arrangement of their contents constitute intellectual creations shall be protected as such. Such protection, which shall not extend to the data or material itself, shall be without prejudice to any copyright subsisting in the data or material itself.[105]

Databases are not protected *per se* but only if they meet the other requirements for being intellectual creations. Importantly, the information in the database is not protected unless rights subsist in the information independently of the rights in the database.[106]

National Folklore

National folklore is one of the defined terms in the ARL 2002. It is any kind of expression of folklore whose distinctive elements reflect the traditional artistic heritage that originated in and continues in the State and is not attributable to a known author.[107]

The only other mention of national folklore in the ARL 2002 is in the definition of a derivative work. Collections of national folklore are to be considered derivative works as long as they are creative as to arrangement or choice of contents. Folkloric works are not mentioned in the indicative list of protected works in article 2. That national folklore is by definition without an author indicates that it is in the public domain and not protected as such. However, that does not mean that it is not regulated.

In order to print, publish, exhibit, or circulate any folkloric work, one must seek permission from the Ministry of Information and Culture. In order to obtain that permission one must have a certificate from the Ministry stating that the work does not contain any distortion or editing of national folklore. The permission can only be issued if the printing, publication, exhibition, or circulation is not for commercial purposes. However, if the

---

104. *See* articles 2, 12, 22, 38 and 39.
105. TRIPs Agreement, article 10.2. *Also see* article 5 of the WCT.
106. Mere facts are denied the protection of the law ARL 2002, article 3.
107. ARL 2002, article 1.

work is registered in the Ministry's deposits register then it may be for commercial purposes. This is what can be understood from article 11 of the 1993 monitoring of protected works regulations.[108] The requirement for the permission is mentioned in both regulations dealing with the registration of works in the deposit register.[109] The subject of national folklore and its preservation is of some importance to the UAE, which has moved from a "traditional" society to a fast-developing Westernized one in a very short time. The protection of national folklore has also grown in international importance and is being debated within WIPO. The first session of the WIPO Intergovernmental Committee on Intellectual Property and Genetic Resources, Traditional Knowledge and Folklore was convened in May 2001.[110] The subject probably deserves more thorough consideration in the UAE's author's rights laws and regulations.

Official Documents

Official documents are denied any protection under the law.[111] As such, the authors of official documents do not have any financial or moral rights in relation to them and the criminal provisions such as those in articles 37 and 38 of the ARL 2002 do not apply to acts done in relation to official documents. The Berne Convention permits member countries to determine what protection is to be granted to "official texts of a legislative, administrative and legal nature."[112] There is no obligation of reciprocal treatment for official documents from other countries because no protection is granted to nationals.[113]

What Is an "Official Document"?

The expression "official document" is illustrated by the list of examples given in article 3.1 of the ARL 2002, which are mostly legal or semi-legal:

(a) texts of laws
(b) regulations
(c) decisions

---

108. Ministerial decision no. 411 of 1993.
109. Ministerial decision no. 412 of 1993, article 6.8 and ministerial no. 131 of 2004, article 7.3.
110. *See* Von Lewinski, *supra* note 44, Chapter 20, "Protection of Folklore," at 527.
111. ARL 2002, article 3.1.
112. Berne Convention, article 2.4.
113. Berne Convention, article 5.

(d) international agreements
(e) judicial rulings
(f) rulings of arbitrators
(g) decisions published by administrative committees with judicial jurisdiction.

The list of examples warrants some discussion from the UAE point of view.

(a) Texts of laws. Federal laws and decrees in the UAE are issued by the President of the UAE and are published in the OFFICIAL GAZETTE. Each of the emirates has certain powers to make laws. Those laws are issued by the ruler of the emirate and published in the official gazette for that emirate. Federal and local laws constitute a clear category of works for which copyright protection is denied. Certain free zones have authority to issue laws. Presumably these fall under this category despite not being "official" in a clear sense. The issue of whether the laws of other countries are also denied protection is discussed below.

(b) Regulations. Unlike the laws that issue from the "legislative function," regulations issue from the executive, the Ministries, the Ministers, and the Cabinet. They could fall under the rubric of legal or administrative.

(c) Decisions. Ministers and the Cabinet issue decisions regularly on matters within their jurisdiction. Regulations are promulgated by means of ministerial decisions. The executive also issues other kinds of decisions. For example, the committees established under the intellectual property laws of the UAE to hear and determine disputes or objections issue decisions. These are probably within the category.

(d) International agreements. The government needs to be able to reproduce these freely to be able comply with them. They are usually published by decree in the OFFICIAL GAZETTE.

(e) Judicial rulings. Generally speaking, only the parties to proceedings can obtain a copy of the judgment from the court file. Some judgments are published in collections prepared and edited by the courts.[114] The names of the parties are usually removed and so are key facts that might identify the parties (such as the trademark the subject of the proceedings).

(f) Rulings of arbitrators. The UAE has a number of centers of arbitration, including the Dubai International Arbitration Centre and the DIFC/LCIA Arbitration Centre.

(g) Decisions published by administrative committees with judicial jurisdiction. See the comments concerning (c) above.

---

114. See the section on collections of works.

The category of official documents denied the protection of the law was probably intended to be coextensive with the Berne Convention category of "official texts of a legislative, administrative and legal nature" despite the fact that the list of documents illustrating the concept has a "legal" flavor. Nevertheless, the documents are those issuing from the three different organs of government: the legislature, the executive, and the judiciary.

The Language of Official Documents and Translations

The "official documents" that are denied the protection of the law include documents in any language, either in their original language or in the language to which they have been transferred.[115] This is clearly a reference to translations of official documents. The UAE would be rightly concerned to be able to translate foreign documents into Arabic without infringing any author's rights. The Berne Convention permits the denial of protection to *official* translations of official texts of a legislative, administrative, or legal nature.[116] It could not have been the intention to deny "unofficial" authors any rights in their translations of official documents. That would be inconsistent with the UAE's Berne Convention obligations. See also the section on translations.

Photographs

Photographs as such are not defined by the ARL 2002 but "photographic and similar works" are mentioned as one of the kinds of protected works.[117]

Rights in Photographs

Leaving aside the issue of photographs of persons for the moment, the law contains no specific provisions relating to photographs, so presumably the usual principles apply:

    (a) photographs are usually considered to be works in the field of the arts and will fall within the definition of a "work" if they are creative in the required sense;[118]

---

115. ARL 2002, article 3.1.
116. Berne Convention, article 2.4.
117. ARL 2002, article 2.
118. ARL 2002, article 1.

(b) the photographer is the "author" because he or she created the work[119] and as the author, the photographer holds the financial and moral rights in the work;[120]

(c) the duration of the author's rights in a photograph is the life of the author plus fifty years;[121]

(d) the position is not altered if the photograph is a commissioned work (unless there is an agreement affecting the rights of the parties) and so the photographer will hold the financial rights in the commissioned photograph with the result that the commissioner of the photograph will not be entitled to reproduce the photograph without the photographer's consent.

Depicting Persons and the Photographer's Rights

Depictions of persons receive special treatment in the ARL 2002, the effect of which is to limit the financial rights of the author. Article 43 permits the person appearing in a photograph or image to authorize publication of the image in the newspapers or media, notwithstanding that the photographer has not licensed or permitted the use of the image.[122]

The law does not give the subject of the photograph the right to demand a copy of the photograph. Equally, the photographer does not have a right to keep or exhibit or publish or distribute photographs depicting persons without the permission of the subject (unless certain conditions apply and unless otherwise agreed). If, for example, a person goes to a studio for passport photos, the studio may not keep a copy of the photograph on its computer system "without the permission of the person who is depicted." If the subject of the photograph does not permit it, no copy may be kept by the photographer, who is the holder of the financial and moral rights in the photograph. What would constitute the subject's permission here is unclear. The law does not say whether it must be express or whether it may be implied. If the subject does not ask the photographer for the original and all copies, does that constitute an implied permission to keep a copy?

This provision has the potential to disable the photographer's financial rights. The photographer cannot exploit the photograph if he or she has no access to the original or any copy or does not have the permission of

---

119. See the definition of "author": ARL 2002, article 1.
120. ARL 2002, articles 5 and 7.
121. ARL 2002, article 20.
122. ARL 2002, article 43. This article deals with images in general. See the comments in the note on the translation of this article in Part A of the Appendices. Although the provision has wider application than to only photographs, I am discussing it in that context because photographs are today probably the most widespread means of producing images of persons.

the subject. There is no express provision in the law for compensation of the photographer in such circumstances.

The moral rights of the photographer must also be affected by the provisions granting rights to the subject. The right to decide when to publish the work for the first time[123] and the right to withdraw the work from circulation[124] cannot operate if the photographer cannot keep a copy of the work and the subject of the photograph has the right to authorize publication against the wishes of the photographer (as expressly provided for in the article).

Limits of the Subject's Rights

The person depicted may give permission to the photographer to save or exhibit or publish or distribute copies of the photograph. And indeed, the effects of the restrictions in the article may be altered by agreement of the parties. However, the subject's permission or any agreement to publish a photograph is not required in the following circumstances:

(a) the publication was done on the occasion of public events; *or*
(b) the photograph is of a person or persons who are official or public personalities or are famous; *or*
(c) the publication was permitted by public authorities as being in the public interest; *and*
(d) the exhibiting or circulating the photograph does not affect the reputation of the person depicted.[125]

The overriding requirement here is that the photograph does not affect the reputation of the person depicted. This effectively ensures that "scandalous" photographs of politicians, businessmen, and other public figures are not published and that the press is limited in its photographic reporting to images that are respectful of public figures' reputations.

The Nationality of the Subject

The article does not limit the nationality of the persons who might seek to rely on its provisions. A foreign celebrity or politician, for example, could seek to prevent the publication and distribution of a reputation-damaging

---

123. ARL 2002, article 5.1.
124. ARL 2002, article 5.4.
125. ARL 2002, article 43.

photograph in the UAE on the basis that he or she had not permitted its publication or distribution. If the photograph appeared, for example, in an international monthly magazine distributed in the UAE, the adverse effect of an order preventing distribution in the UAE would probably not be as significant as the effect on a local magazine whose entire print run has potentially to be recalled and shredded because it contains the offending photograph.

Electronic Circulation of Personal Photographs

The publication of photographs on the Internet is extremely common today. The provisions of article 43 would apply to those who take photographs of persons (whether famous or not) in private contexts and circulate them by means of Web sites and chat rooms, possibly for fun or for other purposes. Such acts are not permitted unless the consent of the subject has been obtained.

The Subject's Remedies

How would a plaintiff proceed in a case of unauthorized publication of a personal photograph? It is potentially both a criminal and a civil matter. The criminal provisions of the law are tied closely to the financial and moral rights of the author. Article 43 is not about these rights but about the rights of the persons depicted in photographs, so the criminal provisions in the ARL 2002 relating to infringement of the author's rights would not apply. However, article 41 of the ARL 2002 addresses "other violations" and permits the punishment of a person who violates any provisions of the law by means of imprisonment or a fine. There may therefore be criminal consequences for the publisher of unauthorized or damaging personal photographs.

The law does not grant any civil rights of action expressly (such as is found in the UAE trademark law,[126] for example). Article 2 of the ARL 2002 says that authors enjoy the protection of the law when their rights are infringed. But here we are concerned with the rights of persons depicted, not authors. Article 34 gives to the court the right to make orders stopping publication, but "based on an application by the author or his successors." Such plaintiffs must therefore look to other laws to enforce their rights, such as the general right to be compensated for loss found in the civil transactions law.[127]

---

126. TML1992A, article 40.
127. Federal law no. 5 of 1985 in relation to civil transactions, article 282.

Titles of Works

The titles of work are not *prima facie* works in themselves—they are not in the indicative list of works in article 2 of the ARL 2002. That would mean, for example, that they could not be recorded as works with the Ministry. The difficulty with titles of works is that they are usually not substantial enough to qualify as works. A title of a work could be a single word or a symbol. However, the ARL 2002 does extend protection to them to the extent that they are creative.[128] Titles such as "Building Regulations in the UAE" or "The History of Seafaring in the Middle East" are probably at the non-creative end of the spectrum. Creative titles are more difficult to identify. To some extent they are usually descriptive of the content of the work, either directly or meta-phorically, whether the work is factual or fictional. The idea of protecting titles appears to have been borrowed from the EGIP, in which titles of works are included under derivative works. In what sense they are derivative is unclear. The question of whether copyright can subsist in titles has been the subject of reported cases in common law jurisdictions.

Translations

Translations are defined in the law as "derivative works."[129] Derivative works are mentioned only once in the ARL 2002 as works in relation to which the author enjoys the protection of the law.[130] The right to translate a work is a form of exploitation of a work and only the holder of the author's rights may grant licenses for such exploitation.[131]

Translations Made with Permission

It is clear that in order to translate a work, the translator must obtain the permission of the holder of the author's rights in the work. Once permission is granted, the translation itself is a new work and the translator is the author of that work.[132] The financial and moral rights in the permitted trans-lation belong to the translator (unless other arrangements have been made

128. ARL 2002, article 2, last paragraph.
129. ARL 2002, article 1. See the definition of a "derivative work."
130. ARL 2002, article 2 "12. Derivative works that do not prejudice the protection of the works from which they are derived."
131. ARL 2002, article 7. The author's right to translate is established by the Berne Convention article 8.
132. This is what follows from articles 1 and 2 of the ARL 2002 and is consistent with article 2.3 of the Berne Convention.

with the holder of the rights in the source work). The translator, in publishing the translation, must respect the author's right of attribution, but is otherwise free to deal with the translation in any way (subject to the terms of any agreement under which the translation was made).

Translations Made without Permission

A translation made without the permission of the holder of the author's rights in the source work is, *prima facie,* an infringement of the financial rights in the source work. The unauthorized translation may also not qualify as a protected work under the ARL 2002 if it can be characterized as prejudicing the protection of the work from which it was derived. A derivative work produced without authorization but which is authorized after it is produced will probably attain the status of a protected work.

Translations with "Amendments"

Article 6 of the ARL 2002 deals with infringements that result from amendments made in the making of translations. It is clear enough that a failure to indicate where a deletion or a change was made is an infringement of the author's rights. The other potential infringement in translating is if the translator's work harms the reputation of the author.

What right is infringed by failing to reference a deletion or change? One of the author's moral rights is to object to certain amendments to his or her work.[133] One of the author's financial rights is the right of amendment.[134] The financial right to permit the alteration or amendment of work is more likely the right that is being referred to. If the translator does not have a right to alter or amend in translating, then alterations or amendments of the work in translation are infringements. The effect then of article 6 of the ARL 2002 may be to limit the author's rights of alteration and amendment in translations to alterations and amendments that are not referenced.[135]

Then there is the further consideration of harm to the reputation of the author resulting from the work of the translator. This provision probably applies whether the amendments made by the translator are referenced or not. If his or her work harms the reputation of the author, the translation has infringed the author's rights.

---

133. ARL 2002, article 5.3.
134. ARL 2002, article 7.
135. I have formed this view with the awareness that article 6 can be traced back to the EGIP, article 143.3, which concern moral rights, not financial rights. However, the moral right of integrity is expressed differently in the EGIP and the ARL 2002.

Some Practical Suggestions for Translators

A translator who wishes to translate another's work must obtain permission to do so from the holder of the financial rights in the work. This may or may not be the author of the work. The permission should include the right to translate the work as well as to amend and alter it, because there may be a fine line between translating and amending or altering. The translator should be sure to reference any deletions or alterations (as practically difficult as this may be). The agreement between the financial rights holder and the translator should address the question of who will own the financial rights in the translation of the work.

The translator should also obtain an authorization to reproduce and publish the translation from the holder of the financial rights in the source work, because these acts done in relation to the translation are potentially an infringement of the financial rights in the source work. The permission to translate a work is only that, nothing more.

Neighboring Rights

Broadcasts

Broadcasting organizations face the problem that some of their broadcast content is lacking in "works" in which rights might subsist. An example might be the live broadcast of a sporting event. Under author's rights principles, it is difficult to see how it could be protected. The neighboring rights given to broadcasters are designed to remedy such deficiencies. The result is that in many cases there may be multiple layers of protection. A live news broadcast for example consists of the script of the news in which the broadcaster may have the author's rights. It will also have neighboring rights in the broadcast program. This is consistent with the opening article of the Rome Convention: "Protection granted under this Convention shall leave intact and shall in no way affect the protection of copyright in literary or artistic works. Consequently, no provision of this Convention may be interpreted as prejudicing such protection."[136]

---

136. Rome Convention, article 1. The UAE became a party to the Rome Convention after the ARL 2002 was issued.

What Is a Broadcast?

The definition of "broadcasting"[137] in the ARL 2002 follows the Rome Convention definition in substance and notably is restricted to broadcasting by wireless means:

> Making an audio or visual or audio-visual transmission to the public by wireless means, of a work or a performance or a sound recording or a program and its recording. Transmitting by means of satellites is also considered to be broadcasting.[138]

The Rome Conventions definition is: "the transmission by wireless means for public reception of sounds or of images and sounds."[139]

Transmitting television programs by means of "wires," such as cable TV operators do in many jurisdictions, will not be broadcasts for the purposes of the ARL 2002. Providing video-on-demand by cable, for example, would not be broadcasting. Equally, all forms of transmission by means of the Internet, which is essentially a wired system, will not be broadcasts according to the ARL 2002. Sending an e-mail is not broadcasting, even if sent to "the public" with images or sounds or both.

Some countries have now amended the definition of a "broadcast" in their law to remove the "wireless" limitation so as to cover broadcasts made by cable to accommodate the distribution of television by this means.[140]

Broadcasting Organizations and Their Rights

Any entity or person making wireless audio or visual or audio-visual broadcast transmissions is a broadcasting organization.[141] This definition would apply to radio stations, free-to-air television stations and satellite television broadcasters. "Wire" or cable broadcasters are not included and must rely on the author's rights they hold, if any, to protect their broadcasts.

---

137. The Arabic term could be translated as either "broadcast" or "broadcasting."
138. ARL 2002, article 1.
139. Rome Convention, article 3 (f).
140. For example, the United Kingdom's Copyright, Patents and Design Act 1988 (as amended), section 6 (1).
141. ARL 2002, article 1.

Broadcasting organizations are granted the following financial rights (in summary):

(a) to grant licenses to exploit their broadcast recordings and programs; and

(b) to prevent any communication of those programs or recordings to the public without a license.[142]

The provision adds that "recording these programs or making copies of them or reproducing their recordings or renting them or rebroadcasting or transmitting them to the public by any means is deemed to be prohibited."

Although the Berne Convention recognizes the broadcast rights of authors,[143] it does not deal with the rights of broadcasters. The UAE's obligations to protect the rights of broadcasters begins with TRIPs Agreement,[144] but as can be seen from the article below, there is no obligation to grant rights specifically to broadcasting organizations if copyright owners are granted certain rights in relation to broadcasts:

> Broadcasting organizations shall have the right to prohibit the following acts when undertaken without their authorization: the fixation, the reproduction of fixations, and the rebroadcasting by wireless means of broadcasts, as well as the communication to the public of television broadcasts of the same. Where Members do not grant such rights to broadcasting organizations, they shall provide owners of copyright in the subject matter of broadcasts with the possibility of preventing the above acts, subject to the provisions of the Berne Convention (1971).[145]

In January 2005, the Rome Convention came into force in the UAE. The obligation to provide rights to broadcasting organizations is set out in article 13 (quoted here in full):

> Broadcasting organizations shall enjoy the right to authorise or prohibit:
>   (a) the rebroadcasting of their broadcasts;
>   (b) the fixation of their broadcasts;
>   (c) the reproduction:
>   (i) of fixations, made without their consent, of their broadcasts;
>   (ii) of fixations, made in accordance with the provisions of article 15, of their broadcasts, if the reproduction is made for purposes different from those referred to in those provisions;

---

142. ARL 2002, article 19.
143. Berne Convention, article 11*bis*.
144. The UAE was required to be TRIPs compliant by January 1, 2000.
145. TRIPs, article 14.3.

(d) the communication to the public of their television broadcasts if such communication is made in places accessible to the public against payment of an entrance fee; it shall be a matter for domestic law of the State where protection of this right is claimed to determine the conditions under which it may be exercised.

The Rome Convention article makes a distinction between the broadcast and fixations, or recordings of broadcasts, and provides for rights in relation to both. This distinction is reflected in the UAE provision which refers to broadcast programs and recordings. Although the term "broadcast" or "broadcasting" is defined, the ARL 2002 also uses the term "broadcast program" in a number of places but this term is not defined.[146] Broadcast recording is also not defined. A program, as distinct from the recording of a program, is perhaps to be understood as a live "performance" such as the reading of the news or the playing of a sporting match or on-location reporting of a political event, an accident, etc. The recording of the program that is broadcast for transmission at a later time would be a "broadcast recording." Of course, broadcast recordings may also qualify as or contain copyright works. Broadcast recordings may be audio-visual works.

The UAE provisions probably give no less than the Rome Convention requires with the exception of the right to prevent fixation or recording of broadcasts. The UAE provisions only prevent the re-communication to the public, or other exploitation, of the recorded broadcast. In any case, given that the UAE is a party to the Rome Convention, the UAE provisions should be given the broadest possible interpretation because the provisions were probably intended to be complaint.

Duration of the Rights of Broadcasting Organizations

The neighboring rights given to broadcast organizations expire twenty years after the year following the year in which the programs were first broadcast.[147] This is the minimum protection period required by the Rome Convention.[148] Importantly, the provision refers to the broadcast of programs and does not refer to recordings. To the extent that the broadcast program contains or consists of other works, other periods of protection may be relevant. If the program for example was pre-recorded, it may also be an audio-visual work. The period of the protection of the recording would be the life of the author (or the last surviving author if a joint work) plus fifty years.

---

146. The term "broadcast program" is used in the definitions of "publishing," "public communication," and "reproduction": ARL 2002, article 1.
147. ARL 2002, article 20.9.
148. Rome Convention, article 14.

Idea for a Broadcast Program

The idea for a broadcast program is stated to be protected by the law if it is creative.[149] Ideas (or thoughts), on the other hand, are denied the protection of the law unless they are given expression in a creative form. It is not the idea that is protected but the creative expression of it.[150] It is unlikely that what is intended here goes against the fundamental requirement in the law for a work to take on a form of expression before it is deemed to be a work. Even if expressed and creative, is it really intended that the ARL 2002 should give protection to an idea rather than the form of expression of that idea? The protection of ideas per se is something that is the domain of patent law. If indeed the provision was intended to give protection to ideas as such, it is an exceptional measure. Why ideas for broadcast programs should receive this special treatment and not ideas for novels or films or plays is not clear.

Problems Faced by Broadcasting Organizations

Broadcasters face a range of problems in protecting the delivery of programming. Signal theft by various means has been a significant problem in the UAE in recent years. The motivation to develop techniques for viewing programming without paying a subscription has probably been the result of relatively high prices for subscriptions from local providers and the possibility of viewing prohibited content (such as adult content) using unauthorized delivery techniques. Various configurations of a set top box, a computer and an Internet connection to an offshore server have been used to deliver unencrypted signals to users. The most evident sign of what amounts to an industry in the UAE is the large number of sellers of set top boxes. These are offered "blank" and after sale (and as part of the deal) they are programmed to function to receive the de-encrypted signal. The sale of the "blank" set top boxes is difficult to characterize as a crime because they could be used for legitimate purposes. Although a number of such traders have been caught, the process of obtaining the evidence is difficult and if a conviction is obtained, the punishments do not constitute a disincentive.[151] As long as the incentives remain, signal theft practices are likely to continue and develop as technologies change.

Footprint problems are of a different species. The geographical area over which a satellite distributes its television signal is known as the "footprint." Due to the nature of the technology, footprints have fuzzy perimeters and

---

149. ARL 2002, article 2, last paragraph.
150. ARL 2002, article 3.
151. In a recent case, a three-month jail sentence for the owner of the shop was dropped on appeal but a 50,000 dirham fine and three-month closure of the shop was maintained.

very often the signal can be detected outside of the license area in ever decreasing levels of strength. This is not in itself a problem unless the set top box and smart card for de-encryption of the signal are available in the country neighboring the territory to which the signal is intended to be limited. A problem arises when, by one means or another, the set top box and smart card become available in the neighboring country. The UAE is one such neighboring country. The incentive exists to import set top boxes and smart cards either because the same programming is available at a lower price than in the UAE or the programming includes content that is banned in the UAE (such as adult content).

What crime is committed by the person who purchases a set top box, smart card, and subscription in the source country and brings it to the UAE to view programming at home that is available in the UAE from other pay TV operators? Although this might be a breach of the subscription agreement that the person entered into in the source country, is it a crime in the UAE to import and view the programming?

Broadcasting organizations have the right to prevent any communication of their programs to the public without a license. The user described above does not have a license for the UAE (only for the source country). But is the user involved in the communication of the programming to the public in any sense? If one were to see the use of the set top box as part of the communication process, then perhaps operating the set top box is communicating the programming. The difficulty is that it is not communication to the public. It is equally difficult to see a crime in an individual bringing the required equipment and subscription (for the source country only) back with them on their return to the UAE from their holidays.

The position is arguably different in relation to traders who offer the set top box and smart card from the source country for sale in the UAE. It is a criminal offense to put a broadcast program within the reach of the public by any means without authorization. By offering these devices to the public, the trader is putting the broadcast program (which would otherwise be unavailable to them) within the reach of the public. Only through the trader's actions in supplying the equipment does the signal become "available" in a meaningful sense.

Performances

Performers are given both financial and moral rights in relation to their performances.[152]

---

152. ARL 2002, articles 16 and 17.

Who Are Performers?

The ARL 2002 definition of performers is largely consistent with the definition given in the WIPO Performances and Phonograms Treaty (WPPT):

> Actors, singers, musicians, dancers or other persons who recite or sing or play or perform in any way, literary or artistic or other works, protected pursuant to the provisions of this law or that are in the public domain.

The WPPT defines performers as:

> performers are actors, singers, musicians, dancers, and other persons who act, sing, deliver, declaim, play in, interpret, or otherwise perform literary or artistic works or expressions of folklore.[153]

Whether or not the performance is of a work protected pursuant to the provisions of the law, it enjoys protection as a performance under the ARL 2002. However, expressions of folklore are not mentioned in the list of works.

Financial Rights of Performers

The WPPT (of which the UAE is a member) gives performers two sets of rights—one set in relation to their unfixed performances and another in relation to the fixations or recordings of their performances. The first set of rights consists of the right to authorize the broadcast and communication of their unfixed performances to the public and to authorize the fixing of their performances.[154]

The second set of rights is in relation to fixations of their performances in "phonograms." Phonograms are defined in the WPPT as "the fixation of the sounds of a performance or of other sounds, or of a representation of sounds, other than in the form of a fixation incorporated in a cinematographic or other audiovisual work."[155] Performers have the exclusive right to authorize the reproduction of their performances in phonograms and to authorize the making available of them to the public, including the right to authorize their commercial rental.[156]

---

153. WPPT, article 2. The Rome Convention definition reads: "Actors, singers, musicians, dancers, and other persons, who act, sing, deliver, declaim, play in, or otherwise perform literary or artistic works" (article 3).
154. WPPT, article 6.
155. WPPT, article 2.
156. WPPT, articles 7, 8 and 9.

Under the ARL 2002, performers enjoy the right to transmit their performances (unrecorded) to the public[157] and to record their performances in a sound recording.[158] These rights were probably intended to embody the first set of rights given to performers under the WPPT. "Transmitting to the public" probably covers broadcasting and communicating. However, the right to fix or record a performance in the WPPT is not limited to fixation in sound recordings, as it is in the ARL 2002.[159] The right of fixation should apply to fixation of sounds or images in any tangible form.[160] What the ARL 2002 gives instead is the right to prevent "the recording of a live performance on any medium."[161] This right to prevent, unlike the right of fixation, is not limited to sound recordings. The granting of a right to prevent instead of a positive right follows article 156.2 of the EGIP.

In relation to the second set of rights established by the WPPT (the right to authorize the reproduction of their performances in phonograms and to authorize the making available to them to the public, including the right to authorize their commercial rental), the ARL 2002 gives performers only the right to reproduce their recorded performances in a sound recording.[162] The right to authorize the making of sound recordings available to the public and the rental right are presented only as forms of prohibited exploitation, but appear not to be limited to sound recordings. In this respect, the ARL 2002 provisions are broader than the WPPT provisions which limit the positive rights to sound recordings of performances. This follows article 156 of the EGIP except that the ARL 2002 provision does not mention the performer's right to *prevent* unauthorized exploitation (as opposed to deeming certain acts to be prohibited exploitation). Presumably, it is to be implied.

As can be seen from the discussion above, the audio aspect of performances is privileged over the visual aspect. Performers that make no sound enjoy only the right to transmit their unrecorded performance to the public. Performers have no positive rights in relation to the visual aspect of their performance but recording live performances of any kind on any medium, and various acts done with those recordings, are deemed to be prohibited exploitation.

The last paragraph of article 17 states: "The provisions of this article apply to the fixing of the performers' performance in an audio-visual work unless otherwise agreed." This provision appears to give back to performers some of what was taken away by the express limitation of their fixation right

---

157. ARL 2002, article 17.1.
158. ARL 2002, article 17.2.
159. Article 7.1.b of the Rome Convention is also not limited to sound recordings.
160. *See* Von Lewinski, *supra* note 44, ¶ 6.39.
161. ARL 2002, article 17, second paragraph.
162. ARL 2002, article 17.3.

to sound recordings. The corresponding final paragraph of the EGIP article dealing with the rights of performer states: "The provisions of this article do *not* apply to the recording of the performers' performance in an audio-visual work unless otherwise agreed."[163] The EGIP provision may be a reference to article 19 of the Rome Convention:

> Notwithstanding anything in this Convention, once a performer has consented to the incorporation of his performance in a visual or audio–visual fixation, article 7 shall have no further application.[164]

The purpose of the provision is to limit the rights of performers over audio-visual works. It not clear that the UAE provisions ultimately limit the performer's rights in audio-visual fixations in the same way. The UAE provisions seem to do no more than merely confirm that the performer's rights in a sound recording are unaffected by incorporation in an audio-visual work. This scenario is referred to in the agreed statement in relation to article 2(b) of the WPPT:

> It is understood that the definition of phonogram provided in Article 2(b) does not suggest that rights in the phonogram are in any way affected through their incorporation into a cinematographic or other audiovisual work.

Moral Rights of Performers

Performers' moral rights are set out in article 16 of the ARL 2002 and are largely consistent with the moral rights of performers established by Article 5 of the WPPT. Performers are granted the right of attribution and a right to prevent damage to reputation from alterations and derogatory treatment.

Duration of Performers' Rights

The Rome Convention establishes a minimum period of twenty years of protection for performances.[165] TRIPs Agreement pushes the period of protection out to fifty years.[166] The UAE follows TRIPs Agreement in establishing that the financial rights of performers are protected for fifty years calculated from

---

163. EGIP, article 156.
164. Article 7 of the Rome Convention grants various rights of prevention to performers. VON LEWINSKI, *supra* note 44, interprets this article to mean that "the minimum protection provided for performers in the visual and audiovisual fields is limited to the possibility of preventing clandestine or otherwise unauthorized visual or audiovisual recordings" (¶ 6.46).
165. Rome Convention, article 14.
166. TRIPs, article 14.5.

the first Gregorian year following the performance.[157] If fixed in an audio recording, protection is calculated from the end of the year it was made.[168]

Sound Recordings

"Sound recording" is a defined term: "Any aural fixation of a group of sounds resulting in a specific performance whatever the manner of fixation or medium used. Sound recordings include the process of fixing sounds with pictures to produce audio-visual works, unless agreed otherwise."[169]

The first part of this definition refers to "a specific performance" which suggests that the definition deals only with sounds that constitute a performance of a work such as a work of music (which is commonly written first and then heard in a specific performance of the work). The definition would not seem to cover a recording of an interview, for example, which is not the specific performance of any work. This may be a drafting lacunae because the definition of a "producer of sound recordings" is someone who records the sound of a performer or "other sounds."[170] Clearly, the kinds of sound recordings that this could encompass are broader than what is encompassed by the first part of the definition of a "sound recording."

The definition of a sound recording, in its second part, also deems the process of fixing sounds with pictures to produce audio-visual works to be sound recordings.[171] Although the language used is open to some interpretation (particularly the use of the expression "the process of" and of how a process can be a work), it appears that at least some audio-visual works are sound recordings for the purposes of the ARL 2002.[172] However, audio-visual works are not encompassed by the definition of a "producer of sound recordings" which refers only to recordings of sounds and not sounds together with pictures.

The definition of a sound recording also contains the qualification: "unless otherwise agreed," which at first suggests that someone—it is not specified who—may agree to alter the meaning of a defined term. Perhaps what is intended is that if anyone uses the term "sound recording" in an agreement,

---

167. The first sentence of article 20.7 of the ARL 2002.
168. The second sentence of article 20.7 of the ARL 2002.
169. ARL 2002, article 1. For comparison, the Rome Convention's definition of a "phonogram" is: "any exclusively aural fixation of sounds of a performance or of other sounds" (article 3).
170. ARL 2002, article 1.
171. Interestingly, the corresponding provision in the EGIP, article 138.13, excludes the process of fixing sounds with images.
172. Perhaps what the drafter had in mind was music videos. Whether it is right to say that their production involves the process of fixing sounds with pictures is questionable. In any case, the definition is much broader than this example.

they can agree that it has a meaning different from the meaning it is given in the ARL 2002. However, that is something normally to be taken for granted.

Summarizing these points, "sound recordings" in the ARL 2002 are recordings of sounds of a specific performance and do not include other kinds of sound recordings but they do include audio-visual recordings where the sounds are fixed with pictures producing an audio-visual work.

Understanding what constitutes a sound recording for the purposes of the ARL 2002 is important because it is a term that appears in, and constitutes part of, other definitions such as the definition of broadcasting, publishing, reproduction, or copying, and is used in the penalty provisions.[173]

The producers of sound recordings enjoy the following financial rights in relation to their works (in summary):

(a) the right to prevent unauthorized exploitation of their works; and
(b) the right to publish their recordings by any means.[174]

The same provision deems to be prohibited exploitation the unauthorized reproduction, renting, broadcasting, re-broadcasting, and making available to the public of the sound recordings. It is curious that the ARL 2002 did not simply follow the drafting of the WPPT, with which it is required, and was probably intended, to comply. The WPPT expresses the rights of producers of sound recordings in positive terms including the right to authorize (a) reproduction,[175] (b) the making of copies of their recordings available to the public,[176] (c) the commercial rental to the public of recordings[177] and (d) the wire or wireless making available of their recordings to the public.[178] The only positive right granted by the ARL 2002 is the right to publish their recordings by any means. "Publish" is defined in the ARL 2002 as making available to the public. This would cover WPPT rights (b) and (d) only. No positive rights are given in relation to reproduction or rental. A question for discussion is whether the granting of a right to prohibit certain acts is equivalent to granting a positive right to authorize those acts.

The producers of sound recordings do not enjoy any rights other than those stated in article 18 of the ARL 2002 (but see the discussion in relation to audio, visual and audio-visual works). They also do not enjoy any moral rights.

---

173. ARL 2002, articles 1 and 34.3.
174. ARL 2002, article 18.
175. WPPT, article 11.
176. WPPT, article 12.
177. WPPT, article 13.
178. WPPT, article 14.

A producer of a sound recording is defined as: "the natural or legal person who records for the first time the sound of a perforner or other sounds."[179] The use of the term "legal person" raises the usual question of how a legal person can act except through the "agency" of natural persons and what relationship that natural person has with the resulting work.[180] Recording the sound for the "first time" is a requirement for being a producer of a sound recording. Presumably every sound occurs only once in time because every sound is different. The performance of a song by a particular singer is different each time and the recording of each performance would be a different recording. Equally one recording of the performance could not be before another (if the requirement is addressing simultaneous recordings of the same performance)—the performance begins and ends at fixed points in time.

Registration of Author's Rights

Is Registration of Author's Rights Mandatory in the UAE?

There is a widespread view in the UAE that works must be registered with the Ministry and that they cannot be dealt with or enforced until they are registered. For example, notaries public may not witness an assignment of rights unless the assignor has a certificate of registration of the work from the Ministry. Local lawyers receiving a letter of demand based on author's rights may also decline, on behalf of their client, to acknowledge any rights in a work until the complainant shows a UAE certificate of registration. The Ministry will often not enforce rights prior to their recordal. What is the legal basis for this view?

The ARL 1992, the UAE's first and now repealed author's rights law, provided that works "are to be" deposited with the Ministry.[181] It is expressed in the passive voice and does not use mandatory language.[182] The two regulations that issued following the ARL 1992 deal with the approval and registration of works.[183]

The language used in the ARL 2002 was diluted considerably. There is now no expression of the idea that works "are to be" deposited. Instead: "The Ministry is to establish a system with the competent authority for

---

179. ARL 2002, article 1.
180. The issue is discussed in the section on "authors."
181. ARL 1992, article 4.
182. A WIPO translation of this provision is: "Works shall be deposited with the competent authority at the Ministry."
183. Ministerial decisions nos. 411 and 412 of 1993.

depositing or registration of rights in works, and for dealing in them that may occur,. . . ."[184] The change made indicates that the drafters wanted to remove any suggestion that the law requires the registration of works. This is confirmed by the article:

> The non-deposit of a work or non-registration of rights or dealings that may occur does not in any way prejudice the rights established by this law.[185]

This provision originates from the "no formalities" provision in the Berne Convention:

> The enjoyment and exercise of these rights shall not be subject to any formality[186]

In 1908, the Berne Convention was amended to abolish completely any requirement to fulfill formalities.[187] Examples of formalities include registration, deposit or filing of copies with an authority, the payment of registration fees, the submission of declarations or the use of copyright notices.[188] The reference to "enjoyment" is a reference to the recognition of the author's rights from creation. That recognition does not require the completion of formalities. The reference to the "exercise" of rights means that the exploitation or enforcement of the author's rights must not be subject to formalities. For example, registration of the rights should not be required in order to commence legal proceedings. Assignments and licenses should also not be subject to formalities.[189]

Despite the introduction of the ARL 2002 and its adoption of what appears to be a purely voluntary system of recordal of works, in 2004 the Ministry issued a new regulation in relation to the registration of works.[190] Although it is not expressed, this regulation probably replaces the 1993 regulation dealing with the same subject.[191] The 1993 regulations required, for example, a certificate from the monitoring department at the Ministry "approving" the work as part of the application for copyright registration.[192] That requirement is not part of the 2004 regulations and presumably is cancelled by the

---

184. ARL 2002, article 4.
185. The third paragraph of article 4 of the ARL 2002.
186. Berne Convention, article 5.
187. *See* Von Lewinski, *supra* note 44, ¶ 5.54.
188. This list is from Von Lewinski, *supra* note 44, ¶ 5.56.
189. See the discussion in Von Lewinski, *supra* note 44, ¶¶ 5.54–5.61.
190. Ministerial decision no. 131 of 2004.
191. Article 18 of Ministerial decision no. 131 of 2004 cancels conflicting provisions.
192. Ministerial decision no. 412 of 1993, article 6.8.

2004 regulations. What appears instead is: "Neither any endorsement in the register nor the issue of a certificate of registration is to be considered to be a permission for the exploitation or circulation or exhibition of the work."[193]

At the same time that the Ministry issued its new regulations in relation to the registration of works, it created a new register: the register of imported and distributed works.[194] Article 3 of the regulation provides:

> It is not permitted for any natural or legal person to practise any activity relating to works including importation or distribution or sale or renting or lending unless it is registered in the Register and having a license from the competent authority in the Ministry.

It is possible that this regulation is an attempt to impose formalities on the enjoyment and exercise of right in works without being in breach of the "no formalities" obligation in the Berne Convention by characterizing the formalities as concerning "the practice of activities relating to works." Although the register is called the register of imported and distributed works, the obligation to register covers the practice of any activity relating to works. On one view, it amounts to an obligation to register a wide range of works under the cover of regulating importation and distribution. On another view, because the register is to contain only the names of the importers and distributors, the scope of the regulation should be read down to imported and distributed works, despite the broader language used. In either case, the regulation appears to be inconsistent with the Berne Convention.

Searching the Works Register

The 2004 regulations cancelled any inconsistent provision in the 1993 regulations. However, there is nothing in the 2004 regulations that is inconsistent with article 36 of ministerial decision no. 412 of 1993

> Any interested person who wishes to review any register referred to in this decision may do so in the presence of the responsible employee in the section and may obtain a certificate of the information that is contained in it in relation to any registered work or disposal.

However, the current practice of the Ministry of Economy is to reject requests made to obtain information about registrations or dealings in works

---

193. Ministerial decision no. 131 of 2004, article 14.
194. Ministerial decision no. 132 of 2004 in relation to the register of imported and distributed works.

unless supported by a court order or a power of attorney from the owner of the registration you are seeking information about.

Requirements for the Registration of Works

The 1993 regulations in relation to the registration of works were quite comprehensive in the sense that they dealt with the procedures in detail, the recordal of dealings in works and annexed the forms to be used. The 2004 regulations dealing with the registration of works do not cover dealings in works and do not have any annexed forms. Yet the Ministry of Economy is receiving applications to record dealings such as licenses (as if the 1993 regulations were still in force). Indeed, the fees for issuing a certificate of disposal of a work were specified in 2004.[195] The forms that are presently being used by the Ministry are different from the 1993 published forms, but not a great deal. The forms change from time to time so the latest forms should be obtained before use. The 1993 regulations required an assignment from the author to the applicant if the applicant is an assignee.[196] That document had to be notarized and legalized.[197] Under the 2004 regulations, the assignment document is not on the list of attachments for the application but the information about the document is to be included in the application form.[198] Despite these different provisions, the Ministry of Economy is requiring an assignment document to be filed. In some cases, a simply signed document has been sufficient. In cases in which the application to record a work is made by a legal person (such as a company), the Ministry will request an assignment document. In response to such a request, the principal of the applicant company may execute an assignment document claiming that the work is a collective work and that he or she directed its creation and therefore is the author and proper assignor. The Ministry will not require the employees who created the work to be identified or to provide any evidence that the assignor principal in fact directed the work.[199] If it is not made in Arabic, it must be accompanied by an official translation.

---

195. Ministerial decision no. 288 of 2004, article 1.
196. Ministerial decision no. 412 of 1993, article 6.5.
197. Ministerial decision no. 412 of 1993, article 7.
198. Ministerial decision no. 131 of 2004, article 4.6.
199. *See* article 26 of the ARL 2002.

Assignments and Licenses

One of the surprising features of the ARL 2002 is that it appears to have no provisions expressly regulating the granting of licenses (other than the provisions on compulsory licenses), although there are several provisions dealing with "transfers" of rights, which one first assumes are about assignments. However, some of the formal requirements for such transfers seem to relate to licenses rather than assignments. For example, the disposal agreement must specify the period of exploitation.[200] Licenses rather than assignments are limited by time. The consideration for the transfer of rights may be based on a percentage of the income resulting from the exploitation.[201] This appears to be a description of a royalty under a license. Furthermore, the court can subsequently review the consideration in light of matters arising after contracting. In view of these provisions, and despite the absence of any mention of licenses, "transfer" of rights in article 9 of the ARL 2002 is very likely a reference to both the assignment of rights as well as the granting of licenses.[202]

Putting assignments and licenses together as if they were the same has the potential for mischief. What is required to regulate one does not necessarily apply to the other and vice versa (as seen in the above examples). Assignments are once-and-for-all disposals of rights. Licenses are generally but not always limited by time and can be given to many different persons at the same time (non-exclusively). They may be so limited in what they grant that they are little more than a contractual permission to do something that the licensee could not otherwise do. Other licenses give the licensee such extensive rights that it is as if it were an assignment (for example, a license granted for a lump sum for the duration of the rights that permits the licensee to take proceedings for infringement in the name of the licensor and retain any damages). In any case, assignments and licenses are different creatures and the language and concepts used to speak about them are distinct. Whether it is more correct to speak of the *grant* of rights or the *transfer* of rights in relation to licenses may be only a matter of terminology, but in this context, a linguistic distinction needs to be maintained between rights that are contractually granted and expire in time and rights that are transferred and disposed of once-and-for-all.

---

200. ARL 2002, article 9.
201. ARL 2002, article 10.
202. Article 149 of the EGIP refers expressly to licenses: ". . . and his license to exploit one of these rights is not to be considered a right to exploit any other financial right he enjoys in the same work." This sentence was not carried over to the UAE provisions. It clearly indicates that the corresponding EGIP provisions dealing with transfers of rights are intended to cover licenses and assignments.

The discussion below proceeds on the assumption that articles 9, 10, and 11 of the ARL 2002 apply to both assignments and licenses. Following the law, I use the term "transfer" to refer to both assignments and licenses. The author, or the author's successors, may transfer all or some of the financial rights in the work to another person, natural or legal.[203] Although article 9 mentions only the author and successors, the provisions apply to holders of neighboring rights by virtue of article 24 of the ARL 2002.

For a transfer of rights to be valid, it must satisfy a number of formal conditions.

Writing and Legalization

Transfers must be in writing. There is no requirement that the document be executed before a notary public. However, as a practical matter, government authorities in the UAE may not recognize the document unless it has been notarized and legalized. For example, the 1993 author's rights regulations require that in order for a transfer of rights to be registered with the Ministry of Information and Culture, the application for registration must be supported by a legalized document.[204] For documents that are executed in the UAE, "legalized" here means executed before a UAE public notary, but for documents executed outside the UAE, it usually means executed before a notary, stamped by the Ministry of Justice in that country, and then by the Ministry of Foreign Affairs and then by the UAE Embassy, and once it arrives in the UAE it must be stamped by the UAE Ministry of Foreign Affairs. There is also a requirement for legalized "transfer" documents in recording works in the register of imported and distributed works.[205]

In summary, all assignments and licenses of author's rights or neighboring rights must be in writing. They should also be legalized if they are intended to be used in dealings with the government authorities including the judicial and enforcement authorities.

Language

There is no requirement in the ARL 2002 that the "writing" of the transfer be in any particular language. However, it may not be possible to use the document for many practical purposes unless it is either in Arabic, the official

---

203. ARL 2002, article 9. The corresponding provision in the ARL 1992 is article 32.
204. Ministerial decision no. 412 of 1993, article 26. *See also* the section in this book on the registration of rights.
205. Ministerial decision no. 132 of 2004, article 5.

language of the UAE, or is accompanied by a translation into Arabic stamped by a government-licensed translator or by a foreign translator and legalized up to the UAE Embassy. It is a requirement for registration of a disposal of rights with the Ministry that the document be accompanied by a translation into Arabic if it is not in written in Arabic.[206]

The Right the Subject of the Disposal

The right the subject of the disposal must be specified. The author or rights holder has no express right under the ARL 2002 to exploit (e.g., to reproduce, translate, etc.) the work in which the rights subsists. The author may license the exploitation of the work.[207] Strictly speaking, the only right that could be assigned is the right to license the exploitation of the work. Nevertheless, there is a good argument for a broader and more workable interpretation. The rights holder must be able to do whatever he or she can license someone else to do. The right to license exploitation of a work then necessarily implies that the rights holder has the right to do those acts that can be licensed.

What then are the specific rights that can be licensed (and therefore can be assigned)? The author's right is the right to license exploitation of the work. The content of the concept is partly determined by the technology of the time (not long ago, broadcasting, and therefore a broadcasting right, did not exist). The ARL 2002 gives some examples of exploitation rights:

    a. reproduction of the work
    b. electronic downloading of the work
    c. electronic storage of the work
    d. the acting of the work by any means
    e. the broadcast or re-broadcast the work
    f. the public performance of the work
    g. the transmission of the work
    h. the translation of the work
    i. the alteration of the work
    j. the amendment of the work
    k. the rental of the work
    l. the lending of the work
    m. any kind of publishing of the work
    n. giving any kind of access to the work including by means of computer or communication networks

---

206. Ministerial decision no. 412 of 1993, article 26.
207. ARL 2002, article 7. See the discussion the section on financial rights.

Broadcasting, publishing, public performance, public communication, and reproduction are defined in the article 1 of the ARL 2002. For the specific financial rights of performers, producers of sound recordings and broadcasting organizations, see the sections dealing with those topics.[208]

There is a consequence if there is ambiguity in the rights being transferred: "The author continues to be the owner of all rights that he does not expressly surrender." The assignee or licensee should beware of making assumptions about the rights that are being transferred. If *all* the rights of exploitation are to be assigned or licensed, the drafter of the document faces the challenge of expressly listing all the rights that subsist in the work. Failing to make a complete list may result in the transfer being only partial. Caution also needs to be exercised in specifying the rights the subject of the transfer because some rights are interconnected, overlap and can be described in different ways. For example, downloading is arguably a kind of reproduction. Broadcasting in some contexts could constitute reproduction and communication to the public. Performing a work may be a reproduction of it. Publishing a work may be a form of communication of it, and so on.

A Statement of the Purpose of the Disposal

A statement of the purpose of the disposal must be in the contract of disposal. It is not clear what is intended to be achieved by including such a statement. From the transferee's point of view, the risk is that such a statement could be interpreted as limiting the scope of the transferred rights. For example, an assignment of the rights to copy and publish might be read down if accompanied by a statement that the purpose of the assignment is to publish the work as a book. A book is just one possible result of the exercise of the rights to copy and publish a work. The purpose of the disposal could be stated broadly to avoid such a limitation if that is what the parties intend. For example, "The purpose of this assignment is to give the assignee the rights to exploit the work in any way he sees fit by means of copying and publishing the work only."

The Period of Exploitation

The requirement to identify the period of exploitation may apply only to transfers that are licenses rather than assignments because the latter are not limited by time. The period of exploitation might be relevant to an assignment when it is accompanied by an agreement to re-assign at a future time.

---

208. ARL 2002, articles 17, 18, and 19.

The Place of Exploitation

The rights of the author can be divided and distributed geographically. There are no limitations in the ARL 2002 on the geographical distribution of rights. The only requirement is that transfers identify the geographical area of the right transferred. For example, the right to copy and print a book might be given to one person for the territory of Lebanon, but the right to make it available to the public might be given to another person for Iraq.

Joint Authors as Transferors

Joint authors must assign or license their rights jointly and not separately if it is not possible to separate out their individual contributions to the work. They may, before creating the work, agree in writing that one of them alone may exercise the joint author's rights. In cases in which the authors participating in a work contribute different kinds of art, they maintain their individual rights in what they contributed and may deal with those rights independently (provided that the dealing does not damage the exploitation of the joint work for the others).[209]

The Author of a Collective Work as Transferor

The author of a collective work may assign or license the author's rights in the work without giving any consideration or reference to the others who participated in the creation of the work because that person alone (the one who directed the creation of the work) may exercise the author's rights.[210] The author of a collective work may be a natural person or a legal person such as a company.

Due Diligence for Transfers from Authors of Joint or Collective Works

From the point of view of an assignee or licensee of a joint work, all the authors who participated in the work should be identified and their contributions ascertained. They will all need to be parties to the agreement if their contributions cannot be distinguished. If their contributions can be distinguished, perhaps because they contributed different kinds of art, it will need

---

209. *See* ARL 2002, article 25. See the discussion above on the subject of joint works.
210. ARL 2002, article 26. See the discussion on the subject of collective works above.

to be determined whether they have already granted any rights to others in their contributions. If they have not, the transferee may want to limit their ability to do so in the future in the contract, in order to get the greatest value from the acquisition of the rights in the joint work. It also needs to be determined whether the authors have appointed one of the authors to exercise the rights in the joint work on the others' behalf.

In relation to collective works, the transferee should receive some assurances from the transferor that the conditions existed during the period of creation of the work for a collective work to come into existence, including warranties that the transferor exercised the required level of "direction" over the creation of the work such that the rights in the work are deemed to be with him or her. Ideally, the authors in fact should be identified and they should confirm that they were directed and waive any right to assert rights in the work at a later time.

Consideration

The consideration for a transfer of rights may be in the form of a lump sum payment or a percentage of income derived from the exploitation of the work. Clearly the former is usually associated with assignments and the latter with licenses. The value of the consideration agreed upon can be the subject of a judicial review if the agreement as to consideration is or becomes detrimental to the rights of the author or of holders of neighboring rights.[211] There is no guidance given in the ARL 2002 as to what the court must or may consider in reviewing the value of the consideration or what would constitute "detriment," and no specific power is given to the court to alter the agreement and the value of the consideration. Presumably the court's power to re-write this aspect of the agreement is implied or derived from elsewhere.

Disposals of Future Works

The EGIP contains a provision that deems any disposal of all of the author's future intellectual production to be null and void.[212] The ARL 2002 contains the same provision but added to it are the words "or more than five of his future works."[213] Of course, "more than five" would cover the case of "all" so the reference to all future works is superfluous. It suggests that the "more than five" idea was simply added to the end of the EGIP provision.

---

211. ARL 2002, article 11.
212. EGIP, article 153.
213. ARL 2002, article 15.

This provision is clearly designed to protect authors from exploitation. Although that may be a noble objective, there are other consequences. First, the limitation applies to performers, producers of sound recordings, and broadcasting organizations by virtue of article 24, and not only to authors. Secondly, five works is an entirely arbitrary number and in some circumstances it may be inconvenient to both the author and the transferee. Thirdly, in certain contexts such as the employment context it is not unreasonable for the employer to expect to own the rights in the works made by employees without the need to assert that the works are collective works (with all of the uncertainties and issues that go with that concept—see the section above on collective works).

Frustration of Exploitation

After a disposal of a right, the author must not do anything that would frustrate the exploitation of the work by the transferee. This obligation is "without prejudice to the moral rights of the author."[214]

This provision appears to be aimed at the practical requirements for exploitation. For example, receiving the right to reproduce a painting is of limited value if the receiver of the right is not given access to the painting to be able to reproduce it. The refusal to give the transferee the practical means to exercise the right would probably constitute frustration of the exploitation of the work.

Ownership of Original Copies

The owner of the physical material in which a work subsists is, however, permitted to frustrate exploitation. Take the example of a painting. The painter might have sold it to a collector. That sale does not in itself result in any transfer of the financial or moral rights in the work.[215] The painter or an assignee or licensee may wish to reproduce the painting (for example, in postcards). The current owner of the painting cannot be compelled to permit the painter, and presumably his successors in title, to "copy, transfer or exhibit" the work.[216] The author or transferee may hold the rights but not be able to exercise them because the owner of the original copy does not wish to cooperate. The result could be that the work cannot be exploited at all—the author cannot get the necessary access and the owner of the original copy has no right to exploit the work.

---

214. ARL 2002, article 9.
215. ARL 2002, article 13, first paragraph.
216. ARL 2002, article 13, second paragraph.

Recordal of Disposals

The recordal or registration of disposals of rights is discussed briefly in the section on the registration of rights.

Infringement of Rights

Authors of works and holders of neighboring rights enjoy the protection of the law, says article 2 of the ARL 2002, if their rights are infringed. Yet, authors are not given any specific right to prevent unauthorized acts which they have the right to do exclusively. The article that gives authors their financial rights does not give them a right to prevent unauthorized acts.[217] The corresponding provision in the EGIP includes a right to prevent unauthorized exploitation.[218] The drafters of the ARL 2002 appear to have decided to omit this fundamental right from the list of author's rights. However, they did decide to give express rights of prevention to producers of sound recordings and broadcasting organizations.[219]

The protection of the law then, as referred to in article 2, appears to be only the protection granted by the criminal provisions. It is in the hands of the State to enforce author's rights. If an author wished to take legal proceedings against an infringer, the action would have to be based on an infringement of the author's exclusive right to license the exploitation of his or her work. Provided that one sees the exclusive right to license exploitation as including the right of the author himself or herself to exploit the work,[220] then the author can allege that the defendant's acts infringe the author's right to exploitation, and not the author's right to *license* the exploitation of the work. The right to license exploitation is only infringed if the defendant, without a license, has licensed another person to exploit the work.

Precautionary Measures and the Main Case

The ARL 2002 certainly contemplates that authors themselves (as opposed to the State) will bring cases of infringement to the court. The precautionary measures provisions speak of the author making an application to the court

---

217. ARL 2002, article 7.
218. EGIP, article 147.
219. ARL 2002, articles 18 and 19.
220. See the discussion in the section on the author's financial rights.

for interim orders and subsequently filing a main case.[221] The only basis for making an application for precautionary measures is an infringement of the author's financial or moral rights. The holders of neighboring rights are not mentioned as having a right to make a precautionary measures application. Whether this was intentional is unclear. To have the right to apply for precautionary measures, the holders of neighboring rights must seek to rely on article 24:

> The rules applying to the financial rights of the author set out in this law also apply to the holders of neighboring rights.

The range of interim orders that can be sought in relation to unauthorized works is one of the strengths of the ARL 2002. They can be summarized as follows:

1. Orders to gather evidence[222]
2. Orders to seize (or attach) works, copies and the means of infringement[223]
3. Orders to stop certain acts[224]
4. Orders to assess financial returns[225]

In the execution of such orders, the court may appoint an expert to assist the court bailiff. The court may also require the applicant to deposit a suitable financial security. Whatever orders are made, they will cease to have effect unless the applicant files a main case within 15 days from the date of the issue of the orders.

There are no provisions in the ARL 2002 dealing with what final orders the court can make.[226] It is reasonable to infer that what the court can order as a precautionary measure it can also order as final relief. There is also no right in the ARL 2002 for the rights holder to seek damages or compensation

---

221. ARL 2002, article 34.
222. ARL 2002, paragraphs 1, 3, 4, and 6 of article 34 refer to orders that might result in the obtaining of relevant evidence.
223. ARL 2002, paragraphs 3 and 5 of article 34 refer to orders to attach (in effect, to seize) originals and copies of a work, the materials used in re-publishing or making copies and the financial returns.
224. ARL 2002, paragraphs 2 and 4 of article 34 refer to orders to stop publication, exhibition and production of a work.
225. ARL 2002, paragraph 5 of article 34 refers to orders to calculate financial returns using an expert if necessary.
226. ARL 2002, article 40 is limited to what the court can order in relation to criminal cases under articles 37, 38 and 39.

for infringement.[227] The applicant must look to the civil transactions law for a right to compensation:

> The doer of any damage to another, even if done unknowingly, is liable for the damage.[228]

Criminal Offenses

The criminal offenses in the ARL 2002 can be seen as falling under the following headings:

(a) offenses arising from the infringement of rights
(b) offenses arising from manufacture and importation
(c) offenses arising from violations of the law and regulations
(d) offenses for interfering with electronic protection

These are discussed below in turn (except for (d) which is discussed briefly in the section on computer programs).

(a) Offenses Arising from the Infringement of Rights

It is a criminal offense to infringe the moral or financial rights of the author or the holder of a neighboring right.[229]

If a person publishes an author's work for the first time without the author's consent, that could be an infringement of the author's moral rights and be deemed to be a criminal act.[230] If a person fails to attribute a work to the author in reproducing it, whether lawfully or otherwise, that could be deemed to be a criminal act.[231] It is less clear how the author's right to object to amendments of his or her work could be infringed by another person.[232] Presumably an author can object to an amendment in any circumstances. Perhaps the offense is in making the amendment, which is damaging to the reputation of the author (for example), and not acting in accordance with the author's objection to it. The offense could also be in not giving the author an opportunity to object to the amendment. In any case, it seems that the offense

---

227. By comparison, article 40 of the TML 1992A gives a right to compensation for damage suffered as a result of the criminal acts proscribed by the law.

228. Federal law no. 5 of 1985 in relation to civil transactions, article 282.

229. ARL 2002, article 37

230. ARL 2002, article 5.1. *See also* article 16.1 concerning performers' right of attribution.

231. ARL 2002, article 5.2.

232. ARL 2002, article 5.3. *See also* article 16.2 concerning performers' rights to prevent certain alterations of their performances.

is committed by omission rather than commission. The right to withdraw a work from circulation is a right that can only be exercised by means of court action. It is difficult to see how it could be infringed by another person and that act be deemed to be criminal.

The infringement of the financial rights of the author and holders of neighboring rights constitutes a criminal offense under article 37.1. Those rights are listed in articles 7, 17, 18, and 19 of the ARL 2002 and are discussed in other sections of this commentary. Offenses can be summarized as follows:

(a) exploitation or the authorization of the exploitation of a protected work without the consent of the author, whether or not the form of exploitation was one listed in article 7 of the ARL 2002

(b) doing without consent any of the acts referred to in article 17 concerning the financial rights of performers

(c) publishing a sound recording without consent[233]

(d) unauthorized exploitation or the authorization of the exploitation of a broadcast recording or program without consent[234]

In addition to these offenses, article 37.2 makes it a crime to sell or rent or make available to the public a work or sound recording or broadcast program without the consent of the rights holder. It is unclear why the drafters of the law added this provision. Selling, renting, and making available to the public copies of a work are all forms of exploitation for which the author has the exclusive right. Perhaps the purpose was to extend the criminal sanctions against certain acts in relation to sound recordings and broadcast programs rather than works. For example, although the producers of sound recordings are given the right to prevent unauthorized exploitation, unauthorized exploitation is not a criminal offense because without a positive right, the criminal provisions do not apply. The only positive right given to producers of sound recordings is to publish their recordings. The effect of article 37.2 is perhaps to fill a gap and give the producers of sound recordings the protection of criminal sanctions against unauthorized sale, rental and circulation of their recordings.

An important feature of article 37 is that is requires written authority from the rights holder in order to avoid liability. The consequence is that in cases in which a legitimate licensee has only a verbal consent or permission to

---

233. ARL 2002, article 18.2. The other right of producers of sound recordings is to prevent exploitation. Arguably such a right cannot be infringed by others.

234. ARL 2002, article 19.1. The other right of broadcasting organization is to prevent communication to the public of their programs and recordings, arguably not a right that can be infringed by others.

exploit a work, the licensee will, strictly speaking, be committing a criminal offense when exploiting the work. It is an indirect way of requiring all licenses and permissions to be in writing.[235]

Many of the persons who deal with works in which author's rights subsist do not have, as a practical matter, written licenses. Take for example a bookseller. There may be a written publishing contract between an author and a publisher giving the publisher the right to copy the work, publish it, offer it for sale, and so on. However, the others down the chain such as distributors, wholesalers, and retailers very likely do not have the written permission from the rights holder that article 37 requires them to have. One implication of this is that publishers and distributors can potentially exercise strict control over who sells books in the market for which they have the rights. Indeed, the provisions are strict enough to create monopoly conditions in the absence of any provisions dealing with the exhaustion of rights in the distribution of authorized copies.

The language of article 37 does not contain any requirement to prove that the defendant had any relevant "knowledge," such as knowledge that copying is a crime or that the work being copied is a protected one.

(b) Offenses Arising from Manufacture and Importation

Article 38 of the ARL 2002 clearly makes unauthorized manufacturing (or producing) and importation of works for the sale, rental, or circulation a criminal offense.[236] The importation offense seems to apply to both the unauthorized importation of authorized copies of a work as well as the importation of unauthorized or counterfeit copies. As such, the provision could potentially be used to control the parallel importation of works. It is also an offense to manufacture or import, for the purpose of sale, rental, or circulation (but not use it seems), any apparatus for manipulating the protection of works.

(c) Offenses Arising from Violations of the Law and Regulations

Article 41 criminalizes any violation of any provision of the ARL 2002 or the regulations and orders implementing it. The potential application of such a general provision is so broad that it is difficult to see how it assists in deterring violations and encouraging compliance.

---

235. See the discussion above on assignments and licenses.

236. ARL 2002, article 38.1. Curiously, a translation issued by the Ministry of Information and Culture omits this offense entirely, yet in the same volume it appears in the Arabic text. *See* ISBN 9948-8500-4-1, page 31.

Orders That the Court Can Make in Criminal Cases

In addition to the punishments that the court may order in relation to crimes committed under article 37, 38, and 39, the court may order confiscation and destruction of seized copies and equipment, and the publication of the judgment in the newspapers. This is similar to the orders a court may make in trademark cases.[237] However, in relation to copyright crimes, the court also has the power to order the closure of the business for up to six months.

Enforcement Authorities for Infringements under ARL 2002

In response to question nos. 36 and 37 put to the UAE by the United States in the WTO review of legislation (June 2001), the UAE described the enforcement procedure for copyright infringements as follows:

> The procedure followed in dealing with such claims use to [sic] start with verifying the claimed cases by the Inspection Division in the Ministry of Information and Culture in order to ensure a minimum of certainty of the elements being claimed. After the inspection action, coordination is made with the Police authorities in order to engage necessary raids and seizure. The case is then presented before the competent court. The Ministry of Information and Culture has also the competency to decide the closing of the establishment taking part in the infringement and piracy under the Law.

The procedure today with the Ministry of Economy is more or less the same as that which is described above. The process begins with a complaint to the Ministry and the Ministry coordinates with the Police in the relevant emirate to carry out a raid. Assuming the raid is successful, the Police transfer the case to the prosecution to investigate and start a criminal prosecution in the court. The complainant may wish to commence a civil case for damages alongside the criminal case.

The rights holder may also go directly to the court with a civil case, perhaps commenced with an application for precautionary measures. Whether going to the Ministry or to the court directly is the better course will depend on the current procedures and the facts of the case.

---

237. Compare article 43 of the TML 1992A with article 40 of the ARL 2002.

In the same response to the questions mentioned above, the UAE also gave the following statistics for complaints received in copyright matters for the period 2000 to June 2001 (using the terminology of the report):

Complaints concerning:	Number of complaints
Vendors	23
Video films	33
Computer programs	18
Smart cards concerning TV broadcasting by satellite	8
Electronic games	6

Permitted Acts

The rights of the author and neighboring rights have the potential to be detrimental to public policy objectives such as ensuring the availability of certain information and developing an educated society. In order to further those objectives, the law permits the doing of certain acts that would otherwise be infringements of the rights in works. The moral rights of the author are intended to remain unaffected. The extent to which exceptions may be made is limited in general terms by the TRIPs Agreement:

> Members shall confine limitations or exceptions to exclusive rights to certain special cases which do not conflict with a normal exploitation of the work and do not unreasonably prejudice the legitimate interests of the right holder.[238]

Personal Use

It is permitted, subject to the exceptions mentioned below, to make a single copy of a published work for the copier's personal use as long as the purpose is not for profit and not for professional use. Such copying is not permitted in relation to:

(a) works of fine art or applied art in private places. If they are in public places, they can be copied with the consent of the rights holder.
(b) architectural works. It is permitted to show architectural works in broadcast programs if they are permanently located in a public place.
(c) computer programs and databases, unless the copying falls within paragraph 2 of article 22.[239]

---

238. TRIPs Agreement, article 13. This parallels article 9.2 of the Berne Convention. *See also* article 10 of the WIPO Copyright Treaty.
239. ARL 2002, article 22.1.

This permission appears to be extremely broad and it is difficult to see the public policy objective that it meets. It has the potential to encourage a culture of "copying is OK." If I buy a novel, I can give it to all my friends for each of them to make a personal copy to read. If I have a music CD, my friends can each make a copy for personal use. It is not clear whether from those personal use copies further copies may be made or whether personal use copies can only be made from an original. With each copy made, the author and all the others in the profit chain suffer loss.

Back-Up Copies of Computer Programs, etc.

This subject is discussed above in the section on computer programs and databases.

Use in Judicial Proceedings

It is permitted to copy protected works for use in judicial and similar proceedings, but only to the extent necessary for the required procedures. The source and author must be mentioned. "Similar proceedings" is open to some interpretation. It might include arbitration proceedings and administrative hearings such as hearings for trademark opposition matters in which the parties may want to produce evidence of the fame of mark by collecting copies of published references to it or to make copies of the other party's advertising—something which would normally require consent.[240]

The Preservation of Documents

If it is not possible to obtain a substitute in reasonable circumstances, and if the copying is done with the knowledge of libraries or archives and not for profit, and if the purpose of the copying is to preserve the original, or to replace it (because it is lost or destroyed or unusable), it is permitted to make a photocopy of a protected work.[241]

---

240. ARL 2002, article 22.3.
241. ARL 2002, article 22.4.a.

Study or Research

Protected works can be copied once or irregularly at libraries or archives for an individual's study or research and not for profit, if it has not been possible to obtain a license to copy. This provision is similar to the personal use exception in the extent to which it has the potential to encourage the idea that copying is acceptable. Most important will be what procedures the libraries and archives implement to limit copying to what is legally permitted.[242]

Criticism or Debate

Quoting short paragraphs or extracts from a protected work for the purpose of criticism and debate or providing news is permitted, provided that it is only to the extent that is customary and the source and author are mentioned.[243]

Certain Performances

Performing protected works such as music and plays for family gatherings is permitted, as is the performance by students of protected works in educational institutes. It must be not for direct or indirect profit.[244] The public policy objectives here are to promote family values and formal and informal education.

Broadcasts Showing Architecture, etc.

It would be difficult for broadcasters to report on public events if they had to avoid filming public buildings, monuments, artworks, and sculptures for fear of infringing author's rights. They are permitted to be shown in broadcast programs if permanently located in a public place.[245]

Education and Cultural Needs

If:
  (a) the copying is for educational, cultural, religious or professional training purposes, and

---

242. ARL 2002, article 22.4.b.
243. ARL 2002, article 22.5.
244. ARL 2002, article 22.6.
245. ARL 2002, article 22.7.

(b) the copying is within reasonable limits and does not exceed its purpose, and

(c) the name of author and the title is mentioned each time it is possible,
and

(d) the copier is obtaining no direct or indirect profit from the copying,
and

(e) it was not possible to obtain a license to copy, then

it is permitted to copy short parts of a work in written, audio or visual recorded form.

Extracts of Publicly Available Works

The press (newspapers, periodicals, and broadcasting organizations) may
reproduce extracts of protected works provided that the work has been
lawfully made available to the public and the extent of copying is justified by
the purpose. It need not be for debate or criticism. The source and author
must be mentioned.[246]

Published Articles on Public Matters

The press (newspapers, periodicals, and broadcasting organizations) may
reproduce protected published articles "relating to debates that have engaged
public opinion" as long as the source and author is mentioned. This is potentially a very broad exception. It would be an extraordinary result if the articles
produced by journalists in other countries, for example, could be reproduced
by the UAE press without their consent or payment of royalties to the rights
holders.

Public Speeches and Discussions

Public speeches, lectures, and discussions such as occur in parliament, the
courts, or public meetings, may be reproduced in the context of current
news reporting.

---

246. ARL 2002, article 23.1.

Customs

The ARL 2002 gives the customs authorities the right to order the non-release of materials that infringe the law for up to a period of twenty days. Customs may make such an order on its own account or based on an application by the rights holder. In cases in which an application is filed by a rights holder, a decision as to the application must be issued to the applicant within three days of filing a complete application.[247]

What appear to be the regulations mentioned in article 36 of the ARL 2002 are part of the ministerial decision in relation to imported and distributed works.[248] The regulations repeat some of what is in the law but add the following:

1. The application of the rights holder must attach documents that prove the right referred to in the application and they must be legalized.[249]
2. The customs authorities are to confirm with the Ministry the correctness of the documents.[250]
3. If the application is not supported by evidence, the applicant must file security being 25% of the value of the materials referred to in the complaint (presumably 25% of the value as if they were not infringements).[251]
4. If the complaint is proved not to be correct, the applicant will forfeit the security.[252]
5. The applicant may be present at the inspection of the materials.[253]

These requirements are potentially so burdensome as to make rights owners rule out customs as an enforcement option. For example, evidencing the rights on which the complaint is based with legalized documents may be impossible or may take months, especially in cases in which there is a chain of ownership. The requirement will in many cases be inconsistent with article 1 of the ARL 2002:

> The author of a work is considered to be the one who puts his name on the work, or to whom the work is attributed upon its publication, unless proven otherwise.[254]

---

247. ARL 2002, article 36.
248. Ministerial decision no. 132 of 2004, article 18.
249. Ministerial decision no. 132 of 2004, article 18.4.
250. Ministerial decision no. 132 of 2004, article 18.4.
251. Ministerial decision no. 132 of 2004, article 18.5.
252. Ministerial decision no. 132 of 2004, article 18.6.
253. Ministerial decision no. 132 of 2004, article 18.7.
254. ARL 2002, article 1, the definition of an author.

There is a presumption in favor of authorship in certain cases for which no documents, legalized or otherwise, should be required (except perhaps a copy of the work with the author's name on it).

The requirement to confirm with the Ministry the correctness of the documents with the complaint raises the question of whether this is another way of saying that the work must be registered with the Ministry.[255] Such a requirement would be contrary to the international conventions to which the UAE is a party.[256]

In relation to the security deposit, article 36 of the ARL 2002 says that it is for ensuring the seriousness of the application. Clearly, the regulations have taken a different view, linking the value of the security to the value of the goods. This raises the question of whether the regulation is enforceable. The practical issue here is that in many cases the information available to the rights holder when filing the complaint does not include details of the quantity of the materials or the value of it. Presumably it is the customs authorities that decide the value and the amount of the security deposit.

The complaint will be based on article 39 of the ARL 2002, which criminalizes the importation of unauthorized works and the unauthorized importation of authorized works.[257] The customs law of the particular emirate concerned may also be relevant. For example, the Dubai customs law penalizes the importation into the emirate of "prohibited goods," which includes goods contravening the laws for the protection of trademarks, intellectual works, author's rights, etc.[258] The GCC Customs law may not be of any assistance unless the case involves duty-free shops or free zones.[259]

Whatever decision is made by Customs in relation to the application, either party can commence a case in the court seeking to establish its rights in the matter.

Compulsory Licenses

Licenses to copy or translate protected works may be granted by the Ministry compulsorily for the specific needs of education, libraries, and archives and only under limited conditions. The empowering provision in the ARL 2002 is article 21. That article refers to implementing regulations. The regulations

---

255. It is a common experience that the Ministry will require registration of a work before taking any enforcement action.
256. See the discussion on the registration of works.
257. See the discussion on infringement of rights.
258. Dubai law no. 4 of 1998, article 114.1 and schedule 1.
259. See the discussion in the customs section of the chapter on trademarks.

were issued in March 2004 under ministerial decision no. 134 of 2004. Article 21 also states that the fees for granting such licenses are to be specified in a decision of the Cabinet. The relevant fees are specified in ministerial decision no. 288 of 2004. The various procedural requirements for applying for and obtaining compulsory licenses are set out in ministerial decision no. 134 of 2004 (see the appendices) and do not need to be repeated here.[260]

Collecting Societies

There were no collecting society provisions in the ARL 1992. Articles 30, 31, 32, and 33 of the ARL 2002, which permit the collective management of author's rights and neighboring rights, are a new initiative. The implementing regulations for the collecting society provisions were issued in March 2004 under ministerial decision no. 133 of 2004. The fees for granting and renewing collective management licenses are specified in ministerial decision no. 288 of 2004.[261]

---

260. *See also* the Appendix to the Berne Convention.
261. No collecting societies have yet been established in the UAE but this is the subject of some discussion (see for example, THE NATIONAL, October 28, 2008, at 6: "Payment of royalties a tough issue as content services boom"). The International Confederation of Societies of Authors and Composers is a useful website for the general subject of collecting societies: http://www.cisac.org.

INTRODUCTION TO THE APPENDICES

The appendices are in two parts: the English translations of a selection of UAE intellectual property laws and regulations are in Part A and the Arabic texts from which the translations were made are in Part B. There are 22 translated texts (Appendices A1 to A22) but 28 Arabic texts (Appendices B1 to B28). One reason for the difference in the number of texts in each is the way that amending legislation and decisions has been handled in the translated texts. For example, the translation of the TML 1992 (Appendix A4) has incorporated into it two amending laws, but in the Arabic texts these are reproduced in full and as separate appendices (Appendices B7 and B8). Another reason is that the Arabic texts also include the FDL 1992 (the repealed patent law) and the ARL 1992 (the repealed author's rights law) (Appendices B1 and B18). There is only one instance in which the Arabic text of amending legislation or decisions has not been reproduced in full as a separate appendix—that of the amendments to the regulations to the law for the prevention of fraud and deception in commercial dealings (Appendix B16). These amendments have been incorporated into the Arabic text of the regulation, as well as into the text of the translation.

A guiding principle in reproducing the Arabic texts has been to reproduce the texts of the laws and regulations as they were published in the official gazette. However, the original texts contain some transcription discrepancies such as the use of the Arabic letter "alif maksura" instead of the letter "ya" or vice versa and the use of "ta marbuta" instead of "ha." These have been corrected in the text without footnoting. A few typographical errors in the spelling of words have been footnoted in the Arabic texts only. Because the laws and regulations were drafted over many years by different government departments, they display a wide range of formatting differences. The texts that appear here have been slightly "regularized" using a consistent formatting but in such a way that should not affect any meaning that might be taken from the structure of paragraphs, etc.

There are some general comments concerning translating in the preface to this book. An important point to reiterate is that none of the translations are in any sense "official" or have any government endorsement. Anything in square brackets has been added by me. The Arabic texts do not generally give a title to each article. It is therefore not possible to cast an eye over the text for specific subjects, so I have added titles in square brackets. Each of the "contents" was compiled based on the added article titles and is not in the original texts.

Arabic has no capital letters. That is not in itself a problem but there is a tradition of defining terms used in laws and identifying those defined terms using an initial capital (such as "the State"). That is not possible in Arabic although terms are often defined in the first article of the law or regulations. The result is that there is no way of knowing when a term that is defined is being used as a defined term or in its undefined sense. Mostly this is does not hinder understanding but, when translating, it is necessary for the translator to make a judgment about whether the term used is a defined one or not and whether to use an initial capital or not for the translated term. After unsuccessfully trying to introduce initial capitals for defined terms into several laws, I realized that the process involved a greater level of interpretation than I was willing to accept and ultimately decided to avoid the problem where possible by not capitalizing defined terms, with the exception of obvious proper names such as "the State," "the Ministry," and "the Minister."

Ultimately, the translations are a guide only and the Arabic text should always be consulted.

Part A. English Translations

Patents and Designs

A1. Federal law no. 17 of 2002 in relation to the regulation and protection of industrial property for patents, industrial drawings and designs [as amended].

A2. Cabinet decision no. 11 of 1993 concerning the implementing regulations for federal law no. 44 of 1992 in relation to the regulation and protection of industrial property for patents, industrial drawings and designs.

A3. Ministerial decision no. 404 of 2000 [concerning pharmaceutical products and patents].

Trademarks

A4. Federal law no. 37 of 1992 in relation to trademarks [with the 2000 and 2002 amendments marked up].

A5. Ministerial decision no. 6 of 1993 concerning the implementing regulations for federal law no. 37 of 1992 in relation to trademarks.

A6. Cabinet decision no. 18 of 1993 in relation to the fees for procedures undertaken pursuant to the provisions of federal law no. 37 of 1992 in relation to trademarks.

A7. Ministerial decision no. 67 of 1998 [in relation to payment of fees for trademark registration].

A8. Ministerial decision no. 67 of 2001 in relation to the collection of fees for the publication of trademarks.

A9. Ministerial decision no. 80 of 2005 in relation to the registration of trademark registration agents.

A10. Federal decree no. 52 of 2007 in relation to the unified trademark law (system) for the Arabian Gulf Cooperation Council Countries.

A11. Federal law no. 4 of 1979 in relation to the prevention of fraud and deception in commercial dealings.

A12. Ministerial decision no. 26 of 1984 concerning the implementing regulations for law no. 4 of 1979 in relation to the prevention of fraud and deception in commercial dealings [as amended].

A13. Ministerial decision no. 418 of 2007 in relation to the use of the trademark "Organic."

Author's Rights

A14. Federal law no. 7 of 2002 in relation to the rights of the author and neighboring rights [as amended].

A15. Ministerial decision no 411 of 1993 in relation to the monitoring of works protected pursuant to the provisions of federal law no. 40 of 1992 in relation to the protection of intellectual works and the rights of the author.

A16. Ministerial decision no 412 of 1993 in relation to the deposit system for protected works and disposals that may occur.

A17. Decision of the Minister of Information and Culture no. 131 of 2004 in relation to the registration of works.

A18. Decision of the Minister of Information and Culture no. 132 of 2004 in relation to the register of importers and distributors of works.

A19. Decision of the Minister of Information and Culture no. 133 of 2004 in relation to administration of collecting societies for the rights of the author and neighboring rights.

A20. Decision of the Minister of Information and Culture no. 134 of 2004 in relation to the compulsory licenses for the copying and translating of works.

A21. Ministerial decision no 288 of 2004 in relation to the fees connected with the rights of the author and neighboring rights.

Customs

A22. Department of Dubai Customs, Customs policy no. DCP 11, titled "The recordal of trademarks for customs purposes," September 6, 2006.

Federal law no. 17 of 2002 in relation to the regulation and protection of industrial property for patents, industrial drawings and designs

Contents

We, Zayed Bin Sultan Al Nahyan, President of the United Arab Emirates,

After reviewing the constitution, and

Federal law no. 1 of 1972 in relation to the jurisdictions of the ministries and powers of the ministers and the laws amending it, and

Federal law no. 5 of 1976 in relation to the federation of chambers of commerce and industry, and

Federal law no. 1 of 1979 in relation to the regulation of the industrial affairs, and

Federal law no. 4 of 1979 in relation to the prevention of fraud and deception in commercial dealings, and

Federal law no. 8 of 1984 in relation to commercial companies and the laws amending it, and

Federal law no. 5 of 1985 in relation to civil transactions and the laws amending it, and

Federal law no. 11 of 1992 in relation to civil procedures, and

Federal law no. 44 of 1992 in relation to the regulation and protection of industrial property for patents, industrial drawings and designs, and

Federal law no. 18 of 1993 in relation to commercial transactions, and

Federal decree no. 21 of 1975 in relation to the accession of the UAE to the World Intellectual Property Organization, and

Federal decree no. 20 of 1996 in relation to the accession of the UAE to the Paris Convention for the protection of the industrial property, and

Federal decree no. 21 of 1997 in relation to the accession of the UAE to The World Trade Organization, and

Federal decree no. 84 of 1998 in relation to the accession of the UAE to the Patent Cooperation Treaty, and

Based on what was presented by the Minister of Finance and Industry, and the approval of the Cabinet of Ministers and the ratification of the Supreme Federation Council,

Issued the following law:

Chapter 1: Definitions and General Provisions

Article 1 [Definitions]

In the application of the provisions of this law, the words and expressions below are intended to have the following meanings unless the context of the text requires otherwise:

The State: The United Arab Emirates.

The Ministry: The Ministry of Economy.[1]

The Minister: The Minister of Economy.[2]

The Department: The Department of Industrial Property at the Ministry and its branches in the State.

The committee: The grievances committee formed by decision by the Minister.

Deed of protection: the document evidencing the Department's grant of protection for an invention or an industrial drawing or a design, such as a patent, a utility certificate, or a registration certificate for an industrial drawing or design.

Invention: An idea arrived at by an inventor and that gives a new technical solution applicable to a specific problem in the domain of technology.[3]

Patent: The deed of protection that is granted by the Department in the name of the State for the invention.

Utility certificate: The deed of protection that is granted by the Department in the name of the State for an invention that results from innovative activity that is insufficient for the grant of a patent.

Registration certificate: Deed of protection that is granted by the Department in the name of the State for an industrial drawing or design.

Know-how: Information or facts or knowledge of a technical nature resulting from experience obtained in the practice of a profession and capable of being practically applied.

---

1. The definition of "Ministry" was amended from the Ministry of Finance and Industry to the Ministry of Economy by article 1 of federal law no. 31 of 2006.
2. The definition of "Minister" was amended from the Minister of Finance and Industry to the Minister of Economy by article 1 of federal law no. 31 of 2006
3. The Ministry of Finance and Industry issued a translation containing a more elaborate translation of this definition as follows: "Any innovative idea relating to a product, a method of manufacture, or an application of a known method of manufacture leading to a practical solution to a technological problem."

Industrial drawing: Any creative[4] composition of lines or colors that has a special appearance and that can be used for an industrial or handicraft product.

Industrial design: Any creative bodily[5] form that has a special appearance and that can be used for an industrial or handicraft product.

Journal: The periodical publication that the Department issues specifically for publishing what is required to be published by this law and its implementing regulations.

International patent application: An application filed with the Department to obtain a patent pursuant to the Patent Cooperation Treaty.

International filing of a patent application: An application filed to obtain a patent with the patent office in one of the countries that is a member of Patent Cooperation Treaty, and which entitles the applicant to a right to protect the invention in the member countries in accordance with the terms and conditions laid down by the convention.

Receiving office for applications: The national office that receives international patent applications and which looks after their transfer to the body specified by the Patent Cooperation Treaty.

Selected office: The office that the person filing an international application chooses for the examination of the application to know whether it satisfies the conditions for the grant of a patent in accordance with the Patent Cooperation Treaty.

Appointed office: The national office that the person filing an international application appoints to issue the patent pursuant to the provisions of this law.

Article 2 [International Agreements and Conventions Respected]

[1.] The provisions of this law are not to violate the international agreements and conventions to which the State is a party and which regulate the rights of nationals of the member states under those agreements and conventions and the rights of persons who are to be treated as they are treated.

[2.] A foreigner who is not covered by the provision in the previous paragraph is to have the rights to which a national is entitled by this law provided that the foreigner carries a nationality of a country that deals with the State reciprocally.

---

4. I have used the word "creative" in relation to industrial drawings and designs and the word "innovative" in relation to patents and utility certificates, although the Arabic text mostly uses one root word and its derivatives: "ibtakara."
5. The Arabic term here, "mujassam," could be translated as "three-dimensional."

Article 3 [Temporary Protection for Exhibited Inventions, Drawings and Designs]

Temporary protection is to be granted to inventions and industrial drawings and designs that are exhibited in exhibitions within the State, subject to the conditions and procedures that the implementing regulations to this law applies to them, and taking into consideration the provisions of international agreements and conventions to which the State is a party or any requirement for reciprocal treatment.

Chapter 2: Inventions

Section 1: Patents and Utility Certificates

Article 4 [Granting of Patents]

[1.] A patent is to be granted to any new invention, resulting from an innovative idea or innovative improvement to an invention, protecting it in all fields of technology, which is founded on a scientific basis and capable of industrial exploitation, whether relating to new industrial products or new ways or methods of manufacturing or a new application of known ways or methods of manufacture.

[2.] An invention is to be deemed capable of industrial application if it is possible to apply it or use it in any kind of industry (in its widest sense) including agriculture, hunting, handicrafts, and services.

[3.] An application must relate to one invention only or a group of interrelated inventions formed on the basis of one general innovative concept.

[4.] If it becomes clear after issue of the patent that the condition of interrelatedness of the inventions mentioned in the previous paragraph has not been met, this is not to be considered as a reason for the invalidity of the patent.

Article 5 [Granting of Utility Certificates]

[1.] A utility certificate is to be given for any new invention capable of industrial application but is the result from innovative activity[6] that is insufficient for the grant of a patent.

---

6. The Arabic expression here is "nashatt ibtikari," meaning literally "creative or inventive activity." The Arabic may be an attempt to translation the English expression "inventive step." "Khattwa ibdaa'ia"—literally, inventive step—is used in article 7.1 of the PDL 2002.

[2.] A utility certificate is also to be granted for any invention complying with the provisions of article 4, upon application by the owner of the invention or the owner's legal representative.

Article 6 [Not Patentable Matter]

1. A patent or utility certificate is not to be granted for the following:

a. Plant or animal research and plant or animal varieties, or biological methods for production of plants or animals, excluding microbiological methods and their products
b. Diagnostic, therapeutic and surgical methods necessary for the treatment of humans or animals
c. Principles and discoveries and scientific theories and mathematic methods
d. Plans or rules or methods followed for carrying on commercial business or performing purely mental activities or games.
e. Inventions whose publication or exploitation would lead to a contravention of public order or morals

2. If it is apparent to the Department during the examination of a patent application that the invention relates to national defense, the procedures stated in the implementing regulations to this law are to be followed.

Article 7 [Right to the Invention; First to File]

1. Without prejudice to the provisions of article 9 of this law, the inventor, or his legal successors, has the right to the invention.
If two persons or more participate in the creation of an invention, they, or their legal successors, are to share between them the right to the invention. The person whose efforts are limited to helping in the implementation of the invention without participating in any inventive step is not to be considered as an inventor or as having the status of an inventor.
2. Without prejudice to the provisions of 8 and 9 of this law, the person who files before others an application for a patent or utility certificate, or who claims priority for the same invention before others, has the right to the patent or utility certificate, according to the circumstances, if his application satisfies the conditions for obtaining it.
3. Anyone with an interest has the right to oppose or appeal against the decision to accept or reject an application pursuant to this law and its implementing regulations.

Article 8 [Misappropriation of an Invention]

If the essential elements of the invention have been obtained from an invention of another person without his agreement to do so or to file an application for protection, the person who suffers damage as a result of this misappropriation may request the transfer of the application, or the patent or the utility certificate (if granted), to himself.

Article 9 [Inventions made by Employees or under Contract]

1. If an invention is created during the execution of a commission contract or a employment contract, the employer has the right to the invention unless there is an agreement to the contrary.

2. If the invention has an economic value above what the parties expected at the time of signing the contract, the inventor is entitled to additional compensation as specified by the court, if a specific amount has not been agreed by the parties.

3. If a worker, whose employment contract does not provide for the doing of innovative activity, creates an invention connected with the field of employment using expertise or documents or tools of the employer or the primary materials he provided to the worker for the purpose of his work, the inventor worker has the right to the invention after the passing of four months from the date of filing the report referred to in paragraph 4 of this article with the employer concerning the invention, or from any date that the employer had knowledge (by other means) of the creation of the invention, if the employer does not make apparent his wish to own the invention by written notice.

4. The inventor worker must inform the employer immediately of his invention by means of a written report.

5. If the employer makes apparent his wish to own the invention within the period specified in paragraph 3 of this article, the right to the invention is to be considered his from the creation of the invention and the inventor worker is entitled to fair compensation taking into account his salary and the economic value of the invention and all benefit from the invention derived by the employer, and if the parties do not agree on the compensation, it is to be specified by the court.

6. Any agreement giving the worker benefits less than what is stated in the provisions of this article is deemed to be void.

Article 10 [Name of the Inventor; Filing Applications]

[1.] The name of the inventor is to be mentioned in the patent or utility certificate unless the inventor declares in writing his wish not to be mentioned.

[2.] The filing of an application for a patent or utility certificate, and the information related to it, is to be done in accordance with what is specified in the implementing regulations to this law.

Article 11 [Priority Claims]

1. An application may contain a request for its priority in filing to be considered to be that of an application previously filed in a country that is a party to an international agreement or convention with the State. The application must state the date and number of the prior application and name of the country in which it has been filed and comply with what is stated in the implementing regulations to this law.
2. The priority period is 12 months from the date of the first filing.

Article 12 [Examination]

[1.] The Department is to examine applications for a patent or a utility certificate in accordance with this law and its implementing regulations. The Department may ask to receive what it considers necessary for the grant of a patent or utility certificate.
[2.] If the Department rejects an application, it must notify the filer of the application of this, who may file an appeal to the committee within sixty days of the date of the notification.

Article 13 [Publication and Opposition]

[1.] Patents and utility certificates are to be granted by decision of the Minister and published in the Journal. Any one who has an interest has the right to oppose the application before the committee within sixty days of the date of publication.
[2.] If an opposition is not filed within the period stated in the previous paragraph, the patent or utility certificate is to be delivered to the owner of the right. After its registration in the register, the patent or certificate must bear a registration number, date of issue, and information as to the payment of the registration fee or renewal or other information in accordance with what is stated in the implementing regulations to this law.

Article 14 [The Patent Term and Annuities]

[1.] The term of a patent is twenty years and the term of a utility certificate is ten years from the filing date.
[2.] Annuities for patents and utility certificates must be paid at the beginning of each year starting from the year following the year in which

the application was filed. If the owner of the patent or utility certificate does not pay the annuity within three months of the beginning of the year, the owner may pay during a further three months starting from the end of the previous period by paying an additional fee pursuant to what is specified in the implementing regulations to this law.

[3.] In any case, it is permitted to pay the annuities in advance of all or some of the period of the patent or utility certificate.

[4.] If the owner of the patent or utility certificate does not pay the annuities within the previous lawful period—six months from when they are due— the patent or utility certificate will be cancelled.

[5.] The provisions of this article apply to applications for patents and utility certificates in the same way that they do to patents and utility certificates.

Article 15 [Rights of the Patentee]

1. A patent gives to its owner:

(a) the right to exploit the invention. In the case of a patent for a product, exploitation of the invention is deemed to be the manufacture of the product, its use, offering it for sale, or selling it, or importing for these purposes. In the case of a patent for an industrial process, or a method to make a specific product, the patentee has the same right in relation to what results directly from the use of this process or method, in addition to his right to use the process or method.

In the case of a patent for a product, the owner has the right to prevent others, who have not obtained his permission, from producing the product and using it and offering it for sale and selling it and importing it for these purposes.

In the case of a patent for an industrial process, the owner has the right to prevent others, who have not obtained his permission, from the effective use of the method or from using the product that is obtained directly by means of the method, and offering the product for sale and selling it and importing it for these purposes.

(b) [the right] to use the method and practice any of the acts referred to in paragraph (a) relating to a product obtained directly by means of the method, in the case of a patent or utility certificate given for a new method or application of a known industrial method or means.

2. The rights referred to in paragraph one of this article, to which the patent or utility certificate gives an entitlement, are limited to the acts that are done for industrial or commercial purposes and do not extend to acts relating to the protected product after its sale.

Article 16 [Scope of Protection]

1. The scope of protection granted by a patent or utility certificate is determined by the application for the deed of protection.
2. The description and engineering drawings are to be used in explaining the content of the application.

Article 17 [Continuation of Prior Acts]

If a person with good intention had produced a product or used the method the subject of the invention or made genuine arrangements for such production or use in the State at the date of filing the protection application by another person, or at the date of priority lawfully claimed for this application, despite the grant of the patent or utility certificate, the first person mentioned has the right to continue doing these acts and practicing the other acts referred to in article 15 of this law in relation to products obtained from them. This right is a personal right and may not be transferred except with the business benefiting from it.

Article 18 [Assignment]

[1.] A patent or utility certificate may be assigned, as may an application for either of them, before they are granted.
[2.] An assignment of a patent or a utility certificate, or an application for either of them, must be in writing, and signed by the contracting parties before a responsible employee in the Department or notarized by a notary public in the State.
[3.] The assignment of a patent or a utility certificate must be recorded in the register specified for this purpose, upon payment of a fee specified in the implementing regulations to this law.

Article 19 [Research Purposes and Transport]

The rights granted by a patent do not apply to the following:

1. Acts for scientific research purposes.
2. Using the subject of the patent in means of transport which enter the region of the State temporarily or accidentally, whether in the body of the transport or its apparatuses or its equipment or devices or in other additional parts, on the condition that the use is limited to the needs of these means.

Article 20 [Joint Patentees]

Joint owners in a patent or utility certificate may separately assign to another their share in the invention protected by the patent or utility certificate, and they may exploit and exercise the rights given by article 15 of this law unless otherwise agreed. However, they may not grant a license to another for the exploitation of the invention except jointly.

Article 21 [Mortgages]

A patent or utility certificate may be mortgaged as security for settlement of a debt, whether independently or with a business. The mortgage is to be indicated in the register of patents or the register of utility certificates, according to the circumstances, and published in the Journal.

Article 22 [Registration of Assignments and Mortgages]

The assignment of a patent or utility certificate or a mortgage of either of them will not be evidence against others[7] until after it is registered in the register of patents or utility certificates and published in the Journal.

Article 23 [Lender Attachments]

[1.] The lender may attach a patent or utility certificate owned by the borrower, or what the borrower has with others, pursuant to the attachment procedures for movable property and according to the circumstances.

[2.] The lender must declare the attachment and the realized price at auction to the Department so that they can be indicated in the specific register. The attachment and the realized price at auction are to be published in the Journal and the required fees are to be paid pursuant to what is specified in the implementing regulations to this law. The attachment or realized price at auction is not to have an effect on others except from the date of its publication.

---

7. The expression in the Arabic text is "hujja 'ala al ghair"—evidence against others. "Hujja" could be evidence, title, proof, or argument.

Section 2: Compulsory Licenses and Loss of Ownership of an Invention

Article 24 [Requirements for a Compulsory License]

1. If the owner of a patent or utility certificate does not exploit the invention contained in the patent or utility certificate at all or insufficiently, any concerned person may request, in accordance with the procedures stated in article 30 of this law, a compulsory license, subject to the following conditions:

(a) At least three years is to have passed since the granting of the patent or utility certificate.

(b) The applicant for the compulsory license is to prove the efforts exerted during a reasonable period to obtain a license from the owner of the patent at a reasonable price and on reasonable commercial terms. The implementing regulations to this law are to specify the required procedures in this regard.

(c) The license may not be unconditional. The terms of the compulsory license may contain obligations and conditions for the licensor and the licensee.

(d) The license is to satisfy the needs of the local market and the applicant for the license must file the necessary sureties that are specified in the implementing regulations to this law. The invention is to be exploited sufficiently to address the lack or satisfy the needs that led to the application to obtain a compulsory license.

(e) The decision to grant the license is to specify the scope and term of the license, considering what is required for the purpose for which the license was granted.

(f) The owner of the patent is to be granted fair compensation.

(g) The exploitation of the patent is limited to the licensee, and the license is not to be transferred to others except if the ownership of the business of the licensee, or the part of it that exploits the patent, is transferred, and on condition that the competent court agrees to the transfer. The provisions of articles 28 and 32 of this law apply to the transfer.

(h) If the invention relates to semiconductors, the license may not be granted except for general non-commercial purposes or to correct practices that have been decided, judicially or administratively, to be anti-competitive.

2. A compulsory license may not be granted if the owner of the patent or utility certificate justifies his position with lawful reasons. Importing the product does not constitute a lawful reason.

Article 25 [Rights of the Compulsory Licensee]

1. A compulsory license entitles the licensee to the r ght to exercise some or all of the acts referred to in article 15 of this law pursuant to the conditions of the license, but excluded from this is the right to import the product.
2. The holder of the license has the right to exercise the civil and penal rights of the owner of the patent or utility certificate to protect the invention and its exploitation if the owner neglects to do so despite having notice or knowledge of an unlawful act.

Article 26 [Compulsory Licenses Non-exclusive]

The grant of a compulsory license does not prevent the grant of other compulsory licenses.

Article 27 [Effect on Patent Owner]

1. The competent court, based on an application by concerned persons, is to consider the extent to which the owner of the patent or utility certificate is deprived of exploiting the invention by himself or granting licenses to exploit it.
2. The competent court may not take into account items (a) and (b) of paragraph 1 of article 24 of this law if the application for the compulsory license was because of a public emergency or urgent public need, or for general non-commercial uses.

Article 28 [Court Application for a Compulsory License]

[1.] An application for a compulsory license is to be filed with the competent court in the form of a petition making the owner of the patent or utility certificate a party and the Department is to be notified to put forward a representative. The court may give the parties a specific period to agree between themselves. The period may be extended if the court considers it justified.
[2.] If the period passes, the court will consider whether to reject the application for a compulsory license, or to grant the license specifying its terms and scope and the compensation for the owner of the patent or utility certificate pursuant to the text of article 24 of this law. The judgment is to be announced to the other party and the Department for noting in the specific register and published in the Journal after payment of the fees. The judgment does not have an effect on others until it has been published.

Article 29 [Compulsory License Issued by the Minister]

1. A compulsory license for the exploitation of an invention protected by a patent or utility certificate may be issued by a decision of the Minister, if the invention is important to the public interest, on the conditions referred to in article 24 excluding items (a) and (b) of paragraph 1.
2. The decision of the Minister concerning a compulsory license or the assessment of compensation may be appealed to the competent court within sixty days of the date of publication of the Minister's decision in the Journal.

Article 30 [Compulsory License Application by a Patent Owner]

1. If it is not possible to exploit the invention protected by a patent or utility certificate in the State without prejudice to the rights granted by a patent or utility certificate based on a prior application, the owner of the later patent or utility certificate may be granted a compulsory license based on an application pursuant to the provisions of item (c) of paragraph 1 of article 24 of this law to the extent necessary for the exploitation of his invention if the invention serves industrial purposes different from the purposes relating to the invention the subject of the prior patent or utility certificate, or if it represents an obvious technical advancement of it.[8]
2. If the two inventions serve the same industrial purpose, the compulsory license is to be granted to the owner of the subsequent patent or utility certificate with the reservation of the right of the owner of the prior patent or utility certificate to obtain a license of the subsequent patent or utility certificate, if he requests.
3. The parties may agree in writing between themselves and notify the Department of their agreement, which is to be noted in the specific register.

Article 31 [Amendment and Cancellation of a Compulsory License]

1. The authority that granted a compulsory license may amend its terms based on an application from the owner of the patent or the utility certificate or the licensee of the compulsory license, if it is justified by new facts, and especially if the owner of the patent or utility certificate has granted a contractual license with terms more favorable than the terms of the compulsory license.

---

8. The meaning here seems to be, "or if it represents an obvious technical advancement of the invention the subject of the earlier patent of utility certificate."

2. The authority that granted a compulsory license has the right to cancel it based on an application by the owner of the patent or utility certificate if the licensee has not complied with the terms of the license or if the reasons that justified the grant of the license no longer exist. If cancelled, the licensee must be given a reasonable period in which to cease exploitation of the invention (if ceasing immediately would cause him substantial damage).

3. The provisions of articles 35 and 36 of this law apply to amending or cancelling compulsory licenses.

Article 32 [Registration of Compulsory Licenses]

1. Compulsory licenses, and what is issued in relation to them, must be registered in the specific register and published in the Journal after payment of the fees established pursuant to what is specified in the implementing regulations to this law.

2. The fees for licenses issued pursuant to article 29 of this law are to be waived if the exploitation of the invention is by a government body.

Section 3: Surrender and Invalidation of Patents or Utility Certificates or Licenses and Cases of Cancellation

Article 33 [Surrender by the Owner]

[1.] The owner of a patent or utility certificate or a compulsory license may surrender it by written notice to the Department and to anyone who has a right related to any one of them.

[2.] The surrender may be limited to one or more rights granted by the patent or utility certificate or compulsory license. The surrender may not damage the rights of another unless that person has given a waiver in writing. The surrender must be registered in the specific register and does not become effective until published in the industrial property Journal.

Article 34 [Cancellation Actions]

[A.] Any person who has an interest may resort to the competent court to request the cancellation of a patent or utility certificate or a compulsory license.

[B.] The owner of the patent or utility certificate or license and the Department and anyone who has a right relating to them must be informed [of the cancellation application] in the following circumstances:

1. If the patent or certificate or license was granted without satisfying the conditions stated for them in this law or its implementing regulations;

2. If the patent or certificate or license was granted without taking into account the priority of prior[9] applications pursuant to article 11 of this law.

[C.] The cancellation application may be limited to a part of a patent or certificate or license, in which case the judgment issued is to be considered as limiting the rights given by the patent, certificate or license.

Article 35 [Effect of Cancellation]

Taking into consideration the provisions of article 31 of this law,[10] the judgment to cancel a patent or certificate or license wholly or partially results in the patent or certificate or license being deemed to be cancelled from the date of grant. The owner is not required to return the compensation he obtained for the exploitation of the invention or compulsory license, if the user's or license holder's benefit is proved. The cancellation judgment must be noted in the specific register and published in the Journal.

Section 4: Special Provisions for Some Inventions

Article 36 [Improvement Patents]

1. The owner of a patent or utility certificate or his legal successors has the right to obtain an additional patent or utility certificate for improvements or changes or additions that may have occurred to the invention after its protection. The application for additional protection is subject to the same conditions that the original protection application was subject to. The additional protection has the same effects that resulted from the original protection.
2. The term of the additional protection ends when the term of the original protection ends. If the original protection is cancelled, this does not result in the cancellation of the additional protection. The implementing regulations are to specify the annuities for the additional protection.
3. Before the grant of the additional protection, the application may be transformed into an application for an independent patent or independent utility certificate.

---

9. The use of the word "prior" may not have been intended here, because the effect of article 11 is that an application does not need to be prior in order to have priority.
10. Article 31 concerns the amendment and cancellation of compulsory licenses.

Section 5: International Patent Application

Article 37 [PCT Applications May be Received]

The Department may receive international patent applications (as a receiving office for applications or an appointed office or a selected office) pursuant to the Patent Cooperation Treaty in force in the State. The implementing regulations to this law are to regulate the conditions and procedures that must be followed in this regard.

Article 38 [PCT Fees]

The fees for the procedures carried out by the Department are specified according to what is established by the Patent Cooperation Treaty and the annuities for a patent application are to be paid starting from the beginning of the year following the date of the international filing of the patent application. The application fails if the applicant does not pay the required fees within six months of the date of filing the application with the Department.

Section 6: Know-how

Article 39 [Know-how Is Protected]

Without prejudice to the rights granted by a patent or a utility certificate, know-how enjoys protection from any unlawful use or disclosure or publication by another as long as it has not been published or not put at the disposal of the pubic. It is a condition of the enjoyment of protection that the holder of the know-how has implemented the necessary arrangements to preserve the secrecy of its elements to the extent set out in the implementing regulations to this law.

Article 40 [Right to Use]

Any person who has gained know-how by his own means or obtained it by lawful means may use it himself or disclose it to another, even if another person has gained the same know-how.

Article 41 [Know-how Contracts]

[1.] A contract in relation to know-how must be in writing and contain the specific elements of the know-how, the purpose of its use and the conditions of its transfer, or otherwise the contract will be void.

[2.] The provisions relating to the exploitation of inventions, and assignments and transfers and licenses of them, apply to contracts in relation to know-how to the extent set out in the implementing regulations to this law.

Article 42 [Unlawful Disclosure]

Any use or disclosure or publication of any element of the know-how without the permission of its owner is to be considered an unlawful act, if done by a person who knows its confidential nature or cannot deny that he knew its confidential nature.

Chapter 3: Industrial Drawings[11] and Designs

Article 43 [Moral and Artistic Rights Preserved]

The provisions for protection stated in this law in relation to industrial drawings and designs are not to contravene the moral or artistic rights connected to them, whether their source is the law or international agreements or conventions to which the State is a party.

Article 44 [Registration of Industrial Drawings and Designs]

Industrial drawings and designs do not enjoy the protection established by this law unless registered in the specific register at the Department. Applications for registration are to be filed and examined pursuant to what is specified as to the procedures and fees in this regard in the implementing regulations to the law.

Article 45 [More Than One Drawing or Design in an Application]

An application for protection may contain more than one industrial drawing or design on the condition that the industrial drawings or designs are connected as to manufacture or use but the number of them may not exceed twenty industrial drawings or designs.

---

11. There are two Arabic words used for "drawings"—one is a normal plural of the word for "drawing" ("rasm/rasoom"), as in the title of the law and in article 50, and the other, as here, is a double plural ("rasoomat"). There seems to be no significance in this. The double plural is not uncommon in Gulf dialects.

Article 46 [Priority Claims]

1. The priority filing provisions stated in article 11 of this law apply to industrial drawings and designs.
2. The priority period is six months from the date of first filing.

Article 47 [Creative or New and Industrially Applicable]

An industrial drawing or design must be creative or new, and must have a possible use as an industrial or handicraft product and must not contravene the public order or morals of the State.

Article 48 [Grant of the Deed and Opposition]

[1.] The grant of a deed of protection for an industrial drawing or design is to be made by a decision of the Minister and published in the Journal with the drawing or design, after payment of the required fees.
[2.] Anyone who has an interest may oppose the decision of the Minister to grant the deed of protection before the committee within sixty days from the date of publication, and if no opposition is filed during the specified period, the certificate of registration is to be delivered to its owner. The registration number, its date, and any other information pursuant to what is stated in the implementing regulations to this law are to be set out in the certificate.

Article 49 [Term of Protection]

The period of protection for an industrial drawing or design is ten years from the date of filing the application for protection.

Article 50 [Annuities]

Taking into account what is stated in articles 49 and 69 of this law, the provisions of article 14 of this law also apply to industrial drawings and designs.

Article 51 [Rights Granted]

[A.] The protection established for industrial drawings and designs pursuant to this law gives an entitlement to the right to prevent others from doing the following acts:

1. Using the industrial drawing or design in the production of any product.

2. Importing any product related to the industrial drawing or design, or possessing it with the purpose of using it or offering it for sale or selling it.

[B.] The acts referred to cannot be made lawful simply by a difference in the domain for which the industrial drawing or design is legally protected or it being related to a product that is different from the industrial drawing or design contained in the deed of protection.

Article 52 [Continuation of Prior Acts]

If a person began, with good intention, to do the acts stated in article 51 of this law, before the filing of an application, it is his right to continue to do what he began in relation to the products he has obtained. His right is to be considered personal and not capable of assignment or transfer to another in any form except as part of the business benefiting from it.

Article 53 [Application of Other Provisions of This Law]

The provisions of articles 7, 9, 17, 18, and 20 and the provisions of section 2 and 3 of chapter 2 of this law also apply to industrial drawings and designs.[12]

Chapter 4: Contractual Licenses

Article 54 [Right to License]

The owner of a deed of protection may license to any person, natural or legal, the use or exploitation of the right the subject of the protection, provided that the duration of the license does not exceed the protection established by the provisions of this law. The license agreement must be in writing and signed by the parties.

---

12. In brief, article 7 concerns the right to an invention and the first to file principle, article 9 concerns inventions made by employees, article 17 concerns continuation of prior acts, article 18 concerns assignment, article 20 concerns joint patentees, and sections 2 and 3 of Chapter 2 concern compulsory licenses and cancellation actions, respectively.

Article 55 [Recordal of Licenses]

The license contract must be recorded and noted in the specific register in relation to the right the subject of the protection upon payment of the required fees. The license is not to have any effect on others except from the date of its publication in the Journal. The recordal may be cancelled based on an application by the parties to the license contract or by the revocation of the contract, or pursuant to a judgment annulling it, or by the expiry of its term.

Article 56 [Non-exclusive]

A contractual license does not prevent the owner of the Deed of Protection from exploiting or using the subject of the protection or from granting licenses to others unless otherwise stated in the license contract.

Article 57 [Licensee Rights]

[1.] The licensee has the right to exploit and use the subject of the protection licensed to him in all the lands of the State during the period of protection in all domains and by all means unless otherwise stated in the contract of the license.

[2.] Whilst the licensee has the right to use the rights that are granted to the owner by the deed of protection, and to prevent infringement or threat or damage to the subject of protection, the licensee must inform the owner of the deed of protection by registered letter of any infringement or threat or damage, and if the owner of the deed of protection neglects or delays and does not undertake the necessary procedures within thirty days of the date of the notice, the licensee may instigate legal and judicial procedures and demand compensation for the damage resulting from either the neglect or delay of the owner of the deed of protection or the action of others.

Article 58 [Licensee Assignments and Sub-licenses]

The licensee may not, except when transferring a business or transferring ownership of it, or the part of it that exploits the license transfer to another the license or grant sub-licenses, unless the license contract states otherwise.

Article 59 [Inspection of Dealings by the Department]

[1.] The license contract, assignment of it, or transfer of ownership of the subject of protection, or any amendment or renewal of these contracts, are to be submitted to the Department for inspection as to the terms and contents and rights that the deeds of protection give.

[2.] The Department may, by arrangement with the concerned parties, request the parties to amend the contracts if they contain an offense against the use of any industrial property right or damage to commercial competition related to the subject of these contracts in the State, and if the parties do not respond, the Department may reject the approval of the contract and not record it in the register, all pursuant to what is specified in the implementing regulations to this law.

Chapter 5: Precautionary Measures, Crimes and Penalties

Article 60 [Precautionary Attachment]

If an act of infringement occurs, or in the event of unlawful acts contravening this law or contracts or licenses granted pursuant to its provisions, the owner of the deed of protection, or the transferee of all or part of the industrial property rights stated in this law, may request the competent court to issue a precautionary attachment order against an invention or industrial drawing or design or a business or the part of it that is using or exploiting any kind of industrial property referred to. What applies to the deed of protection in this regard also applies to applications for a deed of protection.[13]

Article 61 [Security]

[1.] The applicant for a precautionary attachment must deposit a security as assessed by the court before the court issues its attachment order. The attachor[14] must file a substantive case within eight days of the date of issue of the court order, otherwise the order will be deemed not to have been issued.

---

13. It is not clear how this sentence should be interpreted in this context. A translation available from the Ministry of Finance and Industry omits the sentence entirely. This omission has flowed through into other translations such as the one in INTELLECTUAL PROPERTY, UAE LAWS AND TRIPs, Sharjah Chamber of Commerce and Industry (2007) (although the Arabic text in this volume contains the sentence). One view would be that patent applicants, for example, are entitled to seek precautionary measures.

14. To avoid any uncertainty, the attachor is the party seeking the attachment and the attachee is the party against whom the attachment is ordered.

[2.] The attachee may file a case for compensation within ninety days from the expiry of the previous term, or from the date of issue of the final judgment rejecting the substantive case brought by the attachor.
[3.] The security referred to may not be discharged except after a final court judgment in the case brought by the attachor, or in the case for compensation brought by the attachee.

Article 62 [Penalties]

Without prejudice to any greater penalties stated in any other law, anyone who files documents or declares information that is false or forged to obtain a patent or utility certificate or know-how, or anyone whc copies an invention or method of manufacture or any element of know-how, or intentionally infringes any right protected by this law, is to be punished by imprisonment and a fine of not less than 5000 dirhams, and not more than 100,000 dirhams, or either one of them. These penalties apply to matters relating to industrial drawings and designs.

Article 63 [Court Orders]

[1.] The court may order the confiscation of attached items or items that will be attached subsequently, and may order destruction or the removal of the effects of the action contravening the law, and the instruments and tools used in the counterfeiting, and may order any of these in a judgment of innocence.
[2.] The court may order the publication of the Judgment in the Journal or in any of the local daily newspapers at the expense of the defendant.

Chapter 6: The Department of Industrial Property and Concluding Provisions

Article 64 [Establishment of the Department]

[1.] The Ministry is to establish a department called the "Department of Industrial Property." This department and its branches are to be responsible for implementing the provisions of this law and its implementing regulations.
[2.] The Ministry is to issue a decision as to the work arrangements in the Department and its branches and the method of carrying out its responsibilities stated in this law and its implementing regulations.

Article 65 [Department Employees]

Employees of the Department have the title of judicial seizure officers in the implementation of the provisions of this law and its implementing regulations and are not permitted, during or after the end of their service, to disclose the secrets of their work or make public data or information they obtained in the execution of their work or reveal it or use it for their own benefit or for the benefit of others. They may not keep, in a personal capacity, the original or a copy of any document or paper, and are not permitted to work as a registration agent with the Department during their service and for a period of three years following the end of their service.

Article 66 [The Committee]

1. A committee is to be formed by decision of the Minister headed by a judge, nominated by the Minister of Justice and Islamic Affairs and Endowments, and two experts in the field of industrial property rights that are regulated by this law, neither of them being employees of the Department. The Minister is to appoint or delegate a secretary to the committee to be under the administrative supervision of the president of the committee.

2. The committee is to determine grievances that are filed by those concerned with decisions issued in relation to the application of this law and its implementing regulations. The implementing regulations are to specify the system of work of the committee and rewards of the members and the procedures for petitions and their determination and the required fees.

Article 67 [Appeals from the Decisions of the Committee]

An appeal may be made against decisions of the committee to the competent court pursuant to the civil procedures law within thirty days of the date of notice of the decision of the committee. The court may seek the assistance of specialist experts in the field of the dispute and the opinion of the Department.

Article 68 [Registration Agents]

The implementing regulations to this law are to regulate the profession of registration agents with the Department and include specific provisions to be satisfied by agents, their obligations, and the fees required for registration in the list of registration agents, as well as the conditions for cancellation of registration.

Article 69 [Fees]

The implementing regulations are to specify the fees the Department requires for the procedures established pursuant to this law and ts implementing regulations.

Article 70 [Medical Drugs and Pharmaceutical Compounds]

Chemical inventions relating to medical drugs or pharmaceutical compounds are capable of protection by a patent or utility certificate if they satisfy the conditions required by this law and its implementing regulations from January 1, 2005.

Article 71 [Requirements for Applications to Patent Medical Drugs]

Taking into account what is stated in article 70 of this law, the Department is to continue to receive applications for patents to protect chemical inventions relating to medical drugs or pharmaceutical compounds, applying the following provisions:

1. These applications are to be recorded in order of receipt in the patent or utility certificate register (according to the circumstances) and noted in the register pursuant to the provisions of this article.
2. The provisions relating to the novelty of inventions and priority of applications stated in this law and its implementing regulations also apply to these applications.
3. If a patent has been issued in one of the member countries of the World Trade Organization to protect the subject of the mentioned applications and the owner has been licensed to market his invention commercially in that country, the owner of this application enjoys the right to market exclusively the invention from the date of licensing by the relevant authorities in the State of the owner of the application to market his invention commercially.
4. The owner of the application enjoys the exclusive right to market the invention in the State, in accordance with the previous paragraph, for five years, ending when the patent application has been granted or rejected, whichever is earlier.

Article 72 [Implementing Regulations]

The implementing regulations to this law are to be issued by the Cabinet based on the suggestion of the Minister and are to include the distribution of responsibilities, their hierarchy and the delegation of them in the implementation of the provisions of this law, as well as the types of registers, the system of examination of applications, the information and documents required to be filed, fees and expenses, publication fees, and all provisions and rules required for the implementation of the law.

Article 73 [Repeal of Previous Law]

Federal Law no. 44 of 1992 is repealed, as are all provisions contravening or conflicting with the provisions of this law.

Article 74 [Publication of this Law]

This law is to be published in the official gazette and becomes effective from the date of its publication.

Zayed Bin Sultan Al Nahyan
President of the United Arab Emirates

Issued at the Presidential Palace in Abu Dhabi
Date: Ramadan 14, 1423 H.
Corresponding to: November 19, 2002 M

Cabinet decision no. 11 of 1993 concerning the implementing regulations for federal law no. 44 of 1992 in relation to the regulation and protection of industrial property for patents, industrial drawings and designs

Contents

The Cabinet,

After reviewing the provisional constitution, and

Federal law no. 1 of 1972 in relation to the jurisdictions of the ministries and powers of the ministers and the laws amending it, and

Federal law no. 5 of 1976 in relation to the federation of chambers of commerce and industry, and

Federal law no. 1 of 1979 in relation to the regulation of the industrial affairs, and

Federal law no. 4 of 1979 in relation to the prevention of fraud and deception in commercial dealings, and

Federal law no. 8 of 1984 in relation to commercial companies and the laws amending it, and

Federal law no. 44 of 1992 in relation to the regulation and protection of industrial property for patents, industrial drawings and designs, and

Decision of the Cabinet no. 15 of 1991 in relation to the organizational structure for the Ministry of Finance and Industry, and

Based on what was presented by the Minister of Finance and Industry, and the approval of the Cabinet,

Decided:

Chapter 1: Definitions and General Provisions

Section 1—Definitions

Article 1

In the application of the provisions of this decision, the words and expressions below are intended to have the following meanings unless the context of the text requires otherwise:

The State: The United Arab Emirates.

The Ministry: The Ministry of Finance and Industry.

The Minister: The Minister of Finance and Industry.

The Department: The Department of Industrial Property at the Ministry and its branches in the State.

The committee: The grievances committee in the Department of Industrial Property.

The law: Law no. 44 of 1992 in relation to the regulation and protection of industrial property for patents, industrial drawings and designs.

Section 2—Temporary Protection for Inventions and Industrial Drawings and Designs

Article 2 [Application for Temporary Protection for an Invention]

[1.] If a concerned person wishes to protect temporarily an invention that could be the subject of a patent or a utility certificate, or an industrial drawing or design that could be the subject of a registration certificate, for the products that he wishes to exhibit in any exhibition in the State pursuant to article 3 of the law,[15] before exhibiting he must file with the Department an application using Form 1 for inventions, and using Form 2 for industrial drawings and designs, accompanied by summary information of the character of the invention and its drawing, and information about its related products, or two copies of the industrial drawing or design and products belonging to it.

[2.] The Department may require the applicant to file any other information that it considers necessary.

Article 3 [Temporary Protection Register and Its Contents]

The Department is to prepare two temporary protection registers, one for inventions and the other for industrial drawings and designs, in which applications are to be recorded according to serial numbers, and each must contain the following information:

1. Application number
2. The date of filing of the application
3. The name of the applicant, his nationality, his place of residence, or his headquarters and his address

---

15. Article 3 of the PDL 1992 reads: "The implementing regulations of this law are to specify the terms of temporary protection for inventions and industrial drawings and designs for products that are exhibited in exhibitions inside the State, taking into account the provisions of agreements and conventions or the requirement for reciprocal treatment." Article 3 is the corresponding article of the PDL 2002.

4. The name of the agent and his address

5. The chosen place in the State to which letters are to be sent

6. The exhibition and its opening date

7. The name of the invention, or the industrial drawing or design

8. Information about the products relating to the invention or those belonging to the industrial drawing or design

9. The date of entry of the products to the exhibition

10. Number and date of the temporary protection certificate and period of protection

Article 4 [Certificate of Temporary Protection]

Without prejudice to the provisions of agreements and conventions to which the State is a party, and taking into consideration the requirement of reciprocal treatment, the Department is to give to the applicant—after checking the entry of the products into the exhibition—a certificate of temporary protection in accordance with Form 3 for an invention or Form 4 for an industrial drawing or design. This certificate gives to the applicant the rights that result from a deed of protection for a period not exceeding six months from the date of the opening of the exhibition.

Chapter 2: Inventions

Section 1—Patents and Utility Certificates

Firstly: Procedures for Patent or Utility Certificate Applications

Article 5 [One Invention for Each Application]

An application may be filed with the Department using Form 5. The application may not contain more than one invention.

Article 6 [Attachments for Patent and Utility Certificate Applications]

[A.] The following documents are to be attached to an application:
  1. A detailed description of the invention beginning with the name of the invention and addressing the following:

      a. The technical domain to which the invention relates

      b. Prior art information that the applicant is aware of and which is considered useful to understand the invention, to examine it and research it, and preferably mentioning the documents that contain this prior art

c. Disclosure of the invention in words permitting its understanding clearly and completely, in order for any person with a normal level of skill in the art to be able to evaluate the invention and its implementation, and mentioning the beneficial effects of the invention (if any)

d. A description of the figures shown in the drawings (if any)

e. An explanation of the best ways to perform the invention known to the applicant, giving examples when necessary, and referring to the drawings (if any)

f. Clear information about the method of applying the invention industrially, the method of manufacture and use, or the method of its use only, according to the circumstances, and the results that are obtained, supported by examples and statistics, whenever possible

g. Clear and detailed information of the new elements required to be protected and specified in the application

2. The drawings for the invention must be filed when they are necessary for understanding the invention, and they may also be filed if the nature of the invention permits clarification by drawings even if they are not required for understanding the invention.

3. The abstract for the invention may not exceed two hundred words and is to be used only for technical notification and is to consist of the following:

a. A summary of what is disclosed in the description, the elements for protection and the drawings. It must be possible to discern in it the technical domain to which the invention belongs and is to be written so as to permit the formation of a clear idea of the technical problem and the essence of the solution to this problem offered by the invention, and the principal ways of using the invention.

b. When necessary, the chemical form that best identifies the invention when compared with all other forms stated in the application, and attaching to the summary the best explanatory drawing the applicant can provide.

4. An extract from the commercial register or official extract from the establishment contract or instrument of incorporation, according to the circumstances, if the applicant is a legal person.

5. The document indicating the entitlement of the applicant to the invention if the applicant is not the inventor.

6. The agreement of the concerned person if the essential elements of the invention have been obtained from the invention of another person.

7. The power of attorney document, if the application is filed by an agent.

8. A copy of the prior application and attached documents, accompanied by a certificate indicating its filing date and number, and the country in which it was filed, if the application contains a request for priority based on a prior application filed in a country that is a party to an international agreement or convention with the United Arab Emirates pursuant to article 11 of the Law.[16]

9. The temporary protection certificate (if any).

10. A letter from the Israeli boycott office as to the non-existence of any objection to dealing with the applicant.

[B.] The documents referred to in paragraphs 4, 5, 6, 7, and 8 are to be legalized in accordance with the law.

[C.] All supporting documents must be accompanied by an Arabic translation if written in English, or by an Arabic and English translation if written in another language.

[D.] An original and copy of the document mentioned in paragraphs 1, 2, and 3 are to be attached to the application when filed. These and the application are to take in account the conditions stated in articles 7 to 12 of these regulations.

[E.] As to the other documents, if they are not attached to the application, the applicant may undertake in writing using Form 6 to file those of them that must be filed, according to the circumstances, within ninety days of the date of filing the application. If they are not filed during this period, the application will be deemed not to have been filed. From this is excluded the document referred to in paragraph 8, for which the failure to file when required during this period results in the loss of the right to claim priority. Based on a decision of the director of the Department, applications that are deemed not to have been filed, or the loss of the applicant's right to claim priority, are to be noted in the applications register.

Article 7 [The Application Information to Be Typed]

The application information, the description and the abstract, must be typed by typewriter. The symbols, information, chemical or mathematical formulas, and some letters may be written by hand or drawn.

---

16. Article 11 of the PDL 1992 reads: "The registration application may contain a claim for priority in registration based on a previously filed application in a country that is a party to an agreement or convention with the United Arab Emirates. In this case, the application must state the date and number of the previous application and the name of the country in which it was filed, in accordance with what is stated in the implementing regulations for this law."

Article 8 [Nature and Size of the Paper to Be Used]

The application, the description, and the abstract must be filed on strong, white, smooth, non-glossy paper, 29.7 x 21 cms—A4. Drawings must be on drawing paper and satisfy the same conditions, but the Department may accept drawings on paper of a different size.

Article 9 [Numbering of the Papers]

All papers are to be numbered at the top center of the page with consecutive Arabic numbers.

Article 10 [Margins of the Papers]

The margins of the papers must be no smaller than 2 cms.

Article 11 [Copying of the Papers]

All papers must be filed in a way that permits direct copying by means of photocopying, electrostatic means, offset, and microfilm.

Article 12 [The Form of Drawings]

The following must be taken into account in drawings:

1. The preparation of the drawings with fixed, and sufficiently heavy and dark, lines and script, of consistent thickness, and delineated in the best way without the need for coloring.
2. The drawing of diagrams from the top of the drawing paper.
3. The clear writing of the letters and numbers used to refer to parts of the drawings, and using the same letters and numbers in different perspectives for the drawings, and where those letters and numbers are written outside the subject of the drawing, they must be connected to the parts with thin lines.
4. If there is more than one drawing on a page, a sufficient distance must be left between each drawing and be numbered consecutively.
5. No information relating to the title of the invention or its description is to be written on the pages of the drawings.

Article 13 [The Numbering of Applications]

[A.] The applications are to be given consecutive numbers annually according to the date and time of filing, and on the application is to be indicated its filing number, date and time of filing and number and date of receipt of payment of the required fees, and on the attachments to the application is to be indicated the filing number, and the application and its attachment are to be stamped with the stamp of the Department.

[B.] The applicant is to be given a receipt using Form 7 containing the filing number for the application, the date and time of filing, the details of the attached documents, and the number and date of the receipt for the payment of the required fees.

Article 14 [Contents of the Register for Patent and Utility Certificate Applications]

A register for patent and utility certificate applications is to be prepared containing the following information:

1. The filing number of the application
2. The date of filing of the application
3. A statement as to whether a patent or utility certificate is requested
4. The name of the inventor
5. The name of the applicant, his nationality, his chosen location in the State, and his place of residence, or his headquarters
6. The name of the agent and his address
7. The name of the foreign country in which was filed the prior application, its date and number, if the application is filed relying on article 11 of the law[17]
8. The date of issue of the decision rejecting the application (in the case of rejection), and the date of notice of the rejection to the applicant
9. The date of issue of the ministerial decision to grant the patent or the utility certificate, its number and date of publication
10. The number of the patent or utility certificate

Article 15 [Alphabetical Index Cards]

Alphabetical index cards are to be prepared in order of the names of the applicants using Form 8 and stating in them the name of the applicant, the name of the inventor, the filing number for the application, the date and time of filing.

Article 16 [Filing a Sample of the Products]

The Department may require the applicant to file a sample of the products for chemical inventions relating to nutrition or medical drugs or pharmaceutical compounds, in which case the applicant must file the required samples together with a list of them and attach it to the description of the invention and its abstract.

---

17. See the footnote to article 6 for the text of article 11 of the PDL 1992.

Article 17 [Method of Filing Samples]

The samples referred to in article 16 of these regulations are to be filed in glass bottles not higher than 8 cms and 4 cms in diameter and closed by stamped red wax seals and labeled with information indicating the connection between it and the possible production mentioned in the description of the invention.

Article 18 [Inventions Relating to Colored Matter]

If the invention relates to colored matter, a sample of it is to be filed pursuant to the provisions of articles 16 and 17 of these regulations, and a sample of the product printed or dyed with the matter must be attached, and the sample is to be flat and fixed on a card—if capable of this—33 cms long and 21 cms wide, and have written on it detailed information about the method of printing or dying, particularly that which concerns the combination of different acids, their level of concentration and temperature, and the duration of each process and extent of color absorption of the dying acids, as well as the percentage of fixed colored matter on the dyed fabrics and the combination of printing paste. The card is also to carry information indicating the connection between the matter used in printing or dying and what is mentioned in the description of the invention.

Article 19 [Filing of Samples]

[A.] The Department may, in circumstances other than those above, require the applicant to file samples or examples, when necessary, pursuant to the special conditions specified for them.
[B.] In any case, if the samples contain poisonous, caustic or flammable materials, or are capable of exploding, this must be mentioned in the information attached to them.

Secondly: Examination of Patent and Utility Certificate Applications

Article 20 [Objectives of Examination of Patent and Utility Certificate Applications]

The Department's examination of applications and their attachments—pursuant to the system of examination referred to in articles 92 and 93 of these regulations—is to determine the following:

1. That the application has been filed by a natural or legal person enjoying the nationality of the State, or a foreigner who has the right to file an application according to the provision of any international agreement or convention to which the State is a party, or carrying the nationality of a

country that deals with the State reciprocally pursuant to article 2 of the law.[18]

2. That the application has been filed by the owner of the right to the invention.

3. That the application has been filed satisfying the conditions stated in articles 5 to 12 of these regulations.

4. That the samples and the examples filed or required to be filed satisfy the conditions stated in articles 16 to 19 of these regulations.

5. That the invention is not considered to be plant or animal research or biological methods for production of plants or animals, for which patents or utility certificates are not to be granted pursuant to paragraph 1 of article 6 of the law[19], excluding microbiological methods and their products.

6. That the invention is not considered to be a chemical invention relating to nutrition or medical drugs or pharmaceutical preparations for which patents or utility certificates are not to be granted pursuant to paragraph 2 of article 6 of the law.[20]

7. That the invention is not considered to be scientific principles and discoveries pursuant to the text of paragraph 3 of article 6 of the law.[21]

8. That the invention does not relate to national defense pursuant to the text of paragraph 4 of article 6[22] and paragraph 1 of article 38[23] of the law, and if it appears that the invention relates to matters of national defense, the Department must, during the examination of the application, inform the Minister of Defense immediately by written report attaching the application for protection.

9. That the publication or exploitation of the invention will not lead to a contravention of public order or morals pursuant to the text of paragraph 5 of article 6 of the law.[24]

10. If it appears to the Department that the essential elements of the invention have been obtained from the invention of another person, the

---

18. Article 2 of the PDL 1992 is identical in its terms to article 2 of the PDL 2002.

19. Paragraph 1 of article 6 of the PDL 1992 corresponds to article 6.1.a of the PDL 2002.

20. Paragraph 2 of article 6 of the PDL 1992 provided that patents and utility certificates may not be granted for "chemical inventions relating to nutrition or medical drugs or pharmaceutical preparations unless they are made by a specific chemical method, in which case the protection may be given to the methods but not to the products." The PDL 2002 does not contain a corresponding provision. *See* article 70 of the PDL 2002.

21. Paragraph 3 of article 6 of the PDL 1992 corresponds closely to article 6.1.c of the PDL 2002.

22. Paragraph 4 of article 6 of the PDL 1992 corresponds to article 6.2 of the PDL 2002.

23. Paragraph 1 of article 38 of the PDL 1992 reads: "A patent or utility certificate may not be granted for a secret invention. An invention is deemed to be secret if it relates to national defence, unless the Minister of Defence decides otherwise." There is no corresponding provision in the PDL 2002.

24. Paragraph 5 of article 6 of the PDL 1992 corresponds to article 6.1.e of the PDL 2002.

Department must request the applicant to file that person's approval for the applicant to take the essential elements or to file the application pursuant to article 8 of the law.[25]

11. That the invention is new, that is, it has not been anticipated by the prior industrial art. Prior industrial art in this context means any disclosure that has been made to the public in any place or at any time by written or oral description, by use, or any other means of knowing the invention, before the date of the filing of the application or the priority date requested or the commencement of temporary protection on the condition that the application was filed within six months of the date of commencement.

12. That the invention contains an inventive step[26] not obvious to an ordinary man skilled in the art to achieve intuitively based on the prior industrial art relating to the patent application.

13. That the invention is capable of industrial application, that is, it is possible to apply it or use it in any kind of industry, in its widest meaning, including agriculture, hunting, handicrafts, and services.

14. That the inventive elements for which protection is requested are specifically stated in the application and explained clearly in the description and the engineering drawings in accordance with the text of article 16 of the law.[27]

15. That the priority requested is consistent with the provisions of the international agreement or convention that ties the United Arab Emirates with the country in which the priority application has been filed.

Article 21 [Correction and Amendments]

1. The applicant may request the correction of written or calculation errors in what is stated in the application or description.

2. The applicant may request an amendment of any information in the application including the description of the invention or its drawings with a statement of the amendment and the reasons for it, on the condition that it does not result in an essential change to what was in the description and drawings at the time of filing.

3. The correction or amendment referred to in the previous two paragraphs may not be made until after the required fees have been paid and the Department approves them.

---

25. Article 8 of the PDL 1992 corresponds to article 8 of the PDL 2002.
26. The expression here is "nashaat ibtikaari"—literally, inventive activity. *See also* the footnote to article 5 of the PDL 2002.
27. Article 16 of the PDL 1992 corresponds to article 16 of the PDL 2002.

Article 22 [Expert Assistance]

The Department may seek the help of scientific expertise available with any other national or foreign body inside or outside the State when considered necessary.

Thirdly: Determination of Applications for a Patent or Utility Certificate

Article 23 [Rejection of an Application and Right of Appeal]

If it appears from the examination of the application that the conditions stated for it in the law and these regulations have not been satisfied, the Department is to issue a reasoned decision rejecting the application. The applicant is to be notified of the decision by registered letter. The applicant has the right to appeal the decision before the committee within sixty days from the date of receiving the notice.

Article 24 [Acceptance of Applications, Publication, etc.]

1. If it is apparent from the examination of the application that it satisfies the conditions stated for it in the law and these regulations the Department is to accept the application and notify the applicant of the acceptance by registered letter, requesting him to pay the publication fees for the grant of the patent or utility certificate during sixty days from the date of receiving the notice, or his application will be deemed not to have been filed. If the applicant does not pay the publication fees during this period, a record is to be made in the applications register deeming the application not to have been filed based on a decision of the director of the Department.
2. If the publication fees have been paid, the patent or utility certificate is to be granted by a decision of the Minister. This decision is to be published in the official gazette, and anyone with an interest has the right to appeal the decision before the committee during sixty days from the date of publication.
3. After the decision mentioned above has become final because no appeal was made to the committee during the period referred to in the previous paragraph, or because a final decision or judgment has issued supporting it, the Department is to record the patent or utility certificate in the register of patents or of utility certificates referred to in paragraph 5 of this article, according to the circumstances, and to deliver to the applicant the patent or utility certificate pursuant to a delivery receipt.
4. The patent or utility certificate is to contain the following information:

   (a) The application number and the date of its filing.
   (b) The number and date of the ministerial decision issued granting the patent or the utility certificate.

(c) Registration number of the patent or the utility certificate.

(d) The date of issue of the patent or the utility certificate.

(e) A statement of the payment of the fees for recording the application.

(f) The name of the inventor, unless he has declared in writing that he does not wish to have his name mentioned pursuant to article 10 of the law.[28]

(g) The name of the owner, his nationality and address.

(h) The name of the invention.

(i) The classification.

(j) The period of protection and the date of its commencement and its expiry.

(k) The number and date of the priority application and the country in which it was filed, if the patent relies on this priority.

(l) If the patent or utility certificate is additional pursuant to article 37 of the law, it must contain the number of the original patent and the date of expiry of its protection.

(m) If the term of the patent is renewed, the term and date of the renewal and a statement of the payment of the renewal fees must be indicated on the patent.

5. The Department is to prepare two registers, one for patents and one for utility certificates, and each of them is to contain the information referred to in the previous paragraph in addition to the following information:

(a) The number and date of the official gazette in which the Ministerial decision to grant the patent or utility certificate was published.

(b) The name of the agent of the owner of the patent or utility certificate.

(c) The chosen address of the owner of the patent or utility certificate in the State.

[6]. All of what is stated in the law and these regulations as requiring noting in the registers must be indicated in each of the registers.

Fourthly: Renewal of the Term of a Patent

Article 25 [Patent Renewal Applications]

1. Excluding patents that are granted pursuant to the provisions of paragraph 2 of article 6 of the law (whose renewal is not permitted),[29]

---

28. Article 10 of the PDL 1992 corresponds to article 10 of the PDL 2002.

29. Paragraph 2 of article 6 of the PDL 1992 provided that patents and utility certificates may not be granted for "chemical inventions relating to nutrition or medical drugs or pharmaceutical preparations unless they are made by a specific chemical method, in which case the protection may be given to the methods but not to the products." Article 14 of the PDL 1992 gave a ten-year protection period for such methods without any right of renewal.

an application for renewal of the term of the patent may be filed within
the last three months of the original term, accompanied by supporting
documents establishing that the invention the subject of the patent has a
special importance, and that its owner did not obtain from it benefits
proportionate to his efforts and expenses.[30]
2. The applicant must pay the required renewal fees and the Department
must indicate on the application the number and the date of the receipt for
the payment.

Article 26 [Rejection of an Application for Renewal]

The provisions set out in article 23 of these regulations apply to the rejection
of an application for renewal.

Article 27 [Consequences of Renewal]

1. If the renewal application is filed within the statutory period and satisfies
the mandatory conditions for renewal, the Department is to accept the
application and notify the applicant by registered letter requiring the
applicant to pay the publication fees for the renewal within sixty days of the
date of receipt of the notice, and if the applicant does not pay the publication
fees within the period, the application is deemed not to have been filed.
2. If the publication fees are paid, a decision for renewal is to be issued
from the director of the Department and be published in the official gazette.
Anyone who has an interest in appealing the decision before the committee
has a right to do so within sixty days of the date of publication.
3. After the decision to renew has become final because no appeal was
made to the committee during the period referred to in the previous
paragraph, or because a final decision or judgment has issued supporting it,
the Department is to indicate the renewal on the patent and the date of
expiry of the period of renewal, and to record this in the register of patents.

Fifthly: Lapsing of a Patent or a Utility Certificate or an Application

Article 28 [Payment of Annuities]

1. The required annuities are to be paid based on an application filed by the
concerned person indicating the number and date of the patent or utility
certificate application, and the patent or utility certificate number if issued,

---

30. Article 14 of the PDL 1992 gave patents a 15-year term and a 10-year term of utility certificates and allowed for a possible 5-year extension of the term for patents.

and the year or years for which payment is required, and the Department is to indicate on the payment request the number and date of the receipt for the payment and the paid amount, and the year or years paid.

2. The annuities are to be paid within the last three months of each year starting from the year after the year of the date of filing of the patent or utility certificate application.

3. The Department may accept the payment of an annuity if the payment is made within thirty days of the expiry of the period mentioned in the previous paragraph, if the additional required fee is paid.

4. If the required annuities are not paid pursuant to the provisions of the previous two paragraphs, the application or patent or utility certificate lapses and the lapsing is to be published in the official gazette.

5. The Department is to prepare an annuities register for applications for patents and utility certificates, recording in it the following information on a separate page for each application:

> a. The name and address of the applicant
> b. The name and address of the agent
> c. The application number and date of filing
> d. The number and term of the patent or utility certificate and the term of renewal of the patent
> e. The years for which payment is required using consecutive numbers
> f. The date of expiry of the annual period for payment without additional fees
> g. The date of expiry of the annual period for payment with additional fees
> h. The number and the date of the receipt of payment and the amount paid
> i. The date of lapsing

6. The Department is to prepare a card for each application setting out in it the same information referred to in the previous paragraph and to organize these cards according to the date of filing of the applications.

Sixthly: Assignment of a Patent or Certificate, Mortgages and Attachments

Article 29 [Assignment of Applications]

All assignments of applications made pursuant to paragraphs 1 and 2 of article 19 of the law are to be recorded in the register of patent and utility certificate applications.[31]

---

31. Article 19 of the PDL 1992 corresponds to article 18 of the PDL 2002.

Article 30 [Assignment of Patents and Certificates]

Taking into account the text of article 51, all assignment of patents and utility certificates made pursuant to paragraphs 1 and 2 of article 19 of the law are to be recorded in the register of patents or register of certificates, according to the circumstances, and published in the official gazette after payment of the required recordal and publication fees.[32]

Article 31 [Recordal of Mortgages]

Mortgages of patents are to be recorded in the register of patents and published in the official gazette after payment of the required fees.

Article 32 [Attachments]

Attachments on patents or utility certificates are to be recorded in the register of patents or utility certificates, according to the circumstances, as well as the realized price at auction, and each of them are to be published in the official gazette after the lender pays the required publication fees.

Article 33 [Applications for Recordal of Assignments, etc.]

1. The recordals referred to in article 29 of these regulations, and the recordals and publication referred to in articles 30 and 31, are to be made based on an application filed by the concerned person with the Department attaching to it the deed of assignment or mortgage, according to the circumstances.
2. The recordal and publication referred to in article 32 of these regulations are to be done based on a notice from the lender to the Department of the attachment or price realized at auction.

Section 2—Compulsory Licenses and Expropriation of Inventions

Article 34 [Recording License Agreements]

Written agreements that are made in relation to licenses referred to in article 25 of the law[33] are to be noted in the register of patents or utility certificates,

---

32. Article 19 of the PDL 1992 corresponds to article 18 of the PDL 2002.
33. Article 25 of the PDL 1992 corresponds to article 30 of the PDL 2002.

according to the circumstances, based on a notice accompanied by the agreements filed with the Department by those concerned.

Article 35 [Recording Final Judgments and Decisions]

1. All final judgments issued by the competent court rejecting or granting or transferring or cancelling or invalidating, wholly or partially, a compulsory license, are to be noted in the register of patents or utility certificates, according to the circumstances.

The judgment is to be published in the official gazette after notice of the judgment is given to the Department by the concerned person and payment of the required fees has been made.

2. Before issuing the decision of the Minister to expropriate the ownership of an invention, or to issue a compulsory license to exploit it, according to the text of paragraph 1 of article 33 of the law, the Department must notify the owner of the patent or utility certificate to give his point of view concerning the matter.

3. The decision to expropriate ownership is to be noted in the register of patents or utility certificates, according to the circumstances, and to be published in the official gazette, as well as any decision or judgment issued to amend or cancel.

4. Any decision issued by the Minister to grant a compulsory license or to amend it or to cancel it, is to be noted in the register of patents or utility certificates, according to the circumstances, and the decision is to be published in the official gazette after payment of the required fees by the concerned person.

Section 3—Surrender of Patents or Utility Certificates or Licenses and Conditions for Invalidity of a Patent or Utility Certificate

Article 36 [Surrenders to be Recorded, Published, etc.]

[1.] Surrender of a patent or utility certificate or a compulsory license or of one or more rights given by a patent or a utility certificate or a compulsory license is to be recorded in the register of patents or utility certificates, according to the circumstances, and this recordal is to be done by a decision of the director of the Department based on written notice of the surrender from the concerned person to the Department, attaching to it evidence that a copy of the notice has been sent to all those who have a right in relation to the patent or certificate or license, and the Department must notify each of them of the decision mentioned above by registered letter.

[2.] After the decision mentioned above becomes final because no appeal was made during the legal period, or because a final decision or judgment has issued supporting it, the surrender is to be published in the official gazette.

Article 37 [Invalidity Judgments to be Recorded]

All final judgments in relation to the invalidation of a patent or a utility certificate, wholly or partially, are to be noted in the register of patents or utility certificates and published in the official gazette.

Section 4—Patents and Utility Certificates of Addition

Article 38

The provisions stated in sections 1, 2, and 3 of chapter 2 of these regulations apply to patents and utility certificates of addition.

Section 5—Know-how

Article 39 [Conditions for the Protection of Know-how]

The following are the conditions for know-how to enjoy protection against unlawful use or disclosure or publication by others:

1. The know-how must not have been previously published or put at the disposal of the public.

2. The owner of the know-how is to have implemented the necessary arrangements that clearly show his intention to keep its confidentiality, specifically:

a. Keeping the know-how documents in such a way as to ensure that others may not view them without permission.

b. Putting in place a work system so that the workers may not know all elements of the know-how.

c. Not permitting others to visit the place of work without the owner's prior permission and without his presence or that of his delegate, and not including in the visit program what would result in the visitor knowing all elements of the know-how.

d. Including in the contracts of employment a condition of confidentiality that obligates each of them not to disclose or make public any element of the know-how that he obtains in the course of his employment, and not to use or exploit this knowledge for his or others benefit directly or indirectly during the term of his employment contract or after its expiry for any reason without prior permission from the owner of the know-how.

e. Including in the agreements with those whom he grants access to some of the elements of his know-how—such as contractors whom he engages to make some of the ingredients of his products—a confidentiality condition, that obliges them not to disclose or make public any element of the know-how and not to use or exploit these elements for their or other's benefit, directly or indirectly, during the term of the agreements or after their expiry, for any reason without the prior permission of the owner of the know-how.

f. Including in contracts of know-how transfer with those who are to receive it from him a condition of confidentiality that obliges the recipient and his employees not to disclose or make public or reveal the know-how to others without the prior permission of the owner of the know-how.

g. Obtaining confirmation from those he negotiates with in relation to entering into the kinds of contracts referred to in the previous paragraph that includes their commitment to keep the confidentiality of the information relating to the know-how that is disclosed to them and not to disclose or make public or reveal it to others during the negotiations or after them (if they do not result in signing a contract), without the prior permission of the owner of the know-how.

Article 40 [Provisions Applying to Know-how Contracts]

The provisions relating to the exploitation of inventions and their assignments and transfers and licenses for their exploitation apply to know-how contracts as specified in the following articles:

Article 41 [Recordal of Know-how Contracts]

1. Know-how contracts are to be recorded, whether the subject is an assignment of the know-how or a transfer of its ownership or a license for its exploitation, in the register referred to in paragraph 3 of this article, based on an application filed with the Department by any one of the parties, attaching a copy of the notarized contract signed by both parties and translated into Arabic if it is written in another language. The applicant is to pay the required recordal fees.

2. Applications for recordal of know-how contracts are to be given serial numbers according to the date of filing, and to have noted on them the serial number and filing date and the number and date of the receipt for the payment of the recordal fees, and on the copy of the contract is to be noted the serial number of the application, and the application and the copy of the contract is

to be stamped with the Department's stamp. The applicant is to be given a receipt containing the application's serial number and the date of filing and details as to its attachments and the number and date of the receipt for the payment of the recordal fees.

3. The Department is to prepare a register of applications for recordal of know-how contracts which is to contain the following information:

a. The serial number of the application and its date of filing
b. The name and nationality and address of the owner of the know-how and the name and address of his agent, if any
c. The name and nationality and address of the party receiving the know-how and the name and address of his agent, if any
d. The chosen address in the State for each party to the contract
e. The subject of the contract and its duration
f. The date of the decision issued rejecting the recordal and the date of notifying the parties
g. The date of the decision issued accepting the recordal

4. The Department is to prepare a register for know-how contracts that it has approved for recordal, and this register is to contain the following information:

a. The number of the recordal of the contract and its date
b. The date of the decision issued accepting the recordal
c. The serial number of the application and the date t was filed
d. The name and nationality and address of each of the parties to the contract and the name and address of the agent of each of them, if any
e. The chosen address in the State for each of the parties
f. The subject of the contract and its duration

[5.] All amendments or renewals of the contract must be noted in the register after the approval of the Department, and payment of the required amendment or renewal fees.

Article 42 [Checking of Know-how Contracts by the Department]

Know-how contracts, as well as any amendments or renewal of them, are to be submitted for checking to the Department and the Department may request from the parties to the contract to amend the terms or the terms of the amendment or renewal so as to realize the interests of the parties within the framework of the law and the economic interests of the State. If the parties do not comply with the request, the Department may refuse to accept the contract and not record it in the register or refuse the amendment or renewal and not note it in the register.

Article 43 [Rejection of an Application to Record a Contract]

The Department has the right to agree or to refuse to record the contract or to note any amendment or renewal of it pursuant to what it considers necessary for the public good in the following cases:

1. If the know-how the subject of the contract relates to matters for which it is not permitted to grant a patent or utility certificate pursuant to the text of article 6 of the law.

2. If the term of the contract and its renewal exceeds the period stated in article 14 of the law.[34]

3. If the know-how the subject of the contract can be made available locally.

4. If the contract limits the activity of the party receiving the know-how in the domain of research and development or limits his right to export so as to conflict with the interest of the State, or prevents him from receiving or using complementary know-how from other sources.

5. If the contract requires the party receiving the know-how to limit the size of production or price of sale whether to the local or foreign market.

6. If the contract requires the return of the documents containing the know-how that were given to the receiving party pursuant to the contract.

7. If the contract results in financial obligations that are not proportionate to the know-how offered, or that impose an unsuitable burden on the national economy.

8. If the contract requires the receiving party to purchase equipment and machines or spare parts or raw or basic materials from the provider of the know-how or from his agent that can be obtained from different sources on better terms.

The provisions of article 23 of these regulations apply to the issue of decisions of the Department not to accept the contract or any amendment or renewal of it.

Article 44 [Cancellation of Recordals]

Cancellation of recordals of know-how contracts are to be noted in the register of know-how contracts based on an application from both parties filed with

---

34. Article 14 of the PDL 1992 provided that the term of a patent is 15 years and may be renewed for a further 5 years, and that a utility certificate has a term of 10 years without renewal. Article 6.2 patents (for methods of manufacture of nutritional products, medical drugs and pharmaceutical compounds) have only a term of 10 years without renewal.

the Department with the supporting documents, or based on a notice from the Department of a final decision, in the following circumstances:

1. Expiry of the contract
2. Termination of the contract before its expiry by agreement of the parties or by a court judgment
3. Annulment of the contract by a court judgment

Chapter 3: Industrial Drawings and Designs

Article 45 [Applications for Registration]

An application may be filed for a certificate of registration of an industrial drawing or design with the Department using Form 9 and its contents must be typed on A4 paper.

Article 46 [Attachments to the Application for Registration]

[A.] The following are to be attached to the application:

1. Two copies of the drawing or design if it is two-dimensional, or two copies of each perspective if it is three-dimensional, and it is not permitted to substitute a sample of the products relating to the industrial drawing or design.
2. An extract from the commercial register or an official extract of the contract of establishment or instrument of incorporation, according to the circumstances, if the applicant is a legal person.
3. The documents evidencing the right of the applicant to the industrial drawing or design, if the applicant is not the creator.
4. A copy of the prior application and the document attached to it, accompanied by a certificate showing the filing date and number and the country in which it was filed, if the application contains a claim for priority based on a prior application filed in a country that is a party to international agreement or convention with the United Arab Emirates pursuant to article 11 of the law.[35]
5. The power of attorney, if the application was filed by an agent.
6. The certificate of temporary protection, if any.
7. A letter from the Israeli boycott office that there is no objection to dealing with the applicant.

---

35. Article 11 of the PDL 1992 corresponds to article 11 of the PDL 2002, but the priority period for industrial drawings and designs is stated in article 46 of the PDL 2002. The priority period is six months.

[B.] The supporting documents referred to in paragraphs 2, 3, 4, and 5 must be legalized.

[C]. All the documents must be translated into Arabic if they are written in English, or translated into Arabic and English if they are in written any other language.

[D]. The documents referred to in paragraph 1 must be attached when the application is filed and must take into account the conditions set out in the following article.

[E]. As to the other documents, if they are not attached to the application, the applicant may file a written undertaking using Form 6 to file those that are necessary to file, according the circumstances, within ninety days of the date of filing of the application, and if the documents are not filed in this period, the application will be deemed not to have been filed, but excluded from this are the documents referred to in paragraph 4, the non-filing of which when required during this period results only in the loss of the applicant's right to claim priority. The application deemed not to have been filed or the loss of the right to claim priority, according to the circumstances, is to be noted in the register of applications, based on a decision of the director of the Department.

Article 47 [Formal Requirements]

1. The industrial drawing or design may not contain words or letters or numbers unless they are essential elements of the industrial drawing or design.

2. The copies of the industrial drawing or design may be graphic images or drawings or transparencies not exceeding 20 x 10 cms.

3. All of the graphic images or drawings, or transparencies, are to be arranged on A4 cardboard from top to bottom.

4. The graphic images may be colored but the drawings and transparencies must be in black ink.

5. If the drawing or design consists of more than one page, the pages must be numbered in the middle of the top of the page with consecutive Arabic numbers, indicating also whether it represents a complete view or a front view or otherwise.

Article 48 [Examination of Applications]

The Department is to examine the application and its attachments—in accordance with the system of examination referred to in articles 92 and 93 of these regulations to determine the following:

1. That the application has been filed by a natural or legal person enjoying the nationality of the State, or by a foreigner who has the right to file the application pursuant to the provisions of any international agreement or

convention to which the State is a party, or carries the nationality of a state that deals reciprocally with the State pursuant to article 2 of the law.[36]

2. That the application was filed by the owner of the right in the industrial drawing or design.

3. That the application was filed satisfying the conditions and procedures stated in articles 45 to 47 of these regulations.

4. That the industrial drawing or design is new or creative and may be used as a industrial or handicraft product and does not contravene the public order or morals of the State pursuant to article 46 of the law.[37] In order for an industrial drawing or design to be new or creative, it must not have been disclosed to the public at any time or place by any means of publication or use or any other means of knowing the industrial drawing or design, prior to the filing of the application or the priority date claimed, or before the commencement date of any temporary protection on the condition that the application was filed within six months of the date of commencement.

5. That the priority claimed agrees with the provisions of the international agreement or convention that ties the United Arab Emirates with the country in which the prior application was filed.

Article 49 [Other Provisions That Apply]

The provisions of articles 13, 14, 15, 21, 22, 23, 24, 25.2, 26, 27, 28, 29, 30, 33.1, 34, 35, 36, and 37 of these regulations apply to industrial drawings and designs, taking into account the following amendments:

1. Amending Forms 7 and 8 to Forms 10 and 11 respectively.

2. Amending the word "invention" to "industrial drawings or designs."

3. Amending the expression "patent and utility certificate applications" to "applications for industrial drawing and design registration certificates."

4. Amending the word "inventor" to "creator."

5. Deleting what is stated in paragraph "l" of article 24.4 of these regulations.

6. Amending the expression "patent or utility certificate" to "industrial drawing or design registration certificate."

7. Amending the expression "two registers, one for patents and one for utility certificates" in article 24.5 to "two registers, one for certificates for registered drawings and one for certificates for registered industrial designs."

---

36. Article 2 of the PDL 1992 corresponds to article 2 of the PDL 2002.
37. Article 46 of the PDL 1992 corresponds to article 47 of the PDL 2002.

Chapter 4: Contractual Licenses

Article 50 [Recordal of Contractual Licenses]

1. The provisions of articles 41, 42, 43, and 44 of these regulations apply to license contracts for the use or exploitation of the right the subject of protection and any amendment or renewal of them, taking into account the following amendments:

> a. Amending the word "know-how" to "license."
> b. Amending the expressions "the party owning the know-how" and "the party receiving the know-how" to "the licensor" and the "the licensee" respectively.
> c. Deleting what is stated in paragraph 1 of article 43 of these regulations.
> d. Amending what is stated in paragraph 2 of article 43 of these regulations to: "if the term of the contract and its renewals exceeds the term of protection stated in the deed of protection for the right the subject of the contract."
> e. Amending what is stated in paragraph 3 of article 43 of these regulations to: "if the contract grants to the licensee rights that are not granted by the deed of protection to licensor."

2. After recordal of the license contract in the license contracts register, the contract must be noted in the register for the right that is the subject of protection, and all amendments and renewals of the recordal that are noted in the license contracts register are also to be noted in this register.
3. The license contract and any amendment or renewal of it is to be published in the official gazette based on an application from the concerned person after payment of the required publication fees.

Article 51 [Checking of Assignments; Rejection of Recordal Applications]

The provisions of articles 42 and 43 of these regulations apply to assignment or ownership transfer agreements, taking into account the amendments referred to in paragraph 1 of the previous article, changing the word "license" to "assignment" and the word "the licensor" to "the assignor" and the word "licensee" to "the assignee."

Chapter 5: Precautionary Measures, Crimes and Penalties

Article 52 [Use of Falsified Documents]

The Department may implement the necessary measures for the cancellation of a deed of protection or any recordals or notations in its registers, if it is proved by a final penal judgment that a document that was relied on to issue a deed of protection, or to make a recordal or notation in the registers, was falsified.

Chapter 6: The Department of Industrial Property and Concluding Provisions

Section 1—Authorities and Their Hierarchies and Delegation within Them

Article 53 [Issue of Decisions]

Decisions granting deeds of protection are to be issued by the Minister and he may delegate the issuing of all or some of these decisions to the Head of the Department.

Article 54 [Responsibilities of the Head of the Department]

The Head of the Department is responsible for the following:

1. What is delegated to him by the Minister pursuant to article 53 of these regulations, he may not delegate to another.
2. Communicating with international and regional organizations and federations concerned with industrial property and following the conferences on the subject with the purpose of developing and modernizing the Department and its activities and systems in line with international developments.
3. Supervision of the compilation of agreements and conventions relating to industrial property that connects the State with other countries, and of countries that deal with the State reciprocally in this field, and of the preparation of a complete list of these agreements and conventions and countries, and the distribution of it to the examination specialists in the Department.

4. Studying the international agreements and conventions relating to industrial property and suggesting membership of the State to those that are suitable for it.

5. Studying and directing the negotiations in relation to the agreements and conventions with other countries in the field of industrial property to which it is suggested that the State sign.

6. Approving training programs for the employees of the Department and agreeing to the attendance and nomination of those proposed to take part in the training sessions, conferences, and symposiums that are convened within or outside the State in relation to industrial property.

7. Approving requests for assistance from required experts and specifying the periods of their work and rewards.

8. Accepting applications for protection after determining that they satisfy the technical and legal requirements and doing what is necessary to issue the Ministerial decisions concerning them.

9. Approving decisions that are issued pursuant to the text of articles 43, 50, and 51 of these regulations in relation to know-how contracts, contractual licenses, assignment contracts or transfers of ownership of the subject of protection, and any amendments or renewals of them.

10. Presiding over the registration committee responsible for issuing decisions relating to the acceptance or rejection of registration of registration agents with the Department and other decisions relating to them.

11. Issuing decisions relating to the publications referred to in article 90 of these regulations, and specifying the subscription fees, and approving the exchange arrangement in relation to it.

The Head of the Department may delegate some of his responsibilities to the Director of the Department or any of the section heads in the Department, and he may form technical committees to study any subject relating to his responsibilities and to report to him on the subject.

Article 55 [Responsibilities of the Director of the Department]

The Director of the Department is responsible for the following:

1. Carrying out what is delegated to him by the Head of the Department, without delegating it to another.

2. Issuing decisions in relation to the following:

a. Rejecting applications for protection that do not satisfy the technical and legal requirements.

b. Renewing the term of protection.

c. Issuing certificates of temporary protection.

d. All decisions relating to other matters stated in the law and these regulations and that are not mentioned in this article and articles 53 and 54 of these regulations.

The Director of the Department may delegate to the section heads some of his responsibilities as is necessary to benefit the work of the Department and for the nature of the work of each section, according to what is specified in the system of work in the Department that is issued by the Minister pursuant to the text of article 62 of the law.[38]

Article 56 [Responsibilities of the Section Heads]

The section heads are responsible for the matters that are delegated to them by the Director of the Department or for what is contained in system of work in the Department referred to in article 55 of these regulations.

Section 2—The Profession of Registration Agents

Article 57 [Registration Agents Must Be Registered]

It is not permitted to practice the profession of a registration agent without being registered in the list of registration agents with the Department.

Article 58 [Conditions for Registration]

1. It is a condition for registration in the list of registration agents with the Department referred to in article 67.2 of these regulations that the applicant be:

    a. a national of the State or enjoying the nationality of one of the Arab countries
    b. of sound mind
    c. of good reputation
    d. without prior criminal convictions for crimes relating to honor or honesty, unless his moral standing has been restored or was pardoned
    e. a holder of a university or higher degree

2. Companies specializing in the protection of industrial property and that are headquartered in the State or have a branch or registered office in the State may be registered in the list of registration agents.

---

38. Article 62 of the PDL 1992 corresponds to article 64 of the PDL 2002.

Article 59 [Filing of Registration Agent Applications]

1. Applications for registration are to be filed, with supporting documents satisfying the conditions stated in paragraph 1 or 2 of article 58 of these regulations, according to the circumstances, with the registration committee formed by the Head, the Director and the head of the legal section of the Department.

2. The secretary to the registration committee must note on the registration applications the serial numbers according to the date of filing in the register referred in article 67.1 of these regulations, and deliver to the applicant a receipt containing the application serial number, the date of filing, and the details of the attached documents.

Article 60 [The Responsibilities of the Registration Committee]

[1.] The registration committee is to examine the registration applications and attachments, and it may require the applicant to file what it considers outstanding and any clarifications, before issuing its decision.

[2.] The registration committee is to decide—after determining whether the conditions for the application have been satisfied—to register his name in the list of registration agents. The registration is to be for one year and be capable of renewal.

[3.] The registration is to be made in the list with consecutive numbering—after payment of the registration fees—according to the date of payment of the fees, and renewal is to be noted after payment of the renewal fees.

[4.] If the registration committee finds that the conditions for the application have not been satisfied, then the application is to be rejected. Such a decision must be reasoned.

[5.] The registration committee must determine the outcome of applications for registration within three months of the date of filing of the application, and inform the applicant of its decision immediately upon issue by registered letter, accompanied by an acknowledgement of receipt.

[6.] The applicant who has his application rejected may appeal the rejection decision before the grievances committee within sixty days of the date of being notified of the decision.

Article 61 [Annual Publication of Names of Agents]

The Department is to publish annually the schedule of names of registration agents whose names are registered in the list.

Article 62 [Only Registered Agents May Be Authorized]

Applicants for protection or holders of deeds of protection may not authorize anyone to act before the Department except those who are registration agents registered in the list.

Article 63 [Obligations of Registration Agents]

[A.] All those who are registered in the list of registration agents with the Department must:

1. Inform the Department by registered letter of the address of his office within thirty days of the date of registration in the list and of all changes to this address within thirty days of the date of the changes
2. State his name together with his registration number in the list in all correspondence and papers issued by him
3. Perform his work according to the principles of the profession and the provisions of the law and these regulations

Article 64 [Investigation and Cancellation of Registration Agents]

[1.] The registration committee may, of its own volition or based on a complaint filed with it, undertake an investigation in relation to anyone whose name is registered in the list of registration agents, if a contravention of the provisions of the law or these regulations or the principles of the profession has been attributed to him, or one of the required conditions for registration has been lost, or was not satisfied at the time of registration.

[2.] If the investigation proves the truth of what has been attributed to the one whose name is registered in the list, the registration committee is to issue a decision cancelling his registration and to inform him of the decision immediately upon issue by registered letter accompanied by an acknowledgement of receipt.

[3.] The person against whom a decision has issued to cancel his name from the list may object to the decision before the grievances committee within sixty days of the date of receipt of the notice of the decision.

[4.] If it appears to the registration committee that the facts attributed to the one whose name is registered in the list constitute a criminal offense, it must transfer the papers to the public prosecution.

Article 65 [Removal of Names from the List of Agents]

Based on a decision issued by the registration committee, the name of anyone who has died or has had his registration cancelled or who requests his name to be removed is to be removed from the list.

Article 66 [Recordal of Decisions]

1. The secretary to the registration committee must note in the register of applications for registration the decision to accept or reject an application and its date of issue and the date of notifying the applicant.
2. The secretary to the registration committee must note in the list of registration agents the decisions issued to cancel or delete a registration and the date of its issue.

Article 67 [Register for Registration Agent Applications]

1. The Department is to prepare a register for applications for registration of registration agents and this register is to contain the following information:

a. The serial number of the application
b. The date of filing of the application
c. The name of the applicant, his nationality, qualifications, his place of residence and address, and if the applicant is a company, its name, its kind, its purpose and its principal place of business, the address of its branch or its registered office in the State
d. The decision issued concerning the application and its date of issue and the date of notice of it
e. The number and date of the registration in the list of registration agents

2. The Department is to prepare a list of registered registration agents and it must contain the following information:

a. The number and date of registration
b. The number and date of the receipt for the payment of the registration fees
c. The number and date of the receipt for the payment of the renewal fees
d. The date of the decision to cancel or delete the registration

Section 3—Grievances Committee

Article 68 [Objections to Decisions]

1. Objections to decisions issued in relation to the implementation of the law or these regulations may be filed by concerned persons with the grievances

committee referred to in article 64[39] of the law by way of a petition with copies for each of the parties, delivered to the secretary of the committee.
2. The petition must contain the following information:

a. If he is a natural person, the name of the petitioner, his profession, his place of residence, the number, date and source of proof of his identity, or if he is a legal person, his name, his purpose, his headquarters and the number, date and source of registration, specifying h s chosen address in the State, if he does not have residency or a location in the State
b. The information stated in the previous paragraph for the agent of the petitioner—if any—in addition to the number, date, and source of his authorization
c. The name of the defendant, his profession and the place of his residence, if he is a natural person, or his name, his purpose and his headquarters, if he is a legal person
d. The address of the petitioner and his agent, if any, and of the defendant, and the address must contain all the methods that can be used to contact him or write to him including a post office box, a phone number, telex and fax, according to the circumstances
e. A statement of the subject of the objection and requests of the petitioner
f. A statement of the evidence that the petitioner will rely upon
g. A statement of the documents attached to the petit on of the objection
h. The signature of the petitioner or his agent

Article 69 [Functions of the Secretary to the Committee]

1. The secretary of the committee must record the petitions with consecutive numbering annually—after the payment of required fees—in the register referred to in the following paragraph—and deliver to the petitioner or his agent a receipt containing the number and date of the recording of the petition, and a statement of the documents attached, if any.
2. The secretary of the committee is to maintain the register for recordal of the petitions which must contain the following information:

a. The number and date of the recordal of the petition
b. The number and date of the receipt for the payment of the objection fees
c. The information stated in the petition of the object on and referred to in paragraph 2 of article 68 of these regulations, except the signature of the petitioner or his agent
d. The number and date of the notification of the defendant of the objection
e. The date of receiving the reply of the defendant to the objection

---

39. Article 64 of the PDL 1992 corresponds to article 66 of the PDL 2002.

f. The number and date of the notification of the petitioner of the defendant's reply

g. The date of the first hearing set down for considering the objection and the date of notice to the parties

h. The date of issue of the decision concerning the subject of the objection

i. The number and date of notice to the parties of the decision issued concerning the subject of the objection

3. The petition is deemed to be filed with the committee and effective from the date of its recordal.

Article 70 [Notice of the Objection and Replying]

1. The secretary of the committee must deliver to the defendant a copy of the petition of the objection and its attachments by registered post within one week of the date of recordal of the petition.

2. The defendant is to reply to the objection within one month of the date of receiving the notice referred to in the previous paragraph and the reply must be by means of a written memorandum in original and copies sufficient for all the parties.

3. The secretary of the committee must send a copy of the defendant's reply to the petitioner by registered post within one week of the date of receiving the reply.

Article 71 [Setting the Hearing Date]

Within one week of the expiry of the dates set out in article 70 of these regulations, the secretary of the committee must show the complete file for the objection to the chairman of the committee in order to set a date for the hearing of the objection.

Article 72 [Notice of the Hearing Date]

The secretary of the committee must inform the petitioner and the defendant of the date of the hearing for consideration of the objection by registered post not less than ten days prior to the hearing.

Article 73 [Attendance at the Hearing]

The parties may attend the hearing set down for the consideration of the objection by themselves or by means of their legal representatives.

Article 74 [Issuing a Decision]

The committee is to issue its decision concerning the objection after determining that the parties who did not attend were properly notified, and after hearing the submissions of those attending. It may delay the consideration of the objection to another hearing if it considers it justified.

Article 75 [Appointment of an Expert]

If the committee decides to appoint an expert, it must include in its decision the following:

1. A precise statement of the task of the expert
2. A statement as to which of the parties is to be responsible for the costs of the expertise and the method and date of payment
3. The deadline for filing the expert's report
4. The date of the hearing set down for discussion of the expert's report

Article 76 [Assistance of a Translator]

The committee may seek the assistance of a translator if t considers it necessary.

Article 77 [Suspension of the Case]

If the committee considers that its decision in the matter of the objection should be suspended for the determination of another issue outside of its jurisdiction, it may order that the case be suspended pending the determination of the other issue, and as soon as the reason for the suspension ceases, any party may request the continuation of the case within thirty days following the ceasing of the reason for suspension, otherwise the case will be deemed discontinued.

Article 78 [Discontinuation]

[1.] The running of the case is to be discontinued if one of the parties dies or is no longer of sound mind, or if one of the representatives ceases to have the capacity to act in the case, except the agent for the case, unless the parties have started their final submissions and requests.
[2.] The case is to proceed on the date previously specified if someone fills the place of the party who was the reason for the discontinuation of the case.

[3.] Based on an application filed by any concerned person, the case is to proceed and the other parties or their agents are to be informed by registered post accompanied by an acknowledgement of receipt.

Article 79 [Responsibilities of the Chairman and Secretary]

The chairman of the committee is responsible for the conduct of the hearings and the secretary of the committee is responsible for writing the minutes of the hearings, and the minutes of the hearings are to be signed by the chairman and the secretary.

Article 80 [Confidential Deliberations]

The deliberation for its decisions is to be confidential between the chairman of the committee and its gathered members.

Article 81 [Majority Decisions]

The committee is to issue its decisions by unanimous opinion or by a majority, and in any case, the decisions are to be reasoned and signed by the chairman of the committee and its members.

Article 82 [Delivery of Decisions]

The secretary of the committee must send a copy of the decision and its reasons to the parties by registered post within ten days of the date of its issue.

Article 83 [Method of Delivery]

The delivery may be made to the person himself, or his agent, with a receipt signed by him, in place of sending notification to him by registered post.

Article 84 [Correction of Errors]

The committee is responsible for correcting material typographical or calculation errors occurring in its decisions by a decision it issues itself or based on an application from one of the parties. The correction is to be written on the original copy of the decision and signed by the chairman and members.

Article 85 [Clarification of Decisions]

The parties may request from the committee an explanation of what is unclear in the expression of its decision and the explanatory decisions are deemed to be part of the decision explained.

Article 86 [Members' Remuneration]

1. The chairman of the committee is entitled to remuneration in the amount of . . . . . . dirhams for each hearing convened.
2. Each member of the committee is entitled to remuneration in the amount of. . . . . . dirhams for each hearing convened.

Article 87 [Hearings Register]

1. The secretary of the committee is to maintain a register of the hearings recording consecutively each petition put before the committee at each hearing and the decisions issued, as well as the date of the previous hearing that considered the petition and the date of the next hearing to which consideration of the petition has been deferred.
2. The secretary of the committee must note in the register of petitions the decisions issued concerning the petition and the date of issue.

Section 4—Forms, Registers, Publications and Extracts

Article 88 [Forms]

1. The forms referred to in these regulations are the forms specified in the second attached schedule.
2. Without prejudice to the forms referred to in the previous paragraph, the Department may, by a decision from the Head of the Department, issue other forms and amend them as it sees fit for the benefit of the work flow and its development.

Article 89 [Registers and Their Correction]

1. Taking into account the text of article 69.2 of these regulations, the Department must prepare and maintain the registers referred to in these regulations. Each register is to contain the information referred to in these regulations. The Department may, by a decision from the Head of the Department, add other information to these registers or prepare additional registers, as it sees fit for the benefit of the work flow and its development.
2. Any concerned person may request the Department to correct any material error occurring in the register relating to the right the subject of protection, and may request the recordal of any change in the name of the owner or his nationality or his address or his chosen place or the name of the agent or his address in this register, and the applicant must pay the required correction or amendment fees when filing the application.

Article 90 [Periodical Publications]

1. The Department may, by a decision from its Head, issue periodical publications monthly, quarterly or yearly—in Arabic or in English and Arabic, numbered consecutively following the date of issue—publishing in them the news, information, decisions, analyses, and research relating to deeds of protection or applications for them, or the law and these regulations, or registration agents, or the work system in the Department, that it considers necessary for publication.

2. The Department may maintain volumes of the publications referred to in the previous article to refer to when needed, and it may distribute free volumes to government bodies, and anyone may subscribe to the publications after paying the subscription fees specified by the Head of the Department or following the exchange system, whether inside or outside the State.

Article 91 [Viewing and Copying Patents, etc.]

Without payment of fees, anyone may view the patents, utility certificates or certificates of registration for industrial drawings or designs that have been registered with the Department and any information relating to them in the presence of a responsible employee in the Department, and after payment of the required fees, any person has the right to obtain copies of them or of information relating to them, or obtain certificates of what is contained in them or extracts from the registers relating to them.

Section 5—The System of Examination

Article 92 [Formal Examination]

The Department is to examine applications recorded with it as to form, and if it appears from the examination that the conditions set down by the law or these regulations have not been satisfied, it may notify the applicant by registered post requiring him to do what is necessary to complete the application within ninety days of the delivery of the mentioned notice, if he does not do what has been requested during this period, his application will be deemed not to have been filed, and this is to be noted in the register recording his application, based on a decision of the Director of the Department.

Article 93 [Substantive Examination]

If it appears that the application is satisfactory as to form, the Department is to estimate the necessary costs of substantive examination of the application based on a study for evaluating the costs, and then notify the applicant by registered post requiring him to pay these costs within ninety days from delivery of the notice, and if the applicant pays within this period, the application is to be transferred for substantive examination, but if he does not pay during this period, the application is to be deemed not to have been filed, and this is to be noted in the register recording his application, based on a decision of the director of the Department.

Section 6—Fees

Article 94

The fees referred to in the law and these regulations are the fees specified in the first attached schedule.

Article 95 [Publication of this Decision]

This decision is to be published in the official gazette and becomes effective from the date of its publication.

Prime Minister
Issued by us in Abu Dhabi

Dated: Thi Al Qa'da 20, 1413 H
Corresponding to: May 12, 1993 M

First schedule Fees

Fees	*Fee amount in dirhams*	
	Natural person	*Legal person*
1. Application for a deed of protection	400	800
2. Application to correct or amend information	100	200
3. Application for renewal of the protection period	200	400
4. Application for recordal of an assignment of a deed of protection	200	400
5. Application for registration of a know-how contract or license contract	200	400
6. Application to amend or renew a know-how or license contract	100	200
7. Registration in the list of registration agents	400	800
8. Renewal of a registration in the list of registration agents	200	400
9. Objection before the grievances committee	100	200
10. Obtaining a copy of any deed of protection or any papers relating to it or a certificate of the content of any of them or an extract from the register	50	100
11. Publication of any decision or judgment or contract or procedure required by the law or these regulations to be paid before publication	200	400
12. Annuities for deeds of protection and applications for them starting from the second year (the year after the filing of the application) until the expiry of protection		
For the second year	400	800
For the third year	420	840
For the fourth year	440	880
For the fifth year	460	920
For the sixth year	480	960
For the seventh year	500	1000
For the eighth year	520	1040
For the ninth year	540	1080
For the tenth year	560	1120
For the eleventh year	580	1160
For the twelfth year	600	1200

Fees	Fee amount in dirhams	
	Natural person	Legal person
For the fourteenth year	640	1280
For the fifteenth year	660	1320
For the sixteenth year	680	1360
For the seventeenth year	700	1400
For the eighteenth year	720	1440
For the nineteenth year	740	1480
For the twentieth year	760	1520
13. Additional fees for accepting the payment of an annuity within thirty days of the expiry of the payment year	100	200

Second schedule

Forms

Form 1
Application for temporary protection for an invention

The applicant requests the Industrial Property Department to grant a temporary protection certificate pursuant to the following information:	**Official use only** Application number: _____ Filing date and time: _____

1. Invention's name: _____
 _____
 _____

2. Applicant's name: _____
 Address: _____
 _____
 _____

Chosen address in the State: _____
 _____
 _____

Nationality: _____
 _____

Place of residence or headquarters: _____
 _____
 _____

Phone number _____ Telex number _____ Fax number _____
 _____

Number of applicants _____ If there is more than one, their details are to be mentioned on an additional page.

3. Inventor's name: _____
 Address: _____
 _____
 _____

Number of inventors_____ If there is more than one, their details are to be mentioned on an additional page.

4. Agent's name:_____

_____

Number of the power of attorney:_____Date_____Source_____

Address:_____

Phone number_____ Telex number_____ Fax number_____

5. Exhibition and opening date: _____

_____

_____

6. Attachments:

   - Summary of the description of the invention   ☐

   - Invention fees, if any   ☐

   - Details of products relating to the invention   ☐

Applicant Agent

7. Signature:_____

Date:_____

Form 2
Application for temporary protection of an industrial drawing or design

The applicant requests the Industrial Property Department to grant a temporary protection certificate: For a drawing ☐ For an industrial design ☐ pursuant to the following information:	**Official use only** Application number: _____ Filing date and time: _____ _____

1. Name of the industrial drawing or design: _____
_____
_____
_____

2. Applicant's name:_____
Address:_____
_____
_____

Chosen address in the State: _____
_____
_____

Nationality: _____
Place of residence or headquarters:_____
_____
_____

Phone number_____Telex number_____Fax number_____
Number of applicants_____ If there is more than one, their details are to be mentioned on an additional page.

3. Name of the inventor: _____
Address:_____
_____
_____

Number of inventors_____If there is more than one, their details are to be mentioned on an additional page.

4. Name of the agent:_____

_____

Number of the power of attorney:_____Date_____Source_____

Address:_____

_____

Phone number_____ Telex number_____Fax number_____

5. Exhibition and opening date:_____

_____

_____

6. Attachments:

   - Two copies of the industrial drawing or design   ☐

   - Details of the products to which they belong   ☐

Applicant Agent

7. Signature:_____

Date:_____

Form 3
Certificate of temporary protection for an invention

The Director of the Industrial Property Department,

After reviewing article 3 of federal law no. 44 of 1992 in relation to the regulation and protection of industrial property for patents, industrial drawings and designs,

And the implementing regulations of the law,

And application number_____dated_____and the documents relating to it,

Decided

A license of temporary protection be granted, number_____

for the applicant _____his address and nationality _____

for the invention with the name_____

for the products that have been exhibited, being_____

_____

_____

Exhibition name_____

Opening date_____

This certificate grants legal protection to the invention shown above for six months starting from the opening date of the exhibition and ends on_____

Dated_____

Director of the Industrial Property Department

Form 4
Certificate of temporary protection for an
industrial drawing or design

The Director of the Industrial Property Department;

After reviewing article 3 of federal law no. 44 of 1992 in relation to the regulation and protection industrial property for patents, industrial drawings or designs,

And the implementing regulations of the law,

And application number_____dated_____and documents relating to it,

Decided

A license of temporary protection be granted, number_____

for the applicant _____his address and nationality _____

for the invention with the name_____

for the products that have been exhibited, being_____

_____

_____

Exhibition name_____

Opening date_____

This certificate grants legal protection to the invention shown above for six months starting from the opening date of the exhibition and ends on_____

Dated_____

Director of the Industrial Property Department

Form 5
Application for patent or utility certificate

The applicant requested the Industrial Property Department to grant Patent—Original ☐ Additional ☐ Utility certificate—Original ☐ Additional ☐ pursuant to the following information:	**Official use only** Application number _____ Filing date and time_____

1. The name of inventor: _____
_____
_____

2. Applicant name:_____
_____

Address:_____
_____
_____

Chosen address in the State: _____
_____
_____

Nationality: _____
_____

Place of residence or headquarters: _____
_____

Phone number _____ Telex number_____
Fax number_____
Number of applicants_____ If there is more than one, their details are to be mentioned on an additional page.

3. Name of the inventor: _____
Address:_____
_____

Number of inventors_____If there is more than one, their details are to be mentioned on an additional page.

4. Name of the agent:_____
_____

Number of the power of attorney:_____Date_____
Source_____
Address:_____
_____
_____

Phone number_____ Telex number_____
Fax number_____

5. Claim priority based on a prior application:
The name of the state in which the application was filed:_____

Number and date of application:_____

If the priority is based on more than one prior application, the details of the other applications are to be mentioned on an additional page.

6. Number and date of the temporary protection certificate, if any: _____

7. If the application is for an patent or utility certificate of addition, the following should be mentioned: _____
- Number and date of the registration of the original patent or utility certificate application: _____
- Number and date of grant of the original patent or utility certificate: _____

8. The scope of protection (the new elements requiring protection): _____
_____
_____
_____
_____
_____
_____
_____
_____
_____
_____
_____
_____
_____
_____
_____
_____

If this space is not sufficient to specify the scope of protection, the other details may mentioned on an additional page.

| ☐ | ☐ |
| Applicant | Agent |

9. Signature:_____   _____
Date:_____

Information

Attachments for patent or utility certificate applications pursuant to the implementing regulations

The following are to be attached to the application for a patent:

1. A detailed description of the invention.

2. The drawing of the invention when necessary for understanding the invention, or if the nature of the invention permits clarification by drawings.

3. An abstract for the invention may not exceed two hundred words accompanied by the best clarificatory drawing, if any.

4. An extract from the commercial register or an official extract from the establishment contract, if the applicant is a company or legal person.

5. The document indicating the entitlement of the applicant to the invention if the applicant is not the inventor.

6. The agreement of the concerned person if the essential elements of the invention have been obtained from the invention of another person.

7. The power of attorney document, if the application is filed by an agent.

8. A copy of the prior application and attached documents, accompanied by a certificate showing its filing date and number, and the country in which it was filed, if the application contains a request for priority based on a prior application filed in a country that is a party to an international agreement or convention with the United Arab Emirates pursuant to article 11 of the law.

9. The temporary protection certificate, if any.

10. A letter from the Israeli boycott office as to the non-existence of any objection to dealing with the applicant.

The documents referred to in paragraphs 4, 5, 6, 7 and 8 are to be legalized in accordance with the law.

All supporting documents must be accompanied by an Arabic translation if written in English, or by an Arabic and English translation if written in another language.

An original and copy of the document mentioned in paragraphs 1, 2 and 3 are to be attached to the application when filed. These and the application are to take in account the conditions stated in articles 7 to 12 of the implementing regulations.

As to the other documents, if they are not attached to the application, the applicant may undertake in writing using Form 6 to file those of them that must be filed, according to the circumstances, within ninety days of the date of filing of the application. If they are not filed during this period. the application will be deemed not to have been filed. From this is excluding the document referred to in paragraph 8, for which the failure to file when required during this period is the loss of the right to claim priority.

> **For official use**
> Reviewed and required fees of _____AED paid
> according to receipt number _____ dated _____
> Name of the recipient: _____
> Signature: _____
> Date: _____
> Official stamp: _____

Form 6
Undertaking to file documents relating to an application

Patent ☐   **Utility certificate** ☐   **Industrial drawing or design** ☐

Application number:

Date of filing of the application:

Applicant's name:

Agent's name:

I, the undersigned, _____

_____ undertake in my capacity as_____ to file with
the Industrial Property Department the documents mentioned below within ninety
days of the date of filing of the application.

_____

_____

_____

_____

_____

_____

_____

_____

_____

_____

_____

_____

_____

_____

Dated   /   /

Signature

_____

Form 7
Receipt for the receiving of documents

Patent application ☐ **Utility certificate** ☐

Application number:
Time and date of filing of the application:
Applicant name and nationality:

| Fee paid with receipt no: _____ |
| Dated: _____ |

Documents received with the application:

1. A detailed description of the invention/_____ pages
of two copies.   ☐

2. The drawings for the invention/_____ drawings of two copies.   ☐

3. The abstract for the invention/_____pages of two copies.   ☐

4. Extract from the commercial register or official extract from the
establishment contract, according to circumstances, if the applicant
is a legal person.   ☐

5. The document indicating the entitlement of the applicant to the
invention, if the applicant is not the inventor.   ☐

6. The agreement of the concerned person if the essential elements
of the invention have been obtained from the invention of another
person.   ☐

7. The power of attorney document, if the application is filed by an agent.   ☐

8. A copy of the prior application and attached documents accompanied
by a certificate indicating its filing date and number, and the country in
which it was filed, if the application contains a request for priority based
on a prior application filed in a country that is a party to an international
agreement or convention with the United Arab Emirates pursuant to
article 11 of the law.   ☐

9. The temporary protection certificate, if any.   ☐

10. A letter from the Israeli boycott office as to the non-existence of any
objection to dealing with the application.   ☐

11. A written undertaking on Form 6 to file necessary documents
(4 to 10) except the ones attached to the application.   ☐

Official stamp   Total documents received   ☐
                        Recipient:_____
                        Name:_____
                        Signature:_____

Note: a √ mark is to be indicated against documents received.

Form 8
Alphabetical card index for patent and utility
certificate applications

Applicant name: _____

_____

_____

Name of the invention: _____

_____

_____

Application serial number: _____

_____

_____

_____

_____

Time and date of filing of the application:_____

_____

_____

Form 9
Application for registration of an industrial drawing or design

The applicant requests the Industrial Property Department to grant a certificate of registration ⬜ ⬜ For an drawing For industrial design pursuant to the following information:	**Official use only** Application number: _____ Filing date and time: _____ _____

1. Drawing name ⬜   Industrial design name   ⬜

2. Applicant's name:_____ _____

Address:_____ _____ _____

Chosen address in the State: _____ _____ _____

Nationality: _____ _____

Place of residence or headquarters:_____ _____ _____

Phone number_____ Telex number_____

Fax number_____

The number of applicants_____ If there is more than one, their details are to be mentioned on an additional page.

3. Name of the creator: _____ _____

Address:_____ _____ _____

Number of creators_____If there is more than one, their details are to be mentioned on an additional page.

4. Name of the agent:_____
_____
Power of attorney:_____Date_____Source_____   Address:_____   _____   _____
Phone number_____ Telex number_____Fax number_____
5. Priority claim based on a prior application   Name of state in which the application has been filed: _____   _____
Application number and date:_____   _____
If priority is based on more than one application, the details of the other   applications are to be mentioned on an additional page.
6. Number and date of the temporary protection certificate, if any: _____   _____
☐   Applicant   ☐   Agent   7. Signature:_____   _____   Date:_____

Information

Attachments for applications for registration of an industrial drawing or design

The following are to be attached to applications for registration of industrial drawings and designs pursuant to the implementing regulations:

1. Two copies of the drawing or design if it is two-dimensional, or two copies of each perspective if it is three-dimensional. It is not permitted to substitute a sample of the products relating to the industrial drawing or design.

2. An extract from the commercial register or an official extract of the articles of association, if the applicant is a company or legal person.

3. The documents evidencing the right of the applicant to the industrial drawing or design, if the applicant is not the creator.

4. A copy of the prior application and the documents attached to it, accompanied by a certificate showing the filing date and number and the country in which it was filed, if the application contains a claim for priority based on a prior application filed in a country that is a party to international agreement or convention with the United Arab Emirates pursuant to article 11 of the law.

5. The power of attorney, if the application was filed by an agent.

6. The certificate of temporary protection, if any.

7. A letter from the Israeli boycott office that there is no objection to dealing with the applicant.

All the documents must be translated into Arabic if they are written in English, or translated into Arabic and English, if they are in written any other language.

The supporting documents referred to in paragraphs 2, 3, 4 and 5 must be legalized in accordance with the law.

The documents referred to in paragraph 1 must be attached when the application is filed and must take into account the conditions set out in article 47 of the implementing regulations.

As to the other documents, if they are not attached to the application, the applicant may file a written undertaking using Form 6 to file those that are necessary to file, according the circumstances, within ninety days of the date of filing of the application, and if the documents are not filed in this period, the application will be deemed not to have been filed, but excluded from this are the documents referred to in paragraph 4, the non-fi ing of which when required during this period results only in the loss of the applicant's right to claim priority.

For official use

Reviewed and required fees of _____AED paid according to receipt number _____ dated _____

Name of the recipient: _____

Signature: _____

Date: _____

Official stamp: _____

Form 10
Receipt for the receiving of documents

Application for a certificate of registration
Drawing ▭ **Industrial design** ▭

Application number:
Time and date of filing of the application:
Applicant name and nationality:

| Fee paid with receipt no: _____ |
| Time:_____ |
| Dated: _____ |

Documents received with the application:

1. Two copies of the drawing or design if it is two-dimensional, or two copies of each perspective if it is three-dimensional, and it is not permitted to substitute a sample of the products relating to the industrial drawing or design. ▭

2. An extract from the commercial register or an official extract of the articles of association, or instrument of incorporation, according to the circumstances, if the applicant is a legal person. ▭

3. The documents evidencing the right of the applicant to the industrial drawing or design, if the applicant is not the creator. ▭

4. A copy of the prior application and the document attached to it, accompanied by a certificate showing the filing date and number and the country in which it was filed, if the application contains a claim for priority based on a prior application filed in a country that is a party to international agreement or convention with the United Arab Emirates pursuant to article 11 of the law. ▭

5. The power of attorney, if the application was filed by an agent. ▭

6. The certificate of temporary protection, if any. ▭

7. A letter from the Israeli boycott office that there is no objection to dealing with the applicant. ▭

8. A written undertaking using Form 6 to file documents 2 to 7 as required except the ones attached to the application. ▭

Official stamp

Total documents received
Recipient:_____
Name:_____
Signature:_____

Note: a √ mark is to be indicated against the documents received.

Form 11
Alphabetical card index for applications for certificates of registration for industrial drawings and designs

Applicant name: _____
_____
_____

Industrial drawing or design name: _____
_____
_____
_____

Application serial number: _____
_____
_____
_____
_____

Time and date of filing of the application:_____
_____
_____

A3

Ministerial Decision No. 404 of 2000 [Concerning Pharmaceutical Products and Patents]

The Minister of Health,

After considering Federal law no. 1 of 1972 in relation to jurisdictions of the Ministries and powers of the Ministers and the laws amending it, and

Federal law no. 4 of 1983 in relation to the pharmacy profession and pharmaceutical establishments, and

Federal law no. 44 of 1992 in relation to the regulation and protection of industrial property for patents, industrial drawings and designs, and

Federal decree no. 21 of 1998 in relation to the agreement and protocol for the accession of the state to the World Trade Organization and the Uruguay Round document, and

The TRIPs intellectual property rights agreement, and

Based on a letter from the Minister of Finance and Industry received by fax on April 26, 2000,

Decided:

Article 1 [Patent Required]

Any new medicine or pharmaceutical preparation that does not enjoy a patent may not be registered.

Article 2 [Exceptions]

The provisions of the previous article do not apply to medicines and pharmaceutical preparations registered in international drugs registers and obligatory drug lists published by the World Health Organization or by any neutral international scientific body and do not apply to medicines and preparations that have been registered or to those whose period of patent protection for the original product has expired.

Article 3 [Confidentiality]

The concerned departments in the Ministry must keep the confidentiality of the information attached to any application for registration of a medicine or pharmaceutical preparation.

Article 4 [Publication]

This decision is to be published in the official gazette and is considered to be effective from the date of publication.

Article 5 [Implementation]

Those who are to implement this decision are to be informed.

Hamad Abdul Rahman Al Midf'a
Minister of Health

Issued from the Diwan of the Ministry, Abu Dhabi
Dated: Muharram 26 1421 H
Corresponding to: April 30, 2000 M.

A4

Federal Law No. 37 of 1992 in Relation to Trademarks

[This translation incorporates the 2000 and 2002 amendments to the 1992 law, showing the deletions in strike out and the replacement texts in underline. Text shown in italics indicates the areas of difference between the previous text and the replacement text].

Contents

We, Zayed Bin Sultan Al Nahyan, President of the United Arab Emirates,

After considering the provisional constitution, and

Federal law no. 1 of 1972 in relation to the jurisdictions of the Ministries and the powers of the Ministers and the laws amending it, ar d

Federal law no. 4 of 1979 in relation to the prevention of fraud and deception in commercial dealings, and

Federal law no. 5 of 1985 in relation to civil transactions and the laws amending it, and

Federal law no. 3 of 1987 in relation to penalties, and

Based on what was presented by the Minister of Econorr y and Commerce, and the approval of the Cabinet and the ratification of the Supreme Federation Council, Issued the following law:

Chapter 1: Definitions

~~Article 1~~

~~In the application of the provisions of this law, the following words and expressions are intended to have the following meanings, unless the context requires otherwise:~~

~~The State: The United Arab Emirates.~~

~~The Minister: The Minister of Economy & Commerce.~~

~~The Ministry: The Ministry of Economy & Commerce.~~

~~The competent authority: The competent authority in the emirate.~~

~~Drawing: Any design that contains a group of visual elements (any artistic creation).~~

~~Symbol: Any single visual drawing.~~

~~Impressions: Impressed marks.~~

~~Inscriptions: Marks in relief.~~

~~Images: Images of a person whether of the owner of the project or of another.~~
~~The committee: The trademark committee described in this law.~~[40]

~~Article 1~~
~~In the application of the provisions of this law, the following words and~~
~~expressions are intended to have the following meanings, unless the context~~
~~requires otherwise:~~
~~The State: The United Arab Emirates.~~
~~*The Ministry: The Ministry of Economy & Commerce.*~~
~~*The Minister: The Minister of Economy & Commerce.*~~
~~The competent authority: The competent authority in the emirate.~~
~~*The journal: The journal of trademarks that is published by the Ministry.*~~
~~Drawing: Any design that contains a group of visual elements~~
   ~~(any artistic creation).~~
~~Symbol: Any single visual drawing.~~
~~Impressions: Impressed marks.~~
~~Inscriptions: Marks in relief.~~
~~Images: Images of a person whether of the owner of the project or of another.~~
~~The committee: The trademark committee described in this law.~~[41]

Article 1

In the application of the provisions of this law, the following words and
expressions are intended to have the following meanings, unless the context
requires otherwise:

The State: The United Arab Emirates.
The Ministry: The Ministry of Economy & Commerce.
The Minister: The Minister of Economy & Commerce.
The competent authority: The competent authority in the emirate.
The journal: The journal of trademarks that is published by the Ministry.
Drawing: Any design that contains a group of visual elements
   (any artistic creation).
Symbol: Any single visual drawing.
Impressions: Impressed marks.
Inscriptions: Marks in relief.

---

40. Federal law no. 19 of 2000, article 1, replaced this article 1 with a new article 1
   (shown in underline).
41. Although the entirety of article 1 of the TML 1992 was replaced as a consequence of
   the 2000 amendments, the only changes made to it were the addition of a definition
   for "journal" and a reversal of the order of the definitions for "Ministry" and "Minister."
   The entirety of the new article was then replaced as a consequence of the 2002
   amendments.

Images: Images of a person whether of the owner of the project or of another.
The register: The register of trademarks at the Ministry.
The committee: The trademark committee described in this law.[42]

Article 2 [What is a Trademark?]

A trademark is considered to be anything that takes a distinctive form whether names, words, signatures, letters, numbers, drawings, symbols, titles, impressions, stamps, images, inscriptions, advertisements, packaging or any other mark or combination of marks used or intended to be used to distinguish goods or products or services, of whatever origin, or to indicate that the goods or products are those of the owner of the mark because they were manufactured or selected or traded in by the owner, or to indicate the provision of a service.

A sound is considered to be part of a trademark if it accompanies it.

Article 3 [What May Not Be Registered as a Trademark]

The following may not be registered as a trademark or as an element of a trademark:

1. Marks that are devoid of any distinctive attribute or character or that consists of representations that are no more than customary names given to the goods and products and services or conventional drawings or ordinary images of the goods and products.
2. Any mark that contravenes public morals or public order.
3. Public emblems, flags and other symbols of the State, or of Arabic or international organizations, or any of their institutions, or any foreign country, except with their authorization, as well as any imitation of any of them.
4. Symbols of the Red Crescent or Red Cross and any other similar symbols, as well as imitations of any of them.
5. Marks that are identical or similar to symbols of a purely religious nature.
6. Geographic names, if their use would cause confusion in relation to the origin of the good or products or services or their source.
7. The name of another or the name by which he/she is known or his/her image, or emblem, unless the person, or his/her successors, has previously consented to its use.
8. Representations containing honorific titles to which the applicant for registration cannot prove a legal entitlement.

---

42. Federal law no. 7 of 2002 directed the replacement of article 1 of the TML 1992 as amended in 2000 with this new article. However, the only change made was the addition of a definition for "the register."

~~9. Marks that deceive the public or that contain false representations as to the origin or source of the products or the services or their other characteristics, as well as marks that contain an illusory, copied or false commercial name.~~
~~10. Marks owned by natural or legal persons with whom it is forbidden to deal.~~
~~11. Marks whose registration for some classes of products or services would reduce the value of other products or services that are distinguished by the mark.~~
~~12. Marks that contain the following words or expressions: "patent," "patented," "registered," "registered drawing," "copyright," "imitation is counterfeiting" or any words or expressions resembling them.~~

Article 3 [What May Not Be Registered as a Trademark]

The following may not be registered as a trademark or as an element of a trademark:

1. Marks that are devoid of any distinctive attribute or character or that consist of representations that are no more than customary names given to the goods and products and services or conventional drawings or ordinary images of the goods and products
2. Any mark that contravenes public morals or public order
3. Public emblems, flags and other symbols of the State, or of Arabic or international organizations, or any of their institutions, or any foreign country, except with their authorization, as well as any imitation of any of them
4. Symbols of the Red Crescent or Red Cross and any other similar symbols, as well as imitations of any of them
5. Marks that are identical or similar to symbols of a purely religious nature
6. Geographic names, if their use would cause confusion in relation to the origin of the good or products or services or their source
7. The name of another or the name by which he/she is known or his/her image, or emblem, unless the person, or his/her successors, has previously consented to its use
8. Representations containing honorific titles to which the applicant for registration cannot prove a legal entitlement
9. Marks that deceive the public or that contain false representations as to the origin or source of the products or the services or their other characteristics, as well as marks that contain an illusory, copied, or false commercial name
10. Marks owned by natural or legal persons with whom it is forbidden to deal
11. Marks whose registration for some classes of products or services would reduce the value of other products or services that are distinguished by the mark

12. Marks that contain the following words or expressions: "patent," "patented," "registered," "registered drawing," "copyright," "imitation is counterfeiting" or any words or expressions resembling them.[43]

13. Local and foreign medals and coins and paper money

14. Marks that are considered to be not more than translations of a famous mark or another previously registered mark if the registration of the mark would cause confusion amongst consumers in relation to the products that are distinguished by the mark or similar products.[44]

~~Article 4 [Famous Trademarks]~~

~~A foreign trademark that has an international reputation exceeding the borders of the country from which it originates may not be registered except based on an application made by the true owner.~~

Article 4 [Famous Trademarks]

1. A trademark[45] that has an international reputation that exceeds the borders of the country from which it originates to other countries may not be registered except based on an application made by the original owner *or based on an official authorization from the owner.*

2. The extent to which the mark is known by the relevant public as a result of its promotion is to be taken into account in determining whether the mark has a reputation.

3. A mark that has a reputation may not be registered to distinguish goods or services not similar or not identical to those distinguished by the mark, if:

> *a. the use of the mark would indicate a connection between the goods and services required to be distinguished by it and the goods and services of the owner of the original mark; or*[46]
>
> *b. the use of the mark would lead to the possibility of damage to the owner of the original mark.*

---

43. The Arabic terms used here do not correspond with the Arabic terms used in the relevant laws for the matters mentioned. For example, the word for "patent" (if indeed that is how it should be translated) is "imtiyaz"—a word which does not appear in the UAE's patent law. The expression translated here as copyright does not appear in the UAE's author's rights law. Nevertheless, the context suggests that these are the intended concepts.

44. Federal law no. 7 of 2002, article 1, directed the replacement of article 3 of the TML 1992 with this new article. However, the only change made was the addition of paragraphs 13 and 14.

45. The TML 1992 referred to a "foreign trade mark." The word "foreign" was removed.

46. The "or" is an interpretation. In the Arabic text, paragraph (a) ends in a full stop. The interpretation here is based on the use of "or" in article 10 of the TML 1992A.

Chapter 2: Registration of Trademarks and Their Cancellation

Article 5 [The Register]

[A.] The Ministry is to prepare a register called the register of trademarks in which is to be recorded all trademarks and the names of their owners, their addresses, their kind of activity and descriptions of their goods or products or services and any disposal or assignment or transfer of ownership or mortgage or license to use or any other amendments.

[B.] Any person may request a certified copy of what is recorded in this register after payment of the required fees.

Article 6 [Who May Register a Trademark]

The following persons have the right to register their trademarks:

1. Nationals of the State, being natural or legal persons, who carry on any commercial or industrial business or work as artisans or provide services
2. Foreigners, being natural or legal persons, who carry on any commercial or industrial business or work as artisans or provide services in the State
3. Foreigners, being natural or legal persons, who carry on any commercial or industrial business or work as artisans or provide services in any country that deals with the State reciprocally
4. Public legal persons

Article 7 [Entitlement to Apply to Register a Trademark]

Any person who wishes to use a trademark to distinguish a good or products or services may apply to register it pursuant to the provisions of this law.

The application for registration of the mark is to be filed with the Ministry according to the conditions and terms stated in the implementing regulations.

~~Article 8 [Single Class Applications only]~~

~~A trademark may be registered in respect of one or more class of products or services that are specified in the implementing regulations but an application for registration of a mark may not contain more than one class.~~

Article 8 [Single Class Applications Only]

A trademark may be registered in respect of one or more class of products or services *according to the international classification and its rules that are stated in* the implementing regulations to this law but an application for registration of a mark may not contain more than one class.[47]

Article 9 [Series Marks]

A single application may be filed for the registration of a series of marks that are identical in their essential elements and whose differences are limited to matters not affecting the essential identity of the mark, such as the color of the marks or representations of the products or related services on the condition that they fall within one class.

~~Article 10 [Similar Marks May Not Be Registered]~~

~~Taking into account the provision of article 26 of this law, a trademark that is identical or similar to a previously registered mark may not be registered in the same class of products or services.~~

~~If more than one person applies at the same time for the registration of the same mark or marks that are close or similar in one class of products or services, the Ministry must stop the registration of each of the applications until a legalized assignment is filed by the parties in favor of one of them or until a final judgment is issued in favor of one of them.~~

Article 10 [Similar Marks May Not Be Registered]

Taking into account the provision of article 26 of this law, a trademark that is identical or similar to a previously registered mark may not be registered *for the same products or services, or for products or services that are not the same, if the use of the mark for which registration is sought would give rise to the impression of a connection between it and the products or services of the owner of the registered mark or would lead to the possibility of damage to his interests.*

If more than one person applies *on the same date* for the registration of the same mark or marks that are close or similar *for the same products or services or similar products or services falling in the same* class, the Ministry must stop the registration of each of the applications until a legalized assignment is filed by the parties in favor of one of them or until a final judgment is issued in favor of one of them.[48]

---

47. Federal law no. 7 of 2002, article 1, directed the replacement of article 8 of the TML 1992 with this new article. However, the only change made was the inclusion of a reference to the international classification system (the Nice classification system).
48. Federal law no. 7 of 2002, article 1, directed the replacement of article 10 of the TML 1992 with this new article.

~~Article 11 [Imposing Restrictions and Amendments]~~

~~The Ministry may impose such restrictions and amendments as it considers necessary to particularize or clarify the trademark in order to prevent it being confused with another previously registered mark or for any other reason, and if the Ministry rejects the registration of the trademark for some reason, or suspends the registration to comply with restrictions or amendments, the Ministry must inform the applicant for registration in writing of the reasons for its decision.~~

~~In any case, the Ministry must arrive at a decision in relation to the application for registration within 30 days of the date of filing, when it satisfies the terms and conditions stated in this law and its implementing regulations.~~

Article 11 [Imposing Restrictions and Amendments]

[A]. The Ministry may impose such restrictions and amendments as it considers necessary to particularize or clarify the trademark in order to prevent it being confused with another previously registered mark or for any other reason. *The possibility of causing confusion is presumed if the trademark is used to distinguish identical goods or services*
[B]. If the Ministry rejects the registration of the trademark for some reason, or suspends the registration to comply with restrictions or amendments, the Ministry must inform the applicant for registration in writing of the reasons for its decision.
[C]. In any case, the Ministry must arrive at a decision in relation to the application for registration within thirty days of the date of filing, when it satisfies the terms and conditions stated in this law and its implementing regulations.[49]

Article 12 [Appeals against Rejection of an Application]

[A]. The applicant for registration who has had his application rejected, or its acceptance was suspended to satisfy a condition, may appeal the decision to the committee within thirty days of being informed of the rejection or suspension.
[B]. If the committee supports the Ministry's decision in rejecting the application or suspending the acceptance of the application to satisfy some conditions, the applicant for registration may appeal the decision of the committee to the competent civil court within sixty days of being informed of the committee's decision.

---

49. Federal law no. 7 of 2002, article 1, directed the replacement of article 11 of the TML 1992 with this new article.

[C]. The applicant for registration is deemed to have abandoned his application if he does not appeal the decision of the Ministry or appeal the decision of the committee within the period specified in this article or he does not implement the restrictions or conditions imposed by the Ministry within the period specified in the notice sent to him in the matter.

~~Article 13 [Formation of the Trademark Committee]~~

~~A trademark committee is to be formed headed by the undersecretary to the Ministry of Economy and Commerce and is to consist of two representatives from the Ministry chosen by the Minister and a representative from each emirate chosen by the competent authority.~~

Article 13 [Formation of the Trademark Committee]

A trademark committee is to be formed headed by the undersecretary to the Ministry and is to consist of:
   a. Two members from the Ministry nominated by the Minister
   b. A member from the board of directors of the Federation of Chambers of Commerce and Industry in the State, nominated by the Federation of Chambers
   c. A member from the board of directors of each of the chambers of commerce and industry in the State, nominated by the specific chamber

The committee is to choose from its members a deputy president. A quorum is to consist of a majority of its members and its decisions are to be issued by the majority of the members present. If there is a tied vote, the president's vote is to have the greater weigh. The committee is to meet at least once a month.
   The committee is to have a reporter nominated by the Minister.
   The Cabinet is to specify the remuneration of the members of the committee and the reporter.[50]

~~Article 14 [Advertisement, the Right to Oppose and Opposition Procedure]~~

~~[A.] If the Ministry accepts a trademark it must, before registration, advertise it in the official gazette journal[51] and two daily newspapers issued in the State at the expense of the applicant for registration.~~
~~[B.] Any concerned person may oppose the registration of the trademark and file a written opposition with the Ministry or send it by registered post~~

---

50. Federal law no. 7 of 2002, article 1, directed the replacement of article 13 of the TML 1992 with this new article.
51. Amended by Federal law no. 19 of 2000, article 2.

~~within 30 days from the date of the last advertisement. The Ministry must notify the applicant for registration by means of a copy of the opposition to his application within 15 days of the date of the Ministry's receipt of the opposition.~~
~~[C.] The applicant for registration must file with the Ministry a written reply to the opposition within 30 days of the date of being notified of the opposition and if the reply is not received within this period, the applicant is deemed to have abandoned the application.~~

Article 14 [Advertisement, the Right to Oppose and Opposition Procedure]

[A.] If the Ministry accepts a trademark it must, before registration, advertise it in the journal and two daily newspapers issued in the State *in Arabic* at the expense of the applicant for registration.
[B.] Any concerned person may oppose the registration of the trademark and file a written opposition with the Ministry or send it by registered post *or by email* within thirty days from the date of the last advertisement. The Ministry must notify the applicant for registration by means of a copy of the opposition to his application within 15 days of the date of the Ministry's receipt of the opposition.
[C.] The applicant for registration must file with the Ministry a written reply to the opposition within thirty days of the date of being notified of the opposition and if the reply is not received within this period, the applicant is deemed to have abandoned the application.[52]

Article 15 [Opposition—the Ministry's Decision and Appeals]

[A.] The Ministry must, before deciding the oppositions filed with it, hear the submissions of the parties or one of them if any of them requests.
[B.] The Ministry is to issue its decision rejecting or accepting registration and, in the case of acceptance, may impose the restrictions and conditions it considers appropriate.
[C.] Any concerned person may appeal the decision of the Ministry to the committee within 15 days of the date of being informed of the Ministry's decision and may appeal the decision of the committee to the competent civil court within thirty days of being informed of the decision.

---

52. Federal law no. 7 of 2002, article 1, directed the replacement of article 14 of the TML 1992 with this new article.

[D.] Where a decision of the committee to accept the registration of a trademark is appealed, it does not result in the ceasing of the registration procedures unless the competent court decides otherwise.

~~Article 16 [Registration—the Effective Date and the Certificate]~~

~~[A.] If a trademark becomes registered, the effect of registration is retrospective to the date of the filing of the application.~~
~~[B.] The owner of the mark is to be given, as soon as registration is completed, a certificate containing the following information:~~
~~1. The registration number.~~
~~2. The date of filing of the application and the date of registration.~~
~~3. The commercial name or the name of the owner of the mark and his nationality and place of residence.~~
~~4. An identical image of the mark.~~
~~5. A statement of the products or the goods or the services for the mark and their class.~~

Article 16 [Registration—the Effective Date and the Certificate]

[A.] If a trademark becomes registered, the effect of registration is retrospective to the date of the filing of the application.
[B.] The owner of the mark is to be given, as soon as registration is completed, a certificate containing the following information:

1. The registration number
2. The date of filing of the application and the date of registration.
3. The commercial name or the name of the owner of the mark and his nationality and place of residence
4. An identical image of the mark
5. A statement of the products or the goods or the services for the mark and their class
6. *The number and date of the international priority right and the name of the country that is a member of the Paris convention for the protection of industrial property in which the priority application was filed.*[53]

---

53. Federal law no. 7 of 2002, article 1, directed the replacement of article 16 of the TML 1992 with this new article.

Article 17 [Incontestability after Five Years and the Right of
Exclusive Use]

The person who obtains the registration of a mark is deemed to be the
exclusive owner of the mark and no dispute may be raised against the
ownership of the mark if that person has used the mark continuously for at
least five years from the date of registration with no action having been
commenced challenging its validity.

Article 17 [Incontestability after Five Years and the Right of Exclusive Use]

[A]. The person who obtains the registration of a mark is deemed to be the
exclusive owner of the mark and no dispute may be raised against the
ownership of the mark if that person has used the mark continuously for at
least five years from the date of registration with no action having been
commenced *deciding that he does not own the mark.*
[B]. *The owner of a registered mark is to enjoy the right to prevent others
from using the same or a similar mark to distinguish products or services
that are the same or similar or related to the products and services for
which the mark is registered to the extent that it leads to the causing of
confusion amongst consumers.*[54]

Article 18 [Amendments by the Owner]

The owner of a registered trademark may file at any time an application with
the Ministry to make any addition or amendment to the mark that does not
affect its essential identity. The Ministry is to issue a decision in the matter
pursuant to the conditions and rules set down for deciding initial applications
for registration. The decision is able to be opposed and appealed in the same
way [as an initial application for registration].

Article 18 [Amendments by the Owner]

[A]. The owner of a registered trademark may file at any time an application
with the Ministry to make any addition or amendment to *the products or
services distinguished by the mark or to the mark itself provided that the
amendment* does not affect the essential identity of the mark.
[B]. The Ministry is to issue a decision in the matter *of an application to
amend the products or services pursuant to the conditions and rules relating
to the cancellation of marks for some products or services. As to the*

---

54. Federal law no. 7 of 2002, article 1, directed the replacement of article 17 of the TML
    1992 with this new article.

Ministry's decision to amend a mark, it is to be issued pursuant to the
conditions and rules set down for deciding initial registration applications,
and are able to be opposed or appealed in the same way.
[C]. The amendment is to be published in the journal and in two daily
newspapers issued in the State in Arabic at the expense of the applicant
for amendment.[55]

~~Article 19 [Duration and Renewal]~~

~~[A.] The period of protection resulting from the registration of a trademark is~~
~~ten years. The owner of the mark may secure a continuation of the protec-~~
~~tion for successive periods of ten years by filing an application for renewal~~
~~of the registration of the mark within the last year of the current period of~~
~~protection pursuant to the conditions and terms stated in this law and its~~
~~implementing regulations.~~
~~[B.] The renewal of the registration of the mark is to be done without any~~
~~additional examination and without permitting others to oppose the~~
~~renewal. The renewal of the registration of the mark is to be published in~~
~~the official gazette *journal*~~[56]~~and two daily newspapers issued in the State~~
~~at the cost of the owner of the mark.~~
~~[C.] The application for renewal of a registered mark may not introduce~~
~~any change to the mark or add any products or services to the list of~~
~~products or services for which the mark is registered.~~
~~[D.] The Ministry must, within the month following the end of the period~~
~~of protection, notify the owner of the mark in writing at his address as~~
~~recorded in the register of the end of the period of protection, and if the~~
~~owner of the mark does not file an application of renewal within the~~
~~following three months from the end of the period of protection,~~
~~the Ministry is to remove the mark from the register.~~

Article 19 [Duration and Renewal]

[A.] The period of protection resulting from the registration of a trademark
is ten years. The owner of the mark may secure a continuation of the
protection for successive periods of ten years by filing an application for
renewal of the registration of the mark within the last year of the current
period of protection pursuant to the conditions and terms stated in this
law and its implementing regulations.

---

55. Federal law no. 7 of 2002, article 1, directed the replacement of article 18 of the TML
    1992 with this new article.
56. Amended by federal law no. 19 of 2000, article 2.

[B.] The renewal of the registration of the mark is to be done without any additional examination and without permitting others to oppose the renewal. The renewal of the registration of the mark is to be published in the journal and two daily newspapers issued in the State *in Arabic* at the cost of the owner of the mark.

[C.] The application for renewal of a registered mark may not introduce any change to the mark or add any products or services to the list of products or services for which the mark is registered.

[D.] The Ministry must, within the month following the end of the period of protection, notify the owner of the mark in writing at his address as recorded in the register of the end of the period of protection, and if the owner of the mark does not file an application of renewal within the following three months from the end of the period of protection, the Ministry is to remove the mark from the register of its own volition.[57]

Article 20 [A. Cancellation by the Owner]

[1]. The owner of a trademark may apply for the cancellation of its registration from the register, whether in respect of all or some of the products or services for which the mark is registered. The application for cancellation is to be filed pursuant to the conditions and terms stated in the implementing regulations to this law.

[2]. If the use of the mark is licensed pursuant to a contract registered in the trademark register, the registration of the mark may not be cancelled except with the written agreement of the licensee unless the licensee has expressly waived this right in the license contract.

Article 20 [B. Cancellation by the Ministry]

The Ministry may cancel a mark that has been registered without a right after notifying those concerned of the reason for the cancellation and hearing their submissions and considering their defenses. The concerned persons may appeal the cancellation decision to the competent civil court within thirty days from the date of notification of the cancellation.[58]

---

57. Federal law no. 7 of 2002, article 1, directed the replacement of article 19 of the TML 1992 with this new article. The only change made was the addition of the words "in Arabic."

58. Federal law no. 7 of 2002, article 2, directed the addition of a "repeated" article 20 of the TML 1992, leaving the current article 20 in place. To distinguish the two articles 20, I have called the first 20 A and the second 20 B.

~~Article 21 [Cancellation of Trademarks Registered Without a Right]~~

~~Without prejudice to the provision of article 17, the Ministry, and any concerned person, has the right to request a decision cancelling a trademark that has been registered without a right. The Ministry must cancel the registration when a final decision to this effect is filed with it.~~

Article 21 [Cancellation of Trademarks Registered Without a Right]

Without prejudice to the provision of article 17 *of this law, any concerned person* has the right to request a decision cancelling a trademark that has been registered without a right. The Ministry must cancel the registration when a *final signed decision has been filed with it in implementable form.*[59]

~~Article 22 [Cancellation for Non-use]~~

~~The competent civil court may, based on an application by any concerned person, order the cancellation of the registration of a trademark if it is proved before the court that the mark has not been seriously used for five consecutive years, unless the owner of the mark offers a justification for the non-use of the mark.~~

Article 22 [Cancellation for Non-use]

[A]. The competent civil court may, based on an application by any concerned person, order the cancellation of the registration of a trademark if it is proved before the court that the mark has not been *used for five consecutive years,* unless the owner of the mark *proves that the non-use of the mark was for a reason outside of his control. Import restrictions and other government conditions imposed on goods or services distinguished by the mark are deemed to be such reasons.*
[B]. *For the purposes of this article, use of a mark by a person authorized by the owner to do so is deemed to be use of it.*[60]

~~Article 23 [Amendment of the Register]~~

~~The competent civil court may, based on an application by the Ministry or any concerned person, order the addition of any information in the register that~~

---

59. Federal law no. 7 of 2002, article 1, directed the replacement of article 21 of the TML 1992 with this new article.
60. Federal law no. 7 of 2002, article 1, directed the replacement of article 22 of the TML 1992 with this new article.

~~has been omitted from it, or the removal or amendment of any information stated in the register if it was entered unlawfully or it is inconsistent with the truth.~~

Article 23 [Amendment of the Register]

The competent civil court may, based on an application by *a concerned person*, order the addition of any information in the register that has been omitted from it, or the removal or amendment of any information stated in the register if it was entered unlawfully or it is inconsistent with the truth. *The Ministry may do these things of its own volition.*[61]

Article 24 [Cancellation Ordered by the Israeli Boycott Office]

The Ministry must cancel the registration of a trademark if the Israeli Boycott Office in the State decides that the mark resembles or is identical to an Israeli mark or symbol or emblem, or that the mark is owned by persons in relation to whom a decision prohibiting dealing with them has been issued.

~~Article 25 [Publication of Cancellation]~~

~~The cancellation of a trademark from the register must be published in the official gazette *journal.*~~[62]

Article 25 [Publication of Cancellation]

The cancellation of a trademark from the register must be published in the journal *and in two daily newspapers issued in the State in Arabic at the expense of the applicant for cancellation.*[63]

Article 26 [Re-registration of Cancelled Marks]

If the registration of a trademark is cancelled, it is not possible to re-register the mark in the name of any other person for the same products for three years from the date of cancellation.

---

61. Federal law no. 7 of 2002, article 1, directed the replacement of article 23 of the TML 1992 with this new article.
62. Amended by federal law no. 19 of 2000, article 2.
63. Federal law no. 7 of 2002, article 1, directed the replacement of article 25 of the TML 1992 with this new article.

Chapter 3: Transfers and Mortgages of Ownership of Trademarks

Article 27 [Assignments, Mortgages and Attachments]

The ownership of a trademark may be transferred or mortgaged or attached with or without the business or investment project that uses the trademark to distinguish its products or services.

Article 28 [Sale of Business]

[A.] The transfer of the ownership of a business or investment project may include the trademark registered in the name of the transferor of the ownership that has a close connection with the business or investment project unless it has been agreed otherwise.

[B.] If the ownership of a business or investment project is transferred without the mark, the transferor of the ownership may continue to use the mark for the products or services for which the mark has been registered unless it has been agreed otherwise.

Article 29 [Recordal of Assignments and Mortgages]

The transfer of ownership of a trademark or the mortgage of it is not effective against others until after it has been recorded in the register of marks and published in the manner specified in the implementing regulations.

Chapter 4: Contracts for Licensing the Use of a Trademark

Article 30 [Licenses]

[A.] The owner of a trademark may, pursuant to a written and legalized contract, license to one or more persons the use of the mark in relation to all or some of the products or services for which the mark is registered. The owner of the mark may use the mark himself unless it has been agreed otherwise.

[B.] The period of the license to use the mark may not exceed the period set down for the protection of the mark.

Article 31 [Recordal of Licenses]

Contracts licensing the use of trademarks must be recorded in the register of trademarks. The license is not effective against others until after it has been recorded in the register and published in the manner specified in the implementing regulations.

~~Article 32 [Assignment of Licenses]~~

~~The licensee may not assign to another or grant sub-licenses unless the license contract states otherwise.~~

Article 32 [Assignment of Licenses]

The licensee may not assign to another or grant sub-licenses unless the license contract states otherwise.
In no circumstances is it permitted for the exploitation of a trademark to be compelled by a compulsory license.[64]

Article 33 [Cancellation of a License Recordal]

[A.] The recordal of a license is to be cancelled from the register based on an application by the owner of the mark or the licensee after filing proof of the expiry or termination of the license contract.
[B.] The Ministry must inform the other party of the application filed to cancel the license, and that party may oppose the application for cancellation in accordance with the procedures and conditions stated in the implementing regulations.

Article 34 [Permitting Restrictions in Licenses]

The license contract may not contain any terms binding the licensee to restrictions that do not result from the rights granted by trademark registration or that are not necessary for the preservation of those rights, but the license contract may contain the following restrictions:

1. A specification of the geographical area for the marketing of the products or services bearing the mark.

---

64. Federal law no. 7 of 2002, article 1, directed the replacement of article 32 of the TML 1992 with this new article.

2. A specification of the period of the license for use of the mark, taking into account the provisions of article 31 of this law.[65]
3. The conditions by which the owner of the mark ensures the monitoring of the quality of the products to which the license applies.
4. An obligation on the licensee to refrain from all acts that may result in the reduction of, or harm to, the value of the products or services that bear the mark.

Chapter 5: Trademarks for Indicating that Specific Products Have Been Monitored or Examined

Article 35 [Monitoring Marks]

[A.] Legal persons who are responsible for the monitoring or examination of some products or services as to their source, constitutive elements, method of production, quality, identity or any other characteristics, may apply with the Ministry for a license to register the mark that is specifically for indicating the monitoring or examination.
[B.] In any case, this mark may not be registered and its ownership may not be transferred except with the consent of the Minister.

Article 36 [Regulations for Monitoring Marks]

[A.] The implementing regulations are to specify the conditions and rules for the registration of the mark referred to in the previous article and the supporting documents required to be attached to the application for registration.
[B.] The registration of this mark results in all of the consequences stated for it in this law.
[C.] In the event that the mentioned mark is cancelled or not renewed, it may not be registered again for the same or similar products or goods or services.

---

65. The reference to article 31 appears to be an error and should have been a reference to article 30 where the period of the license is mentioned.

Chapter 6: Penalties

~~Article 37 [Counterfeiting]~~

~~A punishment of imprisonment and a fine of not less than 5000 dirhams, or either one of them, is to be imposed on:~~

~~1. Anyone who has counterfeited trademark registered pursuant to the law or has imitated it in a manner leading to the deception of the public, and anyone who has used in bad faith a counterfeited or imitated trademark.~~
~~2. Anyone who has used without a right a registered trademark owned by another.~~
~~3. Anyone who has, in bad faith, put on his products a registered trademark owned by another.~~
~~4. Anyone who has sold, or offered for sale or circulation, or possessed with the intention of selling, products bearing a counterfeited or imitated trademark or a mark placed on them without a right to do so and with knowledge of the fact.~~
~~5. Anyone who has offered to provide services under a counterfeited or imitated trademark or has used it without a right to do so and with knowledge of the fact.~~

Article 37 [Counterfeiting]

A punishment of imprisonment and a fine of not less than 5000 dirhams, or either one of them, is to be imposed on:

1. Anyone who has counterfeited a trademark registered pursuant to the law or has imitated it in a manner that will lead to the deception of the public, *whether in relation to goods and services that the original mark distinguishes, or those that are similar to them, and anyone who has used a counterfeited or imitated trademark with knowledge of that.*
2. Anyone who has, in bad faith, put on his products a registered trademark owned by another or used that mark without a right.
3. Anyone who has sold, or offered for sale or circulation, or possessed with the intention of selling, products bearing a counterfeited or imitated trademark or a mark placed on them without a right to do so and with knowledge of the fact, as well as anyone who has provided or offered to provide services under a counterfeited or imitated trademark or has used it without a right to do so and with knowledge of the fact.[66]

---

66. Federal law no. 7 of 2002, article 1, directed the replacement of article 37 of the TML 1992 with this new article.

~~Article 38 [Using a Mark That May Not Be Registered and~~
~~Misrepresenting That a Mark is Registered]~~

~~A punishment of imprisonment not exceeding one year and a fine of not less~~
~~than 5000 dirhams and not more than 10,000 dirhams, or either one of them,~~
~~is to be imposed on:~~
~~1. Anyone who uses a trademark that is not capable of registration accord-~~
~~ing to what is stated in paragraphs 2, 3, 4, 5, 6, 8, 9, 10, 11 and 12 of~~
~~article 3 of this law.~~
~~2. Anyone who, without a right to do so, puts on his mark or commercial~~
~~papers representations that lead to the belief that the mark is registered.~~

Article 38 [Using a Mark That May Not Be Registered and Misrepresenting That a Mark is Registered]

A punishment of imprisonment not exceeding one year and a fine of not less than 5000 dirhams and not more than 10,000 dirhams, or either one of them, is to be imposed on:

1. Anyone who uses a trademark that is not capable of registration according to what is stated in paragraphs 2, 3, 4, 5, 6, 8, 9, 10, 11, 12, *13, and 14* of article 3 of this law.
2. Anyone who, without a right to do so, puts on his mark or *documents* representations that lead to the belief that the mark is registered, *or distinguishes products or goods other than what is mentioned in the register.*[67]

Article 39 [Penalties for Repeat Offenders]

Anyone who commits any one of the crimes stated in articles 37 and 38 of this law, and who repeats the offense, is to be punished by the same penalties in addition to the closure of the place of business or investment project for not less than 15 days and not more than 6 months with the publication of the judgment at the expense of the defendant pursuant to the procedures specified in the implementing regulations.

Article 40 [Right to Compensation]

Anyone who has suffered damage as a result of any act stated in articles 37 or 38 of this law may raise a case in the competent civil court requesting that the

---

67. Federal law no. 7 of 2002, article 1, directed the replacement of article 38 of the TML 1992 with this new article.

person responsible for the act pay compensation commensurate with the damage suffered.

~~Article 41 [Precautionary Measures]~~

~~[A.] The owner of a trademark may, at any time, even before raising any civil or criminal case, apply for an order from the competent court, based on a petition supported by an official certificate evidencing the registration of the mark, to take the necessary precautionary measures, and in particular the following:~~

~~1. To make a case report and detailed description of the machines and tools used or have been used in the commission of any crime stated in this law, as well as of local or imported products or goods, the addresses of the shops or packaging or papers or other things on which the mark has been put or information the subject of the crime.~~
~~2. To attach the things mentioned in the previous paragraph after the applicant has filed financial security as estimated by the court to compensate the attachee when necessary.~~

~~[B.] The court may appoint one or more experts to cooperate in the implementation of the precautionary measures, and in any case, the precautionary measures that are undertaken by the owner of the mark will be deemed void if they are not followed by a civil or criminal case against the person against whom the procedures were undertaken within 8 days following the issue of the order.~~

Article 41 [Precautionary Measures]

[A.] The owner of a trademark may, at any time, even before raising *any case*, apply for an order from the competent court, based on a petition supported by an official certificate evidencing the registration of the mark, to take the necessary precautionary measures, and in particular the following:

1. To make a case report and detailed description of the machines and tools used or have been used in the commission of any crime stated in this law, as well as of local or imported products or goods, the addresses of the shops or packaging or papers or other things on which the mark has been put or information the subject of the crime.
2. To attach the things mentioned in the previous paragraph after the applicant has filed financial security as estimated by the court to compensate the attachee when necessary.

[B.] The court may appoint one or more experts to assist in the implementation of the precautionary measures.

[C.] The owners of famous marks are not required to file a certificate evidencing registration of the mark.[68]

Article 42 [Seizure Defendant's Right to Compensation]

The attachee may raise a case requesting compensation from the attachor within ninety days beginning from the end of the period stated in the last paragraph of article 41 of this law, if a case is not raised against the attachee, or within ninety days from the issue of a final decision in the case raised against him. In either case, the security is not to be returned to the attachor except after the issue of a final judgment in the case brought by the attachee, or after the end of the period set down for him to raise a case and no case was raised.

~~Article 43 [What the Court May Order]~~

~~In any civil or criminal case, the court may order the confiscation of things that have been attached or that are yet to be attached and the subtraction of their value from the fines or compensation or the disposal of them in any other way the court considers suitable. The court may also order the destruction of the unlawful marks or order when necessary the destruction of the products and wrapping and packaging materials that bear the mark or bear unlawful representations, as well as machines and tools that were used specifically for the counterfeiting operation. The court may also order any of the above in the case of a judgment of innocence. The court may order the publication of the judgment in the official gazette journal[69] or in any one of the daily newspapers at the expense of the defendant.~~

Article 43 [What the Court May Order]

The competent court may order the confiscation of things that have been attached or that are yet to be attached and the subtraction of their value from the fines or compensation or the disposal of them in any other way the court considers suitable. The court may also order the destruction of the unlawful marks or order when necessary the destruction of the products and wrapping and packaging materials that bear the mark or bear unlawful representations, as well as machines and tools that were used specifically for the counterfeiting operation. The court may also order any of the above in the case of a judgment of innocence. The court may order the publication of the judgment *at the*

---

68. Federal law no. 7 of 2002, article 1, directed the replacement of article 41 of the TML 1992 with this new article.
69. Amended by federal law no. 19 of 2000, article 2.

expense of the defendant in the journal or in any one of the newspapers
issued in the State in Arabic.[70]

Chapter 7: General and Transitional Provisions

Article 44 [Transition Procedures]

[A.] Owners of trademarks registered or used in the emirates must, within
one year from this law becoming effective, file an application to record
them in the register of the Ministry in accordance with the provisions and
conditions stated for them in the law.

[B.] Those who did not satisfy the conditions set down in this law must
rectify their circumstances within one year of the law becoming effective
and if the trademark does not satisfy the conditions set down within the
period stated for it in the previous paragraph, it will be considered expired
by force of the law.

[C.] The first user has the right of priority to register his mark within this
period and the date of commencing use, the continuity of the use and the
circumstances surrounding it are to be taken into account in the registration
of the mark.

Article 45 [Ministry to Notify Each Emirate of Trademark Details]

The Ministry must notify the competent authority in each emirate and the
Federal Chamber of Commerce and Industry and the Chambers of the
Commerce and Industry in the State of the names of the owners and details of
trademarks registered with the Ministry, and of changes and amendments and
cancellations that may occur within thirty days from the date of the registration
or change or amendment or cancellation.

Article 46 [Powers of Certain Employees]

Employees responsible for monitoring the implementation of this law and the
decisions implementing it and who are specified in a decision issued by the
Minister of Justice with the agreement of the Minister of Economy and
Commerce and the competent authority, are to have the title of judicial seizure
officers, and the right to enter places in which activities within the scope of

---

70. Federal law no. 7 of 2002, article 1, directed the replacement of article 41 of the TML 1992
    with this new article.

this law are being carried on, excluding places of residence, to ensure compliance with the law and the decisions implementing it and to identify cases of violations. The local authorities in the emirates are to provide to them the facilities necessary to enable them to carry out their work.

Article 47 [Fees]

A decision is to be issued by the Cabinet specifying the fees that are to be paid for the procedures that are to be done pursuant to the provisions of this law.

Article 48 [Conflicting Laws Void]

Any provision violating or contradicting the provisions of this law are repealed.

Article 49 [Regulations]

The Minister is to issue the regulations and decisions necessary to implement the provisions of this law.

Article 50 [Effective Date]

This law is to be published in the official gazette and is to become effective three months after the date of publication.

Zayed Bin Sultan Al Nahyan
President of the United Arab Emirates

Issued from the Presidential Palace in Abu Dhabi
Date: Rabe'a Al Thani 1, 1413 H
Corresponding to: September 28, 1992 M.

Ministerial decision no. 6 of 1993 Concerning the Implementing Regulations for Federal Law No. 37 of 1992 in Relation to Trademarks

Contents

Chapter 8: Marks for Indicating the Monitoring of Specific Products
and Their Examination

The Minister of Economy and Commerce,

After considering Federal law no. 1 of 1972 in relation to the jurisdictions of the Ministries and the powers of the Ministers and the law amending it, and

Federal law no. 37 of 1992 in relation to trademarks,

And based on what was presented by the Undersecretary,

Decided:

Chapter 1: Definitions

Article 1

In the application of the provisions of this decision, the words and expressions below are intended to have the following meanings:

The State: The United Arab Emirates.

The Ministry: The Ministry of Economy and Commerce.

The Minister: The Minister of Economy and Commerce.

The law: The trademarks law.

Mark: Trademark.

The register: The register of trademarks.

The section: The section for the monitoring of trade.

The committee: The trademarks committee referred to in article 13 of the law.

The competent authority: The competent authority in the concerned emirate.

Article 2 [Section Responsible for the Law]

The section in the Ministry is responsible for the application of the trademarks law and its implementing regulations and the collection of the required fees.

Article 3 [Who May File a Trademark Application]

Applications for registration of marks are to be filed with the section by the owner of the mark using the form prepared for this purpose, if he has residency in the State, or by a licensed lawyers' office in the State. An image of the mark for which registration is requested is to be pasted in the space provided for it in the form.

Article 4 [Single Class Applications Only]

The application for registration of a mark is to be limited to one class of products or goods or services shown in attachment 1 to these regulations.

Article 5 [Contents of the Application]

The application for registration must contain the following information:

1. The name of the applicant, his title, his profession and his commercial name, if any, and if the applicant is a company, its name or address, and its type and purpose are to be mentioned
2. The nationality of the applicant, his place of residence and the nature of his business
3. The mark for which registration is requested
4. A statement of the goods or products or services for which registration is requested, together with the number of the class to which they belong
5. The party in whose business or investment project the mark is to be used or is required for use to distinguish its goods or products or services
6. The chosen place in the United Arab Emirates, if any, to which correspondence and documents related to the registration are to be sent
7. The signature of the applicant or his representative, and if the application is filed by a company or establishment, the signature of the person entitled to represent it

Article 6 [Series Marks]

If the applicant for registration has a group of marks that are similar in their essential elements and whose differences are limited to matters that do not affect their essential nature and their registration is requested for goods or products or services falling in one of the classes shown in attachment 1, a single application may be filed for their registration.

Article 7 [Attachments to the Application]

The following are to be attached to the application for registration:

1. Ten images identical to the mark pasted in the application form for registration
2. A legalized power of attorney, if the application is filed by a lawyers' office on behalf of the concerned person
3. Certificate of registration in the commercial register, or its equivalent in or outside of the State
4. Certificate of registration of the mark in any foreign country, if priority is claimed

Article 8 [Translation of the Mark]

If the mark whose registration is requested contains one or more words written in a foreign language, a reliable translation into Arabic must be filed.

Chapter 2: Procedures for Registration

Article 9 [The Register and Filing Receipt]

Applications for registration are to be recorded in a register in the Ministry called "the register of filed applications" by consecutive numbers according to their dates of filing, and the applicant is to be given a receipt for the application containing the following information:

1. The serial number for the application
2. The name of the applicant for registration and his place of residence
3. The date and hour of filing of the application
4. The class of products or goods or services to which the application relates
5. A statement of the documents attached to the application

Article 10 [Examination of the Application]

The section is to examine the application for registration and check it and determine that the mark whose registration is requested is not identical or similar to a mark that was registered previously, or for which an application for registration was previously filed, or that the mark is not banned by the Israeli boycott office in the Ministry, and in relation to marks that are specifically for indicating the monitoring or examination of particular products, the section is to determine that the Minister has approved them.

Article 11 [Requests for Further Information, Conditions and Restrictions and Amendments of the Mark]

Before making a decision in relation to the application for registration, the section may require the applicant or his representative (lawyers' office) to file information that it considers necessary or impose conditions for acceptance of the application, and may require the applicant to make amendments to the mark that it considers necessary to particularize it or clarify it in a way that prevents confusion of it with another mark that has been previously registered or filed.

Article 12 [Rejection or Suspension of an Application]

If the section decides to reject the application for registration or suspend its acceptance because of conditions or amendments, the applicant must be notified in writing of the reasons for the decision. The notice must contain a statement of the right of the applicant to appeal to the committee mentioning the dates and procedures relating to the appeal.

Article 13 [Filing an Appeal]

If an appeal is filed with the committee, the section must inform the applicant for registration of the date of convening of the committee to consider the appeal and request his presence before it to present what information he has. The notice requesting his attendance must be given to him at least ten days before the date of the hearing by registered post, fax or telex.

Article 14 [Rejection of Appeal]

If the committee rejects the appeal, the applicant may appeal the decision of the committee to the competent civil court within sixty days of the date of being informed of the decision.

Article 15 [Abandonment of the Application]

If the applicant does not complete the information or conditions requested by the section with the specified period, or if he does not appeal the decision of the committee within the period specified in the notice addressed to him, the applicant is deemed to have abandoned his application.

Article 16 [Publication of the Application]

If the application is accepted, before registering the mark the section must publish the following information about the application in the official gazette and two daily newspapers issued in the State at the expense of the applicant:

1. The name of the applicant for registration, his nationality, his profession, and his place of residence
2. An identical copy of the mark
3. The serial number of the application for registration
4. The goods or products or services for which registration is requested with the class in which they fall
5. The party in whose business or project the mark is to be used or is required for use to distinguish its goods or products or services

Article 17 [Thirty-day Opposition Period]

Any concerned person may—within thirty days of the date of the last publication of the mark—file a written opposition with the section or send it to the section by registered post.

The section must notify the applicant for registration, with a copy of the opposition to his application, within 15 days of receiving the opposition.

Article 18 [Response to the Opposition]

If the applicant does not file with the section a written response to the opposition mentioned in the previous article within thirty days of the date of being notified of it, the applicant is deemed to have abandoned his application.

Article 19 [Hearing the Opposition]

The section must hear each of the parties to the opposition, if any one of them makes a request to be heard, and must decide the opposition after the hearing and issue its decision rejecting or approving registration or imposing limitations or conditions on acceptance.

Article 20 [Appeal to the Committee and the Court]

Any concerned person may appeal a decision of the section issued pursuant to the previous article to the committee within 15 days of being notified of it, and if the committee does not accept the appeal, he has the right to appeal the decision before a competent court within 30 days of the date of its decision.

Article 21 [Contents of the Register]

The section is to maintain a register of registered trademarks, allocating one page for each trademark and recording in it the following information:

1. The serial number for the mark and an image of it.
2. The date of filing of the application for registration and the date of its registration
3. The name of the owner of the mark, his title, his nationality, his place of residence and his commercial name (if any), and if the owner is a company, its name, address, purpose and headquarters are to be mentioned
4. The goods or products or services for which the mark is registered and the class in which they fall
5. The chosen place in the State to which correspondence and letters relating to the registration are to be sent
6. The party in whose business or project the mark is to be used to distinguish its goods or products or services
7. The conditions that the section requested to obtain registration
8. Any amendment that occurs after registration
9. Transfers of ownership of the mark or mortgages of it
10. Cancellation of mortgages
11. Renewal of marks and cancellation of them
12. Licenses for use of marks, their term and cancellation

Article 22 [Associated Marks and Series Marks]

[A.] In the page for each mark is to be recorded trademarks that are associated with the mark and information as to the association, mentioning the numbers of the associated marks.
[B]. One page is to be allocated to the registration of groups of marks referred to in article 6 of these regulations and the marks constituting the group are to be noted in it, as well as what indicates that the marks are connected.

Article 23 [Registered for All Colors]

If a mark is registered without specifying that it has a specific color, it is deemed to be registered for all colors.

Article 24 [Certificate of Registration]

The owner of the mark—after the completion of registration and paying the fees—is to be provided with a certificate in the form specified for it.

Article 25 [Each Emirate and Others to Be Informed]

The section is to inform the competent authority in each emirate and the federation of chambers of commerce and industry and the chambers of commerce in the State of the name of the owner of the mark and the information indicated in the registration certificate within thirty days of the date of registration. They are to maintain a special register containing the information supplied by the Ministry and set out in the registration certificate referred to in article 24 of these registrations. Each mark is to have its own page in the register.

Chapter 3: Amendments or Additions to the Register

Article 26 [Amending a Mark]

The owner of the mark who wants to enter an amendment or addition to his registered mark not affecting the essential character of it must file an application using the form specified for it with the section attaching ten images of the mark after being amended. The section is to review the application according to the conditions and rules relating to original registration applications. The same objection and appeal avenues and procedures that apply to original applications also apply to the decision in relation to this application.

Article 27 [Other Amendments]

The owner of a registered mark may request the recordal of the following information in the register:

1. A change of name or title of the owner or his profession or his nationality, and in the case of companies, any change that occurs in its name or address or purpose is to be recorded.
2. Cancellation of some of the goods or products or services specified for the mark.
3. A change in the chosen place for letters and correspondence and papers relating to the registration.

If the information requested to be recorded relates to associated marks, it is sufficient to file one application to record the information in the registration pages of these marks.

Article 28 [Court Orders to be Recorded]

Any procedure ordered in a judgment by a competent court is to be recorded in the register.

Article 29 [Responsibilities of the Section]

The section is to be responsible for recording marks in the register and publishing them in the official gazette after paying the publication costs. The register is to contain the mark's serial number, the name of its owner, and the details of amendments and changes that have occurred with a reference to the number of the official gazette in which the registration of the mark was published.

The section is to inform the competent authority in each emirate and the federation of chambers of commerce and industry and the chambers of commerce and industry in the State of the change or amendment within thirty days of its date.

Chapter 4: Renewal of the Registration of a Mark

Article 30 [Renewal Within the Last Year of Protection]

An application for the renewal of the protection period resulting from registration may be filed with the section using the form specified for it within the last year of the period of protection for the mark and attaching to it the certificate of registration and proof of payment of the renewal fees.

Article 31 [Late Renewal]

During the month following the expiry of the period of protection of the mark, the section is to notify the owner in writing at his address as recorded in the register of the expiry of the period of its protection, and the owner must file an application for renewal following the method referred to in the previous article within three months following the date of expiry of the period of protection.

Article 32 [No Examination or Oppositions for Renewals]

Accepted renewal applications are to be approved without any additional examination and without permitting others to oppose the renewal if the application is filed in time and in the circumstances referred to in articles 30 and 31 of these regulations.

Article 33 [Publication of Renewal]

The renewal of the registration of a mark is to be published in the official gazette and in two daily newspapers issued in the State, at the cost of the owner, and must contain the following information:

1. The serial number of the mark
2. The name of the owner, his profession and his place of residence, and if the owner is a company, its name or address and purpose are to be mentioned
3. The date of registration of the mark

Chapter 5: Cancellation of Registration

Article 34 [Cancellation by the Owner]

The owner of a trademark who wishes to cancel its registration for all or some of the goods or products or services for which it is registered must file an application with the section using the specified form, and if it appears from the state of the register that there is a license for the use of the mark, the cancellation may only be made based on written approval from the licensee, unless the license agreement includes a provision by which the licensee expressly consents to his abandonment of the license.

Article 35 [Cancellation by the Section]

The section is to cancel a mark in the following circumstances:

1. If a registration is not renewed pursuant to article 19 of the law
2. Upon application by its owner pursuant to the provisions of article 20 of the law. The cancellation is to be effective from the date of the application
3. Upon the issue of a final judgment from a competent court that the registration of the mark was without a right
4. Upon issue of a judgment from a competent court to cancel the mark because of an unjustified absence of serious use of the mark for a consecutive five year period pursuant to article 22 of the law
5. Upon a decision of the Minister based on a letter from the Israeli boycott office in the United Arab Emirates pursuant to article 24 of the law

Article 36 [Publication of Cancellation]

[A.] The section is to note the cancellation in the register and publish the cancellation in the official gazette. It must contain the following information:

1. The serial number of the mark
2. The name of the owner, his profession and his place of residence, and if the owner is a company, its name or address and purpose are to be mentioned
3. The number of the official gazette in which the registration was published
4. The reason for cancellation and its date

[B.] The section is to inform the competent authority in each emirate and the federation of chambers of commerce and industry and the chambers of commerce and industry in the State of the cancellation within thirty days.

Chapter 6: Transfer of the Ownership of a Mark and Mortgages

Article 37 [Transfers to be Recorded]

Transfers of ownership of a mark that are permitted by the law are to be recorded in the register upon application filed with the section by the assignee or his agent (lawyers' office). The application is to be written on the form prepared for this purpose containing the following information:

1. The serial number of the mark
2. The name, the title and the profession of the party transferring ownership and the party receiving ownership, and his commercial name

and profession, and if either of them is a company, its name or address
and purpose for being established are to be mentioned
3. The place of residence of the applicant and his nationality
4. A statement of the goods or products or services that are distinguished
by the mark, together with the class in which they belong
5. The party whose business or investment project the mark is to protect
6. The document by which the ownership of the mark was transferred
and its date

Article 38 [Proof of the Transfer of Ownership]

The application referred to in the previous article is to have attached to it the
documents proving the transfer of the ownership of mark, and if the applicant
is a company, a copy of the registration page from the commercial register is to
be attached.[71]

Article 39 [Transfer of Associated Marks]

An application may not be filed for the transfer of ownership of one mark that
is deemed to be associated with other marks pursuant to article 6 of these
regulations without the remainder of the other associated marks.

A single application may be filed to record in the register the transfer of
ownership of associated marks.

Article 40 [The Section's Responsibilities]

The section is to record in the register the transfer of the ownership of the
mark, mentioning the name of the new owner, his profession, his address,
the reason for the transfer of ownership and the date of obtaining ownership,
and the date of recording it in the register. The section is to inform the
applicant in writing of the recordal.

Article 41 [Publication of Transfers of Ownership]

The transfer of ownership of the mark is to be published in the official gazette
and in two daily newspapers at the cost of the applicant and is to include the
following information:

1. The serial number of the mark
2. The date of registration and number and date of the official gazette in
which the registration was published

---

71. The requirement for the commercial register extract was removed by article 1 of Ministerial
Decision no. 68 of 2001.

3. The goods or products or services that belong to the mark

4. The name of the previous owner of the mark

5. The name, the nationality and the profession of the assignee

6. The date of transfer of the ownership and the date of its recordal in the register

Article 42 [Mortgages to Be Recorded]

Mortgages of marks are to be recorded in the register under the same procedures and circumstances as transfers of ownership, based on an application filed by the mortgagee using the specified form. The mortgage is to be published in the official gazette and in two daily newspapers with the same information set out in article 41 of these regulations.

Article 43 [Cancellation of Mortgages]

[A.] The mortgage may be cancelled based on an application filed by the owner of the mark with the section using the specified form, accompanied by documents evidencing the expiry of the mortgage.

[B.] The cancellation is to be published in the official gazette at the expense of the applicant and contain the number and date of the official gazette in which the mortgage of the mark was published.

Chapter 7: License Contracts for the Use of a Mark

Article 44 [Licenses to be in Writing]

Licenses for the use of a trademark may be for one or more persons and for all or some of the products or goods or services for which the mark is registered but they must be pursuant to a written and legalized contract for a period not exceeding the period of protection for the mark itself.

Article 45 [Publication of Licenses]

Licenses of a mark are to be published in the official gazette and in two daily newspapers at the cost of the applicant. Publication is to include the following information:

1. The serial number of the mark

2. The date of registration and number and date of the official gazette in which the registration was published

3. The goods or products or services that belong to the mark[72]
4. The name of the owner of the mark, his title, profession, and nationality
5. The name, the title, the profession, and the nationality of the licensee
6. The date of the license for use of the mark and the date of its recordal in the register

Article 46 [Cancellation of a License Recordal]

[A.] Based on an application by the owner of the mark, or the beneficiary of the license, filed with the section using the specified form, a license recordal may be cancelled.

[B.] Evidence of the expiry of the license or its termination must be attached to the application.

Article 47 [Opposition to the Cancellation of Licenses]

The section must hear each of the parties to the opposition if any one of them makes a request to be heard. Within 15 days of receiving the application, it is to notify the other party to the license contract of the contents of the application filed for cancellation, making it clear that he has the right to oppose the application for cancellation within 30 days of receiving this notice, otherwise he loses his right to oppose.[73]

Article 48 [Right to be Heard]

The section must hear any of the parties in the matter of the opposition when one of them requests the hearing of his submissions, and the section will then make a decision rejecting or accepting the opposition.

Article 49 [Appeals]

Each party has the right to appeal the decision of the section to the committee within 15 days of him being notified of it, and any one of them has the right to appeal the decision of the committee to the competent court within 30 days of being notified of the decision of the committee.

---

72. This paragraph was amended by article 2 of ministerial decision no. 68 of 2001 to read: "the goods or products or services registered and licensed for use of the mark."
73. The procedure outlined by the Arabic text of this article is difficult to piece together and may contain an error. The translation here expresses what may have been intended.

Article 50 [After a Final Decision]

If there is no opposition to the cancellation of a license or a final decision to cancel the license has issued, the section is to cancel the license from the register, mentioning the reason for the cancellation and its date, and to inform the applicant in writing of the cancellation.

Article 51 [Publication of Cancellation]

The section is to publish the cancellation of the license in the official gazette at the cost of the applicant, including in the publication the number and date of the official gazette in which the license for use of the mark was published.

Chapter 8: Marks for Indicating the Monitoring of Specific Products and Their Examination

Article 52 [The Application for Registration]

Applications for registration of marks for indicating the monitoring of specific products or their examination may be filed with the section using the form prepared for this purpose accompanied by the following documents:

1. Ten images of the mark identical to the image pasted in the registration application form
2. Two official copies of the constitution of the legal person that will be responsible for the monitoring or examination with a statement of any amendments that may have been made to the articles
3. The Minister's approval for the registration of the mark
4. Two copies of the list of goods or products or services on which the mark will be used once examined, with a statement of their characteristics and types
5. A statement of the persons who will use the mark
6. Two copies of the rules that the applicant for registration will follow in the monitoring and examination processes with a statement of any amendments that may have been made to these rules

Article 53 [Registration Conditions]

The marks referred to in this chapter are to be registered in a special section of the register under the same conditions and rules followed in the registration of other marks.

Article 54 [Publication]

The publication of these marks is to be accompanied by a summary of the rules that the applicant is to follow in the monitoring and examination processes.

Article 55 [Amendments to the Rules]

Any amendment done by the owner of the mark to the rules must be notified to the section and recorded in the register in the section allocated for these marks and published under the same procedures as is followed for other marks.

Article 56 [Right of Owner and Others to Use]

The owner of this mark may use it himself but must permit other persons entitled under the rules to use it if they request.

Article 57 [Transfers of Ownership]

The transfer of ownership of the mark is subject to the approval of the Minister and the Minister may cancel the registration of the mark f it is clear to him that the owner is refusing to permit those who request to use the mark and are entitled to do so under the rules to use it.

Article 58 [Same Rules Apply]

The other conditions and rules for these marks are the same as those stated in these regulations for other marks stated in the law.

Article 59 [Implementation]

The responsible authorities, each according to its jurisdiction, are to implement the provisions of this decision.

Article 60 [Effective Date]

This decision is to be published in the official gazette and to be effective from the date that federal law no. 37 of 1992 relating to trademarks comes into effect.

Sa'eed Ahmad Ghabbash
Minister of Economy and Commerce

Issued in Abu Dhabi
Date: Sha'aban 10, 1413 H
Corresponding to: February 2, 1993 M.

Addendum No. 1

Classes of products

Class (1)
Chemical products used in industry, research, science, photography,
agriculture, horticulture and forestry, fertilizers (natural and chemical);
fire extinguishing compositions; materials for tempering metal and chemical
soldering preparations; chemical substances for preserving foodstuffs,
tanning substances, adhesives used in industry.

Class (2)
Paints, varnishes, lacquers; preservatives against rust and against deterioration
of wood; colorants; mordants; chemical materials for fixing colors; resins;
metals in foil and powder form for engraving and decoration.

Class (3)
Bleaching preparations and other substances for laundry use; cleaning,
polishing, scouring and abrasive preparations; soaps; perfumery, essential oils,
beauty materials (cosmetics), hair lotions, pastes for teeth.

Class (4)
Industrial oils and greases (not including those used in foodstuff or essential
oils); lubricants; dust wetting and absorbing compositions; fuels including
mineral oils (for running engines) and illuminants; candles of all kinds and
wicks for lighting.

Class (5)
Pharmaceutical and veterinary materials; sanitary materials; food for babies
and patients; plasters and materials for dressing; materials for filling teeth,
dental wax; disinfectants; preparations for destroying vermin; fungicides,
herbicides.

Class (6)
Unworked and half-worked metals and their alloys; ships anchors; anvils;
bells; hammered and unhammered metals used in building; railway tracks
and other metallic materials used in railway tracks; chains (except those for
pulling carriages); non-electric cables and wires of metal—that which is
related to the making of locks—pipes and tubes of metal; safes and boxes for

keeping money; balls made from lead; ironmongery, na ls and screws and other products (not stated in other classes) made from common metals; ores.

Class (7)
Machines and machine tools; motors (except motors for land vehicles); machine coupling and transmission components (except for land vehicles); agricultural implements other than hand-operated; incubators for eggs.

Class (8)
Hand tools and implements; cutlery; forks and spoons; swords.

Class (9)
Scientific, nautical, surveying, electrical tools (including wireless), photographic, cinematographic, optical, weighing, measuring, signaling, checking (supervision), life-saving and teaching apparatus and instruments; automatic apparatuses operated by coins or other means—speaking machines—cash registers, calculating machines, fire-extinguishing apparatus.

Class (10)
Surgical, medical, dental and veterinary apparatus and nstruments (including artificial limbs, eyes and teeth).

Class (11)
Apparatus for lighting, heating, steam generating, cooking, refrigerating, drying, ventilating, water supply, and sanitary purposes.

Class (12)
Vehicles—apparatus for locomotion by land, air or water.

Class (13)
Firearms; ammunition and projectiles; explosives; fireworks.

Class (14)
Precious metals and their alloys and goods in precious metals or coated therewith (except cutlery, forks and spoons), jewelry, precious stones; clocks and other instruments for measuring time.

Class (15)
Musical instruments (except speaking and wireless machines).

Class (16)
Paper, cardboard and goods made from these materials; printed matter, newspapers, magazines, books, bookbinding material; photographs; stationery; adhesives for stationery; artists' materials (paint brushes; typewriters and

office requisites (except furniture)); instructional and teaching material (except apparatus); playing cards; printers' type; printing blocks.

Class (17)
Gum, rubber, tiles and their substitutes, and goods made from these materials and not included in other classes; materials for use in packing, stopping and insulating; asbestos and mica and their products; flexible pipes (not of metal).

Class (18)
Tanned and finished natural leathers, and imitations of leather, and goods made of these materials and not included in other classes; hides; trunks and bags; umbrellas, parasols and walking sticks; whips, harnesses and saddleries.

Class (19)
Building materials; natural and manufactured stones; cements: lime; flexible [pipes]; gypsum; gravel; ceramic and cement pipes; materials used for making roads, asphalt, bitumen; transportable buildings; monuments made from stone and chimneys.

Class (20)
Furniture, mirrors, picture frames; goods (not included in other classes) made of wood, cork, reed, cane, wicker, horn, bone, ivory, whalebone, shell, oyster, amber, mother of pearl, meerschaum, celluloid, and substitutes for all these materials.

Class (21)
Small household utensils and containers (except those made of precious metals or coated therewith); combs and sponges; brushes (except paint brushes); brush-making materials; tool and apparatus for cleaning purposes (steel wool); glassware, Chinese glass, earthenware (not included in other classes).

Class (22)
Ropes, string, nets, tents, awnings (tarpaulins), oilcloths not including linoleum, (sails and bags, upholstering and stuffing materials, hair; "qabouq," feathers, sea weeds and others); raw fibrous textile materials.

Class (23)
Yarns and threads.

Class (24)
Textiles, bed and table covers, textile goods not included in other classes.

Class (25)
Clothing including all the kinds of footwear and slippers.

Class (26)
Lace and embroidery, ribbons, buttons, thimbles, hooks, pins and needles; artificial flowers.

Class (27)
Carpets, "baleett," mats, linoleum and other materials used in covering stone floors; wall hangings (not of textile materials).

Class (28)
Games and playthings; gymnastic and sporting articles (except clothes); decorations for Christmas trees.

Class (29)
Meat, fish, poultry; animals and game; meat extracts; preserved, dried and cooked fruit and vegetables; jellies, all kinds of jams; eggs, milk and milk products; edible oils and fats; preserved and picked food.

Class (30)
Coffee, tea, cocoa, sugar, rice, tapioca, sago, artificial coffee; flour and preparations made from cereals, bread, biscuit, pastry, pies, sweets and ices; honey, treacle; yeast, baking-powder; salt, mustard; pepper, vinegar, sauces; spices; ice.

Class (31)
Agricultural, horticultural and forestry products and grains (not included in other classes); live animals; fresh fruits and vegetables; seeds, natural plants and flowers; foodstuffs for animals; malt.

Class (32)
Mineral and aerated waters and other non-alcoholic drinks; syrups and other materials for making non-alcoholic drinks.

Class (33)
Tobacco, raw and prepared; smokers' articles; matches.

Class (34)
Advertising; business functions.

Class (35)
Insurance; financial affairs.

Class (36)
Building construction; installation services; repair.

Class (37)
Communications and telecommunications.

Class (38)
Transport; storage.

Class (39)
Treatment of materials.

Class (40)
Education; training; entertainment.

Class (41)
Miscellaneous

Cabinet Decision No. 18 of 1993 in Relation to the Fees for Procedures Undertaken Pursuant to the Provisions of Federal Law No. 37 of 1992 in Relation to Trademarks

The Cabinet,

After considering the provisional constitution, and

Federal law no. 1 of 1972 in relation to the jurisdictions of the Ministries and the powers of the Ministers and the laws amending t, and

Federal law no. 37 of 1992 in relation to trademarks, and

Cabinet decision no. 15 of 1992 in relation to the fees for procedures undertaken pursuant to the provisions of federal law no. 37 in relation to trademarks, and

Based on what was presented by the Minister of Economy and Commerce, and with the approval of the Cabinet,

Decided:

Article 1 [Fees for Procedures Listed]

The fees in the attached list are required for the procedures undertaken pursuant to the provisions of federal law no. 37 of 1992 in relation to trademarks.

Article 2 [Cancellation of Decision No. 15 of 1992]

Ministerial decision no. 15 of 1992 in relation to the fees for the procedures undertaken pursuant to the provisions of federal law no. 37 of 1992 in relation to trademarks is cancelled.

Article 3 [Implementation]

Each competent authority is to implement this decision and it is to become effective from January 1, 1994 and to be published in the official gazette.

Deputy Prime Minister

Issued in Abu Dhabi
Dated: Rajab 6, 1414 H
Corresponding to: December 19, 1993 M.

List of Required Fees for the Registration of Trademarks

No.	Procedures	Fees
1	Application to register a trademark or a series of trademarks for goods or products or services in one class	500 dirhams
2	Application to register a monitoring mark for goods or products or services in one class	500 dirhams
3	Appeal against the rejection of the registration of a mark or against conditional acceptance	250 dirhams
4	Opposition to the registration of a mark	250 dirhams
5	Application to be heard before a decision in oppositions	250 dirhams
6	Registration of a mark or series of marks for goods or products or services in one class	5000 dirhams
7	Registration of a monitoring mark for goods or products or services in one class	5000 dirhams
8	Application to note in the register of trademarks an associated mark registered before the date of registration of the first	250 dirhams
9	Application to note in the register a transfer of ownership of a trademark or a monitoring mark or an associated mark or the grant of a right to use a mark:	
	a. if the application is filed before the passing of three months from the date of the transfer or right to use and for each mark of the associated marks after the first mark	250 dirhams
	b. if the application is filed after the passing of three months but before 6 months from the date of the transfer of ownership or the right to use and for each mark of the associated marks after the first mark	500 dirhams
	c. if the application is filed after the passing of 6 months from the date of the transfer of ownership or the right to use and for each mark of the associated marks after the first mark	750 dirhams
10	Application to note in the register a mortgage of a trademark or of associated marks pursuant to the following:	
	a. if the application is filed before the passing of three months from the date of the mortgage and for each mark of the associated marks after the first mark	250 dirhams

No.	Procedures	Fees
	b. if the application is filed after the passing of three months but before six months from the date of the mortgage and for each mark of the associated marks after the first mark	500 dirhams
	c. if the application is filed after the passing of six months from the date of the mortgage and for each mark of the associated marks after the first mark	750 dirhams
11	Application to record information stated in article 27 of the implementing regulations in the trademark register	250 dirhams
12	Application to make any addition or amendment to the mark	250 dirhams
13	Appeal against a refusal to make an addition or amendment to the mark	250 dirhams
14	Application to renew the period of protection of a registered mark or series of marks, or a monitoring mark according to the following:	
	a. if the application is filed in the last year of the period of protection and for each of the marks composing the series after the first mark	250 dirhams
	b. if the application is filed during the three months following the end of the period of protection and for each of the marks composing the series after the first mark	500 dirhams
15	Renewal of the registration of a trademark or of a series of marks for goods or products or services in one class	5000 dirhams
16	Renewal of the registration of a monitoring mark for goods or products or services in one class	5000 dirhams
17	Application to amend the system for use of a registered monitoring mark	250 dirhams
18	Application to obtain temporary protection in local or international exhibitions	250 dirhams
19	Application for a certified copy of what is recorded in the register of trademark or of any application or document filed with or issued by the department responsible for trademarks	100 dirhams
20	Application to study or search a trademark	250 dirhams
21	Application to note in the register the cancellation of a mark, whether for all or some goods and products and services	250 dirhams

No.	Procedures	Fees
22	Application to note in the register the cancellation of a mortgage of a mark or associated marks	250 dirhams
23	Application to note in the register the cancellation of the recordal of a license to use a mark	250 dirhams
24	Opposition to an application to note a cancellation of a recordal of a license to use a mark	250 dirhams

A7

Ministerial Decision no. 67 of 1998 [In Relation to the Payment of Fees for Trademark Registration]: Repealed by Ministerial decision no. 12 of 2002

The Minister of Economy and Commerce,

After considering federal law no. 1 of 1972 in relation to the jurisdictions of the Ministries and the powers of the Ministers and the laws amending it, and

Federal law no. 37 of 1992 in relation to trademarks, and

Cabinet decision no. 18 of 1993 in relation to the fees for procedures undertaken pursuant to the provisions of the trademarks law, and

Ministerial decision no. 6 of 1993 with the implementing regulations for the trademarks law, and

Ministerial decision no. 5 of 1996 in relation to the payment of fees required to complete the registration of trademarks, and

Based on the letter of the Minister of Finance and Industry no. m.a.d/98/496 dated 28 February 1998 and on the acceptance of what was put forward by the Minister for the collection of fees for the registration of trademarks after acceptance by the Trademarks Section and before advertisement in the local newspapers and official gazette, and

Based on what was presented by the deputy undersecretary,

Decided:

Article 1 [Registration Fees to be Paid upon Filing]

The fees for the registration of a trademark or a series of marks for goods or products or services in one class are to be collected at the time of filing the application with the Trademark Section.

Article 2 [Decision Applies to Filed Applications]

This decision is to apply to applications for registration of trademarks filed with the Trademark Section and the Section must undertake the necessary procedures to notify the owners of these trademarks to pay the registration fees within thirty days of the date of notice, or otherwise the application will be deemed to be abandoned.

Article 3 [Return of Registration Fees]

Arrangements are to be made with the Department of Revenues at the Ministry of Finance and Industry to put in place a mechanism and rules for those cases in which the registration fees should be returned.

Article 4 [Cancellation of Ministerial Decision no. 5 of 1996]

Ministerial decision no. 5 of 1996 is cancelled.

Article 5 [Publication]

This decision is to be published in the official gazette and to become effective from the date of its issue.

Fahim Bin Sultan Al Qasimi
Minister of Economy and Commerce.

Issued in Abu Dhabi
Dated: 07/08/1998 M
Corresponding to: 03/14/1419 H.[74]

---

74. The Gregorian date (8 July 1998) was put first, followed by the Islamic date (14 Rabi' Al Awwal 1419).

Ministerial Decision no. 67 of 2001 in Relation to the Collection of Publication Fees for Trademark Registration

The Minister of Economy and Commerce,

After considering:

Federal law no. 1 of 1972 in relation to the jurisdictions of the Ministries and the powers of the Ministers and the laws amending it, and

Federal law no. 37 of 1992 in relation to trademarks and the laws amending it, and

Cabinet decision no. 18 of 1993 in relation to the fees for procedures undertaken pursuant to the provisions of federal law no. 37 in relation to trademarks, and

Ministerial decision no. 6 of 1993 with the implementing regulations for the law of trademarks and the decisions amending it, and

Ministerial decision no. 25 of 2001 in relation to the fees for publication of trademarks in the journal that is issued by the Ministry;

Based on what was presented by the deputy undersecretary,

Decided:

Article 1 [60 Days to Collect Publication Fees]

The fees for the publication of trademarks in the journal that is published by the Ministry are to be collected within sixty days of the date of notifying the filer of the application of the acceptance for registration of the mark, otherwise the application will be deemed to be abandoned.

Article 2 [Publication of Additions and Amendments]

[A] The publication fee for applications for entry of any addition or amendment to a mark not affecting its essential character is to be collected within sixty days of the date of notifying the filer of the application of acceptance of the addition or amendment, otherwise the application will be deemed to be abandoned.
[B] The publication fee for applications for entry of any amendment to the goods or services that the mark distinguishes is to be collected during the same period, otherwise the application will be deemed to be abandoned.

Article 3 [Publication of renewal, transfers, etc]

The publication fee is to be collected upon filing the application in the following cases:

1. Applications for renewal of the registration of a trademark
2. Applications for the transfer of ownership of a trademark or for putting a mortgage or a attachment on it
3. Applications for licensing the use of a trademark to another for all or some of the goods or services for which it is registered
4. Applications for cancellation of the recordal of a license to another to use a trademark
5. Applications to indicate in the register the cancellation of a mark for all or some of the goods or services for which it is registered

Article 4 [Informing Concerned Persons of Obligation to Pay]

The concerned persons are to be informed of the obligation to pay the publication fees within sixty days of the day of being notified in circumstances where the law and implementing regulations makes publication necessary and where an application has been filed with the trademark section before the issue of this decision and where otherwise the application would be deemed not to have been filed.

Article 5 [Cancellation of Ministerial Decision No. 25 of 2001]

Ministerial decision no. 25 of 2001 is cancelled, as is any provision stated in the text of previous ministerial decisions that contravenes the provisions of this decision.

Article 6 [Publication]

This decision is to be published in the official gazette and is effective from the date of its publication.

Fahim Bin Sultan Al Qasimi
Minister of Economy and Commerce.

Issued in Abu Dhabi
Dated: Safar 8, 1422 H
Corresponding to: May 2, 2001 M.

Ministerial Decision No. 80 of 2005 in Relation to Trademark Registration Agents

The Minister of Economy and Planning,

After considering:

Federal law no. 1 of 1972 in relation to the jurisdictions of the Ministries and the powers of the Ministers and the laws amending it, and

Federal law no. 37 of 1992 (and its amendments) in relation to trademarks, and

Cabinet decision no. 30 of 2004 in relation to the introduction and amendment of some fees for services offered by the Ministry of Economy and Planning, and

Ministerial decision no. 6 of 1993 concerning the implementing regulations for federal law no. 37 of 1992 in relation to trademarks, and

Ministerial decision no. 21 of 1998 in relation to the amendment of some provisions of Ministerial decision no. 6 of 1993, and

Based on what was presented by the Undersecretary,

Decided:

Article 1 [Definitions]

In the application of the provisions of this decision, the words and expressions below are intended to have the following meanings, unless the context of the text requires otherwise:
   The State: The United Arab Emirates.
   The Ministry: The Ministry of Economy and Planning.
   The responsible department: The department of commercial registration.

The responsible section: The trademark section.

Register: The register of registered trademark registration agents at the Ministry of Economy and Planning.

Registration agent: The person who is authorized by the owner of a trademark to register trademarks in the register of trademarks at the Ministry of Economy and Planning.

Article 2 [Who May File Trademark Applications]

The owner of a trademark who has residence in the State or an office of a "trademark registration agent" registered in the register may file an application for registration of any trademark in the State with the responsible section.

Article 3 [Registration as Agent Required]

It is not permitted for any person to carry on the activity of a "trademarks registration agent" unless his name is registered in the register.

It is not permitted for any person to hold out in his papers or publicity or advertising that he is a trademarks registration agent without his name being registered in the register.

Article 4 [Natural Persons as Agents]

The conditions for natural persons who wish to register in the Register are as follows:

1. To have legal capacity
2. To hold a university certificate notarized and legalized according to the law
3. To have experience of not less than two years in working with one of the offices or companies registered in the register or which has a commercial license from a responsible authority to practice this activity before the issue of this decision
4. To be of good fame and character and no judgments issued against him in crimes contrary to honor or trust unless his moral standing has been restored

Article 5 [Legal Persons as Agents]

The conditions for legal persons who wish to register in the register are as follows:

1. That the responsible director in the company established in the State, whether he is one of the partners or not, satisfy the conditions stated in article 4 of this law

2. That the company established outside the State be licensed to carry on the activity of trademarks registration agent in the country of its incorporation

Article 6 [Application and Attachments—Natural Persons]

An application for the registration of natural persons in the register is to be filed with the responsible section using the form prepared for this purpose attaching the following supporting documents:

1. A copy of the registration summary or passport
2. An official certificate stating that the applicant for registration has not previously had a conviction against him for crimes against honor or trust
3. Certificates of academic expertise
4. Rent contract for the office in which the activity is carried on
5. Identification of the emirate or emirates in which it is desired to carry on the activity
6. A sample of the authorized signature
7. The names of the authorized representative of the registration agent

Article 7 [Application and Its Attachments—Legal Persons]

An application for the registration of legal persons in the register is to be filed with the responsible section using the form prepared for this purpose, attaching the following supporting documents:

1. A true copy of the articles of association of the company
2. A true copy of the company's certificate of registration in the commercial register
3. The rent contract for the location of the company
4. Identification of the emirate or emirates in which it is desired to carry on the activity
5. Official certificates from the official authorities in the country in which the foreign company is registered, showing that the company is established, registered, and licensed to carry on this activity in the country in which the company is established pursuant to the provisions of the applicable laws
6. A true copy of the decision issued by the parent company if a foreign company is opening a branch or branches in the State
7. The supporting documents required from the responsible director of the company in accordance with articles 4 and 5 of this decision
8. A sample of the authorized signature
9. The names of the authorized representative of the registration agent

Article 8 [Acceptance or Rejection Within 2 Months]

The responsible section must notify the applicant for registration of the acceptance or rejection decision within two months from the date of filing the application by registered letter or direct delivery and the notice must include reasons if the application is rejected.

Article 9 [Certificate of Registration]

If the application is accepted, the responsible section must register the name of the applicant and details of the application in the register and deliver to the applicant the certificate of registration indicating the achieving of registration and the number and date of registration. The certificate is to be effective for one year from the date of registration in the register.

Article 10 [Notifying of Amendments or Changes]

Trademark registration agents must notify the responsible section of any amendment or change that may occur in the registration application information or supporting documents. The notice is to be made pursuant to an application indicated to be for that purpose and is to be filed with the responsible section within thirty days of the occurrence of the amendment or change, attaching documents supporting the correctness of the information stated in the application.

Article 11 [Acceptance or Rejection of Amendments, etc.]

If the responsible section accepts the notice, it is to enter the new information in the register, indicating in the margin of the register the date of entry and the supporting documents for the entry, and to give the applicant a copy of the application indicating on it the acceptance of the amendment or change and its date. The responsible section may reject an application for amendment or change by notifying the applicant of the decision by registered letter within thirty days of the date of filing the notice of amendment or change.

Article 12 [Annual Renewal]

Registration agents who are registered in the register must file with the Ministry an annual registration renewal.

The renewal application is to be filed with the responsible section using the specified form thirty days before the expiry of the certificate of registration each year.

Article 13 [Registration Number to Be Used]

Each person who has his name registered in the register must use his name with his registration number in all correspondence and certificates and reports issued by him.

Article 14 [Offices in Other Emirates]

Any registration agent who obtains a license to open an office in an emirate must file with the responsible section, within a period not exceeding three months, the license from the responsible authority in the emirate.

Article 15 [Disciplinary Measures]

Without prejudice to civil and criminal liability, when necessary, the registration agent who fails to comply with his duties in carrying on this activity is to be punished with the following disciplinary measures:

1. A warning
2. Ceasing to practice the activity for a period not exceeding one year and in the case of a repetition of the offense, a period not exceeding two years
3. Cancellation of registration

A person who has had his registration cancelled may not file a new application for registration within three years from the date of the cancel of registration.

Article 16 [Investigation of Agents]

Of its own accord, or based on an application from the responsible section, or based on a complaint filed with it, the Ministry may undertake an investigation into a registration agent as to the offenses that have been imputed to him in the carrying on of this activity. If it is apparent to the Ministry that what has been imputed to the registration agent constitutes a criminal offense, it is to refer the matter to the public prosecution.

Article 17 [Agent's Right to Present a Defense]

Before issuing a decision to cancel, the responsible section must notify the registration agent by registered letter to present his defense within thirty days from the date of the notice. If the registration agent does not present his defense within the mentioned period, or does not convince the responsible section of his defense, the undersecretary must make a decision in relation to the cancellation of his registration from the register and notify him of the decision by registered letter.

Article 18 [Fees]

The fees that are to be collected for the procedures done pursuant to the provisions of this decision are as follows:

1. Fees for registration of a trademarks registration agent for each office—3000 dirhams
2. Fees for renewal of a registration of a trademarks registration agent for each office—1000 dirhams
3. A fine of 100 dirhams for each month in delaying renewal of a registration of a trademarks registration agent (no more than 1000 dirhams per year and any part of a month is to be calculated as a full month).

Article 19 [Cancellation of Prior Regulations]

Ministerial decision no. 21 of 1997 is cancelled.

Article 20 [Publication]

This decision is to be published in the official gazette and is deemed to be effective from the date of its issue.

Lubna Bint Khalid Al Qasimi
Minister of Economy and Planning

Issued in Abu Dhabi
Date: Muharam 28, 1426 H
Corresponding to: March 9, 2005 M.

A10

Federal Decree No. 52 of 2007 in Relation to the Unified Trademark Law (System) for the Arabian Gulf Cooperation Council Countries

We, Khalifa Bin Zayed Al Nahyan, President of the United Arab Emirates, after considering the Constitution, and

Federal law no. 1 of 1972 in relation to the jurisdictions of the Ministries and the powers of the Ministers and the laws amending it, and

Based on what was presented by the Minister of Economy, and the approval of the Cabinet of Ministers, and the ratification of the Supreme Federation Council,

Decreed as follows:

Article 1

The unified trademark law (system) for the Arabian Gulf Cooperation Council Countries has been approved, the text of which is attached.

Article 2

The Minister of Economy is to implement this decree and publish it in the official gazette.

Khalifa Bin Zayed Al Nahyan
President of the United Arab Emirates

Issued from the Presidential Palace in Abu Dhabi
Date: Jumaada Al Akhira 5, 1428 H
Corresponding to: June 20, 2007 M.

[Attachment:]

The unified trademark law (system) of the Arabian Gulf Cooperation Council Countries

Contents

Chapter 1: General provisions

Article 1 Definitions

The following terms are to have the meanings shown beside them unless the context requires otherwise:

Countries of the council: The countries of the cooperation council for the Arabian Gulf countries.

Competent authority: The ministry that is responsible for commercial matters in each of the countries of the council and that is authorized with the implementation of this law (system).

Implementing regulations: The regulations put in place by the commercial cooperation committee implementing this system.

Register: The register of trademarks.

Article 2 [What Is a Trademark?]

A trademark is anything that takes a distinctive form, whether names, words, signatures, letters, symbols, numbers, titles, stamps, drawings, images, inscriptions, packaging, graphic elements, shapes, groups of colors, or combinations of these, or any sign or group of signs capable of being visually perceived, used or intended to be used to distinguish the goods or services of one undertaking from the goods and services of another, or to indicate the provision of a service, or the monitoring or examination of goods or services.

A mark with the character of a sound or a smell may be considered to be a trademark.

Chapter 2: Procedures

Section 1: Procedures for the Registration of Trademarks

Article 3 [What May Not Be Registered as a Trademark]

The following are not to be considered as trademarks or part of them, and may not be registered as trademarks:

1. Marks that are devoid of any distinctive characteristic or that consists of representations that are no more than customary names given to the goods and services or conventional drawings or ordinary images for the goods
2. Any expression or drawing or mark that contravenes public morals or public order
3. Public emblems, flags, military and honorific insignia, national and foreign medals, coins and paper money, and other symbols belonging to the state, or to any other state, or to Arab or international organizations, or to any of their institutions, or any imitation of any of them
4. Symbols of the Red Crescent or Red Cross and any other similar symbols, as well as marks being imitations of any of them
5. Marks that are identical or similar to symbols of a purely religious nature
6. Geographic names and representations, if their use would cause confusion in relation to the source or origin of the good or services
7. The name of another or the name by which he/she is known or his/her image or emblem, unless the person, or his/her heirs, has previously consented to its use
8. Representations relating to honorific titles or university degrees to which the applicant for registration cannot prove a legal entitlement
9. Marks that deceive the public or that contain false representations as to the origin or source of the products or the services or their other characteristics, as well as marks that contain an illusory, copied or false commercial name
10. Marks owned by natural or legal persons with whom it is forbidden to deal pursuant to a decision issued in this matter by the competent authority
11. Any trademark the same or similar to a mark previously filed or registered by others for the same or similar goods or services, if the use of the mark for which registration is sought would give rise to an impression of a connection between it and the products or services of the owner of the registered mark, or would lead to damage of his interests

12. Marks whose registration for some goods or services would reduce the value of other goods or services that are distinguished by the prior mark

13. Marks that are considered to be not more than translations of a famous mark or another previously registered mark if the registration of the mark would cause confusion amongst consumers in relation to the products or services that are distinguished by the mark or similar products

14. Marks that contain the following words or expressions: "patent," "patented," "registered," "registered drawing," "copyright." or any words or expressions resembling them

Article 4 [Famous Trademarks]

1. A famous trademark whose reputation exceeds the borders of the country of origin to other countries may not be registered for the same or similar goods or services, except based on an application filed by the owner of the famous mark or with his express consent to do so.

2. In determining whether the mark is famous, the extent to which the mark is known to the relevant public as a result of its promotion is to be taken into account.

3. Marks that are famous may not be registered to distinguish goods or services not similar or not identical to those distinguished by the famous mark, if:

> a. the use of the mark would indicate a connection between the goods and services required to be distinguished by it and the goods and services of the owner of the famous mark; and[75]
>
> b. the use of the mark would lead to the possibility of damage to the interests of the owner of the famous mark.

Article 5 [Geographical Indications]

Any concerned person may apply for registration of a trademark bearing a geographical indication to protect the origin of his specific product, but acceptance for registration does not result in any exclusive right for the applicant and anyone who carries on a business in this geographical place may use the indication.

Article 6 [Who May Register a Trademark]

The following classes of persons have the right to register their trademarks:

---

75. The "and" here is an interpretation. In the Arabic text, paragraph (a) ends in a full stop, leaving it unclear as to whether the two paragraphs should be understood as linked by an "or" or an "and."

1. Any natural or legal person who is the owner of a factory or producer or trader or artisan or owner of a private services venture, and enjoying the nationality of any of the countries of the council.
2. Foreigners who are resident in any of the countries of the council and are authorized to carry on commercial or industrial or handicraft or service activities.
3. Foreigners who belong to a country that deals reciprocally with the countries of the council in any one of which the mark is to be registered.
4. Public organizations.

Article 7 [The Trademark Register]

The competent authority is to prepare a register called the register of trademarks in which is to be recorded all trademarks and the names of their owners, their addresses and descriptions of their goods or services, and any transfer of ownership or assignment or license to use or mortgage or renewal or cancellation or any other amendments that may occur. Any person with an interest has the right to inspect the register and take a certified extract from it after paying the required fees.

Article 8 [Exclusive Ownership, Incontestability and Prior Use]

1. The person who registers a trademark is deemed to be the exclusive owner unless proven otherwise. No dispute may be raised against the ownership of the mark if the person who registered the mark has used it continuously for at least five years from the date of registration with no action having been commenced in relation to its validity.
2. The one who has earlier use of the mark as against the one who registered it in his name may request the competent court to cancel the registration within five years of the date of registration, unless it is proved that the first user agreed expressly or impliedly to the use of the mark by the one who registered it in his name.

Article 9 [Applications for Registration]

An application for registration of a mark may be filed with the competent authority for the registration of trademarks using the specific form for that purpose by a concerned person or the one who is authorized by him, in accordance with the conditions and terms stated in the implementing regulations for this system (law).

Article 10 [Single Class Applications Only]

A trademark may be registered in respect of one or more classes of goods or services specified in the implementing regulations to this law but an application for registration of a mark may not contain more than one class.

Article 11 [Series Marks]

A single application may be filed for the registration of a series of marks that are identical in their essential elements and whose differences relate to elements not affecting the essential identity of the mark, such as the color of the marks or representations of related products or services on the condition that they fall within one class.

Article 12 [Similar Marks Applied for at the Same Time]

If two or more persons apply at the same time for the registration of the same mark, or marks that are close or similar, in one class of products or services, each of the applications must be suspended until an executed assignment, legalized by the competent authority, is filed by the parties in favor of one of them or until a final judgment is issued in the dispute.

Article 13 [Claiming Priority]

If the applicant or his successor wishes to enjoy a priority right relying on a prior application filed in a country that deals reciprocally with the countries of the council, he must attach to his application a statement showing the date of the prior application, its number and the country in which the application was filed. The applicant must also file a copy of the prior application within six months of filing the registration application for which he claims the right of priority, otherwise his right is deemed to have lapsed.

Article 14 [Imposing Restrictions and Amendments]

1. The competent authority may impose such restrictions and amendments as it considers necessary to particularize or clarify the trademark in order to prevent it being confused with another previously registered or filed mark or for any other reason.
2. If the applicant for registration does not comply with the request of the competent department to satisfy the conditions within ninety days of the date of being informed of them, he is deemed to have abandoned his application.
3. If the competent authority rejects the registration of the trademark for some reason, or suspends the registration to comply with restrictions or

amendments, it must inform the applicant or his agent in writing of the reasons for its decision.

4. In any case, the competent authority must arrive at a decision in relation to the application for registration within ninety days of the date of filing, once the application has satisfied the terms and conditions stated in this law and its implementing regulations.

Article 15 [Appeals from Decisions of the Competent Authority]

1. The applicant for registration or his agent may appeal any decision issued by the competent authority rejecting registration or conditionally suspending it to a committee specified in the implementing regulations to this law within thirty days of being informed of the rejection or suspension. The applicant may appeal the decision of the committee to the competent court within sixty days of being informed of the committee's decision.

2. If the applicant does not appeal the decision in the specified period, or does not implement the restrictions imposed by the competent authority within this period, he is deemed to have abandoned his application.

Article 16 [Advertisement, Right to Oppose and Opposition Procedure]

1. If the competent authority accepts a trademark, it must, before registration, advertise it in any means of publication specified in the implementing regulations to this law and the applicant for registration must bear the costs of publication.

2. Any concerned person may, within sixty days from the date of advertisement, file with the competent authority, a written opposition to the registration of the trademark. The competent authority must notify the applicant for registration by means of a copy of the notice of opposition within thirty days of the date of its filing. The applicant must file, with the competent authority within sixty days from the date of being notified, a written reply to the opposition, otherwise the applicant for registration will be deemed to have abandoned his application.

3. The competent authority may, if it is apparent that the opposition to the registration of the mark is not serious, carry out the registration procedures, and notify the opponent of its reasoned decision.

The opponent may appeal the decision to the court within thirty days of the date of being notified.

Article 17 [Opposition—the Competent Authority's Decision and Appeals]

1. The competent authority is to decide the opposition filed with it after hearing the parties or one of them.

2. The competent authority is to issue its decision accepting or rejecting registration and, in the case of acceptance, it may decide the restrictions it considers necessary.

3. Any concerned person may appeal the decision of the competent authority to the court within thirty days of the date of being informed of its decision.

Article 18 [Registration—the Effective Date, the Certificate and the Owner's Right]

1. If a trademark becomes registered, the effect of registration is retrospective to the date of the filing of the application and the owner of the mark is to be given, as soon as registration is completed, a certificate containing the following information:

a. The registration number

b. The number and date of priority and the country in which the application was filed

c. The date of filing of the application and the date of registration and the date of the expiry of protection

d. The name of the owner of the mark, his title, place of residence and nationality

e. An identical image of the mark

f. A statement of the goods or the services for the mark and their class

2. The registered owner has the right to request the competent authority to prevent others from using his mark or using any sign similar to it that causes deception of the public in relation to similar products or services.

Article 19 [Amendments by the Owner]

The owner of a registered trademark may file at any time an application with the competent authority to make any addition or amendment to the mark that does not affect its essential identity. The competent authority is to issue a decision in the matter pursuant to the conditions set down for deciding initial applications for registration and the decision is able to be appealed in the same way.

Article 20 [Amendment of the Register]

The competent authority may add any information to the register that has been omitted from it, or remove or amend any information, if it was entered in the register unlawfully or is inconsistent with the truth. Any concerned person may appeal any action taken in this regard to the competent court.

Section 2: Period of Protection of Trademarks

Article 21 [Duration and Renewal]

1. The period of protection resulting from the registration of a trademark is ten years. The owner of the mark may secure a continuation of the protection for periods of the same duration by filing an application for renewal within the last year pursuant to the conditions and terms stated in this law and its implementing regulations.
2. The competent authority may, within three months following the end of the period of protection, notify the owner of the mark in writing of the end of the period of protection and send the notice to his address as recorded in the register. If the owner of the mark does not file an application for renewal within six months following the end of the period of protection, the competent authority is to remove the mark from the register.
3. The renewal of the registration of the mark is to be done without any new examination and without considering any opposition from others.

Article 22 [Temporary Protection for Trademarks During Exhibitions]

Trademarks that satisfy the conditions for registration stated in this law are to enjoy temporary protection during the period of their exposure in exhibitions that are undertaken within or outside the countries of the council and that are specified in a decision issued by the competent authority.

The implementing regulations are to specify the terms and conditions and procedures for granting this protection.

Section 3: Cancellation of Trademark Registrations

Article 23 [Court-ordered Cancellation]

Without prejudice to the provisions of article 8 of this law, the competent authority and any concerned person may resort to the court to request a decision cancelling a trademark that has been unlawfully registered.

The competent authority must cancel the registration when a final decision has been filed with it.

Article 24 [Cancellation by the Owner and Recorded Users]

The owner of a trademark may apply to the competent authority to cancel a mark from the register, whether in respect of all or some of the goods or services for which the mark is registered. The application for cancellation is to be filed pursuant to the conditions and procedures specified in the implementing regulations. If the use of the mark is licensed pursuant to a contract recorded in the register, the registration of the mark may not be cancelled except based on a written consent from the licensee unless the licensee has expressly waived this right in the license.

Article 25 [Cancellation for Non-use]

The court may, based on an application by any concerned person, order the cancellation of a registration if it is proved before it that the mark has not been used in a serious manner for five consecutive years, unless the owner of the mark provides a justification for the non-use.

Article 26 [Re-registration of Cancelled Marks]

If the registration of a trademark is cancelled, it is not possible to re-register the mark for the benefit of another person for the same or similar goods or services for three years from the date of cancellation unless the cancellation was based on a judgment from the court, in which case the judgment may specify a shorter period.

Article 27 [Publication of Cancellations and Renewals]

The cancellation or renewal of a registration must be published by any means specified in the implementing regulations.

Section 4: Transfer of the ownership of a mark, mortgages and attachments

Article 28 [Transfers, Mortgages, Attachments, etc. and Their Recordal]

1. The ownership of a trademark may be transferred—with or without consideration—or mortgaged or attached, with the business or investment

project that uses the trademark to distinguish its goods or services, unless otherwise agreed.

2. The ownership of a trademark may be transferred by inheritance, will or gift.

3. In any case, the transfer of ownership of a mark or the mortgage or attachment of it is not effective against others until after it has been recorded in the register of trademarks and published in the manner specified in the implementing regulations.

Article 29 [Transfers of Marks and Businesses]

1. The transfer of the ownership of a business or investment project includes the trademark registered in the name of the transferor of the ownership that may be considered to have a close connection with the business or project unless it has been agreed otherwise.

2. If the ownership of a business or project is transferred without transferring the ownership of the mark, the transferor of the ownership may continue to produce the same goods or provide the same services for which the mark has been registered and to trade in them, unless it has been agreed otherwise.

Chapter 3: License Contracts

Article 30 [Licenses and Their Duration]

The owner of a mark may license any person, natural or legal, to use the mark in relation to all or some of the goods or services for which the mark is registered. The owner of the mark has the right to license other persons to use the same mark, and may use the mark himself unless it has been agreed otherwise. The period of the license to use the mark may not exceed the period set down for the protection of the mark.

Article 31 [Restrictions in Licenses]

The license contract may not contain any terms binding the licensee to restrictions that do not result from the rights granted by trademark registration or that are not necessary for the preservation of those rights, but the license contract may contain the following restrictions:

1. A specification of the geographical area or duration for the use of the mark

2. Conditions that the requirements for effective monitoring of the quality of the goods or services necessitate

3. Obligations imposed on the licensee to refrain from all acts that may result in harm to the trademark

Article 32 [Licenses to Be in Writing; Recordal not Required]

The taking of a license contract to use a trademark must be in writing. There is no requirement to record it in the register.

Article 33 [No License Assignments or Sub-licenses]

The licensee may not assign the license to another or grant sub-licenses unless the license contract states otherwise.

Article 34 [Cancellation of License Recordals]

A recordal of a license can be cancelled from the register based on an application by the owner of the mark or the licensee after filing proof of the expiry or termination of the license.

The competent authority must inform the other party of the application to cancel the license, and that party may oppose the application for cancellation in accordance with the procedures and conditions stated in the implementing regulations.

Chapter 4: Collective Marks, Monitoring Marks and the Marks of Non-profit Organizations and Professional Establishments

Article 35 [Collective Marks]

a. Collective marks that are used to distinguish the goods or services of businesses that are members of a specific entity that has a legal personality may be registered.

An application for registration of a collective mark to be used by the members may be filed by a representative of the entity pursuant to the terms and conditions specified by the representative and are to be approved by the competent authority.

b. The applicant for registration of a collective mark must indicate in the application for registration that it is for a collective mark, and attach to the application a copy of the conditions for use of the mark.

In any case, the owner of the registered collective mark is to notify the competent authority of any changes to these conditions. The changes are not to be effective until after they have been approved by the competent authority.

c. A collective mark may not be re-registered for the benefit of another for the same or similar goods or services after it has been cancelled.

d. The competent court may, based on an application by any concerned person, order the cancellation of the registration of a collective mark if it is proved before it that the registered owner is using the collective mark alone, or that he is using it or permitting its use in a way that contravenes the conditions referred to in paragraph (b) of this article, or he is using it in a way that causes the deception of the public as to the origin of the goods or any characteristic shared by the goods or services for which the collective mark is registered.

Article 36 [Monitoring Marks]

a. Legal persons who are responsible for the monitoring or examination of some goods or services as to their source, constitutive elements, method of production, quality, identity or any other characteristics, may apply with the competent authority for registration of the mark that is specifically for indicating the monitoring or examination.

In any case, this mark may not be registered and its ownership may not be transferred except with the consent of the competent authority.

b. The applicant for registration of a monitoring mark must indicate in the application for registration that it is for a monitoring or examination mark, and attach to the application a copy of the conditions for use of the marks for which registration is sought.

In any case, the owner of the registered mark is to notify the competent authority of any changes to these conditions. The changes are not to be effective until after they have been approved by the competent authority.

Article 37 [Non-commercial Marks]

Marks for non-commercial purposes such as the logos adopted by non-profit organizations or used by professional establishments to distinguish their correspondence or to be an indication for its members may be registered.

Article 38 [Regulations for Collective Marks, Monitoring Marks and Non-Commercial Marks]

The implementing regulations are to specify the conditions and rules for the registration of the marks referred to in articles 35, 36, and 37 and the supporting documents required to be filed for registration, and the other organizational matters relating to them. The registration of any of these marks results in all of the effects stated in this law.

Chapter 5: Penalties

Article 39 [Offenses and Their Punishments]

a. Without prejudice to any harsher punishment provided for in any other law, a punishment of imprisonment for a period of not more than five years and a fine of not more than 1,000,000 Saudi riyals, or its equivalent in the currencies of the countries of the council, or either one of them, is to be imposed on:

> 1. Anyone who has counterfeited a lawfully registered mark or has imitated it in a manner leading to the deception of the public and anyone who has used in bad faith a counterfeited or imitated trademark.
> 2. Anyone who has, in bad faith, put on his goods or used in relation to his services a mark owned by another.

b. Without prejudice to any harsher punishment provided for in any other law, a punishment of imprisonment for a period of not more than three years and a fine of not more than 100,000 Saudi riyals, or its equivalent in the currencies of the countries of the council, or either one of them, is to be imposed on:

> 1. Anyone who has sold, or offered for sale or circulation, or possessed with the intention of selling, goods bearing a counterfeited or an imitated trademark or such a mark that is placed on them or used without the right to do so and with his knowledge of that, as well as anyone who has offered services under this mark.
> 2. Anyone who has used an unregistered mark in the circumstances stated for them in paragraphs 2 to 11 in article 3.
> 3. Anyone who, without a right to do so, has put with his mark or on his commercial papers or documents representations that lead to the belief that the mark is registered.
> 4. Anyone who intentionally and in bad faith omits to put his registered trademark on the goods or services that are distinguished by it.
> 5. Anyone who makes or possesses tools or materials with the intention of using them to counterfeit a registered or famous trademark.

Article 40 [Penalties for Repeat Offenders]

In the case of the repetition [of an offense], the repeat offender is to be punished by not more than double the maximum penalty set down for the offense, in addition to the closure of the place of business or project for not less than 15 days and not more than 6 months, with the publication of the judgment at the expense of the offender, pursuant to the procedures specified in the implementing regulations.

In the application of this law, a repeat offender is deemed to be someone who has been judged to have committed one of the offenses stated in this law and who repeated the commission of another similar offense within three years of the date of the final judgment against him in the previous offense.

Article 41 [Right to Compensation]

Anyone who has suffered damage as a result of the commission of any offense stated in this system may demand from the person responsible for this offense appropriate compensation for the damage resulting from the offense.

Article 42 [Precautionary Measures]

1. The owner of a trademark may, at any time, even before raising any case, apply for an order from the competent court, based on a petition supported by an official certificate evidencing the registration of the mark or based on the fame of his mark, to take the necessary precautionary measures, and in particular, an attachment of machines and any tools being used or that have been used in the commission of the crime, as well as the goods and the addresses of the shops, the packaging, the papers, the documents or other things on which the mark has been put or information the subject of the crime.

2. This attachment may be made on the importation of goods from outside.

3. The order issued by the court may contain an order to appoint one or more experts to assist the one making the attachment and to oblige the applicant to file financial security as estimated by the court to compensate the attachee when necessary. The security may not be released except by an order from the court.

4. After signing the attachment, the owner of the goods may dispute before the court the sufficiency of the value of the financial security filed by the attachor.

Article 43 [10 Days to Commence the Main Case]

The attachment procedures stated in the previous article are deemed to be void if a case is not raised against the attachee within ten days following the signing of the attachment.

Article 44 [What the Court May Order]

1. The court may order, in any case, the confiscation of things that have been attached or that are yet to be attached, the subtraction of their value

from the compensation or fines or the disposal of them, in any other way the court considers suitable.

2. The court may also order the destruction of the unlawful marks and order when necessary the destruction of the goods and wrapping and packaging materials and other things that bear the mark or bear unlawful representations, as well as the destruction of machines and tools that were used specifically for the counterfeiting operation. The court may also order any of the above even in the case of a judgment of innocence.

3. The court may order the publication of the judgment in the official gazette or in any one of the daily newspapers at the expense of the defendant.

Article 45 [Five-year Limitation Period]

After the passing of five years from the commission of an offense without any investigation or prosecution having been undertaken, the public right to bring a case is extinguished. The loss of the public right does not have any effect on private rights.

Article 46 [Attachee's Right to Compensation]

The defendant may undertake procedures to require a plaintiff with bad faith to pay the compensation that he may deserve resulting from the procedures undertaken by the plaintiff and stated in article 42 of this system within ninety days from [a] the date of the end of the period stated in article 43 of this law (system), if the attachor does not raise a case against the attachee, or [b] the date of the issue of a final decision in the case raised by the attachor relating to the trademark. In any case, the financial security is not to be returned to the attachor, except after the issue of a final judgment finding against the attachee, or after the end of the period set down for him without him raising a case, unless the judgment issued in the attachor's case decides on the subject of the financial security.

Chapter 6: Concluding Provisions

Article 47 [Judicial Seizure Officers]

Employees appointed by the competent Minister in relation to the implementation of the provisions of this system (law) and to proving crimes that occur contravening it are to have the title of judicial seizure officers.

Article 48 [Fees]

The implementing regulations are to specify the fees relating to this system (law).

Article 49 [Commercial Cooperation Committee]

The Commercial Cooperation Committee has the right to explain and suggest amendments to this law "system."

Article 50 [The Implementing Regulations]

The Commercial Cooperation Committee is to publish the implementing regulations for this law "system."

A11

Federal Law No. 4 of 1979 in Relation to the Prevention of Fraud and Deception in Commercial Dealings

We, Zayed Bin Sultan Al Nahyan, president of the United Arab Emirates,

After considering the provisional constitution, and

Federal law no. 1 of 1972 in relation to the jurisdictions of the Ministries and the powers of the Ministers and the laws amending it, and

Based on what was presented by the Minister of Economy and Commerce, and the approval of the Cabinet and the Federation National Council and ratification of the Supreme Federation Council,

Issued the following law:

Article 1 [Deception in Commercial Dealings]

Any person who deceives or attempts to deceive the person with whom he is contracting in any way as to any of the following matters is to be punished by imprisonment not exceeding a period of two years and a fine of not less than 500 dirhams and not more than 10,000 dirhams, or either one of them:

1. the number of products sold, their quantity, their size, their measurements, their weight, their capabilities, their standard or their specifications;
2. the identity of the products, if what was delivered is not what was contracted for;
3. the substance of the products, or their nature, or their essential characteristics, or the useful elements they contain and in general the internal elements of their composition;

4. the type, the origin or the source of the products in those cases in which the type of product or its origin or its source was clearly important in entering into the contract for them;
5. making illusory reductions in the price of the goods or products offered for sale in seasonal or non-seasonal clearance sales.

If the crime was committed or attempted to be committed by use of counterfeit or different weights or measures or gauges or hallmarks or stamps or other examination apparatus, or by use of ways or methods that make the process of weighing or measuring or gauging or examination of the goods to be incorrect, the punishment is to be imprisonment for a period of not more than three years and a fine of not less than 4000 dirhams, and not more than 20,000 dirhams, or either one of them.

Article 2 [Falsification or Corruption of Goods]

Anyone who:

1. falsifies or attempts to falsify human or animal food, medical drugs, agricultural or natural products or any other materials prepared for sale;
2. puts forward or offers for sale or sells human or animal food, medical drugs, agricultural or natural products or any other materials knowing that they are false or corrupt. The knowledge of the falsification or corruption [of the products] is to be presumed if the defendant is someone who works in trade or is a hawker, unless he proves his good faith and reveals the source of the materials the subject of the crime;
3. prepares or puts forward or offers for sale or sells materials with the intention of using them to falsify human or animal food, medical drugs, agricultural or natural products or any other materials, or who encourages the use of these materials in fraud by any means of publication is to be punished by imprisonment not exceeding a period of two years and a fine of not less than 500 dirhams and not more than 10,000 dirhams, or either one of them.

If the foods or medical drugs or agricultural products or other products or materials referred to in the previous two paragraphs[76] are harmful to the health of humans or animals, the punishment is to be imprisonment for a period of not more than three years and a fine of not less than 1000 dirhams, and not more than 20,000 dirhams, or either one of them.

The punishments stated in the previous paragraph are to be applied even if the purchaser or consumer knew of the falsification or corruption of the products.

---

76. The reference here is probably to paragraph nos. 1 and 2.

Article 3 [Possession of Falsified or Corrupted Goods]

Anyone who possesses food or medical drugs or agricultural or other products or materials of those referred to in the first paragraph of the previous article knowing of their falsification or corruption is to be punished by imprisonment for a period not more than six months and a fine not exceeding 500 dirhams, or either one of them, unless he proves that his possession of them is for a legitimate reason.

If the foodstuffs or medical drugs or agricultural products or natural products or other materials that were found in his possession are harmful to the health of humans or animals, the punishment is to be imprisonment for a period of not more than one year and a fine of not more than 2000 dirhams, or either one of them.

Article 4 [Importation of falsified or corrupted goods]

The importation of any human or animal food or medical drugs or agricultural products or natural products or any other materials that are falsified or corrupted is not permitted.

The Minister of Economy and Commerce may order the re-export of these goods to their source within the period specified by him. If the re-export is not completed within this period, the Minister may order their destruction at the expense of their importer.

However, the Minister of Economy and Commerce may allow the entry of these goods and their circulation if they are to be used for another purpose for which they are suitable, pursuant to conditions specified in the decision he issues.

Article 5 [Jurisdiction of the Ministry of Economy and Commerce]

The following matters are to be regulated by decisions of the Ministry of Economy and Commerce:

1. The use of specific vessels or containers or wrapping in the preparation of foodstuffs and medical drugs and agricultural produce or products or other materials and the means of bottling, packing, preserving, distributing or transporting them for the purpose of putting them forward for sale or selling them with a statement of the method of use of these materials and the means of preserving or possessing them and the circumstances in which they are or will become unsuitable for consumption and of their name, source and place of manufacture, and the name of manufacturer and other necessary statements in order to define them.

2. The keeping of the registers and books relating to the products and the method of their review and the giving of certificates for the products and their use.

3. The specification of the elements or the percentages that must exist in the composition of the materials mentioned above to be able to sell or offer them for sale.

4. Matters relating to the import, export, manufacture, sale, possession and circulation of products to which the provisions of this law apply.

Without prejudice to the punishments stated in this law, anyone who violates the provisions of these decisions is to be punished by imprisonment for a period of not more than six months and by a fine not less than 500 dirhams and not more than 5000 dirhams, or either one of them.

Article 6 [Role of Ministry Employees]

The proving of the crimes that occur in violation of the provisions of this law and regulations issued to implement it is to be carried out by the employees who are entrusted by the Minister of Economy and Commerce with that task by agreement with the competent authorities in the member emirates of the federation.

These employees are to be judicial seizure officers, and for the purpose of controlling violations of the provisions of this law, they may enter all shops and places that foodstuffs, medical drugs or produce and products and other materials to which the provisions of this law are subject are put forward or offered for sale or stored.

They may also take a sample of these materials pursuant to what is determined by this law and regulations issued implementing it.

Article 7 [Seizure of Products]

If the employees referred to in the previous article have strong reasons to believe that there is a violation of the provisions of this law, they may temporarily seize the suspected materials.

In this case, the concerned persons are to be invited to attend while at least three samples are taken from the seized materials for analysis and identification of the extent of their conformity to the elements and specifications required to be in them, and each of them is to be stamped with red wax and one of the samples is to be delivered to the concerned person and a report is to be prepared including all the necessary information to prove that the sample and materials are those taken from the seized materials. The analysis of the materials and products that are capable of being damaged or spoiled is to be carried out expeditiously. A decision of the Ministry of Economy and Commerce is to be issued for the regulation of the taking of samples, their preservation and analysis.

Without prejudice to the right of the defendant to request the release of the seized products from the competent court, the goods are to be released by force of law if an order from the court supporting the seizure within the 15 days following the day of the seizure is not issued.

If it is proved that the accusation attributed to him is incorrect, the concerned person is entitled to restitution and just compensation for the damage he has suffered.

Article 8 [Obstruction of Employees]

Anyone who obstructs the employees referred to in article 6 of this law from doing their work whether by preventing them from entering factories or stores or shops or other places in which there are materials the subject of a contravention or from obtaining samples from them or by any other means is to be punished by imprisonment for a period of not more than six months and a fine not less than 500 dirhams and not more than 5000 dirhams, or either one of them.

Article 9 [Confiscation of Falsified or Corrupted Goods]

The court must, when deciding to convict in the case of one of the crimes stated in articles 2 and 3 of this law, order the confiscation of the food or drugs or produce or products or other materials that are the subject of the crime.

In such a case, the court may also order the publication of the judgment in one or two local newspapers at the cost of the convicted person.

Article 10 [Other Penalties]

The competent court may, when deciding to convict the owner of a commercial shop or establishment or business or workshop for one of the crimes stated in articles 2 and 3 of this law, order the closure of the place for a period of not more than six months.

The court may also, in the case of a repetition of the crime, order the cancellation of the trade license.

If the holder of the license is not a United Arab Emirates national, the court may order his expulsion from the country.

Article 11 [Repeat Offenses]

In the case of a repeat of the offense, the accused is to be penalized by both imprisonment and a fine.

For the purpose of determining whether a crime has been repeated, the crimes stated in the previous articles and those stated in any other law relating to the prevention of fraud and deception are to be deemed to be the same.

Article 12 [Implementation]

The Minister of Economy and Commerce is to issue the necessary decisions to implement the provisions of this law.

Article 13 [Publication]

The Ministers, each according to his jurisdiction, and the competent authorities in the emirates that are members of the federation, must implement the provisions of this law which is to be published in the official gazette and is to become effective three months after the date of publication.

Zayed Bin Sultan Al Nahyan
President of the United Arab Emirates

Issued from the presidential palace in Abu Dhabi
Date: 3/20/1399 H
Corresponding to: 3/19/1979 M.

A12

Ministerial Decision no. 26 of 1984 Concerning the Implementing Regulations for Law no. 4 of 1979 in Relation to the Prevention of Fraud and Deception in Commercial Dealings

The Minister of Economy and Commerce,

After considering federal law no. 1 of 1972 in relation to the jurisdictions of the Ministries and the powers of the Ministers and the laws amending it, and

Federal law no. 4 of 1979 in relation to the prevention of fraud and deception in commercial dealings, and

Federal law no. 5 of 1979 in relation to agricultural quarantine, and

Federal law no. 6 of 1979 in relation to veterinary quarantine, and

Federal law no. 4 of 1983 in relation to the pharmacy profession and pharmaceutical establishments, and

Based on what was presented by the Undersecretary,

Decided:

Chapter 1: Unlawful Competitive Commercial Information

Article 1 [What is Commercial Information?]

In the application of the provisions of law no. 4 of 1979 and of the provisions of this regulation, any representation, direct or indirect, relating to the following is deemed to be commercial information:

1. The number of products sold, their quantity, their size, their measurements, their weight, their capabilities, their standard, or their specifications

2. The entity or country in which the product was made or produced and the date of manufacture or production and the expiry date[77]

3. The method of manufacture or production of the product

4. The constitutive ingredients in the composition of the product

5. The kind of product or its origin or its provenance or its source

6. The name or characteristics of the producer or manufacturer

7. The existence of patent or trademark or other industrial property right or any distinctions or prizes or commercial or industrial advantages

Article 2 [Commercial Information Must Be True]

Commercial information must be identical to the truth in all its aspects, whether the information has been put on the products themselves or on the shop or inside it or on packaging or invoices or correspondences or advertisements or on other means used to offer the products to the public.

Article 3 [Country and Producer Information]

The name of the seller or the importer or his address may not be put on the goods or products unless it is accompanied by accurate information written using prominent script about the country in which they were made or the entity that produced them.

Article 4 [Dissemination of False Information]

The trader may not disseminate information in consistent with the truth or publish false information relating to the provenance of goods or their characteristics or their worth, and may not advertise contrary to the fact that he possesses degrees or medals or awards and may not resort to any other means of deception of the public.

Article 5 [Incorrect or Deceptive Statements]

Traders, manufacturers, and producers may not do any of the following acts:

1. Use, directly or indirectly, an incorrect or deceptive statement about the provenance of the goods or their source or their character or the producer or manufacturer supplying the goods

---

77. The words "and the expiry date" were added by ministerial decision no. 8 of 1988 amending some of the provisions of ministerial decision no. 26 of 1984 concerning the implementing regulations for law no. 4 of 1979 in relation to the prevention of fraud and deception in commercial dealings.

2. Use, directly or indirectly, an incorrect or deceptive appellation of origin, or copy of an appellation of origin, even if the true origin of the goods is mentioned or if a translation of the appellation is used or if it is accompanied by expressions such as "type" or "style" or "copy" or any similar expression

3. Use a counterfeit or copied trademark, or knowingly use a mark without a right to do so, or changing the truth in any circumstances, and by a "trademark" is meant any visible means used to distinguish the products of one business from others

4. Any act that leads to the creation of obscurity or confusion by any means as to competitors' commercial names or their products or their industrial or commercial activity

Article 6 [Imported Goods]

All imported goods are to be subject to proof of their orig n, and their entry into the State is prohibited if they carry a mark or statement that is false or deceptive as to their origin or source, whether or not the marks or statements are on the goods themselves or on their packaging or on their wrapping.

In the application of the provision of these regulations, the expression "origin" of the goods is intended to mean the country of their production, and the expression "source" of the goods is intended to mean the country from which they were imported directly.

Article 7 [Importation of Certain Goods Prohibited]

The entry of imported goods that have not satisfied the conditions stated for them in the laws and systems for the protection of origin and industrial property is prohibited, but the Minister of Economy and Commerce may remove this prohibition for specific cases based on a report from the committee referred to in article 44 of these regulations.

Chapter 2: The Regulation of the Importation of Materials Subject to the Provisions of the Law

Article 8 [Re-export of Falsified or Corrupted Products]

It is not permitted to import or bring into the State any kind of foodstuff for humans or animals or medical drugs or agricultural produce or natural products or any other material that is falsified or corrupted. The importer must re-export them to their source within one week from the date of being notified, if the goods are perishable, and within two weeks for other goods, and may be extended when necessary.

If the importer delays or refuses to re-export the goods within the specified period, the goods are to be destroyed at his expense whether he attends or not. This is without prejudice to the right of the competent department of customs or ports to demand from the importer fees for storage and handling and services rendered for the re-export or destruction of the goods.

The Minister of Economy and Commerce may, based on an application by a concerned person, and the consent of the committee stated in article 44 of these regulations, decide to permit the entry of falsified or corrupted goods into the State for use for any other purpose for which it is suitable. The decision is to specify the conditions for the circulation of these goods and the domain of their use and their circulation.

Chapter 3: Monitoring Foodstuffs

Article 9 [Suitable for Human Consumption]

Foodstuffs must be have a nutritional value and be suitable for human consumption and be permitted religiously and legally. They must also satisfy the specifications and stipulations issued by the decision of the Minister of Economy and Commerce in agreement with the competent ministries and government departments.

In the application of the provisions of law no. 4 of 1979 and these regulations, the word "foodstuffs" is intended to mean any food or drink consumed by humans excluding medical preparations.

Article 10 [Food Additives]

Food additives must not be harmful to health and be permitted religiously and legally and must satisfy the specifications and stipulations issued by the decision of the Minister of Economy and Commerce in agreement with the competent ministries and government departments.

In the application of the provisions of these regulations, "food additives" is intended to mean any matter added to foodstuffs with the intention of coloring them, or improving their taste and flavor, or preserving them, or stabilizing their ingredients, or for any other permitted manufacturing or preparation or packaging purpose. Food additives are not in themselves considered to be foodstuffs or natural ingredients for any foodstuffs.

Article 11 [Dumping and Land Transiting of Imported Foodstuffs]

It is not permitted to empty any imported foodstuffs into any sea or air ports of the State. It is also not permitted to authorize their transiting through land points of entry in the State unless they have been examined and declared to have been examined by the quarantine inspectors or the competent health department in the port or entry point. These employees may request that the transporter or his representative produce the following documents:

1. A certified copy of the manifest
2. A certified copy of the plan of the arrangement of the products
3. A declaration that during the trip the foodstuffs will not be put with poisonous or health damaging materials
4. Any other documents stated in laws and regulations in force whose production is required

In any case, these employees have the right to view the originals of any documents produced.

Article 12 [Quarantine or Health Declaration]

It is not permitted to release any imported foodstuffs unless it has a declaration from competent quarantine or health department, as the case may be.

Article 13 [Registers of Foodstuff Importers and Traders]

Anyone importing or trading in foodstuffs must maintain orderly registers in which is recorded the kinds of foodstuffs in his possession, their quantities, their packaging, their weights, their sources, the date on which possession began, the quantity of them sold, and the date of sale with the name of the purchaser, if the purchaser is a wholesaler or retailer.

Article 14 [Compliance with Public Health Rules]

Factories, warehouses, kitchens and in general all shops that manufacture or prepare or make ready or sell or store foodstuffs must satisfy the health and technical specifications and stipulations set down by the responsible municipality department in agreement with the ministries and the competent government departments. Such places must also comply with public health rules in the manufacture or preparation or making ready of foodstuffs or medicinal materials and containers used.

Article 15 [Post-expiry Foodstuffs]

It is not permitted to sell any foodstuffs or offer them for sale or possess them for the purpose of sale when the period in which they are suitable for consumption has expired, and anyone who deals in manufacture, trade or storage of foodstuffs must notify the competent municipal ty department of the foodstuffs in his possession whose period for being suitable for consumption has expired in order that they may be destroyed.

Article 16 [Rules of Islamic Law]

The selling of frozen or cold or processed meat and poultry or offering it for sale or possessing it with the intention of sale is prohibited unless it is slaughtered in accordance with the rules of Islamic law.

Article 17 [Frozen Meats]

The selling of frozen or vacuum sealed meat, poultry, or fish or offering it for sale as if it is fresh is prohibited. It is also prohibited to defrost them.

Butcher shops are prohibited from selling frozen meat without a license from the competent municipality department.

Article 18 [Transport of Foodstuffs]

Means of transport of foodstuffs must satisfy the health and technical specifications and stipulations issued by a decision of the Minister of Economy and Commerce in agreement with the ministries and the competent government departments.

It is not permitted to transport any foodstuffs except those that have been declared in the license issued for the means of transport.

Article 19 [Health Certificate Required for Workers]

Anyone who works in the manufacture, preparation, sale, circulation, storage, transport, or cooking of foodstuffs must obtain a health certificate from the Ministry of Health, and must renew the certificate on the dates set down.

The employer may not permit any employee to undertake work referred to in the previous paragraph except after obtaining this certificate, and he must prevent workers from undertaking their work immediately upon knowing that one of them is suffering from a contagious disease that is specified by the Ministry of Health or when the health certificate has not been renewed. The employer must also supply the workers with the uniforms decided upon by the competent municipality department and prevent them undertaking their work unless they are wearing the uniform.

Article 20 [Pork and Alcohol Products]

Shops and entities licensed to trade in foodstuffs must separate pork meat, foodstuffs in which there are pork products, or alcoholic materials, and isolate them in a special place, and write on them in clear and prominent script the expression "pork meats and foodstuffs with pork products or alcoholic materials for non-Muslims," according to the circumstances.

Chapter 4: Foodstuff Labels

Article 21 [Untrue, Misleading and Deceptive Labels]

It is not permitted to describe goods or offer them with explanatory labels or statements which are untrue or misleading or deceptive or that suggest, in a direct or indirect way, that the goods are another material, or leading to any form of wrong impression as to their nature or their characteristics, or to confuse between them and other products.

In the application of the provisions of these regulations, "label" is intended to mean any statement, explanation, sign or illustrative or written or required[78] or pasted or engraved descriptive material on the package of the goods or what is attached to it. "Explanatory statements" is intended to mean labels or any written, printed or drawn material accompanying the goods or having a relation to them.

Article 22 [Various Requirements for Foodstuff Labels]

Statements written on the labels of packaged foodstuff or accompanying them must be prominent and clear so as to make it easy for consumers to read them in the ordinary circumstances of purchase and use and it is not permitted to hide these statements with any other drawn, written or printed thing. The statements must be written in a color different from the color of the background in a good and fixed manner so that it is difficult to remove or make any change in it and the alphabetical letters by which the name of the foodstuff are written must have a reasonable size compared to the other statements made on the label.

---

78. It is possible that the word "required" is an error in the text.

If the packaging is covered with an external covering, the covering must bear all the necessary statements and must not conceal the packaging label or prevent the reading of the statements with ease.

The name of the foodstuff and its net size must always be prominent in a part of the label prepared for showing to the consumer at the time of sale.

In the application of the provisions of these regulations, "packaged" is intended to mean anything that has been filled in advance to be ready for retail sale in containers and "container" is intended to mean any form in which foodstuffs are put for sale as a separate unit whether it contains all or part of it and including wrappings and coverings.

Article 23 [Meat Derivatives and Alcohol]

If foodstuffs contain fats or meats or enzymes or blood or gelatin or any other animal extracts, the label must mention the names and kinds of animals from which the mentioned materials have been extracted. If the foodstuffs contain any alcoholic materials, the label must contain a statement of that.

Article 24 [Special Purpose Foodstuffs]

If foodstuffs are prepared for special purposes or are stated to contain vitamins or minerals or otherwise, the label must give an explanatory statement and necessary information indicating the foodstuff that corresponds to what is described and its suitability for the purpose for which it was prepared.

For foodstuffs that cure by means of mild radiation, it is necessary to mention this on the labels of the containers.

Article 25 [Name of the Foodstuff]

The name of the foodstuff must be one that specifies the true nature of the product and be one that belongs to it and not to another. If one of the reliable standardized specifications determines a name or names for the foodstuff, then at least one of them must be used, otherwise the common or usual name is to be used if one exists, and if there is no such name, a suitable descriptive name may be used.

A created name may be used for this foodstuff on the condition that it is not deceptive and be accompanied by a suitable descriptive name.

Article 26 [List of Ingredients]

A list of ingredients must be written on the label in descending order of percentage of each of them except in following circumstances:

1. If the foodstuff is dried and prepared to be ready by adding water, it is permitted to order the ingredients in descending order according to the percentage of prepared nutritional material after the water under the heading "Ingredients after preparation."

2. If the composition of the foodstuff is known, and not mentioning its ingredients does not lead to the deception of the consumer, on the condition that explanatory statements on the label of the container enables to the consumer to understand the nature of the foodstuff.

3. If one of the reliable standardized specifications states otherwise.

Article 27 [Elements of Ingredients in Foodstuffs]

If one of the ingredients of the foodstuff contains a number of elements, the list of ingredients must contain the names of the elements except in those cases where the ingredient is a foodstuff whose reliable standardized specifications do not state the necessity of mentioning its elements in the complete list of ingredients.

Article 28 [Added Water]

Except in those cases in which water is a part of one of the ingredients of the foodstuff, the added water must be mentioned in the list of ingredients if this explanation leads to a better understanding of the composition of the product.

Article 29 [Preservatives, etc.]

If a foodstuff contains one of the permitted preservatives, whitening, coloring or other additives, the list of ingredients must contain a statement of them.

Article 30 [Instructions for storage, transport, and use]

The label for foodstuffs must set out instructions for the conditions for storage, for transport, and for the means of use.

Article 31 [Net Ingredients]

A statement of net ingredients must be separately written in metric units on the label of foodstuffs so that it is clear and distinctive and parallel to the base of the container, and specifying the net ingredients according to the nature of each foodstuff as follows:

1. The volume, in the case of liquid foodstuffs
2. The weight, in the case of solid foodstuffs, except foodstuffs that are sold by number, in which case the number is to be mentioned

3. The weight and volume, in the case of glutinous or semi-solid foodstuffs

In those cases in which the foodstuff is in a liquid medium which is to be removed before use, the statement of net ingredients must specify the net weight of the container and the liquid.

Article 32 [Frozen, Cold and Preserved Foodstuffs]

The net ingredients of the container must be equivalent to the weight and volume of the foodstuff when prepared according to its state as follows:

1. For frozen foodstuffs, the net weight and volume are to be specified at the point of freezing.
2. For cold foodstuffs, the net weight and volume are to be specified at 4 degrees Celsius.
3. For preserved foodstuffs, the net weight and volume are to be specified at 20 degrees Celsius.

Article 33 [Country of Origin, Manufacturer and Packager]

The name of the country of origin of the foodstuff and the name and address of the manufacturer or packager must be written on the label of the container. It is permitted to write the name of the importer or seller on the label in accordance with the conditions stated for this in the third article of these regulations.

If the foodstuff is subjected to preparation that changes its basic nature in another country, that country is deemed to be the country of origin in relation to the label and accompanying explanatory statements.

Article 34 [Production and Expiry Dates]

For foodstuffs in relation to which a decision has issued from the Minister of Economy and Commerce, the label of the foodstuff must state the date of production or manufacture or packaging and the date of expiry of its suitability for use.

Article 35 [Arabic Language]

The Arabic language must be one of the languages used on the label of foodstuffs and accompanying statements. If one or more languages are used beside the Arabic language, all statements in the other languages must be identical to the statements made in Arabic.

Article 36 [Two-month Grace Period]

After the passing of two months from the effective date of these regulations, it is not permitted to import, produce, circulate, or sell any packaged foodstuffs unless its label satisfies the conditions stated in these regulations.

Chapter 5: Seizure—Sample—Investigation

Article 37 [Customs Examination]

The customs departments in the emirates, each in its jurisdiction, must examine imported goods before their release to confirm the absence of any contraventions under the provisions of law no. 4 of 1979 or the provisions of these regulations, and in the event of a contravention, they must seize the goods and not release them if the contravention is one that requires the prevention of the entry of the goods into the State.

The contravention is to be evidenced by a report, which is to be sent to the director of the customs department together with the documents related to the goods in the event that the importer refuses to re-export the contravening goods to their source in the period stated in article 8 of these regulations.

Article 38 [Customs to Examine Imported Materials][79]

The customs departments inspectors in the ports and land and air entry points must fully or partially examine imported materials before allowing their release, and if they suspect the existence of a contravention of the provisions of law no. 4 of 1979 or the provisions of the regulations, they must take samples from the goods for analysis and prepare the necessary report in this matter, and inform the competent customs department to keep the goods and not release them.

In the case that the contravention is proven and the importer refuses to re-export the contravening goods to their source in the period stated in article 8 of the regulations, the report together with the documents relating to the goods is to be transferred to the director of the competent customs department and the commercial monitoring department in the Ministry is to be informed of the procedures taken in the matter.

---

79. This article is as amended by article 1 of ministerial decision no. 126 of 2003 amending ministerial decision no. 26 of 1984 concerning the implementing regulations for law no. 4 of 1979 in relation to the prevention of fraud and deception in commercial dealings.

Article 39 [Inspectors to Prove Crimes][80]

The inspectors representing the following authorities are to prove the crimes that occur contravening the provisions of the law for the prevention of fraud and deception in commercial dealings and its implementing regulations:

1. The Ministry of Economy and Commerce
2. The Ministry of Agriculture, Animal and Fish Resources
3. The Ministry of Finance and Industry—Department of Industrial Property
4. The Ministry of Information—Intellectual works and the rights of the author
5. The Ministry of Health
6. The departments of health and foodstuff monitoring in the municipalities in relation to foodstuffs
7. The organization for standards and measurements
8. The trade license authorities in the competent local authorities

These inspectors, each in their jurisdiction, are to be judicial seizure officers and are to have, in the process of identifying contraventions of the provisions of the law and the ministerial decisions implementing it, the right to enter all shops and places where goods, the subject of the provisions of the law, are offered or stored, and take the necessary samples for analysis. These inspectors are to be responsible for the making of the seizure report and taking samples in accordance with the procedures stated in the implementing regulations for the law and for the transfer of the report and its attachments to the department of commercial monitoring in the Ministry to consider bringing it before the national committee for the combating of commercial fraud formed pursuant to ministerial decision no. 295 of 2002 and its amendments in order to take the necessary decision in the matter.

Article 40 [Taking Samples]

The samples are to be taken at random and mixed well according to the kind of goods. This is to be done in the presence of the owner of the shop or the goods, or his representative. They are then to be divided into three parts and put inside a container sealed with red wax and labelled with the following information:

1. The date the sample was taken
2. The type of sample and its quantity

---

80. This article is as amended by article 2 of ministerial decision no. 126 of 2003 amending ministerial decision no. 26 of 1984 concerning the implementing regulations for law no. 4 of 1979 in relation to the prevention of fraud and deception in commercial dealings.

3. The name of the owner of the goods from whom the samples were taken, and his address

One of the samples is to be given to the owner and the second sample is to be kept with the party that took the samples and third is to be sent for analysis.

Article 41 [Samples Report]

A report evidencing the taking of the samples is to be prepared, and is to contain, in addition to the information stated in the previous article, the following:

1. Date and time of writing the report in numbers and letters
2. The address of the shop from which the samples were taken
3. The number of samples and the quantity of each
4. The quantity of goods from which the samples were taken and the approximate value
5. The circumstances in which the samples were taken with information as to the trademarks and the name of the material from which they were taken, and all other information that is useful in identifying the samples and the material from which they were taken

Article 42 [Seizure Report]

The seized goods are to be isolated and marked as such and kept with the owner and under his responsibility. A report is to be prepared containing the following information:

1. The place and date and time of the making of the seizure report in numbers and letters
2. The name of the writer of the seizure report, his title, his position, and signature
3. The names of the employees who made the seizure, their titles, their positions, and their signatures
4. The name of the owner of the seized goods, his title, profession, and his address
5. The goods seized, their kinds, their quantities, and approximate value
6. The goods that were not seized as far as known or inferred
7. The statements of the owner of the goods or his representative and his signature, and in the event of his refusal to sign, evidence of that in the report
8. All other useful facts and evidence of the presence of defendants at the time of making the inventory or of their refusal to attend
9. The date and time of the end of the making of the report

Article 43 [Matter to be Closed if the Owner Cooperates]

The owner of the goods must be notified of the result of the analysis and, if the analysis shows that the seized goods are unfit and it is apparent to the director of the authority that seized the goods in its jurisdiction that the owner of the goods had good intentions and agrees to destroy the goods at his expense, the matter is to be closed and the Minister of Economy and Commerce is to be notified of the decision in the matter.

In all other cases, after completing the investigation and receiving the results of the analysis, the papers are to be transferred to the public prosecution to raise a public case against the owner of the goods.

Article 44 [Investigation Committee]

A committee is to be formed by a decision of the Minister of Economy and Commerce headed by the undersecretary of the Ministry of Economy and Commerce and consisting of a representative from each of the Ministry of Economy and Commerce, the Ministry of Health and the Ministry of Agriculture and Fisheries, chosen by the competent Minister, and a representative from the general secretariat of the Municipalities, chosen by the general secretary, and a representative of the Customs Council chosen by the president of the Council, and a representative of the Federal Chambers of Commerce and Industry chosen by the general secretary. The committee is to be joined by a representative of each of the Customs departments and the Municipality department that identified the contravention in the domain of their jurisdiction, chosen by the head of the department, and a representative of the concerned Chamber of Commerce and Industry, chosen by the head of the Chamber.

The jurisdiction of the committee is the investigation of contraventions of the provisions of the federal law no. 4 of 1979 and these regulations that are transferred to it by the Minister of Economy and Commerce and the competent government departments. The committee must complete the investigation within 15 days from the transfer of the matter to it and produce its report to the Minister of Economy and Commerce to take what steps he deems suitable in the matter.

Article 45 [Publication]

This decision is to be published in the official gazette and is to come into force from the date of publication.

Saif Ali Al Jarwan
Minister of Economy and Commerce

Issued in Abu Dhabi
Date: Ramadhan 14, 1404 H
Corresponding to: June 14, 1984 M.

A13

Ministerial decision no. 418 of 2007 in relation to the approval of the trademark "Organic"

The Minister of Environment and Water,

After considering:

Federal law no. 1 of 1972 in relation to the jurisdictions of the Ministries and the powers of the Ministers and the laws amending it, and

Decree for federal law no. 1 of 2006 amending some of the provisions of federal law no. 1 of 1972 in relation to the jurisdictions of the Ministries and the powers of the Ministers, and

Cabinet decision no. 5 of 2006 in relation to the transfer of some of ministerial functions, and

Ministerial decision no. 100 of 2004 in relation to the establishment of units attached to the Department of Agricultural Research and Advice, and

In view of the importance of developing organic farming in the State and of monitoring organic products throughout the processes of production and marketing, and of curbing acts of fraud and deception, and

Based on the approval of the Minister of Economy to register a trademark in the name of the Minister of Environment and Water for organic products of the State and which was registered under number 82214 on 13 June 2007 in class 42,[81] and

Based on the needs of the public interest,

Decided as follows:

Article 1 [ORGANIC Trademark Registered]

The trademark "Organic, 'Udhwee [in Arabic characters]" registered with the Ministry of Economy under no. 82214 on 13 June 2007 in class 42 has been

---

81. This registration resulted from application no. 83855 filed on August 2, 2006, published in trademark journal no. 67.

approved and is for organic agricultural products. The mark is owned by the Ministry of Environment and Water in the United Arab Emirates, and has the following appearance:

[image of the mark—an oval divided horizontally by a curved line with ORGANIC below the line and 'Udhwee in Arabic characters above the line]

Article 2 [Conditions of Use]

The conditions of use of the trademark are:

1. It is not permitted to use the trademark except with the approval of the Ministry of Environment and Water and the user must enter into a contract with the Ministry before beginning use pursuant to conditions and for a specified period.

2. The trademark is to be used for organic products that have been inspected, certified, and approved by the Ministry of Environment and Water.

3. The original user of the trademark must inform the Ministry of Environment and Water of all secondary users of the mark and is to be responsible for any wrong that may result from the use of the mark.

4. It is prohibited to use the trademark with other similar marks without the approval of the Ministry of Environment and Water.

5. It is permitted to put the "Organic" trademark with the mark that distinguishes the producer.

6. It is not permitted to use the mark as a trademark for reasons other than those issued for it.

7. When putting the trademark on products that are not packaged, it is necessary to indicate that the products have been certified and approved by the Ministry of Environment and Water.

8. It is not permitted to change the color of the mark or its size when printing it on the products except with the prior approval of the Ministry of Environment and Water.

Article 3 [Publication]

This decision is deemed to be effective from the date it is issued and all those who are concerned with the matter are to do what is necessary to implement it and publish it in the official gazette.

Dr. Muhammad Saeed Al Kindi
Minister of Environment and Water

Date: Shawwal 18, 1428 H
Corresponding to: October 29, 2007 M.

APPENDIX

A14

Federal Law No. 7 of 2002 in Relation to the Rights of the Author and Neighboring Rights

Contents

We, Zayed Bin Sultan Al Nahyan, President of the United Arab Emirates, after considering:

The constitution, and

Federal law no. 1 of 1972 in relation to the jurisdictions of the Ministries and the powers of the Ministers and the laws amending it, and

Federal law no. 15 of 1980 in relation to printed matter and publishing, and

Federal law no. 40 of 1992 in relation to the protection of intellectual works and the rights of the author, and

Based on what was presented by the Minister of Information and Culture, and the approval of the Cabinet, and the ratification of the Supreme Federal Council,

Issued the following law:

Article 1 [Definitions]

In the application of the provisions of this law, the words and expressions below are intended to have the following meanings unless the context of the text requires otherwise:

The State:	The United Arab Emirates.
The Ministry:	The Ministry of Economy.[82]
The Minister:	The Minister of Economy.[83]
Work:	Any creative[84] work in the field of literature, or the arts, or the sciences, of whatever kind or manner of expression, or whatever its importance or its purpose.[85]

---

82. Federal law no. 32 of 2006 amending federal law no. 7 of 2002 in relation to the rights of the author and neighboring rights, directed the replacement of "Ministry of Information and Culture" with "Ministry of Economy."

83. Federal law no. 32 of 2006 amending federal law no. 7 of 2002 in relation to the rights of the author and neighboring rights, directed the replacement of "Minister of Information and Culture" with "Minister of Economy."

84. The Arabic word here is "mubtakar," which comes from the verb "ibtakara," to invent, create or to originate, but also to be the first person to do something. In other contexts, it might be more appropriate to translate it as "inventive" or "innovative."

85. This definition appears to be an adaptation of article 1 of the Berne Convention: "The expression 'literary and artistic works' shall include every production in the literary, scientific and

Author:	A person who creates a work. The author of a work is considered to be the one who puts his name on the work, or to whom the work is attributed upon its publication, unless proven otherwise.[86]
	The author of a work is also considered to be the one who publishes a work without a name or under a pseudonym or in any other way, on the condition that there is no doubt in knowing the true identity of the author. If there is such a doubt, the publisher or producer of the work, whether or not a natural or legal person, is deemed to be the representative of the author in exercising his rights until the real identity of the author is known.
Creativity:[87]	The creative[88] characteristic that gives to the work originality and distinctiveness.
Holders of neighboring rights:	Performance artists, producers of sound recordings, broadcasting organizations, as defined by this law.
Performers:	Actors, singers, musicians, dancers or other persons who recite or sing or play or perform in any way, literary or artistic or other works, protected pursuant to the provisions of this law or that are in the public domain.
Producer of sound recordings:	A natural or legal person who records for the first time the sounds of a performer or other sounds.[89]
Broadcasting organization:	Any entity making wireless audio or visual or audio-visual broadcast transmissions.
Broadcasting:	Making an audio or visual or audio-visual transmission to the public by wireless means, of a work or a performance or a sound recording or a program and its recording. Transmitting by means of satellites is also considered to be broadcasting.

---

artistic domain, whatever may be the mode or form of its expression." The Arabic text is substantially the same as article 138.1 of the IPEG.

86. The Arabic text for this definition is identical to article 138.3 of the IPEG.

87. The Arabic word here is "Ibtikaar" and comes from the same root as the word for "creative" in the definition of a "work." The Arabic text for this definition follows article 138.2 of the IPEG but adds the concept of "distinctiveness."

88. The Arabic word here is "ibdaa'e, a possible synonym for the word "mubtakar" that is used in the definition of a "work."

89. The Arabic word here is "asswaat" and is generally used to mean both "sounds" and "voices" depending on the context. I have translated both uses of the word in this sentence as "sounds" to capture the broader meaning in English.

Publishing:	Making available to the public a work or a sound recording or a broadcast program or any performance, in any way.
Public performance:	An action that leads to the direct communication of a work to the public such as acting a theatrical work or offering or performing artistic works, or showing audio-visual works, and playing musical works, and reciting literary works, it making no difference whether the performance is live or recorded.
Public communication:	Transmission, by wire or wirelessly, of a work, or a performance of a sound recording, or broadcast program, the receiving of which is possible by means of the transmission alone, other than a transmission to family members and close friends, in any place other than the place from which the transmission starts, regardless of the time or place or manner of receiving.
Reproduction:	Making one or more copies of a work, or a sound recording, or a broadcast program, or any performance, in any manner or form, including permanent or temporary electronic downloading or storage, regardless of the method or device used in the reproduction.
Sound recording:	Any aural fixation of a group of sounds resulting in a specific performance whatever the manner of fixation or medium used. Sound recordings include the process of fixing sounds with pictures to produce audio-visual works, unless agreed otherwise.[90]
Producer of audio-visual works:	The natural or legal person who provides the necessary conditions to produce an audio-visual work, and who takes on the responsibility of its production.
Collective work:	A work created by a group of authors under the direction of a natural or legal person who is responsible for the work's publication in his name and under his supervision. The contributions of the authors to the work are incorporated into the work for the general purpose intended by the person who directed the work and are not able to be separated or distinguished.[91]
Joint work:	A work in whose creation a number of persons participated, whether or not it is possible to separate

---

90. The expression "unless otherwise agreed" seems out of place here. Statutory definitions are not usually open to the agreement of those to whom the law applies.
91. The Arabic text here is almost identical to IPEG article 138.4.

	each person's share, and which is not classified as a collective work.[92]
Derivative work:	A work whose existence relies on the existence of a prior work such as translations. Collections of literary and artistic works and collections of folkloric expressions are to be considered as derivative works as long as they are creative as to their arrangement or choice of contents.[93]
National folklore:	Any expression of oral, musical, dynamic, or tangible popular folklore containing distinctive elements reflecting traditional artistic heritage originating and continuing in the State, and not attributable to a known author.[94]
Public domain:	All those works that are from the beginning excluded from protection or those for which the period of protection for the financial rights has expired.[95]

Chapter 1: The Scope of Protection

Article 2 [Works and Rights Protected from Infringement]

The protection established by this law is to be enjoyed by the authors of works and the holders of neighboring rights, if their rights are infringed within the State,[96] especially in relation to the following works:

1. Books, pamphlets, articles and other written works
2. Computer programs and their applications, databases and such similar works as are determined by a decision of the Minister
3. Lectures, speeches, addresses, and other works that have a similar nature
4. Dramatic works, including those with music and those without sound
5. Musical works with and without words
6. Audio, visual, and audio-visual works

---

92. The Arabic text here is almost identical to IPEG article 138.5 but the word order has been changed.
93. Compare EGIP, article 138.6.
94. Article 138.7 of the EGIP contains explanations of the meanings of some of the terms used here. The term "dynamic folklore," for example, includes dance and theatre.
95. The definition here is almost identical to IPEG article 138.8.
96. It is unclear why the enjoyment of rights under the law has been made contingent upon infringement occurring. This expression is not in the corresponding provision of the EGIP—article 140.

7. Architectural works and engineering drawings and plans.

8. Works of drawing by means of lines or colors, sculpture, engraving, printing on stone, on fabric, on wood and on metals, and any similar works in the field of the fine arts.

9. Photographic and similar works

10. Works of applied art and plastic art

11. Illustrative pictures, geographical maps, diagrams. three-dimensional works relating to geography, topography and architectural designs, etc.

12. Derivative works, without prejudice to the protection of the works from which they are derived[97]

The protection of the law extends to the title of a work if it is creative[98] and to the written creative idea for a broadcast program.

Article 3 [Limits of Protection]

The protection [of the law] does not extend to thoughts, procedures, methods of operation, mathematical concepts, principles and mere facts unless a creative form of expression is given to them. Specifically, protection does not extend to:

1. Official documents, whatever language they were originally in or were transferred to, such as texts of laws, regulations, decisions, international agreements, judicial rulings, rulings of arbitrators and decisions published by administrative committees with judicial jurisdiction

2. Reports and information about events and current affairs that are purely informational

3. Works that have fallen into the public domain

However, collections of what is referred to in paragraphs 1, 2, and 3 of this article enjoy the protection of the law if the collecting or arrangement of them or any efforts that have gone into them are distinguished by creativity.[99]

Article 4 [Registration of Rights in Works]

The Ministry is to establish a system with the competent authority for the depositing or registration of rights in works and for dealings that may occur pursuant to what is set down in the implementing regulations to this law.

The records of the deposit or registration of rights with the Ministry are a reference for the particulars of the work.

---

97. The Arabic text of this list is substantially the same as the list in article 140 of the EGIP.
98. The Arabic text here is identical to the last phrase of article 140.13 of the EGIP.
99. Compare EGIP, article 141.

The non-deposit of a work or non-registration of rights or of dealings that may occur does not in any way prejudice to the rights established by this law.

Chapter 2: Rights of the Author

Article 5 [Moral Rights of the Author]

The author and his successors are to enjoy moral rights in the work, and such rights may not be limited by time or alienated, including the following:

1. The right to decide to publish the work for the first time.
2. The right to have the work attributed to him.
3. The right to object to any amendment of the work if the amendment would be denigrating to or a distortion of the work or would be damaging to the reputation of the author.
4. The right to withdraw his work from circulation, if serious reasons arise justifying it. This right is to be exercised through the competent court, with an obligation to pay fair compensation to the one to whom the financial rights of exploitation have been transferred and in the time specified for it by the court and before the execution of the order to withdraw, otherwise any effect of the order is terminated.

Article 6 [Amendments in Translating]

Amendment in the domain of translation is not to be considered infringement unless the translator omitted a reference to the places of deletion or change or his work harms the reputation of the author.[100]

Article 7 [Who May License a Work]

The author alone and his successors after him, or the holder of the right of the author, may license, in any way, the exploitation of the work, especially by means of reproduction including electronic downloading and storing, or acting by any method, or broadcasting, or re-broadcasting, or public performance or transmission, or translation, or alteration, or amendment, or rental, or lending, or publishing in any way, including giving access to the work by means of a computer or information and communication networks, or by other means.

---

100. The Arabic text of this article is identical to part of paragraph 143.3 of the EGIP.

Article 8 [Renting Works]

There is no right to rent computer programs unless the program itself is the subject of the rental. Similarly, there is no right to rent audio-visual works unless the rental is for the ordinary exploitation of the work.

Article 9 [Transfers of Rights]

The author or his successors may transfer to others, whether natural or legal persons, all or some of his financial rights set out in this law. It is a condition of making any disposal of rights that it be in writing and the right the subject of the disposal be specified, with a statement of the purpose of the disposal, the period and place of exploitation. The author continues to be the owner of all rights that he does not expressly assign.

Without prejudice to the moral rights of the author stated in this law, the author may not do anything that would frustrate the exploitation of the work the subject of the disposal.

Article 10 [Consideration for Transfers of Rights]

The author or his successors may be paid in cash or its equivalent for his transfer of one or more of his financial rights to another to exploit the work that is based on a shared percentage of the income resulting from the exploitation. He may also contract to receive a lump sum payment, or to receive both a lump sum and a percentage of income.[101]

Article 11 [Judicial Review of Consideration]

If it is apparent that the agreement referred in article 10 of this law is detrimental to the right of the author or to any holders of neighboring rights, or becomes detrimental because of circumstances that arise after contracting, the author or his successors may resort to the competent court to request a review of the value of the payment that was agreed upon.[102]

Article 12 [Transfers of Rights in Computer Programs]

Without prejudice to the provisions of article 9 of this law, the transfer of financial rights in relation to computer programs and applications or databases is subject to the license contract that is stated on or affixed to the program

---

101. The Arabic text of this article is almost identical to article 150 of the EGIP.
102. The Arabic text of this article is almost identical to most of article 151 of the EGIP.

whether appearing on the disc[103] or on the screen when downloading or storing the program. The purchaser or user of the program is obliged to comply with the conditions stated in the license.

Article 13 [Disposal of Original Copies]

Any disposal by the author of the author's original copy of the work does not result in a transfer of the author's financial rights, unless otherwise agreed.

However, the transferee of the property in the original copy of the work is not obliged—without prior agreement—to permit the author to copy the work, transfer it or exhibit it.[104]

Article 14 [Attachment of Financial Rights]

The financial rights of authors in their published works may be attached. However, the unpublished works of a dead author cannot be attached unless it is proven with certainty that he intended to publish the works before his death.[105]

Article 15 [Future Copyright Works]

Any disposal by the author of all of the author's future intellectual production or more than five of his future works is null and void.[106]

Chapter 3: The Scope of Protection for Holders of Neighboring Rights

Article 16 [Moral Rights of Performers]

Performers and their successors enjoy a moral right that cannot be assigned or be subject to limitations, entitling them to:

1. The right to attribute the performance to themselves whether it was live or recorded
2. The right to prevent any alteration, distortion, or derogatory treatment or modification of their performance in any way that damages their reputation

---

103. The meaning here could be broader than "disc" to include anything that carries the program.
104. This article corresponds to article 152 of the EGIP.
105. This article corresponds to article 154 of the EGIP.
106. The Arabic text here is identical to article 153 of the EGIP except that the concept of "more than five works" has been added in the UAE version of the article.

The Ministry is to exercise this moral right after the end of the period of protection of the financial rights stated in this law in order to preserve the manner in which the performance was created.[107]

Article 17 [Financial Rights of Performers]

Performers alone enjoy the following financial rights:

1. The right to transmit their unrecorded[108] performance and transfer it to the public
2. The right to fix their performance in a sound recording
3. The right to reproduce their recorded[109] performance in a sound recording

The recording of a live performance on any medium or renting it with the purpose of obtaining a direct or indirect commercial return or transmitting it or making it available to the public without the consent of the owner of the right is to be considered prohibited exploitation.

The provisions of this article apply to the fixing of the performers' performance in an audio-visual work unless otherwise agreed.[110]

Article 18 [Rights of Producers of Sound Recordings]

Producers of sound recordings alone enjoy the following financial rights:

1. The right to prevent any exploitation of their recordings by any means without a license from them (reproducing or renting or broadcasting or re-broadcasting or making their recording available to the public by computer or other means is to be considered prohibited exploitation).
2. The right to publish their recordings by wire or wireless means or by computer or other means.[111]

Article 19 [Rights of Broadcasting Organizations]

Broadcasting organizations alone enjoy the following financial rights:

1. The right to grant licenses to exploit its broadcast recordings and programs.

---

107. The Arabic text here is substantially similar to article 155 of the EGIP.
108. Or "unfixed."
109. Or "fixed."
110. This article corresponds to article 156 of the EGIP.
111. This article corresponds to article 157 of the EGIP.

2. The right to prevent any communication of its programs or recordings to the public without a license from it (recording these programs or making copies of them or reproducing their recordings or renting them or re-broadcasting or transmitting them to the public by any means is deemed to be prohibited).[112]

Chapter 4: Term of Protection and Licensing the Use of Works

Article 20 [Terms of Protection]

1. The financial rights of the author stated in this law are protected for the life of the author and fifty years from the first Gregorian year following his death.[113]

2. The financial rights of authors of joint works are protected for the lives of the authors and fifty years from the first Gregorian year following the death of the last author that remains alive.[114]

3. In relation to collective works, if the author is a legal person, the financial rights of the author—with the exception of authors of works of applied art—are protected for fifty years from the first Gregorian year following the year of first publication, but if the author is a natural person, the financial rights are protected for the periods referred to in paragraphs 1 and 2 of this article.

 The financial rights in works published for the first time after the death of the author expire fifty years from the first Gregorian year following the year in which the work was first published. [115]

4. The financial rights in works published without the name of the author or under a pseudonym are protected for fifty years from the first Gregorian year following the year in which the work was first published. However, if the author is known and identifiable or he reveals his identity, then the period of protection is calculated according to the principle stated in paragraph 1 of this article.[116]

5. The financial rights of the authors of works of applied art expire 25 years from the first Gregorian year following the year of first publication.[117]

---

112. This article corresponds to article 158 of the EGIP.
113. The Arabic text of this paragraph is substantially identical to article 160 of the EGIP.
114. The Arabic text of this paragraph is substantially identical to article 161 of the EGIP.
115. The Arabic text of these two paragraphs is substantially identical to article 162 of the EGIP.
116. The Arabic text of this paragraph is substantially identical to article 153 of the EGIP.
117. The Arabic text of this paragraph is substantially identical to article 164 of the EGIP.

6. In the cases where the period of protection is calculated from the date of first publication, the date of first publication is taken as the basis for calculating the period regardless of any subsequent re-publication, unless on re-publication the author made essential amendments such that the work can be considered as a new work.

If the work consists of several parts or volumes published separately and over a period, each part or volume is to be considered as an independent work for the purposes of calculating the period of protection.[118]

7. The financial rights of performers are protected for fifty years calculated from the first Gregorian year following the year of the performance. If the performance is fixed in a sound recording, the period of protection is calculated from the end of the year in which the performance was fixed.[119]

8. The financial rights of producers of recordings are protected for a period of fifty Gregorian years calculated from the first Gregorian year following the year in which the recording was published or, if the recording has not been published, from the first year in which the recording was fixed.[120]

9. The rights of broadcasting organizations are protected for a period of twenty years from the first Gregorian year following the year in which the programs were first broadcast.[121]

Article 21 [Compulsory Licenses]

Any person may apply to the Ministry for the grant of a compulsory license to copy or translate or both any work protected pursuant to the provisions of this law, but in relation to licenses to translate, only after the passing of three years from the date of publication of the work. The license is to be issued by means of a reasoned decision specifying the time and place of exploitation and the fair payment to which the author is entitled. The purpose of the issue of the license must always be restricted to educational needs of any kind or level, or the needs of public libraries or archives. Such licenses are to be granted pursuant to the conditions, constraints, and terms specified in the implementing regulations of this law, and in a way that does not cause unjustifiable damage to the lawful interests of the author or his successors or prejudice the normal exploitation of the work. The fees to be charged for granting such licenses are to be specified in a decision of the Cabinet.[122]

---

118. The Arabic text of these two paragraphs is substantially identical to article 165 of the EGIP.
119. This paragraph corresponds to article 166 of the EGIP.
120. This paragraph corresponds to article 167 of the EGIP.
121. This paragraph corresponds to article 168 of the EGIP.
122. Article 21 of the ARL 2002 corresponds to article 170 of the EGIP.

Article 22 [Permitted Acts]

Without prejudice to the moral rights of the author set out in this law, the author, after the publication of his work, may not prevent others from doing any of the following acts:

1. Making a single copy of the work for the copier's personal use for purely non-profit and non-professional purposes, but excluded from this are [a] works of fine art or applied art unless they are located in a public place and the owner of the rights or his successors has consented, and [b] architectural works not covered by paragraph (7) of this article, and [c] computer programs and applications and databases not mentioned in paragraph (2) of this article

2. Making a single copy of a computer program or its applications or a database with the knowledge of the lawful possessor, who has the right to adapt it, but only within the limits of the licensed purpose, for the purpose of back-up, or as a replacement for when the original copy is lost or destroyed or unusable, on the condition that the substitute or adapted copy is destroyed as soon as the copier no longer has the right to possess the original copy, even if the copy is carried or stored on a computer

3. Copying protected works for use in judicial or similar procedures within the limits of what is necessary for such procedures and with mention of the source and author's name

4. Photocopying a single copy of the work with the knowledge of the documentation office, archives, libraries or documentary centers, not being for any direct or indirect profit, in either of the following two circumstances:

> a. The copying is for the purpose of preserving the original, or to replace a lost or destroyed copy or one that has become unsuitable for use, and it is not possible to obtain a substitute in reasonable circumstances.
> b. The purpose of the copying is to answer a request from a natural person to use the copy in study or research but only once or at irregular intervals, but only if it has not been possible to obtain a license to copy pursuant to the provisions of this law.

5. Quoting short paragraphs or extracts or analyses within the limits of what is customary for such a work, with the intention of criticism or debate or news, mentioning the source and the name of the author.

6. Performing the work in family gatherings or, if performed by students, performing the work in educational institutes, provided that the performance is not for direct or indirect payment.

7. Showing works of fine art, applied art, plastic art or architecture in broadcast programs if the work is permanently located in a public place.

8. Copying short parts of a work in written form or in an audio or visual recording for educational, or cultural, or religious, or professional training

purposes, provided that the copying is within reasonable limits, and does not exceed its purpose, and the name of the author and the title of the work are mentioned each time it is possible, and that the copier is not aiming to obtain a direct or indirect profit, and on condition that it was not possible to obtain a license to copy pursuant to the provisions of this law.[123]

Article 23 [Rights of the Press]

Without prejudice to the moral rights of the author pursuant to this law, the author may not prevent reproduction by newspapers periodicals, or broadcasting organizations for the purpose of publishing any of the following within the limits that are justified by that purpose:

1. Extracts of the author's works that have been lawfully made available to the public. This provision applies to also to works that have been seen or heard during current events or broadcasts of the work or any other transmission of the work to the public.
2. The author's published articles relating to debates on subjects that have engaged public opinion at particular times, as long as at the time of publication such articles have not been declared to be prohibited.
   In the cases mentioned in paragraphs 1 and 2, the source and the name of the author must be mentioned.
3. Speeches, lectures and discussions in public parliamentary or judicial sessions, or in public meetings, as long as they are addressed to the public and reproduced in the context of current news reporting.
   The author alone, or his successors, continues to have the right to collect any of these works in collections attributed to him.[124]

Article 24 [Same Rules for Holders of Neighboring Rights]

The rules applying to the financial rights of the author set out in this law also apply to the holders of neighboring rights.[125]

---

123. Article 22 of the ARL 2002 corresponds to article 171 of the EGIP.
124. Article 23 of the ARL 2002 corresponds to article 172 of the EGIP.
125. Article 24 of the ARL 2002 is almost identical to article 173 of the EGIP.

Chapter 5: Provisions Relating to Some Works

Article 25 [Joint Authors]

If a number of persons participated in the creation of a work and it is not possible to separate the contribution of each of them, all of the participants are considered to be authors of the work equally, unless otherwise agreed in writing. Only if the participants agree in writing prior to creating the work may one of them alone exercise the author's rights.

If each of the authors participated in the work contributing different kinds of art, each of them has the right to exploit the part that he alone contributed, on the condition that the exploitation does not damage the exploitation of the work for the others, unless otherwise agreed in writing. Each of them has the right to raise a case of infringement of any one of the author's rights protected by this law.

If one of the participating authors dies without a successor, his share in the work passes to the remaining participants or their successors after them, unless otherwise agreed in writing.[126]

Article 26 [Authors of Collective Works]

The natural or legal person who directed the creation of a collective work may alone exercise the financial and moral rights in relation to it, unless there is an agreement to the contrary.[127]

Article 27 [Audio and Visual Works]

1. The following are considered to be joint authors of an audio-visual, audio or visual work:

   a. The author of the scenario
   b. The person who adapted an existing literary work such that it is suitable for an audio-visual use
   c. The author of the dialogue
   d. The composer of music that is made especially for the work
   e. The director, if he exercised effective control over the production of the work

---

126. The Arabic text of article 25 of the ARL 2002 is substantially the same as article 174 of the EGIP.
127. Article 26 of the ARL 2002 corresponds to article 175 of the EGIP.

If the work is taken or derived from another prior work. the author of the prior work is deemed to be one of the authors participating in the new work.

2. The author of the literary or musical part has the right to publish what is his in any way other than the way in which the joint work is published, unless agreed in writing to the contrary.

3. If one of the participants in the creation of an audio-visual or audio or visual work refrains from completing his part of the work, the rest of the participants are not prevented from exploiting the part of the work created by them, but without prejudice to the rights in the creation resulting from the participation of the one who refrained.

4. The producer, during the agreed period for the exploitation of the audio-visual, audio or visual work, is to be the representative of the authors of the work and their successors, in agreeing to the exploitation of the work, without prejudice to the rights of the authors of the literary works, or extracted or adapted musical works, unless otherwise agreed in writing.

The producer is deemed to be the publisher of this work and has the rights of the publisher for it and for its reproductions, within the limits of the purposes of financial exploitation.[128]

Article 28 [Anonymous and Pseudonymous Works]

The author of a work that does not carry the name of the author or carries a pseudonym is deemed to have appointed the publisher as his representative in exercising the rights set out in this law, unless he appoints another representative or declares his identity or confirms his role as author or there is no doubt as to the truth of his identity.[129]

Article 29 [Attachment of Infringing Buildings]

Buildings may not be attached and an order may not be issued for the destruction, change of features or confiscation of a building, with the purpose of preserving the rights of the architectural author whose engineering designs and drawings or plans have been unlawfully used, but that does not prejudice his right to just compensation.

---

128. Article 27 of the ARL 2002 corresponds to 177 of the EGIP.
129. The Arabic text of article 28 of the ARL 2002 is substantially the same as article 176 of the EGIP.

Chapter 6: Collecting Society Management of the Author's Rights and Neighboring Rights

Article 30 [Assignment to Collecting Societies]

The holders of the rights of the author and of neighboring rights may assign their financial rights to a professional collecting society that specializes in their management, or may authorize other persons to exercise these rights.

Contracts executed by the collecting society or other persons in relation to this matter are considered to be civil contracts.

Article 31 [Discrimination by Collecting Societies]

The collecting society or other persons mentioned in article 30 of this law may not discriminate between applicants seeking to contract with it for the exploitation of works entrusted to it.

The grant of licenses by the collecting society or other persons for reduced payment is not to be considered discrimination in the following two circumstances if based on a reasoned decision:

1. Exploitation of works for public celebrations by means of live performance
2. Exploitation of works in the context of educational or cultural activities that do not produce a direct or indirect financial return

Article 32 [Collecting Society Licenses]

The collecting society or other persons who are responsible for the management of the rights of the author and neighboring rights may not practice their activities except with an annual license from the Ministry and the Ministry may put into the implementing regulations any rules organizing the work of the collecting society or persons and make the necessary amendments to the rules and the system of licensing and the carrying out of its work.

The Cabinet is to issue a decision specifying the fees for the grant of licenses.

Article 33 [Register of Collecting Society Members]

The collecting societies and those responsible for the management of the rights of the author and neighboring rights must hold registers with the names of its members and their titles and the acts for which they have contracted, explaining the kind of act and duration and the payment agreed. They must inform the Ministry of any changes in the registers, and must abide by administrative decisions issued by the Ministry. The Ministry has the right to withdraw the license if the collecting society or other persons do not comply with the provisions of the law and regulations and administrative decisions implementing the law.

Chapter 7: Precautionary Procedures and Penalties

Article 34 [Interim Court Orders]

The President of the First Instance Court may, based on an application by the author or his successors and, consistent with the orders sought in the pleadings, order the following procedures in relation to any works published or exhibited without the written permission of the author or his successors:

1. To make a detailed description of the work
2. To stop publication, exhibition or production of the work
3. To attach the original work or its copies (whether books, pictures, drawings, performances, photographs, sound recordings or broadcast programs or other works) and also the materials used in re-publishing the work or extracting copies from it, on the condition that these materials are suitable only for re-publishing the work
4. To record the public performance of the playing, the acting or the recitation of the work to the public, and prevent the continuation of the present exhibition or prohibit it in the future
5. To calculate the financial return produced by the publication or exhibition, if necessary by means of an expert appointed for this purpose, and attach the financial return in any case
6. To obtain proof of the fact of infringement of any of the rights protected pursuant to the provisions of this law

The President of the First Instance Court may, in any case, order the appointment of an expert to assist the court bailiff who has been charged with execution of the order, and may order the applicant to deposit a suitable security. The applicant must file the main case in relation to the dispute within fifteen days after the issue of the order, and if the applicant does not file the case within this period, the order is to cease to have effect.[130]

---

130. Article 34 of the ARL 2002 corresponds to article 179 of the EGIP.

Article 35 [Right to Challenge Interim Court Orders]

The person against whom the order has been issued may challenge the order before the President of the Court that issued the order within twenty days of the issue of the order, and in this case, the President of the Court may either confirm the order, or wholly or partially cancel it, or appoint a guardian whose role it is to re-publish the work the subject of the dispute, or to exploit it, or to exhibit it, or to manufacture it or to extract copies of it, and deposit the financial return produced in the treasury of the court until the main case has been decided.[131]

Article 36 [Customs Seizure]

The customs authorities may order, on their own account or upon application by the author or the right holder or their successors, based on a reasoned decision, the non-release from customs, for a period of not more than twenty days, of any copied material infringing the provisions of this law. The implementing regulations are to specify the circumstances, conditions and procedures for a non-release application, and what supporting documents should be attached to it, and the value of what is necessary for the applicant to deposit as suitable financial security to ensure the seriousness of the application. Three days from the date on which the application is filed satisfying all requirements, the applicant will be informed of the decision immediately upon its issue.

In any case, the customs authorities may not prevent interested parties from examining the materials in respect of which the non-release order has been made, pursuant to the conditions that are specified in the implementing regulations.

Article 37 [Infringement and Its Penalties]

Without prejudice to any harsher punishment stated in any other law, any person who, without the written permission of the author or the holder of neighboring rights, or their successors, does any of the following acts, is to be punished by imprisonment for a period of at least two months and a fine not less than 10,000 dirhams and not exceeding 50,000 dirhams or either one of these:

1. Infringes any of the moral or financial rights of the author or holder of a neighboring right as set out in this law, including putting any work or performance or sound recording or broadcast program that is protected by

---

131. Article 35 of the ARL 2002 corresponds to article 180 of the EGIP.

this law within the reach of the public whether by means of computer or the Internet or information networks or communication networks or any other means

2. Sells or rents or makes available for circulation in any way a work or sound recording or broadcast program protected pursuant to the provisions of this law

The punishment set out in this article is to be multiplied according to the number of works or performances or broadcasts or recordings the subject of the crime.

If the crime is committed again, imprisonment for not less than six months and a fine of not less than 50,000 dirhams are to be imposed.[132]

Article 38 [Manufacturing and Importing for Sale, etc.]

Without prejudice to any harsher punishment stated in any other law, any person who commits the following acts is to be punished by imprisonment for a period of at least three months and a fine not less than 50,000 dirhams and not exceeding 500,000 dirhams:

1. Manufacturing or importing, without a right to do so, and with the purpose of selling or renting or circulating, any work or counterfeit copies or any apparatus or means or tools designed or prepared especially for manipulating protection or techniques used by the author or the holder of a neighboring right to transmit or offer for circulation or to regulate or to manage these rights or to preserve a specific clarity of quality of reproduction

2. Disabling or impairing, without a right to do so, any technical protection or electronic information intended to regulate and manage the rights set out in this law

3. Computer downloading or storing of any copy of computer programs or applications or databases without a license from the author or right holder or their successors

If the crime is committed again, imprisonment for not less than nine months and a fine of not less than 200,000 dirhams is to be imposed.

Article 39 [Computer Program Infringements]

Aside from the provisions of article 37 of this law, any person who uses a computer program or applications or databases without a prior license from the author or his successors is to be punished by a fine of not less than

---

132. Article 37 of the ARL 2002 corresponds to part of article 181 of the EGIP.

10,000 dirhams and not more than 30,000 dirhams for each program or application or database.

If the crime is committed again, a fine of not less than 30,000 dirhams is to be imposed.

If the crime is committed in the name of, or on account of, a legal person, or a commercial or professional business, the court may order its closure for a period of not less than three months.

Article 40 [Orders the Court May Make]

Without prejudice to the punishments set out in articles 37, 38, and 39 of this law, the court may order the confiscation of the counterfeit copies the subject of the crime or obtained from it and the destruction of them. The court may also order the confiscation of the equipment and tools used in the commission of the crime that are not suitable for any other purpose, and the closure of the business that committed the crime of counterfeiting for not more than six months and publish a summary of the judgment issued in one or more daily newspaper at the expense of the defendant.

Article 41 [Violations of Other Provisions]

Without prejudice to the penalties that are stated in this law, any person who violates any provision of this law or regulations or orders issued implementing it is to be punished by imprisonment not exceeding six months and a fine, or by either one of them.

Chapter 8: General and Final Provisions

Article 42 [Intestate Authors]

The Ministry is to exercise the moral and financial rights of the author in the event that there is no heir or testator. The Ministry is to continue to exercise the moral rights set out in this law with the purpose of preserving the work even after the expiry of the prescribed period of protection for the financial rights in the work.

Article 43 [Images of People]

A person who makes a image of another, by any means, does not have the right to save or exhibit or publish or distribute the original or copies of it without the permission of the person who is depicted, unless otherwise agreed, or unless publication of the image was done on the occasion of public events, or it relates to persons who are official or public personalities or are famous, or the publication was permitted by the public authorities as being in the public interest, but on the condition that the exhibiting of the image or its circulation does not affect the reputation of the person that is represented.

The person appearing in the image may authorize publication of it in newspapers or other media, even if the creator did not permit the publication, unless otherwise agreed.[133]

Article 44 [Works of Foreigners—Reciprocal Treatment]

In the domain of conflicts of laws, the provisions of this law apply to the works and performances and sound recordings and broadcast programs of foreigners, on the condition that there is reciprocal treatment, and without prejudice to the provisions of international agreements in force in the State.

Article 45 [Law Officers]

The Minister of Justice and Islamic Affairs and Endowments, in agreement with the Minister of Economy[134], is to issue a decision specifying the employees who have the role of judicial seizure officers in the implementation of the provisions of this law.

Article 46 [Fees]

The specific fees for undertaking the procedures pursuant to this law are to be published by a decision of the Cabinet.

Article 47 [Regulations]

The Minister is to issue the regulations and decisions necessary for the implementation of this law.

---

133. The Arabic text of article 43 is substantially the same as part of article 178 of the EGIP. The EGIP article also contains the paragraph: "These provisions apply to any images however they are made including by drawing or engraving or any other means." Seen in the context from which the article was probably adopted, it should be interpreted broadly and not as limited to, for example, photographs.
134. Federal law no. 32 of 2006 amending federal law no. 7 of 2002 in relation to the rights of the author and neighboring rights, directed the replacement of "Minister of Information and Culture" with "Minister of Economy."

Article 48 [Repeal of the 1992 Law]

Federal law no. 40 of 1992, and all provisions inconsistent with the provisions of this law, are repealed.

Article 49 [Regulations Previously in Force]

Applicable regulations and decisions remain in force, to the extent that they do not contradict the provisions of this law, until such time as implementing regulations and decisions are issued.

Article 50 [Publication of this Law]

This law is to be published in the official gazette and will come into force on the date of its publication.

Zayed Bin Sultan Al Nahyan
President of the United Arab Emirates

Issued at the Presidential Palace in Abu Dhabi
Date: Rabi'a 20, 1423 H
Corresponding to: July 1, 2002 M.

A15

Ministerial Decision no. 411 of 1993 in Relation to the Monitoring of Protected Works Pursuant to the Provisions of Federal Law no. 40 of 1992 in Relation to Protection of Intellectual Works and the Author's Rights

Minister of Information and Culture.

After considering federal law no. 1 of 1972 in relation to the jurisdictions of the Ministries and the powers of the Ministers and the law amending it, and

Federal law no. 15 of 1980 in relation to printed matter and publishing and the laws amending it, and

Federal law no. 40 of 1992 in relation to the protection of intellectual works and the rights of the author, and

Cabinet decision no. 12 of 1975 in relation to the system of the Ministry of Information and Culture, and

Ministerial decision no. 412 of 1993 in relation to the system for the depositing of protected works and disposals of them that may occur.

Decided:

Chapter 1: General Provisions

Article 1 [Definitions]

In the application of the provisions of this decision, the words and expressions below are intended to have the following meanings, unless the context of the text requires otherwise:
  The State: The United Arab Emirates.
  The Ministry: The Ministry of Information and Culture.

The Minister: The Minister of Information and Culture.

The department: The department of monitoring in the ministry.

The law: Federal law no. 40 of 1992 in relation to the protection of intellectual works and the rights of the author.

Work: Any intellectual works enjoying the protection established by the law.

Author: Author or the authors of joint works.

Article 2 [Decision Applies to Protected Works]

The provisions of this decision apply to the works protected by the law.

Article 3 [Department to Implement Decision]

The department is empowered to implement the provisions of this decision.

Chapter 2: Approval of Works for the Purpose of Depositing Them

Article 4 [Approval of Work for Registration]

The owner of the work or the author or the official agent in the State of either of them may request the department to give him a certificate including an approval of the work or that it has the approval pursuant to the printed matter and publishing law no. 15 of 1980 referred to in that law, for the purpose of registration in the register of deposits that has been established pursuant to the law and decision of the Minister of Information and Culture no. 412 of 1993 relating to the system for depositing of protected works and disposals of them that may occur.

It is not permitted to include more than one work in the application.

Article 5 [Who May Apply for Approval]

An application to obtain a certificate referred to in article 4 of this decision may only be accepted if it is from the holders of the moral or financial rights in the work or from the official agent in the State for any of them and they are:

1. The author
2. The author's heir or his successors after his death
3. The author's assignee for the exploitation of the work or his heir or his successors after his death
4. The natural or legal person who realized the work pursuant to the text of article 24 of the law

5. The producer of a theatrical or cinematic or broadcast or television work who looks after the execution of the cassette[135] and bears the responsibility for this execution and puts in the reach of the authors of the work the material and financial means enabling its making and the realization of its production pursuant to the text of article 29 of the law

Article 6 [Contents of Approval Application]

The application for a certificate referred to in articles 4 and 5 of this decision must include the following information:

1. The name of the applicant, his nationality and standing
2. The place of residence of the applicant or his headquarters or his chosen place in the State if this place of residence or headquarters is outside the State
3. The subject of the work, its kind and its name, if one exists

Article 7 [Attachments to the Approval Application]

The following are to be attached to the application:

1. Proof of the standing of the applicant if he is not the author or if the application is filed by an agent
2. Two copies of the work from which it is possible to extract copies by means of printing or any other similar means, if copies have not previously been deposited with the department pursuant to the law of printed matter and publishing no. 15 of 1980

Article 8 [Examination of the Approval Application]

The department will examine the application to determine the following:

1. That the application satisfies the conditions stated in articles 5, 6, and 7 of this decision
2. That the work is approved or has previously been approved by the department or there is no prohibition against its approval pursuant to the provisions of the law of printed matter and publishing no. 15 of 1980

Article 9 [Certificate of Approval]

If it appears to the department from the examination of the application that it satisfies the conditions referred to in article 8 of this decision, the department will give the applicant a certificate including approval of the work or that it is

---

135. Literally, "tape."

approved pursuant to the law of printed matter and publishing no. 15 of 1980 for the purpose of presenting the certificate to the department of culture in the Ministry with the application for deposit of the work, and the certificate must have attached to it a copy of the work stamped with the stamp of the department.

Chapter 3: Declaration of Publication or Exhibition or Circulation of Works

Article 10 [Permission to Publish, Exhibit, etc.]

Without prejudice to the provisions of the law of printed matter and publishing no. 15 of 1980 and decisions issued implementing it, in order to permit the publication or exhibition or circulation of any work, the following must be attached:

1. Birth certificate of the author showing his name or of the assignee of the right of exploitation
2. Approval from the supplier or the owner of the work to be exhibited or circulated stating the permitted geographical area for exhibition or circulation
3. Certificate from the supplier notifying of the grant of the rights of publication, whether it is by a public performance or by means of making samples of the work or a copy for distribution

These supporting documents must be legalized according to the law and attach a translation into Arabic if they are written in another language.

Article 11 [Permission for Folkloric Works]

Without prejudice to the provisions of article 10 of this decision, in order to permit the printing or publication or exhibition or circulation of any folkloric work, the following is required:

1. That the applicant provide a certificate from the department of culture in the Ministry stating that the work does not contain any distortion or editing of national folklore
2. That the printing or publication or exhibition or circulation not be for commercial exploitation unless the applicant provides a certificate from the department of culture in the Ministry stating that the work is registered in the Ministry's register of deposits

Chapter 4: Necessary Document for Businesses[136] to Maintain

Article 12 [Documents to be Kept]

Each business that is licensed to copy or distribute or se l works in the State must keep the following documents:

1. The letter issued from the Ministry approving to the business carrying on this activity.
2. The license issued to the business from the municipality of the emirate in which the activity is carried on.
3. A written and legalized permission or agreement issued by any of the holders of the right to exploit the work referred to in article 5 of this decision entitling the business to a right to copy or distribute or sell each of the works according to the circumstances whethe⁻ the work is from inside or outside the State.
4. The permission of the department for each of the works that requires permission pursuant to the provisions of the law of printed matter and publishing no. 15 of 1980 and decisions issued implementing it.
5. A statement provided by the department specifyirg the works prepared outside of the State and stating the source of each of them and the permission or agreement which entitles the business to copy or distribute or sell.
6. Any other documents that should be maintained pursuant to the law of printed matter and publishing no. 15 of 1980 anc decisions issued implementing it.

Article 13 [Reporting Works for Which Documents Are Not Available]

Each business referred to in article 12 of this decision must provide to the department within two weeks from the date that this decision enters into force, an original list and a copy both signed by the owner of the business and the responsible manager containing all the works existing in the business for which the documents referred to in paragraphs 3 and 5 of article 12 of this decision are not available. The following information for each work must be attached to the list:

1. Name and type of work
2. Source of the work whether from within or from outside the State

---

136. Or shops.

3. Number of copies of the work existing in the business including the original copy

4. Which of the works has previously been approved by the department and the date of approved

Each page of the original and copy of this list is to be stamped with the stamp of the department which will keep the original and return the copy to the person filing it.

Article 14 [One-year Grace Period]

The businesses referred to in this chapter are granted a one-year grace period from the effective date of this decision in which to remove all works stated in the list referred to in article 13 of this decision.

Article 15 [Publication]

This decision is to be published in the official gazette and becomes effective from the date of its publication.

Khalfan Muhammad Al Rumi
Minister of Information and Culture

Date: 3/15/1414 H
Corresponding to: 9/1, 1993 M.

A16

Ministerial Decision No. 412 of 1993 in Relation to the System for Depositing Protected Works and Disposals of Them That Occur

Minister of Information and Culture,

After considering federal law no. 1 of 1972 in relation to the jurisdictions of the Ministries and the powers of the Ministers and the law amending it, and

Federal law no. 15 of 1980 in relation to printed matter and publishing and the law amending it, and

Federal law no. 40 of 1992 in relation to the protection of intellectual works and the rights of the author, and

Cabinet decision no. 12 of 1975 in relation to the system of the Ministry of Information and Culture,

Decided:

Chapter 1: General Provisions

Article 1 [Definitions]

In the application of the provisions of this decision, the words and expressions below are intended to have the following meanings, unless the context of the text requires otherwise:

The State: The United Arab Emirates.
The Ministry: The Ministry of Information and Culture.
The Minister: The Minister of Information and Culture.
The department: The department of culture in the Ministry.
Section: Deposit and intellectual property section in the department.

The law: The federal law no. 40 of 1992 in relation to the protection of intellectual works and the rights of the author.

Work: Any intellectual work enjoying the protection established by the law.

Derivative work: A work in a new form that has come from a previous work whether by translating it into another language or by summarizing it or by modifying it or by amending it or by explaining it or by any other means pursuant to article 5 of the law.

Author: Author or the authors of joint works.

Article 2 [Decision Applies to Protected Works]

The provisions of this decision apply to the works protected by the law.

Article 3 [Department to Implement Decision]

The department is empowered to implement the provisions of this decision.

Chapter 2: Depositing of Works

Section 1—Filing Deposit Applications

Article 4 [Application for Registration]

An application for registration of the work in the deposit register is to be filed with the section by the owner of the work or its author or the official agent or whichever one of them is in the State using Form 1 attached to this decision and it is not permitted for the application to include more than one work.

Article 5 [Contents of the Application]

An application for registration must include the following information:

1. The name of the applicant and his nationality and place of residence or his headquarters out of the State.
2. The name and the address of the agent in the State and the number and the date and the source of the agency if the application is filed by an agent.
3. The author's name and nationality and his place of residence or his headquarters.
4. The subject of the work, its type and its name if one exists.
5. The way in which the author or his successors—if the author is dead—chose to publish the work.

Article 6 [Application Attachments]

The following are to be attached to the application for registration:

1. A complete statement of the specifications of the work
2. The document proving the position of the applicant if he is not the author or if the application is filed by an agent
3. A written declaration from the author or his successors—if the author is dead—of his or their ownership of the work
4. A written declaration from the author or his successors—if the author is dead—including a description of the way in which the author chose or willed the work to be published or of the way in which the successors chose to publish the work if the author did not leave any instructions in relation to the publication of the work
5. A written assignment from the author or his successors—if the author is dead—of his or their right to exploit the work pursuant to the provisions of articles 32 and 37 of the law if the application is filed by an assignee of the right
6. Written permission from the author of the original work or from his successors—if he is dead—if the work the subject of the application is derived from an original work by any means of derivation that gives it a new form pursuant to the provisions of 5 of the law
7. A legalized contract between the author of the work and the natural or legal person who made the work based on his instructions and is responsible for its publication under his direction and in his name pursuant to the provisions of article 24 of the law if the application is filed by this person
8. A certificate from the monitoring department at the Ministry including its permission for the work or that it is permitted pursuant to the law of printed matter and publishing
9. Two copies of the work from which can be extracted many copies by means of printing or any other similar means

Article 7 [Legalization and Translation Required]

The documents referred to in paragraphs 2, 3, 4, 5, 6, and 7 of article 6 of this decision must be legalized in accordance with the law and they, together with the document referred to in paragraph 1 of article 6, are to be accompanied by a translation into Arabic if they are written in another language.

Article 8 [Undertaking to File Required Documents]

1. To receive the application it must contain all the required information—according to the circumstances—pursuant to article 5 of this decision, and must have attached to it the documents referred to in paragraphs 1, 8, and 9 of article 6 of this decision, and as for the other documents, if they are not attached to the application, the applicant may give a written undertaking, using Form 2 attached to this decision, to file the necessary documents according to the circumstances within sixty days of the date of filing of the application.

2. If the applicant does not file the documents which he undertook to file within the period specified in paragraph 1 of this article, his application will be deemed not to have been filed, unless he requests before the end of the period to be granted another extension of time based on serious justifications accepted by the director of the department who in these circumstances can grant the applicant another and final extension of time in which he must file the documents or he will be considered to have abandoned his application.

Article 9 [Numbering of Applications]

The applications are to be given annual serial numbers according to the date of filing, and the serial number is to be indicated on the application as well as the date of filing, and the application and its attachments are to be stamped with the stamp of the department, and the applicant is to be given a receipt using Form 3 attached to this decision including the applicant's serial number and the date of filing and a statement of the attached documents.

Article 10 [Register of Applications]

The section will prepare a register of applications for registration in which the following will be recorded:

1. Serial number of the application
2. Date of filing of the application
3. All information stated in the application and referred to in article 5 of this decision
4. Decision of the department in relation to the application and its date
5. Date of informing the applicant of the decision in the case of the rejection of the application
6. Date and number of registration of the work in the type register for depositing and the date of delivery of the certificate of registration to the applicant in the case of its acceptance

Article 11 [File for Each Work]

The section is to prepare a file for each work for which registration has been sought, placing in it the application and the supporting documents and all papers and decisions relating to it, and writing on it the serial number of the application, the date of filing, the name of the applicant, the name of the author, the subject of the work and its type.

Article 12 [Card Index]

The section is to prepare an alphabetical card index organized according to the names of the applicants using Form 4 attached to this decision and is to write on it the information set out in article 11 of this decision, and the decision of the department concerning the application.

Section 2—Examination of Deposit Applications

Article 13 [Examination of Applications]

The department is to examine applications for registration in the deposit registers in light of the information stated in them and the necessary documents filed pursuant to the texts of articles 6, 7 and 8 of this decision, after their filing is complete.

For the purpose of examining the application, the department may seek assistance from anyone it considers it necessary to seek assistance from of the specialists inside the State or outside the State for a fee or without a fee according to the circumstances pursuant to the rules established for that.

Article 14 [Requests for Further Documents]

The department may require the applicant to file any documents or other information it considers necessary to determine the existence of the conditions necessary for accepting the application, and the applicant is to be notified of this in writing, specifying the period for filing what has been requested, and if the applicant does not file what has been requested during this period, his application will be deemed not to have been filed, unless he requests before the end of the period to be granted another extension of time based on serious justifications accepted by the director of the department who in these circumstances can grant the applicant another and final extension of time in which he must file the documents or information or he will be considered to have abandoned his application.

Article 15 [Matters for Examination]

The department must determine the following:

1. That the work has not been previously registered in the type deposit registers

2. That the work falls under one of the classes set out in article 3 of the law, which are:

> (a) that the author of the work is a citizen of the United Arab Emirates whether he published the work inside or outside the State;
> (b) that the author of the work is a citizen of a foreign country and is publishing the work inside the United Arab Emirates for the first time;
> (c) that the author of the work is a citizen of a foreign country and is publishing the work there, on the condition that the law of that country protects the works of United Arab Emirates citizens that are published inside the United Arab Emirates.

3. That the work is one of the kinds of work that enjoys protection pursuant to the provisions of articles 2 and 5 of the law.

4. That the work is not one of the kinds of works that does not enjoy protection pursuant to the provisions of article 6 of the law.

5. That the work is not a folkloric work that is no more than chosen collections of national folklore that are not distinguished by creativity or arrangement or any other personal efforts deserving protection or not a work that includes any denigration or distortion of previous folkloric works.

6. That twenty-five Gregorian years have not passed since the first publication of the work, if it is one of the following:

> (a) cinematic films and works of applied art;
> (b) works that have realized by legal persons;
> (c) works published for the first time after the death of the author;
> (d) works that are published under a pseudonym or without mention of the name of the author unless the author reveals his identity before the end of this period.

7. That ten Gregorian years have not passed since the date of publication if the work is a photographic work

8. That twenty-five Gregorian years have not passed since the date of the death of the author or the death of the last remaining joint author, if the work was published during the life of the author or one of them, unless the work is one of the works referred to in paragraphs 6, 7, and 8 of this article

9. That the applicant is one of the holders of the moral or financial rights in the work, being:

> (a) The author
> (b) The inheritors of the author or his successors after his death
> (c) The assignee from the author or his inheritors or his successors after his death for the exploitation of the work

(d) The natural or legal person who realized the work in accordance with the text of article 24 of the law

(e) The producer of a theatrical or cinematic or broadcast or televisual work who look after execution of the tape and bears the responsibility for its execution and who made available to the authors of the work the financial and material means securing its making and realizing its production according to the text of article 29 of the law

10. That the agent who filed the application on behalf of the holder of the right in the application is entitled to file it according to a lawfully legalized authorization

Section 3—The Determination of Deposit Applications

Article 16 [Rejection of an Application]

If it is apparent from the examination of the application that the requirements set out in the law and this decision have not been met, the department is to issue a reasoned decision rejecting the application and is to notify the applicant of this decision by registered letter.

If the reason for this decision is that the period of protection referred to in article 20 of the law and paragraphs 6, 7, 8, and 9 of article 15 of this decision has passed, it has no effect on any moral right of the author that does not expire pursuant to the provisions of the law.

Article 17 [Acceptance]

If it is apparent from the examination of the application that the requirements as set out in the law and this decision have been met, the department is to issue a decision accepting the application.

Article 18 [Sixty Days to Decide; New Application after Rejection]

1. The director of the department is to issue a decision rejecting or accepting the application after reviewing the examination report during the period of no more than sixty days from the date that the documents and information for the application are completed pursuant to the provisions of articles 5, 6, 7, 8, and 14 of this decision.

2. The director of the department is to issue a decision deeming the application not to exist or to have been abandoned, applying the provisions of articles 8 and 14 of this decision.

3. Anyone whose application has been deemed not to exist or to have been abandoned may file with the section at any time a new application, and in

order for the application to be received, it must include all the necessary documents and information to be completed according to the provisions of this decisions, including the documents and information that the department requested from the applicant before and that he did not complete and that was the reason for issuing a decision deeming his previous application not to exist or to be abandoned.

Section 4—Registration of Works in the Deposit Registers

Article 19 [Registration and the Certificate]

Each work for which a decision of acceptance for its registration has issued is to be registered in the type deposit register and the applicant is to be given a certificate of registration of the work pursuant to the provisions of articles 20, 21, 22, and 23 of this decision.

Article 20 [Registers]

The department is to prepare type deposit registers registering in them the accepted works according to their type and to the division that it deems suitable for the types of works.

The registers are to be given serial numbers and they are to be written on their covers, together with the type of the works that are registered in them, and each work is to be registered in the type register belong to it following the serial numbers.

Article 21 [Contents of Registers]

Each of the registers is to contain the following information:

1. Number and date of the registration of the work
2. Application number and date of filing
3. Number and date of the decision of the director of the department accepting the application for registration
4. Subject of the work and its type and its name if one exists
5. The author's name and nationality and address
6. The applicant's name and nationality and position and address if he is not the author
7. The way in which the author or his successors—if the author is dead—chose to publish the work and the date and place of first publication
8. The number and date of the monitoring department certificate in the Ministry permitting the work
9. The number of copies of the work deposited

10. The date of issue of the certificate of registration of the work and the number and date of the receipt the applicant received for it

11. The period of protection decided for the work pursuant to the provisions of the law

Article 22 [Contents of Certificate]

The department is to issue a certificate of registration of the work using Form 5 attached to this decision including the following information:

1. The number and date of the decision of the director of the department accepting the application for registration

2. The date and number of registration of the work in the type deposit register

3. The subject of the work and its type and its name, if one exists, and its author's name

4. The name of the owner or owners of the work

5. The name of the person who received the certificate and his position

Article 23 [Original and Copy Certificate]

The certificate of registration of the work is to be issued in an original and a copy. The original is given to the person who applied for registration, acknowledging receipt using Form 6 attached to this decision, and the copy of the certificate with a copy of the receipt of delivery is to be put in the file of the work.

Chapter 3: Depositing Disposals

Article 24 [Application to Register a Disposal]

An application for registration of any disposals that occur of works registered in the registers of deposited works may be filed with the section by the transferor or the transferee or any of their successors, depending on the circumstances, or by the official agent registered in the State of any one of them using Form 7 attached to this decision.

Article 25 [Contents of Application]

The application for registration must include the following information:

1. The name of the applicant, his nationality, his position, his place of residence or his headquarters, and his chosen place in the State if his place of residence or his headquarters are out of the State

2. The name and the address of the agent in the State and the number and date and source of his authority if the application is filed by an agent

3. The subject of the work that the disposal concerns, its type, the number and date of its registration in the type register

4. The date of the disposal whose registration is requested and its type, the right or rights that are included

Article 26 [Application Attachments]

The application must have attached to it the following documents:

1. A written and lawfully legalized disposal document accompanied by an Arabic translation if it is written in another language, specifying clearly and separately each right of the financial rights that is the subject of the disposal and the period of this disposal and its method and its quantity and its purpose and its place

2. The document evidencing the position of the applicant if he is not the author or if the application is filed by an agent

Article 27 [Application Numbering]

The applications are to be given annual serial numbers according to the date of filing and the application is to be marked with its serial number and the date of filing, and stamped with the stamp of the department and a receipt is to be given to the applicant using Form 8 attached to this decision including the application serial number and the date of filing and the documents attached to it.

Article 28 [Disposal Applications Register]

The section is to prepare a register for applications for the registration of disposals with the following information to be written in it:

1. The application serial number and the date of filing

2. All the information stated in the application and referred to in article 25 of this decision

3. The decision of the department in relation to the application and its date

4. The date of informing the applicant of the decision in the case of rejection of the application

5. The date and registration number of the disposal in the register of deposited disposals in the case of acceptance of the application

Article 29 [The File for the Work]

The application for registration of the disposal is to be deposited with all related papers and decisions in the file of the work the subject of the disposal.

Article 30 [Examination]

The department is to examine the application for registrat on of the disposal to determine the following:

1. That the work the subject of the disposal is registered in one of the type deposit registers
2. The disposal the subject of the application does not conflict with any previously registered disposal in the deposit disposals register referred to in article 32 of this decision
3. That the application satisfies all the conditions stated in articles 25 and 26 of this decision

Article 31 [Rejection and Acceptance]

If it is apparent from the examination of the application that the conditions referred to in articles 25, 26, and 30 of this decision have not been met, the department is to issue a reasoned decision rejecting the application and inform the applicant of the decision by registered letter, and if it is apparent that the application has satisfied the conditions, it will issue a decision accepting the application, and in both cases the director of department is to issue the decision after reviewing the examination report.

Article 32 [Register of Deposited Disposals]

The section is to prepare a register for deposit of disposals recording in it disposals whose registration has been accepted. The register must include the following information:

1. The number of the application for registration and ts date of filing.
2. The name of the assignor, his nationality, his position and his address
3. The name of the assignee, his nationality, his position and his address
4. The date of the disposal and its duration
5. An identification of each right of the financial rights the subject of the disposal and the duration of the disposal and its method and its quantity and its purpose and its place
6. The number and date of decision of the director of the department accepting the application for registration
7. The subject of the work being disposed of and its type and its name, if one exists
8. The number and the date of registration of the work in the type register

Article 33 [Information Concerning the Work]

Each disposal registered in the register referred to in article 32 of this decision is to be marked with the information concerning the work disposed of that is recorded in the type deposit register for that work.

Chapter 4: Concluding Provisions

Article 34 [Distribution of Copies]

The department must maintain in the section at least one copy of the copies of the works that are filed with it pursuant to article 6 of this decision and must distribute the remaining copies to the public libraries and other parties that the department chooses.

Article 35 [Cancellations and Amendments]

Final judgments, whose implementation requires the making of a cancellation or amendment of any registered information in all or some of the registers, are to be noted in the type deposit registers or in the disposals deposit register, if [a] the judgment is issued against the Ministry, or [b] the concerned persons file with the Ministry an official copy of the judgment. A copy of the judgment is to be put in the file for the work.

Article 36 [Review of Registers]

Any interested person who wishes to review any register referred to in this decision may do so in the presence of the responsible employee in the section and may obtain a certificate of the information that is contained in it in relation to any registered work or disposal.

Article 37 [Additional Registers]

The section may with the approval of the director of the department prepare registers additional to those registers referred to in this decision pursuant to what he considers necessary for good workflow.

Article 38 [Material Errors]

Any interested person may request the section to correct any material error made in any register referred to in this decision.

Article 39 [Publication]

This decision is to be published in the official gazette and is effective from the date of publication.

Khalfan Muhammad Al Roumi
Minister of Information and Culture

Date: 3/15/1414 H
Corresponding to: 9/1/1993 M.[137]

---

137. The Islamic date is 15 Rabi' Al Awwal 1414 and the Gregorian date is September 1, 1993.

United Arab Emirates
Ministry of Information and Culture
Department of Culture

Form 1
Application for registration of a work in the deposit register

The applicant requests the registration of the work, the subject of the application, in the type deposit register and to be granted a registration certificate pursuant to the following information:	**Official use only** Application number:_____ _____ Filing date:_____

1. Applicant's information:

A. Applicant's name, nationality and title:_____
_____
_____
_____
_____

B. Applicant's place of residence or headquarters: _____
_____
_____
_____
_____

C. Applicant's chosen address in the State if his place of residence or headquarters is out of the State: _____
_____
_____
_____
_____

D. Phone number_____ Fax number_____Telex number_____

2. Author's information:

A. Author's name and nationality:_____
_____
_____
_____

B. Author's place of residence or headquarters in or out of the State: _____

_____

_____

_____

3. Agent's information if the application is filed by an agent:

A. Agent's name and address in the State:_____

_____

_____

_____

_____

B. The number of power of attorney:_____

Date_____Source_____

C. Phone number_____Fax number_____

Telex number_____

The following are to be attached to the application for registration:

1. A complete statement of the specifications of the work.

2. The document proving the position of the applicant if he is not the author or if the application is filed by an agent.

3. A written declaration from the author or his successors—if the author is dead—of his or their ownership of the work.

4. A written declaration from the author or his successors—if the author is dead—including the way in which the author chose or willed the work to be published or of the way in which the successors chose to publish the work if the author did not leave any instructions in relation to the publication of the work.

5. A written assignment from the author or his successors—if the author is dead—of his or their right to exploit the work pursuant to the provisions of articles 7.3 and 32 of the law if the application is filed by an assignee of the right.

6. Written permission from the author of the original work or from his successors—if he is dead—if the work the subject of the application is derived from an original work by any means of derivation that gives it a new form pursuant to the provisions of 5 of the law.

7. A legalized contract between the author of the work and the natural or legal person who made the work based on his instructions and is responsible for its publication under his direction and in his name pursuant to the provisions of article 24 of the law if the application is filed by this person.

8. A certificate from the monitoring department at the Ministry including its permission for the work or that it is permitted pursuant to the law of printed matter and publishing.

9. Ten copies of the work from which can be extracted many copies by means of printing or any other similar means.

10. A written undertaking using Form 2 to file the necessary documents from 2 to 7 other than those attached to the application.

Note:

1. Documents 1 to 7 must be accompanied by a translation into Arabic done by a reliable translator if they are written in another language.

2. Documents 2 to 7 must be legalized in accordance with the law.

4. Information about the work:

A. Name of the work, if any: _____

_____

B. Subject and type of the work: _____

_____

_____

_____

_____

_____

_____

_____

_____

_____

_____

_____

_____

_____

_____

_____

C. The way in which the author or his successors—if the author is dead—chose to publish the work: _____

_____

_____

☐   ☐
Applicant   Agent

9. Signature: _____   _____

Date: _____

Note: if there is more than one applicant or author, their information is to be mentioned on an additional page attached to this form.

United Arab Emirates
Ministry of Information and Culture
Department of Culture

Form 2
Undertaking to file documents relating to the application to deposit a work

Application number: _____

Date of filing the application: _____

Applicant's name: _____

Agent's name: _____

I, the undersigned, _____

_____ undertake in my capacity as: _____

_____ to file with the department

of culture the documents mentioned below within **sixty** days of the date of filing

the application:

1) _____
_____

2) _____
_____

3) _____
_____

4) _____
_____

5) _____
_____

6) _____
_____

Dated   /   /

Signature

_____

United Arab Emirates
Ministry of Information and Culture
Department of Culture

Form 3
Receipt for receiving an application for
registration of a work and its attachments

Application number:

Date of filing the application:

Applicant's name, nationality and title:

Information of the documents filed with the work: ☐

1. A complete statement of the specifications of the work.

2. The document proving the position of the applicant if he is not the author or if the application is filed by an agent.   ☐

3. A written declaration from the author or his successors—if the author is dead—of his or their ownership of the work.   ☐

4. A written declaration from the author or his successors—if the author is dead—including the way in which the author chose or willed the work to be published or of the way in which the successors chose to publish the work if the author did not leave any instructions in relation to the publication of the work.   ☐

5. A written assignment from the author or his successors—if the author is dead—of his or their right to exploit the work pursuant to the provisions of articles 7.3 and 32 of the law if the application is filed by an assignee of the right.   ☐

6. Written permission from the author of the original work or from his successors—if he is dead—if the work the subject of the application is derived from the original work by any means of derivation that gives it a new form pursuant to the provisions of 5 of the law.   ☐

7. A legalized contract between the author of the work and the natural or legal person who made the work based on his instructions and is responsible for its publication under his direction and in his name pursuant to the provisions of article 24 of the law if the application is filed by this person.   ☐

8. A certificate from the monitoring department at the Ministry including its permission for the work or that it is permitted pursuant to the law of printed matter and publishing.   ☐

9. Ten copies of the work from which can be extracted many copies by means of printing or any other similar means.

10. A written undertaking using Form 2 to file necessary documents 2 to 7 other than those attached to this application.

Official stamp Total documents received

Recipient:_____

Name:_____

Signature:_____

Note: a √ mark is to be indicated against the documents received.

United Arab Emirates
Ministry of Information and Culture
Department of Culture

Form 4
Alphabetical card index for applications for
registration of a work

1. Applicant's name and title:_____

_____

_____

2. Application serial number: _____

3. Date of filing the application: _____

4. Author's name:_____

_____

5. Subject and type of work: _____

_____

_____

_____

_____

_____

_____

_____

6. Department's decision: _____

Date of the department's decision: _____

United Arab Emirates
Ministry of Information and Culture
Department of Culture

Form 5
Certificate for registration of a work in the type deposit register

The Department of the Culture witnesses that the work the subject of this
certificate has been registered in the type deposit register number (###)
for_____pursuant to the following information:
1. Date of registration of the work in the type deposit register: _____
2. Number of the registration: _____

3. Subject of the work: _____

4. Type of the work: _____

5. Name of the work: _____
6. Name of the author of the work or authors: _____

7. Name of the owner of the work or owners: _____

and this certificate has been delivered to Mr: _____

in his capacity as:
Author   ☐   his successors   ☐
Owner of work   his successors   Agent   ☐
Without any responsibility on the Department.
Written on   /   /   ☐   ☐
_____
Manager of the Department

United Arab Emirates
Ministry of Information and Culture
Department of Culture

Form 6
Receipt for receiving the certificate for the
registration of a deposited work

I, the undersigned, _____

_____received in my capacity as: _____

_____a certificate

for the registration of a deposited work in the type deposit register number

(_____) registered on / / number_____

Dated   /   /

Recipient's name and title_____

Signature_____

United Arab Emirates
Ministry of Information and Culture
Department of Culture

Form 7
Application for registration of disposal on registered work

The applicant request the acceptance of the registration of the disposal the subject of the application in the register for depositing disposals of the registered works pursuant to the following information:	**Official use only** Application number:_____ Filing date:_____

1. Applicant's information:

A. Applicant's name, nationality and title:_____
_____
_____
_____
_____

B. Applicant's place of residence or headquarters in the State: _____
_____
_____
_____
_____

C. Applicant's chosen address in the State if his place of residence or headquarters is out of the State: _____
_____
_____
_____
_____

D. Phone number_____ Fax number_____ Telex number_____

2. Information relating to the deposited work:

A. The name of the work, if any: _____
_____
_____

B. The type and subject of the work: _____
_____
_____
_____

C. Date and number of the registration of the work in the type deposit register: ___
_____
_____

3. Agent's information, if the application is filed by an agent:

A. Agent's name and address in the State _____
_____
_____
_____
_____**B.** The number of power
of attorney: _____Date_____Source_____
C. Phone number_____ Telex number_____
Fax number_____

The application must have attached to it the following documents:
1. A written and lawfully legalized assignment document accompanied by an
Arabic translation if it is written in another language, specifying clearly and
separately each right of the financial rights the subject of the disposal and the
period of this disposal and its method and its quantity and its purpose and its
place.
2. The document evidencing the position of the applicant if he is not the author
or if the application is filed by an agent.

4. Information relating to the disposal the subject of the application:

A. The type of the disposal for which registration is requested_____
B. The date of the written assignment document proving the disposal for which
registration is requested and the date of legalization _____
_____
C. A nature of the right or rights included in the disposal (in detail)_____
_____
_____

☐	☐
Applicant	Agent

9. Signature:_____   _____
Date:_____

Note: if there is more than one applicant, their information is to be mentioned on an
additional page attached to this form.

United Arab Emirates
Ministry of Information and Culture
Department of Culture

Form 8
Receipt for receiving an application for
registration of a disposal

Application serial number: _____

Date of filing the application: _____

Applicant's name, nationality and title: _____

1. Written disposal dated   /   /_____ ☐

2. The document evidencing the position of the applicant if he is not the author or
if the application is filed by an agent:_____ ☐

Dated   / /

Signature

Decision of the Minister of Information and Culture No. 131 of 2004 in Relation to the Registration of Works

The Minister of Information and Culture,

After considering federal law no. 1 of 1972 in relation to the jurisdictions of the Ministries and the powers of the Ministers and the laws amending it, and

Federal law no. 7 of 2002 in relation to the rights of the author and neighboring rights, and

Based on what was presented by the Undersecretary,

Decided:

Article 1 [Definitions]

In the application of the provisions of this decision, the words and expressions below are intended to have the following meanings, unless the context of the text requires otherwise:

The State: The United Arab Emirates.

The Ministry: The Ministry of Information and Culture.

The Minister: The Minister of Information and Culture.

The law: Federal law no. 7 of 2002 in relation to the rights of the author and neighboring rights.

The office: The office of intellectual works.

The register: The register in which is recorded information about the work including the rights or disposals that occur.

Article 2 [Register of Works]

A register is to be created in the office to record the details of works and certificates of registration of the work are to be obtained according to those details.

Article 3 [Application to Register]

The author or any of the holders of rights or holders of neighboring rights or any of their successors may file an application to register a work pursuant to the provisions of this decision.

Article 4 [Application Contents and Attachments]

Firstly: the application for registration must contain the following information:

1. The title of the work, its type, description and language
2. The applicant's name, his nationality, capacity and address, and a copy of the power of attorney
3. The name of the author, pseudonym, and name of renown (if one exists), his nationality and address and date of death (if one exists)
4. The name of the party that directed the work (if one exists), its address and the document that evidences the relationship between it and the author
5. The name and address of the publisher, and the date and place of first publication, and the international number (if one exists)
6. The name, address and nationality of the assignee, the kind of assignment, its term and geographical scope, details of the financial rights that were acquired by means of the assignment and the document that evidences the assignment from the author or the right holder

Secondly: The following must be attached to the application for registration:

1. A copy of the passport or identity of the person filing the application for registration and the author and the assignee
2. Two copies of the work or two photographic images 20 x 20 centimeters, depending on the nature of the work

Article 5 [One Work per Application]

The application for registration may not seek registration for more than one work, taking into consideration the nature of the works.

Article 6 [Application Numbering]

The applicant will be given a serial number according to the date of filing and a receipt of filing mentioning the attachments filed with the application.

Article 7 [Matters for Determination]

The office will study the application to determine the following:

1. That the work has not been registered previously
2. That the work is not one of the works that does not enjoy protection pursuant to article 3 of the law
3. That the work is not a folkloric work that contains a denigration or distortion or that requires a permission from the competent authority in the State
4. The information and documents set out in article 4 of this decision have been received
5. That the work has reached its final form and is not only a draft or a preliminary work in preparation

Article 8 [E-mail and Electronic Registers]

The office may receive applications by means of e-mail when the work system allows it. The office may specify any additional requirements for maintaining the electronic registers and any other procedures connected with it after the delivery of the work and payment of the required fees.

Article 9 [Other Documents or Information]

The office may require the applicant to file any documents or other information it considers necessary to determine whether the application satisfied the conditions necessary for its acceptance by a written notice sent to the applicant.

Article 10 [Sixty Days to Comply]

If the applicant does not provide the requested documents and information within sixty days of being notified, the application will be deemed to be rejected.

Article 11 [Assistance of Specialists]

For the purpose of examination of applications for registration, the office may seek the assistance of any of the specialists in the State or outside it, and the opinion offered by the specialist to the office is to be considered as advisory.

Article 12 [Rejection of Application]

The office will issue a reasoned decision rejecting the application if it is apparent that the work does not satisfy the conditions stated in the law or that the application contravenes the provisions of this decision, and will inform the applicant of it.

Article 13 [New Application after Rejection]

Anyone who has received a decision rejecting his application or deeming it to be rejected may file with the office at any later time a new application after providing the documents and information that caused the rejection decision to issue.

Article 14 [Registration Not a Permission]

Neither any endorsement in the register nor the issue of a certificate of registration is to be considered as a permission for the exploitation or circulation or exhibition of the work. The concerned person must consult the competent authority at the Ministry for permission as to the subject of the work.

Article 15 [Material Errors]

Any interested person may request that the office correct any material error occurring in the information in the register.

Article 16 [Cancellation and Amendment]

Cancellation of registered information from the register or registration of it for another person is not permitted except based on a final court judgment requiring it to be done.

Article 17 [Organization of the Registers]

The office may make necessary changes in the organization of the register according to what it considers appropriate to carry on its work. Such changes are not to conflict with the provisions of this decision.

Article 18 [Cancellation of Conflicting Provisions]

Any provision conflicting with the provisions of this decision is cancelled.

Article 19 [Publication]

This decision is to be published in the official gazette and is effective from the date of publication.

Abdullah Bin Zayed Al Nahyan
Minister of Information and Culture

Issued on: 2/1/1425 H
Corresponding to: 3/22/2004 M.[138]

---

138. The Islamic date is 1 Safar 1425 and the Gregorian date is March 22, 2004.

A18

Decision of the Minister of Information and Culture No. 132 of 2004 in Relation to the Register of Imported and Distributed Works

The Minister of Information and Culture,

After considering federal law no. 1 of 1972 in relation to the jurisdictions of the Ministries and the powers of the Ministers and the laws amending it, and

Federal law no. 7 of 2002 in relation to the rights of the author and neighboring rights, and

Based on what was presented by the Undersecretary,

Decided:

Article 1 Definitions

In the application of the provisions of this decision, the words and expressions below are intended to have the following meanings, unless the context of the text requires otherwise:

The State: The United Arab Emirates.

The Ministry: The Ministry of Information and Culture.

The Minister: The Minister of Information and Culture.

The law: Federal law no. 7 of 2002 in relation to the rights of the author and neighboring rights.

The office: The office of intellectual works.

The register: The register of imported and distributed works.

Article 2 [Register of Imported and Distributed Works]

A register called the imported and distributed works register is to be established in the office and in it is to be registered the names of the importers and distributors and the basis of their rights to import or distribute the works in the State, and information about their activities and parties who authorized them to import or distribute the works as shown in the register.

Article 3 [Acts Prohibited Without a License]

It is not permitted for any natural or legal person to practice any activity relating to works including importation or distribution or sale or renting or lending unless he is registered in the register and he has a license from the competent authority in the Ministry.

Article 4 [Application for Registration]

The application for registration in the register is to be filed with the office by the importer or the distributor or the legal agent for either of them using the form prepared for that purpose.

Article 5 [Contents of the Register and Applications for Registration]

Firstly: The Register will contain the following information and documents:
  1. The name of the applicant for registration, his nationality, his title, place of residence, address and the name of the person authorized to sign on his behalf.
  2. The name of the natural or legal person requesting registration, his nationality, his address and activity.
  3. The following documents are required to be provided with the application and must be filed once a year and are to be current and to be legalized copies:

  a. A license to practice the activity issued by the competent authority in the Ministry.
  b. A certificate from the Chamber of Commerce and Industry in the emirate in which the center of activity of the legal person is located
  c. A license from the Municipality or Economic Development Department or any competent authority in the emirate in which the center of activity of the legal person is located

Secondly: the application for registration of the rights of importation and distribution of works in the register is to contain the following information and documents:
  1. The title of the work, its kind and language
  2. The name of the producing party and his address and place of production

3. The documents that prove the legal relationship that permits importation or distribution showing the following:

a. The agreed geographical area for distribution of the work
b. The period of financial exploitation of the work
c. The means of financial exploitation of the work
d. The place and date of the signing of the document referred to
e. The official legalization of the document pursuant to the followed legal principles

4. A legal translation of the document into Arabic if it is written in a foreign language.

Article 6 [Identification Code]

The person who files an application for registration of his rights to import or distribute the work is to be given an identification code number by the office, and is to be given a number for each request he files pursuant to article 5 of this decision, and he must refer to this number each time he files an application for registration of this rights to import and/or distribute works that have a relationship with the specific request.

Article 7 [Serial Numbers]

Applications for registration of rights to import or distribute works are to be given serial numbers and the applicant is to be given a receipt containing the following information:

1. The code number
2. Request number
3. Date and time
4. Information about the documents attached to the application

Article 8 [Sixty Days to Complete Information]

If the office accepts an application with incomplete information or documents, the applicant is to be informed of this stating the information or papers or documents that are required to be clarified or attached, and he must file them within sixty days from the date of being informed or otherwise the application will be deemed cancelled. The office may not accept to register any of his subsequent applications for sixty days.

Article 9 [Further Information]

The office may require the applicant to file any information or documents or clarifications that it considers appropriate to support the application and documents attached. The office may also request any authority to determine the accuracy of the documents or information filed.

Article 10 [Rejection]

The office must reject the application if it contravenes any of the provisions of the law or of this decision and the applicant is to be informed of this.

Article 11 [Acceptance]

If the application is accepted, the kind of rights granted, and their duration, and the number of works and their names and language and geographical domain of exploitation are to be registered.

   The office is to inform the competent authority in the Ministry of the applicant's registration of these rights, as well as inform the applicant of the decision of the office to accept his application, and must present the application to the competent authority in the Ministry for substantive approval.

Article 12 [Permission Required from Competent Authority]

The licensee is not permitted to import or distribute the works recorded in the register or exploit them financially or distribute them or offer them for circulation until after obtaining the permission of the competent authority in the Ministry.

Article 13 [Withdrawal of License]

The competent authority in the Ministry may, by means of a reason decision, withdraw the license to offer the work for circulation.

Article 14 [More Than One Importer or Distributor]

The registration in the register may include the name of more than one importer or distributor for the one work if justifications for such registration are given in the application.

Article 15 [Amendments and Changes]

The persons who have registered their names in the register must inform the office of any amendment or change occurring in the information of the register or attached documents within twenty days of the date of the amendment or change, and the notice is to be by them by means of a letter. The office may make in the register any amendments or changes required.

Article 16 [Documents to be Kept]

Those who obtain licenses to import and distribute works are required to keep in the place of conduct of the activity the following documents and licenses:

1. The license issued by the competent authority in the Ministry to purse the activity of importation or distribution or exploitation of the works
2. The license issued by the municipality of the emirate or the competent authority in it for pursuing the activity
3. A written document of the relationship with any of the right holders for the exploitation of the work and which gives the party the right to import or exploit or distribute or sell the work, legalized according to the law, and whatever will assist the registration of the right with the office
4. A circulation permission from the competent authority in the Ministry to circulate the work

The concerned persons must produce these documents to the persons authorized to carry out inspections when requested.

Article 17 [The Register and Changes]

The office is to prepare the register and make in it the changes required according to what it considers appropriate for the workflow.

Article 18 [Customs]

1. The author or the right holder or their successors may file with the customs authorities a request for the temporary non-release from customs of intellectual works before their release from customs control and the customs authorities must decide on the request within three days from its satisfactory filing and inform the applicant of the decision upon its issue.
2. The customs authorities may, of their own volition, temporarily not release [the intellectual works] if there is a doubt as to the accuracy of any of the documents filed with them.
3. The decision of customs authorities temporarily not to release [intellectual works] must in all cases be reasoned and for a period of not more than twenty days.

4. The applicant must attach to his application the documents that prove the right referred to in his application, legalized according to the law. The customs authorities must confirm the correctness of these documents with the cooperation of the Ministry.

5. The applicant is to file financial security or a conditional bank guarantee to the value of 25 percent of the value of the materials mentioned in the application and the customs authorities have the right to renew it or cash it upon its request. The applicant is only required to file financial security if he does not have evidence supporting his application.

6. The applicant's security is not to be returned to him if it is decided by the competent court to cancel the customs non-release decision or the importer or exporter files official documents proving the inaccuracy of the application.

7. The customs authorities must make it possible for the applicant to be present—if he wants—at the inspection of the materials stated in the application, and must issue an attendance permission specifying in it the name and title of the person whose attendance is permitted and is to be valid for one time only.

Article 19 [6 month grace period]

Anyone who practices the activity of importing or distributing works in the State at the time of the issue of this decision must bring his circumstances into line with its provisions within six months from the date of its operation.

Article 20 [Conflicting Provisions Cancelled]

Any provision conflicting with or contradicting the provisions of this decision are cancelled.

Article 21 [Publication]

This decision is to be published in the official gazette and is effective from the date of publication.

Abdullah Bin Zayed Al Nahyan
Minister of Information and Culture

Issued: 2/1/1425 H
Corresponding to: 3/22/2004 M.[139]

---

139. The Islamic date is 1 Safar 1425 and the Gregorian date is March 22, 2004.

A19

Decision of the Minister of Information and Culture No. 133 of 2004 in Relation to the Collective Management of the Rights of the Author and Neighboring Rights

The Minister of Information and Culture,

After considering federal law no. 1 of 1972 in relation to the jurisdictions of the Ministries and the powers of the Ministers and the laws amending it, and

Federal law no. 7 of 2002 in relation to the rights of the author and neighboring rights, and

Based on what was presented by the Undersecretary,

Decided:

Article 1 [Definitions]

In the application of the provisions of this decision, the words and expressions below are intended to have the following meanings, unless the context of the text requires otherwise:

The State: The United Arab Emirates.

The Ministry: The Ministry of Information and Culture.

The Minister: The Minister of Information and Culture

The law: Federal law no. 7 of 2002 in relation to the rights of the author and neighboring rights.

The office: The office of intellectual works.

Collective management license: The approval issued by the Ministry to collecting societies or other competent entities to manage and exercise the rights of the author and neighboring rights.

Article 2 [License to be Obtained]

Collecting societies and other entities that wish to be responsible for the collective management of the rights of the author and neighboring rights must obtain a license from the Ministry before practicing this activity.

Article 3 [Approval Required Prior to Applying for a License]

Collecting societies and other entities filing an application for a collective management license must obtain, before filing the application, the necessary approval from the competent authorities in the State, pursuant to the conditions set down for this matter.

Article 4 [Application Contents and Attachments]

The following documents and information must be filed as a condition of obtaining a collective management license:

1. Copy of the articles of association of the applicant for the license and its contract of incorporation
2. Copy of the study qualifications and of the passport or identity card of the responsible director of the applicant for the license
3. A statement of the percentage of national employees in the entity applying for the license
4. A license from the country of origin evidencing the practice of the activity of the applicant for the license in the domain of collective management, if the applicant for the license is a subsidiary of a legal person located outside the State
5. A statement of the number of authors and holders of neighboring rights that have contracted with the legal person filing the application, if any
6. A copy of the signed contract between the legal person and the contracting authors and neighboring rights holders, if any

Article 5 [Obligations on Licensees]

The legal person to whom the license is issued must do the following:

1. Prepare the necessary registers that contain the names of the persons, their titles, addresses, their information, their works and the acts that they have contracted in relation to, and the period of the contract and its value, and notify the Ministry of any change that may occur in the information in these registers
2. Keep the document of the signed agreement between the legal person and the ones who are exploiting the financial rights in which is specified the agreed costs of the funds collection

3. Undertake all administrative and legal procedures to protect the rights of the contracting parties

4. Prepare audited accounts and distribution of profits to the contracting parties at least once a year

5. Allow the contracting parties to view the audited accounts and the methods of distribution of profits at any time

6. Prepare regular reports for the owners of the rights showing in them the parties that used their works and the funds that were obtained

7. File with the Ministry the information and documents referred to in this decision whenever requested

Article 6 [Fees]

The applicant for the license must, after satisfying the license conditions, pay to the competent authority in the Ministry the required fees to practice the activity, and annually renew the license after paying the required fees.

Article 7 [Non-compliance and License Cancellation]

The Ministry may cancel the license after its issue in the event of the licensee's non-compliance with the provisions of the law or its implementing decisions.

Article 8 [Obligation to Manage Unless Justified]

The licensee may not refuse to manage the rights of authors or of holders of neighboring rights without a justifying reason.

Article 9 [Publication]

This decision is to be published in the official gazette and is to be effective from the date of its publication.

Abdullah Bin Zayed Al Nahyan
Minister of Information and Culture

Issued: 2/1/1425 H
Corresponding to: 3/22/2004 M.[140]

---

140. The Islamic date is 1 Safar 1425 and the Gregorian date is March 22, 2004.

A20

Decision of the Minister of Information and Culture No. 134 of 2004 in Relation to Compulsory Licensing for Copying and Translating Works

The Minister of Information and Culture,

After considering federal law no. 1 of 1972 in relation to the jurisdictions of the Ministries and the powers of the Ministers and the aws amending it, and

Federal law no. 7 of 2002 in relation to the rights of the author and neighboring rights, and

Based on what was presented by the Undersecretary,

Decided:

Article 1 [Definitions]

In the application of the provisions of this decision, the words and expressions below are intended to have the following meanings, unless the context of the text requires otherwise:

The State: The United Arab Emirates.
The Ministry: The Ministry of Information and Culture.
The Minister: The Minister of Information and Culture.
The law: Federal law no. 7 of 2002 in relation to the rights of the author and neighboring rights.
The office: The office of intellectual works.
License: A compulsory license granted pursuant to the law.

Article 2 [Application for a License]

Any person may file an application with the office to obtain a license to copy or to translate a work protected by the law to satisfy the needs education of any kind or any level, or the needs of public libraries or archives, pursuant to the conditions stated in this decision.

Article 3 [Proof of Attempts to License to be Filed]

1. The applicant for a license to copy or translate must file proof that he requested that the author or the owner of the right permit him to copy the work or translate it and to publish the copied or translated edition and he refused the request or that it was impossible to contact the author or owner of the right to exploit the work.
2. If the applicant for the license is not able to contact the author or the owner of the right to exploit the work, then he must communicate with the publisher whose name appears on the work and file proof that he followed the procedures set out in the previous paragraph.

Article 4 [Conditions for Grant of a License to Copy]

Without prejudice to the provisions of article 3 of this decision, it is a condition of issuing a license to copy a work that:

1. Five years from the date of first publication of the work have passed and no copy of the work licensed by the author or the owner of the right of exploitation of the work is available in the markets of the State, or the needs of education or public libraries or archives have not been satisfied at a price approximating the usual price in the State in relation to similar works, except in the following circumstances:

(a) if the work contains subjects related to mathematics or the natural or technical sciences, then only three years is required to pass from the date of first publication of the work;
(b) if the work contains subjects relating to the world of the imagination such as novels and poetic or theatrical or musical works, or are books of art, then seven years must pass from the date of first publication of the work.

2. Three months following the period of five and seven years referred to in this article must pass following the date of first communication with the author or the owner of the right to exploit the work, or six months must pass following the end of the three years referred to in this article.

Article 5 [Conditions for Grant of a License to Translate]

Without prejudice to the provisions of article 3 of this decision, it is a condition of the issue of a license to translate that:

1. Three years have passed from the date of first publication of the work without a copy of the work being available translated into Arabic or into a

language in common circulation in the State that satisfies the needs of education or public libraries or archives, or if the translated copies of the work have been consumed in that period.

2. Six months have passed from the first communication with the author or the owner of the right to exploit the work following the end of the three years referred to in paragraph 1 of this article, and if the work contains explanatory pictures the holder of the license to translate must comply with the provisions of article 4 of this decision.

Article 6 [License to be Denied]

A license must not be given in the following circumstances:

1. If the work is withdrawn from circulation based on a request by the author or the owner of the right to exploit the financial rights
2. If the author or the owner of the right to exploit the financial rights put the work into circulation during the additional period referred to in articles 4.2 and 5.2 of this decision satisfying the needs of education or public libraries or archives at a price approximating the usual price in the State in relation to similar works

Article 7 [Obligations on the Licensee]

The holder of the license must comply with the following:

1. To mention the name of the author on the translated or copied edition, putting the title of the work as it is stated in the original language
2. To ensure the faithful transfer of the work to the concerned edition including to copy it or translate it in an accurate way
3. To mark on each copied or translated edition that t is are suitable for circulation inside the State only, and to mention that the issued edition is based on a compulsory license
4. To use the license to satisfy the needs of education or public libraries or archives
5. To pay to the author or the owner of the right to exploit the work fair financial compensation to be specified in the decision granting the license, with the guidance of the international standards applied in this domain
6. To file with the office before receiving the license proof that the financial compensation referred to in the previous paragraph corresponds to the transfer into the currency of the country in which the original work was published, and that the author or owner of the right in it received the compensation
7. Not to export the licensed work outside the State

Article 8 [License Not Assignable]

The license to copy or to translate is to be issued in the name of the applicant and may not be assigned to anyone else.

Article 9 [End of Validity of the License]

The validity of the license to copy or to translate ends if the author or the owner of the right to exploit the work makes a copy or translation of the work available at a price approximating the usual price in the State in relation to similar works.

An edition for which a license to copy or translate has issued is to circulate until it is used up.

Article 10 [Communicating with International Organizations]

The office may communicate with the international organization working in the domain of the rights of the author and neighboring rights to know the ways of communicating with the author or the owner of the right or to estimate the fair reward or determine that it was received by the author or the owner of the right.

Article 11 [Publication]

This decision is to be published in the official gazette and is effective from the date of publication.

Abdullah Bin Zayed Al Nahyan
Minister of Information and Culture

Issued: 2/1/1425 H
Corresponding to: 3/22/2004 M.[141]

---

141. The Islamic date is 1 Safar 1425 and the Gregorian date is March 22, 2004.

A21

Ministerial Decision No. 288 of 2004 in Relation to the Fees Relating to the Rights of the Author and Neighboring Rights

Minister of Information and Culture,

After considering federal law no. 1 of 1972 in relation to the jurisdictions of the Ministries and the powers of the Ministers and the laws amending it, and

Federal law no. 7 of 2002 in relation to the rights of the author and neighboring rights, and

Cabinet decision no. 14 of 1999 in relation to commercial media licenses fees that are issued by the Ministry of Information and Culture, and

After cooperating with the Ministry of Finance and Industry,

Decided:

Article 1 [Fees for Licenses]

The fees for licenses and certificates for works that are issued by the Ministry of Information and Culture are as follows [in UAE dirhams]:

	Type of license	Required fee	Annual renewal	Replacement
1	Collective management license	10,000	5,000	100
2	License to translate a work	100	-	50
3	License to copy a work	100	-	50
4	License to translate and copy a work	200	-	100
5	Issue of a certificate of registration of a work	30	-	15
6	Issue of a certificate of disposal of a work	30	-	15

Article 2 [Fees Due on Acceptance]

The fees are to be collected upon acceptance of the application.

Article 3 [Publication]

This decision is to be published in the official gazette and is effective from the date of publication.

Abdullah Bin Zayed Al Nahyan
Minister of Information and Culture

Issued: Jumaada Al Akhira 9, 1425 H.
Corresponding to: 7/26/2004 M.

APPENDIX
A22

United Arab Emirates
Department of Dubai Customs

General Director's Office
Date: September 6, 2006

Customs Policy

Policy code: DCP 11

Policy name: trademark recordal for customs purposes
Details of the policy

Article (1) [IPR Department to Record Trademarks]

For the purposes of strengthening, supporting, and facilitating Customs control and protecting intellectual property rights, and to facilitate the establishment of an administrative unit charged with informing trademark owners of the detention, confiscation, requisition, or destruction of any shipments related to his registered trademark and any infringement of it, the Intellectual Property Rights Department will record trademarks that have been registered with the competent authority.

Article (2) [The Register and Its Purpose]

A register called "The register for recording trademarks" will be created at the Department for the purpose of compiling and archiving data, information and documents relating to trademarks published by the competent authority and submitted by the trademark owner or his legal agent.

Article (3) [Fee for Trademark Recordal]

The trademarks will be recorded for an administrative fee of 200 dirhams for each class for each trademark according to the internat onal specification of classes. These fees will be collected by the Intellectual Property Rights Protection Department for services and protection rendered by the Department to trademarks owners.

Article (4) [Recordal Fee not Reimbursable]

The administrative fees are collected upon the receipt of the documents and the completion of the recordal applications and conditions for opening a file in the name of the trademark owner. These fees are not reimbursable even if the recordal application is rejected.

Article (5) [Complaint and Security Deposit]

The Intellectual Property Rights Department will begin its operational procedures in relation to customs control in the field of intellectual property rights protection after receiving and studying the complaint and statement from the trademark owner, and will follow the trademark infringement case, for a fee of 2000 dirhams, in addition to the amount of 5000 dirhams as a security deposit to cover the possible inspection, transportation, and follow-up expenses that is reimbursable if the complaint is correct and that is not reimbursable if it is apparent that the complaint is incorrect.

Article (6) [Urgent and Other Complaints]

The owner of the trademark will be responsible for additional fees of 500 dirhams in case of an urgent complaint and for further fees of 1000 dirhams if the complaint coincides with a vacation day, official holidays, or a weekend.

Article (7) [Responsibility for Other Fees and Expenses]

If the complaint proves to be incorrect and the shipment is free of any contravening goods, the mark owner will be responsible for all the expenses and fees resulting from the stopping of the shipment the subject of the complaint and the required fees for stopping or delaying the means of transport carrying the goods, and also the fees for storage, offloading, handling and transportation, or any expenses or fees resulting from his complaint. The trademark owner is to submit a written undertaking to this effect when submitting the complaint and the statement.

Article (8) [Responsibility for Technical Inspection Cost]

The trademark owner is responsible for the fees for technical examination performed by the laboratory in case a specialised technical examination is necessary to prove the infringement of the trademark or its counterfeiting.

Article (9) [Responsibility for Transportation and Destruction Costs]

The person the subject of the complaint being the owner of the shipment or the carrier will be responsible for the expenses of the transportation and destruction if the seized goods are proved to be infringing. after the issuance of the confiscation and destruction decision.

Article (10) [Effective Date]

This customs policy is applicable from the first of October 2006.

Ahmad Buti Ahmad

Part B. Arabic texts

Patents and designs

B1. Federal law no. 44 of 1992 in relation to the regulation and protection of industrial property for patents, industrial drawings and designs.

B2. Federal law no. 17 of 2002 in relation to the regulation and protection of industrial property for patents, industrial drawings and designs.

B3. Federal law no. 31 of 2006 amending federal law no. 17 of 2002 in relation to the regulation and protection of industrial property for patents, industrial drawings and designs

B4. Cabinet decision no. 11 of 1993 concerning the implementing regulations for federal law no. 44 of 1992 in relation to the regulation and protection of industrial property for patents, industrial drawings and designs.

B5. Ministerial decision no. 404 of 2000 [concerning pharmaceutical products and patents].

Trade marks

B6. Federal law no. 37 of 1992 in relation to trade marks.

B7. Federal law no. 19 of 2000 amending some of the provisions of federal law no. 37 of 1992 in relation to trade marks.

B8. Federal law no. 8 of 2002 amending some of the provisions of federal law no. 37 of 1992 in relation to trade marks.

B9. Ministerial decision no. 6 of 1993 concerning the implementing regulations for federal law no. 37 of 1992 in relation to trade marks.

B10. Cabinet decision no. 18 of 1993 in relation to the fees for procedures undertaken pursuant to the provisions of federal law no. 37 of 1992 in relation to trade marks.

B11. Ministerial decision no. 67 of 1998 [in relation to payment of fees for trade mark registration].

B12. Ministerial decision no. 67 of 2001 in relation to the collection of fees for the publication of trade marks.

B13. Ministerial decision no. 80 of 2005 in relation to the registration of trade mark registration agents.

B14. Federal decree no. 52 of 2007 in relation to the unified trade mark law (system) for the Arabian Gulf Cooperation Council Countries.

B15. Federal law no. 4 of 1979 in relation to the prevention of fraud and deception in commercial dealings.

B16. Ministerial decision no. 26 of 1984 concerning the implementing regulations for law no. 4 of 1979 in relation to the prevention of fraud and deception in commercial dealings [as amended].

B17. Ministerial decision no. 418 of 2007 in relation to the use of the trade mark "Organic".

Author's rights

B18. Federal law no. 40 of 1992 in relation to the protection of intellectual works and the rights of the author.

B19. Federal law no. 7 of 2002 in relation to the rights of the author and neighbouring rights.

B20. Federal law no. 32 of 2006 amending federal law no. 7 of 2002 in relation to the rights of the author and neighbouring rights.

B21. Ministerial decision no 411 of 1993 in relation to the monitoring of works protected pursuant to the provisions of federal law no. 40 of 1992 in relation to the protection of intellectual works and the rights of the author.

B22. Ministerial decision no. 412 of 1993 in relation to the deposit system for protected works and disposals that may occur.

B23. Decision of the Minister of Information and Culture no. 131 of 2004 in relation to the registration of works.

B24. Decision of the Minister of Information and Culture no. 132 of 2004 in relation to the register of importers and distributers of works.

B25. Decision of the Minister of Information and Culture no. 133 of 2004 in relation to administration of collecting societies for the rights of the author and neighbouring rights.

B26. Decision of the Minister of Information and Culture no. 134 of 2004 in relation to the compulsory licences for the copying and translating of works.

B27. Ministerial decision no. 288 of 2004 in relation to the fees connected with the rights of the author and neighbouring rights.

Customs

B28. Department of Dubai Customs, Customs policy no. DCP 11, titled "The recordal of trade marks for customs purposes", September 6, 2006.

قانون اتحادي رقم (٤٤) لسنة ١٩٩٢
في شأن تنظيم وحماية الملكية الصناعية لبراءات الاختراع والرسوم والنماذج
الصناعية

نحن زايد بن سلطان آل نهيان، رئيس دولة الامارات العربية المتحدة،

بعد الاطلاع على الدستور المؤقت،

وعلى القانون الاتحادي رقم (١) لسنة ١٩٧٢ بشأن اختصاصات الوزارات وصلاحيات
الوزراء والقوانين المعدلة له،

وعلى القانون الاتحادي رقم (٥) لسنة ١٩٧٦ في شأن اتحاد غرف التجارة والصناعة،

وعلى القانون الاتحادي رقم (١) لسنة ١٩٧٩ في شأن تنظيم شئون الصناعة،

وعلى القانون الاتحادي رقم (٤) لسنة ١٩٧٩ في شأن قمع الغش والتدليس في
المعاملات التجارية،

وعلى القانون الاتحادي رقم (٨) لسنة ١٩٨٤ في شأن الشركات التجارية والقوانين
المعدلة له،

وبناءً على ماعرضه وزير المالية والصناعة، وموافقة مجلس الوزراء، وتصديق
المجلس الاعلى للاتحاد،

أصدرنا القانون الآتي:

الباب الأول
تعريفات وأحكام عامة

المادة (١)

في تطبيق أحكام هذا القانون يكون للكلمات والعبارات التالية، المعاني الموضحة قرين كل منها ما لم يدل سياق النص على غير ذلك:

الوزير:	وزير المالية والصناعة.
الإدارة:	إدارة الملكية الصناعية بوزارة المالية والصناعة وفروعها في الإمارات.
اللجنة:	لجنة التظلمات بإدارة الملكية الصناعية.
المحكمة المختصة:	المحكمة الابتدائية المدنية.
سند الحماية :	الوثيقة الدالة على تسجيل الملكية الصناعية لبراءة الاختراع أو شهادة المنفعة أو الرسم والنموذج الصناعي.
براءة الأختراع:	سند الحماية الذي تمنحه إدارة الملكية الصناعية باسم الدولة عن الاختراع.
الدراية العملية:	المعلومات أو البيانات أو المعارف الناجمة عن الخبرة المكتسبة من المهنة ذات الطبيعة التقنية والقابلة للتطبيق عملياً.
النموذج الصناعي:	كل تكوين للخطوط أو للألوان، أو كل شكل مجسم يرتبط أو لا يرتبط بالخطوط أو الألوان، بشرط أن يعطي مظهراً خاصاً ويمكن استخدامه كنموذج لمنتج صناعي أو حرفي.
علامة المنشأ:	التعبير أو الرمز المستخدم للدلالة على أصل المنتج سواء كانت دولة أو مجموعة دول أو ولاية أو اقليماً.

المادة (٢)

لاتخل احكام هذا القانون بما تنص عليه الاتفاقيات والمعاهدات الدولية التي تكون دولة الامارات العربية المتحدة طرفاً فيها، والتي تنظم حقوق مواطني الدول الأطراف في تلك الاتفاقيات والمعاهدات وحقوق الاشخاص الذين يعاملون معاملتهم.

ويكون للاجنبي الذي لا يشمله حكم الفقرة السابقة حقوق المواطن التي يخولها هذا القانون اذا كان يحمل جنسية دولة تعامل دولة الامارات العربية المتحدة معاملة المثل.

المادة (٣)

تحدد اللائحة التنفيذية لهذا القانون احكام الحماية المؤقتة للاختراعات والرسوم والنماذج الصناعية بالنسبة الى المنتجات التي يتم عرضها في المعارض داخل الدولة وذلك بمراعاة احكام الاتفاقيات والمعاهدات أو شرط المعاملة بالمثل.

الباب الثاني
الاختراعات

الفصل الأول
براءة الاختراع وشهادة المنفعة

المادة (٤)

تمنح براءة الاختراع عن كل اختراع جديد ناتج عن فكرة مبتكرة أو تحسين مبتكر لاختراع تحميه براءة، ويكون كل منهما قائماً على اسس علمية وقابلاً للاستغلال الصناعي، سواء تعلق ذلك بمنتجات صناعية جديدة أو بطرق أو وسائل صناعية مستحدثة أو بتطبيق جديد لطرق أو وسائل صناعية معروفة.

ويعتبر الاختراع قابلاً للتطبيق الصناعي اذا أمكن تطبيقه أو استعماله في أي نوع من الصناعة بمعناها الواسع بما في ذلك الزراعة والصيد والحرف اليدوية والخدمات.

المادة (٥)

تمنح شهادة المنفعة عن كل اختراع جديد قابل للتطبيق الصناعي ولكنه لا ينتج عن نشاط ابتكاري كاف لمنح براءة اختراع عنه.

المادة (٦)

لاتمنح براءة الاختراع أو شهادة المنفعة عما يأتي:

١. الابحاث النباتية أو الحيوانية أو الطرق البيولوجية لانتاج النبات أو الحيوان ويستثنى من ذلك طرق علم الاحياء الدقيقة ومنتجاتها.

٢. الاختراعات الكيميائية المتعلقة بالاغذية أو العقاقير الطبية أو المركبات الصيدلية الا اذا كانت هذه المنتجات تصنع بطرق كيميائية خاصة وفي هذه الحالة لاتنصرف الحماية الى المنتجات ذاتها بل تنصرف الى طريقة صنعها.

٣. المبادى والاكتشافات لعلمية.

٤. الاختراعات المتعلقة بالدفاع الوطني.

٥. الاختراعات التي ينشأ عن نشرها أو استغلالها اخلال بالنظام العام أو الآداب.

المادة (٧)

١. مع عدم الاخلال بأحكام المادة (٩) من هذا القانون يكون الحق في الاختراع للمخترع أو لخلفه القانوني.

٢. واذا اشترك شخصان أو أكثر في انجاز اختراع، يكون الحق في الاختراع لهم أو لخلفائهم القانونيين شركة فيما بينهم. ولا يعتبر مخترعاً أو في مرتبة المخترع ذلك الذي تقتصر جهوده على المساعدة في تنفيذ الاختراع دون الاسهام في أية خطوة ابتكارية.

٣. ومع عدم الاخلال بأحكام المادتين (٨) و (٩) من هذا القانون يعتبر مخترعاً أو خلفاً للمخترع الشخص الذي يودع طلباً قبل غيره عن براءة اختراع أو شهادة منفعة أو الذي يطالب قبل غيره بأسبقية عن ذات الاختراع.

٤. ويكون لكل ذي مصلحة حق التظلم والطعن في قرار قبول أو رفض الطلب وفقاً لاحكام هذا القانون ولائحته التنفيذية.

المادة (٨)

اذا كانت العناصر الجوهرية للاختراع قد تم الحصول عليها من اختراع شخص اخر دون موافقته على ذلك أو على ايداع طلب الحماية، فيجوز لمن أصيب بضرر نتيجة لهذا الاغتصاب المطالبة بنقل الطلب اليه أو بنقل البراءة أو شهادة المنفعة اذا كانت قد منحت الى المغتصب.

المادة (٩)

١. إذا انجز الاختراع من خلال تنفيذ عقد مقاولة أو عقد عمل يكون الحق في الاختراع لصاحب العمل مالم ينص الاتفاق على غير ذلك.

٢. واذا كان للاختراع قيمة اقتصادية تفوق تصورات الطرفين عند توقيع العقد، يستحق المخترع تعويضاً اضافياً تحدده المحكمة اذا لم يتفق الطرفان على مبلغ معين.

٣. واذا أنجز العامل الذي لا ينص عقد عمله على القيام بنشاط ابتكاري اختراعاً يتصل بمجال نشاط صاحب العمل مستخدماً في ذلك خبرات أو وثائق أو أدوات صاحب العمل أو مواده الاولية الموضوعة تحت تصرفه من خلال العمل فيكون الحق في ذلك الاختراع للعامل المخترع بانقضاء أربعة شهور من تاريخ تقديمه التقرير المشار اليه في الفقرة (٤) من هذه المادة لصاحب العمل عن الاختراع أو اعتباراً من أي تاريخ علم من

خلاله صاحب العمل بصورة أخرى عن تحقق الاختراع، ولم يبد صاحب العمل استعداده لتملك الاختراع باعلان كتابي.

٤. وعلى العامل المخترع أن يخطر صاحب العمل فوراً بتقرير كتابي عن اختراعه.

٥. واذا أبدى صاحب العمل استعداده لتملك الاختراع خلال المدة المحددة في الفقرة (٣) من هذه المادة يعتبر الحق في الاختراع عائداً له منذ نشوء الاختراع ويستحق العامل المخترع تعويضاً عادلاً يؤخذ فيه بعين الاعتبار مرتبه والقيمة الاقتصادية للاختراع وكل فائدة تعود منه على صاحب العمل، واذا لم يتفق الطرفان على التعويض تحدده المحكمة.

٦. وكل اتفاق يعطي للعامل مزايا أقل مما تنص عليه أحكام هذه المادة يعتبر باطلاً.

المادة (١٠)

يذكر اسم المخترع في براءة الاختراع أو شهادة المنفعة، ما لم يعلن المخترع كتابة عن رغبته في عدم ذكر اسمه. ويتم تقديم طلب تسجيل الاختراع وبياناته وفقاً لما تحدده اللائحة التنفيذية لهذا القانون.

المادة (١١)

يجوز أن يتضمن طلب التسجيل الرغبة في اعتبار الاولوية في التسجيل لطلب سبق تقديمه في دولة تكون طرفاً في اتفاقية أو معاهدة مع دولة الامارات العربية المتحدة. وفي هذه الحالة، يجب أن يوضح في الطلب تاريخ ورقم قيد الطلب السابق واسم الدولة التي قدم اليها، وذلك وفقاً لما تنص عليه اللائحة التنفيذية لهذا القانون.

المادة (١٢)

تقوم الادارة بفحص طلبات التسجيل وفقاً لاحكام القانون ولائحته التنفيذية ولها ان تطلب استيفاء ماتراه لازماً لمنح البراءة أو شهادة المنفعة.

وعلى الادارة في حالة رفض التسجيل اخطار مقدم الطلب بذلك ويجوز له أن يتظلم الى اللجنة خلال ستين يوماً من تاريخ الاخطار.

المادة (١٣)

تمنح براءات الاختراع وشهادات المنفعة بقرار من الوزير وتنشر في الجريدة الرسمية. ولكل ذي مصلحة الحق في التظلم امام اللجنة خلال ستين يوماً من تاريخ النشر.

وتسلم البراءة أو شهادة المنفعة الى صاحب الحق فيها، اذا لم يقدم في شأنها أي تظلم خلال الميعاد المنصوص عليه في الفقرة السابقة، وذلك بعد قيدها في السجل الخاص.

ويجب ان تحمل البراءة أو الشهادة رقم القيد وتاريخ الاصدار وبيان دفع رسم القيد أو التجديد وغير ذلك من البيانات وفقاً لما تنص عليه اللائحة التنفيذية لهذا القانون.

المادة (١٤)

مدة براءة الاختراع خمس عشرة سنة ومدة شهادة المنفعة عشر سنوات تبدأ كل منهما من تاريخ تقديم طلب التسجيل ويجوز تجديد المدة مرة واحدة بما لايجاوز خمس سنوات بالنسبة الى البراءة ويجب تقديم طلب التجديد خلال ثلاثة الاشهر الاخيرة من المدة الاصلية ويشترط للتجديد أن يثبت المخترع ان للاختراع أهمية خاصة وأنه لم يجن منه ثمرة تتناسب مع جهوده ونشاطه.

أما البراءات التي تمنح وفقاً لاحكام الفقرة (٢) من المادة (٦) من هذا القانون فتكون مدتها عشر سنوات غير قابلة للتجديد.

وتحدد اللائحة التنفيذية رسوم التسجيل والتجديد ورسماً متصاعداً سنوياً يبدأ سداده من السنة التالية لتاريخ ايداع طلب التسجيل. ويجب اداء الرسم السنوي خلال ثلاثة الاشهر الاخيرة من كل سنة والا سقطت البراءة او الشهادة. ويجوز قبول الرسم اذا تم دفعه خلال ثلاثين يوماً من انقضاء المدة السابقة وذلك مقابل رسم اضافي تحدده اللائحة التنفيذية. وفي جميع الاحوال يجوز سداد الرسوم السنوية مقدماً عن كل او بعض مدة البراءة أو الشهادة.

المادة (١٥)

تخول البراءة أو شهادة المنفعة لمالكها الحق في منع الغير من الاعمال الآتية:

١. تصنيع المنتج واستيراده وعرضه للبيع وبيعه واستعماله أو الاحتفاظ به بهدف العرض للبيع أو للاستعمال، وذلك عندما تمنح البراءة أو شهادة المنفعة عن منتج.

٢. استعمال الطريقة ومباشرة أي من الأعمال المشار اليها في الفقرة (١) من هذه المادة بخصوص منتج يتم الحصول عليه بوساطة الطريقة مباشرة، وذلك عندما تمنح البراءة أو شهادة المنفعة عن طريقة.

المادة (١٦)

١. يحدد نطاق الحماية التي تخولها البراءة أو شهادة المنفعة بطلب التسجيل.

٢. ويستخدم الوصف والرسومات الهندسية في تفسير مضمون طلب التسجيل.

المادة (١٧)

تقتصر الحقوق التي تخولها البراءة أو شهادة المنفعة على الأعمال التي تتم لأغراض صناعية أو تجارية. ولا تمتد هذه الحقوق الى الاعمال الخاصة بالمنتج الذي تحميه بعد بيعه في دولة الامارات العربية المتحدة. ومع ذلك اذا كانت البراءة أو شهادة المنفعة تتعلق ايضاً باستعمال خاص للمنتج، فيكون لمالكها حق الاحتفاظ بهذا الاستعمال.

المادة (١٨)

اذا قام شخص بحسن نية بتصنيع المنتج أو باستعمال الطريقة موضوع الاختراع أو اتخاذ ترتيبات جدية لهذا التصنيع أو الاستعمال في دولة الامارات العربية المتحدة في تاريخ ايداع طلب طلب الحماية من شخص آخر، أو في تاريخ الأسبقية المطالب بها قانوناً بالنسبة لهذا الطلب، يكون للاول بالرغم من منح البراءة أو شهادة المنفعة، الحق في مواصلة القيام بهذه الأعمال ومباشرة الاعمال الأخرى المشار اليها في المادة (١٥) من هذا القانون بالنسبة للمنتجات المتحصلة منهما، وهذا الحق شخصي، لا يقبل الانتقال الا مع المنشأة المستفيدة منه.

المادة (١٩)

١. يجوز التنازل عن البراءة أو شهادة المنفعة أو عن طلبها قبل المنح للغير.

٢. ويجب أن يتم التنازل عن البراءة أو شهادة المنفعة أو عن طلبها كتابة وأن يوقع من الأطراف المتعاقدة أمام الموظف المسؤول في الادارة أو أن يصادق على توقيعاتهم الكاتب العدل.

٣. ويجب قيد التنازل عن البراءة أو شهادة المنفعة في السجل المخصص لذلك مقابل رسم تحدده اللائحة التنفيذية.

٤. ولا يكون التنازل عن البراءة أو شهادة المنفعة حجة على الغير الا بعد قيده في سجل البراءات أو سجل شهادات المنفعة والاشهار عنه في الجريدة الرسمية.

المادة (٢٠)

يجوز للمالكين المشتركين في البراءة او شهادة المنفعة، كل على انفراد، أن يتنازلوا للغير عن حصتهم في الاختراع المحمي بالبراءة أو شهادة المنفعة وأن يستغلوه وأن يباشروا الحقوق التي تخولها المادة (١٥) من هذا القانون ما لم يتفق على خلاف ذلك، ولكن لايجوز لهم أن يمنحوا ترخيصاً للغير باستغلال الاختراع الا مجتمعين.

المادة (٢١)

يجوز رهن براءة الاختراع ضماناً للوفاء بدين سواء بصورة مستقلة أو مع المحل التجاري ويؤشر بالرهن في سجل براءات الاختراع وينشر في الجريدة الرسمية.

المادة (٢٢)

يجوز للدائنين أن يحجزوا على براءات الاختراع أو شهادات المنفعة المملوكة لمدينيهم وفقاً لاجراءات الحجز على المنقول أو حجز ما للمدين لدى الغير حسب الاحوال. وتعفي الادارة من اقرار المحجوز لديه بما في ذمته للمحجوز عليه.

ويجب على الدائن ان يعلن الحجز وحكم مرسى المزاد للادارة للتأشير بهما في السجل الخاص. وينشر الحجز وحكم مرسى المزاد في الجريدة الرسمية وتحصل الرسوم المقررة وفقاً لما تحدده اللائحة التنفيذية ولا يكون للحجز أو حكم مرسى المزاد اثر بالنسبة الى الغير الا من تاريخ النشر.

الفصل الثاني
التراخيص الاجبارية ونزع ملكية الاختراع

المادة (٢٣)

١. يجوز لكل ذي شأن في أي وقت بعد انقضاء أربع سنوات من تاريخ ايداع طلب البراءة أو ثلاث سنوات من تاريخ منحها، وكذلك يجوز لكل ذي شأن في أي وقت بعد انقضاء ثلاث سنوات من تاريخ طلب شهادة المنفعة أو سنتين من تاريخ منحها، أن يطلب وفقاً للاجراءات المبينة في المادة (٢٩) من هذا القانون الحصول على ترخيص اجباري لسبب أو لاكثر من الأسباب الآتية:

أ) ان الاختراع الذي تحميه البراءة أو شهادة المنفعة والذي يمكن استغلاله في دولة الامارات العربية المتحدة لايستغل وفقاً لأحكام الفقرة (٣) من هذه المادة.
ب) ان استغلال الاختراع الذي تحميه البراءة أو شهادة المنفعة في دولة الامارات العربية المتحدة لايفي بالطلب على المنتج بشروط معقولة.
ج) ان استغلال الاختراع الذي تحميه البراءة أو شهادة المنفعة في دولة الامارات العربية المتحدة قد توقف من قبل المستثمر سنتين متتاليتين.
د) ان رفض مالك البراءة أو شهادة المنفعة الترخيص عليها عقدياً بشروط عادلة قد ادى الى اخلال أساسي باقامة أو تنمية الأنشطة الصناعية أوالتجارية في دولة الامارات العربية المتحدة.

٢. ولا يمنح الترخيص الاجباري في جميع الحالات المتقدمة اذا برر مالك البراءة أو شهادة المنفعة موقفه بأسباب مشروعة. ولا يشكل استيراد المنتج سبباً مشروعاً.

٣. ولغايات هذه المادة يقصد باستغلال اختراع تحميه براءة أو شهادة منفعة تصنيع منتج محمي أو استعمال طريقة محمية أو استخدام آلة محمية في التصنيع من قبل منشاة قائمة جدياً وفعالة في دولة الامارات العربية المتحدة.

المادة (٢٤)

١. يخول الترخيص الاجباري المرخص له الحق في مباشرة بعض أو كل الاعمال المشار اليها في المادة (١٥) من هذا القانون وفقاً لشروط الترخيص ويستثنى من ذلك حق استيراد المنتج.

٢. ويكون لصاحب الترخيص الحق في استعمال الحقوق المدنية والجزائية لصاحب براءة الاختراع أو شهادة المنفعة لحماية الاختراع واستغلاله اذا قصر احدهما في ذلك رغم اخطاره أو علمه بأي عمل غير مشروع.

المادة (٢٥)

١. اذا كان من غير الممكن استغلال اختراع تحميه براءة أو شهادة منفعة في دولة الامارات العربية المتحدة دون الاخلال بحقوق مستمدة من براءة أو شهادة منفعة منحت بناءً على طلب سابق، فانه يجوز منح مالك البراءة أو شهادة المنفعة الأخيرة ترخيصاً اجبارياً بناءً على طلبه ووفقاً للشروط المبينة في المادة (٢٨) من هذا القانون بالقدر اللازم لاستغلال اختراعه اذا كان هذا الاختراع يخدم أغراضاً صناعية مختلفة عن تلك الاغراض الخاصة بالاختراع موضوع البراءة أو شهادة المنفعة السابقة أو يشكل تقدماً تقنياً ملحوظاً بالنسبة اليه.

٢. واذا كان الاختراعان يخدمان ذات الغرض الصناعي، يمنح الترخيص الاجباري لمالك البراءة أو شهادة المنفعة اللاحقة مع حفظ الحق لصاحب البراءة أو شهادة المنفعة السابقة في الحصول على ترخيص عن البراء[1] أو شهادة المنفعة اللاحقة، اذا طلب ذلك.

٣. ومع ذلك يجوز للطرفين الاتفاق كتابة فيما بينهما واخطار الادارة باتفاقهما للتأشير به في السجل الخاص.

المادة (٢٦)

لايجوز منح ترخيص اجباري باستغلال الاختراع الا بعد أن يقدم طالب الترخيص مايثبت اخطار صاحب الاختراع بذلك بكتاب مسجل وعدم توصله الى اتفاق خلال وقت معقول وبشروط عادلة.

---

[1]. وردت هذه الكلمة في نص الجريدة الرسمية "البراء" والأصح ان تكون "البراءة" فاقتضى التنويه.

المادة (٢٧)

يقتصر منح الترخيص الاجباري على الطالب الذي يقدم الضمانات اللازمة لاستغلال الاختراع استغلالاً كافياً لمعالجة أوجه النقص أو لمقابلة الاحتياجات التي أدت الى طلب الحصول على الترخيص الاجباري.

المادة (٢٨)

١. لايجوز أن يكون الترخيص الاجباري مطلقاً.

٢. ويجوز أن تتضمن شروط الترخيص الاجباري التزامات وقيوداً على كل من المرخص أو المرخص له بترخيص اجباري.

المادة (٢٩)

يقدم طلب الترخيص الاجباري الى المحكمة المختصة في صورة دعوى يختصم فيها صاحب براءة الاختراع أو شهادة المنفعة وتعلن بها الادارة لحضور ممثل عنها، وللمحكمة ان تعطي الطرفين مهلة تحددها للاتفاق فيما بينهما، ويجوز مد المهلة اذا رأت المحكمة مبرراً لذلك.

فاذا انقضت المهلة، نظرت المحكمة في الطلب برفض منح الترخيص الاجباري، أو بمنحه مع تحديد شروطه ومجاله وتحديد التعويض لصاحب براءة الاختراع أو شهادة المنفعة وفقاً لنص المادة (٢٣) من هذا القانون، ويعلن الحكم الى الطرف الآخر والى الادارة للتأشير به في السجل الخاص وينشر في الجريدة الرسمية بعد اداء الرسم المقرر، ولا يكون للحكم اثر بالنسبة الى الغير الا من تاريخ النشر.

المادة (٣٠)

١. لايجوز انتقال الترخيص الاجباري الا مع منشأة المرخص له أو مع ذلك الجزء من منشأته الذي يستغل الاختراع. ويتم الانتقال بموافقة السلطة التي منحت الترخيص الاجباري والا كان باطلاً. وتسري على الانتقال أحكام المادتين (٢٩) و(٣٢) من هذا القانون.

٢. ولا يجوز لمن منح ترخيصاً اجبارياً أن يمنح بدوره تراخيص من الباطن.

المادة (٣١)

١. يجوز للسلطة التي منحت الترخيص الاجباري أن تعدل شروطه بناءً على طلب مالك البراءة أو شهادة المنفعة أو المرخص له بترخيص اجباري، إذا كان ذلك مبرراً بوقائع جديدة، وبوجه خاص إذا منح مالك البراءة أو شهادة المنفعة ترخيصاً تعاقدياً بشروط أفضل من شروط الترخيص الاجباري.

٢. ويجوز للسلطة التي منحت الترخيص الاجباري أن تقرر الغاءه بناءً على طلب مالك البراءة أو شهادة المنفعة اذا لم يتبع المرخص له شروط الترخيص أو اذا زالت الاسباب التي بررت منحه وفي هذه الحالة يجب منح المرخص له مهلة معقولة ليكف عن استغلال الاختراع إذا كان التوقف الفوري يسبب له ضرراً جسيماً.

٣. وتسري أحكام المادتين (٣٦) و(٣٧) من هذا القانون على تعديل والغاء التراخيص الاجبارية.

المادة (٣٢)

يجب قيد التراخيص الاجبارية وما يصدر في شأنها بالسجل الخاص ونشرها في الجريدة الرسمية وذلك بعد أداء الرسوم المقررة وفقاً لما تحدده اللائحة التنفيذية لهذا القانون.

المادة (٣٣)

يجوز بقرار من الوزير، نزع ملكية الاختراع أو اصدار ترخيص اجباري باستغلاله دون التقيد بالمواعيد المنصوص عليها في المادة (٢٣) من هذا القانون، إذا كان للاختراع أهمية للمنفعة العامة أو الدفاع أو الاقتصاد الوطني، ويجوز أن يشمل ذلك جميع الحقوق المترتبة على الاختراع أو جزءاً منها ولا يخل ذلك بحق صاحب براءة الاختراع أو شهادة المنفعة في التعويض الذي تقدره اللجنة.

ويجب قبل اصدار القرار اخطار صاحب براءة الاختراع أو شهادة المنفعة لابداء وجهة نظره في هذا الشأن ويتم التأشير بقرار نزع الملكية أو الترخيص الاجباري في السجل وينشر في الجريدة الرسمية.

ويجوز الطعن في قرار نزع الملكية أو الترخيص الاجباري أو تقدير التعويض أمام المحكمة المختصة خلال ستين يوماً من تاريخ اخطار صاحب براءة الاختراع أو شهادة المنفعة.

الفصل الثالث
التخلي عن براءة الاختراع أو شهادة المنفعة أوالترخيص وحالات إبطال كل منها

المادة (٣٤)

يجوز لصاحب براءة الاختراع أو شهادة المنفعة او الترخيص الاجباري أن يتخلى عنها بموجب اخطار كتابي الى الادارة والى كل من تعلق له حق بأي منها.

ويجوز أن يقتصر التخلي على حق أو اكثر مما تخوله براءة الاختراع أو شهادة المنفعة أو الترخيص الاجباري ولا يجوز ان يضر التخلي بحقوق الغير، مالم يكن قد تم التخلي عنها كتابة.

ويقيد التخلي في السجل الخاص، ولا يصبح نافذاً الا من تاريخ نشره في الجريدة الرسمية.

المادة (٣٥)

يجوز لكل ذي مصلحة ان يلجأ الى المحكمة المختصة لطلب ابطال براءة الاختراع أو شهادة المنفعة او الترخيص الاجباري.

ويجب إعلان صاحب براءة الاختراع أو شهادة المنفعة أو الترخيص والادارة وكل من تعلق له حق بأي منها، وذلك في الحالات الآتية:

١. اذا منحت البراءة أو الشهادة او الترخيص دون توفر الشروط المنصوص عليها في هذا القانون أو لائحته التنفيذية.

٢. اذا منحت البراءة او الشهادة او الترخيص دون مراعاة اولوية الطلبات السابقة وفقاً للمادة (١١) من هذا القانون.

ويجوز ان يقتصر طلب الابطال على جزء من البراءة أو الشهادة أو الترخيص وفي هذه الحالة يعتبر الحكم الصادر تقييداً لما تخوله من حقوق.

المادة (٣٦)

مع مراعاة حكم المادة (٣١) من هذا القانون يترتب على الحكم ببطلان براءة الاختراع او الشهادة او الترخيص كلياً او جزئياً، اعتبار البطلان من تاريخ منح البراءة أو الشهادة أو الترخيص ومع ذلك لايلزم صاحبها برد التعويضات التي حصل عليها مقابل استغلال الاختراع او الترخيص الاجباري، اذا ثبت استفادة المستغل أو صاحب الترخيص.

ويجب التأشير بحكم البطلان في السجل الخاص، ونشره في الجريدة الرسمية.

الفصل الرابع
أحكام خاصة ببعض الاختراعات

المادة (٣٧)

١. لمالك البراءة أو شهادة المنفعة أو لخلفه القانوني الحق في الحصول على براءة اختراع اضافية أو شهادة منفعة اضافية تمنح على التحسينات أو التغييرات أو الاضافات التي طرأت على الاختراع بعد حمايته. ويخضع طلب الحماية الاضافية إلى ذات الشروط التي يخضع لها طلب الحماية الأصلية. وتترتب على الحماية الاضافية ذات الآثار المترتبة على الحماية الاصلية.

٢. وتنتهي مدة الحماية الاضافية بانتهاء مدة الحماية الاصلية. ومع ذلك، فإن بطلان الحماية الأصلية لا يترتب عليه حتماً بطلان الحماية الاضافية. وتحدد اللائحة التنفيذية الرسوم السنوية للحماية الاضافية.

٣. ويجوز قبل منح الحماية الاضافية تحويل الطلب الخاص بها إلى طلب براءة مستقلة أو شهادة منفعة مستقلة.

المادة (٣٨)

١. لا يجوز منح براءة اختراع أو شهادة منفعة عن اختراع سري. ويعد الاختراع سرياً عندما يكون متعلقاً بالدفاع الوطني إلا إذا قرر وزير الدفاع غير ذلك.

٢. ويجب على الادارة من خلال فحص طلب الحماية أن تخطر فوراً وزير الدفاع بتقرير كتابي مرفق بطلب الحماية، إذا تبين ان الاختراع يتعلق بأمور الدفاع الوطني.

٣. وبناءً على قرار وزير الدفاع يعتبر الاختراع سرياً أو يسمح بحمايته حسب الاجراءات العادية.

٤. وإذا اعتبر الاختراع سرياً فلا يجوز الاشهار عنه.

٥. ويتنازل مالك الاختراع عن اختراعه لوزارة الدفاع لقاء تعويض عادل.

الفصل الخامس
الدراية العملية

المادة (٣٩)

مع عدم الاخلال بالحقوق التي تخولها براءة الاختراع أو شهادة المنفعة، تتمتع الدراية العملية بالحماية من أي استعمال أو إفشاء أو إعلان غير مشروع من قبل الغير، ما دامت لم تنشر أو توضع تحت التصرف العام للكافة، ويشترط للتمتع بالحماية أن يكون صاحب الدراية العملية قد اتخذ التدابير اللازمة للمحافظة على سرية عناصرها على النحو الذي تبينه اللائحة التنفيذية لهذا القانون.

المادة (٤٠)

يكون لكل شخص توصل بوسائله الخاصة إلى تطوير طريقة صناعية أو دراية عملية متعلقة باستخدام الاساليب والوسائل الصناعية، أو حصل على ذلك بطريق مشروع ان يستعمل هذه الطريقة أو الدراية العملية بنفسه أو اعلانها للغير، حتى ولو كان شخص آخر قد توصل إلى ذات الطريقة أو الدراية العملية.

المادة (٤١)

يجب أن يكون عقد الدراية العملية ثابتاً بالكتابة، وان يتضمن تحديد عناصرها والغرض من استعمالها وشروط نقلها، وإلا اعتبر العقد باطلا.

وتسري على عقود الدراية العملية الاحكام الخاصة باستغلال الاختراعات والتنازل عنها ونقلها والترخيص باستغلالها على النحو الذي تحدده اللائحة التنفيذية لهذا القانون.

المادة (٤٢)

يعتبر عملاً غير مشروع كل استعمال او افشاء او اعلان اي عنصر من عناصر الدراية العملية دون موافقة صاحبها، وإذا وقع ذلك من شخص يعلم طبيعتها السرية او لا يمكن لمثله ان يجهل هذه الطبيعة.

الباب الثالث
الرسومات والنماذج الصناعية

المادة (٤٣)

لا تخل احكام الحماية المنصوص عليها في هذا القانون بالنسبة الى الرسومات والنماذج الصناعية بالحقوق الادبية والفنية المتصلة بها، سواء كان مصدرها القانون او الاتفاقيات والمعاهدات الدولية انتي تكون الدولة طرفاً فيها.

المادة (٤٤)

لا يتمتع الرسم او النموذج الصناعي بالحماية المقررة في هذا القانون، الا بتسجيله في السجل الخاص لدى الادارة، ويقدم طلب التسجيل ويتم فحصه وفقاً لما تحدده اللائحة التنفيذية لهذا القانون من اجراءات ورسوم في هذا الشأن.

المادة (٤٥)

تسري في شأن الرسومات والنماذج الصناعية احكام اولوية التسجيل المنصوص عليها في المادة (١١) من هذا القانون.

المادة (٤٦)

يجب ان يكون الرسم او النموذج الصناعي جديداً او مبتكراً ويمكن استخدامه كمنتج صناعي او حرفي، ومع ذلك لايجوز تسجيل اى رسم او نموذج صناعي يخل بالنظام العام او الآداب في الدولة.

المادة (٤٧)

يتم تسجيل الرسم او النموذج الصناعي بقرار من الوزير وينشر في الجريدة الرسمية مع الرسم او النموذج بعد اداء الرسوم المقررة.

ويجوز لكل ذي مصلحة ان يتظلم من قرار التسجيل امام اللجنة خلال ستين يوما من تاريخ النشر فاذا لم يقدم اي تظلم خلال الميعاد المشار اليه، تسلم شهادة التسجيل الى صاحبها موضحا فيها رقم القيد وتاريخه واية بيانات اخرى وفقاً لما تنص عليه اللائحة التنفيذية لهذا القانون.

المادة (٤٨)

مدة تسجيل الرسم او النموذج الصناعي خمس سنوات من تاريخ تقديم طلب التسجيل ويجوز تجديدها مدتين جديدتين على التوالي، ويجب تقديم طلب التجديد خلال ثلاثة الاشهر الاخيرة من المدة الاصلية. وتحدد اللائحة التنفيذية رسوم التسجيل والتجديد ورسماً سنوياً متصاعداً يبدأ سداده من السنة التالية لتاريخ ايداع طلب التسجيل، ويجب سداد الرسم السنوي خلال ثلاثة الاشهر الاخيرة من كل سنة والا سقط التسجيل، ويجوز قبول الرسم اذا تم اداؤه خلال ثلاثين يوما من انقضاء المدة السابقة، وذلك مقابل رسم اضافي تحدده اللائحة التنفيذية وينشر قرار التجديد وما سقط من تسجيلات في الجريدة الرسمية.

وفي جميع الاحوال، يجوز اداء الرسوم السنوية مقدماً عن كل او بعض مدة الحماية.

المادة (٤٩)

تخول الحماية المقررة للتصميم او النموذج الصناعي بمقتضى هذا القانون، الحق في منع الغير من ممارسة الاعمال الاتية:

١. استعمال التصميم او النموذج الصناعي في صناعة أي منتج.

٢. استيراد اي منتج يتعلق بالرسم او النموذج الصناعي او حيازته بغرض عرضه للبيع او بيعه.

ولا تنقلب الاعمال المشار اليها مشروعة، لمجرد اختلاف مجالها عن مجال استعمال الرسم او النموذج الصناعي الذى يحميه القانون، او انها تتعلق بمنتج يختلف عن الرسم أو النموذج المسجل.

المادة (٥٠)

اذا بدأ شخص بحسن نية في ممارسة الاعمال المنصوص عليها في المادة السابقة قبل تقديم طلب التسجيل، كان من حقه الاستمرار فيما بدأه منها بالنسبة الى المنتجات التي

حصل عليها ويعتبر هذا الحق شخصياً غير قابل للتنازل عنه او نقله الى الغير بأية صورة الا كجزء من المنشآت المستفيدة منه.

المادة (٥١)

تسرى على الرسم او النموذج الصناعي أحكام المواد (٧ و٩ و١٥ و١٨ و١٩ و٢٠) واحكام الفصلين الثاني والثالث من الباب الثاني من هذا القانون.

الباب الرابع
التراخيص التعاقدية

المادة (٥٢)

يجوز لصاحب سند الحماية أن يرخص لاي شخص طبيعي او اعتباري في استعمال او استغلال الحق موضوع الحماية، على الا تجاوز مدة الترخيص الحماية المقررة بموجب أحكام هذا القانون. ويجب ان يكون عقد الترخيص مكتوباً وموقعاً من الاطراف.

المادة (٥٣)

يجب قيد عقد الترخيص والتأشير به في السجل الخاص بالحق موضوع الحماية مقابل الرسم المقرر ولا يكون للترخيص اثر بالنسبة الى الغير الا من تاريخ نشره في الجريدة الرسمية.

ويشطب القيد بناءً على طلب اطراف عقد الترخيص، او بفسخه، او بمقتضى حكم ببطلانه، او بانقضاء مدته.

المادة (٥٤)

الترخيص التعاقدي لا يمنع صاحب سند الحماية من استغلال او استعمال موضوع الحماية بنفسه او منح تراخيص اخرى للغير مالم ينص عقد الترخيص على خلاف ذلك.

المادة (٥٥)

للمرخص له حق استغلال واستعمال موضوع الحماية المرخص به في جميع اراضي الدولة طوال مدة الحماية القانونية في كل المجالات وبجميع الوسائل مالم ينص عقد الترخيص على خلاف ذلك.

كما يكون للمرخص له الحق في استخدام الحقوق التي يمنحها سند الحماية لصاحبه، والتي من شأنها منع التعدي او التهديد او الاضرار بموضوع الحماية، ويجب على المرخص له ان يخطر صاحب سند الحماية بكتاب مسجل بالتعدي او التهديد او الضرر،

فاذا اهمل او تراخى صاحب سند الحماية ولم يتخذ الاجراءات اللازمة خلال ثلاثين يوماً من تاريخ الاخطار، كان للمرخص له اتخاذ الاجراءات القانونية والقضائية والمطالبة بالتعويض عن الاضرار التي لحقته سواء من اهمال او تراخي صاحب سند الحماية او من افعال الغير.

المادة (٥٦)

لايجوز للمرخص له في غير حالة التنازل او انتقال ملكية المنشأة او جزئها الذى يستغل الترخيص، ان يتنازل الى الغير عن الترخيص او منح تراخيص من الباطن، مالم ينص عقد الترخيص على خلاف ذلك.

المادة (٥٧)

يخضع عقد الترخيص او التنازل او نقل ملكية موضوع الحماية، واي تعديل او تجديد لهذه العقود، لرقابة الادارة من حيث الشروط والضمانات والحقوق التي تخولها سندات الحماية. وللادارة ان تطلب من الاطراف تعديل العقود بما يحقق مصلحة الطرفين في اطار القانون والمصالح الاقتصادية للدولة، فاذا لم يستجب الاطراف كان للادارة رفض الموافقة على العقد وعدم قيده في السجل وذلك كله وفقاً لما تحدده اللائحة التنفيذية لهذا القانون.

الباب الخامس
الاجراءات التحفظية والجرائم والجزاءات

المادة (٥٨)

يجوز لصاحب سند الحماية او لمن انتقلت اليه كل او بعض حقوق الملكية الصناعية المنصوص عليها في هذا القانون، ان يطلب من المحكمة المختصة اثناء نظر اية دعوى مدنية او جزائية او قبل رفعها، اصدار امر بالحجز التحفظي على الاختراع او الرسم او النموذج الصناعي او المنشأة او جزئها الذى يستعمل او يستغل اي نوع من انواع الملكية الصناعية المشار اليها وذلك في حالة وقوع فعل من افعال التعدي او الاعمال غير المشروعة بالمخالفة لهذا القانون او العقود او التراخيص الممنوحة وفقاً لأحكامه.

المادة (٥٩)

يجب على طالب الحجز التحفظي ان يودع كفالة تقدرها المحكمة قبل اصدار امرها بالحجز ويجب على الحاجز رفع الدعوى الموضوعية خلال ثمانية أيام من تاريخ صدور امر المحكمة والا اعتبر الامر كأن لم يكن.

ويجوز للمحجوز عليه ان يرفع دعوى بالتعويض خلال ستين يوماً من تاريخ انقضاء المهلة السابقة او من تاريخ صدور حكم نهائي برفض الدعوى الموضوعية التي رفعها الحاجز.

ولا يجوز صرف الكفالة المشار اليها الا بعد صدور حكم نهائي في دعوى الحاجز او دعوى التعويض المرفوعة من المحجوز عليه.

المادة (٦٠)

مع عدم الاخلال بأية عقوبة اشد ينص عليها قانون آخر، يعاقب بالحبس مدة لا تقل عن ثلاثة اشهر ولا تزيد على سنتين وبغرامة لا تقل عن (٥٠٠٠) خمسة الاف درهم او باحدى هاتين العقوبتين، كل من تقدم بمستندات او ادلى بمعلومات غير صحيحة او مزورة للحصول على براءة اختراع او شهادة منفعة أو دراية عملية، وكذلك كل من قلد اختراعاً او طريقة صنع او عنصراً من عناصر الدراية العملية، او اعتدى عمداً على اي حق يحميه هذا القانون.

وتطبق ذات العقوبة اذا كان الامر متعلقاً برسم او نموذج صناعي.

المادة (٦١)

يجوز للمحكمة في أية دعوى مدنية او جزائية ان تحكم بمصادرة الاشياء المحجوز عليها او التي تحجز عليها فيما بعد واستنزال ثمنها من الغرامات أو التعويضات أو التصرف فيها بأية طريقة اخرى تراها المحكمة مناسبة ويجوز للمحكمة ايضاً ان تأمر باتلاف او ازالة آثار الفعل المخالف للقانون وكذلك الآلات والادوات التي استعملت في التزوير، ولها ان تأمر بكل ما سبق حتى في حالة الحكم بالبراءة.

ويجوز للمحكمة كذلك ان تأمر بنشر الحكم في الجريدة الرسمية أو في احدى الصحف اليومية على نفقة المحكوم عليه.

الباب السادس
ادارة الملكية الصناعية والاحكام الختامية

المادة (٦٢)

تنشأ في وزارة المالية والصناعة ادارة تسمى (ادارة الملكية الصناعية) وتتولى هذه الادارة وفروعها تنفيذ احكام هذا القانون ولائحته التنفيذية.

ويصدر الوزير قراراً بنظام العمل في الادارة وفروعها وكيفية ممارستها الاختصاصات المنصوص عليها في هذا القانون ولائحته التنفيذية.

المادة (٦٣)

يكون لموظفي الادارة صفة الضبطية القضائية في مجال تنفيذ احكام هذا القانون ولائحته التنفيذية ويحظر عليهم في اثناء مدة خدمتهم وبعد انتهائها افشاء اسرار عملهم او الادلاء ببيانات او معلومات اتصلوا بها بحكم وظائفهم او الكشف عنها او استعمالها لمصلحتهم أو لمصلحة الغير، ولا يجوز لهم الاحتفاظ بصفة شخصية باصل اى مستند او ورقة او بصور من ذلك، كما يحظر عليهم طوال مدة خدمتهم وخلال ثلاث سنوات تالية لانتهائها ممارسة مهنة وكلاء التسجيل لدى الادارة.

المادة (٦٤)

تشكل بقرار من الوزير لجنة برئاسة احد اعضاء السلطة القضائية واربعة اعضاء يمثلون وزارة المالية والصناعة ووزارة الاقتصاد والتجارة واتحاد غرف التجارة والصناعة والامانة العامة لبلديات الدولة، يختار كلا منهم الوزير المختص او رئيس اتحاد غرف التجارة والصناعة او الامين العام للبلديات حسب الاحوال.

ولا يجوز ان يكون ممثل وزارة المالية والصناعة من موظفي الادارة ويجوز ان يكون ممثل اتحاد غرف التجارة والصناعة وممثل الامانة العامة للبلديات من موظفي احدى الغرف او موظفي بلدية سارة من امارات الدولة.

وتختص اللجنة بالفصل في التظلمات التي يقدمها ذوو الشأن من القرارات الصادرة في مجال تطبيق هذا القانون ولائحته التنفيذية.

وتحدد اللائحة التنفيذية نظام عمل اللجنة ومكافأة اعضائها واجراءات التظلم والفصل فيه والرسوم المستحقة.

المادة (٦٥)

يجوز الطعن في قرارات اللجنة امام المحكمة المختصة وفقاً لنظام الاجراءات امام هذه المحكمة وذلك خلال ثلاثين يوماً من تاريخ الاخطار بقرار اللجنة.

ويجوز للمحكمة ان تستعين بالخبراء المتخصصين في مجال المنازعة وبرأي الادارة.

المادة (٦٦)

تنظم اللائحة التنفيذية للقانون مهنة وكلاء التسجيل لدى الادارة وتتضمن تحديد الشروط اللازم توفرها في الوكلاء وواجباتهم والرسوم المستحقة للقيد في جدول وكلاء التسجيل وحالات الغاء القيد وشطبه.

المادة (٦٧)

تصدر اللائحة التنفيذية لهذا القانون من مجلس الوزراء بناءً على اقتراح الوزير متضمنة توزيع الاختصاصات وتدرجها والتفويض فيها في مجال تنفيذ احكام هذا القانون، وكذلك انواع السجلات ونظام فحص الطلبات والبيانات والمستندات الواجب تقديمها والرسوم والنفقات ومقابل النشر وجميع الاحكام والقواعد التي يقتضيها تنفيذ القانون.

المادة (٦٨)

يلغى كل حكم يخالف او يتعارض مع احكام هذا القانون.

المادة (٦٩)

ينشر هذا القانون في الجريدة الرسمية، ويعمل به بعد ثلاثة اشهر من تاريخ نشره.

زايد بن سلطان آل نهيان
رئيس دولة الإمارات العربية المتحدة

صدر عنا بقصر الرئاسة في أبو ظبي
بتاريخ: ١٥ ربيع الثاني ١٤١٣هـ.
الموافق: ١٢ اكتوبر ١٩٩٢م.

قانون اتحادي رقم (١٧) لسنة ٢٠٠٢م
في شأن تنظيم وحماية الملكية الصناعية لبراءات الاختراع والرسوم
والنماذج الصناعية.

نحن زايد بن سلطان آل نهيان، رئيس دولة الإمارات العربية المتحدة،

بعد الإطلاع على الدستور،

وعلى القانون الاتحادي رقم (١) لسنة ١٩٧٢ بشأن اختصاصات الوزارات وصلاحيات
الوزراء والقوانين المعدلة له،

وعلى القانون الاتحادي رقم (٥) لسنة ١٩٧٦ في شأن اتحاد غرف التجارة والصناعة،

وعلى القانون الاتحادي رقم (١) لسنة ١٩٧٩ في شأن تنظيم شئون الصناعة،

وعلى القانون الاتحادي رقم (٤) لسنة ١٩٧٩ في شأن قمع الغش والتدليس في
المعاملات التجارية،

وعلى القانون الاتحادي رقم (٨) لسنة ١٩٨٤ في شأن الشركات التجارية والقوانين
المعدلة له،

وعلى قانون المعاملات المدنية الصادر بالقانون الاتحادي رقم (٥) لسنة ١٩٨٥
والقوانين المعدلة له،

وعلى قانون الإجراءات المدنية الصادر بالقانون الاتحادي رقم (١١) لسنة١٩٩٢،

وعلى القانون الاتحادي رقم (٤٤) لسنة ١٩٩٢ في شأن تنظيم وحماية الملكية الصناعية
لبراءات الاختراع والرسوم والنماذج الصناعية،

وعلى قانون المعاملات التجارية الصادر بالقانون الاتحادي رقم (١٨) لسنة ١٩٩٣،

وعلى المرسوم الاتحادي رقم (٢١) لسنة ١٩٧٥ بشأن انضمام دولة الإمارات العربية
المتحدة إلى المنظمة العالمية للملكية الفكرية،

وعلى المرسوم الاتحادي رقم(٢٠) لسنة ١٩٩٦ في شأن انضمام دولة الإمارات العربية المتحدة إلى اتفاقية باريس لحماية الملكية الصناعية،

وعلى المرسوم الاتحادي رقم (٢١) لسنة ١٩٩٧ بانضمام دولة الإمارات العربية المتحدة إلى منظمة التجارة العالمية،

وعلى المرسوم الاتحادي رقم (٨٤) لسنة ١٩٩٨ في شأن انضمام دولة الإمارات العربية المتحدة إلى معاهدة التعاون بشأن براءات الاختراع،

وبناءً على ما عرضه وزير المالية والصناعة، وموافقة مجلس الوزراء، وتصديق المجلس الأعلى للاتحاد،

أصدرنا القانون الآتي:

الباب الاول
تعريفات وأحكام عامة

المادة (١)

في تطبيق أحكام هذا القانون يكون للكلمات والعبارات التالية المعاني الموضحة قرين كل منها ما لم يدل سياق النص على غير ذلك:

الدولة:	دولة الإمارات العربية المتحدة.
الوزارة:	وزارة المالية والصناعة.
الوزير:	وزير المالية والصناعة.
الإدارة:	إدارة الملكية الصناعية بالوزاره وفروعها في الدولة.
اللجنة:	لجنة التظلمات المشكلة بقرار من الوزير.
سند الحماية:	الوثيقة الدالة على منح الإدارة حماية لاختراع أو رسم أو نموذج صناعي، والمتمثلة في براءة اختراع أو شهادة منفعة أو شهادة تسجيل رسم أونموذج صناعي.
الاختراع:	الفكرة التي يتوصل إليها أي مخترع وتتيح عملياً حلاً فنياً جديداً لمشكلة معينة في مجال التكنولوجيا.
براءة الاختراع:	سند الحماية الذي تمنحه الإدارة باسم الدولة عن الاختراع.
شهادة المنفعة:	سند الحماية الذي تمنحه الإدارة باسم الدولة عن اختراع لا ينتج عن نشاط ابتكاري كاف لمنح براءة اختراع عنه.
شهادة التسجيل:	سند الحماية الذي تمنحه الإدارة باسم الدولة عن الرسم أو النموذج الصناعي.

الدراية العملية:	المعلومات أو البيانات أو المعارف الناجمة عن الخبرة المكتسبة من المهنة ذات الطبيعة التقنية والقابلة للتطبيق عملياً.
الرسم الصناعي:	أي تكوين مبتكر للخطوط أو للألوان ، يعطي كل منهما أو كلاهما مظهراً خاصاً يمكن استخدامه كمنتج صناعي أو حرفي.
النموذج الصناعي:	أي شكل مجسم مبتكر ، يعطي مظهراً خاصاً يمكن استخدامه كمنتج صناعي أو حرفي.
النشرة:	النشرة الدورية التي تصدرها الإدارة وتخصصها لنشر كل ما يوجب هذا القانون أو اللائحة التنفيذية نشره.
طلب البراءة الدولي:	الطلب المقدم للإدارة للحصول على براءة اختراع طبقاً لمعاهدة التعاون بشأن براءات الاختراع.
الايداع الدولي لطلب براءة الاختراع:	الطلب المقدم للحصول على براءة اختراع إلى مكتب البراءات في إحدى الدول الأعضاء في معاهدة التعاون بشأن براءات الاختراع، والذي يخول صاحبه حق حماية الاختراع في الدول الأعضاء طبقاً لشروط وبمراعاة الإجراءات المقررة في هذه المعاهدة.
مكتب استلام الطلبات:	المكتب الوطني الذي يسلم فيه طلب براءة اختراع دولية والذي يتولى احالته إلى أي جهة أخرى تتحدد طبقاً لمعاهدة التعاون بشأن براءات الاختراع.
مكتب مختار:	المكتب الذي يختاره مودع الطلب الدولي للقيام بفحص الطلب لمعرفة مدى استيفائه لشروط منح البراءة طبقاً لمعاهدة التعاون بشأن براءات الاختراع.
مكتب معين:	المكتب الوطني الذي يعينه مودع الطلب الدولي باعتباره الجهة المعنية بإصدار براءات الاختراع طبقاً لأحكام هذا القانون.

المادة (٢)

لا تخل أحكام هذا القانون بما تنص عليه الاتفاقيات والمعاهدات الدولية التي تكون الدولة طرفاً فيها، والتي تنظم حقوق مواطني الدول الأطراف في تلك الاتفاقيات والمعاهدات وحقوق الأشخاص الذين يعاملون معاملتهم.

ويكون للأجنبي الذي لا يشمله حكم الفقرة السابقة حقوق المواطن التي يخولها هذا القانون إذا كان يحمل جنسية دولة تعامل الدولة معاملة المثل.

المادة (٣)

تمنح حماية مؤقتة للاختراعات وللرسوم والنماذج الصناعية التي تعرض في معارض داخل الدولة، وذلك طبقاً للشروط والإجراءات التي تنظمها اللائحة التنفيذية لهذا القانون، وبمراعاة أحكام الاتفاقيات والمعاهدات الدولية التي تكون الدولة طرفاً فيها أو بشرط المعاملة بالمثل.

الباب الثاني
الاختراعات

الفصل الاول
براءة الاختراع وشهادة المنفعة

المادة (٤)

تمنح براءة الاختراع عن كل اختراع جديد ناتج عن فكرة مبتكرة أو تحسين مبتكر لاختراع تحميه براءة في كافة مجالات التقنية ويكون كل منهما قائماً على أسس علمية وقابلاً للاستغلال الصناعي، سواء تعلق ذلك بمنتجات صناعية جديدة أو بطرق أو وسائل صناعية مستحدثة أو بتطبيق جديد لطرق أو وسائل صناعية معروفة.

ويعتبر الاختراع قابلاً للتطبيق الصناعي إذا أمكن تطبيقه أو استعماله في اي نوع من الصناعة بمعناها الواسع بما في ذلك الزراعة والصيد والحرف اليدوية والخدمات.

ويجب أن يتعلق الطلب باختراع واحد فقط أو بمجموعة من الاختراعات المرتبطة فيما بينها على نحو تشكل فيه مفهوماً ابتكارياً عاماً واحداً.

وإذا اتضح بعد صدور البراءة، تخلف شرط ترابط الاختراعات طبقاً لما ورد في الفقرة السابقة، فإن هذا التخلف لا يعتبر سبباً لإسقاط البراءة.

المادة (٥)

تمنح شهادة المنفعة عن كل اختراع جديد قابل للتطبيق الصناعي ولكنه لا ينتج عن نشاط ابتكاري كاف لمنح براءة اختراع عنه.

كما تمنح شهادة منفعة عن كل اختراع تنطبق عليه احكام المادة (٤) بناءً على طلب صاحب الاختراع أو من يمثله قانونا.

المادة (٦)

١. لا تمنح براءة الاختراع أو شهادة المنفعة عما يأتي:

أ) الأبحاث والأنواع النباتية أو الحيوانية أو الطرق البيولوجية لإنتاج النبات أو الحيوان ويستثنى من ذلك طرق علم الأحياء الدقيقة ومنتجاتها.

ب) طرق التشخيص والعلاج والجراحة اللازمة لمعالجة البشر أو الحيوانات.

ج) المبادئ والاكتشافات والنظريات العلمية والطرائق الرياضية.

د) المخططات أو القواعد أو الطرائق المتبعة لمزاولة الأعمال التجارية أو ممارسة الأنشطة الذهنية المحضة أو لعبة من اللعب.

هــ) الاختراعات التي ينشأ عن نشرها أو استغلالها إخلال بالنظام العام أو الآداب.

٢. إذا تبين للإدارة عند فحصها طلب البراءة تعلق الاختراع بالدفاع الوطني تتبع الإجراءات المنصوص عليها في اللائحة التنفيذية لهذا القانون.

المادة (٧)

١. مع عدم الإخلال بأحكام المادة (٩) من هذا القانون يكون الحق في الاختراع للمخترع أو لخلفه القانوني.

وإذا اشترك شخصان أو أكثر في إنجاز اختراع، يكون الحق في الاختراع لهم أو لخلفائهم القانونيين شركة فيما بينهم، ولا يعتبر مخترعاً أو في مرتبة المخترع ذلك الذي تقتصر جهوده على المساعدة في تنفيذ الاختراع دون الإسهام في أية خطوة ابتكارية.

٢. مع عدم الإخلال بأحكام المادتين (٨) و(٩) من هذا القانون فإنه يكون للشخص الذي يودع قبل غيره طلباً عن براءة اختراع أو شهادة منفعة، أو الذي يطالب قبل غيره بأسبقية عن ذات الاختراع، الحق في براءة الاختراع أو شهادة المنفعة حسب الأحوال، إذا توفرت في طلبه شروط الحصول عليها.

٣. يكون لكل ذي مصلحة حق التظلم والطعن في قرار قبول أو رفض الطلب وفقاً لأحكام هذا القانون ولائحته التنفيذية.

المادة (٨)

إذا كانت العناصر الجوهرية للاختراع قد تم الحصول عليها من اختراع شخص آخر دون موافقته على ذلك أو على إيداع طلب الحماية، فيجوز لمن أصيب بضرر نتيجة لهذا الاغتصاب المطالبة بنقل الطلب إليه أو بنقل البراءة أو شهادة المنفعة إذا كانت قد منحت إلى المغتصب.

المادة (٩)

١. إذا أنجز الاختراع من خلال تنفيذ عقد مقاولة أو عقد عمل يكون الحق في الاختراع لصاحب العمل ما لم ينص الاتفاق على غير ذلك.

٢. إذا كان للاختراع قيمة اقتصادية تفوق تصورات الطرفين عند توقيع العقد ، يستحق المخترع تعويضاً إضافياً تحدده المحكمة إذا لم يتفق الطرفان على مبلغ معين.

٣. إذا أنجز العامل الذي لا ينص عقد عمله على القيام بنشاط ابتكاري اختراعاً يتصل بمجال نشاط صاحب العمل مستخدماً في ذلك خبرات أو وثائق أو أدوات صاحب العمل أو مواده الأولية الموضوعة تحت تصرفه من خلال العمل فيكون الحق في ذلك الاختراع للعامل المخترع بانقضاء أربعة شهور من تاريخ تقديمه التقرير المشار إليه في البند (٤) من هذه المادة لصاحب العمل عن الاختراع أو اعتباراً من أي تاريخ علم من خلاله صاحب العمل بصورة أخرى عن تحقق الاختراع، ولم يبد صاحب العمل استعداده لتملك الاختراع بإعلان كتابي.

٤. على العامل المخترع أن يخطر صاحب العمل فوراً بتقرير كتابي عن اختراعه.

٥. إذا أبدى صاحب العمل استعداده لتملك الاختراع خلال المدة المحددة في البند (٣) من هذه المادة يعتبر الحق في الاختراع عائداً له منذ نشوء الاختراع ويستحق العامل المخترع تعويضاً عادلاً يؤخذ فيه بعين الاعتبار مرتبه والقيمة الاقتصادية للاختراع وكل فائدة تعود منه على صاحب العمل، وإذا لم يتفق الطرفان على التعويض تحدده المحكمة.

٦. كل اتفاق يعطي لعامل مزايا أقل مما تنص عليه أحكام هذه المادة يعتبر باطلا.

المادة (١٠)

يذكر اسم المخترع في براءة الاختراع أو شهادة المنفعة ما لم يعلن المخترع كتابة عن رغبته في عدم ذكر اسمه.

ويتم تقديم طلب تسجيل براءة الاختراع وبياناته أو شهادة المنفعة وفقاً لما تحدده اللائحة التنفيذية لهذا القانون.

المادة (١١)

١. يجوز أن يتضمن طلب الايداع الرغبة في اعتبار الاولوية في الايداع لطلب سبق تقديمه في دولة تكون طرفاً في اتفاقية أو معاهدة مع الدولة. وفي هذه الحالة يجب أن يوضح في الطلب تاريخ ورقم قيد الطلب السابق واسم الدولة التي قدم اليها، وذلك وفقاً لما تنص عليه اللائحة التنفيذية لهذا القانون.

٢. مدة الأولوية اثنا عشر شهراً من تاريخ الايداع الاول.

المادة (١٢)

تقوم الإدارة بفحص طلب براءة الاختراع أو شهادة المنفعة وفقاً لأحكام هذا القانون ولائحته التنفيذية، ولها أن تطلب استيفاء ما تراه لازماً لمنح براءة الاختراع أو شهادة المنفعة.

وعلى الإدارة – في حالة رفض الطلب – إخطار مقدم الطلب بذلك. ويجوز له أن يتظلم إلى اللجنة خلال ستين يوماً من تاريخ الإخطار.

المادة (١٣)

تمنح براءات الاختراع وشهادات المنفعة بقرار من الوزير وتنشر في النشرة. ولكل ذي مصلحة الحق في التظلم مام اللجنة خلال ستين يوماً من تاريخ النشر.

وتسلم براءة الاختراع أو شهادة المنفعة إلى صاحب الحق فيها، إذا لم يقدم في شأنها أي تظلم خلال الميعاد المنصوص عليه في الفقرة السابقة، وذلك بعد قيدها في السجل، ويجب أن تحمل البراءة أو الشهادة رقم القيد وتاريخ الإصدار وبيان دفع رسم القيد أو التجديد وغير ذلك من البيّنات وفقاً لما تنص عليه اللائحة التنفيذية لهذا القانون.

المادة (١٤)

مدة براءة الاختراع عشرون سنة ومدة شهادة المنفعة عشر سنوات تبدأ كل منهما من تاريخ تقديم الطلب.

ويستحق على براءة الاختراع وعلى شهادة المنفعة رسم سنوي يتعين سداده في بداية كل سنة اعتباراً من السنة التالية لتاريخ تقديم طلب براءة الاختراع أو شهادة المنفعة، وإذا لم يقم مالك براءة الاختراع أو شهادة المنفعة بسداد الرسم السنوي في موعد أقصاه ثلاثة أشهر من بداية السنة جاز ـ'ه أن يدفع الرسم خلال ثلاثة أشهر أخرى تبدأ من انقضاء المدة السابقة مع سداد رسم إضافي وفقاً لما تحدده اللائحة التنفيذية لهذا القانون.

وفي جميع الأحوال يجوز سداد الرسوم السنوية مقدماً عن كل أو بعض مدة براءة الاختراع أو شهادة المنفعة.

فإذا لم يقم مالك البراءة أو شهادة المنفعة بسداد الرسم السنوي خلال المهلة القانونية السابقة – ستة أشهر من تاريخ الاستحقاق– سقطت براءة الاختراع أو شهادة المنفعة.

ويسري على طلب براءة الاختراع أو شهادة المنفعة في حكم هذه المادة ما يسري على البراءة أو شهادة المنفعة.

المادة (١٥)

١. تعطي براءة الاختراع لصاحبها:

أ) حق استغلال الاختراع. ويعتبر استغلالاً للاختراع – إذا كان موضوع براءة الاختراع منتجاً – صناعته واستخدامه وعرضه للبيع أو بيعه أو استيراده لهذه الأغراض. وإذا كان الاختراع عملية صناعية أو طريقة صنع منتج معين، فإن لمالك البراءة ذات الحق بالنسبة لما ينتج مباشرة عن استخدام هذه العملية أو الطريقة، إضافة إلى حقه في استخدام تلك العملية أو الطريقة.

ولصاحب براءة الاختراع، إذا كان موضوع البراءة منتجاً، الحق في منع الغير، الذي لم يحصل على موافقته، من صنع المنتج واستخدامه وعرضه للبيع وبيعه واستيراده لهذه الاغراض.

أما إذا كان موضوع البراءة عملية صناعية، فله منع الغير الذي لم يحصل على موافقته من الاستخدام الفعلي للطريقة ومن استخدام المنتج الذي يتم الحصول عليه مباشرة بهذه الطريقة ومن عرضه للبيع ومن بيعه ومن استيراده لهذه الأغراض.

ب) إستعمال الطريقة ومباشرة أي من الأعمال المشار إليها في الفقرة (أ) بخصوص منتج يتم الحصوٰل عليه بواسطة الطريقة مباشرة، وذلك عندما تمنح براءة الاختراع أو شهادة المنفعة عن طريقة أو عن تطبيق جديد لطريقة أو وسيلة صناعية معروفة.

٢. تقتصر الحقوق المشار إليها في البند (١) من هذه المادة والتي تخولها براءة الاختراع أو شهادة المنفعة على الأعمال التي تتم لأغراض صناعية أو تجارية ولا تمتد هذه الحقوق إلى الأعمال الخاصة بالمنتج الذي تحميه بعد بيعه.

المادة (١٦)

١. يحدد نطاق الحماية التي تخولها براءة الاختراع أو شهادة المنفعة بطلب سند الحماية.

٢. ويستخدم الوصف والرسومات الهندسية في تفسير مضمون الطلب.

المادة (١٧)

إذا قام شخص بحسن نية بتصنيع المنتج أو باستعمال الطريقة موضوع الاختراع أو اتخاذ ترتيبات جدية لهذا التصنيع أو الاستعمال في الدولة في تاريخ إيداع طلب الحماية من شخص آخر، أو في تاريخ الأسبقية المطالب بها قانوناً بالنسبة لهذا الطلب، يكون للأول بالرغم من منح براءة الاختراع أو شهادة المنفعة، الحق في مواصلة القيام بهذه الأعمال ومباشرة الأعمال الأخرى المشار إليها في المادة (١٥) من هذا القانون بالنسبة للمنتجات المتحصلة منهما، وهذا الحق شخصي، لا يقبل الانتقال إلا مع المنشأة المستفيدة منه.

المادة (١٨)

يجوز التنازل للغير عن براءة الاختراع أو شهادة المنفعة أو عن طلب أي منهما قبل المنح.

ويجب أن يتم التنازل عن البراءة أو شهادة المنفعة أو عن طلب أي منهما كتابة وأن يوقع كل من الأطراف المتعاقدة أمام الموظف المسؤول في الإدارة أو أن يصادق على توقيعاتهم الكاتب العدل في الدولة.

ويجب قيد التنازل عن براءة الاختراع أو شهادة المنفعة في السجل المخصص لذلك مقابل رسم تحدده اللائحة التنفيذية لهذا القانون.

المادة (١٩)

لا تسري الحقوق التي تحولها براءة الاختراع على الآتي:

١. الأعمال الخاصة بأغراض البحث العلمي.

٢. استعمال موضوع براءة الاختراع في وسائل النقل التي تدخل اقليم الدولة بصفة مؤقتة أو عرضية سواء كان في جسم وسيلة النقل أو في آلاتها أو أجهزتها أو عُددها أو في الأجزاء الإضافية الأخرى على أن يكون الاستعمال قاصراً على احتياجات تلك الوسائل.

المادة (٢٠)

يجوز للمالكين المشتركين في براءة الإختراع أو شهادة المنفعة، كل على انفراد، أن يتنازلوا للغير عن حصتهم في الاختراع المحمي ببراءة الإختراع أو شهادة المنفعة وأن يستغلوه وأن يباشروا الحقوق التي تخولها المادة (١٥) من هذا القانون ما لم يتفق على خلاف ذلك، ولكن لا يجوز لهم أن يمنحوا ترخيصاً للغير باستغلال الاختراع إلا مجتمعين.

المادة (٢١)

يجوز رهن براءة الاختراع أو شهادة المنفعة ضماناً للوفاء بدين سواء بصورة مستقلة أو مع المحل التجاري، ويؤشر بالرهن في سجل براءات الاختراع أو سجل شهادات المنفعة حسب الأحوال، وينشر في النشرة.

المادة (٢٢)

لا يكون التنازل عن براءة الإختراع أو شهادة المنفعة أو رهنهما حجة على الغير إلا بعد قيد التنازل أو الرهن حسب الأحوال في سجل براءات الإختراع أو سجل شهادات المنفعة والإشهار عنه في النشرة.

المادة (٢٣)

يجوز للدائن أن يحجز على براءة الاختراع أو شهادة المنفعة المملوكة لمدينه وفقاً لإجراءات الحجز على المنقول أو حجز ما للمدين لدى الغير حسب الأحوال.

ويجب على الدائن أن يعلن الحجز وحكم مرسى المزاد للإدارة للتأشير بهما في السجل الخاص. وينشر الحجز وحكم مرسى المزاد في النشرة، وتحصل الرسوم المقررة وفقاً لما تحدده اللائحة التنفيذية لهذا القانون، ولا يكون للحجز أو حكم مرسى المزاد أثر بالنسبة إلى الغير إلا من تاريخ النشر.

الفصل الثاني
التراخيص الإجبارية ونزع ملكية الاختراع

المادة (٢٤)

١ . إذا لم يستغل مالك البراءة أو شهادة المنفعة الاختراع المشمول بالبراءة أو شهادة المنفعة على الإطلاق أو استغله على وجه غير كاف، جاز لكل ذي شأن أن يطلب وفقاً للإجراءات المبينة في المادة (٣٠) من هذا القانون الحصول على ترخيص اجباري وفق الشروط التالية:

أ) أن يكون قد مضى على منح البراءة أو شهادة المنفعة ثلاث سنوات على الأقل.

ب) أن يثبت طالب الترخيص بذله جهوداً خلال فترة معقولة، للحصول على ترخيص من مالك البراءة بسعر معقول وبشروط تجارية معقولة، وتحدد اللائحة التنفيذية لهذا القانون الاجراءات المطلوبة في هذا الشأن.

ج) ألا يكون الترخيص مطلقاً، ويجوز أن تتضمن شروط الترخيص الاجباري التزامات وقيوداً على كل من المرخص والمرخص له بترخيص اجباري.

د) أن يكون الترخيص لسد احتياجات السوق المحلية، ويلتزم طالب الترخيص بتقديم الضمانات اللازمة التي تحددها اللائحة التنفيذية لهذا القانون وذلك لإستغلال الاختراع استغلالاً كافياً لمعالجة أوجه النقص أو لمقابلة الاحتياجات التي أدت الى طلب الحصول على الترخيص الاجباري.

هـ) أن يحدد قرار الترخيص نطاق ومدة الترخيص بما يقتضيه الغرض الذي منح من أجله.

و) أن يمنح مالك براءة الإختراع تعويضاً عادلاً.

ز) أن يقتصر استغلال براءة الاختراع على المرخص له، ولا ينتقل الترخيص الى الغير إلا في حالة نقل ملكية منشأة المرخص له أو الجزء من منشأته الذي يستغل البراءة، وبشرط موافقة المحكمة المختصة على هذا الانتقال، وتسري على الانتقال أحكام المادتين (٢٨) و(٣٢) من هذا القانون.

ح) إذا كان الاختراع يتعلق بتقنية أشباه الموصلات، لايجوز الترخيص إلا للأغراض العامة غير التجارية أو لتصحيح ممارسات تقرر قضائياً أو إدارياً أنها غير تنافسية.

٢. ولا يمنح الترخيص الاجباري إذا برر مالك براءة الاختراع أو شهادة المنفعة موقفه بأسباب مشروعة، ولا يشكل استيراد المنتج سبباً مشروعاً.

المادة (٢٥)

١. يخول الترخيص الإجباري المرخص له الحق في مباشرة بعض أو كل الأعمال المشار إليها في المادة (١٥) من هذا القانون وفقاً لشروط الترخيص، ويستثنى من ذلك حق استيراد المنتج.

٢. ويكون لصاحب الترخيص الحق في استعمال الحقوق المدنية والجزائية لصاحب براءة الاختراع أوشهادة المنفعة لحماية الاختراع واستغلاله إذا قصر أحدهما في ذلك رغم إخطاره أو علمه بأي عمل غير مشروع.

المادة (٢٦)

لا يترتب على منح الترخيص الإجباري عدم منح تراخيص إجبارية أخرى.

المادة (٢٧)

١. تنظر المحكمة المختصة، بناءً على طلب ذوي الشأن في مدى حرمان مالك براءة الاختراع أو شهادة المنفعة من استغلال الاختراع بذاته أو منحه تراخيص أخرى باستغلاله.

٢. يجوز للمحكمة المختصة عدم مراعاة الفقرتين (أ) و(ب) من البند (١) من المادة (٢٤) من هذا القانون إذا كان طلب الترخيص الإجباري بسبب حالة طوارئ عامة أو حاجة عامة ملحة، أو كان لاستخدامات عامة غير تجارية.

المادة (٢٨)

يقدم طلب الترخيص الإجباري إلى المحكمة المختصة في صورة دعوى يختصم فيها صاحب براءة الاختراع أو شهادة المنفعة وتعلن بها الإدارة لحضور ممثل عنها، وللمحكمة أن تعطي الطرفين مهلة تحددها للاتفاق فيما بينهما، ويجوز مد المهلة إذا رأت المحكمة مبرراً لذلك.

فإذا انقضت المهلة، نظرت المحكمة في الطلب برفض منح الترخيص الإجباري، أو بمنحه مع تحديد شروطه ومجاله وتحديد التعويض لصاحب براءة الاختراع أو شهادة المنفعة وفقاً لنص المادة (٢٤) من هذا القانون، ويعلن الحكم إلى الطرف الآخر والى الإدارة للتأشير به في السجل الخاص وينشر في النشرة بعد أداء الرسم المقرر، ولا يكون للحكم أثر بالنسبة إلى الغير إلا من تاريخ النشر.

المادة (٢٩)

١. يجوز بقرار من الوزير إصدار ترخيص إجباري باستغلال إختراع مشمول بحماية براءة اختراع أو شهادة منفعة إذا كان للاختراع أهمية للمصلحة العامة، وذلك بالشروط المذكورة في المادة (٢٤) باستثناء الفقرتين (أ) و(ب) من البند (١) منها.

٢. يجوز الطعن في قرار الوزير بالترخيص الإجباري أو تقدير التعويض أمام المحكمة المختصة خلال ستين يوماً من تاريخ نشر قرار الوزير في النشرة.

المادة (٣٠)

١. إذا كان من غير الممكن استغلال اختراع تحميه براءة إختراع أو شهادة منفعة في الدولة دون الإخلال بحقوق مستمدة من براءة الاختراع أو شهادة منفعة منحت بناءً على طلب سابق، فإنه يجوز منح مالك براءة الاختراع أو شهادة المنفعة الأخيرة ترخيصاً إجبارياً بناءً على طلبه وفقاً لأحكام الفقرة (ج) من البند (١) من المادة (٢٤) من هذا القانون بالقدر اللازم لاستغلال اختراعه إذا كان هذا الاختراع يخدم أغراضاً صناعية مختلفة عن تلك الأغراض الخاصة بالاختراع موضوع براءة الاختراع أو شهادة المنفعة السابقة أو يشكل تقدماً تقنياً ملحوظاً بالنسبة إليه.

٢. وإذا كان الاختراعان يخدمان ذات الغرض الصناعي، يمنح الترخيص الإجباري لمالك براءة الاختراع أو شهادة المنفعة اللاحقة مع حفظ الحق لصاحب براءة الاختراع أو شهادة المنفعة السابقة في الحصول على ترخيص عن براءة الاختراع أو شهادة المنفعة اللاحقة، إذا طلب ذلك.

٣. ومع ذلك يجوز للطرفين الاتفاق كتابة فيما بينهما واخطار الإدارة باتفاقهما للتأشير به في السجل الخاص.

المادة (٣١)

١. يجوز للسلطة التي منحت الترخيص الإجباري أن تعدل شروطه بناءً على طلب مالك براءة الاختراع أو شهادة المنفعة أو المرخص له بترخيص اجباري، إذا كان ذلك مبرراً بوقائع جديدة، وبوجه خاص إذا منح مالك براءة الاختراع أو شهادة المنفعة ترخيصاً تعاقدياً بشروط أفضل من شروط الترخيص الاجباري.

٢. ويجوز للسلطة التي منحت الترخيص الإجباري أن تقرر إلغاءه بناءً على طلب مالك براءة الاختراع أو شهادة المنفعة إذا لم يتبع المرخص له شروط الترخيص أو إذا زالت الأسباب التي بررت منحه وفي هذه الحالة يجب منح المرخص له مهلة معقولة ليكف عن استغلال الاختراع إذا كان التوقف الفوري يسبب له ضرراً جسيماً.

٣. وتسري أحكام المادتين (٣٥) و(٣٦) من هذا القانون على تعديل وإلغاء التراخيص الإجبارية.

المادة (٣٢)

١. يجب قيد التراخيص الإجبارية وما يصدر في شأنها بالسجل الخاص ونشرها في النشرة وذلك بعد أداء الرسوم المقررة وفقاً لما تحدده اللائحة التنفيذية لهذا القانون.

٢. تعفى التراخيص الصادرة طبقا للمادة (٢٩) من هذا القانون من الرسوم إذا قامت الجهات الحكومية باستغلال الاختراع.

الفصل الثالث
التخلي عن براءة الاختراع أو شهادة المنفعة أو الترخيص وحالات إبطال كل منها

المادة (٣٣)

يجوز لصاحب براءة الاختراع أو شهادة المنفعة أو الترخيص الإجباري أن يتخلى عنها بموجب إخطار كتابي إلى الإدارة والى كل من تعلق له حق بأي منها.

ويجوز أن يقتصر التخلي عن حق أو أكثر مما تخوله براءة الاختراع أو شهادة المنفعة أو الترخيص الإجباري، ولا يجوز أن يضر التخلي بحقوق الغير، ما لم يكن الغير قد تخلى عنها كتابة، ويقيد التخلي في السجل الخاص، ولا يصبح نافذاً إلا من تاريخ نشره في نشرة الملكية الصناعية.

المادة (٣٤)

يجوز لكل ذي مصلحة أن يلجأ إلى المحكمة المختصة لطلب إبطال براءة الاختراع أو شهادة المنفعة أو الترخيص الإجباري.

ويجب إعلان صاحب براءة الاختراع أو شهادة المنفعة أو الترخيص والإدارة وكل من تعلق له حق بأي منها، وذلك في الحالات الآتية:

١. اذا منحت البراءة أو الشهادة أو الترخيص دون توفر الشروط المنصوص عليها في هذا القانون أو لائحته التنفيذية.

٢. إذا منحت البراءة أو الشهادة أو الترخيص دون مراعاة أولوية الطلبات السابقة وفقاً للمادة (١١) من هذا القانون.

ويجوز أن يقتصر طلب الإبطال على جزء من البراءة أو الشهادة أو الترخيص وفي هذه الحالة يعتبر الحكم الصادر تقييداً لما تخوله من حقوق.

المادة (٣٥)

مع مراعاة حكم المادة (٣١) من هذا القانون يترتب على الحكم ببطلان براءة الاختراع أو شهادة المنفعة أو الترخيص كلياً أو جزئيا، اعتبار البطلان من تاريخ منح البراءة أو الشهادة أو الترخيص ومع ذلك لا يلزم صاحبها برد التعويضات التي حصل عليها مقابل استغلال الاختراع أو الترخيص الإجباري، إذا ثبت استفادة المستغل أو صاحب الترخيص، ويجب التأشير بحكم البطلان في السجل الخاص، ونشره في النشرة.

الفصل الرابع
احكام خاصة ببعض الاختراعات

المادة (٣٦)

١. لمالك براءة الاختراع أو شهادة المنفعة او لخلفه القانوني الحق في الحصول على براءة اختراع إضافية أو شهادة منفعة إضافية تمنح على التحسينات او التغيرات او الإضافات التي طرأت على الاختراع بعد حمايته. ويخضع طلب الحماية الإضافية إلى ذات الشروط التي يخضع لها طلب الحماية الأصلية. وتترتب على الحماية الإضافية ذات الآثار المترتبة على الحماية الأصلية.

٢. تنتهي مدة الحماية الإضافية بإنتهاء مدة الحماية الأصلية. ومع ذلك، فإن بطلان الحماية الأصلية لا يترتب عليه حتماً بطلان الحماية الإضافية. وتحدد اللائحة التنفيذية الرسوم السنوية للحماية الإضافية.

٣. يجوز قبل منح الحماية الإضافية تحويل الطلب الخاص بها إلى طلب براءة اختراع مستقلة أو شهادة منفعة مستقلة.

الفصل الخامس
طلب براءة الاختراع الدولي

المادة (٣٧)

تتلقى الإدارة طلبات براءات الاختراع الدولية (باعتبارها: مكتب استلام الطلبات أو مكتب معين أو مكتب مختار) طبقاً لمعاهدة التعاون بشأن براءات الاختراع النافذة في

الدولة، وتنظم اللائحة التنفيذية لهذا القانون الشروط والإجراءات التي يجب مراعاتها في هذا الشأن.

المادة (٣٨)

تتحدد الرسوم عن الإجراءات التي تقوم بها الإدارة طبقاً لما تنظمه معاهدة التعاون بشأن براءات الاختراع، وتستحق الرسوم السنوية عن طلب براءة الاختراع اعتباراً من تاريخ بداية السنة التالية لتاريخ الإيداع الدولي لطلب البراءة، ويسقط الطلب إذا لم يقم مقدمه بسداد الرسوم المستحقة عنه خلال ستة أشهر اعتباراً من تاريخ تقديمه إلى الإدارة.

الفصل السادس
الدراية العملية

المادة (٣٩)

مع عدم الإخلال بالحقوق التي تخولها براءة الاختراع أو شهادة المنفعة، تتمتع الدراية العملية بالحماية من أي استعمال أو إفشاء أو اعلان غير مشروع من قبل الغير، ما دامت لم تنشر أو توضع تحت التصرف العام للكافة، ويشترط للتمتع بالحماية أن يكون صاحب الدراية العملية قد اتخذ التدابير اللازمة للمحافظة على سرية عناصرها على النحو الذي تبينه اللائحة التنفيذية لهذا القانون.

المادة (٤٠)

لكل شخص توصل بوسائله الخاصة إلى درايه عملية، أو حصل على ذلك بطريق مشروع أن يستعمل هذه الدراية العملية بنفسه أو يعلنها للغير، حتى ولو كان شخص آخر قد توصل إلى ذات الدراية العملية.

المادة (٤١)

يجب أن يكون عقد الدراية العملية ثابتاً بالكتابة، وأن يتضمن تحديد عناصرها والغرض من استعمالها وشروط نقلها، وإلا اعتبر العقد باطلاً.

وتسري على عقود الدراية لعملية الأحكام الخاصة باستغلال الاختراعات والتنازل عنها ونقلها والترخيص باستغلالها على النحو الذي تحدده اللائحة التنفيذية لهذا القانون.

المادة (٤٢)

يعتبر عملاً غير مشروع كل استعمال أو إفشاء أو اعلان أي عنصر من عناصر الدراية العملية دون موافقة صاحبها. إذا وقع ذلك من شخص يعلم طبيعتها السرية أو لا يمكن لمثله أن يجهل هذه الطبيعة.

الباب الثالث

الرسوم والنماذج الصناعية

المادة (٤٣)

لا تخل أحكام الحماية المنصوص عليها في هذا القانون بالنسبة إلى الرسومات والنماذج الصناعية بالحقوق الأدبية والفنية المتصلة بها، سواء كان مصدرها القانون أو الاتفاقيات والمعاهدات الدولية التي تكون الدولة طرفاً فيها.

المادة (٤٤)

لا يتمتع الرسم أو النموذج الصناعي بالحماية المقررة في هذا القانون، إلا بتسجيله في السجل الخاص لدى الإدارة، ويقدم طلب التسجيل ويتم فحصه وفقاً لما تحدده اللائحة التنفيذية لهذا القانون من إجراءات ورسوم في هذا الشأن.

المادة (٤٥)

يجوز أن يتضمن طلب الحماية أكثر من رسم أو نموذج صناعي شريطة أن تكون هذه الرسوم أو النماذج الصناعية مرتبطة من حيث التصنيع والاستخدام وألا يجاوز عددها عشرين رسماً أو نموذجاً صناعياً.

المادة (٤٦)

١. تسري في شأن الرسومات والنماذج الصناعية أحكام أولوية الإيداع المنصوص عليها في المادة (١١) من هذا القانون.

٢. مدة الأولوية ستة أشهر من تاريخ الإيداع الأول.

المادة (٤٧)

يجب أن يكون الرسم أو النموذج الصناعي مبتكراً أو جديداً، ويمكن استخدامه كمنتج صناعي أو حرفي، وألا يخل بالنظام العام أو الآداب في الدولة.

المادة (٤٨)

يتم منح سند الحماية للرسم أو النموذج الصناعي بقرار من الوزير وينشر في النشرة مع الرسم أو النموذج بعد اداء الرسوم المقررة.

ويجوز لكل ذي مصلحة أن يتظلم من قرار الوزير بمنح سند الحماية أمام اللجنة خلال ستين يوماً من تاريخ النشر، فإذا لم يقدم أي تظلم خلال الميعاد المشار إليه، تسلم شهادة

التسجيل إلى صاحبها موضحاً فيها رقم القيد وتاريخه وأية بيانات أخرى وفقاً لما تنص عليه اللائحة التنفيذية لهذا القانون.

المادة (٤٩)

مدة حماية الرسم أو النموذج الصناعي عشر سنوات من تاريخ تقديم طلب الحماية.

المادة (٥٠)

مع مراعاة ما ورد في المادتين (٤٩) و(٦٩) من هذا القانون تسري في شأن الرسوم والنماذج الصناعية أحكام المادة (١٤) من هذا القانون.

المادة (٥١)

تخول الحماية المقررة للرسم أو النموذج الصناعي بمقتضى هذا القانون، الحق في منع الغير من ممارسة الأعمال الآتية:

١. استعمال الرسم أو النموذج الصناعي في صناعة أي منتج.

٢. استيراد أي منتج يتعلق بالرسم أوالنموذج الصناعي أو حيازته بغرض استخدامه أو عرضه للبيع أو بيعه.

ولا تنقلب الأعمال المشار إليها مشروعة، لمجرد اختلاف مجالها عن مجال استخدام الرسم أو النموذج الصناعي الذي يحميه القانون، أو كونها تتعلق بمنتج يختلف عن الرسم أو النموذج الصناعي المشمول بسند الحماية.

المادة (٥٢)

إذا بدأ شخص بحسن نية في ممارسة الأعمال المنصوص عليها في المادة (٥١) من هذا القانون قبل تقديم طلب الإيداع، كان من حقه الاستمرار فيما بدأه منها بالنسبة إلى المنتجات التي حصل عليها، ويعتبر هذا الحق شخصياً غير قابل للتنازل عنه أو نقله إلى الغير بأية صورة إلا كجزء من المنشآت المستفيدة منه.

المادة (٥٣)

تسري على الرسم أو النموذج الصناعي أحكام المواد (٧)، (٩)، (١٧)، (١٨)، (٢٠) وأحكام الفصلين الثاني والثالث من الباب الثاني من هذا القانون.

الباب الرابع
التراخيص التعاقدية

المادة (٥٤)

يجوز لصاحب سند الحماية أن يرخص لأي شخص طبيعي أو اعتباري في استعمال أو استغلال الحق موضوع الحماية، على ألا تجاوز مدة الترخيص الحماية المقررة بموجب أحكام هذا القانون. ويجب أن يكون عقد الترخيص مكتوباً وموقعاً من الأطراف.

المادة (٥٥)

يجب قيد عقد الترخيص والتأشير به في السجل الخاص بالحق موضوع الحماية مقابل الرسم المقرر ولا يكون للترخيص أثر بالنسبة إلى الغير إلا من تاريخ نشره في النشرة. ويشطب القيد بناءً على طلب أطراف عقد الترخيص، أو بفسخه، أو بمقتضى حكم ببطلانه، أو بانقضاء مدته.

المادة (٥٦)

الترخيص التعاقدي لا يمنع صاحب سند الحماية من استغلال أو استعمال موضوع الحماية بنفسه أو منح تراخيص أخرى للغير مالم ينص عقد الترخيص على خلاف ذلك.

المادة (٥٧)

للمرخص له حق استغلال واستعمال موضوع الحماية المرخص به في جميع أراضي الدولة طوال مدة الحماية القانونية في كل المجالات وبجميع الوسائل ما لم ينص عقد الترخيص على خلاف ذلك.

كما يكون للمرخص له الحق في استخدام الحقوق التي يمنحها سند الحماية لصاحبه، والتي من شأنها منع التعدي أو التهديد أو الاضرار بموضوع الحماية، ويجب على المرخص له أن يخطر صاحب سند الحماية بكتاب مسجل بالتعدي أو التهديد أو الضرر، فإذا أهمل أو تراخى صاحب سند الحماية ولم يتخذ الإجراءات اللازمة خلال ثلاثين يوماً من تاريخ الإخطار، كان للمرخص له اتخاذ الإجراءات القانونية والقضائية والمطالبة بالتعويض عن الأضرار التي لحقته سواء من إهمال او تراخي صاحب سند الحماية أو من أفعال الغير.

المادة (٥٨)

لا يجوز للمرخص له في غير حالة التنازل عن المنشأة أو انتقال ملكيتها أو جزئها الذي يستغل الترخيص، أن يتنازل إلى الغير عن الترخيص أو منح تراخيص من الباطن، ما لم ينص عقد الترخيص على خلاف ذلك.

المادة (٥٩)

يخضع عقد الترخيص أو التنازل عنه أو نقل ملكية موضوع الحماية، وأي تعديل أوتجديد لهذه العقود، لرقابة الإدارة من حيث الشروط والضمانات والحقوق التي تخولها سندات الحماية.

وللإدارة – بالتنسيق مع الجهات المعنية – أن تطلب من الأطراف تعديل العقود إذا تضمنت إساءة لاستخدام حق من حقوق الملكية الصناعية او الإضرار بالمنافسة التجارية المتصلة بموضوع هذه العقود في الدولة فإذا لم يستجب الأطراف كان للإدارة رفض الموافقة على العقد وعدم قيده في السجل وذلك كله وفقاً لما تحدده اللائحة التنفيذية لهذا القانون.

الباب الخامس
الإجراءات التحفظية والجرائم والجزاءات

المادة (٦٠)

يجوز لصاحب سند الحماية أو لمن انتقلت إليه كل أو بعض حقوق الملكية الصناعية المنصوص عليها في هذا القانون، أن يطلب من المحكمة المختصة إصدار أمر بالحجز التحفظي على الاختراع أو الرسم أو النموذج الصناعي أو المنشأة أو جزئها الذي يستخدم أو يستغل أي نوعٍ من أنواع الملكية الصناعية المشار إليها وذلك في حالة وقوع فعل من أفعال التعدي أو الأعمال غير المشروعة بالمخالفة لهذا القانون أو العقود أو التراخيص الممنوحة وفقاً لأحكامه. ويسري على طلب سند الحماية ما يسري على سند الحماية في هذا الشأن.

المادة (٦١)

يجب على طالب الحجز التحفظي أن يودع كفالة تقدرها المحكمة قبل إصدار أمرها بالحجز ويجب على الحاجز رفع الدعوى الموضوعية خلال ثمانية ايام من تاريخ صدور امر المحكمة وإلا اعتبر الأمر كأن لم يكن.

ويجوز للمحجوز عليه أن يرفع دعوى بالتعويض خلال تسعين يوماً من تاريخ انقضاء المهلة السابقة أو من تاريخ صدور حكم نهائي برفض الدعوى الموضوعية التي رفعها الحاجز.

ولا يجوز صرف الكفالة المشار إليها إلا بعد صدور حكم نهائي في دعوى الحاجز أو دعوى التعويض المرفوعة من المحجوز عليه.

المادة (٦٢)

مع عدم الإخلال بأية عقوبة أشد ينص عليها قانون آخر، يعاقب بالحبس وبغرامة لا تقل عن (٥٠٠٠) خمسة آلاف درهم ولا تزيد على (١٠٠٠٠٠) مائة ألف درهم أو بإحدى هاتين العقوبتين، كل من تقدم بمستندات أو أدلى بمعلومات غير صحيحة أو مزورة للحصول على براءة اختراع أو شهادة منفعة أو دراية عملية، وكذلك كل من قلد اختراعاً أو طريقة صنع أو عنصراً من عناصر الدراية العملية، أو اعتدى عمداً على أي حق يحميه هذا القانون. وتطبق ذات العقوبة إذا كان الأمر متعلقاً برسم أو نموذج صناعي.

المادة (٦٣)

يجوز للمحكمة أن تحكم بمصادرة الأشياء المحجوز عليها أو التي تحجز عليها فيما بعد، كما يجوز للمحكمة أيضاً أن تأمر بإتلاف أو إزالة آثار الفعل المخالف للقانون وكذلك الآلات والأدوات التي استعملت في التزوير، ولها أن تأمر بكل ما سبق حتى في حالة الحكم بالبراءة.

ويجوز للمحكمة كذلك أن تأمر بنشر الحكم في النشرة أو في احدى الصحف المحلية اليومية على نفقة المحكوم.

الباب السادس
إدارة الملكية الصناعية والأحكام الختامية

المادة (٦٤)

تنشأ في الوزارة إدارة تسمى (إدارة الملكية الصناعية) وتتولى هذه الإدارة وفروعها تنفيذ أحكام هذا القانون ولائحته التنفيذية.

ويصدر الوزير قراراً بنظام العمل في الإدارة وفروعها وكيفية ممارستها الاختصاصات المنصوص عليها في هذا القانون ولائحته التنفيذية.

المادة (٦٥)

يكون لموظفي الإدارة صفة الضبطية القضائية في مجال تنفيذ أحكام هذا القانون ولائحته التنفيذية ويحظر عليهم في أثناء مدة خدمتهم وبعد إنتهائها إفشاء أسرار عملهم أو الإدلاء ببيانات أو معلومات اتصلوا بها بحكم وظائفهم أو الكشف عنها أو استعمالها لمصلحتهم أو لمصلحة الغير، ولا يجوز لهم الاحتفاظ بصفة شخصية بأصل أي مستند أو ورقة أو بصور من ذلك، كما يحظر عليهم طوال مدة خدمتهم وخلال ثلاث سنوات تالية لانتهائها ممارسة مهنة وكلاء التسجيل لدى الإدارة.

المادة (٦٦)

١. تشكل بقرار من الوزير لجنة برئاسة قاض يرشحه وزير العدل والشؤون الاسلامية والأوقاف واثنين من ذوي الخبرة في مجال حقوق الملكية الصناعية التي ينظمها هذا القانون على ألا يكون من بينهما موظف بالإدارة، ويعين الوزير أو يندب أمين سر للجنة يتبع في عمله رئيس اللجنة إدارياً.

٢. تختص اللجنة بالفصل في التظلمات التي يقدمها ذوو الشأن من القرارات الصادرة في مجال تطبيق هذا القانون ولائحته التنفيذية. وتحدد اللائحة التنفيذية نظام عمل اللجنة ومكافأة اعضائها وإجراءات التظلم والفصل فيه والرسوم المستحقة.

المادة (٦٧)

يجوز الطعن في قرارات اللجنة أمام المحكمة المختصة وفقاً لقانون الإجراءات المدنية وذلك خلال ثلاثين يوماً من تاريخ الإخطار بقرار اللجنة. ويجوز للمحكمة أن تستعين بالخبراء المتخصصين في مجال المنازعة وبرأي الإدارة.

المادة (٦٨)

تنظم اللائحة التنفيذية للقانون مهنة وكلاء التسجيل لدى الإدارة وتتضمن تحديد الشروط اللازم توفرها في الوكلاء وواجباتهم والرسوم المستحقة للقيد في جدول وكلاء التسجيل وحالات إلغاء القيد وشطبه.

المادة (٦٩)

تحدد اللائحة التنفيذية لهذا القانون الرسوم التي تتقاضاها الإداره عن الاجراءات المقررة طبقاً لهذا القانون ولائحته التنفيذية.

المادة (٧٠)

تكون الاختراعات الكيميائية المتعلقة بالعقاقير الطبية أو المركبات الصيدلية قابلة للحماية بموجب براءة اختراع أو شهادة منفعة إذا استوفت الشروط المقررة في هذا القانون وفي لائحته التنفيذية، وذلك اعتبارا من تاريخ ١ / ١ / ٢٠٠٥.

المادة (٧١)

مع مراعاة ما ورد في المادة (٧٠) من هذا القانون تستمر الإدارة في تلقي طلبات البراءة لحماية الاختراعات الكيميائية المتعلقة بالعقاقير الطبية أو المركبات الصيدلية، وتطبق في شأنها الأحكام التالية:

١. تقيد هذه الطلبات حسب ورودها في سجل براءات الاختراع أو شهادة المنفعة حسب الأحوال، ويؤشر في السجل بما يفيد قيدها وفقاً لأحكام هذه المادة.

٢. تطبق على هذه الطلبات عند فحصها الأحكام المتعلقة بجدة الاختراع وأسبقية الطلب المنصوص عليها في هذا القانون ولائحته التنفيذية.

٣. إذا صدرت براءة اختراع في إحدى الدول الأعضاء في منظمة التجارة العالمية لحماية موضوع أحد الطلبات المذكورة ورخص لصاحبه بتسويق اختراعه تجارياً في تلك الدولة، فإن صاحب هذا الطلب يتمتع بحق التسويق الحصري لهذا الاختراع، وذلك اعتباراً من تاريخ ترخيص الجهات المعنية بالدولة لصاحب الطلب بتسويق اختراعه تجارياً.

٤. يتمتع صاحب الطلب بحق التسويق الحصري للاختراع في الدولة بموجب البند السابق، لمدة خمس سنوات، وتنتهي هذه المدة بمنح أو رفض طلب البراءة أي الفترتين أقصر.

المادة (٧٢)

تصدر اللائحة التنفيذية لهذا القانون من مجلس الوزراء بناءً على اقتراح الوزير متضمنة توزيع الاختصاصات وتدرجها والتفويض فيها في مجال تنفيذ أحكام هذا القانون، وكذلك أنواع السجلات ونظام فحص الطلبات والبيانات والمستندات الواجب تقديمها والرسوم والنفقات ومقابل النشر وجميع الأحكام والقواعد التي يقتضيها تنفيذ القانون.

المادة (٧٣)

يلغى القانون الاتحادي رقم (٤٤) لسنة ١٩٩٢ المشار إليه، كما يلغى كل حكم يخالف أو يتعارض مع أحكام هذا القانون.

المادة (٧٤)

ينشر هذا القانون في الجريدة الرسمية، ويعمل به من تاريخ نشره.

زايد بن سلطان آل نهيان
رئيس دولة الإمارات العربية المتحدة

صدر عنا في قصر الرئاسة بأبوظبي.
بتاريخ: ١٤ رمضان ١٤٢٣هـ.
الموافق: ١٩ نوفمبر ٢٠٠٢م.

قانون اتحادي رقم (٣١) لسنة ٢٠٠٦م
بتعديل القانون الاتحادي رقم (١٧) لسنة ٢٠٠٢م
بشأن تنظيم وحماية الملكية الصناعية لبراءات الاختراع والرسوم
والنماذج الصناعية

نحن خليفة بن زايد آل نهيان رئيس دولة الإمارات العربية المتحدة،

بعد الإطلاع على الدستور،

وعلى القانون الاتحادي رقم (١) لسنة ١٩٧٢ بشأن اختصاصات الوزارات وصلاحيات الوزراء والقوانين المعدلة له،

وعلى القانون الاتحادي رقم (٥) لسنة ١٩٧٦ في شأن اتحاد غرف التجارة والصناعة،

وعلى القانون الاتحادي رقم (١) لسنة ١٩٧٩ في شأن تنظيم شئون الصناعة،

وعلى القانون الاتحادي رقم (٤) لسنة ١٩٧٩ في شأن قمع الغش والتدليس في المعاملات التجارية،

وعلى القانون الاتحادي رقم (٨) لسنة ١٩٨٤ في شأن الشركات التجارية والقوانين المعدلة له،

وعلى قانون المعاملات المدنية الصادر بالقانون الاتحادي رقم (٥) لسنة ١٩٨٥ والقوانين المعدلة له،

وعلى قانون الإجراءات المدنية الصادر بالقانون الاتحادي رقم (١١) لسنة ١٩٩٢ والقوانين المعدلة له،

وعلى قانون المعاملات التجارية الصادر بالقانون الاتحادي رقم (١٨) لسنة ١٩٩٣،

وعلى القانون الاتحادي رقم (١٧) لسنة ٢٠٠٢ في شأن تنظيم وحماية الملكية الصناعية لبراءات الاختراع والرسوم والنماذج الصناعية،

وعلى المرسوم الاتحادي رقم (٢١) لسنة ١٩٧٥ بشأن انضمام دولة الإمارات العربية المتحدة إلى المنظمة العالمية للملكية الفكرية،

وعلى المرسوم الاتحادي رقم (٢٠) لسنة ١٩٩٦ في شأن انضمام دولة الإمارات العربية المتحدة إلى منظمة التجارة العالمية،

وعلى المرسوم الاتحادي رقم (٨٤) لسنة ١٩٩٨ في شأن انضمام دولة الإمارات العربية المتحدة إلى معاهدة التعاون بشأن براءات الاختراع،

وبناءً على ما عرضته وزيرة الاقتصاد، وموافقة مجلس الوزراء، وتصديق المجلس الأعلى للاتحاد،

أصدرنا القانون الآتي:

المادة (١)

تستبدل عبارة "وزارة الاقتصاد" وعبارة "وزير الاقتصاد" بعبارتي "وزارة المالية والصناعة" و"وزير المالية والصناعة" أينما وردتا في القانون الاتحادي رقم (١٧) لسنة ٢٠٠٢ المشار إليه.

المادة (٢)

يلغى كل حكم يخالف أحكام هذا القانون أو يتعارض معه.

المادة (٣)

ينشر هذا القانون في الجريدة الرسمية، ويعمل به اعتباراً من تاريخ نشره.

خليفة بن زايد آل نهيان
رئيس دولة الإمارات العربية المتحدة

صدر عنا في قصر الرئاسة بأبو ظبي
بتاريخ: ٩ رمضان ١٤٢٧هـ.
الموافق: ١ اكتوبر ٢٠٠٦م.

قرار مجلس الوزراء رقم (١١) لسنة ١٩٩٣م
باللائحة التنفيذية للقانون الاتحادي رقم (٤٤) لسنة ١٩٩٢ م
في شأن تنظيم وحماية الملكية الصناعية لبراءات الاختراع
والرسوم والنماذج الصناعية

مجلس الوزراء،

بعد الاطلاع على الدستور المؤقت،

وعلى القانون الاتحادي رقم (١) لسنة ١٩٧٢م بشأن اختصاصات الوزارات وصلاحيات الوزراء والقوانين المعدلة له،

وعلى القانون الاتحادي رقم (٥) لسنة ١٩٧٦م في شأن اتحاد غرف التجارة والصناعة،

وعلى القانون الاتحادي رقم (١) لسنة ١٩٧٩م في شأن تنظيم شؤون الصناعة،

وعلى القانون الاتحادي رقم (٤) لسنة ١٩٧٩م في شأن منع الغش والتدليس في المعاملات التجارية،

وعلى القانون الاتحادي رقم (٨) لسنة ١٩٨٤م في شأن الشركات التجارية والقوانين المعدلة له،

وعلى القانون الاتحادي رقم (٤٤) لسنة ١٩٩٢م في شأن تنظيم وحماية الملكية الصناعية لبراءات الاختراع والرسوم والنماذج الصناعية،

وعلى قرار مجلس الوزراء رقم (١٥) لسنة ١٩٩١م في شأن الهيكل التنظيمي لوزارة المالية والصناعة،

وبناءً على ما عرضه وزير المالية والصناعة، وموافقة مجلس الوزراء،

قرر:

الباب الأول
تعريفات وأحكام عامة

الفصل الأول
تعريفات

المادة (١)

في تطبيق أحكام هذا القرار يكون للكلمات والعبارات التالية المعاني الموضحة قرين كل منها ما لم يدل سياق النص على غير ذلك:

الدولة: دولة الإمارات العربية المتحدة.

الوزارة: وزارة المالية والصناعة.

الوزير: وزير المالية والصناعة.

الإدارة: إدارة الملكية الصناعية بوزارة المالية والصناعة وفروعها في الامارات.

اللجنة: لجنة التظلمات بإدارة الملكية الصناعية.

القانون: قانون تنظيم وحماية الملكية الصناعية لبراءات الاختراع والرسوم والنماذج الصناعية رقم (٤٤) لسنة ١٩٩٢م.

الفصل الثاني
الحماية المؤقتة للاختراعات والرسوم والنماذج الصناعية

المادة (٢)

إذا رغب صاحب الشأن في الحماية المؤقتة للاختراع الذي يمكن أن يكون موضوعاً لبراءة أو شهادة منفعة، او للرسم أو النموذج الصناعي الذي يمكن أن يكون موضوعاً لشهادة تسجيل، بالنسبة للمنتجات التي يرغب في عرضها في أي معرض يقام داخل الدولة وفقاً للمادة (٣) من القانون، يجب عليه ان يتقدم قبل العرض إلى الإدارة بطلب على النموذج رقم (١) بالنسبة للاختراع أو رقم (٢) بالنسبة للرسم او النموذج الصناعي مصحوباً ببيان موجز عن وصف الاختراع ورسمه، وبيان بالمنتجات المتعلقة به، أو صورتين من الرسم او النموذج الصناعي والمنتجات المخصص لها.

ويجوز للادارة ان تكلف الطالب بتقديم اي بيان اخر تراه ضرورياً.

المادة (٣)

تعد الادارة سجلين للحماية المؤقتة أحدهما للاختراعات والاخر للرسوم والنماذج الصناعية، تقيد فيهما الطلبات بارقام متتابعة، ويجب ان يشتمل كل منهما على البيانات الآتية:

١. رقم الطلب.

٢. تاريخ تقديم الطلب.

٣. اسم الطالب وجنسيته ومحل إقامته أو مركزه وعنوانه.

٤. اسم الوكيل وعنوانه.

٥. المحل المختار بالدولة الذي ترسل إليه المكاتبات.

٦. المعرض وتاريخ افتتاحه.

٧. اسم الاختراع، او الرسم او النموذج الصناعي.

٨. بيان المنتجات المتعلقة بالاختراع او المخصص لها الرسم او النموذج الصناعي.

٩. تاريخ ادخال المنتجات إلى المعرض.

١٠. رقم وتاريخ شهادة الحماية المؤقتة ومدة الحماية.

المادة (٤)

مع عدم الاخلال بأحكام الاتفاقيات والمعاهدات التي تكون الدولة طرفاً فيها، ومراعاة شرط المعاملة بالمثل، تعطي الإدارة للطالب – بعد التحقق من إدخاله المنتجات إلى المعرض – شهادة الحماية المؤقتة على النموذج رقم (٣) بالنسبة للاختراع أو رقم (٤) بالنسبة للرسم أو النموذج الصناعي وتكفل هذه الشهادة للطالب الحقوق التي تترتب على سند الحماية لمدة لا تتجاوز ستة أشهر من تاريخ افتتاح المعرض.

الباب الثاني
الاختراعات

الفصل الأول
براءات الاختراع وشهادات المنفعة

أولاً: اجراءات طلب البراءة او شهادة المنفعة

المادة (٥)

يقدم الطلب إلى الإدارة على النموذج رقم (٥) ولا يجوز أن يتضمن الطلب أكثر من اختراع واحد.

المادة (٦)

يرفق بالطلب المستندات الآتية:

١. وصف تفصيلي للاختراع يبدأ بذكر اسم الاختراع ثم يراعى فيه ما يأتي:

أ) تحديد المجال التقني الذي يتعلق به الاختراع.

ب) بيان خلفية الفن التي يكون صاحب الطلب على علم بها والتي قد تعد مفيدة لفهم الاختراع وفحصه وبحثه، ويستحسن ذكر الوثائق التي تتضمن هذا الفن.

ج) الكشف عن الاختراع بكلمات تسمح بفهمه وبطريقة واضحة وكاملة لكي يتمكن أي شخص من ذوي المهارات العادية بالفن من تقييم الاختراع وتنفيذه، مع ذكر الآثار المفيدة للاختراع إن وجدت.

د) وصف الاشكال الواردة في الرسومات باختصار ان وجدت.

هـ) شرح أفضل الوسائل التي فكر فيها صاحب الطلب لتنفيذ الاختراع، على ان يتم ذلك بسرد الامثلة عند الاقتضاء وبالاشارة إلى الرسومات إن وجدت.

و) بيان واضح لطريقة تطبيق الاختراع صناعياً، ولطريقة صنعه واستعماله أو طريقة استعماله فقط على حسب الاحوال، والنتائج التي تم التوصل إليها مدعمة بالامثلة والاحصائيات كلما امكن ذلك.

ز) بيان واضح ومفصل للعناصر الجديدة المطلوب حمايتها والمحددة في الطلب.

٢. الرسومات الخاصة بالاختراع، ويجب تقديمها عندما تكون ضرورية لادراك الاختراع، كما يجوز تقديمها إذا كان طابع الاختراع يسمح بإيضاحه بالرسم حتى إذا لم يكن ذلك ضرورياً لإدراك الاختراع.

٣. ملخص للاختراع لا يزيد على ٢٠٠ كلمة، يستعمل لمجرد الاعلام التقني، ويتكون مما يأتي:

أ) موجز ما هو مكشوف عنه في الوصف وعناصر الحماية والرسومات، ويجب أن يبين فيه المجال التقني (الفني) الذي ينتمي إليه الاختراع، وأن يحرر بشكل يسمح بتكوين فكرة واضحةً عن المشكلة التقنية وجوهر حل هذه المشكلة بواسطة الاختراع، وكذلك أوجه استعمال الاختراع الرئيسية.

ب) وعند الاقتضاء، الصيغة الكيميائية التي تميز الاختراع على افضل وجه بالمقارنة بكل الصيغ الاخرى الواردة في الطلب.

ويرفق بالملخص افضل رسم توضيحي يقدمه الطالب.

٤. مستخرج من السجل التجاري او مستخرج رسمي من عقد التأسيس أو اداة الانشاء على حسب الاحوال إذا كان الطالب شخصاً اعتبارياً.

٥. المستند الدال على احقية الطالب في الاختراع اذا كان الطالب غير المخترع.

٦. موافقة صاحب الشأن اذا كانت العناصر الجوهرية للاختراع قد تم الحصول عليها من اختراع شخص آخر.

٧. سند الوكالة إذا أودع الطلب بواسطة وكيل.

٨. صورة من الطلب السابق والمستندات المرفقة به مصحوبة بشهادة تبين تاريخ ورقم ايداعه والدولة التي أودع فيها، إذا كان الطلب يتضمن الرغبة في اعتبار الأولوية في التسجيل لطلب سبق تقديمه في دولة تكون طرفاً في اتفاقية أو معاهدة دولية مع دولة الامارات العربية المتحدة وفقاً للمادة (١١) من القانون.

٩. الشهادة الصادرة بالحماية المؤقتة إن وجدت.

١٠. كتاب من مكتب مقطعة اسرائيل بعدم حظر التعامل مع الطالب.

ويجب أن تكون المستندات المشار إليها في البنود ٤ و٥ و٦ و٧ و٨ مصدقاً عليها حسب الاصول.

ويجب أن تكون جميع المستندات مصحوبة بترجمة إلى اللغة العربية إذا كانت محررة باللغة الانجليزية أو بترجمة إلى اللغتين العربية والانجليزية إذا كانت محررة بلغة اخرى.

ويتعين ان ترفق المستندات المشار إليها في البنود ١ و٢ و٣، من اصل وصورة بالطلب عند تقديمه، ويجب أن يراعى فيها وفي الطلب الشروط المبينة في المواد من (٧) إلى (١٢) من هذه اللائحة.

أما المستندات الاخرى فيجوز حال عدم ارفاقها بالطلب ان يقدم الطالب تعهداً كتابياً على النموذج رقم (٦) بتقديم ما يلزم تقديمه منها على حسب الاحوال خلال تسعين يوماً من تاريخ تقديم الطلب، وإذا لم يقدمها خلال هذه المهلة يعتبر الطلب كأن لم يكن، وذلك باستثناء المستند المشار إليه في البند (٨) فإنه يترتب على عدم تقديمه – عند لزومه – خلال هذه المهلة سقوط حق الطالب في المطالبة بالاولوية، ويتم التأشير في سجل الطلبات باعتبار الطلب كأن لم يكن أو سقوط حق الطالب في المطالبة بالاولوية – على حسب الاحوال – بناءً على قرار من مدير الإدارة.

المادة (٧)

يجب طباعة بيانات الطلب والوصف والملخص على الآلة الكاتبة، أما الرموز والبيانات والصيغ الكيميائية أو الحسابية وبعض حروف الكتابة فإنه يجوز كتابتها باليد أو رسمها.

المادة (٨)

يجب أن يقدم الطلب والوصف والملخص على ورق متين وأبيض واملس وغير براق من مقاس (A4 – ٧،٢٩ سم × ٢١سم)، ويجب ان تكون الرسوم على ورق رسوم تتوافر فيه تلك الشروط، ويجوز للإدارة أن تقبل اوراق الرسم من قياس آخر.

المادة (٩)

يجب ترقيم كل الاورق في وسط اعلى الصفحة بأرقام عربية متتالية.

المادة (١٠)

يجب أن يكون الحد الادنى لهوامش الاوراق (٢سم).

المادة (١١)

يجب تقديم كل الاوراق بشكل يسمح بنسخها مباشرة بالتصوير الفوتوغرافي والوسائل الالكتروستاتية والاوفست والميكروفيلم.

المادة (١٢)

يجب أن يراعى في لرسومات ما يلي:

١. اعداد الرسومات بسطور وخطوط ثابتة، وكثيفة وداكنة بما فيه الكفاية، وسميكة على نسق واحد ومحددة على احسن وجه دون الحاجة إلى تلوينها.

٢. رسم الاشكال في وضع رأسي بالنسبة إلى ورق الرسم.

٣. كتابة الحروف والارقام المستخدمة في الاشارة إلى اجزاء الرسم بشكل واضح، واستخدام ذات الحروف والارقام في الاوضاع المختلفة للرسم، وفي حالة كتابة تلك الحروف و الارقام خارج الشكل يجب وصلها بالاجزاء التي تشير إليها بخطوط رفيعة.

٤. في حالة رسم أكثر من شكل في الورقة الواحدة، يجب ترك مسافة كافية بين كل شكل واخر واعطاء الاشكال ارقام متتابعة.

٥. عدم كتابة أي بيان يتعلق بتسمية الاختراع أو وصفه على اوراق الرسم.

المادة (١٣)

تعطى الطلبات ارقاماً متتابعة سنوياً حسب تاريخ وساعة تقديمها، ويؤشر على الطلب بالرقم المتتابع له وتاريخ وساعة تقديمه ورقم وتاريخ ايصال سداد الرسم المقرر، ويؤشر على مرفقات الطلب بالرقم المتتابع له ويختم الطلب ومرفقاته بخاتم الإدارة.

ويسلم للطالب ايصال على النموذج رقم (٧) يتضمن الرقم المتتابع للطلب وتاريخ وساعة تقديمه، وبيان المستندات المرفقة به ورقم وتاريخ ايصال سداد الرسم المقرر.

المادة (١٤)

يعد سجل لطلبات البراءات وشهادات المنفعة، فيه البيانات الآتية:

١. الرقم المتتابع للطلب.

٢. تاريخ تقديم الطلب.

٣. بيان ما إذا كان المطلوب براءة أو شهادة منفعة.

٤. اسم الاختراع.

٥. اسم الطالب وجنسيته، ومحله المختار في الدولة، ومحل اقامته او مركزه الرئيسي.

٦. اسم وعنوان الوكيل.

٧. اسم الدولة الاجنبية التي قدم إليها طلب سابق وتاريخه ورقم قيده إذا كان الطلب مقدماً استناداً للمادة (١١) من القانون.

٨. تاريخ القرار الصادر برفض الطلب في حالة رفضه وتاريخ إخطار الطالب به.

٩. تاريخ القرار الوزاري الصادر بمنح البراءة أو شهادة المنفعة ورقمه وتاريخ نشره.

١٠. رقم البراءة أو شهادة المنفعة.

المادة (١٥)

تعد بطاقات مفهرسة ابجدياً وفقاً لاسماء الطالبين على النموذج رقم (٨) ويدون بها اسم الطالب واسم الاختراع والرقم المتتابع للطلب وتاريخ وساعة تقديمه.

المادة (١٦)

يجوز للادارة ان تكلف الطالب بتقديم عينة من المنتجات الخاصة بالاختراعات الكيميائية المتعلقة بالاغذية أو العقاقير الطبية أو المركبات الصيدلية، وفي هذه الحالة يجب على الطالب تقديم العينات المطلوبة وتحرير قائمة بها وإلحاق هذه القائمة بوصف الاختراع وملخصه.

المادة (١٧)

تقدم العينات المنصوص عليها في المادة (١٦) من هذه اللائحة في زجاجات لا يزيد ارتفاعها عن (٨ سم) وقطرها الخارجي على (٤ سم) وتغلق باحكام بسدادات وتختم بالشمع الاحمر ويلصق على العينات بيان يشير إلى الصلة بينها وبين الانتاج الوارد ذكره في وصف الاختراع.

المادة (١٨)

إذا تعلق الاختراع بمادة ملونة قدمت عينة منها وفقاً لاحكام المادتين (١٦) و(١٧) من هذه اللائحة وجب ان تشفع العينة بنماذج من سلع طبعت أو صبغت بهذه المادة، وتكون النماذج – بقدر الامكان – مسطحة ومثبتة على بطاقات بمقاس (٣٣ سم طولاً و ٢١ سم عرضاً) يكتب عليها بيان تفصيلي عن عملية الطبع أو الصباغة، وعلى الاخص ما يتعلق بتركيب محاليل الاحماض المختلفة ودرجة تركيزها ودرجة الحرارة ومدة كل عملية ومدى امتصاص اللون في احماض الصباغة، كما تبين على البطاقة نسبة المواد الملونة الثابتة على الاقمشة المصبوغة، ويبين عليها كذلك تركيب عجينة الطباعة، وتحمل البطاقة بياناً يشير إلى الصلة بين المادة التي استخدمت في الطبع أو الصباغة وبين ما ذكر عنها في وصف الاختراع.

المادة (١٩)

يجوز للادارة في غير الاحوال السابقة تكليف الطالب بتقديم عينات أو نماذج عند الاقتضاء وذلك طبقاً للاشتراطات الخاصة التي تعينها.

في جميع الأحوال إذا كانت العينات تحتوي على مواد سامة أو كاوية أو سريعة الاشتعال أو قابلة للانفجار يجب ذكر ذلك في البيان الملصق عليها.

ثانياً: فحص طلب البراءة أو شهادة المنفعة

المادة (٢٠)

تفحص الادارة الطلب ومرفقاته وفقاً لنظام الفحص المشار إليه في المادتين ٩٢ و٩٣ من هذه اللائحة للتحقق مما يأتي:

١. ان الطلب مقدم من شخص طبيعي أو معنوي يتمتع بجنسية الدولة، أو أجنبي يحق له التقدم بالطلب وفقاً لأحكام اية اتفاقية أو معاهدة دولية تكون الدولة طرفاً فيها أو يحمل جنسية دولة تعامل الدولة معاملة المثل طبقاً للمادة (٢) من القانون.

٢. ان الطلب مقدم من صاحب الحق في الاختراع.

٣. ان الطلب قدم مستوفياً للشروط المنصوص عليها في المواد من (٥) إلى (١٢) من هذه اللائحة.

٤. ان العينات والنماذج المقدمة أو المطلوب تقديمها مستوفية للشروط المنصوص عليها في المواد من (١٦) إلى (١٩) من هذه اللائحة.

٥. ان الاختراع لا يعد من الابحاث النباتية أو الحيوانية أو الطرق البيولوجية لانتاج النبات أو الحيوان التي لا يمنح عنها براءة اختراع أو شهادة منفعة طبقاً لنص الفقرة (١) من المادة (٦) من القانون والتي لا يستثنى منها إلا طرق علم الاحياء الدقيقة ومنتجاتها.

٦. ان الاختراع لا يعد من الاختراعات الكيميائية المتعلقة بالاغذية أو العقاقير الطبية أو المركبات الصيدلية التي لا تمنح عنها براءة اختراع أو شهادة منفعة طبقاً للفقرة (٢) من المادة (٦) من القانون.

٧. ان الاختراع لا يعد من المبادئ والاكتشافات العلمية طبقاً لنص الفقرة (٣) من المادة (٦) من القانون.

٨. ان الاختراع ليس من الاختراعات المتعلقة بالدفاع الوطني طبقاً لنص الفقرة (٤) من المادة (٦) والفقرة (١) من المادة (٣٨) من القانون، ويجب على الادارة من خلال فحص الطلب ان تخطر فوراً وزير الدفاع بتقرير[2] كتابي مرفق بطلب الحماية إذا تبين ان الاختراع يتعلق بأمور الدفاع الوطني.

٩. ان الاختراع لا ينشأ عن نشره أو استغلاله اخلال بالنظام العام أو الآداب طبقاً لنص الفقرة (٥) من المادة (٦) من القانون.

---

[2] . وردت هذه الكلمة في نص الجريدة الرسمية "بتفرير" والأصح ان تكون "بتقرير" فاقتضى التنويه.

١٠. إذا تبين للادارة ان العناصر الجوهرية للاختراع تم الحصول عليها من اختراع شخص آخر، فيجب عليها ان تطلب من الطالب تقديم موافقة ذلك الشخص على حصول الطالب على تلك العناصر الجوهرية أو على ايداع الطلب طبقاً للمادة (٨) من القانون.

١١. ان الاختراع جديد أي لم يسبق من حيث التقنية الصناعية السابقة، ويقصد بالتقنية الصناعية السابقة في هذا المجال كل ما تحقق الكشف عنه للجمهور في أي مكان أو زمان بالوصف المكتوب، أو الشفوي، أو بطريق الاستعمال، أو بأية وسيلة أخرى من الوسائل التي يتحقق بها العلم بالاختراع، وذلك قبل تاريخ تقديم الطلب أو تاريخ الأولوية المطالب بها أو قبل تاريخ بدء الحماية المؤقتة بشرط أن يكون الطلب قد قدم خلال ستة اشهر من تاريخ بدئها.

١٢. ان الاختراع ينطوي على نشاط ابتكاري لا يتيسر لرجل المهنة العادي التوصل إليه بصورة بديهية نتيجة التقنية الصناعية السابقة المتصلة بطلب البراءة.

١٣. ان الاختراع قابل للتطبيق الصناعي أي يمكن تطبيقه أو استعماله في أي نوع من الصناعة بمعناها الواسع بما في ذلك الزراعة والصيد والحرف اليدوية والخدمات.

١٤. ان العناصر المبتكرة المطلوب حمايتها واردة في الطلب بطريقة محددة ومفسرة تفسيراً واضحاً في الوصف والرسومات الهندسية طبقاً لنص المادة (١٦) من القانون.

١٥. ان الاولوية المطالب بها تتفق مع أحكام الاتفاقية أو المعاهدة الدولية التي تربط دولة الامارات العربية المتحدة مع الدولة التي قدم فيها الطلب السابق.

المادة (٢١)

١. يجوز للطالب ان يطلب تصحيح ما ورد في الطلب أو الوصف من أخطاء كتابية أو حسابية.

٢. يجوز للطالب أن يطلب تعديل أي بيان في الطلب بما في ذلك وصف الاختراع أو رسمه مع بيان ماهية التعديل وأسبابه بشرط ألا يترتب على ذلك أي تغيير جوهري لما كان عليه الوصف والرسم وقت تقديم الطلب.

٣. لا يتم التصحيح أو التعديل المشار إليهما في الفقرتين السابقتين إلا بعد سداد الرسم المقرر وموافقة الادارة على ذلك.

المادة (٢٢)

للادارة أن تستعين بالخبرة العلمية المتوفرة لدى أية جهة أخرى وطنية كانت أم اجنبية داخل الدولة أو خارجها متى رأت ضرورة لذلك.

ثالثاً: البت في طلب البراءة أو شهادة المنفعة

المادة (٢٣)

اذا تبين من فحص الطلب انه لا تتوافر فيه الشروط المنصوص عليها في القانون وهذه اللائحة تصدر الادارة قراراً مسبباً برفض الطلب، وتخطر الطالب بهذا القرار بكتاب مسجل، ويحق للطالب التظلم من هذا القرار إلى اللجنة خلال ستين يوماً من تاريخ استلام الاخطار .

المادة (٢٤)

١. إذا تبين من فحص الطلب انه تتوافر فيه الشروط المنصوص عليها في القانون وهذه اللائحة تقبل الادارة الطلب، وتخطر الطالب بذلك بكتاب مسجل تكلفه فيه بسداد رسم النشر عن منح البراءة أو شهادة المنفعة خلال ستين يوماً من تاريخ استلامه هذا الاخطار وإلا اعتبر طلبه كأن لم يكن، فإذا لم يسدد الطالب رسم النشر خلال تلك المهلة يتم التأشير في سجل الطلبات باعتبار الطلب كأن لم يكن بناءً على قرار من مدير الادارة.

٢. إذا تم سداد رسم النشر تمنح براءة الاختراع أو شهادة المنفعة بقرار من الوزير، وينشر هذا القرار في الجريدة الرسمية، ويحق لكل ذي مصلحة التظلم من هذا القرار امام اللجنة خلال ستين يوماً من تاريخ النشر.

٣. بعد صيرورة القرار المذكور نهائياً بعدم التظلم منه أمام اللجنة خلال الميعاد المشار إليه في الفقرة السابقة، أو بصدور قرار أو حكم نهائي بتأييده، تقوم الادارة بقيد البراءة أو شهادة المنفعة في سجل البراءات أو سجل شهادات المنفعة المشار إليهما في الفقرة (٥) من هذه المادة على حسب الاحوال، ثم تسلم الطالب البراءة أو شهادة المنفعة بموجب ايصال استلام.

٤. يجب أن تشتمل براءة الاختراع أو شهادة المنفعة على البيانات الآتية:

أ) رقم الطلب وتاريخ تقديمه.
ب) رقم وتاريخ القرار الوزاري الصادر بمنح البراءة أو شهادة المنفعة.
ج) رقم قيد البراءة أو شهادة المنفعة.
د) تاريخ اصدار البراءة أو شهادة المنفعة.
هـ) بيان دفع رسم قيد الطلب.
و) اسم المخترع ما لم يكن قد اعلن كتابة عن عدم رغبته في ذكر اسمه طبقاً للمادة (١٠) من القانون.
ز) اسم المالك وجنسيته وعنوانه.
ح) اسم الاختراع.
ط) التصنيف.
ي) مدة الحماية وتاريخ بدءها ونهايتها.

ك) رقم وتاريخ طلب الاولوية والدولة التي قدم فيها في حالة استناد البراءة إلى هذه الاولوية.

ل) إذا كانت البراءة أو شهادة المنفعة اضافية طبقاً للمادة (٣٧) من القانون فيجب أن تشتمل على رقم البراءة الاصلية وتاريخ انتهاء مدة حمايتها.

م) إذا جددت مدة البراءة فيجب التأشير على البراءة بمدة وتاريخ التجديد وبيان دفع رسم التجديد.

٥. تعد الادارة سجلين احدهما لبراءات الاختراع والاخر لشهادات المنفعة، ويجب ان يشتمل كل منهما على البيانات المشار إليها في الفقرة السابقة بالاضافة إلى البيانات الآتية:

أ) رقم وتاريخ عدد الجريدة الرسمية المنشور فيه القرار الوزاري بمنح البراءة أو شهادة المنفعة.

ب) اسم وكيل مالك البراءة أو شهادة المنفعة.

ج) المحل المختار لمالك البراءة أو شهادة المنفعة في الدولة.

ويجب ان يتم التأشير في كل سجل منهما بكل ما نص القانون أو هذه اللائحة على وجوب التأشير به فيه.

رابعاً: تجديد مدة البراءة

المادة (٢٥)

١. فيما[3] عدا البراءات الممنوحة وفقاً لاحكام الفقرة (٢) من المادة (٦) من القانون والتي لا يجوز تجديدها، يقدم طلب تجديد مدة البراءة خلال ثلاثة الاشهر الاخيرة من المدة الاصلية مصحوباً بالمستندات التي تثبت ان للاختراع موضوع البراءة اهمية خاصة، وان مالكه لم يجن منه ثمرة تتناسب مع جهوده ونفقاته.

٢. يجب على الطالب سداد رسم التجديد المقرر، وعلى الادارة التأشير على الطلب برقم وتاريخ ايصال سداد الرسم.

المادة (٢٦)

تسري في حالة رفض طلب التجديد الاحكام المبينة في المادة (٢٣) من هذه اللائحة.

المادة (٢٧)

١. إذا قدم طلب التجديد في الموعد القانوني مستوفياً للشروط اللازمة لتجديده تقبل الادارة الطلب وتخطر الطالب بذلك بكتاب مسجل فيه بتكلفه بسداد رسم النشر عن

---

[3] . . وردت هذه الكلمة في نص الجريدة الرسمية "قيما" والأصح ان تكون "فيما" فاقتضى التنويه.

التجديد خلال ستين يوماً من تاريخ استلامه هذا الاخطار، وإذا لم يسدد الطالب رسم النشر خلال تلك المهلة اعتبر طلبه كأن لم يكن.

٢. اذا تم سداد رسم النشر يصدر قرار التجديد من مدير الادارة، وينشر في الجريدة الرسمية، ويحق لكل ذي مصلحة التظلم من هذا القرار امام اللجنة خلال ستين يوماً من تاريخ النشر.

٣. بعد صيرورة قرار التجديد نهائياً بعدم التظلم منه امام اللجنة خلال الميعاد المشار إليه في الفقرة السابقة، او بصدور قرار أو حكم نهائي بتأييده، تقوم الادارة بالتأشير على البراءة بتجديدها وتاريخ انتهاء مدة التجديد، والتأشير بذلك في سجل براءات الاختراع.

خامساً: سقوط البراءة أو شهادة المنفعة أو الطلب

المادة (٢٨)

١. يسدد الرسم السنوي المتصاعد المقرر، بناءً على طلب بقدم من صاحب الشأن يبين فيه رقم وتاريخ طلب البراءة أو شهادة المنفعة، ورقم البراءة أو شهادة المنفعة حال صدورها، والسنة أو السنوات المطلوب السداد عنها، وتؤشر الادارة على طلب السداد برقم وتاريخ ايصال السداد والمبلغ المسدد والسنة او السنوات المسدد عنها.

٢. يجب ان يتم سداد الرسم السنوي المتصاعد خلال ثلاثة الأشهر الاخيرة من كل سنة اعتباراً من السنة التالية لتاريخ تقديم طلب البراءة أو شهادة المنفعة.

٣. يجوز للإدارة ان تقبل سداد الرسم السنوي المتصاعد اذا تم دفعه خلال ثلاثين يوماً من انقضاء المدة المشار إليها في الفقرة السابقة وذلك مقابل دفع الرسم الاضافي المقرر.

٤. يسقط الطلب او البراءة أو شهادة المنفعة على حسب الاحوال إذا لم يتم سداد الرسم السنوي المتصاعد وفقاً لأحكام الفقرتين السابقتين، وينشر عن السقوط في الجريدة الرسمية.

٥. تعد الإدارة سجلاً للرسوم السنوية المتصاعدة لطلبات البراءات وشهادات المنفعة، تقيد فيه البيانات التالية في صفحة مستقلة لكل طلب:

أ) اسم الطالب وعنوانه.
ب) اسم الوكيل وعنوانه.
ج) رقم الطلب وتاريخ تقديمه.
د) رقم ومدة البراءة أو شهادة المنفعة، ومدة تجديد البراءة.
هـ) سنوات استحقاق الرسوم بأرقام متسلسلة.
و) تاريخ نهاية الموعد السنوي للسداد بدون رسم اضافي.
ز) تاريخ نهاية الموعد السنوي للسداد برسم اضافي.

ح) رقم وتاريخ ايصال السداد والمبلغ المسدد.

ط) تاريخ السقوط.

٦. تعد الادارة بطاقة لكل طلب تدون فيها ذات البيانات المشار إليها في الفقرة السابقة، وترتب هذه البطاقات وفقاً لتواريخ تقديم الطلبات.

سادساً: التنازل عن البراءة أو الشهادة ورهنها والحجز عليها

المادة (٢٩)

يؤشر في سجل طلبات البراءات وشهادات المنفعة بكل تنازل للغير عن الطلب يتم وفقاً لنص الفقرتين (١) و(٢) من المادة (١٩) من القانون.

المادة (٣٠)

مع مراعاة نص المادة (٥١)، يقيد في سجل البراءات أو سجل شهادات المنفعة على حسب الاحوال كل تنازل للغير عن البراءة أو الشهادة يتم وفقاً لنص الفقرتين (١) و(٢) من المادة (١٩) من القانون، وينشر هذا التنازل في الجريدة الرسمية وذلك بعد اداء رسم القيد ورسم النشر المقرر.

المادة (٣١)

يؤشر في سجل البراءات برهن البراءة، وينشر عنه في الجريدة الرسمية بعد أداء رسم النشر المقرر.

المادة (٣٢)

يؤشر في سجل البراءات أو سجل شهادات المنفعة على حسب الاحوال بالحجز على البراءة أو شهادة المنفعة، وبحكم مرسى المزاد، وينشر عن كل منهما في الجريدة الرسمية بعد أن يؤدي الدائن رسوم النشر المقررة.

المادة (٣٣)

١. يتم التأشير المشار إليه في المادة (٢٩) من هذه اللائحة والقيد أو التأشير والنشر المشار إليهما في المادتين (٣٠) و(٣١) منها بناءً على طلب يقدمه صاحب الشأن إلى الإدارة ويرفق به سند التنازل أو سند الرهن على حسب الأحوال.

٢. يتم التأشير والنشر المشار إليهما في المادة (٣٢) من هذه اللائحة بناءً على اعلان الدائن للإدارة بالحجز أو حكم مرسى المزاد.

الفصل الثاني
التراخيص الإجبارية ونزع ملكية الاختراع

المادة (٣٤)

يؤشر في سجل البراءات أو سجل شهادات المنفعة على حسب الاحوال بالاتفاقات الكتابية التي تتم بشأن التراخيص المشار إليها في المادة (٢٥) من القانون بناءً على إخطار مصحوب بهذه الاتفاقات يوجهه ذوو الشأن إلى الإدارة.

المادة (٣٥)

١. يؤشر في سجل البراءات أو سجل شهادات المنفعة على حسب الاحوال بكل حكم نهائي يصدر من المحكمة المختصة برفض منح الترخيص الاجباري أو بمنحه أو انتقاله أو تعديله أو إلغائه أو إبطاله كلياً أو جزئياً.

وينشر الحكم في الجريدة الرسمية، وذلك بعد اعلان صاحب الشأن الادارة بالحكم، وقيامه بسداد الرسوم المقررة.

٢. على الإدارة قبل صدور قرار الوزير بنزع ملكية الاختراع أو إصدار ترخيص إجباري باستغلاله وفقاً لنص الفقرة (١) من المادة (٣٣) من القانون، أن تخطر صاحب براءة الاختراع أو شهادة المنفعة لإبداء وجهة نظره في هذا الشأن.

٣. يؤشر في سجل البراءات أو سجل شهادات المنفعة على حسب الاحوال، بقرار نزع الملكية وينشر هذا القرار في الجريدة الرسمية، كما يؤشر في السجل بكل قرار أو حكم يصدر بتعديله أو إلغائه، وينشر القرار أو الحكم المعني بالجريدة الرسمية.

٤. يؤشر في سجل البراءت أو سجل شهادات المنفعة على حسب الاحوال، بكل قرار يصدر من الوزير بمنح الترخيص الاجباري أو تعديله أو إلغائه، وينشر القرار في الجريدة الرسمية بعد أداء صاحب المصلحة الرسم المقرر.

الفصل الثالث
التخلي عن براءة الاختراع أو شهادة المنفعة أو الترخيص
وحالات ابطال البراءة أو شهادة المنفعة

المادة (٣٦)

يقيد في سجل البراءات أو سجل شهادات المنفعة على حسب الاحوال التخلي عن براءة الاختراع أو شهادة المنفعة أو الترخيص الاجباري أو عن حق او اكثر مما تخوله البراءة أو شهادة المنفعة أو الترخيص الاجباري، ويتم هذا القيد بقرار من مدير الادارة يصدر بناءً على اخطار كتابي بالتخلي موجه من صاحب الشأن للإدارة ومرفق به ما يدل على توجيه نسخة منه إلى كل من تعلق له حق بأي منها، ويجب على الإدارة اخطار كل من تعلق له حق بأي منها بالقرار المذكور بكتاب مسجل.

وينشر عن التخلي بالجريدة الرسمية بعد صيرورة القرار المذكور نهائياً بعدم التظلم منه في الموعد القانوني أو بصدور قرار أو حكم نهائي بتأييده.

المادة (٣٧)

يؤشر في سجل البراءات أو سجل شهادات المنفعة على حسب الاحوال بكل حكم نهائي ببطلان البراءة أو شهادة المنفعة كلياً أو جزئياً، وينشر هذا الحكم في الجريدة الرسمية.

الفصل الرابع
البراءة أو شهادة المنفعة الاضافية

المادة (٣٨)

تسري الاحكام الواردة في كل من الفصول الاول والثاني والثالث من الباب الثاني من هذه اللائحة على البراءة أو شهادة المنفعة الاضافية.

الفصل الخامس
الدراية العملية

المادة (٣٩)

يشترط لتمتع الدراية العملية بالحماية من أي استعمال أو افشاء أو اعلان غير مشروع من قبل الغير ما يأتي:

١. عدم سبق نشرها أو وضعها تحت التصرف العام للكافة.

٢. قيام صاحب الدراية العملية باتخاذ التدابير اللازمة التي تظهر بوضوح اتجاه ارادته للحفاظ على سريتها ومنها على وجه الخصوص التدابير الآتية:

أ) حفظ وثائق الدراية العملية بطريقة تكفل عدم اطلاع الغير عليها دون إذنه.

ب) وضع نظام عمله على اسس تضمن عدم المام أي عامل من عماله بكل عناصر الدراية العملية.

ج) عدم السماح للغير بزيارة اماكن عمله دون اذن سابق منه ودون مرافقته أو من يفوض من قبله وعدم تضمين برنامج الزيارة ما يؤدي إلى المام الزائر بكل عناصر الدراية العملية.

د) تضمين عقود العمل التي تربطه بعماله شرط السرية الذي يوجب على كل منهم الالتزام بعدم افشاء أو اعلان أي عنصر من عناصر الدراية العملية التي اكتسب معرفتها بمناسبة عمله، وبعدم استعمال أو استغلال هذه المعرفة لحسابه الخاص أو لحساب الغير بطريقة مباشرة أو غير مباشرة خلال مدة قيام عقد العمل أو بعد انقضائه لأي سبب من الأسباب دون اذن سابق من صاحب الدراية العملية.

هـ) تضمين الاتفاقات التي تربطه بمن يدخل معهم في علاقات من شأنها أن تتيح لهم التعرف على بعض عناصر درايته العملية – مثل المقاولين الذين يعهد إليهم بتصنيع بعض مكونات انتاجه– شرط السرية الذي يوجب عليهم الالتزام بعدم افشاء أو اعلان أي عنصر من عناصر هذه الدراية العملية وبعدم استعمال أو استغلال هذه العناصر لحسابهم الخاص أو لحساب الغير بطريقة مباشرة أو غير مباشرة خلال مدة هذه الاتفاقات أو بعد انقضائها لأي سبب من الاسباب دون اذن سابق من صاحب الدراية العملية.

و) تضمين عقود نقل الدراية العملية التي تربطه بمتلقيها عنه شرط السرية الذي يلتزم بموجبه المتلقي بعدم القيام هو او العاملين لديه من افشاء أو اعلان أو الكشف عن تلك الدراية العملية للغير دون اذن سابق من صاحب الدراية العملية.

ز) الحصول على اقرار ممن يتفاوض معهم بشأن ابرام عقد من العقود المشار إليها في البند السابق يتضمن التزامهم بسرية المعلومات المتعلقة بالدراية العملية التي يتم الكشف لهم عنها وعدم افشائها أو اعلانها أو الكشف عنها للغير اثناء المفاوضات أو بعد انتهائها دون التوصل إلى ابرام العقد بغير اذن سابق من صاحب الدراية العملية.

المادة (٤٠)

تسري على عقود الدراية العملية الاحكام الخاصة باستغلال الاختراعات والتنازل عنها ونقلها والترخيص باستغلالها على النحو المحدد في المواد الآتية:

المادة (٤١)

١. يجب قيد عقد الدراية العملية سواء كان موضوعه التنازل عن هذه الدراية العملية أو نقل ملكيتها أو الترخيص باستغلالها في السجل المشار إليه في الفقرة (٣) من هذه المادة، وذلك بناءً على طلب يقدم للادارة من أي من طرفي العقد مرفقاً به نسخة من العقد مصدقاً على توقيعات الطرفين عليها حسب الاصول ومترجمة إلى اللغة العربية ان كانت محررة بلغة اخرى، ويجب على الطالب سداد رسم القيد المقرر.

٢. تعطى طلبات قيد عقود الدراية العملية ارقاماً متتابعة حسب تاريخ تقديمها، ويؤشر على الطلب بالرقم المتتابع له وتاريخ تقديمه ورقم وتاريخ ايصال سداد رسم القيد ويؤشر على نسخة العقد بالرقم المتتابع للطلب ويختم الطلب ونسخة العقد بخاتم الادارة، ويسلم للطالب ايصال يتضمن الرقم المتتابع للطلب وتاريخ تقديمه وبيان المستندات المرفقة به ورقم وتاريخ ايصال سداد رسم القيد.

٣. تعد الادارة سجلاً لطلبات قيد عقود الدراية العملية، ويجب أن يشتمل هذا السجل على البيانات الآتية:

أ) الرقم المتتابع للطلب وتاريخ تقديمه.

ب) اسم وجنسية وعنوان الطرف المالك للدراية العملية واسم وعنوان وكيله ان وجد.

ج) اسم وجنسية وعنوان الطرف المتلقي للدراية العملية واسم وعنوان وكيله ان وجد.

د) المحل المختار في الدولة لكل من طرفي العقد.

هـ) موضوع العقد ومدته.

و) تاريخ القرار الصادر برفض القيد وتاريخ اخطار الطرفين به.

ز) تاريخ القرار الصادر بالموافقة على القيد.

٤. تعد الادارة سجلاً لعقود الدراية العملية التي وافقت على قيدها، ويجب ان يشتمل هذا السجل على البيانات الآتية:

أ) رقم قيد العقد وتاريخ القيد.

ب) تاريخ القرار الصادر بالموافقة على القيد.

ج) الرقم المتتابع للطلب وتاريخ تقديمه.

د) اسم وجنسية وعنوان كل من طرفي العقد واسم وعنوان وكيل كل منهما ان وجد.

هـ) المحل المختار في الدولة لكل منهما.

و) موضوع العقد ومدته.

ويجب ان يتم التأشير في هذا السجل بكل تعديل أو تجديد للعقد بعد موافقة الادارة عليه، وسداد رسم التعديل أو التجديد المقرر.

المادة (٤٢)

يخضع عقد الدراية العملية واي تعديل أو تجديد له لرقابة الادارة، وللإدارة ان تطلب من طرفي العقد تعديل شروطه أو شروط تعديله أو تجديده بما يحقق مصلحة الطرفين في اطار القانون والمصالح الاقتصادية للدولة فإذا لم يستجب الطرفان لذلك كان للإدارة رفض الموافقة على العقد وعدم قيده في السجل أو رفض الموافقة على التعديل أو التجديد وعدم التأشير به في السجل.

المادة (٤٣)

للإدارة الحق في الموافقة على قيد العقد أو التأشير بأي تعديل أو تجديد له أو رفض الموافقة على و ذلك فقاً لما تقتضيه اعتبارات الصالح العام وضلك في الحالات الآتية:

١. اذا كانت الدراية العملية موضوع العقد متعلقة بالامور التي لا يجوز ان يمنح عنها براءة اختراع أو شهادة منفعة طبقاً لنص المادة (٦) من القانون.

٢. إذا كانت مدة العقد وتجديداته تزيد عن المدد الواردة في المادة (١٤) من القانون.

٣. اذا كانت الدراية العملية موضوع العقد يمكن اتاحتها محلياً.

٤. اذا كان العقد يحد من نشاط الطرف المتلقي للدراية العملية في مجال البحث والتطوير أو يحد من حقه في مجال التصدير بما يتعارض مع مصالح الدولة، أو يمنعه من تلقي او استخدام دراية عملية مكملة من مصادر اخرى.

٥. اذا كان العقد يفرض على الطرف المتلقي للدراية العملية قيوداً تتعلق بحجم الانتاج أو بسعر البيع سواء للسوق المحلي أو الاجنبي.

٦. اذا كان العقد يشترط استرداد وثائق الدراية العملية التي سلمت للطرف المتلقي بموجب العقد.

٧. اذا كان العقد يرتب التزامات مالية لا تتناسب مع الدراية العملية المقدمة، أو ان يكون من شأنه القاء عبء غير مناسب على الاقتصاد الوطني.

٨. اذا كان العقد يلزم المتلقي بشراء المعدات والالات أو قطع الغيار أو المواد الخام أو الوسيطة من مورد الدراية العملية أو من يعينه والتي يمكن الحصول عليها من مصادر اخرى بشروط افضل.

وتسري احكام المادة (٢٣) من هذه اللائحة في حالة صدور قرار الادارة بعدم الموافقة على العقد أو أي تعديل أو تجديد له.

المادة (٤٤)

يؤشر في سجل عقود الدراية العملية بشطب قيد عقد الدراية العملية بناءً على طلب من طرفيه يقدم للإدارة مع المستندات المؤيدة، أو بناءً على اعلان الادارة بحكم نهائي في الحالات الآتية:

١. انقضاء مدة العقد.

٢. فسخ العقد قبل انقضاء مدته باتفاق الطرفين او بحكم قضائي.

٣. بطلان العقد بموجب حكم قضائي.

الباب الثالث
الرسوم والنماذج الصناعية

المادة (٤٥)

يقدم طلب شهادة تسجيل الرسم أو النموذج الصناعي إلى الادارة على النوذج رقم (٩) ويجب أن تطبع بياناته على الآلة الكاتبة، وأن تكون جميع أوراقه من مقاس (A4).

المادة (٤٦)

يرفق بالطلب المستندات الآتية:

١. نسختان من الرسم أو النموذج إذا كان ثنائي الابعاد أو نسختان من كل جانب منه إذا كان ثلاثي الابعاد، ولا يجوز ان يستعاض عن ذلك بعينة من المنتجات المخصص لها ذلك الرسم أو النموذج الصناعي.

٢. مستخرج من السجل التجاري أو مستخرج رسمي من عقد التأسيس أو أداة الانشاء على حسب الاحوال إذا كان الطالب شخصاً اعتبارياً.

٣. المستند الدال على احقية الطالب في الرسم أو النموذج الصناعي اذا كان الطالب غير المبتكر.

٤. صورة من الطلب السابق والمستندات المرفقة به مصحوبة بشهادة تبين تاريخ ورقم ايداعه والدولة التي اودع فيها، اذا كان الطلب يتضمن الرغبة في اعتبار الاولوية في التسجيل لطلب سبق تقديمه في دولة تكون طرفاً في اتفاقية أو معاهدة دولية مع دولة الامارات العربية المتحدة وفقاً للمادة (١١) من القانون.

٥. سند الوكالة اذا اودع الطلب بواسطة وكيل.

٦. الشهادة الصادرة بالحماية المؤقتة ان وجدت.

٧. كتاب من مكتب مقاطعة اسرائيل بعدم حظر التعامل مع الطالب.

ويجب ان تكون المستندات المشار إليها في البنود ٢ و٣ و٤ و٥ مصدقاً عليها حسب الاصول.

ويجب ان تكون جميع المستندات مصحوبة بترجمة إلى اللغة العربية اذا كانت محررة باللغة الانجليزية أو بترجمة إلى اللغتين العربية والانجليزية إذا كانت محررة بلغة اخرى.

ويتعين ان يرفق المستند المشار إليه في البند (١) بالطلب عند تقديمه ويجب أن يراعى فيه الشروط المبينة في المادة التالية.

اما المستندات الأخرى فيجوز – في حالة عدم ارفاقها بالطلب – ان يقدم الطالب تعهداً كتابياً على النموذج رقم (٦) بتقديم ما يلزم تقديمه منها حسب الاحوال خلال تسعين يوماً من تاريخ تقديم الطلب، واذا لم يقدمها خلال هذه المهلة يعتبر الطلب كأن لم يكن، وذلك باستثناء المستند المشار إليه في البند (٤) فانه يترتب على عدم تقديمه – عند لزومه – خلال هذه المهلة سقوط حق الطالب في المطالبة بالأولوية، ويتم التأشير في سجل الطلبات باعتبار الطلب كأن لم يكن أو سقوط حق الطالب في المطالبة بالأولوية – على حسب الاحوال – بناءً على قرار من مدير الإدارة.

المادة (٤٧)

١. لا يجوز ان يشتمل للرسم أو النموذج الصناعي على كلمات أو حروف أو أرقام إلا إذا كانت من العناصر الجوهرية للرسم أو النموذج الصناعي.

٢. يجوز أن تكون نسخ الرسم أو النموذج الصناعي صوراً تخطيطية أو رسوماً، أو رسوماً استشفافية على ألا يتجاوز مقاس أي منها (١٠سم × ٢٠سم).

٣. يجب وضع كل من لصور التخطيطية أو الرسوم، أو الرسوم الاستشفافية في وضع رأسي على ورقة من الورق المقوى مقاس (A4).

٤. يجوز أن تكون الصور التخطيطية بالألوان، أما الرسوم، والرسوم الاستشفافية فيجب ان تكون بالحبر الأسود.

٥. إذا كان الرسم أو النموذج مكون من أكثر من ورقة فيجب ترقيم الأوراق في وسط أعلى الورقة بأرقام عربية متتالية، والاشارة فيها إلى ما إذا كانت تمثل منظراً كاملاً أو أمامياً أو غير ذلك.

المادة (٤٨)

تفحص الادارة الطلب ومرفقاته – وفقاً لنظام الفحص المشار إليه في المادتين (٩٢) و(٩٣) من هذه اللائحة لتحقق مما يأتي:

١. ان الطلب مقدم من شخص طبيعي أو معنوي يتمتع بجنسية الدولة، أو أجنبي يحق له التقدم بالطلب وفقاً لاحكام أية اتفاقية أو معاهدة دولية تكون الدولة طرفاً فيها، أو يحمل جنسية دولة تعامل الدولة معاملة المثل وفقاً للمادة (٢) من القانون.

٢. ان الطلب مقدم من صاحب الحق في الرسم أو النموذج الصناعي.

٣. ان الطلب قدم مستوفيً للشروط والاجراءات المنصوص عليها في المواد من (٤٥) إلى (٤٧) من هذه اللائحة.

٤. ان الرسم أو النموذج الصناعي جديد أو مبتكر، ويمكن استخدامه كمنتج صناعي أو حرفي، ولا يخل بالنظام انعام أو الآداب في الدولة طبقاً للمادة (٤٦) من القانون، ويقصد بكون الرسم أو النموذج الصناعي جديداً أو مبتكراً انه لم يتحقق الكشف عنه للجمهور في أي زمان أو مكان بأي طريقة من طرق النشر أو الاستعمال أو بأية وسيلة اخرى من الوسائل التي يتحقق بها العلم بالرسم أو النموذج الصناعي، وذلك قبل تاريخ تقديم الطلب أو تاريخ الأولوية لمطالب بها، أو قبل تاريخ بدء الحماية المؤقتة بشرط ان يكون الطلب قد قدم خلال ستة أشهر من تاريخ بدئها.

٥. ان الأولوية المطالب بها تتفق مع أحكام الاتفاقية أو المعاهدة الدولية التي تربط دولة الامارات العربية المتحدة مع الدولة التي قدم فيها الطلب السابق.

المادة (٤٩)

تسري على الرسومات والنماذج الصناعية احكام المواد (١٣ و١٤ و١٥ و٢١ و٢٢ و٢٣ و٢٤ و٢/٢٥ و٢٦ و٢٧ و٢٨ و٢٩ و٣٠ و١/٣٣ و٣٤ و٣٥ و٣٦ و٣٧) من هذه اللائحة وذلك مع مراعاة التعديلات الآتية:

١. تعديل النموذج رقم (٧) والنموذج رقم (٨) إلى النموذج رقم (١٠) والنموذج رقم (١١) على التوالي.

٢. تعديل كلمة "اختراع" إلى عبارة "الرسومات أو النماذج الصناعية".

٣. تعديل عبارة "طلبات البراءات وشهادات المنفعة" إلى عبارة "طلبات شهادات تسجيل الرسومات والنماذج الصناعية".

٤. تعديل كلمة "المخترع" إلى كلمة "المبتكر".

٥. حذف البيان الوارد في البند (ل) من المادة (٤/٢٤) من هذه اللائحة.

٦. تعديل عبارة "البراءة أو شهادة المنفعة" إلى عبارة "شهادة تسجيل الرسم أو النموذج الصناعي".

٧. تعديل عبارة "سجلين احدهما لبراءات الاختراع والآخر لشهادات المنفعة" الواردة في المادة (٥/٢٤) إلى عبارة "سجلين احدهما لشهادات تسجيل الرسومات والآخر لشهادات تسجيل النماذج الصناعية".

الباب الرابع
التراخيص التعاقدية

المادة (٥٠)

١. تسري على عقود الترخيص في استعمال أو استغلال الحق موضوع الحماية وأي تعديل أو تجديد لها احكام المواد (٤١ و٤٢ و٤٣ و٤٤) من هذه اللائحة مع مراعاة التعديلات الآتية:

أ) تعديل كلمة "الدراية العملية" إلى كلمة "الترخيص".

ب) تعديل عبارتي "الطرف المالك للدراية العملية" و"الطرف المتلقي للدراية العملية" إلى "المرخص" و"المرخص له" على التوالي.

ج) حذف الحالة الواردة في نص الفقرة (١) من المادة (٤٣) من هذه اللائحة.

د) تعديل الحالة المنصوص عليها في الفقرة (٢) من المادة (٤٣) من هذه اللائحة إلى ما يأتي:

"إذا كانت مدة العقد وتجديداته تزيد عن مدة الحماية المقررة في سند الحماية للحق موضوع العقد".

هـ) تعديل الحالة المنصوص عليها في الفقرة (٣) من المادة (٤٣) من هذه اللائحة إلى ما يأتي:

"إذا كان العقد يخول للمرخص له حقوقاً لا يخولها سند الحماية للمرخص".

٢. يجب بعد قيد عقد الترخيص في سجل عقود الترخيص ان يتم التأشير به في السجل الخاص بالحق موضوع الحماية، كما يجب التأشير في هذا السجل ايضاً بكل تعديل أو تجديد للقيد يتم التأشير به في سجل عقود الترخيص.

٣. ينشر عن عقد الترخيص وعن أي تعديل أو تجديد له في الجريدة الرسمية بناءً على طلب صاحب الشأن بعد سداد رسم النشر المقرر.

المادة (٥١)

تسري على عقد التنازل أو نقل ملكية موضوع الحماية احكام المادتين (٤٢) و(٤٣) من هذه اللائحة مع مراعاة التعديلات المشار إليها في الفقرة (١) من المادة السابقة وتغيير لفظ "الترخيص" إلى "التنازل" ولفظ "المرخص" إلى "المتنازل" ولفظ "المرخص له" إلى "المتنازل له".

الباب الخامس
الاجراءات التحفظية والجرائم والجزاءات

المادة (٥٢)

للادارة اتخاذ الاجراءات اللازمة لإلغاء سند الحماية أو إلغاء اي قيود أو تأشيرات في سجلاتها اذا ثبت بموجب حكم جزائي نهائي تزوير أي من المستندات التي صدر بناءً عليها سند الحماية أو تم بناءً عليها القيد أو التأشير في السجلات.

الباب السادس
ادارة الملكية الصناعية والاحكام الختامية

الفصل الأول
الاختصاصات وتدرجها والتفويض فيها

المادة (٥٣)

تصدر قرارات بمنح سندات الحماية من الوزير، وله ان يفوض رئيس الادارة في اصدار كل او بعض هذه القرارات.

المادة (٥٤)

يختص رئيس الادارة بما يأتي:

١. ما يفوضه الوزير فيه وفقاً للمادة (٥٣) من هذه اللائحة، ولا يجوز لرئيس الادارة ان يفوض غيره فيه.

٢. الاتصال بالمنظمات والاتحادات الإقليمية والعالمية المتخصصة في مجال الملكية الصناعية ومتابعة المؤتمرات المتعلقة بهذا المجال، وذلك بهدف تطوير وتحديث الادارة وانشطتها ونظمها لمسايرة التطور العالمي.

٣. الاشراف على حصر الاتفاقيات والمعاهدات المتعلقة بحماية الملكية الصناعية التي تربط الدولة بغيرها من الدول، وحصر الدول التي تعامل الدولة معاملة المثل في هذا المجال، وإعداد بيان شامل بهذه الاتفاقيات والمعاهدات وتلك الدول وتوزيعه على المختصين بالفحص في الادارة.

٤. دراسة الاتفاقات والمعاهدات الدولية المتعلقة بحماية الملكية الصناعية واقتراح انضمام الدولة إلى المناسب منها.

٥. دراسة وادارة للمفاوضات بشأن الاتفاقيات والمعاهدات المقترح ابرامها بين الدولة وغيرها من الدول في مجال الملكية الصناعية.

٦. اعتماد برنامج تدريب العاملين بالادارة والموافقة على التحاق أو تسمية من يرشح منهم بالدورات التدريبية وحضور المؤتمرات والندوات التي تعقد داخل أو خارج الدولة بشأن حماية الملكية الصناعية.

٧. الموافقة على الاستعانة بمن يلزم من الخبراء وتحديد مدد عملهم ومكافآتهم.

٨. قبول طلبات الحماية بعد التحقق من توافر الشروط الفنية والقانونية واتخاذ اللازم لاصدار القرارات الوزارية بشأنها.

٩. اعتماد القرارات التي تصدر وفقاً لنص المواد (٤٣) و(٥٠) و(٥١) من هذه اللائحة بشأن عقود الدراية العملية والتراخيص التعاقدية وعقود التنازل أو نقل ملكية موضوع الحماية وأي تعديل أو تجديد لها.

١٠. رئاسة لجنة القيد المختصة باصدار القرارات المتعلقة بقبول أو رفض تسجيل وكلاء التسجيل لدى الادارة وغير ذلك من القرارات المتعلقة بهم.

١١. اصدار القرارات المتعلقة باصدار النشرات المشار إليها في المادة (٩٠) من هذه اللائحة، وتحديد رسوم الاشتراك بها، واعتماد انظمة التبادل بشأنها.

ويجوز لرئيس الإدارة تفويض مدير الادارة أو أي من رؤساء الاقسام بالادارة في بعض اختصاصاته، كما يجوز له تشكيل لجان فنية لدراسة أي موضوع من الموضوعات الداخلة في اختصاصه ورفع تقرير له بشأنها.

المادة (٥٥)

يختص مدير الادارة بما يلي:

١. ما يفوضه فيه رئيس الادارة من اعمال، ولا يجوز لمدير الادارة تفويض غيره فيه.

٢. اصدار القرارات المتعقة بما يأتي:

أ) رفض طلبات الحماية التي لا تتوافر فيها الشروط الفنية والقانونية.
ب) تجديد مدد الحماية.
ج) اصدار شهادات الحماية المؤقتة.
د) جميع القرارات المتعلقة بالامور الاخرى المنصوص عليها في القانون وهذه اللائحة والتي لم يرد النص عليها في هذه المادة والمادتين (٥٣) و(٥٤) من هذه اللائحة.

ويجوز لمدير الادارة ان يفوض رؤساء الاقسام في بعض اختصاصاته وفقاً لما يقتضيه صالح العمل بالادارة وطبيعة عمل كل قسم من هذه الاقسام حسبما يحدده نظام العمل في الادارة الذي يصدر من الوزير وفقاً لنص المادة (٦٢) من القانون.

المادة (٥٦)

يختص رؤساء الاقسام بالامور التي يفوضهم فيها مدير الادارة أو التي يتضمنها نظام العمل في الادارة المشار إليه في المادة (٥٥) من هذه اللائحة.

الفصل الثاني
مهنة وكلاء التسجيل

المادة (٥٧)

لا يجوز ان يزاول مهنة وكلاء التسجيل إلا من كان اسمه مقيداً في جدول وكلاء التسجيل لدى الادارة.

المادة (٥٨)

١. يشترط للقيد في جدول وكلاء التسجيل لدى الادارة المشار إليه في المادة (٢/٦٧) من هذه اللائحة ان يكون الطالب:

أ) من مواطني الدولة أو متمتعاً بجنسية احدى الدول العربية.
ب) كامل الأهلية المدنية.
ج) محمود السيرة وحسن السمعة.
د) ألا يكون قد سبق الحكم عليه بعقوبة جنائية في جريمة مخلة بالشرف أو الأمانة ما لم يكن قد رد إليه اعتباره أو صدر عفو عنه.
هـ) حاصلاً على مؤهل جامعي أو عال.

٢. يجوز ان يقيد في جدول وكلاء التسجيل لدى الادارة الشركات المتخصصة في مجال حماية الملكية الصناعية التي يكون مركزها الرئيسي الدولة او يكون لها فرع أو مكتب مسجل في الدولة.

المادة (٥٩)

١. تقدم طلبات القيد مع المستندات المثبتة لتوافر الشروط المنصوص عليها في الفقرة (١) أو الفقرة (٢) من المادة (٥٨) من هذه اللائحة على حسب الاحوال على لجنة تسمى لجنة القيد وتشكل من رئيس الادارة ومدير الادارة ورئيس القسم القانوني بالادارة.

٢. يجب على أمين سر لجنة القيد تدوين طلبات القيد بأرقام متتابعة حسب تاريخ تقديمها في السجل المشار إليه في المادة (١/٦٧) من هذه اللائحة وتسليم الطالب ايصالاً يتضمن الرقم المتتابع للطلب، وتاريخ تقديمه، وبيان المستندات المرفقة به.

المادة (٦٠)

تفحص لجنة القيد طلبات القيد والمستندات المرفقة بها، ولها ان تكلف الطالب بتقديم ما تراه من استيفاءات أو ايضاحات قبل اصدار قرارها.

وتقرر لجنة القيد – بعد تحققها من توافر الشروط في الطالب – قيد اسمه في جدول وكلاء التسجيل ويكون القيد لمدة سنة قابلة للتجديد.

ويتم القيد في الجدول بأرقام متتابعة – بعد سداد رسم القيد – وفقاً لتاريخ سداد الرسم، ويتم التأشير بالتجديد بعد سداد رسم التجديد.

اما إذا رأت لجنة القيد عدم توافر الشروط في الطالب فتقرر رفض الطلب ويجب ان يكون هذا القرار مسبباً.

وعلى لجنة القيد ان تفصل في طلبات القيد خلال مدة لا تزيد على ثلاثة اشهر من تاريخ تقديم الطلب، وان تخطر الطالب بقرارها فور صدوره بكتاب مسجل مصحوب بعلم الوصول.

ولمن رفض طلبه ان يتظلّم من قرار الرفض امام لجنة التظلمات خلال ستين يوماً من تاريخ تسلمه الاخطار بهذا القرار.

المادة (٦١)

تقوم الادارة بنشر بيان سوي باسماء المزاولين لمهنة وكلاء التسجيل لديها المقيد اسماؤهم في الجدول.

المادة (٦٢)

لا يجوز لطالبي الحماية أو أصحاب سندات الحماية ان يوكلوا عنهم امام الادارة إلا أحد وكلاء التسجيل المقيدين في الجدول.

المادة (٦٣)

يجب على كل من يقيد اسمه في جدول وكلاء التسجيل لدى الادارة ما يأتي:

١. ان يخطر الادارة بكتاب مسجل بعنوان مكتبه خلال ثلاثين يوماً من تاريخ قيده في الجدول وبكل تغيير في هذا العنوان خلال ثلاثين يوماً من تاريخ التغيير.

٢. ان يقرن اسمه برقم قيده بالجدول في جميع المكاتبات والاوراق الصادرة عنه.

٣. ان يؤدي عمله وفقاً لاصول المهنة واحكام القانون وهذه اللائحة.

المادة (٦٤)

للجنة القيد من تلقاء نفسها أو بناءً على شكوى تقدم إليها ان تجري تحقيقاً مع من قيد اسمه في جدول وكلاء التسجيل إذا نسب إليه مخالفة احكام القانون أو هذا اللائحة أو اصول المهنة، أو فقد شرطاً من الشروط الواجب توافرها للقيد، أو انه كان فاقداً لأي منها عند القيد.

فإذا اسفر التحقيق عن ثبوت الواقعة المنسوبة للمقيد اسمه في الجدول تصدر لجنة القيد قراراً بإلغاء قيده وتخطره بهذا القرار فور صدوره بكتاب مسجل مصحوب بعلم الوصول.

ويجوز لمن صدر قرار بإلغاء قيد اسمه من الجدول، التظلم من هذا القرار امام لجنة التظلمات خلال ستين يوماً من تاريخ تسلمه الاخطار بهذا القرار.

وإذا تبين للجنة القيد ان الواقعة المنسوبة للمقيد اسمه في الجدول تكون جريمة جنائية فعليها احالة الاوراق إلى النيابة العامة.

المادة (٦٥)

يشطب من الجدول اسم من توفى او الغي قيده او من طلب شطب اسمه وذلك بناءً على قرار يصدر من لجنة القيد.

المادة (٦٦)

١. على أمين سر لجنة القيد ان يؤشر في سجل طلبات القيد بقرار رفض أو قبول الطلب وتاريخ صدوره وتاريخ اخطار الطالب به.

٢. على أمين سر لجنة القيد ان يؤشر في جدول وكلاء التسجيل بالقرارات الصادرة بإلغاء أو شطب القيد وتاريخ صدورها.

المادة (٦٧)

١. تعد الادارة سجلاً لطلبات قيد وكلاء التسجيل، ويجب ان يشتمل هذا السجل على البيانات الآتية:

أ) الرقم المتتابع للطلب.
ب) تاريخ تقديم الطلب.
ج) اسم الطالب وجنسيته ومؤهلاته ومحل اقامته وعنوانه، وإذا كان الطالب شركة يذكر اسمها ونوعها وغرضها ومحل مركزها الرئيسي وعنوان فرعها أو مكتبها المسجل في الدولة.

د) القرار الصادر في الطلب وتاريخ صدوره وتاريخ الاخطار به.

هـ) رقم وتاريخ القيد في جدول وكلاء التسجيل.

٢. تعد الادارة جدولاً لقيد وكلاء التسجيل، ويجب ان يشتمل هذا الجدول على البيانات الآتية:

أ) رقم وتاريخ القيد

ب) رقم وتاريخ ايصال سداد رسم القيد.

ب) رقم وتاريخ ايصال سداد رسم التجديد

د) تاريخ قرار الغاء أو شطب القيد.

الفصل الثالث
لجنة التظلمات

المادة (٦٨)

١. تقدم تظلمات ذوي الشأن من القرارات الصادرة في مجال تطبيق القانون وهذه اللائحة إلى لجنة التظلمات المشار إليها في المادة (٦٤) من القانون بعريضة من اصل وعدد من الصور بقدر عدد المتظلم ضدهم، ويسلم الاصل والصور إلى أمين سر اللجنة.

٢. يجب ان تشتمل عريضة التظلم على البيانات الآتية:

أ) اسم المتظلم ومهنته ومحل اقامته ورقم وتاريخ ومصدر اثبات شخصيته ان كان شخصاً طبيعياً، أو اسمه وغرضه ورقم مركزه ورقم وتاريخ ومصدر تسجيله ان كان شخصاً معنوياً، وتعيين محل مختار له في الدولة ان لم يكن له محل اقامة او مقر فيها.

ب) البيانات الواردة في الفقرة السابقة لوكيل المتظلم – ان وجد – بالاضافة إلى رقم وتاريخ ومصدر التوكيل.

ج) اسم المتظلم ضده ومهنته ومحل اقامته ان كان شخصاً طبيعياً او اسمه وغرضه ومقر مركزه ان كان شخصاً معنوياً.

د) عنوان المتظلم، ووكيله ان وجد، والمتظلم ضده، على ان يشتمل عنوان كل منهم على جميع الوسائل التي يمكن مخاطبته بها أو مراسلته عليها بما في ذلك صندوق البريد ورقم الهاتف والتلكس والفاكس على حسب الاحوال.

هـ) بيان موضوع التظلم وطلبات المتظلم.

و) بيان الأدلة التي يستند إليها المتظلم.

ز) بيان المستندات المرفقة بعريضة التظلم.

ح) توقيع المتظلم أو وكيله.

المادة (٦٩)

١. على امين سر اللجنة ان يقيد التظلمات بأرقام متتابعة سنوياً – بعد سداد الرسوم المقررة – في السجل المشار إليه في الفقرة التالية – وان يسلم للمتظلم او وكيله ايصالاً يتضمن رقم وتاريخ قيد المتظلم وبيان المستندات المرفقة به ان وجدت.

٢. يمسك امين سر اللجنة سجلاً لقيد التظلمات، ويجب ان يشتمل هذا السجل على البيانات الآتية:

أ) رقم وتاريخ قيد التظلم.

ب) رقم وتاريخ ايصال سداد رسم التظلم.

ج) البيانات الواردة في عريضة التظلم والمشار إليها في الفقرة (٢) من المادة (٦٨) من هذه اللائحة عدا توقيع المتظلم أو وكيله.

د) رقم وتاريخ اخطار المتظلم ضده بالتظلم.

هـ) تاريخ ورود رد المتظلم ضده على التظلم.

و) رقم وتاريخ اخطار المتظلم برد المتظلم ضده.

ز) تاريخ اول جلسة حددت لنظر التظلم وتاريخ اخطار الطرفين بها.

ح) تاريخ القرار الصادر في موضوع التظلم.

ط) رقم وتاريخ اخطار الخصوم بالقرار الصادر في موضوع التظلم.

٣. يعتبر التظلم مقدماً للجنة ومنتجاً لآثاره من تاريخ قيده.

المادة (٧٠)

١. على امين سر اللجنة ان يخطر المتظلم ضده بصورة من عريضة التظلم ومن المستندات المرفقة بها بالبريد المسجل خلال اسبوع من تاريخ قيد التظلم.

٢. للمتظلم ضده ان يرد على التظلم خلال شهر من تاريخ استلامه الاخطار المشار إليه في الفقرة السابقة، ويجب ان يكون الرد بمذكرة مكتوبة من اصل وعدد من الصور بقدر عدد الخصوم.

٣. يرسل امين سر اللجنة صورة من رد المتظلم ضده إلى المتظلم بالبريد المسجل خلال اسبوع من تاريخ تسلمه الرد.

المادة (٧١)

على امين سر اللجنة ان يقوم خلال اسبوع من تاريخ انتهاء المواعيد المبينة في المادة (٧٠) من هذه اللائحة بعرض ملف التظلم كاملاً على رئيس اللجنة لتحديد جلسة لنظر التظلم.

المادة (٧٢)

على امين سر اللجنة ان يخطر المتظلم والمتظلم ضده بموعد الجلسة المحددة لنظر التظلم بالبريد المسجل قبل موعد الجلسة بعشرة ايام على الاقل.

المادة (٧٣)

للخصوم ان يحضروا بانفسهم أو بواسطة من يمثلونهم قانوناً في الجلسة المحددة لنظر التظلم.

المادة (٧٤)

تصدر اللجنة قرارها في التظلم بعد التحقق من صحة اخطار من لم يحضر من الخصوم، وبعد سماع اقوال من يحضر منهم، ولها ان تؤجل نظر التظلم إلى جلسة اخرى إذا رأت مبرراً لذلك.

المادة (٧٥)

اذا قررت اللجنة ندب خبير وجب ان يتضمن قرارها ما يأتي:

١. بياناً دقيقاً لمأمورية الخبير.

٢. تحديد من يتحمل من الخصوم نفقات الخبرة وطريقة وموعد دفعها.

٣. الاجل المضروب لإيداع تقرير الخبير.

٤. تاريخ الجلسة التي تعين لمناقشة تقرير الخبير.

المادة (٧٦)

للجنة ان تستعين بمترجم من اية جهة اذا رأت ضرورة لذلك.

المادة (٧٧)

اذا رأت اللجنة ان قرارها في موضوع التظلم يتوقف على الفصل في مسألة أخرى تخرج عن ولايتها امرت بوقف الخصومة إلى أن يتم الفصل في هذه المسألة من جهة الاختصاص، وبمجرد زوال سبب الوقف يكون لأي من الخصوم طلب الاستمرار في الخصومة خلال الثلاثين يوماً التالية لزوال سبب الوقف وإلا اعتبرت الخصومة كأن لم تكن.

المادة (٧٨)

ينقطع سير الخصومة حكماً بوفاة احد الخصوم أو بفقده أهلية الخصومة أو بزوال صفة من كان يباشر الخصومة عنه من النائبين عدا الوكيل بالخصومة إلا إذا كان الخصوم قد ابدوا اقوالهم وطلباتهم الختامية.

وتستأنف الخصومة سيرها إذا حضر من يحل محل الخصم الذي انقطعت الخصومة بسببه في الموعد الذي حدد سابقاً.

كما تستأنف الخصومة سيرها بناءً على طلب يقدم من أي من اصحاب الشأن يتم ابلاغه للاطراف الاخرين أو من يقوم مقامهم بالبريد المسجل المصحوب بعلم الوصول.

المادة (٧٩)

يتولى رئيس اللجنة ادارة الجلسات، ويتولى امين سر اللجنة تحرير محاضر الجلسات، ويجب توقيع هذه المحاضر من رئيس اللجنة وأمين سرها.

المادة (٨٠)

تكون المداولة في القرارات سرية بين رئيس اللجنة واعضائها مجتمعين.

المادة (٨١)

تصدر اللجنة قراراتها باجماع الاراء أو بأغلبيتها، وفي كل الاحوال تكون القرارات مسببة وموقعة من رئيس اللجنة واعضائها.

المادة (٨٢)

على امين سر اللجنة ان يخطر الخصوم بصورة من قرار اللجنة واسبابه بالبريد المسجل خلال عشرة ايام من تاريخ صدوره.

المادة (٨٣)

في جميع الاحوال يقوم التسليم للشخص نفسه أو وكيله بموجب ايصال استلام موقع منه مقام ارسال الاخطار له بالبريد المسجل.

المادة (٨٤)

تتولى اللجنة تصحيح ما يقع في القرارات من اخطاء مادية، كتابية او حسابية، بقرار تصدره من تلقاء نفسها، او بناءً على طلب احد الخصوم، ويدون التصحيح على نسخة القرار الاصلية ويوقع عليه من الرئيس والاعضاء.

المادة (٨٥)

يجوز للخصوم ان يطلبوا من اللجنة تفسير ما وقع في منطوق قرارها من غموض، وتعد قرارات التفسير متممة للقرار الذي تفسره.

المادة (٨٦)

١. يتقاضى رئيس اللجنة مكافأة قدرها ----- درهم عن كل جلسة يتم انعقادها.

٢. يتقاضى كل عضو من اعضاء اللجنة مكافأة وقدرها ----- درهم عن كل جلسة يتم انعقادها.

المادة (٨٧)

١. يمسك امين سر اللجنة سجلاً للجلسات يدون فيه اولاً بأول التظلمات المعروضة على اللجنة في كل جلسة والقرارات الصادرة فيها، وتاريخ الجلسة السابقة التي نظر فيها كل تظلم وتاريخ الجلسة اللاحقة التي يؤجل اليها نظر اي تظلم.

٢. على امين سر اللجنة ان يؤشر في سجل قيد التظلمات بالقرارات الصادرة في التظلم وتاريخ صدورها.

الفصل الرابع
النماذج والسجلات والنشرات والمستخرجات

المادة (٨٨)

١. النماذج المشار إليها في هذه اللائحة هي النماذج المحددة في الجدول الثاني المرفق.

٢. مع عدم الاخلال بالنماذج المشار إليها في الفقرة السابقة، يجوز للادارة بقرار من رئيسها اصدار نماذج اخرى وتعديلها وفقاً لما تراه مناسباً لحسن سير العمل وتطوره.

المادة (٨٩)

١. مع مراعاة نص المادة (٦٩/٢) من هذه اللائحة يجب على الادارة القيام باعداد وامساك السجلات المشار إليها في هذه اللائحة مع مراعاة ان يشتمل كل سجل منها على البيانات المشار إليها في هذه اللائحة، ويجوز للادارة بقرار من رئيسها اضافة بيانات اخرى إلى هذه السجلات أو اعداد سجلات اضافية وفقاً لما تراه مناسباً لحسن سير العمل وتطوره.

٢. يجوز لكل ذي شأن ان يطلب من الادارة تصحيح اي خطأ مادي يقع في السجل الخاص بالحق موضوع الحماية، كما يجوز له ان يطلب تدوين اي تغيير يحصل في اسم

المالك او جنسيته او عنوانه او محله المختار او اسم الوكيل او عنوانه في ذلك السجل، ويجب على الطالب سداد رسم التصحيح أو التعديل المقرر عند تقديم الطلب.

المادة (٩٠)

١. للادارة بقرار من رئيسها ان تصدر نشرات دورية شهرية او ربع سنوية او سنوية – باللغة العربية او باللغتين العربية والانجليزية بأرقام مسلسلة وفقاً لتاريخ اصدارها – تنشر فيها كل ما ترى لزوماً لنشره من اخبار وبيانات وقرارات وتحاليل وابحاث تتعلق بسندات الحماية أو طلباتها أو بالقانون وهذه اللائحة أو بوكلاء التسجيل أو بنظام العمل في الادارة.

٢. للادارة الاحتفاظ باعداد من النشرات المشار إليها في الفقرة السابقة وذلك للرجوع إليها عند الحاجة، ولها تزويد الجهات الحكومية بأعداد مجانية منها، ويجوز الاشتراك في هذه النشرات بعد سداد مقابل الاشتراك الذي يحدده رئيس الادارة أو طبقاً لنظام التبادل سواء داخل الدولة أو خارجها.

المادة (٩١)

يجوز الاطلاع بدون مقابل على البراءات أو شهادات المنفعة أو شهادات تسجيل الرسوم أوالنماذج الصناعية المسجلة لدى الادارة وأية بيانات متعلقة بها، بحضور الموظف المسؤول بالادارة، ويحق لأي شخص بعد دفع الرسوم المقررة ان يحصل على صور منها أو من البيانات المتعلقة بها أو على شهادات بمضمونها او مستخرجات من السجل الخاص بها.

الفصل الخامس
نظام الفحص

المادة (٩٢)

تقوم الادارة بفحص الطلبات المقيدة لديها من الناحية الشكلية، وإذا تبين من الفحص عدم استيفاء بعض الشروط المقررة في القانون أو هذه اللائحة فلها ان توجه اخطاراً بالبريد المسجل إلى الطالب تكلفه فيه باجراء اللازم لاستيفاء الطلب خلال تسعين يوماً على الاكثر من تاريخ استلامه الاخطار المذكور، وإذا لم يتم تنفيذ ما طلب منه خلال تلك الفترة اعتبر طلبه كأن لم يكن، ويتم التأشير بذلك في السجل المقيد به الطلب بناءً على قرار من مدير الادارة.

المادة (٩٣)

إذا تبين ان الطلب مستوف من الناحية الشكلية، تقوم الادارة بتقدير النفقات اللازمة للفحص الموضوعي للطلب بناءً على دراسة تقديرية لهذه النفقات، ثم توجه اخطاراً بالبريد المسجل إلى الطالب تكلفه فيه بسداد هذه النفقات خلال تسعين يوماً من تاريخ

تسلمه هذا الاخطار، فإن سددها الطالب خلال تلك المهلة يحال الطلب للفحص الموضوعي، اما إذا لم يسددها خلال تلك المهلة فيعتبر الطلب كأن لم يكن، ويتم التأشير بذلك في السجل المقيد به الطلب بناءً على قرار من مدير الادارة.

الفصل السادس
الرسوم

المادة (٩٤)

الرسوم المشار إليها بالقانون وهذه اللائحة هي الرسوم المحددة بالجدول الأول المرفق.

المادة (٩٥)

ينشر هذا القرار في الجريدة الرسمية، ويعمل به من تاريخ نشره.

رئيس مجلس الوزراء

صدر عنا في أبو ظبي
بتاريخ: ٢٠ ذي القعدة ١٤١٣هـ.
الموافق: ١٢ مايو ١٩٩٣ م.

الجدول الأول

الرسوم

مقدار الرسم بالدرهم		نوع الرسم
الاشخاص الاعتبارية	الأشخاص الطبيعيون	
٨٠٠	٤٠٠	١- رسم طلب سند الحماية
٢٠٠	١٠٠	٢- رسم طلب تصحيح أو تعديل بيانات
٤٠٠	٢٠٠	٣- رسم طلب تجديد مدة الحماية
٤٠٠	٢٠٠	٤- رسم طلب قيد تنازل عن سند الحماية
٤٠٠	٢٠٠	٥- رسم طلب قيد عقد دراية عملية أو عقد ترخيص
٢٠٠	١٠٠	٦- رسم طلب تعديل أو تجديد عقد دراية عملية أو عقد ترخيص
٨٠٠	٤٠٠	٧- رسم قيد في جدول وكلاء التسجيل
٤٠٠	٢٠٠	٨- رسم تجديد قيد في جدول وكلاء التسجيل
٢٠٠	١٠٠	٩- رسم تظلم امام لجنة التظلمات
١٠٠	٥٠	١٠- رسم الحصول على صورة من اي سند من سندات الحماية او اية اوراق اخرى متعلقة به او شهادة بمضمون اي منها او مستخرج من السجل الخاص به
٤٠٠	٢٠٠	١١- رسم النشر عن اي قرار او حكم او عقد او اجراء وجب القانون او هذه اللائحة سداده قبل النشر
		١٢- الرسم السنوي المتصاعد عن سندات الحماية وطلباتها اعتباراً من السنة الثانية (التالية لتاريخ تقديم الطلب) وحتى انتهاء مدة الحماية
٨٠٠	٤٠٠	– عن السنة الثانية
٨٤٠	٤٢٠	– عن السنة الثالثة
٨٨٠	٤٤٠	– عن السنة الرابعة
٩٢٠	٤٦٠	– عن السنة الخامسة
٩٦٠	٤٨٠	– عن السنة السادسة
١٠٠٠	٥٠٠	– عن السنة السابعة

١٠٤٠	٥٢٠	– عن السنة الثامنة
١٠٨٠	٥٤٠	– عن السنة التاسعة
١١٢٠	٥٦٠	– عن السنة العاشرة
١١٦٠	٥٨٠	– عن السنة الحادية عشر
١٢٠٠	٦٠٠	– عن السنة الثانية عشر
١٢٤٠	٦٢٠	– عن السنة الثالثة عشر
١٢٨٠	٦٤٠	– عن السنة الرابعة عشر
١٣٢٠	٦٦٠	– عن السنة الخامسة عشر
١٣٦٠	٦٨٠	– عن السنة السادسة عشر
١٤٠٠	٧٠٠	– عن السنة السابعة عشر
١٤٤٠	٧٢٠	– عن السنة الثامنة عشر
١٤٨٠	٧٤٠	– عن السنة التاسعة عشر
١٥٢٠	٧٦٠	– عن السنة العشرين
٢٠٠	١٠٠	١٣– الرسم الاضافي في حالة قبول سداد الرسم السنوي المتصاعد خلال ثلاثين يوماً من انتهاء سنة السداد

الجدول الثاني
النماذج
نموذج رقم ١
طلب شهادة بالحماية المؤقتة للاختراع

للاستعمال الرسمي فقط	يلتمس الطالب من ادارة الملكية الصناعية منحه شهادة بالحماية المؤقتة للاختراع وفقاً للبيانات التالية
رقم الطلب: ـــــــــــــــــــــــ	
تاريخ وساعة تقديمه: ـــــــــــــــــــــــ	

١- اسم الاختراع: ـــ
ـــ

٢- اسم الطالب: ـــ

العنوان: ـــ
ـــ

المحل المختار في الدولة: ـــــــــــــــــــــــــــــــــ
ـــ

الجنسية: ـــ

محل الاقامة أو المركز الرئيسي للاعمال: ـــــــــــــــــ
ـــ
ـــ

رقم الهاتف: ـــــــــــــ رقم التلكس ـــــــــــــ رقم الفاكس ـــــــــــــ

عدد الطالبين ـــــــــــــ اذا كان الطالبون اكثر من واحد تذكر بيانات الباقين في ورقة تابعة

٣- اسم المخترع: ————— ----------------------

العنوان: ——— ----------------------------------

عدد المخترعين ————— اذا كان المخترعون اكثر من واحد يذكر بيانات الباقين في ورقة تابعة

٤- اسم الوكيل: —— --------------------------------

رقم الوكالة: ———— تاريخها ————— مصدرها —————

العنوان: ——— ----------------------------------

رقم الهاتف ————— رقم التلكس ————— رقم الفاكس —————

٥- المعرض وتاريخ افتتاحه: ——— ----------------------

٦- المرفقات:

- موجز عن وصف الاختراع ☐

- رسم الاختراع ان وجد ☐

- بيان بالمنتجات المتعلقة بالاختراع ☐

الوكيل   الطالب

٧– التوقيع: ————————   ————————————

التاريخ: ————————————

نموذج رقم ٢
طلب شهادة بالحماية المؤقتة للرسم أو النموذج الصناعي

للاستعمال الرسمي فقط	يلتمس الطالب من ادارة الملكية الصناعية منحه
رقم الطلب: ــــــــــــــــــ	للرسم □
تاريخ وساعة تقديمه: ــــــــــــــ	شهادة بالحماية المؤقتة
	للنموذج الصناعي □
	وفقاً للبيانات التالية:

١– اسم الرسم أو النموذج الصناعي: –––––––––––––––––––––––––––

٢– اسم الطالب: –––––––––––––––––––––––––––––

العنوان: ––– ––––––––––––––––––––––––
––––––––––––––––––––––––––––––––––

المحل المختار في الدولة: ––– ––––––––––––––––––––––––
––––––––––––––––––––––––––––––––––

الجنسية: ––– –––––––––––––––––––––––––

محل الاقامة أو المركز الرئيسي للاعمال: ––– ––––––––––––––––
––––––––––––––––––––––––––––––––––
––––––––––––––––––––––––––––––––––

رقم الهاتف: ––––––– رقم التلكس –––––––– رقم الفاكس ––––––––

عدد الطالبين ––––––––– اذا كان الطالبون اكثر من واحد تذكر بيانات الباقين في ورقة تابعة

٣- اسم المبتكر : ------------------------------

العنوان: ---------------------------------

عدد المبتكرين ----- اذا كان عدد المبتكرون اكثر من واحد يذكر بيانات الباقين
في ورقة تابعة

٤- اسم الوكيل: ------------------------------

رقم الوكالة: ------- تاريخها --------- مصدرها -------

العنوان: ---------------------------------

رقم الهاتف -------- رقم التلكس -------- رقم الفاكس --------

٥- المعرض وتاريخ افتتاحه: ------- ---------

٦- المرفقات:

- صورتان من الرسم أو النموذج

- بيان بالمنتجات المخصص لها

الوكيل

الطالب

٧- التوقيع: ------------ -------------

التاريخ: ------------ -------------

نموذج رقم ٣
شهادة بالحماية المؤقتة للاختراع

مدير ادارة الملكية الصناعية

بعد الاطلاع على المادة ٣ من القانون الاتحادي رقم ٤٤ لسنة ١٩٩٢م. في شأن تنظيم وحماية الملكية الصناعية لبراءات الاختراع والرسوم والنماذج الصناعية،

وعلى اللائحة التنفيذية للقانون المذكور،

وعلى الطلب رقم _____ بتاريخ _____ والمستندات المتعلقة به،

قرر

تمنح شهادة بالحماية المؤقتة برقم _____

للطالب _____

وعنوانه وجنسيته _____

عن اختراع باسم _____

بالنسبة للمنتجات التي تم عرضها وهي _____

_____

اسم المعرض _____

تاريخ افتتاح المعرض _____

وتكفل هذه الشهادة الحماية القانونية للاختراع المبين اعلاه لمدة ستة اشهر تبدأ من تاريخ افتتاح المعرض وتنتهي في _____

تحريراً في _____

مدير ادارة الملكية الصناعية

نموذج رقم ٤
شهادة بالحماية المؤقتة للرسم أو النموذج الصناعي

مدير ادارة الملكية الصناعية

بعد الاطلاع على المادة ٣ من القانون الاتحادي رقم ٤٤ لسنة ١٩٩٢م. في شأن تنظيم وحماية الملكية الصناعية لبراءات الاختراع والرسوم والنماذج الصناعية،

وعلى اللائحة التنفيذية للقانون المذكور،

وعلى الطلب رقم _____ بتاريخ _____ والمستندات المتعلقة به،

قرر

تمنح شهادة بالحماية المؤقتة برقم _____

للطالب _____

وعنوانه وجنسيته _____

عن رسم / نموذج صناعي باسم _____

بالنسبة للمنتجات التي تم عرضها وهي _____

_____

اسم المعرض _____

تاريخ افتتاح المعرض _____

وتكفل هذه الشهادة الحماية القانونية للرسم أو النموذج الصناعي المبين اعلاه لمدة ستة اشهر تبدأ من تاريخ افتتاح المعرض وتنتهي في _____

تحريراً في _____

مدير ادارة الملكية الصناعية

نموذج رقم ٥
طلب براءة أو شهادة منفعة

للاستعمال الرسمي فقط	يلتمس الطالب من ادارة الملكية الصناعية منحه
رقم الطلب: _____	[ ] براءة اختراع (اصلية [ ] اضافية [ ])
تاريخ وساعة تقديمه: _____	[ ] شهادة منفعة (اصلية [ ] اضافية [ ])
	وفقاً للبيانات التالية:

١- اسم الاختراع: –––––––––––––––––––––––––––––

٢- اسم الطالب: ––––––––––––––––––––––––––––

العنوان: ––––––––––––––––––––––––
–––––––––––––––––––––––––––––––––

المحل المختار في الدولة: ––––––––––––––––
–––––––––––––––––––––––––––––––––

الجنسية: ––––––––––––––––––––––

محل الاقامة أو المركز الرئيسي للاعمال: –––––––
–––––––––––––––––––––––––––––––––
–––––––––––––––––––––––––––––––––

رقم الهاتف: ––––––––– رقم التلكس ––––––– رقم الفاكس –––––––

عدد الطالبين ––––––––– اذا كان الطالبون اكثر من واحد تذكر بيانات الباقين في ورقة تابعة

٣– اسم المخترع: ————————————————————
————————————————————————

العنوان: ——————————————————————
————————————————————

عدد المخترعين ———— اذا كان المخترعون اكثر من واحد يذكر بيانات الباقين في ورقة تابعة

٤– اسم الوكيل: ——————————————————————
————————————————————

رقم الوكالة: ———————— تاريخها ————— مصدرها ————————

العنوان: ——————————————————————
————————————————————

رقم الهاتف ————— رقم التلكس ————— رقم الفاكس ————————

٥– المطالبة بالاولوية استناداً إلى طلب سابق:

اسم الدولة التي قدم إليها الطلب: ————————————————

رقم وتاريخ الطلب: ————————————————

إذا كانت الأولوية تستند إلى أكثر من طلب سابق تذكر بيانات باقي الطلبات في ورقة تابعة

٦– رقم وتاريخ شهادة الحماية المؤقتة إن وجدت ——————————————

٧– إذا كان الطلب عن براءة أو شهادة منفعة اضافية يذكر:

– رقم وتاريخ قيد طلب البراءة أو شهادة المنفعة الأصلية: ——————————

- رقم وتاريخ منح البراءة أو شهادة المنفعة الأصلية: ————— ——————————————

٨– نطاق الحماية (العناصر الجديدة المطلوب حمايتها): ——— ——————————————
————————————————————————————————
————————————————————————————————
(إذا لم يكف هذا الاطار ——————————————————————
لتحديد نطاق الحماية يتم تحديد العناصر الباقية في ورقة تابعة)

الوكيل [   ]   الطالب [   ]

٩– التوقيع: ——————————   ————————————

التاريخ: ———   ————————————————

بيان
بمرفقات طلب براءة أو شهادة منفعة

طبقاً للائحة التنفيذية يرفق بطلب براءة الاختراع ما يأتي:

١. وصف تفصيلي للاختراع.

٢. الرسم الخاص بالاختراع إذا كان ضرورياً لإدراك الاختراع أو كان طابع الاختراع يسمح بذلك.

٣. ملخص للاختراع لا يزيد على ٢٠٠ كلمة مصحوباً بأفضل رسم توضيحي إن وجد.

٤. مستخرج من السجل التجاري أو مستخرج رسمي من عقد التأسيس إذا كان الطالب شركة أو هيئة.

٥. المستند الدال على أحقية الطالب في الاختراع إذا كان الطالب غير المخترع.

٦. موافقة صاحب الشأن إذا كانت العناصر الجوهرية للاختراع قد تم الحصول عليها من اختراع شخص اخر.

٧. سند الوكالة إذا اودع الطلب بواسطة وكيل.

٨. صورة من الطلب السابق والمستندات المرفقة به مصحوبة بشهادة تبين تاريخ ورقم ايداعه والدولة التي اودع فيها، إذا كان الطلب يتضمن الرغبة في اعتبار الأولوية في التسجيل لطلب سبق تقديمه في دولة تكون طرفاً في اتفاقية أو معاهدة دولية مع دولة الامارات العربية المتحدة وفقاً للمادة ١١ من القانون.

٩. الشهادة الصادرة بالحماية المؤقتة إن وجدت.

١٠. كتاب من مكتب مقاطعة اسرائيل بعدم حظر التعامل مع الطالب.

ويجب أن تكون المستندات المشار إليها في البنود ٤، ٥، ٦، ٧، ٨ مصدقاً عليها حسب الأصول.

ويجب ان تكون كافة المستندات مصحوبة بترجمة إلى اللغة العربية إذا كانت محررة باللغة الانجليزية أو بترجمة إلى اللغتين العربية والانجليزية إذا كانت محررة بلغة اخرى.

ويتعين ان ترفق المستندات المشار إليها في البنود ١، ٢، ٣ من اصل وصورة بالطلب عند تقديمه ويجب ان يراعى فيها وفي الطلب الشروط المادية المبينة في المواد من ٧ إلى ١٢ من اللائحة التنفيذية.

اما المستندات الاخرى فيجوز حال عدم ارفاقها بالطلب أن يقدم الطالب تعهداً كتابياً على النموذج رقم ٦ بتقديم ما يلزم تقديمه منها على حسب الاحوال خلال تسعين يوماً من تاريخ تقديم الطلب. وإذا لم يقدمها خلال هذه المهلة يعتبر الطلب كأن لم يكن، وذلك باستثناء المستند المشار ليه في البند ٨ فإنه يترتب على عدم تقديمه – عند لزومه – خلال هذه المهلة سقوط حق الطالب في المطالبة بالأولوية.

للاستعمال الرسمي

تمت المراجعة وسداد الرسم المقرر وقدره _____درهم
بموجب ايصال رقم _____ بتاريخ _____
اسم المستلم _____
التوقيع_____
التاريخ _____
الختم الرسمي _____

نموذج رقم ٦
تعهد بتقديم مستندات متعلقة بطلب

براءة ⬜ شهادة منفعة ⬜ رسم او نموذج صناعي ⬜

رقم الطلب:

تاريخ تقديم الطلب:

اسم الطالب:

اسم الوكيل:

اتعهد انا الموقع ادناه _____

بصفتي : _____

بأن اقدم لإدارة الملكية الصناعية المستندات المبينة ادناه خلال تسعين يوماً من تاريخ تقديم الطلب

_____

تحريراً في   /   /

التوقيع

_____

نموذج رقم ٧
ايصال استلام مستندات

شهادة منفعة [   ]   طلب براءة [   ]

رقم الطلب:

ساعة وتاريخ تقديم الطلب:

| سدد الرسم بايصال رقم: _____ |
| بتاريخ: _____ |

اسم الطالب وجنسيته:

بيان المستندات المستلمة مع الطلب:

١. الوصف التفصيلي للاختراع / عدد ———————— صفحة من نسختين. [   ]

٢. الرسم الخاص بالاختراع / عدد ———————— لوحة من نسختين. [   ]

٣. الوصف المختصر للاختراع / عدد —————— صفحة من نسختين. [   ]

٤. مستخرج من السجل التجاري أو مستخرج رسمي من عقد التأسيس
أو أداة الانشاء على حسب الاحوال إذا كان الطالب شخصاً اعتبارياً. [   ]

٥. المستند الدال على أحقية الطالب في الاختراع إذا كان الطالب
غير المخترع. [   ]

٦. موافقة صاحب الشأن إذا كانت العناصر الجوهرية للاختراع قد تم
الحصول عليها من اخترع شخص اخر. [   ]

٧. سند الوكالة إذا اودع الطلب بواسطة وكيل. [   ]

٨. صورة من الطلب السابق والمستندات المرفقة به مصحوبة بشهادة تبين
تاريخ ورقم ايداعه والدولة التي اودع فيها، إذا كان الطلب يتضمن الرغبة
في اعتبار الأولوية في التسجيل لطلب سبق تقديمه في دولة تكون طرفاً في
اتفاقية أو معاهدة دولية مع دولة الامارات العربية المتحدة وفقاً للمادة ١١
من القانون. [   ]

٩. الشهادة الصادرة بالحماية المؤقتة ان وجدت. [   ]

١٠. كتاب من مكتب مقاطعة اسرائيل بعدم حظر التعامل مع الطالب. [ ]

١١. تعهد كتابي على النموذج رقم ٦ بتقديم اللازم من المستندات
(من ٤-١٠) عدا المرفق منها مع الطلب. [ ]

الخاتم الرسمي   مجموع المستندات المستلمة [ ]

المستلم: _____

الاسم: _____

التوقيع: _____

ملاحظة: يؤشر بعلامة √ امام المستندات المستلمة.

نموذج رقم ٨
بطاقة الفهرس الابجدي
لطلبات البراءات وشهادات المنفعة

اسم الطالب: ------------------------------------

اسم الاختراع: ------------------------------------

الرقم المتتابع للطلب: ------------------------------------

تزريخ وساعة تقديم الطلب: ------------------------------------

نموذج رقم ٩
طلب شهادة تسجيل رسم أو نموذج صناعي

للاستعمال الرسمي فقط	يلتمس الطالب من ادارة الملكية الصناعية منحه
رقم الطلب: _____	رسم ☐
تاريخ وساعة تقديمه: _____	شهادة تسجيل: نموذج صناعي ☐
	وفقاً للبيانات التالية:

١– اسم الرسم ☐ النموذج الصناعي ☐ ـــــــــــــــــــــــ

٢– اسم الطالب: ـــــــــــــــــــــــــــــــــــــ

العنوان: ـــــــــــــــــــــــــــــــــ
ـــــــــــــــــــــــــــــــــ

المحل المختار في الدولة: ـــــــــــــــــــــــــ
ـــــــــــــــــــــــــــــــــ

الجنسية: ـــــــــــــــــــــــــــــــــ

محل الاقامة أو المركز الرئيسي للاعمال: ـــــــــــــــــ
ـــــــــــــــــــــــــــــــــ
ـــــــــــــــــــــــــــــــــ

رقم الهاتف: ـــــــــــ رقم التلكس ـــــــــ رقم الفاكس ـــــــ

عدد الطالبين ـــــــــــ اذا كان الطالبون اكثر من واحد تذكر بيانات الباقين في ورقة تابعة

٣– اسم المبتكر: ـــــــــــــــــــــــــــــــ
ـــــــــــــــــــــــــــــــــ

العنوان: ————————————————————————
————————————————————————————————

عدد المبتكرين ———— اذا كان المبتكرون اكثر من واحد يذكر بيانات الباقين في ورقة تابعة

٤ – اسم الوكيل: ————————————————————
————————————————————————————————

رقم الوكالة: ———— تاريخها ———— مصدرها ————

العنوان: ——————————————————————————
————————————————————————————————

رقم الهاتف ———— رقم التلكس ———— رقم الفاكس ————

٥ – المطالبة بالأولوية استناداً إلى طلب سابق:

الدولة التي قدم إليها الطلب: ——————————————

رقم وتاريخ الطلب: ——————————————————

إذا كانت الأولوية تستند إلى أكثر من طلب سابق تذكر بيانات باقي الطلبات في ورقة تابعة

٦ – رقم وتاريخ شهادة الحماية المؤقتة ان وجدت: ——————————

الوكيل	الطالب

٧ – التوقيع: ———————— ————————

التاريخ: ————————

بيان
بمرفقات طلب شهادة تسجيل رسم أو نموذج صناعي

طبقاً للائحة التنفيذية يرفق بطلب شهادة تسجيل الرسم أو النموذج الصناعي ما يأتي:

١. نسختان من الرسم أو النموذج إذا كان ثنائي الابعاد أو نسختان من كل جانب منه إذا كان ثلاثي الأبعاد ولا يجوز أن يستعاض عن ذلك بعينة من المنتجات المخصص لها ذلك الرسم أو النموذج الصناعي.

٢. مستخرج من السجل التجاري أو مستخرج رسمي من عقد التأسيس إذا كان الطالب شركة أو هيئة.

٣. المستند الدال على احقية الطالب في الرسم أو النموذج الصناعي إذا كان الطالب غير المبتكر.

٤. صورة من الطلب السبق والمستندات المرفقة به مصحوبة بشهادة تبين تاريخ ورقم ايداعه والدولة التي اودع فيها، إذا كان الطلب يتضمن الرغبة في اعتبار الأولوية في التسجيل لطلب سبق تقديمه في دولة تكون طرفاً في اتفاقية أو معاهدة دولية مع دولة الامارات العربية المتحدة وفقاً للمادة ١١ من القانون.

٥. سند الوكالة إذا اودع الطلب بواسطة وكيل.

٦. الشهادة الصادرة بالحماية المؤقتة إن وجدت.

٧. كتاب من مكتب مقاطعة اسرائيل بعدم حظر التعامل مع الطالب.

ويجب ان تكون كافة المستدات مصحوبة بترجمة إلى اللغة العربية إذا كانت محررة باللغة الانجليزية أو بترجمة إلى اللغتين العربية والانجليزية إذا كانت محررة بلغة اخرى.

ويجب أن تكون المستندات المشار إليها في البنود ٢، ٣، ٤، ٥ مصدقاً عليها حسب الاصول.

ويتعين ان يرفق المستند المشار إليه في البند ١ بالطلب عند تقديمه ويجب ان يراعى في الشروط المادية المبينة في المادة ٤٧ من اللائحة التنفيذية.

اما المستندات الاخرى فيجوز في حال عدم ارفاقها بالطلب أن يقدم الطالب تعهداً كتابياً على النموذج رقم ٦ بتقديم ما يلزم تقديمه منها على حسب الاحوال خلال تسعين يوماً من تاريخ تقديم الطلب. وإذا لم يقدمها خلال هذه المهلة يعتبر الطلب كأن لم يكن، وذلك باستثناء المستند المشار إليه في البند ٤ فإنه يترتب على عدم تقديمه – عند لزومه – خلال هذه المهلة سقوط حق الطالب في المطالبة بالأولوية.

للاستعمال الرسمي فقط

تمت المراجعة وسداد الرسم المقرر وقدره ––– درهم
بموجب ايصال رقم ––––– بتاريخ –––––––––
اسم المستلم ––––––––––––––––––
التوقيع ––––––––––––––––––
التاريخ –––––––––––––––––––
الختم الرسمي ––––––––––––––––––

نموذج رقم ١٠

ايصال استلام مستندات

طلب شهادة تسجيل رسم ☐   نموذج صناعي ☐

رقم الطلب:

ساعة وتاريخ تقديم الطلب:

اسم الطالب وجنسيته:

سدد الرسم بايصال رقم: ــــــــــــــــ
بتاريخ: ــــــــــــــــــــــ

بيان المستندات المستلمة مع الطلب:

١. نسختان من الرسم أو النموذج إذا كان ثنائي الابعاد أو نسختان من كل جانب إذا كان ثلاثي الأبعاد ولا يجوز أن يستعاض عن ذلك بعينة من المنتجات المخصص لها ذلك الرسم أو النموذج الصناعي. ☐

٢. مستخرج من السجل لتجاري أو مستخرج رسمي من عقد التأسيس أو أداة الانشاء على حسب الاحوال إذا كان الطالب شخصاً اعتبارياً. ☐

٣. المستند الدال على احقية الطالب في الرسم أو النموذج الصناعي إذا كان الطالب غير المبتكر. ☐

٤. صورة من الطلب السبق والمستندات المرفقة به مصحوبة بشهادة تبين تاريخ ورقم ايداعه والدولة التي اودع فيها، إذا كان الطلب يتضمن الرغبة في اعتبار الأولوية في التسجيل لطلب سبق تقديمه في دولة تكون طرفاً في اتفاقية أو معاهدة دولية مع الدولة وفقاً للمادة ١١ من القانون. ☐

٥. سند الوكالة إذا اودع الطلب بواسطة وكيل. ☐

٦. الشهادة الصادرة بالحمية المؤقتة إن وجدت. ☐

٧. كتاب من مكتب مقاطعة اسرائيل بعدم حظر التعامل مع الطالب. ☐

٨. تعهد كتابي على النموذج رقم ٦ بتقديم اللازم من المستندات (من ٢ إلى ٧) عدا المرفق منها بالطلب ☐

مجموع المستندات المستلمة	
المستلم: ــــــــــــــــــــ	
الخاتم الرسمي	الاسم: ــــــــــــــــــــ
التوقيع: ــــــــــــــــــــ	
ملاحظة: يؤشر بعلامة √ امام المستندات المستلمة.	

نموذج رقم ١١
بطاقة الفهرس الابجدي
لطلبات شهادات تسجيل الرسوم والنماذج الصناعية

اسم الطالب: ـــ ـــ
اسم الرسم أو النموذج الصناعي: ـــــــــــــــــــــــــــــــــ ــ
الرقم المتتابع للطلب: ــــــــــــــــــــــــــــــــــــ ـــ ــ
تاريخ وساعة تقديم الطلب: ــــــــــــــــــــــــــــــــــــ ــ

قرار وزاري رقم (٤٠٤) لسنة ٢٠٠٠م

وزير الصحة

بعد الاطلاع على القانون الاتحادي رقم (١) لسنة ١٩٧٢م بشأن اختصاصات الوزارات و صلاحيات الوزراء والقوانين المعدلة له،

وعلى القانون الاتحادي رقم (٤) لسنة ١٩٨٣م في شأن مهنة الصيدلة والمؤسسات الصيدلانية،

وعلى القانون الاتحادي رقم (٤٤) لسنة ١٩٩٢م في شأن تنظيم وحماية الملكية الصناعية لبراءات الاختراع ورسوم والنماذج الصناعية،

وعلى المرسوم الاتحادي رقم (٢١) لسنة ١٩٩٧م في شأن اتفاقية وبروتوكول انضمام الدولة إلى منظمة التجارة العالمية ووثيقة جولة ارجواي.

وعلى اتفاقية حقوق الملكية الفكرية TRIPS ،

وعلى كتاب وزارة المالية ءالصناعة الوارد بالفاكس بتاريخ ٢٠٠٠/٤/٢٦،

قرر:

المادة (١)

يحظر تسجيل أي دواء أو مستحضر صيدلاني جديد لا يتمتع ببراءة اختراع.

المادة (٢)

لا تسري احكام المادة السابقة على الادوية والمستحضرات الصيدلانية المسجلة بدساتير الادوية العالمية وكذلك قائمة الادوية الضرورية الصادرة من منظمة الصحة العالمية أو من أي جهة علمية عالمية محايدة كذلك لا تسري على الأدوية والمستحضرات التي تم تسجيلها كما لا تسري على الأدوية والمستحضرات التي انتهت مدة حماية براءة الاختراع للمنتج الأصلي.

المادة (٣)

على الادارات المعنية بالوزارة ضرورة الحفاظ على سرية المعلومات المرفقة بأي طلب تسجيل دواء أو مستحضر صيدلاني.

المادة (٤)

ينشر هذا القرار بالجريدة الرسمية ويسري اعتباراً من تاريخ نشره.

المادة (٥)

يبلغ هذا القرار من يلزم لتنفيذه.

حمد عبد الرحمن المدفع
وزير الصحة

صدر بديوان الوزارة / أبو ظبي
بتاريخ: ٢٦ / محرم / ١٤٢١ هـ.
الموافق: ٣٠ / ٤ / ٢٠٠٠ م.

قانون اتحادي رقم (٣٧) لسنة ١٩٩٢م
في شأن العلامات التجارية

نحن زايد بن سلطان آل نهيان، رئيس دولة الإمارات العربية المتحدة،

بعد الاطلاع على الدستور المؤقت،

وعلى القانون الاتحادي رقم (١) لسنة ١٩٧٢م في شأن اختصاصات الوزارات وصلاحيات الوزراء والقوانين المعدلة له،

وعلى القانون الاتحادي رقم (٤) لسنة ١٩٧٩م في شأن قمع الغش والتدليس في المعاملات التجارية،

وعلى القانون الاتحادي رقم (٥) لسنة ١٩٨٥م بإصدار قانون المعاملات المدنية، والقوانين المعدلة له،

وعلى القانون الاتحادي رقم (٣) لسنة ١٩٨٧م بإصدار قانون العقوبات،

وبناءً على ماعرضه وزير الاقتصاد والتجارة وموافقة مجلس الوزراء وتصديق المجلس الأعلى للاتحاد،

أصدرنا القانون الآتي:

الباب الأول
تعاريف

المادة (١)

في تطبيق أحكام هذا القانون يقصد بالكلمات والعبارات التالية المعاني الموضحة قرين كل منها مالم يقض سياق النص بغير ذلك:

الدولة: دولة الإمارات العربية المتحدة.

الوزير: وزير الاقتصاد والتجارة.

الوزارة: وزارة الاقتصاد والتجارة.

السلطة المختصة: السلطة المختصة في الامارة.

الرسم: كل تصميم يتضمن مجموعة من المرئيات (أي تكوين فني).

الرمز: كل رسم مرئي واحد.

الدمغات: العلامات المحفورة.

النقوش: العلامات البارزة.

الصور: صور الإنسان سواء كانت صورة صاحب المشروع أو صورة غيره.

اللجنة: لجنة العلامات التجارية المنصوص عليها في هذا القانون.

المادة (٢)

تعتبر علامة تجارية كل ما يأخذ شكلاً مميزاً من أسماء أو كلمات أو إمضاءات أو حروف أو أرقام أو رسوم أو رموز أو عناوين أو دمغات أو أختام أو صور أو نقوش أو اعلانات أو عبوات أو أية علامة أخرى أو أي مجموع منها إذا كانت تستخدم أو يراد أن تستخدم اما في تمييز بضائع أو منتجات أو خدمات أياً كان مصدرها وإما للدلالة على أن البضائع أو المنتجات تعود لمالك العلامة بسبب صنعها أو انتقائها أو الاتجار بها أو للدلالة على تأدية خدمة من الخدمات.

ويعتبر الصوت جزءاً من العلامة التجارية إذا كان مصاحباً لها.

المادة (٣)

لايسجل كعلامة تجارية أو كعنصر منها ما يأتي:

١. العلامة الخالية من أية صفة أو طابع مميز أو العلامة المكونة من بيانات ليست إلا التسمية التي يطلقها العرف على البضائع والمنتجات والخدمات أو الرسوم المألوفة والصور العادية للبضائع والمنتجات.

٢. أية علامة تخل بالآداب العامة أو تخالف النظام العام.

٣. الشعارات العامة والأعلام وغيرها من الرموز الخاصة بالدولة أو المنظمات العربية أو الدولية أو احدى مؤسساتها أو أية دولة أجنبية إلا بتفويض منها، وكذلك أي تقليد لتلك الشعارات أو الأعلام أو لرموز.

٤. رموز الهلال الاحمر أو الصليب الاحمر وغيرها من الرموز الأخرى المشابهة وكذلك العلامات التي تكون تقليداً لها.

٥. العلامات المماثلة أو لمشابهة للرموز ذات الصبغة الدينية المحضة.

٦. الاسماء الجغرافية اذا كان من شأن استعمالها أن يحدث لبساً فيما يتعلق بمنشأ البضاعة أو المنتجات أو الخدمات أومصدرها.

٧. اسم الغير أو لقبه أو صورته أو شعاره مالم يوافق هو أو ورثته مقدماً على استعماله.

٨. البيانات الخاصة بدرجات الشرف التي لا يثبت طالب التسجيل استحقاقه لها قانوناً.

٩. العلامات التي من شأنها أن تضلل الجمهور أو التي تتضمن بيانات كاذبة عن منشأ أو مصدر المنتجات أو الخدمات أو عن صفاتها الأخرى وكذلك العلامات التي تحتوي على اسم تجاري وهمي أو مقلد أو مزور.

١٠. العلامات المملوكة لأشخاص طبيعيين أو معنويين يكون التعامل معهم محظوراً.

١١. العلامة التي ينشأ عن تسجيلها لبعض فئات المنتجات أو الخدمات الحط من قيمة المنتجات أو الخدمات الأخرى التي تميزها تلك العلامة.

١٢. العلامات التي تشمل الألفاظ أو العبارات الآتية:

(امتياز) أو (ذو امتياز) أو (مسجل) أو (رسم مسجل) أو (حقوق الطبع) أو (التقليد يعتبر تزويراً) أو ما شابه ذلك من الألفاظ والعبارات.

المادة (٤)

لا يجوز تسجيل العلامات التجارية الأجنبية ذات الشهرة العالمية التي تجاوز حدود البلد الاصلي للعلامة إلى البلاد الاخرى الا بناءً على طلب مالكها الأصلي.

الباب الثاني
تسجيل العلامات وشطبها

المادة (٥)

يعد في الوزارة سجل يسمى سجل العلامات التجارية تدون فيه جميع العلامات التجارية وأسماء أصحابها وعناوينهم ونوع نشاطهم وأوصاف بضائعهم أو منتجاتهم أو خدماتهم ومايطرأ على العلامات من تحويل أو تنازل أو نقل للملكية أو رهن أو ترخيص بالاستعمال أو أية تعديلات أخرى.

ولكل شخص أن يطلب صورة طبق الأصل مما هو مدون في هذا السجل بعد دفع الرسوم المقررة.

المادة (٦)

للأشخاص التالي ذكرهم الحق في تسجيل علاماتهم التجارية:

١. مواطنو الدولة من الاشخاص الطبيعيين أو الاعتباريين الذين يزاولون أي عمل من الاعمال التجارية أو الصناعية أو الحرفية أو الخدمية.

٢. الأجانب من الاشخاص الطبيعيين أو الاعتباريين الذين يزاولون أي عمل من الأعمال التجارية أو الصناعية أو الحرفية أو الخدمية في الدولة.

٣. الأجانب من الاشخاص الطبيعين أو الاعتباريين الذين يزاولون أي عمل من الأعمال التجارية أو الصناعية أو الحرفية أو الخدمية في أية دولة من الدول التي تعامل الدولة معاملة المثل.

٤. الاشخاص الاعتبارية العامة.

المادة (٧)

لكل من يرغب في استعمال علامة تجارية لتمييز بضاعة أو منتجات أو خدمات أن يطلب تسجيلها وفقًا لاحكام هذا القانون.

ويقدم طلب تسجيل العلامة إلى الوزارة بالأوضاع والشروط المنصوص عليها في اللائحة التنفيذية.

المادة (٨)

يجوز تسجيل العلامة التجارية عن فئة واحدة أو اكثر من فئات المنتجات أو الخدمات التي تحددها اللائحة التنفيذية ومع ذلك لايجوز أن يشتمل طلب تسجيل العلامة على أكثر من فئة واحدة.

المادة (٩)

يجوز تقديم طلب واحد لتسجيل مجموعة من العلامات المتماثلة في عناصرها الجوهرية والتي يقتصر اختلافها على أمور لا تمس ذاتيتها مساساً جوهرياً كلون العلامات أو بيانات المنتجات أو الخدمات المرتبطة بها ، على أن تكون هذه المنتجات أو الخدمات تابعة لفئة واحدة.

المادة (١٠)

مع مراعاة حكم المادة (٢٦) من هذا القانون لايجوز تسجيل أية علامة تجارية مطابقة أو مشابهة لعلامة سبق تسجيلها عن ذات فئات المنتجات أو الخدمات.

واذا طلب شخص أو أكثر في وقت واحد تسجيل العلامة ذاتها أو علامات متقاربة أو متشابهة عن فئة واحدة من المنتجات أو الخدمات ، وجب على الوزارة وقف تسجيل جميع الطلبات إلى أن يقدم تنازل مصدق عليه من المتنازعين لمصلحة أحدهم أو إلى أن يصدر حكم نهائي لمصلحة واحد منهم.

المادة (١١)

يجوز للوزارة أن تفرض ماتراه لازماً من القيود والتعديلات لتحديد العلامة التجارية وتوضيحها على وجه يمنع التباسها بعلامة أخرى سبق تسجيلها أو لأي سبب أخر تراه، وإذا رفضت الوزارة تسجيل العلامة التجارية لسبب ما أو علق التسجيل على قيود أو تعديلات وجب عليها أن تخطر طالب التسجيل كتابة بأسباب قرارها.

وفي جميع الاحوال يتعين على الوزارة أن تبت في طلب التسجيل خلال ثلاثين يوماً من تاريخ تقديمه متى كان مستوفياً للشروط والأوضاع المنصوص عليها في هذا القانون ولائحته التنفيذية.

المادة (١٢)

يجوز لطالب التسجيل الذي رفض طلبه أو علق قبوله على شرط أن يتظلم من هذا القرار إلى اللجنة خلال ثلاثين يوماً من تاريخ إبلاغه به.

وإذا أيدت اللجنة قرار الوزارة القاضي برفض الطلب أو تعليق قبوله على استيفاء بعض الشروط جاز لطالب التسجيل أن يطعن في قرار اللجنة أمام المحكمة المدنية المختصة خلال ستين يوماً من تاريخ إبلاغه به.

ويعتبر طالب التسجيل متنازلاً عن طلبه إذا لم يتظلم من قرار الوزارة أو لم يطعن في قرار اللجنة خلال المواعيد المحددة في هذه المادة أو لم يقم بتنفيذ ما فرضته الوزارة من قيود أو شروط في الميعاد الذي يحدده الاخطار الموجه إليه في هذا الشأن.

المادة (١٣)

تشكل لجنة العلامات التجارية برئاسة وكيل وزارة الاقتصاد والتجارة وعضوية ممثلين عن الوزارة يختارهما الوزير ، وممثل عن كل امارة تختاره السلطة المختصة.

المادة (١٤)

إذا قبلت الوزارة العلامة التجارية وجب عليها قبل تسجيلها أن تعلن عنها في الجريدة الرسمية وفي صحيفتين يوميتين تصدران في الدولة وذلك على نفقة طالب التسجيل.

ولكل ذي شأن أن يعترض على تسجيل العلامة، ويقدم الاعتراض كتابة إلى الوزارة أو يرسل إليها بالبريد المسجل خلال ثلاثين يوماً من تاريخ آخر اعلان، وعلى الوزارة أن تخطر طالب التسجيل بصورة من الاعتراض على طلبه خلال خمسة عشر يوماً من تاريخ إستلامها له.

وعلى طالب التسجيل أن يقدم إلى الوزارة رداً مكتوباً على هذا الاعتراض خلال ثلاثين يوماً من تاريخ إبلاغه به فإذا لم يصل الرد في الميعاد المذكور اعتبر أن طالب التسجيل متنازلاً عن طلبه.

المادة (١٥)

يتعين على الوزارة قبل أن تفصل في الاعتراضات المقدمة إليها أن تسمع أقوال الطرفين أو أحدهما إذا طلب اي منهما ذلك.

وتصدر الوزارة قرارها برفض التسجيل أو بقبوله ولها أن تفرض في الحالة الأخيرة ماتراه من قيود أو شروط.

ولكل ذي شأن أن يتظلم من قرار الوزارة خلال خمسة عشر يوماً من تاريخ إخطاره به أمام اللجنة وله أن يطعن في قرار اللجنة أمام المحكمة المدنية المختصة خلال ثلاثين يوماً من تاريخ إبلاغه بالقرار.

ولا يترتب على الطعن في القرار الصادر بقبول تسجيل العلامة التجارية وقف إجراءات التسجيل مالم تقرر المحكمة المختصة غير ذلك.

المادة (١٦)

إذا سجلت العلامة التجارية انسحب أثر التسجيل إلى تاريخ تقديم الطلب.

ويعطى لمالك العلامة بمجرد إتمام تسجيلها شهادة تشمل البيانات الآتية:

١. رقم تسجيل العلامة.

٢. تاريخ تقديم الطلب وتاريخ التسجيل.

٣. الاسم التجاري أو اسم مالك العلامة وجنسيته ومحل إقامته.

٤. صورة مطابقة للعلامة.

٥. بيان بالمنتجات أو بالبضائع أو بالخدمات المخصصة لها العلامة وبيان فئتها.

المادة (١٧)

يعتبر من قام بتسجيل العلامة مالكاً لها دون سواه ولا تجوز المنازعة في ملكية العلامة إذا استعملها من قام بتسجيلها بصفة مستمرة خمس سنوات على الاقل من تاريخ التسجيل دون أن ترفع عليه دعوى تقضي بصحتها.

المادة (١٨)

يجوز لمالك علامة تجارية سبق تسجيلها أن يقدم في أي وقت طلباً إلى الوزارة لإدخال أية إضافة أو تعديل على علامته لايمس ذاتيتها مساساً جوهرياً، ويصدر قرار الوزارة في هذا الشأن وفقاً للشروط والقواعد المقررة للبت في طلبات التسجيل الاصلية ويكون قابلاً للتظلم والطعن بالطرق ذاتها.

المادة (١٩)

مدة الحماية المترتبة على تسجيل العلامة التجارية عشر سنوات، ولصاحب العلامة أن يكفل استمرار الحماية لمدد متتالية كل منها عشر سنوات إذا قدم طلباً بتجديد تسجيل العلامة خلال السنة الأخيرة من مدة الحماية السارية وفقاً للأوضاع والشروط المنصوص عليها في هذا القانون ولائحته التنفيذية.

ويتم تجديد تسجيل العلامة دون أي فحص إضافي ودون أن يسمح للغير بالمعارضة في التجديد، ويشهر تجديد تسجيل العلامة في الجريدة الرسمية وفي صحيفتين يوميتين تصدران في الدولة على نفقة صاحب العلامة.

ولا يجوز في حالة طلب تجديد تسجيل العلامة ادخال أي تغيير على العلامة أو اضافة أية منتجات أو خدمات على قائمة المنتجات أو الخدمات التي سجلت عنها العلامة.

وعلى الوزارة خلال الشهر التالي لانتهاء مدة الحماية أن تقوم بإخطار صاحب العلامة كتابة على عنوانه المقيد في السجل بانتهاء مدة حمايتها، وإذا لم يقم صاحب العلامة بتقديم طلب التجديد خلال الثلاثة أشهر التالية لتاريخ انتهاء مدة الحماية قامت الوزارة من تلقاء نفسها بشطب العلامة من السجل.

المادة (٢٠)

يجوز لصاحب العلامة التجارية أن يطلب شطب تسجيلها من السجل سواء عن كل المنتجات أو الخدمات التي سجلت عنها العلامة أو عن جزء منها فقط ويقدم طلب الشطب وفقاً للأوضاع والشروط التي تنص عليها اللائحة التنفيذية لهذا القانون.

وإذا كانت العلامة مرخصاً باستعمالها وفقاً لعقد مقيد في سجل العلامات التجارية فلا يجوز شطب تسجيل هذه العلامة إلا بناءً على موافقة كتابية من المستفيد من الترخيص مالم يتنازل المستفيد عن هذا الحق صراحة في عقد الترخيص.

المادة (٢١)

مع عدم الإخلال بحكم المادة (١٧) يكون للوزارة ولكل ذي شأن الحق في طلب الحكم بشطب العلامة التجارية التي تكون قد سجلت بغير حق، وعلى الوزارة أن تقوم بشطب التسجيل متى قدم لها حكم نهائي بذلك.

المادة (٢٢)

للمحكمة المدنية المختصة أن تحكم بناءً على طلب كل ذي شأن بشطب تسجيل العلامة التجارية إذا ثبت لديها أنها لم تستعمل بصفة جدية خمس سنوات متتالية إلا إذا قدم مالك العلامة ما يبرر به عدم استعمالها.

المادة (٢٣)

للمحكمة المدنية المختصة أن تحكم بناءً على طلب الوزارة أو كل ذي شأن بإضافة أي بيان للسجل يكون قد أغفل تدوينه به أو بحذف أو بتعديل أي بيان وارد بالسجل إذا كان قد دون بدون وجه حق أو كان غير مطابق للحقيقة.

المادة (٢٤)

على الوزارة أن تقوم بشطب تسجيل العلامات التجارية التي يقرر مكتب مقاطعة إسرائيل في الدولة أنها مشابهة أو مطابقة لعلامة أو رمز أو شعار اسرائيلي، وكذلك العلامات المملوكة لاشخاص يصدر في شأنهم قرار بحظر التعامل معهم.

المادة (٢٥)

يجب إشهار شطب العلامة التجارية من السجل في الجريدة الرسمية.

المادة (٢٦)

إذا شطب تسجيل العلامة التجارية فلا يجوز إعادة تسجيلها لصالح الغير عن ذات المنتجات إلا بعد إنقضاء ثلاث سنوات من تاريخ الشطب.

الباب الثالث
انتقال ملكية العلامة ورهنها

المادة (٢٧)

يجوز نقل ملكية العلامة التجارية أو رهنها أو الحجز عليها مع الحل التجاري أو مشروع الاستغلال التي تستخدم العلامة في تمييز منتجاته أو خدماته أو بدونهما.

المادة (٢٨)

يشمل انتقال ملكية المحل التجاري أو مشروع الاستغلال العلامات التجارية المسجلة باسم ناقل الملكية التي يمكن اعتبارها ذات ارتباط وثيق بالمحل أو بالمشروع مالم يتفق على غير ذلك.

وإذا انتقلت ملكية المحل النجاري أو مشروع الاستغلال من غير العلامة جاز لناقل الملكية الاستمرار في استعمال العلامة بالنسبة للمنتجات أو الخدمات التي سجلت من أجلها مالم يتفق على غير ذلك.

المادة (٢٩)

لايكون نقل ملكية العلامة التجارية أو رهنها حجة على الغير إلا بعد التأشير به في سجل العلامات وإشهاره بالكيفية التي تحددها اللائحة التنفيذية.

الباب الرابع
عقود الترخيص باستعمال العلامة

المادة (٣٠)

يجوز لمالك العلامة التجارية، بموجب عقد مكتوب وموثق لشخص أو أكثر باستعمال العلامة عن كل أو بعض المنتجات أو الخدمات المسجلة عنها العلامة ، ويكون لمالك العلامة أن يستعملها بنفسه مالم يتفق على غير ذلك.

ولا يجوز أن تزيد مدة الترخيص باستعمال العلامة عن المدة المقررة لحمايتها.

المادة (٣١)

يجب قيد عقد الترخيص باستعمال العلامة التجارية في سجل العلامات، ولايكون للترخيص أثر قبل الغير إلا بعد قيده في السجل والإشهار عنه بالكيفية التي تحددها اللائحة التنفيذية.

المادة (٣٢)

لايجوز للمستفيد من الترخيص التنازل عنه لغيره أو منح تراخيص من الباطن مالم ينص عقد الترخيص على خلاف ذلك.

المادة (٣٣)

يشطب قيد الترخيص من السجل بناءً على طلب مالك العلامة أو المستفيد من الترخيص بعد تقديم ما يثبت انتهاء أو فسخ عقد الترخيص.

وعلى الوزارة أن تخطر الطرف الاخر بالطلب المقدم لشطب الترخيص ، ولهذا الطرف أن يعترض على طلب الشطب وفقاً للإجراءات والأوضاع التي تنص عليها اللائحة التنفيذية.

المادة (٣٤)

لايجوز أن يتضمن عقد الترخيص أية نصوص تقيد المستفيد من الترخيص بقيود غير مترتبة على الحقوق التي يخولها تسجيل العلامة التجارية أو غير ضرورية للمحافظة على هذه الحقوق، ومع ذلك يجوز أن يتضمن عقد الترخيص القيود الاتية:

١. تحديد نطاق المنطقة الجغرافية لتسويق المنتجات أو الخدمات التي تحمل العلامة.

٢. تحديد مدة الترخيص باستعمال العلامة على أن يراعى في هذا الشان أحكام المادة (٣١) من هذا القانون.

٣. الشروط التي تكفل لمالك العلامة مراقبة جودة المنتجات التي ينطبق عليها الترخيص.

٤. الزام المستفيد من الترخيص بالامتناع عن جميع الأعمال التي قد يترتب عليها الحط من قيمة المنتجات أو الخدمات التي تحمل العلامة أو الإساءة إليها.

الباب الخامس
العلامات التي تخصص للدلالة على مراقبة منتجات معينة أو فحصها

المادة (٣٥)

يجوز للأشخاص الاعتباريين الذين يتولون مراقبة أو فحص بعض المنتجات أو الخدمات من حيث مصدرها أو عناصر تركيبها أو طريقة صنعها أو جودتها أو ذاتيتها أو أية خاصية أخرى أن يطلبوا من الوزارة الترخيص لهم بتسجيل علامة تكون مخصصة للدلالة على إجراء المراقبة والفحص.

وفي جميع الأحوال لا يجوز تسجيل هذه العلامة أو نقل ملكيتها إلا بموافقة الوزير.

المادة (٣٦)

تحدد اللائحة التنفيذية الشروط والقواعد الخاصة بتسجيل العلامة المشار إليها في المادة السابقة والمستندات المطلوب إرفاقها بطلب التسجيل.

ويترتب على تسجيل هذه العلامة جميع الآثار المنصوص عليها في هذا القانون.

ولا يجوز إعادة تسجيل العلامة المذكورة في حالة شطبها أو عدم تجديدها بالنسبة إلى منتجات أو بضائع أو خدمات مماثلة أو متشابهة.

الباب السادس
العقوبات

المادة (٣٧)

يعاقب بالحبس وبالغرامة التي لا تقل عن (٥٠٠٠) خمسة الاف درهم أو بإحدى هاتين العقوبتين:

١. كل من زور علامة تجارية تم تسجيلها طبقاً للقانون أو قلدها بطريقة تدعو إلى تضليل الجمهور وكل من استعمل بسوء القصد علامة تجارية مزورة أو مقلدة.

٢. كل من استعمل بغير حق علامة تجارية مسجلة مملوكة لغيره.

٣. كل من وضع بسوء القصد على منتجاته علامة تجارية مسجلة مملوكة لغيره.

٤. كل من باع أو عرض للبيع أو للتداول أو حاز بقصد البيع منتجات عليها علامة تجارية مزورة أو مقلدة أو موضوعة بغير حق مع علمه بذلك.

٥. كل من عرض تقديم خدمات تحت علامة تجارية مزورة أو مقلدة أو مستعملة بغير حق مع علمه بذلك.

المادة (٣٨)

يعاقب بالحبس مدة لا تجاوز سنة وبالغرامة التي لاتقل عن (٥٠٠٠) خمسة آلاف درهم ولا تزيد على (١٠٠٠٠) عشر آلاف درهم أو بإحدى هاتين العقوبتين:

١. كل من استعمل علامة غير قابلة للتسجيل وفقاً لما هو منصوص عليه في البنود ٢ و٣ و٤ و٥ و٦ و٨ و٩ و١٠ و١١ و١٢ من المادة (٣) من هذا القانون.

٢. كل من دون بغير حق على علامته أو أوراقه التجارية بيان يؤدي إلى الاعتقاد بحصول تسجيلها.

المادة (٣٩)

يعاقب كل من ارتكب إحدى الجرائم المنصوص عليها في المادتين (٣٧) و(٣٨) من هذا القانون في حالة العود بذات العقوبة علاوة على إغلاق المحل التجاري أو مشروع الاستغلال مدة لا تقل عن خمسة عشر يوماً ولا تزيد على ستة أشهر مع نشر الحكم على نفقة المحكوم عليه وفقاً للإجراءات التي تحددها اللائحة التنفيذية.

المادة (٤٠)

يجوز لكل من أصابه ضرر نتيجة لاي من الأفعال المنصوص عليها في المادتين (٣٧) أو (٣٨) من هذا القانون أن يرفع دعوى أمام المحكمة المدنية المختصة لمطالبة المسئول عن الفعل بتعويض مناسب عما لحقه من اضرار.

المادة (٤١)

يجوز لمالك العلامة التجارية في أي وقت ولو كان ذلك قبل رفع أية دعوى مدنية أو جنائية أن يستصدر بناءً على عريضة مشفوعة بشهادة رسمية دالة على تسجيل العلامة أمراً من المحكمة المختصة باتخاذ الإجراءات التحفظية اللازمة وعلى الأخص يأتي:

١. إجراء محضر حصر ووصف تفصيلي للآلات والأدوات التي تستخدم أو التي استخدمت في ارتكاب أي من الجرائم المنصوص عليها في هذا القانون، وكذلك المنتجات أو البضائع المحلية أو المستوردة وعناوين المحلات أو الأغلفة أو الأوراق أو غيرها تكون قد وضعت عليها العلامة أو البيان موضوع الجريمة.

٢. توقيع الحجز على الاشياء المذكورة في البند السابق وذلك بعد أن يقدم الطالب تأميناً مالياً تقدره المحكمة لتعويض المحجوز عليه عند الاقتضاء.

ويجوز للمحكمة ندب خبير أو أكثر للمعاونة في تنفيذ الإجراءات التحفظية، وفي جميع الأحوال تعتبر الإجراءات التحفظية التي اتخذها مالك العلامة كأن لم تكن إذا لم يتبعها رفع دعوى مدنية أو جنائية على من اتخذت ضده هذه الإجراءات وذلك خلال الثمانية أيام التالية لصدور الأمر.

المادة (٤٢)

للمحجوز عليه أن يرفع دعوى لمطالبة الحاجز بالتعويض خلال تسعين يوماً تبدأ من تاريخ انقضاء الميعاد المنصوص عليه في الفقرة الأخيرة من المادة (٤١) من هذا القانون، اذا لم ترفع الدعوى ضد المحجوز عليه، أو من تاريخ صدور الحكم النهائي في الدعوى المرفوعة ضده. وفي الحالتين لا يرد التأمين للحاجز إلا بعد صدور الحكم النهائي في دعوى المحجوز عليه أو بعد انقضاء الميعاد المقرر له دون رفعها.

المادة (٤٣)

يجوز للمحكمة في أية دعوى مدنية أو جنائية أن تحكم مصادرة الأشياء المحجوز عليها أو التي يحجز عليها فيما بعد واستنزال ثمنها من الغرامات أو التعويضات أو التصرف فيها بأية طريقة أخرى تراها المحكمة مناسبة ويجوز للمحكمة أيضا أن تأمر بإتلاف العلامات غير القانونية أو أن تأمر عند الاقتضاء بإتلاف المنتجات والأغلفة ومعدات الحزم وغيرها من الأشياء التي تحمل تلك العلامات أو تحمل بيانات غير قانونية وكذلك الآلات والأدوات التي استعملت بصفة خاصة في عملية التزوير ولها أن تأمر بكل ما

سبق حتى في حالة الحكم بالبراءة. ويجوزللمحكمة كذلك أن تأمر بنشر الحكم في الجريدة الرسمية أو في إحدى الصحف اليومية على نفقة المحكوم عليه.

الباب السابع
احكام عامة وانتقالية

المادة (٤٤)

على أصحاب العلامات التجارية المسجلة أو المستعملة في الإمارات عند العمل بأحكام هذا القانون أن يتقدموا بطلب قيدها في سجل الوزارة طبقاً للأحكام والشروط المنصوص عليها فيه خلال سنة من تاريخ العمل بأحكامه.

وعلى الذين لم يستوفوا الشروط المقررة في هذا القانون أن يعدلوا أوضاعهم خلال سنة من تاريخ العمل به و إذا لم تستوف العلامة التجارية الشروط المقررة لها خلال المدة المنصوص عليها في الفقرة السابقة اعتبرت منقضية بقوة القانون.

ويكون للمستعمل الأول حق الأولوية في تسجيل علامته خلال هذه الفترة ويراعى في تحديد الاستعمال الأول تاريخ البدء به واستمراريته والظروف المحيطة به وواقعة تسجيل العلامة.

المادة (٤٥)

على الوزارة إخطار السلطة المختصة في كل إمارة واتحاد غرف التجارة والصناعة وغرف التجارة والصناعة في الدولة بأسماء أصحاب العلامات التجارية المسجلة بالوزارة وبياناتها وما يطرأ عليها من تغيير أو تعديل أو شطب وذلك خلال ثلاثين يوماً من تاريخ التسجيل أو التغيير أو التعديل أو الشطب.

المادة (٤٦)

يكون للموظفين المختصين بمراقبة تنفيذ أحكام هذا القانون والقرارات المنفذة له والذين يصدر بتحديدهم قرار من وزير العدل بالاتفاق مع وزير الاقتصاد والتجارة والسلطة المختصة صفة مأموري الضبط القضائي ولهم بهذه الصفة حق الدخول إلى الأماكن التي يدخل نشاطها في نطاق أحكام هذا القانون عدا الأماكن المخصصة للسكن وذلك بغرض التأكد من تنفيذ أحكامه والقرارات المنفذة له وضبط الحالات المخالفة وعلى السلطات المحلية بالإمارات تقديم التسهيلات اللازمة لهؤلاء الموظفين لتمكينهم من القيام بعملهم.

المادة (٤٧)

يصدر بتحديد الرسوم التي تستوفى عن الاجراءات التي تتم بموجب أحكام هذا القانون قرار من مجلس الوزراء.

المادة (٤٨)

يلغى كل حكم يخالف أو يتعارض مع أحكام هذا القانون.

المادة (٤٩)

يصدر الوزير اللوائح والقرارات اللازمة لتنفيذ أحكام هذا القانون.

المادة (٥٠)

ينشر هذا القانون في الجريدة الرسمية ويعمل به بعد ثلاثة أشهر من تاريخ نشره.

زايد بن سلطان آل نهيان
رئيس دولة الامارات العربية المتحدة

صدر عنا في قصر الرئاسة بأبو ظبي
بتاريخ: ١ ربيع الثاني ١٤١٣هـ.
الموافق: ٢٨ سبتمبر ١٩٩٢م.

قانون اتحادي رقم (١٩) لسنة ٢٠٠٠م
بتعديل بعض أحكام القانون الإتحادي رقم (٣٧) لسنة ١٩٩٢م
في شأن العلامات التجارية

نحن زايد بن سلطان آل نهيان رئيس دولة الإمارات العربية المتحدة،

بعد الإطلاع على الدستور،

وعلى القانون الاتحادي رقم (١) لسنة ١٩٧٢ بشأن اختصاصات الوزارات وصلاحيات الوزراء والقوانين المعدلة له،

وعلى القانون الاتحادي رقم (٤) لسنة ١٩٧٩ في شأن قمع الغش والتدليس في المعاملات التجارية،

وعلى قانون المعاملات المدنية الصادر بالقانون الاتحادي رقم (٥) لسنة ١٩٨٥ والقوانين المعدلة،

وعلى قانون العقوبات الصادر بالقانون الاتحادي رقم (٣) لسنة ١٩٨٧،

وعلى القانون الاتحادي رقم (٣٧) لسنة ١٩٩٢ في شأن العلامات التجارية،

وعلى قانون المعاملات التجارية الصادر بالقانون الاتحادي رقم (١٨) لسنة ١٩٩٣،

وبناءً على ما عرضه وزير الاقتصاد والتجارة، وموافقة مجلس الوزراء، والمجلس الوطني الاتحادي، وتصديق المجلس الأعلى للاتحاد،

أصدرنا القانون الآتي:

المادة الأولى

يستبدل بنص المادة (١) من القانون الاتحادي رقم (٣٧) لسنة ١٩٩٢ المشار إليه النص الآتي:

مادة (١)

في تطبيق أحكام هذا القانون يقصد بالكلمات والعبارات التالية المعاني الموضحة قرين كل منها ما لم يقض سياق النص بغير ذلك:

الدولة: دولة الإمارات العربية المتحدة.

الوزارة: وزارة الاقتصاد والتجارة.

الوزير: وزير الاقتصاد والتجارة.

السلطة المختصة: السلطة المختصة في الإمارة.

النشرة: نشرة العلامات التجارية التي تصدرها الوزارة.

الرسم: كل تصميم يتضمن مجموعة من المرئيات (أي تكوين فني).

الرمز: كل رسم مرئي واحد.

الدمغات: العلامات المحفورة.

النقوش: العلامات البارزة.

الصور: صور الإنسان سواء كانت صورة صاحب المشروع أو صورة غيره.

اللجنة: لجنة العلامات التجارية المنصوص عليها في هذا القانون.

المادة الثانية

يستبدل بعبارة (الجريدة الرسمية) عبارة (النشرة) في المواد (١٤، ١٩، ٢٥، ٤٣) من القانون الاتحادي رقم (٣٧) لسنة ١٩٩٢ المشار إليه.

المادة الثالثة

ينشر هذا القانون في الجريدة الرسمية، ويعمل به من تاريخ نشره.

زايد بن سلطان آل نهيان
رئيس دولة الإمارات العربية المتحدة

صدر عنا في قصر الرئاسة بأبو ظبي:
بتاريخ: ١٨ جمادى الآخرة ١٤٢١هـ.
الموافق: ١٦ سبتمبر ٢٠٠٠م.

قانون اتحادي رقم (٨) لسنة ٢٠٠٢م
بتعديل بعض أحكام القانون الاتحادي رقم (٣٧) لسنة ١٩٩٢م
في شأن العلامات التجارية

نحن زايد بن سلطان آل نهيان رئيس دولة الإمارات العربية المتحدة،

بعد الإطلاع على الدستور،

وعلى القانون اتحادي رقم (١) لسنة ١٩٧٢ في شأن اختصاصات الوزارات وصلاحيات الوزراء والقوانين المعدلة له،

وعلى القانون اتحادي رقم (٤) لسنة ١٩٧٩ في شأن قمع الغش والتدليس في المعاملات التجارية،

وعلى قانون المعاملات المدنية الصادر بالقانون اتحادي رقم (٥) لسنة ١٩٨٥ والقوانين المعدلة له،

وعلى قانون العقوبات الصادر بالقانون اتحادي رقم (٣) لسنة ١٩٨٧.

وعلى القانون الاتحادي رقم (٣٧) لسنة ١٩٩٢ في شأن العلامات التجارية،

وعلى قانون المعاملات التجارية الصادر بالقانون الاتحادي رقم (١٨) لسنة ١٩٩٣،

وعلى المرسوم الاتحادي رقم (٢٠) لسنة ١٩٩٦ بشأن المصادقة على انضمام دولة الإمارات العربية المتحدة إلى اتفاقية باريس لحماية الملكية الصناعية،

وعلى المرسوم اتحادي رقم (٢١) لسنة ١٩٩٧ في شأن اتفاقية وبروتوكول انضمام الدولة إلى منظمة التجارة العالمية ووثيقة جولة (أورجواي)،

وبناءً على ما عرضه وزير الاقتصاد والتجارة، وموافقة مجلس الوزراء والمجلس الوطني الاتحادي، وتصديق المجلس الأعلى للاتحاد،

أصدرنا القانون الآتي:

المادة الاولى

يستبدل بنصوص المواد (۱) و(۳) و(٤) و(۸) و(۱۰) و(۱۱) و(۱۳) و(۱٤) و(۱٦) و(۱۷) و(۱۸) و(۱۹) و(۲۱) و(۲۲) و(۲۳) و(۲٥) و(۳۲) و(۳۷) و(۳۸) و(٤۱) و(٤۳) من القانون الاتحادي رقم (۳۷) لسنة ۱۹۹۲ المشار إليه النصوص الآتية:

مادة (۱)

في تطبيق أحكام هذا القانون يقصد بالكلمات والعبارات التالية المعاني الموضحة قرين كل منها ما لم يقض سياق النص بغير ذلك:

الدولة:	دولة الإمارات العربية المتحدة.
الوزارة:	وزارة الاقتصاد والتجارة.
الوزير:	وزير الاقتصاد والتجارة.
السلطة المختصة:	السلطة المختصة في الإمارة.
النشرة:	نشرة العلامات التجارية التي تصدرها الوزارة.
الرسم:	كل تصميم يتضمن مجموعة من المرئيات (أي تكوين فني).
الرمز:	كل رسم مرئي واحد.
الدمغات:	العلامات المحفورة.
النقوش:	العلامات البارزة.
الصور:	صور الإنسان سواء كانت صورة صاحب المشروع أو صورة غيره.
السجل:	سجل العلامات التجارية لدى الوزارة.
اللجنة:	لجنة العلامات التجارية المنصوص عليها في هذا القانون.

مادة (۳)

لا يسجل كعلامة تجارية أو كعنصر منها ما يأتي:

۱. العلامة الخالية من أية صفة أو طابع مميز أو العلامة المكونة من بيانات ليست إلا التسمية التي يطلقها العرف على البضائع والمنتجات والخدمات أو الرسوم المألوفة والصور العادية للبضائع و لمنتجات.

۲. أية علامة تخل بالآداب العامة أو تخالف النظام العام.

۳. الشعارات العامة والأعلام وغيرها من الرموز الخاصة بالدولة أو المنظمات العربية أو الدولية أو إحدى مؤسساتها أو أية دولة أجنبية إلا بتفويض منها، وكذلك أي تقليد لتلك الشعارات أو الأعلام أو الرموز.

٤. رموز الهلال الأحمر أو الصليب الأحمر وغيرها من الرموز الأخرى المشابهة وكذلك العلامات التي تكون تقليداً لها.

٥. العلامات المماثلة أو المشابهة للرموز ذات الصبغة الدينية المحضة.

٦. الأسماء والبيانات الجغرافية إذا كان من شأن استعمالها أن يحدث لبساً فيما يتعلق بمنشأ البضاعة أو المنتجات أو الخدمات أو مصدرها.

٧. اسم الغير أو لقبه أو صورته أو شعاره ما لم يوافق هو أو ورثته مقدماً على استعماله.

٨. البيانات الخاصة بدرجات الشرف التي لا يثبت طالب التسجيل استحقاقه لها قانوناً.

٩. العلامات التي من شأنها أن تضلل الجمهور أو التي تتضمن بيانات كاذبة عن منشأ أو مصدر المنتجات أو الخدمات أو عن صفاتها الأخرى، وكذلك العلامات التي تحتوي على اسم تجاري وهمي أو مقلد أو مزور.

١٠. العلامات المملوكة لأشخاص طبيعيين أو معنويين يكون التعامل معهم محظوراً.

١١. العلامة التي ينشأ عن تسجيلها لبعض فئات المنتجات أو الخدمات الحط من قيمة المنتجات أو الخدمات الأخرى التي تميزها العلامة.

١٢. العلامات التي تشمل الألفاظ أو العبارات الآتية: (امتياز) أو (ذو امتياز) أو (مسجل) أو (رسم مسجل) أو (حقوق الطبع) أو (التقليد يعتبر تزويرا) أو ما شابه ذلك من الألفاظ والعبارات.

١٣. الأوسمة الوطنية والأجنبية، و العملات المعدنية أو الورقية.

١٤. العلامة التي تعتبر مجرد ترجمة لعلامة مشهورة أو لعلامة أخرى سبق تسجيلها إذا كان من شأن التسجيل أن يحدث لبساً لدى جمهور المستهلكين بالنسبة للمنتجات التي تميزها العلامة أو المنتجات المماثلة.

مادة (٤)

١. لا يجوز تسجيل العلامات التجارية ذات الشهرة العالمية التي تجاوز حدود البلد الأصلي للعلامة إلى البلاد الأخرى، إلا بناءً على طلب مالكها الأصلي أو بناءً على توكيل رسمي منه.

٢. ولتحديد ما إذا كانت العلامة ذات شهرة يراعى مدى معرفتها لدى الجمهور المعني نتيجة ترويجها.

٣. ولا يجوز تسجيل العلامات ذات الشهرة لتمييز سلع أو خدمات غير مماثلة أو مطابقة لتلك التي تميزها هذه العلامات إذا:

أ– دل استخدام العلامة على صلة بين السلع والخدمات المطلوب تمييزها وسلع أو خدمات صاحب العلامة الأصلية.

ب– أدى استخدام العلامة لاحتمال الإضرار بمصالح صاحب العلامة الأصلية.

مادة (٨)

يجوز تسجيل العلامة التجارية عن فئة واحدة أو أكثر من فئات المنتجات أو الخدمات بحسب التصنيف الدولي وقواعده الواردة في اللائحة التنفيذية لهذا القانون ، ولا يجوز أن يشتمل طلب تسجيل العلامة على أكثر من فئة واحدة.

مادة (١٠)

مع مراعاة حكم المادة (٢٦) من هذا القانون، لا يجوز تسجيل أية علامة تجارية مطابقة أو مشابهة لعلامة سبق تسجيلها عن ذات المنتجات أو الخدمات، أو عن منتجات أو خدمات غير مماثلة إذا كان من شأن استعمال العلامة المطلوب تسجيلها أن يولد انطباعاً بالربط بينها وبين منتجات أو خدمات مالك العلامة المسجلة أو أن يؤدي لاحتمال الإضرار بمصالحه.

وإذا طلب شخص أو أكثر في تاريخ واحد تسجيل العلامة ذاتها أو علامات متقاربة أو متشابهة عن ذات المنتجات أو الخدمات أو عن منتجات أو خدمات مماثلة لها تقع في ذات الفئة، وجب على الوزارة وقف تسجيل جميع الطلبات إلى أن يقدم تنازل مصدق عليه من المتنازعين لمصلحة أحدهم أو إلى أن يصدر حكم نهائي لمصلحة أي منهم.

مادة (١١)

يجوز للوزارة أن تفرض ما تراه لازماً من القيود والتعديلات لتحديد العلامة التجارية وتوضيحها على وجه يمنع التباسها بعلامة أخرى سبق تسجيلها أو لأي سبب آخر تراه. ويفترض احتمال حدوث التباس في حالة استخدام علامة تجارية لتمييز سلع أو خدمات متطابقة.

وإذا رفضت الوزارة تسجيل العلامة التجارية لسبب ما، أو علق التسجيل على قيود أو تعديلات وجب عليها أن تخطر طالب التسجيل كتابة بأسباب قرارها.

وفي جميع الأحوال يتعين على الوزارة أن تبت في طلب التسجيل خلال ثلاثين يوماً من تاريخ تقديمه متى كان مستوفياً للشروط والأوضاع المنصوص عليها في هذا القانون ولائحته التنفيذية.

مادة (١٣)

تشكل لجنة العلامات التجارية برئاسة وكيل الوزارة وعضوية كل من:

– عضوين يمثلان الوزارة يرشحهما الوزير.
– عضو مجلس إدارة من اتحاد غرف التجارة والصناعة في الدولة يرشحه اتحاد الغرف.
– عضو مجلس إدارة عن كل غرفة من غرف التجارة والصناعة في الدولة ترشحه الغرفة المعنية.

وتختار اللجنة من بين أعضائها نائباً للرئيس، ويكون اجتماعها صحيحا بحضور أغلبية أعضائها، وتصدر القرارات بأغلبية الأعضاء الحاضرين وفي حالة التساوي في الأصوات يرجح الجانب الذي فيه الرئيس، وتجتمع مرة على الأقل شهرياً.

ويكون للجنة مقرر ترشحه الوزارة.

وتحدد بقرار من مجلس الوزراء مكافآت أعضاء اللجنة والمقرر.

مادة (١٤)

إذا قبلت الوزارة العلامة التجارية وجب عليها قبل تسجيلها أن تعلن عنها في النشرة وفي صحيفتين يوميتين تصدران في الدولة باللغة العربية ، وذلك على نفقة طالب التسجيل.

ولكل ذي شأن أن يعترض على تسجيل العلامة، ويقدم الاعتراض كتابة إلى الوزارة أو يرسل إليها بالبريد المسجل أو البريد الإلكتروني خلال ثلاثين يوماً من تاريخ آخر إعلان، وعلى الوزارة أن تخطر طالب التسجيل بصورة من الاعتراض على طلبه خلال خمسة عشر يوماً من تاريخ تسلمها له.

وعلى طالب التسجيل أن يقدم إلى الوزارة رداً مكتوباً على هذا الاعتراض في خلال ثلاثين يوماً من تاريخ إبلاغه به، فإذا لم يصل الرد في الميعاد المذكور اعتبر طالب التسجيل متنازلاً عن طلبه.

مادة (١٦)

إذا سجلت العلامة التجارية انسحب أثر التسجيل إلى تاريخ تقديم الطلب.

ويعطى لمالك العلامة بمجرد إتمام تسجيلها شهادة تشمل البيانات الآتية:

١. رقم تسجيل العلامة.

٢. تاريخ تقديم الطلب وتاريخ التسجيل.

٣. الاسم التجاري أو إسم مالك العلامة وجنسيته ومحل إقامته.

٤. صورة مطابقة للعلامة.

٥. بيان بالمنتجات أو بالبضائع أو بالخدمات المخصصة لها العلامة وبيان فئتها.

٦. رقم وتاريخ حق الأسبقية الدولي واسم الدولة العضو في اتفاقية باريس لحماية الملكية الصناعية التي أودع فيها طلب الأسبقية.

مادة (١٧)

يعتبر من قام بتسجيل العلامة مالكاً لها دون سواه ولا تجوز المنازعة في ملكية العلامة إذا استعملها من قام بتسجيلها بصفة مستمرة خمس سنوات على الأقل من تاريخ التسجيل دون أن ترفع عليه دعوى تقضي بعدم ملكيته للعلامة.

ويتمتع صاحب العلامة المسجلة بحق منع الغير من استعمال علامة مطابقة أو مشابهة لتمييز منتجات أو خدمات مطابقة أو مشابهة أو مرتبطة بالمنتجات والخدمات التي سجلت عنها العلامة على نحو يؤدي لإحداث لبس لدى جمهور المستهلكين.

مادة (١٨)

يجوز لمالك علامة تجارية سبق تسجيلها أن يقدم في أي وقت طلباً إلى الوزارة لإدخال أية إضافة أو تعديل على المنتجات أو الخدمات التي تميزها العلامة، أو على العلامة ذاتها على ألا يمس التعديل ذاتية العلامة مساساً جوهرياً.

ويصدر قرار الوزارة في شأن طلب التعديل على المنتجات أو الخدمات وفقاً للشروط والقواعد المتعلقة بشطب تسجيل العلامة عن بعض المنتجات أو الخدمات. أما قرارها في شأن التعديل على العلامة فيصدر وفقاً للشروط والقواعد المقرره للبت في طلبات التسجيل الأصلية، ويكون قابلاً للتظلم والطعن فيه بالطرق ذاتها.

ويعلن عن التعديل في النشرة وفي صحيفتين يوميتين تصدران في الدولة باللغة العربية، وذلك على نفقة طالب التعديل.

مادة (١٩)

مدة الحماية المترتبة على تسجيل العلامة التجارية عشر سنوات، ولصاحب العلامة أن يكفل استمرار الحماية لمدد متتالية كل منها عشر سنوات إذا قدم طلباً بتجديد تسجيل العلامة خلال السنة الأخيرة من مدة الحماية السارية وفقاً للأوضاع والشروط المنصوص عليها في هذا القانون ولائحته التنفيذية.

ويتم تجديد تسجيل العلامة دون أي فحص إضافي ودون أن يسمح للغير بالمعارضة في التجديد.

ويشهر تجديد تسجيل العلامة في النشرة وفي صحيفتين يوميتين تصدران في الدولة باللغة العربية على نفقة صاحب العلامة.

ولا يجوز في حالة طلب تجديد تسجيل العلامة إدخال أي تغيير عليها أو شطب أو إضافة أية منتجات أو خدمات على قائمة المنتجات أو الخدمات التي سجلت عنها العلامة.

وعلى الوزارة خلال الشهر التالي لانتهاء مدة الحماية أن تقوم بإخطار صاحب العلامة كتابة على عنوانه المقيد في السجل بانتهاء مدة حمايتها، وإذا لم يقم صاحب العلامة بتقديم طلب التجديد خلال الثلاثة أشهر التالية لتاريخ انتهاء مدة الحماية قامت الوزارة من تلقاء نفسها بشطب العلامة من السجل.

مادة (٢١)

مع عدم الإخلال بحكم المادة (١٧) من هذا القانون يكون لكل ذي شأن الحق في طلب الحكم بشطب العلامة التجارية التي تكون قد سجلت بغير حق، وعلى الوزارة أن تقوم بشطب التسجيل متى قدم لها حكم بات مذيل بالصيغة التنفيذية.

مادة (٢٢)

للمحكمة المدنية المختصة أن تحكم بناءً على طلب كل ذي شأن بشطب تسجيل العلامة التجارية إذا ثبت لديها أنها لم تستعمل خمس سنوات متتالية إلا إذا أثبت مالك العلامة أن عدم استعمالها كان لسبب أجنبي عنه، ويعتبر سبباً اجنبياً ، قيود الاستيراد والشروط الحكومية الأخرى التي تفرض على السلع والخدمات التي تميزها العلامة.

ولغايات هذه المادة، يعتبر استعمال العلامة من قبل شخص مخول بذلك من مالكها استخداماً لها.

مادة (٢٣)

للمحكمة المدنية المختصة، بناءً على طلب ذي الشأن، الأمر بإضافة أي بيان للسجل يكون قد أغفل تدوينه به، أو بحذف أو بتعديل أي بيان وارد في السجل، إذا كان قد دون بدون وجه حق أو كان غير مطابق للحقيقة، وللوزارة أن تقوم بذلك من تلقاء نفسها.

مادة (٢٥)

يجب إشهار شطب العلامة التجارية من السجل في النشرة وفي صحيفتين يوميتين تصدران في الدولة باللغة العربية، وذلك على نفقة طالب إشهار الشطب.

مادة (٣٢)

لا يجوز للمستفيد من الترخيص التنازل عنه لغيره أو منح تراخيص من الباطن ما لم ينص عقد الترخيص على خلاف ذلك.

ولا يجوز الإلزام بالترخيص الإجباري لاستغلال العلامة التجارية في أي حال من الأحوال.

مادة (٣٧)

يعاقب بالحبس وبالغرامة التي لا تقل عن خمسة آلاف درهم أو بإحدى هاتين العقوبتين:

١. كل من زور علامة تجارية تم تسجيلها طبقاً للقانون أو قلدها بطريقة تدعو إلى تضليل الجمهور سواء بالنسبة للسلع والخدمات التي تميزها العلامة الأصلية أو تلك التي تماثلها، وكل من استعمل علامة تجارية مزورة أو مقلدة مع علمه بذلك.

٢. كل من وضع بسوء نية على منتجاته علامة تجارية مسجلة مملوكة لغيره أو استعمل تلك العلامة بغير حق.

٣. كل من باع أو عرض للبيع أو للتداول أو حاز بقصد البيع منتجات عليها علامة تجارية مزورة أو مقلدة أو موضوعة بغير حق مع علمه بذلك. وكذلك كل من قدم أو عرض تقديم خدمات تحت علامة تجارية مزورة أو مقلدة أو مستعملة بغير حق مع علمه بذلك.

مادة (٣٨)

يعاقب بالحبس مدة لا تجاوز سنة وبالغرامة التي لا تقل عن خمسة آلاف درهم ولا تزيد على عشرة آلاف درهم أو بإحدى هاتين العقوبتين:

١. كل من استعمل علامة غير قابلة للتسجيل وفقاً لما هو منصوص عليه في البنود (٢) و(٣) و(٤) و(٥) و(٦) و(٨) و(٩) و(١٠) و(١١) و(١٢) و(١٣) و(١٤) من المادة (٣) من هذا القانون.

٢. كل من دون بغير حق على علامته أو مستنداته بياناً يؤدي إلى الاعتقاد بحصول تسجيلها أو بتمييزها لمنتجات أو سلع غير تلك المذكورة في السجل.

مادة (٤١)

يجوز لمالك العلامة التجارية، في أي وقت ولو كان ذلك قبل رفع أية دعوى أن يستصدر، بناءً على عريضة مشفوعة بشهادة رسمية دالة على تسجيل العلامة، أمراً من المحكمة المختصة باتخاذ الإجراءات التحفظية اللازمة وعلى الأخص ما يأتي:

١. إجراء محضر حصر ووصف تفصيلي للآلات والأدوات التي تستخدم أو التي استخدمت في ارتكاب أي من الجرائم المنصوص عليها في هذا القانون، وكذلك المنتجات أو البضائع المحلية أو المستوردة وعناوين المحلات أو الأغلفة أو الأوراق أو غيرها تكون قد وضعت عليها العلامة أو البيان موضوع الجريمة.

٢. توقيع الحجز على الأشياء المذكورة في البند السابق، وذلك بعد أن يقدم الطالب تأميناً مالياً تقدره المحكمة لتعويض المحجوز عليه عند الاقتضاء.

ويجوز للمحكمة ندب خبير أو أكثر للمعاونة في تنفيذ الإجراءات التحفظية.

ويستثنى أصحاب العلامات المشهورة من شرط تقديم الشهادة الدالة على تسجيل العلامة.

مادة (٤٣)

للمحكمة المختصة أن تحكم بمصادرة الأشياء المحجوزة عليها أو التي يحجز عليها فيما بعد واستنزال ثمنها من الغرامات أو التعويضات أو التصرف فيها بأية طريقة أخرى تراها المحكمة مناسبة ويجوز للمحكمة أيضا أن تأمر بإتلاف العلامات غير القانونية أو أن تأمر عند الاقتضاء بإتلاف المنتجات والأغلفة ومعدات الحزم وغيرها من الأشياء التي تحمل تلك العلامات أو تحمل بيانات غير قانونية وبمصادرة الآلات والأدوات التي استعملت بصفة خاصة في عملية التزوير ولها أن تأمر بكل ما سبق حتى في حالة الحكم بالبراءة.

ويجوز للمحكمة كذلك أن تأمر بنشر الحكم على نفقة المحكوم عليه في النشرة أو في إحدى الصحف التي تصدر في الدولة باللغة العربية.

المادة الثانية

تضاف مادة جديدة برقم (٢٠) مكرراً للقانون الاتحادي رقم (٣٧) لسنة ١٩٩٢ المشار إليه يكون نصها الآتي:

"للوزارة أن تقوم بشطب العلامة التي سجلت دون وجه حق بعد إخطار ذوي الشأن بسبب الشطب وسماع أقوالهم والوقوف على أوجه دفاعهم.

ولذوي الشأن الطعن في قرار الشطب لدى المحكمة المدنية المختصة خلال ثلاثين يوماً من تاريخ الإخطار بالشطب."

المادة الثالثة

ينشر هذا القانون في الجريدة الرسمية ، ويعمل به من تاريخ نشره.

زايد بن سلطان آل نهيان
رئيس دولة الامارات العربية المتحدة

صدر عنا في قصر الرئاسة بأبو ظبي:
بتاريخ ١٤ جمادى الأول ١٤٢٣هـ
الموافق: ٢٠٠٢/٧/٢٤م.

قرار وزاري رقم (٦) لسنة ١٩٩٣م
باللائحة التنفيذية للقانون الاتحادي رقم (٣٧) لسنة ١٩٩٢م
في شأن العلامات التجارية

وزير الاقتصاد والتجارة،

بعد الاطلاع على القانون الاتحادي رقم (١) لسنة ١٩٧٢م في شأن اختصاصات
الوزارات وصلاحيات الوزراء والقوانين المعدلة له،

وعلى القانون الاتحادي رقم (٣٧) لسنة ١٩٩٢م في شأن العلامات التجارية.

وبناءً على عرضه وكيل الوزارة.

قرر ما يلي:

الباب الاول
تعريفات

المادة (١)

في تطبق احكام هذا القرار يقصد بالعبارات والالفاظ الاتية المعاني الموضحة قرين كل
منها:

الدولة:	دولة الامارات العربية المتحدة.
الوزارة:	وزارة الاقتصاد والتجارة.
الوزير:	وزير الاقتصاد والتجارة.
القانون:	قانون العلامات التجارية.
العلامة:	العلامة التجارية.
السجل:	سجل العلامات التجارية.
القسم:	قسم الرقابة التجارية.

اللجنة: لجنة العلامات التجارية المنصوص عليها في المادة (١٣) من القانون.

السلطة المختصة: السلطة المختصة في الامارة المعنية.

المادة (٢)

يختص القسم في الوزارة بتطبيق قانون العلامات التجارية ولائحته التنفيذية وتحصيل الرسوم المقررة.

المادة (٣)

يقدم طلب تسجيل العلامة على النموذج المعد لذلك الى القسم من قبل صاحب العلامة اذا كان له موطن في الدولة، او من قبل مكتب محاماة مرخص في الدولة، وتلصق صورة من العلامة المطلوب تسجيلها في الفراغ المخصص لها بالنموذج.

المادة (٤)

يجب ان يكون الطلب قاصراً على تسجيل العلامة عن فئة واحدة من فئات المنتجات او البضائع او الخدمات المبينة بالملحق رقم (١) المرفق بهذه اللائحة.

المادة (٥)

يجب ان يشتمل طلب التسجيل على البيانات الاتية:

١. اسم الطالب ولقبه ومهنته واسمه التجاري – ان وجد – واذا كان الطالب شركة ذكر اسمها او عنوانها وشكلها وغرضها.

٢. جنسية الطالب ومحل اقامته ونوع تجارته.

٣. العلامة المطلوب تسجيلها.

٤. بيان البضائع او المنتجات او الخدمات المطلوب تسجيل العلامة عنها مع ذكر رقم فئة المنتجات التي تتبعها.

٥. الجهة التي يوجد بها المحل التجاري او مشروع الاستغلال الذي تستخدم العلامة او يراد لها ان تستخدم في تمييز بضائعه او منتجاته او خدماته.

٦. المحل المختار في دولة الامارات العربية المتحدة – ان وجد – الذي توجه اليه المكاتبات والمستندات المتعلقة بالتسجيل.

٧. توقيع الطالب او ممثله، واذا كان الطلب مقدماً من شركة او مؤسسة فتوقيع صاحب الصفة في تمثيلها.

المادة (٦)

اذا كان لطلب التسجيل مجموعة من العلامات المتماثلة في عناصرها الجوهرية والتي يقتصر اختلافها على امور لا تمس ذاتيتها مساساً جوهرياً ومطلوب تسجيلها عن بضائع او منتجات او خدمات تابعة لفئة واحدة من الفئات المبينة بالملحق رقم (١) فيجوز تقديم طلب واحد لتسجيلها.

المادة (٧)

يرفق بطلب التسجيل ما يلي:

١. عشر صور مطابقة لنموذج العلامة الملصق على طلب التسجيل.

٢. سند الوكالة – موثق حسب الاصول – اذا كان الطلب مقدماً من مكتب محاماة عن صاحب الشأن.

٣. شهادة بالقيد في السجل التجاري، أو ما يقوم مقامها داخل الدولة او خارجها.

٤. شهادة تسجيل العلامة في أي بلد اجنبي اذا كان مطالباً بأولوية خاصة – ان وجدت.

المادة (٨)

اذا اشتملت العلامة المطلوب تسجيلها على لفظ او اكثر مكتوب بلغة اجنبية وجب تقديم ترجمة معتمدة باللغة العربية معها.

الباب الثاني
اجراءات التسجيل

المادة (٩)

تقيد طلبات التسجيل في سجل خاص بالوزراة يسمى (سجل ايداع الطلبات) بأرقام مسلسلة حسب تواريخ ايداعها، ويسلم الطالب ايصالاً باستلام الطلب يشتمل على البيانات التالية:

١. الرقم المسلسل للطلب.

٢. اسم طالب التسجيل ومحل اقامته.

٣. تاريخ وساعة ايداع الطلب.

٤. فئة المنتجات او البضائع او الخدمات المتعلق بها الطلب.

٥. بيان المستندات المرفقة بالطلب.

المادة (١٠)

يقوم القسم بفحص طلب التسجيل ومراجعته والتحقق من ان العلامة المطلوب تسجيلها ليست مطابقة او مشابهة لعلامة سبق تسجيلها، او سبق تقديم طلب بشأن تسجيلها، او انها محظورة من مكتب مقاطعة اسرائيل بالوزارة وبالنسبة للعلامات التي تخصص للدلالة على مراقبة منتجات معينة او فحصها يقوم القسم بالتحقق من موافقة الوزير عليها.

المادة (١١)

يجوز للقسم قبل البت في طلب التسجيل تكليف الطالب او ممثله (مكتب المحاماة) بتقديم مايراه لازماً من بيانات أو يفرض ما يراه من شروط لقبول الطلب كما يجوز له تكليف الطالب بادخال ما يراه لازماً من تعديلات على العلامة لتحديدها وتوضيحها على وجه يمنع التباسها بعلامة اخرى سبق تسجيلها او تقديم طلب بشأن تسجيلها.

المادة (١٢)

اذا قرر القسم رفض طلب التسجيل او تعليق قبوله على قيود او تعديلات وجب اخطار الطالب كتابة باسباب القرار. ويجب ان يشتمل الاخطار على بيان حق الطالب في التظلم الى اللجنة مع ذكر المواعيد والاجراءات المتعلقة بالتظلم.

المادة (١٣)

اذا قدم تظلم للجنة يقوم القسم باخطار طالب التسجيل بميعاد انعقاد اللجنة لنظر التظلم وتكليفه بالحضور امامها لابداء ما لديه من بيانات على ان يصله الاخطار قبل موعد انعقاد الجلسة بعشرة ايام على الاقل ويكون التكليف بالحضور بخطاب موصى عليه او بالفاكس او التلكس.

المادة (١٤)

اذا رفضت اللجنة التظلم فللطالب الطعن في قرار اللجنة امام المحكمة المدنية المختصة خلال ستين يوماً من تاريخ ابلاغه بقرارها في التظلم المقدم منه.

المادة (١٥)

يعتبر الطالب متنازلاً عن طلبه اذا لم يقم خلال الميعاد المحدد باستيفاء البيانات او الشروط التي طلبها القسم او اذا لم يطعن في قرار اللجنة خلال الميعاد الذي يحدده الاخطار الموجه اليه في هذا الشأن.

المادة (١٦)

في حالة قبول الطلب يلتزم القسم قبل تسجيله العلامة بنشر البيانات التالية عنها في الجريدة الرسمية وفي صحيفتين يوميتين تصدران في الدولة وذلك على نفقة الطالب.

١. اسم طالب التسجيل وجنسيته ومهنته وموطنه.

٢. صورة مطابقة للعلامة.

٣. الرقم المتتابع لطلب التسجيل.

٤. البضائع او المنتجات او الخدمات التي طلب تسجيل العلامة عنها مع بيان فئة المنتجات التي تتبعها.

٥. الجهة[4] التي يوجد بها المحل التجاري او المشروع الذي يستخدم العلامة او يريد استخدامها في تمييز بضائعه او منتجاته او خدماته.

المادة (١٧)

لكل ذي شأن خلال ثلاثين يوماً من تاريخ اخر اعلان عن العلامة ان يقدم بشخصه اعتراضاً مكتوباً للقسم او يرسله اليه بالبريد المسجل.

وعلى القسم اخطار طالب التسجيل بصورة من الاعتراض على طلبه خلال خمسة عشر يوماً من تلقي الاعتراض.

المادة (١٨)

يعتبر طالب التسجيل متنازلاً عن طلبه اذا لم يقدم للقسم رداً مكتوباً على الاعتراض المذكور في المادة السابقة خلال ثلاثين يوماً من تاريخ اخطاره به.

---

[4]. وردت هذه الكلمة في نص الجريدة الرسمية "الجنة" والأصح ان تكون "الجهة" فاقتضى التنويه.

المادة (١٩)

يتعين على القسم سماع اي من الطرفين في موضوع الاعتراض اذا طلب سماع اقواله ويفصل القسم في الاعتراض بعد هذا السماع، ويصدر قراره برفض التسجيل او قبوله او تقييد القبول بما يراه من قيود او شروط.

المادة (٢٠)

لكل ذي شأن ان يتظلم للجنة من قرار القسم الصادر وفقاً للمادة السابقة خلال خمسة عشر يوماً من تاريخ اخطاره به، واذا لم تقبل اللجنة تظلمه فله حق الطعن في قرارها امام المحكمة المختصة خلال ثلاثين يوماً من تاريخ ابلاغه بذلك القرار.

المادة (٢١)

يحتفظ القسم بسجل لتسجيل العلامات التجارية تخصص منه صفحة لكل علامة من العلامات التجارية تدون فيه البيانات التالية:

١. الرقم المسلسل للعلامة وصورتها.

٢. تاريخ تقديم طلب تسجيل العلامة وتاريخ التسجيل.

٣. اسم مالك العلامة ولقبه وجنسيته ومحل اقامته واسمه التجاري – ان وجد – واذا كان المالك شركة ذكر اسمها او عنوانها وغرضها ومركز ادارتها.

٤. البضائع او المنتجات او الخدمات التي سجلت عنها العلامة وفئتها.

٥. المحل المختار في الدونة الذي توجه اليه المكاتبات والمراسلات المتعلقة بالتسجيل.

٦. الجهة التي يوجد بها المحل التجاري او المشروع المخصص للعلامة لتمييز بضائعه او منتجاته او خدماته.

٧. القيود التي يطلبها القسم لحصول التسجيل.

٨. اية تعديلات تطرأ على العلامة بعد التسجيل.

٩. انتقال ملكية العلامة او رهنها.

١٠. شطب الرهن.

١١. تجديد تسجيل العلامة وشطبها.

١٢. الترخيص بالانتفاع بالعلامة ومدته وشطبه.

المادة (٢٢)

يدون في نفس الصفحة كل علامة من العلامات المرتبطة معها مع بيان ما يدل على الارتباط وتذكر ارقام العلامات الاخرى المرتبطة بها.

وتخصص لتسجيل مجموعة العلامات المنصوص عليها في المادة السادسة من هذه اللائحة صفحة واحدة يشار فيها للعلامات المكونة للمجموعة والى ما يفيد بأنها علامات مرتبطة.

المادة (٢٣)

اذا تم تسجيل علامة دون تخصيص لون معين لها او لجزء منها اعتبر تسجيلها شاملاً لجميع الالوان.

المادة (٢٤)

يزود صاحب العلامة – بعد اتمام التسجيل وسداد الرسوم – بشهادة وفق النموذج المعد لذلك.

المادة (٢٥)

يخطر القسم السلطة المختصة في كل امارة واتحاد غرف التجارة والصناعة وغرف التجارة والصناعة في الدولة باسم صاحب العلامة والبيانات الواردة في شهادة التسجيل خلال ثلاثين يوماً من تاريخ التسجيل وتحتفظ الجهات المذكورة بسجل خاص تدون فيه البيانات الواردة من الوزارة والمبينة في شهادة التسجيل المشار اليها في المادة (٢٤) من هذه اللائحة ويكون لكل علامة صفحة خاصة في ذلك السجل.

الباب الثالث
التعديلات او الاضافات التي تطرأ على التسجيل

المادة (٢٦)

على صاحب العلامة الذي يريد ادخال اي تعديل او اضافة على علامته المسجلة لا يمس ذاتيتها مساساً جوهرياً ان يتقدم بطلب على النموذج المعد لذلك الى القسم ويرفق به عشر صور للعلامة بعد تعديلها وينظر القسم في هذا الطلب وفقاً للشروط والقواعد

المتعلقة بطلبات التسجيل الاصلية كما يخضع هذا الطلب من حيث البت فيه والتظلم والطعن لنفس الطرق والإجراءات المتعلقة بالطلب الاصلي.

المادة (٢٧)

يجوز لصاحب العلامة المسجلة ان يطلب قيد البيانات التالية في السجل:

١. تغيير اسم ولقب المالك أو مهنته او جنسيته، وفي حالة الشركات يدون كل تغيير يطرأ على اسمها أو عنوانها أو غرضها.

٢. شطب بعض البضائع او المنتجات او الخدمات المخصصة لها العلامة.

٣. تغيير المحل المختار للمراسلات والمكاتبات والاوراق المتعلقة بالتسجيل.

واذا كانت البيانات المطلوب تدونيها متعلقة بعلامات مرتبطة اكتفى بتقديم طلب واحد للقيد بمقتضاه في صفحات تسجيل تلك العلامات.

المادة (٢٨)

يقيد في السجل كل اجراء يصدر به حكم من المحكمة المختصة.

المادة (٢٩)

يتولى القسم قيد العلامات في السجل واشهارها في الجريدة الرسمية بعد سداد مصاريف الاعلان ويشتمل القيد على الرقم المسلسل للعلامة واسم مالكها وبيان التعديلات او التغييرات التي طرأت مع الاشارة الى رقم الجريدة الرسمية التي تم بها اشهار تسجيل العلامة.

ويخطر القسم السلطة المختصة في كل امارة واتحاد غرف التجارة والصناعة وغرف التجارة والصناعة في الدولة بالتغيير او التعديل خلال ثلاثين يوماً من تاريخه.

الباب الرابع
تجديد تسجيل العلامة

المادة (٣٠)

يقدم طلب تجديد مدة الحماية المترتبة على التسجيل الى القسم على النموذج المعد لذلك خلال السنة الاخيرة من مدة حماية العلامة وترفق بالنموذج شهادة التسجيل وما يفيد اداء رسم التجديد.

المادة (٣١)

يقوم القسم خلال الشهر التالي لانتهاء مدة حماية العلامة بإخطار مالكها كتابة على عنوانه المقيد في السجل بانتهاء مدة حمايتها، وعليه تقديم طلب التجديد وفقاً للكيفية المشار اليها في المادة السابقة خلال الثلاثة اشهر التالية لتاريخ انتهاء مدة الحماية.

المادة (٣٢)

تتم الموافقة على طلبات التجديد المقبوله دون اي فحص اضافي ودون ان يسمح للغير بالمعارضة في التجديد اذا قدمت في المواعيد وبالاوضاع المشار اليها في المادتين (٣٠ و ٣١) من هذه اللائحة.

المادة (٣٣)

يشهر تجديد تسجيل العلامة في الجريدة الرسمية وفي صحيفتين يوميتين تصدران في الدولة وذلك على نفقة صاحبها على ان يتضمن ذلك البيانات التالية:

١. الرقم المسلسل للعلامة.

٢. اسم مالكها ومهنته ومحل اقامته، واذا كان المالك شركة ذكر اسمها او عنوانها وغرضها.

٣. تاريخ تسجيل العلامة.

الباب الخامس
شطب التسجيل

المادة (٣٤)

على صاحب العلامة التجارية الذي يرغب في شطب تسجيلها عن كل البضائع او المنتجات او الخدمات التي سجلت عنها او عن بعضها ان يتقدم بطلب الى القسم على النموذج المعد لذلك واذا تبين من واقع السجل سبق الترخيص باستعمال العلامة فلا يتم الشطب الا بناءً على موافقة كتابية من المرخص له باستعمالها ما لم يتضمن عقد الترخيص نصاً يقضي بموافقة المرخص له صراحة بتنازله عن الترخيص.

المادة (٣٥)

يقوم القسم بشطب العلامة في الاحوال التالية:

١. اذا لم يتم تجديد التسجيل وفقاً للمادة (١٩) من القانون.

٢. بناءً على طلب صاحبها وفقاً لاحكام المادة (٢٠) من القانون ويكون للشطب اثره من تاريخ الطلب.

٣. بناءً على حكم نهائي صادر من المحكمة المختصة بأن تسجيل العلامة كان بغير حق.

٤. بناءً على حكم من المحكمة المختصة صادر بشطب العلامة بسبب عدم الاستعمال الجدي غير المبرر لخمس سنوات متتالية وفقاً للمادة (٢٢) من القانون.

٥. بناءً على قرار من الوزير مبني على كتاب من مكتب مقاطعة اسرائيل في دولة الامارات العربية المتحدة وفقاً للمادة (٢٤) من القانون.

المادة (٣٦)

يقوم القسم بالتأشير بالشطب في السجل، ويشهر الشطب في الجريدة الرسمية على ان يشمل الاشهار البيانات التّالية:

١. الرقم المسلسل للعلامة.

٢. اسم مالكها ومهنته ومحل اقامته. واذا كان المالك شركة ذكر اسمها او عنوانها وغرضها.

٣. رقم الجريدة الرسمية التي اشهر فيها التسجيل.

٤. سبب الشطب وتاريخ حصوله.

ويخطر القسم السلطة المختصة في كل امارة واتحاد غرف التجارة والصناعة وغرف التجارة والصناعة في الدولة بالشطب خلال ثلاثين يوماً من تاريخ حصوله.

الباب السادس
انتقال ملكية العلامة ورهنها

المادة (٣٧)

يحصل التأشير في السجل بانتقال ملكية العلامة التي يسمح القانون ينقل ملكيتها بناءً على طلب يقدم للقسم ممن نتقلت اليه الملكية او من وكيله (مكتب محاماه).

ويحرر الطلب على النموذج المعد لذلك ويتضمن البيانات التالية:

١. الرقم المسلسل للعلامة.

٢. اسم ولقب ومهنة كل من ناقل الملكية ومن انتقلت اليه الملكية واسمه التجاري ومهنته واذا كان احدهما او كلاهما شركة ذكر اسمها او عنوانها والغرض من تأسيسها.

٣. محل اقامة الطالب وجنسيته.

٤. البضائع او المنتجات او الخدمات التي تميزها العلامة مع ذكر فئاتها.

٥. الجهة التي يوجد بها المحل التجاري او مشروع الاستغلال الذي تحميه العلامة.

٦. السند الذي حصل بموجبه انتقال الملكية وتاريخه.

المادة (٣٨)

ترفق بالطلب المشار اليه في المادة السابقة المستندات الدالة على انتقال ملكية العلامة، واذا كان الطالب شركة ارفق بالطلب كذلك صورة من صحيفة قيدها في السجل التجاري.

المادة (٣٩)

لا يجوز تقديم طلب لنقل ملكية علامة ما من العلامات التي تعتبر مرتبطة وفقاً للمادة السادسة من هذه اللائحة دون بقية العلامات الاخرى المرتبطة بها.

ويجوز تقديم طلب واحد للتأشير في السجل بنقل ملكية تلك العلامات.

المادة (٤٠)

يقوم القسم بالتأشير في السجل بما يفيد انتقال ملكية العلامة مع ذكر اسم المالك الجديد ومهنته وعنوانه وسبب انتقال الملكية وتاريخ حصوله وتاريخ التأشير به في السجل ويخطر القسم الطالب كتابة بحصول التأشير.

المادة (٤١)

يتم اشهار انتقال ملكية العلامة في الجريدة الرسمية وفي صحيفتين يوميتين بموجب اعلان على نفقة الطالب يتضمن البيانات التالية:

١. الرقم المسلسل للعلامة.

٢. تاريخ تسجيلها ورقم وتاريخ الجريدة الرسمية التي اشهر فيها التسجيل.

٣. البضائع او المنتجات او الخدمات المخصصة لها العلامة.

٤. اسم ومالك العلامة اسابق.

٥. اسم من انتقلت اليه الملكية وجنسيته ومهنته.

٦. تاريخ انتقال الملكية وتاريخ التأشير به في السجل.

المادة (٤٢)

يحصل التأشير في السجل برهن العلامة في السجل وفقاً للاجراءات والاوضاع الخاصة بانتقال ملكيتها وذلك بناءً على طلب يقدم من الدائن المرتهن على النموذج المعد لذلك ويشهر الرهن في الجريدة الرسمية وفي صحيفتين يوميتين بموجب اعلان بذات البيانات المنصوص عليها في المادة (٤١) من هذه اللائحة.

المادة (٤٣)

يشطب الرهن بناءً على طلب يقدم من مالك العلامة للقسم على النموذج المعد لذلك مصحوباً بالمستندات الدالة على انقضاء الرهن.

ويجب شهر الشطب بنشره في الجريدة الرسمية على نفقة الطالب يتضمن رقم وتاريخ الجريدة الرسمية التي تم فيها اشهار رهن العلامة.

الباب السابع
عقود الترخيص باستعمال العلامة

المادة (٤٤)

يكون الترخيص باستعمال العلامة التجارية لشخص او اكثر عن كل او بعض المنتجات او البضائع او الخدمات المسجلة عنها على ان يتم ذلك بموجب عقد مكتوب وموثق ولمدة لا تزيد عن المدة المقررة لحماية العلامة نفسها.

المادة (٤٥)

يتم اشهار الترخيص بالنشر عن العلامة في الجريدة الرسمية وفي صحيفتين يوميتين على نفقة الطالب وتتضمن النشرة البيانات التالية:

١. الرقم المتتابع للعلامة.

٢. تاريخ تسجيلها ورقم وتاريخ الجريدة الرسمية التي اشهر فيها التسجيل.

٣. البضائع او المنتجات او الخدمات المخصصة لها العلامة.

٤. اسم مالك العلامة ولقبه ومهنته وجنسيته.

٥. اسم المرخص له ولقبه ومهنته وجنسيته.

٦. تاريخ الترخيص باستعمال العلامة وتاريخ التأشير به في السجل.

المادة (٤٦)

يتم شطب قيد الترخيص بناءً على طلب من مالك العلامة او المستفيد من الترخيص يقدم للقسم على النموذج المعد لذلك.

ويرفق بالطلب ما يثبت انتهاء الترخيص او فسخه.

المادة (٤٧)

يتعين على القسم سماع اي من الطرفين في موضوع الاعتراض اذا طلب سماع اقواله خلال خمسة عشر يوماً من تلقي الطلب باخطار الطرف الاخر في عقد الترخيص بمضمون الطلب المقدم للشطب، مبيناً ان له حق الاعتراض على طلب الشطب خلال ثلاثين يوماً من تلقيه هذا الاخطار والا سقط حقه في الاعتراض.

المادة (٤٨)

يتعين على القسم سماع اي من الطرفين في موضوع الاعتراض متى طلب سماع اقواله ويفصل القسم في الاعتراض بعد ذلك ويصدر قراره برفض الاعتراض او قبوله.

المادة (٤٩)

لاي من الطرفين حق التظلم امام اللجنة من قرار القسم خلال خمسة عشر يوماً من تاريخ اخطاره به، ولاي منهما كذلك حق الطعن في قرار اللجنة امام المحكمة المختصة خلال ثلاثين يوماً من تاريخ ابلاغه بقرارها.

المادة (٥٠)

في حالة عدم الاعتراض على شطب الترخيص او صدور قرار نهائي بإقرار الشطب يقوم القسم بشطب الترخيص من السجل مع ذكر سبب الشطب وتاريخ حصوله ويخطر الطالب كتابة بحصول الشطب.

المادة (٥١)

يقوم القسم بشهر شطب الترخيص بموجب نشره في الجريدة الرسمية على نفقة الطالب يتضمن رقم وتاريخ الجريدة الرسمية التي تم فيها اشهار الترخيص باستعمال العلامة.

الباب الثامن
العلامات التي تخصص للدلالة على مراقبة منتجات معينة او فحصها

المادة (٥٢)

تقدم طلبات تسجيل العلامات المخصصة للدلالة على مراقبة منتجات معينة او فحصها للقسم على النموذج المعد لذلك مصحوبة بالمستندات التالية:

١. عشر صور للعلامة مطابقة للصورة الملصقة على نموذج طلب التسجيل.

٢. نسختين رسميتين من النظام الاساسي للشخص الاعتباري الذي يتولى المراقبة او الفحص مع بيان التعديلات التي تكون قد ادخلت على ذلك النظام.

٣. موافقة الوزير على تسجيل العلامة.

٤. نسختين من قائمة البضائع او المنتجات او الخدمات التي تستخدم العلامة في فحصها مع بيان خصائصها او نوعيتها.

٥. بيان الاشخاص الذين سيستخدمون العلامة.

٦. نسختين من القواعد التي يتبعها طالب التسجيل في عمليات المراقبة او الفحص مع بيان التعديلا ت التي قد تكون ادخلت على تلك القواعد.

المادة (٥٣)

تسجيل العلامات المنصوص عليها في هذا الفصل في قسم خاص من السجل بنفس الشروط والقواعد المتبعة في تسجيل العلامات الاخرى.

المادة (٥٤)

يكون النشر عن هذه العلامات مصحوباً بموجز للقواعد التي يتبعها الطالب في عمليات المراقبة او الفحص.

المادة (٥٥)

اي تعديل يجريه مالك هذه العلامة على تلك القواعد يجب ان يبلغ إلى القسم ويقيد في السجل في القسم المخصص لهذه العلامات ويشهر بنفس الاجراءات المتبعة في العلامات الاخرى.

المادة (٥٦)

يجوز لصاحب هذه العلامة استعمالها بنفسه كما يجب عليه السماح لغيره من الاشخاص المخولين وفقاً لتلك القواعد باستعمالها اذا ما طلبوا ذلك.

المادة (٥٧)

يخضع انتقال ملكية العلامة لموافقة الوزير كما يجوز للوزير الغاء تسجيل العلامة اذا ما اتضح له ان مالكها يرفض السماح لمن يطلب من الغير المخولين بموجب تلك القواعد باستعمالها.

المادة (٥٨)

تكون الشروط والقواعد الاخرى الخاصة بهذه العلامات هي ذات الشروط والقواعد التي نصت عليها هذه اللائحة بالنسبة للعلامات الاخرى المنصوص عليها في القانون.

المادة (٥٩)

على الجهات المختصة كل فيما يخصه تنفيذ احكام هذا القرار.

المادة (٦٠)

ينشر هذا القرار في الجريدة الرسمية ويعمل به من تاريخ سريان القانون الاتحادي رقم (٣٧) لسنة ١٩٩٢ م في شأن العلامات التجارية.

سعيد أحمد غباش
وزير الاقتصاد والتجارة

صدر في أبو ظبي
بتاريخ: ١٠ شعبان ١٤١٣هـ.
الموافق: ٢ فبراير ١٩٩٣م.

ملحق رقم (١)
فئات المنتجات

الفئة (١)

المنتجات الكيماوية التي تستخدم في الصناعة والابحاث والتجارب العلمية والتصوير الفوتوغرافي والزراعة وفلاحة البساتين وغرس الغابات الاسمدة (الطبيعية والصناعية)، مواد اطفاء الحريق ومواد سقي المعادن والمستحضرات الكيماوية الخاصة باللحام، المواد الكيماوية الخاصة بحفظ الاغذية، مواد الدباغة، مواد اللصق التي تستخدم في الصناعة.

الفئة (٢)

الدهانات والورنيش واللاكيه، المواد التي تستخدم لوقاية المعادن من الصدأ والخشب من التلف، المواد الملونة ومواد الصباغة، المواد الكيماوية الخاصة بتثبيت الالوان، الراتنج، المعادن المتخذة شكل الواح أو المسحوقة التي تستخدم في النقش والزخرفة.

الفئة (٣)

المستحضرات الخاصة بتبييض الاقمشة وغيرها من المواد التي تستخدم في غسيل الملابس ومستحضرات التنظيف والصقل وازالة الاوساخ والكشط، الصابون المواد العطرية والزيوت الطيارة ومواد التزيين (الكوزموتيك) ومحاليل الشعر ومعاجين الاسنان.

الفئة (٤)

الزيوت والشحوم التي تستخدم في الصناعة (غير الزيوت والمواد الدهنية التي تستخدم في التغذية والزيوت الطيارة)، مواد التشحيم، المستحضرات التي تستخدم لترسيب الاتربة وأمتصاصها، الوقود بما في ذلك الزيوت المعدنية (الخاصة بإدارة المحركات) ومواد الاضاءة، شموع الاضاءة بجميع أنواعها وفتائل الاضاءة.

الفئة (٥)

مواد الصيدلة والطب البيطري والمواد الصحية، أغذية الاطفال والمرضى، اللصق (اللزق) الطبية ومواد التضميد، المواد الخاصة بحشو الاسنان والشمع المستخدم في طب الانسان، المواد المطهرة، المستحضرات المستخدمة في ابادة الحشائش والاعشاب والحيوانات والحشرات الضارة.

الفئة (٦)

المعادن غير المشغولة ونصف المشغولة وكل خليط منها، مراسي المراكب (الهلب) السندانات والاجراس والمعادن المطروقة وغير المطروقة التي تستخدم في البناء، القضبان وغيرها من المواد المعدنية التي تستخدم في الطرق الحديدية، السلاسل (عدا السلاسل الخاصة بجر العربات) الحبال المعدنية والأسلاك (غير الكهربائية) – مايتعلق بصناعة الاقفال– المواسير والانابيب المعدنية، الخزائن وصناديق حفظ النقود، الكرات المصنوعة من الصلب، الحدادى، المسامير العادية واللولبية (القلاوظ) المنتجات الاخرى (غير الواردة ضمن فئات أخرى) المصنوعة من معادن غير نفيسة، خامات المعادن.

الفئة (٧)

الآلات وعدد الآلات، المحركات (عدا محركات السيارات) وصلات وسيور الآلات (عدا الخاصة بالسيارات)، الآلات والادوات الزراعية الكبيرة، أجهزة التفريخ.

الفئة (٨)

العدد والآلات اليدوية، أدوات القطع والشوك والملاعق، الاسلحة البيضاء.

الفئة (٩)

الاجهزة والعدد العلمية والبحرية والخاصة بمسح الاراضي والاجهزة والعدد الكهربائية (بما في ذلك اللاسلكية) وكذلك الاجهزة والعدد الفوتوغرافية والسينما توغرافية والاجهزة الخاصة بصناعة النظارات وعمليات الوزن والقياس وأعطاء الاشارات والضبط (المراقبة) والانقاذ والتعليم، والاجهزة الاتوماتيكية التي تعمل بوضع قطعة من النقود أو غيرها –الآلات المتكلمة _الخزائن الراصدة للنقود، الآلات الحاسبة، أجهزة أطفاء الحريق.

الفئة (١٠)

العدد والاجهزة التي تستخدم في الجراحة والطب البشري وطب الاسنان والطب البيطري (بما في ذلك اطراف الجسم والعيون والاسنان الصناعية).

الفئة (١١)

أجهزة الانارة والتدفئة وتوليد البخار والطهي والتبريد والتجفيف والتهوية وتوزيع المياه والتركيبات الصحية.

الفئة (١٢)

السيارات –أجهزة النقل البري أو الجوي أو المائي.

الفئة (١٣)

الاسلحة النارية، الذخائر والمقذوفات والمواد المفرقعه، الالعاب النارية.

الفئة (١٤)

المعادن النفيسة وأي خليط منها والمنتجات المصنوعة من تلك المعادن أو المطلاة بها (عدا أدوات القطع والشوك والملاعق)، المجوهرات والاحجار الكريمة، الساعات وغيرها من العدد الخاصة بقياس الوقت.

الفئة (١٥)

الآلات الموسيقية (عدا الآلات المتكلمة أو الاجهزة اللاسلكية).

الفئة (١٦)

الورق والاصناف المصنوعة منه والورق المقوى والاصناف المصنوعة منه، والمطبوعات والجرائد والدوريات والكتب، مواد التجليد، الصور الفتوغرافية، الادوات الكتابية، مواد اللصق الخاصة بالادوات الكتابية، الادوات الخاصة بالفنانين (فرش التلوين والآلات الكاتبة ولوازم المكاتب "عدا الاثاث")، الادوات التي تستخدم في التهذيب والتعليم (عدا الاجهزة)، ورق اللعب، حروف الطباعة، الاكلشيهات.

الفئة (١٧)

الصمغ والمطاط والبلاط ومايقوم مقامها والاصناف المصنوعة منها غير الواردة ضمن فئات أخرى، المواد التي تستخدم في التغليف أو السد أو العزل، الحرير الصخري (الاسبستوس) والميكا ومتجاتهما، المواسير المرنة (غير المعدنية).

الفئة (١٨)

الجلود المدبوغة والمصقولة الطبيعية والجلود الصناعية والاصناف المصنوعة منها غير الواردة ضمن فئات أخرى، والجلود الخام الصناديق والحقائب، الشماسي والمظلات والعصي والسياط وأطقم الخيل والسروج.

الفئة (١٩)

مواد البناء والاحجار الطبيعية والصناعية والاسمنت والجير والمونة والجبس والحصى، المواسير من الفخار أو الأسمنت، المواد التي تستخدم في إنشاء الطرق، الاسفلت والزفت والقطران (القار)، المساكن المتنقلة الاثار المصنوعة من الحجر، المداخن.

الفئة (٢٠)

الاثاث والمرايا والبراويز، الاصناف (غير الواردة ضمن فئات أخرى) المصنوعة من الخشب أو الفلين أو الغاب أو الخيزران أو المفصاف أو القرون أو العظم أو العاج أو عظم الحوت أو قشر السمك والمحار أو الكهرمان أو الصدف أو رغوة البحر أو السلولويد أو مما يقوم مقام تلك المواد.

الفئة (٢١)

الادوات والاوعية المنزلية الصغيرة (غير المصنوعة من معادن نفسية أو المطلاة بها)، الامشاط والاسفنج، الفرش (عدا فرش التلوين)، المواد التي تستعمل في صناعة الفرش، الادوات والآلات التي تستخدم في التنظيف، (السلك الدقيق المستعمل في التنظيف)، المصنوعة الزجاجية والصيني والفخار (غير الواردة ضمن فئات أخرى).

الفئة (٢٢)

الحبال والدوبار والشباك والخيام والمظلات (تندات القماش السميك) والمشمع غير المستخدم في فرش أرضية الحجر (القلوع والاكياس مواد التنجيد والحشو والشعر والقابوق والريش وأعشاب البحر وغيرها)، المواد الليفية الخام التي تستخدم في النسيج.

الفئة (٢٣)

الغزل[5] والخيوط.

الفئة (٢٤)

المنسوجات، أغطية الفراش والمائد، الاصناف المنسوجة غير الواردة فئات أخرى.

الفئة (٢٥)

الملابس بما في ذلك الاحذية بجميع أنواعها والشباشب.

الفئة (٢٦)

الدنتله والمطرزات والشرائط والازرار والكبسون والشناكل والدبابيس والابر والزهور الصناعية.

الفئة (٢٧)

---

[5]. . وردت هذه الكلمة في نص الجريدة الرسمية "الفزل" والأصح ان تكون "الغزل" فاقتضى التنويه.

الابسطة والبليط والحصير والمشمع وغيرها من المواد التي تستخدم لتغطية أرضية الحجر، مايستخدم لتزيين الحائط (غير المواد المنسوجة).

الفئة (٢٨)

اللعب وأدوات اللعب، أدوات الالعاب البدنية والادوات الرياضية (عدا الملابس) الزخارف والزينات الخاصة وشجرة عيد الميلاد.

الفئة (٢٩)

اللحوم، الاسماك، الطيور الداجنة، حيوانات وطيور الصيد، مستخرجات اللحوم، الفواكه والخضروات المحفوظة والمجففة والمطهية، والهلام (الجلي)، المربيات بأنواعها، البيض، اللبن وغيره من منتجات الالبان، الزيوت والشحوم المعدة للتغذية، الاغذية المحفوظة والمخللات.

الفئة (٣٠)

البن، الشاي، الكاكاو، السكر، الارز، التابيوكا والساجو، ومايقوم مقام البن، الدقيق والمستحضرات المصنوعة من الحبوب، الخبز، البسكويت والكعك والفطائر والحلويات والمثلجات، عسل النحل والعسل الاسود (الدبس)، الخميرة ومسحوق الخميرة، الملح، الخردل، الفلفل والخل والصلصة، البهارات التوابل، الثلج.

الفئة (٣١)

الحاصلات الزراعية، منتجات البساتين والغابات والحبوب (غير الواردة ضمن فئات أخرى)، الحيوانات الحية، الفواكه والخضروات الطازجة، البذور، النباتات الحية والزهور الطبيعية، المواد الغذائية للحيوانات، شعير البيرة.

الفئة (٣٢)

المياه المعدنية والغازية وغيرها من المشروبات غير الكحولية، والشراب، وغيرها من المستحضرات لعمل المشروبات غير الكحولية.

الفئة (٣٣)

التبغ الخام أو المصنوع، أدوات التدخين، الكبريت.

فئات الخدمات

الفئة (٣٤)

الاعلان والاعمال التجارية.

الفئة (٣٥)

التأمين والأعمال المالية.

الفئة (٣٦)

أعمال البناء والانشاء والتصليح.

الفئة (٣٧)

المواصلات والاتصالات.

الفئة (٣٨)

النقل والتخزين.

الفئة (٣٩)

معالجة المواد.

الفئة (٤٠)

التربية والتعليم والترفيه.

الفئة (٤١)

متنوعات.

قرار مجلس الوزراء رقم (١٨) لسنة ١٩٩٣م
في شأن رسوم الاجراءات التي تتم بموجب احكام القانون الاتحادي رقم (٣٧)
لسنة ١٩٩٢م بشأن العلامات التجارية

مجلس الوزراء،

بعد الاطلاع على الدستور المؤقت،

وعلى القانون الاتحادي رقم (١) لسنة ١٩٧٢م في شأن اختصاصات الوزارات
وصلاحيات الوزراء والقوانين المعدلة له،

وعلى القانون الاتحادي رقم (٣٧) لسنة ١٩٩٢م في شأن العلامات التجارية،

وعلى قرار مجلس الوزراء رقم (١٥) لسنة ١٩٩٢م في شأن رسوم الاجراءات التي تتم
بموجب احكام القانون الاتحادي رقم (٣٧) لسنة ١٩٩٢م المذكور،

وبناءً على ما عرضه وزير الاقتصاد والتجارة، وموافقة مجلس الوزراء،

قرر:

المادة (١)

تفرض الرسوم المرفق بيانها على الاجراءات التي تتم بموجب احكام القانون الاتحادي
رقم (٣٧) لسنة ١٩٩٢م بشأن العلامات التجارية.

المادة (٢)

يلغى قرار مجلس الوزراء رقم (١٥) لسنة ١٩٩٢م في شأن رسوم الاجراءات التي تتم
بموجب احكام القانون الاتحادي رقم (٣٧) لسنة ١٩٩٢م بشأن العلامات التجارية.

المادة (٣)

على جميع الجهات المختصة تنفيذ هذا القرار، ويعمل به اعتباراً من ١٩٩٤/١/١م،
وينشر في الجريدة الرسمية.

نائب رئيس مجلس الوزراء

صدر عنا في ابو ظبي:
بتاريخ ٦ رجب ١٤١٤هـ.
الموافق: ١٩ ديسمبر ١٩٩٣م.

قائمة الرسوم المفروضة على تسجيل العلامات التجارية

الرسوم	الاجراءات	رقم
٥٠٠ درهم	طلب تسجيل علامة تجارية أو مجموعة علامات عن بضائع أو منتجات أو خدمات تابعة لفئة واحدة.	١
٥٠٠ درهم	طلب تسجيل علامة مخصصة للدلالة على اجراء المراقبة أو الفحص عن بضائع أو منتجات أو خدمات تابعة لفئة واحدة.	٢
٢٥٠ درهم	التظلم من رفض طلب تسجيل علامة أو من تعليق قبول الطلب على شرط.	٣
٢٥٠ درهم	اعتراض الغير على تسجيل العلامة	٤
٢٥٠ درهم	طلب سماع اقوال الطرفين أو احدهما قبل الفصل في الاعتراضات.	٥
٥٠٠٠ درهم	رسم تسجيل علامة أو مجموعة علامات عن بضائع أو منتجات أو خدمات تابعة لفئة واحدة.	٦
٥٠٠٠ درهم	رسم تسجيل علامة مخصصة للدلالة على اجراء المراقبة أو الفحص عن بضائع أو منتجات أو خدمات تابعة لفئة اخرى واحدة.	٧
٢٥٠ درهم	طلب التأشير في صفحة تسجيل علامة تجارية بأنها مرتبطة بعلامة اخرى سجلت بعد تاريخ تسجيل الاولى.	٨
٢٥٠ درهم ٥٠٠ درهم ٧٥٠ درهم	طلب التأشير في السجل بانتقال ملكية علامة تجارية أو علامة مخصصة للدلالة على اجراء المراقبة أو الفحص أو بانتقال ملكية علامة مرتبطة أو بمنح حق الانتفاع بها وفقاً للتفصيل التالي: أ- إذا قدم الطلب قبل مضي ثلاثة اشهر من تاريخ انتقال الملكية أو حق الانتفاع وعن كل علامة من العلامات المرتبطة بعد العلامة الاولى. ب- اذا قدم الطلب بعد مضي ثلاثة اشهر ولكن خلال ستة اشهر من تاريخ انتقال الملكية أو حق الانتفاع وعن كل علامة من العلامات المرتبطة بعد العلامة الاولى. ج- إذا قدم الطلب بعد مضي ستة اشهر من تاريخ انتقال الملكية أو حق الانتفاع وعن كل علامة من العلامات المرتبطة بعد العلامة الاولى.	٩

	طلب التأشير في السجل برهن علامة تجارية أو برهن علامات مرتبطة وفقاً للتفصيل التالي:	١٠
٢٥٠ درهم	أ– اذا قدم الطلب قبل مضي ثلاثة اشهر من تاريخ الرهن وعن كل علامة مرتبطة بعد العلامة الاولى.	
٥٠٠ درهم	ب– اذا قدم الطلب بعد مضي ثلاثة اشهر ولكن خلال ستة اشهر من تاريخ الرهن وعن كل علامة من العلامات المرتبطة بعد العلامة الاولى.	
٧٥٠ درهم	ج– اذا قدم الطلب بعد مضي ستة اشهر من تاريخ الرهن وعن كل علامة من العلامات المرتبطة بعد العلامة الاولى.	
٢٥٠ درهم	طلب قيد البيانات المنصوص عليها في المادة ٢٧ من اللائحة التنفيذية في سجل العلامات التجارية.	١١
٢٥٠ درهم	طلب ادخال أية اضافة أو تعديل على العلامة ذاتها.	١٢
٢٥٠ درهم	التظلم من رفض ادخال أية اضافة أو تعديل على العلامة.	١٣
	طلب تجديد مدة حماية علامة أو مجموعة علامات مسجلة، أو علامة مخصصة للدلالة على اجراء المراقبة أو الفحص طبقاً لما يلي:	١٤
٢٥٠ درهم	أ– اذا قدم الطلب خلال السنة الاخيرة من مدة الحماية وعن كل علامة من العلامات المكونة للمجموعة بعد العلامة الاولى.	
٥٠٠ درهم	ب– اذا قدم الطلب خلال الشهور الثلاثة التالية لانتهاء مدة الحماية وعن كل علامة من العلامات المكونة للمجموعة بعد العلامة الاولى.	
٥٠٠٠ درهم	رسم تجديد قيد علامة تجارية أو مجموعة علامات عن بضائع او منجات او خدمات تابعة لفئة واحدة.	١٥
٥٠٠٠ درهم	رسم تجديد قيد علامة تجارية مخصصة للدلالة على اجراء المراقبة أو الفحص عن بضائع أو منتجات أو خدمات تابعة لفئة واحدة.	١٦
٢٥٠ درهم	طلب تعديل نظام استخدام علامة مسجلة مخصصة للدلالة على اجراء المراقبة أو الفحص.	١٧
٢٥٠ درهم	طلب الحصول على الحماية الوقتية في المعارض الاهلية والدولية.	١٨

١٠٠ درهم	طلب صورة طبق الاصل مما هو مدون في سجل العلامات التجارية أو من أي طلب أو مستند مقدم إلى الادارة المختصة بالعلامات التجارية أو صادر منها.	١٩
٢٥٠ درهم	طلب التقصي أو البحث عن علامة تجارية.	٢٠
٢٥٠ درهم	طلب التأشير في السجل بشطب العلامة سواء عن كل البضائع والمنتجات والخدمات ام عن بعضها.	٢١
٢٥٠ درهم	طلب التأشير في السجل بشطب رهن علامة أو علامات مرتبطة.	٢٢
٢٥٠ درهم	طلب التأشير في السجل بشطب قيد الترخيص باستعمال العلامة.	٢٣
٢٥٠ درهم	الاعتراض على طلب التأشير بشطب قيد الترخيص باستعمال العلامة.	٢٤

قرار وزاري رقم (٦٧) لسنة ١٩٩٨م.

وزير الاقتصاد والتجارة،

بعد الاطلاع على القانون الاتحادي رقم (١) لسنة ١٩٧٢م في شأن اختصاصات الوزارات وصلاحيات الوزراء والقوانين المعدلة له،

وعلى القانون الاتحادي رقم (٣٧) لسنة ١٩٩٢م في شأن العلامات التجارية،

وعلى قرار مجلس الوزراء رقم (١٨) لسنة ١٩٩٣م في شأن رسوم الاجراءات التي تتم بموجب احكام قانون العلامات التجارية،

وعلى القرار الوزاري رقم (٦) لسنة ١٩٩٣م باللائحة التنفيذية لقانون العلامات التجارية،

وعلى القرار الوزاري رقم (٥) لسنة ١٩٩٦م بشأن دفع الرسوم المقررة لاتمام تسجيل العلامات التجارية،

وبناءً على كتاب وزارة المالية والصناعة المرقم م.أ.د/٩٨/٤٩٦ والمؤرخ في ٢٨ فبراير ١٩٩٨م بالموافقة على اقتراح الوزارة بتحصيل رسوم تسجيل العلامات التجارية بعد قبولها من جانب قسم العلامات التجارية، وقبل الاعلان عنها في الصحف المحلية والجريدة الرسمية،

وبناءً على ما عرضه وكيل الوزارة بالإنابة،

قرر:

المادة (١)

يتم تحصيل رسم تسجيل علامة تجارية أو مجموع علامات عن بضائع أو منتجات أو خدمات تابعة لفئة وذلك عند ايداع الطلب لدى قسم العلامات التجارية.

المادة (٢)

يسري أثر هذا القرار على طلبات تسجيل العلامات التجارية المودعة لدى قسم العلامات التجارية، وعلى القسم اتخاذ الاجراءات اللازمة لاخطار أصحاب تلك العلامات لسداد رسوم تسجيلها خلال ثلاثين يوماً من تاريخ الاخطار، وإلا اعتبر متنازلاً عن طلبه.

المادة (٣)

يتم بالتنسيق مع إدارة الايرادات بوزارة المالية والصناعة لوضع آلية وضوابط للحالات التي يتعين بموجبها رد رسوم التسجيل.

المادة (٤)

يلغى القرار الوزاري رقم (٥) لسنة ١٩٩٦م.

المادة (٥)

ينشر هذا القرار في الجريدة الرسمية ويعمل به من تاريخ صدوره.

فاهم بن سلطان القاسمي
وزير الاقتصاد والتجارة

صدر في أبو ظبي
بتاريخ: ١٩٩٨/٧/٨م.
الموافق: ١٤١٩/٣/١٤هـ.

قرار وزراي رقم (٦٧) لسنة ٢٠٠١م
بشأن تحصيل رسوم النشر عن العلامات التجارية

وزير الاقتصاد والتجارة،

بعد الاطلاع على القانون الاتحادي رقم (١) لسنة ١٩٧٢م في شأن اختصاصات الوزارات وصلاحيات الوزراء والقوانين المعدلة له،

وعلى القانون الاتحادي رقم (٣٧) لسنة ١٩٩٢م في شأن العلامات التجارية والقوانين المعدلة له،

وعلى قرار مجلس الوزراء رقم (١٨) لسنة ١٩٩٣م في شأن رسوم الاجراءات التي تتم بموجب احكام قانون العلامات التجارية،

وعلى القرار الوزاري رقم (٦) لسنة ١٩٩٣م باللائحة التنفيذية لقانون العلامات التجارية والقرارات المعدلة له،

وعلى القرار الوزاري رقم (٢٥) لسنة ٢٠٠١م بشأن رسوم النشر عن العلامة التجارية في النشرة التي تصدرها الوزارة،

وبناءً على ما عرضه وكيل الوزارة بالإنابة،

قرر،

المادة (١)

يتم تحصيل رسم النشر عن العلامة التجارية في النشرة الخاصة التي تصدرها الوزارة خلال (٦٠) يوماً من تاريخ إخطار مقدم الطلب بقبول تسجيل العلامة وإلا اعتبر متنازلاً عن طلبه.

المادة (٢)

يتم تحصيل رسم النشر عن طلب إدخال أية إضافة أو تعديل على العلامة لا يمس
ذاتيتها مساساً جوهرياً خلال (٦٠) يوماً من تاريخ إخطار مقدم الطلب بالموافقة على
الاضافة أو التعديل وإلا اعتبر متنازلاً عن طلبه.

ويتم تحصيل رسم النشر عن طلب إدخال اية تعديلات على المنتجات أو الخدمات التي
تميزها العلامة خلال نفس الفترة، وإلا اعتبر مقدم الطلب متنازلاً عن طلبه.

المادة (٣)

يتم تحصيل رسم النشر عند تقديم الطلب في الحالات الآتية:

١. طلب تجديد تسجيل العلامة التجارية.

٢. طلب نقل ملكية العلامة أو رهنها أو الحجز عليها.

٣. طلب الترخيص للغير باستعمال العلامة التجارية عن كل أو بعض المنتجات أو
الخدمات المسجلة عنها العلامة.

٤. طلب شطب قيد الترخيص للغير باستعمال العلامة التجارية.

٥. طلب التأشير في السجل بشطب العلامة عن كل أو بعض المنتجات أو الخدمات
المسجلة عنها العلامة.

المادة (٤)

يُخطر ذوو الشأن بوجوب المبادرة خلال ستين يوماً من تاريخ الاخطار إلى سداد رسوم
النشر في الحالات التي أوجب القانون واللائحة التنفيذية إشهارها والمودعة لدى قسم
العلامات التجارية قبل صدور هذا القرار وإلا اعتبرت تلك الطلبات كأن لم تكن.

المادة (٥)

يُلغى القرار الوزاري رقم (٢٥) لسنة ٢٠٠١م وأي حكم مخالف لاحكام هذا القرار ورد
النص عليه في قرارات وزارية سابقة.

المادة (٦)

يُنشر هذا القرار في الجريدة الرسمية ويُعمل به من تاريخ نشره.

فاهم بن سلطان القاسمي
وزير الاقتصاد والتجارة

صدر في ابو ظبي:
بتاريخ: ٨ صفر ١٤٢٢هـ.
الموافق: ٢٠٠١/٥/٢م.

قرار وزاري رقم ٨٠ لسنة ٢٠٠٥م
في شأن قيد وكلاء تسجيل علامات تجارية

وزيرة الاقتصاد والتخطيط،

بعد الاطلاع على القانون الاتحادي رقم (١) لسنة ١٩٧٢م في شأن اختصاصات الوزارات وصلاحيات الوزراء والقوانين المعدلة له،

وعلى القانون الاتحادي رقم (٣٧) لسنة ١٩٩٢م في شأن العلامات التجارية وتعديلاته،

وعلى قرار مجلس الوزراء رقم (٣٠) لسنة ٢٠٠٤م بشأن استحداث وتعديل بعض رسوم الخدمات التي تقدمها وزارة الاقتصاد والتخطيط،

وعلى القرار الوزاري رقم ٦ لسنة ١٩٩٣م باللائحة التنفيذية للقانون الاتحادي رقم (٣٧) لسنة ١٩٩٢ في شأن العلامات التجارية وتعديلاته،

وعلى القرار الوزاري رقم (٢١) لسنة ١٩٩٧م في شأن تعديل بعض احكام القرار الوزاري رقم (٦) لسنة ١٩٩٣م،

وبناءً على ما عرضه وكيل الوزارة،

قرر :

المادة (١)

في تطبيق احكام هذا القرار يقصد بالعبارات والألفاظ التالية المعاني الموضحة قرين كل منها ما لم يدل سياق النص على خلاف ذلك:

الدولة:	دولة الامارات العربية المتحدة.
الوزارة:	وزارة "الاقتصاد والتخطيط.
الإدارة المختصة:	إدارة التسجيل التجاري.
القسم المختص:	قسم العلامات التجارية.

السجل: سجل قيد وكلاء تسجيل العلامات التجارية بوزارة الاقتصاد والتخطيط.

وكيل تسجيل: الشخص الذي يوكل من قبل صاحب العلامة التجارية لقيد علامة تجارية بسجل العلامات التجارية بوزارة الاقتصاد والتخطيط.

المادة (٢)

يقدم طلب تسجيل أي علامة تجارية في الدولة للقسم المختص إما من قبل صاحب العلامة التجارية اذا كان له موطن في الدولة أو من قبل مكتب "وكيل تسجيل علامات تجارية" مقيد في السجل.

المادة (٣)

لا يجوز لأي شخص مزاولة نشاط "وكيل تسجيل علامات تجارية" ما لم يكن اسمه مقيداً في السجل.

ولا يجوز لأي شخص أن يثبت في اوراقه أو وسائل الدعاية والإعلان انه وكيل تسجيل علامات تجارية دون ان يكون اسمه مقيداً بالسجل.

المادة (٤)

يشترط فيمن يقيد اسمه في السجل من الاشخاص الطبيعيين ما يلي:

١. ان يكون كامل الأهلية.

٢. أن يكون حاصلاً على شهادة جامعية موثقة ومصدقة حسب الاصول.

٣. ان يكون لديه خبرة لا تقل عن سنتين بالعمل في أحد (المكاتب / الشركات) المقيدة بالسجل أو التي (لديه / لديها) رخصة تجارية من السلطة المختصة لممارسة هذا النشاط قبل صدور هذا القرار.

٤. ان يكون حسن السيرة والسلوك ولم تصدر ضده احكام في جرائم مخلة بالشرف أو الامانة ما لم يكن قد رد إليه اعتباره.

المادة (٥)

يشترط فيمن يقيد اسمه في السجل من الاشخاص الاعتباريين ما يلي:

١. ان تتوافر في المدير المسؤول في الشركة المؤسسة في الدولة سواء كان من الشركاء أو من غيرهم كافة الشروط المنصوص عليها في المادة ٤ من هذا القانون.

٢. ان تكون الشركة المؤسسة خارج الدولة مرخصاً لها بمزاولة نشاط وكيل تسجيل علامات تجارية في نفس الدولة التي تحمل جنسيتها.

المادة (٦)

يقدم طلب قيد الاشخاص الطبيعيين في السجل إلى القسم المختص على النموذج المعد لذلك مرفقاً به المستندات الآتية:

١. صورة خلاصة القيد أو جواز السفر.

٢. شهادة رسمية من الجهات المعنية تفيد بأن طالب القيد لم يسبق الحكم عليه بعقوبة في جريمة مخلة بالشرف أو الامانة.

٣. شهادة الخبرة العملية مصدقة حسب الاصول.

٤. عقد ايجار المكتب الذي يزاول فيه نشاطه.

٥. تحديد الامارة او الامارات التي يرغب في مزاولة النشاط فيها.

٦. نموذج التوقيع المعتمد.

٧. اسماء المندوبين المعتمدين من وكيل التسجيل.

المادة (٧)

يقدم طلب قيد الاشخاص الاعتبارية في السجل إلى القسم المختص على النموذج المعد لذلك مرفقاً به المستندات الآتية:

١. صورة طبق الاصل من عقد الشركة أو نظامها الاساسي.

٢. صورة طبق الاصل من شهادة قيد الشركة في السجل التجاري.

٣. عقد ايجار مقر الشركة.

٤. تحديد الامارة او الامارات التي ترغب الشركة في مزاولة النشاط فيها.

٥. شهادة رسمية من الجهات الرسمية في الدولة المسجلة فيها الشركة الاجنبية تبين انها مؤسسة ومسجلة ومرخص لها بمزاولة هذا النشاط في الدولة التي تحمل جنسيتها وفقاً لأحكام القوانين المعمول بها.

٦. صورة طبق الاصل من القرار الصادر من الشركة الام في حالة قيام الشركة الاجنبية بفتح فرع او فروع لها داخل الدولة.

٧. المستندات المطلوبة من مدير الشركة المسؤول وفقاً للمادتين (٤ و٥) من هذا القرار.

٨. نموذج التوقيع المعتمد.

٩. اسماء المندوبين المعتمدين من وكيل التسجيل.

المادة (٨)

على القسم المختص ان يخطر طالب القيد بقرار القبول أو الرفض خلال شهرين من تاريخ تقديم الطلب بموجب كتاب مسجل أو بالتسليم المباشر ويجب ان يتضمن الاخطار في حالة رفض الطلب اسباب الرفض.

المادة (٩)

على القسم المختص في حالة قبول الطلب قيد اسم مقدم الطلب وبيانات الطلب في السجل وتسليم الطالب شهادة قيد مؤشراً عليها بحصول القيد ورقمه وتاريخه وتكون الشهادة سارية لمدة سنة واحدة اعتباراً من تاريخ القيد في السجل.

المادة (١٠)

على وكلاء تسجيل العلامات التجارية اخطار القسم المختص بكل تعديل أو تغيير يطرأ على بيانات طلب القيد أو المستندات المرفقة به ويكون الاخطار بموجب طلب تأشير على النموذج المخصص لذلك ويقدم إلى القسم المختص خلال ثلاثين يوماً من تاريخ حدوث التعديل أو التغيير ويرفق به المستندات المؤيدة لصحة البيانات الواردة فيه.

المادة (١١)

يقوم القسم المختص في حالة قبول الاخطار بتدوين البيانات الجديدة في السجل والتأشير في هامش السجل بتاريخ التأشير والمستندات المؤيدة له ويعطى الطالب صورة من الطلب مؤشراً عليها بحصول التأشير بالتعديل أو التغيير وتاريخه، وللقسم المختص ان يرفض طلب التعديل او التغيير على ان يخطر الطالب بقرار الرفض بكتاب مسجل وذلك خلال ثلاثين يوماً من تاريخ تقديم الاخطار بالتعديل او التغيير.

المادة (١٢)

على كل وكيل تسجيل مقيد في السجل ان يتقدم للوزارة لتجديد قيده سنوياً.

ويقدم طلب التجديد الى القسم المختص على النموذج المخصص لذلك قبل ثلاثين يوماً من تاريخ انتهاء صلاحية شهادة القيد من كل سنة.

المادة (١٣)

على كل من قيد اسمه في السجل ان يقرن اسمه برقم قيده في السجل في جميع المكاتبات والشهادات والتقارير الصادرة عنه.

المادة (١٤)

على وكيل التسجيل الذي حصل على ترخيص بفتح مكتب في امارة ما ان يقدم للقسم المختص خلال مدة اقصاها ثلاثة اشهر ترخيص السلطة المختصة بالامارة.

المادة (١٥)

مع عدم الاخلال بالمسؤولية المدنية او الجزائية عند الاقتضاء يعاقب وكيل التسجيل الذي يخل بواجباته في مزاولة هذا النشاط بالعقوبات التأديبية الآتية:

١. الانذار.

٢. الوقف عن ممارسة النشاط لمدة لا تجاوز سنة و في حالة تكرار المخالفة لمدة لا تجاوز سنتين.

٣. شطب القيد.

ولا يجوز لمن شطب قيده التقدم بطلب اعادة القيد قبل مضي ثلاث سنوات من تاريخ شطب القيد.

المادة (١٦)

للوزارة من تلقاء نفسها او بناءً على طلب من السلطة المختصة او بناءً على شكوى تقدم اليها ان تجري تحقيقاً مع وكيل التسجيل فيما ينسب إليه من مخالفات في مزاولة هذا النشاط. فإذا تبين للوزارة ان الواقعة المنسوبة لوكيل التسجيل تكون جريمة جزائية أحالت الموضوع إلى النيابة العامة.

المادة (١٧)

على القسم المختص قبل صدور قرار الشطب ان يخطر وكيل التسجيل بكتاب مسجل لتقديم أوجه دفاعه وذلك خلال ثلاثين يوماً من تاريخ الاخطار فإذا لم يقدم وكيل التسجيل أوجه دفاعه خلال الميعاد المذكور أو لم يقتنع القسم المختص بدفاعه عرض الامر على

وكيل الوزارة لاتخاذ قرار بشأن شطب قيده من السجل واخطاره بهذا القرار بكتاب مسجل.

المادة (١٨)

تحدد الرسوم التي تستوفى عن الاجراءات التي تتم بموجب احكام هذا القرار على الوجه الآتي:

الاجراء	الرسم المقرر بالدرهم
١- رسوم قيد وكيل تسجيل علامة تجارية لكل مكتب	٣٠٠٠
٢- رسوم تجديد قيد وكيل تسجيل علامة تجارية لكل مكتب	١٠٠٠
٣- رسوم غرامة تأخير عن تجديد قيد وكيل تسجيل علامة تجارية. وبحد اقصى ١٠٠٠ درهم سنوياً ويحسب جزء الشهر شهراً كاملاً.	١٠٠ درهم شهرياً

المادة (١٩)

يلغى القرار الوزاري رقم ٢١ لسنة ١٩٩٧م.

المادة (٢٠)

ينشر هذا القرار في الجريدة الرسمية ويعمل به اعتباراً من تاريخ صدوره.

لبنى بنت خالد القاسمي
وزيرة الاقتصاد والتخطيط

صدر في ابو ظبي
بتاريخ ٢٨ محرم ١٤٢٦هـ.
الموافق ٢٠٠٥/٣/٩م.

مرسوم اتحادي رقم ٥٢ لسنة ٢٠٠٧م
في شأن قانون (نظام) العلامات التجارية الموحد
لدول مجلس التعاون لدول الخليج العربي

نحن خليفة بن زايد آل نهيان، رئيس دولة الإمارات العربية المتحدة،

بعد الاطلاع على الدستور،

وعلى القانون الاتحادي رقم (١) لسنة ١٩٧٢ في شأن اختصاصات الوزارات وصلاحيات الوزراء والقوانين المعدلة له،

وبناءً على ماعرضته وزيرة الاقتصاد، وموافقة مجلس الوزراء، وتصديق المجلس الأعلى للاتحاد،

رسمنا بما هو آت :

المادة (١)

صُودق على قانون (نظام) العلامات التجارية الموحد لدول مجلس التعاون لدول الخليج العربي، والمرفق نصه.

المادة (٢)

على وزيرة الاقتصاد تنفيذ هذا المرسوم و ينشر في الجريدة الرسمية.

خليفة بن زايد آل نهيان
رئيس دولة الامارات العربية المتحدة

صدر عنا في قصر الرئاسة بأبو ظبي :
بتاريخ : ٥ جمادى الآخرة ١٤٢٨هـ
الموافق: ٢٠ يونيو ٢٠٠٧ م

قانون (نظام) العلامات التجارية
لدول مجلس التعاون لدول الخليج العربية

الباب الأول
أحكام عامة

المادة (١)

تعريفات

يكون لكل من المصطلحات التالية المعنى الموضح قرين كل منها ما لم يقضِ سياق النص خلاف ذلك:

دول المجلس: دول مجلس التعاون لدول الخليج العربية.

الجهة المختصة: الوزارة التي تكون شؤون التجارة من اختصاصها في كل دولة من دول المجلس وهي المختصة بتنفيذ هذا القانون (النظام).

اللائحة التنفيذية : هي التي تضعها لجنة التعاون التجاري تنفيذاً لهذا النظام .

السجل: سجل العلامات التجارية.

المادة (٢)

العلامة التجارية هي: كل ما يأخذ شكلاً مميزاً من أسماء أو كلمات أو إمضاءات أو حروف أو رموز أو أرقام أو عناوين أو أختام أو رسوم أو صور أو نقوش أو تغليف أو عناصر تصويرية أو أشكال أو مجموعات ألوان أو مزيج من ذلك أو أية اشارة أو مجموعة اشارات قابلة للادراك بالنظر إذا كانت تستخدم أو يراد استخدامها في تمييز سلع أو خدمات منشأة ما عن سلع أو خدمات المنشآت الأخرى أو للدلالة على تأدية خدمة من الخدمات، أو على اجراء المراقبة أو الفحص للسلع أو الخدمات.

ويجوز اعتبار العلامة الخاصة بالصوت أو الرائحة علامة تجارية.

الباب الثاني
الاجراءات

الفصل الأول
اجراءات تسجيل العلامات التجارية

المادة (٣)

لا تعد علامة تجارية أو جزء منها، و لا يجوز أن يسجل بهذا الوصف ما يأتي:

١. العلامة الخالية من اية صفة مميزة، او العلامات المكونة من بيانات ليست الا التسمية التي يطلقها العرف على السلع و الخدمات، أو الرسوم المألوفة و الصور العادية للسلع.

٢. أي تعبير أو رسم أو علامة تخل بالآداب العامة أو تخالف النظام العام.

٣. الشعارات العامة والأعلام والشارات العسكرية والشرفية والاوسمة الوطنية والأجنبية والعملات المعدنية والورقية وغيرها من الرموز الخاصة بالدولة أو أي دولة أخرى، أو بالمنظمات العربية او الدونية أو احدى مؤسساتها، أو أي تقليد لأي من ذلك.

٤. رموز الهلال الأحمر أو الصليب الأحمر وغيرها من الرموز الأخرى المشابهة، وكذلك العلامات التي تكون تقليداً لها.

٥. العلامات المطابقة أو المشابهة للرموز ذات الصبغة الدينية المحضة.

٦. الأسماء و البيانات الجغرافية اذا كان من شأن استعمالها ان يحدث لبساً فيما يتعلق بمصدر أو أصل السلع أو الخدمات.

٧. اسم الغير أو لقبه أو صورته أو شعاره، ما لم يوافق هو أو ورثته مقدماً على استعماله.

٨. البيانات الخاصة بدرجات الشرف او الدرجات العلمية التي لا يثبت طالب التسجيل استحقاقه لها قانوناً.

٩. العلامات التي من شأنها أن تضلل الجمهور، او التي تتضمن بيانات كاذبة عن منشأ أو مصدر المنتجات أو الخدمات أو عن صفاتها الأخرى و كذلك العلامات التي تحتوي على اسم تجاري وهمي أو مقلد أو مزور.

١٠. العلامات المملوكة لأشخاص طبيعيين أو معنويين يكون التعامل معهم محظوراً وفقاً لقرار صادر في هذا الشأن من الجهة المختصة.

١١. أي علامة تجارية مطابقة او مشابهة لعلامة سبق ايداعها أو تسجيلها من قبل الآخرين عن ذات السلع أو الخدمات أو عن سلع او خدمات مشابهة اذا كان من شأن استعمال العلامة المطلوب تسجيلها ان يولد الانطباع بالربط بينها وبين منتجات أو خدمات مالك العلامة المسجلة او أن يؤدي الى الاضرار بمصالحه.

١٢. العلامات التي ينشأ عن تسجيلها بالنسبة لبعض السلع أو الخدمات الحط من قيمة السلع أو الخدمات التي تميزها العلامة السابقة.

١٣. العلامة التي تعتبر مجرد ترجمة لعلامة مشهورة أو لعلامة أخرى سبق تسجيلها اذا كان من شأن التسجيل ان يحدث لبساً لدى جمهور المستهلكين بالنسبة للمنتجات أو الخدمات التي تميزها العلامة أو المنتجات المشابهة.

١٤. العلامات التي تشمل الألفاظ أو العبارات الآتية:

امتياز "ذو امتياز"، مسجل أو "رسم مسجل" أو حقوق الطبع او ما شابه ذلك من الألفاظ والعبارات.

المادة (٤)

١. لا يجوز تسجيل العلامة التجارية المشهورة التي تجاوزت شهرتها حدود البلد الأصلي لأي البلاد الأخرى على سلع أو خدمات مطابقة أو مشابهة إلا إذا قدم طلب من مالك العلامة المشهورة أو بموافقة صريحة منه .

٢. ولتحديد ما اذا كانت العلامة مشهورة يراعى مدى معرفتها لدى الجمهور المعني نتيجة ترويجها.

٣. ولا يجوز تسجيل العلامات المشهورة لتمييز سلع أو خدمات غير مطابقة أو مشابهة لتلك التي تميزها هذه العلامات اذا:

أ) كان استخدام العلامة يدل على صلة بين السلع أو الخدمات المطلوب تمييزها وسلع أو خدمات صاحب العلامة المشهورة .
ب) أدى استخدام العلامة الى احتمالية الإضرار بمصالح صاحب العلامة المشهورة.

المادة (٥)

لكل ذي شأن أن يطلب تسجيل علامة تجارية تحمل مؤشر جغرافي لحماية منشأ سلعته بعينها، و لا يترتب على قبول التسجيل أي حق استئثاري للطالب، فيجوز استخدامه ممن يباشر نشاطه في هذا المنشأ الجغرافي.

المادة (٦)

للفئات التالية الحق في تسجيل علاماتهم التجارية:

١. كل شخص طبيعي أو معنوي يكون صاحب مصنع أو منتج او تاجر أو حرفي او صاحب مشروع خاص بالخدمات و متمتع بجنسية أي من دول المجلس.

٢. الأجانب الذين يقيمون في أي من دول المجلس و يكون مصرحاً لهم مزاولة عمل من الاعمال التجارية أو الصناعية أو الحرفية أو الخدمية.

٣. الاجانب الذين ينتمون الى دولة تعامل دول المجلس التي تسجل بأي منها العلامة بالمثل.

٤. المصالح العامة.

المادة (٧)

يعد سجل في الجهة المختصة يسمى سجل العلامات التجارية، تدون فيه جميع العلامات وأسماء أصحابها وعناوينهم وأوصاف سلعهم أو خدماتهم، ومما يطرأ على العلامات من نقل الملكية أو التنازل أو الترخيص بالاستعمال أو الرهن أو التجديد أو الشطب أو أي تعديلات أخرى، و لكل ذي مصلحة حق الاطلاع على هذا السجل، و أخذ مستخرج مصدق منه بعد دفع الرسوم المقررة.

المادة (٨)

١. يعتبر من قام بتسجيل علامة تجارية مالكاً لها دون سواه، ما لم يثبت العكس، ولا تجوز المنازعة في ملكية العلامة اذا استعملها من قام بتسجيلها بصفة مستمرة خمس سنوات على الأقل من تاريخ التسجيل، دون أن ترفع عليه دعوى بشأن صحتها.

٢. يجوز لمن كان اسبق الى استعمال العلامة ممن سجلت باسمه أن يطلب من المحكمة المختصة الغاء هذا التسجيل خلال خمس سنوات من تاريخ التسجيل، ما لم يثبت رضاء الأول صراحة أو ضمناً باستعمال العلامة من قبل من سجلت باسمه.

المادة (٩)

يقدم طلب تسجيل العلامة إلى الجهة المختصة لتسجيل العلامات التجارية على الاستمارة المحددة لذلك من صاحب الشأن أو من ينوب عنــه، بالأوضاع والشروط المنصوص عليها في اللائحة التنفيذية لهذا النظام (القانون).

المادة (١٠)

يجوز تسجيل العلامة التجارية عن فئة واحدة أو أكثر من فئات السلع أو الخدمات التي تحددها اللائحة التنفيذية لهذا القانون ومع ذلك لا يجوز أن يشتمل طلب تسجيل العلامة على أكثر من فئة واحدة.

المادة (١١)

يجوز تقديم طلب واحد لتسجيل مجموعة من العلامات المتطابقة من حيث عناصرها الجوهرية، اذا كان اختلافها يتعلق بعناصر لا تمس ذاتها مساساً جوهرياً، كلون العلامات أو بيانات المنتجات أو الخدمات المرتبطة بها، على أن تكون هذه المنتجات أو الخدمات تابعة لذات الفئة.

المادة (١٢)

إذا طلب شخصان أو أكثر في وقت واحد تسجيل العلامة ذاتها أو علامات متقاربة أو متشبهة عن فئة واحدة من المنتجات أوالخدمات، وجب وقف جميع الطلبات الى أن يقدم تتنازل موقع من المتنازعين ومصدق عليه من الجهة المختصة لمصلحة أحدهم، أو الى أن يصدر حكم نهائي في النزاع.

المادة (١٣)

إذا رغب طالب تسجيل علامة أو خلفه في التمتع في حق الأولوية استناداً الى طلب سابق مودع في دولة تعامل دول المجلس معاملة المثل فعليه أن يرفق بطلبه إقراراً يبين فيه تاريخ الطلب السابق ورقمه والدولة التي أودع فيها هذا الطلب، كما يتعين على الطالب أن يودع صورة من الطلب السابق في الدولة التي أودع فيها وذلك خلال الستة أشهر من تاريخ طلب التسجيل الذي يدعي من أجله حق الأولوية و الا سقط حقه في المطالبة بها.

المادة (١٤)

١. يجوز للجهة المختصة أن تفرض ما تراه لازماً من القيود والتعديلات لتحديد العلامة التجارية وتوضيحها على وجه يمنع التباسها بعلامة أخرى سبق تسجيلها أو سبق ايداع طلب تسجيلها، أو لأي سبب آخر ترتئيه.

٢. اذا لم يستجب طالب التسجيل لطلبات الادارة المختصة باستيفاء الشروط خلال تسعين يوماً من تاريخ ابلاغه بذلك اعتبر متنازلاً عن طلبه.

٣. اذا رفضت الجهة المختصة تسجيل العلامة التجارية لسبب ارتأته ، أو علقت التسجيل على قيود أو تعديلات، وجب عليها أن تخطر صاحب الطلب أو من ينوب عنه كتابة بأسباب قرارها.

٤. و في جميع الأحوال يتعين على الجهة المختصة أن تبت في طلب التسجيل خلال فترة تسعين يوماً من تاريخ تقديمه متى ما كان مستوفياً للشروط والأوضاع المنصوص عليها في هذا القانون ولائحته التنفيذية.

المادة (١٥)

١. كل قرار تصدره الجهة المختصة برفض التسجيل أو تعليقه على شرط يجوز لطالب التسجيل أو من ينيبه أن يتظلم منه خلال ثلاثين يوماً من تاريخ إبلاغه به أمام لجنة تحددها اللائحة التنفيذية لهذا القانون. ويجوز له خلال ستين يوماً من تاريخ إبلاغه بقرار اللجنة أن يطعن فيه أمام المحكمة المختصة.

٢. واذا لم يتظلم الطالب على القرار في المواعيد المحددة، او لم يقم بتنفيذ ما فرضته الجهة المختصة من القيود في هذا الميعاد اعتبر متنازلاً عن طلبه.

المادة (١٦)

١. اذا قبلت الجهة المختصة العلامة التجارية، وجب عليها قبل تسجيلها أن تعلن عنها بأي وسيلة نشر تحددها اللائحة التنفيذية لهذا القانون ويلزم طالب التسجيل بتكاليف الاشهار.

٢. ولكل ذي شأن، خلال ستين يوماً من تاريخ النشر، أن يقدم للجهة المختصة اعتراضاً مكتوباً على تسجيل العلامة. وعلى الجهة المختصة ان تبلغ طالب التسجيل بصورة من إخطار الاعتراض خلال ثلاثين يوماً من تاريخ تقديمه. وعلى طالب التسجيل أن يقدم للجهة المختصة خلال ستين يوماً من تاريخ اخطاره رداً مكتوباً على هذا الاعتراض، وإلا اعتبر طالب التسجيل متنازلاً عن طلبه.

٣. وللجهة المختصة اذا تبين لها أن الاعتراض في تسجيل العلامة غير جدي أن تباشر في اجراءات تسجيلها، واخطار المعترض بقرارها مسبباً، و له الطعن ضد القرار أمام المحكمة خلال ثلاثين يوماً من تاريخ اخطاره به.

المادة (١٧)

١. تفصل الجهة المختصة في الاعتراض المحال اليها، بعد سماع الطرفين أو أحدهما.

٢. تصدر الجهة المختصة قراراً بقبول التسجيل أو رفضه، وفي الحالة الأولى يجوز أن تقرر ما تراه لازماً من قيود.

٣. ولكل ذي شأن الطعن في قرار الجهة المختصة أمام المحكمة في خلال ثلاثين يوماً من تاريخ إخطاره به.

المادة (١٨)

١. اذا سجلت العلامة انسحب أثر التسجيل الى تاريخ تقديم الطلب ويعطى لمالك العلامة، بمجرد اتمام تسجيلها شهادة تشتمل على البيانات الآتية:

أ) رقم تسجيل العلامة.

ب) رقم وتاريخ الأولوية وجنسية الدولة التي اودع فيها الطلب.

ج) تاريخ تقديم الطلب وتاريخ التسجيل وتاريخ انتهاء مدة الحماية.

د) اسم مالك العلامة ولقبه ومحل اقامته وجنسيته.

هـ) صورة مطابقة للعلامة.

و) بيان بالسلع أو الخدمات المخصصة لها العلامة، وبيان فئتها.

٢. لمالك العلامة المسجلة الحق في الطلب من الجهة المختصة منع الغير من استعمال علامته أو استعمال أية اشارة مشابهة لها يكون من شأنها أن تضلل الجمهور بالنسبة للمنتجات أو الخدمات المشابهة

المادة (١٩)

يجوز لمالك علامة سبق تسجيلها أن يقدم في أي وقت طلباً الى الجهة المختصة لادخال أي اضافة أو تعديل على علامته لا تمس ذاتيتها مساساً جوهرياً و تصدر الجهة المختصة قراراً في ذلك وفقاً للشروط الموضوعة للقرارات الخاصة بطلبات التسجيل الأصلية، ويكون قابلاً للطعن بالطرق ذاتها.

المادة (٢٠)

يجوز للجهة المختصة اضافة أي بيان للسجل يكون قد أغفل تدوينه، أو حذف أو تعديل أي بيان اذا كان مدون في السجل بدون وجه حق أو كان غير مطابق للحقيقة.

كما يجوز لكل ذي شأن الطعن لدى المحكمة المختصة على أي إجراء قامت به الجهة المذكورة بهذا الشأن.

الفصل الثاني
مدة حماية العلامة التجارية

المادة (٢١)

١. مدة الحماية المترتبة عن تسجيل العلامة عشر سنوات، ولصاحب الحق فيها أن يكفل استمرار الحماية لمدد مماثلة اذا قدم طلباً بالتجديد خلال السنة الأخيرة بالأوضاع والشروط المنصوص عليها في هذا القانون ولائحته التنفيذية.

٢. يجوز للجهة المختصة أن تقوم خلال الثلاثة أشهر التالية لانتهاء مدة الحماية باخطار صاحب العلامة كتابة بانتهاء مدة حمايتها، ويرسل إليه الاخطار بالعنوان المقيد في السجل، فاذا انقضت ستة الأشهر التالية لتاريخ إنتهاء مدة الحماية دون أن يقدم صاحب العلامة طلب التجديد قامت الجهة المختصة بشطب العلامة من السجل.

٣. يتم التجديد دون أي فحص جديد و دون اعتداد بأي اعتراض من الغير.

المادة (٢٢)

تتمتع بحماية مؤقتة العلامات، التي تتوافر فيها شروط التسجيل المنصوص عليها في هذا القانون، خلال مدة عرضها في المعارض التي تقام داخل دول المجلس أو خارجها والتي يصدر بتحديده قرار من الجهة المختصة.

وتحدد اللائحة التنفيذية شروط وأوضاع واجراءات منح تلك الحماية.

الفصل الثالث
شطب تسجيل العلامة التجارية

المادة (٢٣)

مع عدم الاخلال بأحكام المادة (٨) من هذا القانون يكون للجهة المختصة و لكل ذي شأن، اللجوء إلى المحكمة بطلب الحكم بشطب العلامة التجارية التي قد تكون سجلت بغير وجه حق وتقوم الجهة المختصة بشطب التسجيل متى قدم لها حكم نهائي بذلك.

المادة (٢٤)

لمالك العلامة التجارية أن يطلب من الجهة المختصة شطب تسجيل العلامة من السجل سواء عن كل السلع أو الخدمات التي سجلت عنها العلامة أو عن جزء منها فقط ويقدم طلب الشطب وفقاً للأوضاع والاجراءات التي تحددها اللائحة التنفيذية. واذا كانت العلامة مرخصاً باستعمالها وفقاً لعقد مؤشر به في السجل، فلا يجوز شطب تسجيل هذه العلامة إلا بناءً على موافقة كتابية من المستفيد من الترخيص ما لم يتنازل المستفيد عن هذا الحق صراحة عن هذا الترخيص.

المادة (٢٥)

للمحكمة، بناءً على طلب أي ذي شأن، أن تأمر بشطب التسجيل اذا ثبت لديها أن العلامة لم تستعمل بصفة جدية خمس سنوات متتالية، الا اذا قدم مالك العلامة ما يسوغ به عدم استعمالها.

المادة (٢٦)

إذا شطب تسجيل العلامة، فلا يجوز أن يعاد تسجيلها لصالح الغير عن ذات السلع أو الخدمات أو على خدمات أو سلع مشابهة، الا بعد مضي ثلاث سنوات من تاريخ الشطب ما لم يكن الشطب قد تم بناءً على حكم من المحكمة و في هذه الحالة يجوز أن ينص الحكم على مدة أقل.

المادة (٢٧)

يجب إشهار شطب التسجيل أو تجديده بأي وسيلة نشر تحددها اللائحة التنفيذية.

الفصل الرابع
نقل ملكية العلامة ورهنها والحجز عليها

المادة (٢٨)

١. يجوز نقل ملكية العلامة التجارية بعوض أو بغير عوض أو رهنها أو الحجز عليها مع المحل التجاري أو مشروع الاستغلال الذي تستخدم العلامة في تمييز سلعه أو خدماته ما لم يتفق على خلاف ذلك.

٢. يجوز نقل ملكية العلامة التجارية بالارث أو بالوصية أو بالهبة.

٣. وفي جميع الأحوال لا يكون نقل ملكية العلامة أو رهنها أو الحجز عليها حجة على الغير الا بعد التأشير به في سجل العلامات التجارية، واشهاره بأي وسيلة نشر تحددها اللائحة التنفيذية.

المادة (٢٩)

١. يتضمن انتقال ملكية المحل التجاري أو مشروع الاستغلال العلامات المسجلة باسم ناقل الملكية والتي يمكن اعتبارها ذات ارتباط وثيق بالمحل التجاري أو المشروع، ما لم يتفق على غير ذلك.

٢. وإذا نقلت ملكية المحل التجاري أو المشروع دون نقل ملكية العلامة ذاتها، جاز لناقل الملكية الاستمرار في صناعة ذات السلع أو تقديم ذات الخدمات التي سجلت العلامة من أجلها أو الاتجار فيها، ما لم يتفق على غير ذلك.

الباب الثالث
عقود الترخيص

المادة (٣٠)

يجوز لمالك العلامة أن يرخص لأي شخص طبيعي أو معنوي باستعمالها عن كل أو بعض السلع أو الخدمات المسجلة عنها العلامة ويكون لمالك العلامة الحق في أن يرخص لأشخاص آخرين باستعمال ذات العلامة كما يكون له أن يستعملها بنفسه ما لم يتفق على غير ذلك. و لا يجوز أن تزيد مدة الترخيص عن المدة المقررة لحماية العلامة.

المادة (٣١)

لا يجوز أن تفرض على المستفيد من الترخيص قيود غير مترتبة على الحقوق التي يخولها تسجيل العلامة أو غير ضرورية للمحافظة على هذه الحقوق.

ومع ذلك يجوز أن يتضمن عقد الترخيص القيود الآتية:

١. تحديد نطاق المنطقة أو فترة استخدام العلامة.

٢. الشروط التي تستلزمها متطلبات الرقابة الفعالة لجودة السلع والخدمات.

٣. الالتزامات المفروضة على المستفيد من الترخيص بالامتناع عن كافة الأعمال التي قد ينتج عنها الاساءة إلى العلامة التجارية.

المادة (٣٢)

يجب للاعتداد بعقد الترخيص باستعمال العلامة التجارية أن يكون مكتوباً ولا يشترط التأشير به في السجل.

المادة (٣٣)

لا يجوز للمستفيد من الترخيص التنازل عنه لغيره أو منح تراخيص من الباطن ما لم يتفق على خلاف ذلك.

المادة (٣٤)

يشطب قيد عقد الترخيص من السجل بناءً على طلب مالك العلامة أو المستفيد من الترخيص بعد تقديم ما يثبت انتهاء أو فسخ الترخيص.

وعلى الجهة المختصة أن تخطر الطرف الآخر بطلب شطب الترخيص وله في هذه
الحالة الاعتراض على ذلك وفقاً للإجراءات والأوضاع المنصوص عليها في اللائحة
التنفيذية.

الباب الرابع
العلامات الجماعية وعلامات المراقبة
وعلامات الهيئات ذات النفع العام والمؤسسات المهنية

المادة (٣٥)

أ. يجوز تسجيل العلامات الجماعية التي تستخدم لتمييز سلع أو خدمات منشآت أعضاء
ينتمون إلى كيان معين يتمتع بشخصية قانونية.

ويقدم طلب تسجيل العلامة الجماعية من قبل ممثل هذا الكيان ليستخدمه الاعضاء فيه
وفقاً للشروط والاوضاع التي يحددها على ان يعتمد ذلك على الجهة المختصة.

ب. يتعين على طالب تسجيل العلامات الجماعية أن يشير في طلب التسجيل الى أنه
يخص علامة جماعية، وأن يرفق بالطلب نسخة من اشتراطات استعمال العلامة
المطلوب تسجيلها.

وفي جميع الأحوال يلتزم مالك العلامة الجماعية المسجلة باخطار الجهة المختصة بأية
تغييرات على تلك الاشتراطات، ولا يكون التغير نافذاً الا بعد موافقة الجهة المختصة
عليه.

ج. لا يجوز إعادة تسجيل العلامة الجماعية لصالح الغير في حالة شطبها بالنسبة لسلع أو
خدمات متطابقة أو مشابهة .

د. للمحكمة المختصة بناءً على طلب أي ذي شأن أن تأمر بشطب تسجيل علامة جماعية
اذا ثبت لديها أن المالك المسجل يستعمل العلامة الجماعية بمفرده، أو أنه يستعملها أو
يسمح باستعمالها بشكل مخالف للاشتراطات المشار لها في البند (ب) من هذه المادة، أو
يستعملها بطريقة من شأنها أن تضلل الجمهور من حيث منشأ السلعة أو أية صفة
مشتركة للسلع أو الخدمات المسجلة بشأنها العلامة الجماعية.

المادة (٣٦)

أ. يجوز للأشخاص الاعتباريين الذين يتولون مراقبة أو فحص بعض السلع أو الخدمات
من حيث مصدرها أو عناصر تركيبها أو طريقة صنعها أوجودتها أو ذاتيتها أو أية
خاصية أخرى أن يطلبوا من الجهة المختصة لهم بتسجيل علامة تكون مخصصة للدلالة
على إجراء المراقبة أو الفحص.

وفي جميع الأحوال لا يجوز تسجيل هذه العلامة أو نقل ملكيتها إلا بموافقة الجهة المختصة.

ب. يتعين على طالب تسجيل علامة المراقبة ان يشير في طلب التسجيل إلى أنه يخص علامة مراقبة أو فحص وأن يرفق بالطلب نسخة من اشتراطات استعمال العلامات المطلوب تسجيلها.

وفي جميع الاحوال يلتزم مالك العلامة المسجلة باخطار الجهة المختصة بأية تغيرات تلك الاشتراطات، ولا يكون أي تغيير نافذ إلا بعد موافقة الجهة المختصة عليه.

المادة (٣٧)

يجوز تسجيل علامة لغايات غير تجارية كالشعار الذي تتخذه هيئة ذات نفع عام أو تستعمله مؤسسة مهنية لتمييز مراسلاتها أو ليكون شارة لأعضائها.

المادة (٣٨)

تحدد اللائحة التنفيذية الشروط والقواعد الخاصة بتسجيل العلامات المنصوص عليها في المواد (٣٥) و(٣٦) و(٣٧) والمستندات التي يتعين تقديمها للتسجيل، وسائر الأمور التنظيمية المتعلقة بها، ويترتب على تسجيل أي من تلك العلامات جميع الآثار المنصوص عليها في هذا القانون.

الباب الخامس
العقوبات

المادة (٣٩)

أ. مع عدم الاخلال بأي عقوبة أشد منصوص عليها في قانون آخر يعاقب بالحبس مدة لا تزيد عن خمس سنوات وبغرامة لا تزيد عن مليون ريال سعودي أو ما يعادلها بعملات دول المجلس أو باحدى هاتين العقوبتين:

١. كل من زور علامة تم تسجيلها طبقاً للقانون، أو قلدها بطريقة تدعو إلى تضليل الجمهور وكل من استعمل وهو سيء النية علامة مزورة أو مقلدة.

٢. كل من وضع وهو سيء النية على سلعه أو استعمل فيما يتعلق بخدماته علامة مملوكة لغيره.

ب. مع عدم الاخلال بأي عقوبة أشد منصوص عليها في قانون آخر يعاقب بالحبس مدة لاتزيد عن ثلاث سنوات وبغرامة لاتزيد عن مائة ألف ريال سعودي أو ما يعادلها بعملات دول المجلس أو باحدى هاتين العقوبتين:

١. كل من باع أو عرض للبيع أو للتداول أو حاز بقصد البيع سلع عليها علامة مزورة أو مقلدة أو موضوعة أو مستعملة بغير حق مع علمه بذلك و كذلك كل من عرض خدمات في ظل هذه العلامة.

٢. كل من استعمل علامة غير مسجلة في الأحوال المنصوص عليها في الفقرات (من "٢" الى "١١") من المادة (٣).

٣. كل من دون بغير حق على علامته أو أوراقه أو مستنداته التجارية ما يؤدي إلى الاعتقاد بحصول تسجيل العلامة.

٤. كل من تعمد وهو سيء النية إغفال وضع علامته التجارية المسجلة على السلع أو الخدمات التي تميزها.

٥. كل من وضع أو حاز أدوات أو مواد بقصد إستعمالها بتقليد العلامات التجارية المسجلة أو المشهورة.

المادة (٤٠)

في حالة العود يعاقب العائد بعقوبة لاتزيد عن ضعف الحد الاقصى للعقوبة المقررة للمخالفة مع إغلاق المحل التجاري أو المشروع لمدة لاتقل عن خمسة عشر يوماً و لا تزيد عن ستة أشهر مع نشر الحكم على نفقة المخالف وفقاً للاجراءات التي تحددها اللائحة التنفيذية.

ويعتبر عائداً في تطبيق أحكام هذا القانون من حكم عليه في مخالفة من المخالفات المنصوص عليها فيه وعاد إلى إرتكاب مخالفة أخرى مماثلة خلال ثلاث سنوات من تاريخ الحكم عليه نهائياً في المخالفة السابقة.

المادة (٤١)

يجوز لكل من أصابه ضرر نتيجة إرتكاب إحدى المخالفات المنصوص عليها في هذا النظام أن يطالب المسؤول عن هذه المخالفة بالتعويض المناسب عما لحقه من ضرر.

المادة (٤٢)

١. يجوز لمالك العلامة في أي وقت، ولو كان ذلك قبل رفع اية دعوى، ان يستصدر، بناءً على عريضة مشفوعة بشهادة رسمية دالة على تسجيل العلامة أو بناءً على شهرة علامته، امراً من المحكمة المختصة باتخاذ الاجراءات التحفظية اللازمة، وعلى وجه الخصوص حجز الآلات أو أية ادوات تستخدم أو تكون قد استخدمت في ارتكاب الجريمة وكذا السلع وعناوين المحال أو الأغلفة أو الأوراق أو المستندات أو غيرها مما تكون وضعت عليها العلامة أو البيانات موضوع الجريمة.

٢. ويجوز إجراء هذا الحجز عند استيراد البضائع من الخارج.

٣. ويجوز أن يشمل الأمر الصادر من المحكمة ندب خبير أو أكثر لمعاونة القائم بالحجز على عمله، وإلزام الطالب بتقديم ضمان مالي تقدره المحكمة لتعويض المحجوز عليه عند الاقتضاء ولا يتم الافراج عن الضمان إلا بأمر من المحكمة.

٤. بعد توقيع الحجز لمالك البضاعة أن ينازع أمام المحكمة في مدى كفاية قيمة الضمان المالي الذي قدمه الحجز.

المادة (٤٣)

تعتبر اجراءات الحجز المنصوص عليها في المادة السابقة كأن لم تكن إذا لم ترفع دعوى على من اتخذت بشأنه هذه الاجراءات، وذلك خلال ١٠ أيام من توقيع الحجز.

المادة (٤٤)

١. يجوز للمحكمة، في اية دعوى، ان تقضي بمصادرة الأشياء المحجوزة أو التي تحجز فيما بعد، لاستنزال ثمنها من التعويضات أو الغرامات، أو للتصرف فيها بأية طريقة أخرى تراها المحكمة مناسبة.

٢. ويجوز لها كذلك ان تأمر بإتلاف العلامات الغير قانونية، وأن تأمر عند الاقتضاء بإتلاف السلع والأغلفة ومعدات الحزم وغيرها من الأشياء التي تحمل هذه العلامات أو تحمل بيانات غير قانونية، وكذلك إتلاف الآلات والأدوات التي استعملت بصفة خاصة في عملية التزوير، ولها أن تأمر بكل ما سبق حتى في حالة الحكم بالبراءة.

٣. ويجوز للمحكمة أن تأمر بنشر الحكم في الجريدة الرسمية أو في إحدى الصحف اليومية على نفقة المحكوم عليه.

المادة (٤٥)

تسقط دعوى الحق العام بمضي خمس سنوات من تاريخ ارتكاب المخالفة دون اتخاذ أي من إجراءات التحقيق أو المحاكمة، ولا يترتب على سقوط دعوى الحق العام أي مساس بالحقوق الخاصة.

المادة (٤٦)

للمدعى عليه أن يتخذ اجراءات مطالبة المدعي السيء النية بالتعويض الذي قد يستحق له نتيجة اتخاذه للإجراءات المنصوص عليها في المادة "الثانية والأربعين" من هذا النظام وذلك خلال تسعين يوماً من تاريخ انتهاء الميعاد المنصوص عليه في المادة "الثالثة والأربعين" من هذا القانون (النظام) إذا لم يرفع الحاجز دعواه أو من تاريخ صدور الحكم النهائي في دعوى الحاجز المتعلقة في العلامة التجارية، وفي جميع الاحوال لا

يجوز صرف الضمان المالي للحاجز إلا بعد صدور الحكم النهائي في دعوى المحجوز عليه بإدانته، أو بعد انقضاء الميعاد المقرر له دون رفعها ما لم يتضمن الحكم الصادر في دعوى الحاجز الفصل في موضوع الضمان المالي.

الباب السادس

أحكام ختامية

المادة (٤٧)

يكون للموظفين الذين يعينهم الوزير المختص صفة مأموري الضبط القضائي فيما يتعلق بتطبيق أحكام هذا النظام (القانون) واثبات الجرائم التي تقع بالمخالفة له.

المادة (٤٨)

تحدد اللائحة التنفيذية الرسوم المتعلقة بهذا النظام (القانون).

المادة (٤٩)

للجنة التعاون التجاري حق تفسير واقتراح تعديل هذا القانون (النظام).

المادة (٥٠)

تصدر لجنة التعاون التجاري اللائحة التنفيذية لهذا القانون (النظام).

قانون اتحادي رقم (٤) لسنة ١٩٧٩
في شأن قمع الغش والتدليس في المعاملات التجارية

نحن زايد بن سلطان آل نهيان رئيس دولة الامارات العربية المتحدة،

بعد الاطلاع على احكام الدستور المؤقت،

وعلى القانون رقم (١) لسنة ١٩٧٢ في شأن اختصاصات الوزارات وصلاحيات الوزراء والقوانين المعدلة له،

وبناءً على ما عرضه وزير الاقتصاد والتجارة،

وموافقة مجلس الوزراء والمجلس الوطني الاتحادي، وتصديق المجلس الأعلى للاتحاد،

اصدرنا القانون الآتي:

المادة (١)

يعاقب بالحبس لمدة لا تجاوز سنتين، وبغرامة لا تقل عن خمسمائة درهم ولا تجاوز عشرة آلاف درهم أو بإحدى هاتين العقوبتين كل من خدع أو شرع في أن يخدع المتعاقد معه بأية طريقة من الطرق في احدى الأمور الآتية:

١. عدد البضاعة المباعة أو مقدارها أو مقاسها أو كيلها أو وزنها أو طاقاتها أو عيارها أو مواصفاتها.

٢. ذاتية البضاعة اذا كان ما سلم منها غير ما تم التعاقد عليه.

٣. حقيقة البضاعة أو طبيعتها أو صفاتها الجوهرية أو ما تحتويه من عناصر نافعة وعلى وجه العموم العناصر الداخلة في تركيبها.

٤. نوعها أو أصلها أو مصدرها في الاحوال التي يكون فيها لنوع البضاعة أو لأصلها أو لمصدرها اعتبار ملحوظ عند التعاقد عليها.

725

٥. اجراء تخفيضات وهمية في اسعار السلع والبضائع المعروضة للبيع في التصفيات الموسمية أو غير الموسمية.

وتكون العقوبة الحبس لمدة لا تجاوز ثلاث سنوات وغرامة لا تقل عن أربعة آلاف درهم ولا تجاوز عشرين ألف درهم، أو إحدى هاتين العقوبتين إذا ارتكبت الجريمة أو شرع في ارتكابها باستعمال موازين أو مقاييس أو مكاييل أو دمغات أو اختام أو آلات فحص اخرى مزيفة او مختلفة أو باستعمال طرق أو وسائل من شأنها جعل عملية وزن البضاعة أو قياسها أو كيلها أو فحصها غير صحيحة.

المادة (٢)

يعاقب بالحبس مدة لا تجاوز سنتين وبغرامة لا تقل عن خمسمائة درهم ولا تجاوز عشرة آلاف درهم أو باحدى هاتين العقوبتين:

١. كل من غش أو شرع في ان يغش اغذية للانسان أو الحيوان أو عقاقير طبية أو حاصلات زراعية أو منتجات طبيعية أو أية مواد اخرى معدة للبيع.

٢. كل من طرح أو عرض للبيع أو باع اغذية للانسان أو الحيوان أو عقاقير طبية أو حاصلات زراعية أو منتجات طبيعية أو مواد اخرى مع علمه بغشها أو فسادها.

ويفترض العلم بالغش أو الفساد اذا كان المخالف من المشتغلين بالتجارة أو من الباعة الجائلين ما لم يثبت حسن نيته ويرشد عن مصدر المواد موضوع الجريمة.

٣. كل من اعد او طرح او عرض للبيع او باع مواد بقصد استعمالها في غش اغذية الانسان او الحيوان او العقاقير او الحاصلات الزراعية او المنتجات الطبيعية او المواد الاخرى.

وكذلك كل من حرض بأية وسيلة من وسائل النشر على استعمال هذه المواد في الغش.

وتكون العقوبة الحبس لمدة لا تجاوز ثلاث سنوات وغرامة لا تقل عن ألف درهم ولا تجاوز عشرين ألف درهم أو احدى هاتين العقوبتين، إذا كانت الأغذية أو العقاقير الطبية أو الحاصلات الزراعية أو المنتجات أو المواد الاخرى المشار [6] إليها في الفقرتين السابقتين ضارة بصحة الانسان او الحيوان.

وتطبق العقوبات المنصوص عليها في الفقرة السابقة ولو كان المشتري أو المستهلك عالماً بغش البضاعة أو فسادها.

---

[6]. . وردت هذه الكلمة في نص الجريدة الرسمية "المشاير" والأصح ان تكون "المشار" فاقتضى التنويه

المادة (٣)

يعاقب بالحبس مدة لا تجاوز ستة أشهر، وبغرامة لا تجاوز خمسمائة درهم أو بإحدى هاتين العقوبتين كل من حاز اغذية او عقاقير طبية او حاصلات او منتجات او مواد اخرى مما هو مشار اليه في الفقرة الاولى من المادة السابقة وهو عالم بغشها او فسادها وذلك ما لم يثبت ان حيازته لها لسبب مشروع.

وتكون العقوبة الحبس لمدة لا تجاوز سنة وغرامة لا تجاوز ألفي درهم أو بإحدى هاتين العقوبتين اذا كانت المواد الغذائية أو العقاقير الطبية او الحاصلات الزراعية او المنتجات الطبيعية والمواد الاخرى التي وجدت في حوزته ضارة بصحة الانسان او الحيوان.

المادة (٤)

لا يجوز استيراد اي شيء من أغذية الانسان أو الحيوان أو العقاقير الطبية أو الحاصلات الزراعية أو امنتجات الطبيعية أو أي مواد اخرى تكون مغشوشة أو فاسدة.

ويأمر وزير الاقتصاد والتجارة باعادة تصدير تلك البضائع الى مصدرها في الميعاد الذي يحدده. فإذا لم تتم اعادة تصديرها في هذا الميعاد كان للوزير ان يأمر باعدامها على نفقة مستوردها.

على انه يجوز لوزير الاقتصاد والتجارة ان يسمح بادخال تلك البضائع وتداولها وذلك لاستعمالها في أي غرض آخر تكون صالحة له وذلك طبقاً للشروط التي يحددها بقرار يصدره.

المادة (٥)

تنظم بقرارات من وزير الاقتصاد والتجارة المسائل الآتية:

أولاً: استعمال أوان أو أوعية أو أغلفة معينة في تجهيز المواد الغذائية والعقاقير الطبية والحاصلات والمنتجات والمواد الأخرى وكيفية تعبئتها أو حزمها أو حفظها أو توزيعها أو نقلها بقصد طرحها للبيع أو بيعها مع بيان كيفية استعمال هذه المواد وطرق حفظها وحيازتها والحالات التي تكون أو تصبح فيها غير صالحة للاستهلاك وايضاح اسمها ومصدرها ومحل صنعها واسم صانعها وغير ذلك من البيانات اللازمة للتعريف بها.

ثانياً: مسك السجلات والدفاتر الخاصة بهذه البضائع وطريقة مراجعتها واعطاء الشهادات الخاصة بها أو اعتمادها.

ثالثاً: تحديد العناصر أو النسب الواجب توافرها في تركيب المواد سالفة الذكر وذلك لامكان بيعها أو عرضها للبيع.

رابعاً: الامور المتعلقة باستيراد وتصدير وصنع وبيع وحيازة وتداول البضائع التي تنطبق عليها احكام هذا القانون.

مع عدم الاخلال بالعقوبات المنصوص عليها في هذا القانون يعاقب من يخالف احكام هذه القرارات بالحبس لمدة لا تجاوز ستة اشهر وبغرامة لا تقل عن خمسمائة درهم ولا تجاوز خمسة آلاف درهم أو باحدى هاتين العقوبتين.

المادة (٦)

يقوم باثبات الجرائم التي تقع بالمخالفة لاحكام هذا القانون واللوائح الصادرة تنفيذاً له الموظفون الذين يكلفون بذلك من وزير الاقتصاد والتجارة بالاتفاق مع السلطات المختصة بالامارات الاعضاء في الاتحاد.

ويكون لهؤلاء الموظفين صفة الضبطية القضائية ولهم في سبيل ضبط ما يقع من مخالفات لاحكام هذا القانون ان يدخلوا جميع المحال والاماكن المطروحة أو المعروضة فيها للبيع أو المودعة فيها المواد الغذائية أو العقاقير الطبية والحاصلات والمنتجات وغيرها من المواد الخاضة لاحكامه.

ولهم ان يأخذوا عينات من تلك المواد وفقاً لما يقرره هذا القانون واللوائح الصادرة لتنفيذه.

المادة (٧)

اذا وجدت لدى الموظفين المشار إليهم في المادة السابقة اسباب قوية تحملهم على الاعتقاد بأن ثمة مخالفة لاحكام هذا القانون جاز لهم ضبط المواد المشتبه فيها بصفة مؤقتة.

وفي هذه الحالة يدعى اصحاب الشأن للحضور وتؤخذ ثلاث عينات على الاقل من المواد المضبوطة لتحليلها وتحديد مدى مطابقتها للعناصر والمواصفات الواجب توافرها فيها وتختم جميعها بالشمع الاحمر وتسلم احدى هذه العينات لصاحب الشأن ويحرر بذلك محضراً مشتملاً على جميع البيانات اللازمة للتثبت من ذات العينات والمواد التي أخذت منها، ويجب الاسراع في تحليل المواد والسلع القابلة للتلف أو العطب، ويصدر بتنظيم أخذ العينات وحفظها وتحليلها قرار من وزير الاقتصاد والتجارة.

ومع عدم الاخلال بحق المخالف في طلب الافراج عن البضاعة المضبوطة من المحكمة المختصة يفرج عنها بحكم القانون اذا لم يصدر امر من المحكمة بتأييد الضبط خلال الخمسة عشر يوماً التالية ليوم الضبط.

ويرد لصاحب الشأن اعتباره وتعويضه تعويضاً عادلاً عما اصابه من أضرار اذا ثبت عدم صحة التهمة المنسوبة اليه.

المادة (٨)

يعاقب بالحبس مدة لاتجاوز ستة اشهر وبغرامة لا تقل عن خمسمائة درهم ولا تجاوز خمسة آلاف درهم أو باحدى هاتين العقوبتين كل من حال دون تأدية الموظفين المشار إليهم في المادة السادسة من هذا القانون اعمال وظائفهم سواء بمنعهم من دخول المصانع أو المخازن أو المتاجر أو غيرها من المحال التي توجد بها المواد موضوع المخالفة أو من الحصول على عينات منها أو بأية طريقة اخرى.

المادة (٩)

على المحكمة متى قضت بالادانة في جريمة من الجرائم المنصوص عليها في المادتين الثانية والثالثة من هذا القانون ان تقضي بمصادرة الاغذية أو العقاقير أو الحاصلات أو المنتجات أو المواد الاخرى التي تكون جسم الجريمة.

وللمحكمة في هذه الحالة ايضاً ان تأمر بنشر الحكم في جريدة أو جريدتين محليتين على نفقة المحكوم عليه.

المادة (١٠)

للمحكمة المختصة عند الحكم بالادانة على صاحب المحل التجاري أو المنشأة أو المهنة أو الحرفة في احدى الجرائم المنصوص عليها في المادتين الثانية والثالثة من هذا القانون ان تأمر باغلاق المحل لمدة لا تجاوز ستة اشهر.

ويجوز لها في حالة العود ان تأمر بسحب الترخيص.

واذا كان صاحب الترخيص من غير ابناء دولة الامارات العربية المتحدة جاز لها ان تأمر بابعاده عن البلاد.

المادة (١١)

يحكم على المتهم في حالة العود بعقوبتي الحبس والغرامة.

وتعتبر الجرائم المنصوص عليها في المواد السابقة والجرائم المنصوص عليها في اي قانون اخر خاص بقمع الغش والتدليس متماثلة بالنسبة الى العود.

المادة (١٢)

على وزير الاقتصاد والتجارة ان يصدر القرارات اللازمة لتنفيذ احكام هذا القانون.

المادة (١٣)

على الوزراء كل فيما يخصه والسلطات المختصة في الامارات الاعضاء في الاتحاد تنفيذ احكام هذا القانون، وينشر في الجريدة الرسمية ويعمل به بعد ثلاثة اشهر من تاريخ نشره.

زايد بن سلطان آل نهيان
رئيس دولة الامارات العربية المتحدة

صدر عنا بقصر الرئاسة بأبو ظبي
بتاريخ: ١٣٩٩/٤/٢٠هـ
الموافق: ١٩٧٩/٣/١٩م.

قرار وزاري رقم (٢٦) لسنة ١٩٨٤ م
باللائحة التنفيذية للقانون رقم (٤) لسنة ١٩٧٩م
في شأن قمع الغش والتدليس في المعاملات التجارية

وزير الاقتصاد والتجارة.

بعد الاطلاع على القانون الاتحادي رقم (١) لسنة ١٩٧٢ في شأن اختصاصات الوزارات وصلاحيات الوزراء والقوانين المعدلة له،

وعلى القانون الاتحادي رقم (٤) لسنة ١٩٧٩ في شأن قمع الغش والتدليس في المعاملات التجارية،

وعلى القانون الاتحادي رقم (٥) لسنة ١٩٧٩ في شأن الحجر الزراعي،

وعلى القانون الاتحادي رقم (٦) لسنة ١٩٧٩ في شأن الحجر البيطري،

وعلى القانون الاتحادي رقم (٤) لسنة ١٩٨٣ في شأن مهنه الصيدلة والمؤسسات الصيدلانية،

وبناءً على ما عرضه وكيل الوزارة،

قرر:

الفصل الأول
البيانات التجارية المنافسة غير المشروعة

المادة (١)

يعتبر بياناً تجارياً في تطبيق احكام القانون رقم (٤) لسنة ١٩٧٩ المشار اليه واحكام هذه اللائحة كل ايضاح يتعلق بصفة مباشرة أو غير مباشرة بما يأتي:

١. عدد البضاعة المباعة أو مقدارها أو مقاسها أو كيلها أو وزنها أو طاقتها أو عيارها أو مواصفاتها.

٢. الجهة أو البلد الذي صنعت فيه البضاعة أو انتجت وتاريخ الصنع أو الانتاج وتاريخ انتهاء الصلاحية.[7]

٣. طريقة صنع البضاعة أو انتاجها.

٤. العناصر الداخلة في تركيب البضاعة.

٥. نوع البضاعة أو اصلها أو منشئها أو مصدرها.

٦. اسم أو صفات المنتج أو الصانع.[8]

٧. وجود براءات اختراع أو علامات تجارية أو غير ذلك من حقوق الملكية الصناعية أو اي امتيازات أو جوائز أو ميزات تجارية أو صناعية.

المادة (٢)

يجب ان يكون البيان التجاري مطابقاً للحقيقة من جميع الوجوه سواء كان موضوعاً على نفس المنتجات أو على المحال أو بداخلها أو على الاغلفة أو الفواتير أو المكاتبات أو وسائل الاعلان أو غير ذلك مما يستعمل في عرض البضائع على الجمهور.

المادة (٣)

لا يجوز وضع اسم البائع أو المستورد أو عنوانه على بضائع أو منتجات مالم يكن ذلك مقترناً ببيان دقيق مكتوب بحروف ظاهرة عن البلد أو الجهة التي صنعت أو انتجت فيها.

المادة (٤)

لا يجوز للتاجر ان يذيع معلومات مغايرة للحقيقة أو ينشر بيانات كاذبة تتعلق بمنشأ البضاعة أو اوصافها أو اهميتها ولا ان يعلن خلافاً للواقع انه حائز لمرتبة أو ميدالية أو مكافأة ولا ان يلجأ الى اية طريقة اخرى تنطوي على تضليل للجمهور.

---

[7]. تم تعديل هذه الفقرة من المادة (١) بموجب القرار الوزاري رقم (٨) لسنة ١٩٨٨ المعدل للقرار الوزاري رقم (٢٦) لسنة ١٩٨٤ حيث تم اضافة عبارة "وتاريخ انتهاء الصلاحية".

[8]. وردت هذه الكلمة في نص الجريدة الرسمية "المصانع" والأصح ان تكون "الصانع" فاقتضى التنويه.

المادة (٥)

يحظر على التاجر أو الصانع أو المنتج القيام بأي عمل من الاعمال الآتية:

١. الاستعمال المباشر أو غير المباشر لبيان غير صحيح أو مضلل عن منشأ البضاعة أو مصدرها أو عن شخصية المنتج أو الصانع المورد لها.

٢. الاستعمال المباشر أو غير المباشر لتسمية الاصل غير الصحيحة أو المضللة أو تقليد تسمية الاصل حتى ولو ذكر الاصل الحقيقي للبضاعة أو استعملت التسمية مترجمة أو كانت مصحوبة بالفاظ مثل نوع أو طراز أو تقليد أو ما شابه ذلك.

٣. استعمال علامة تجارية مزورة أو مقلدة أو موضوعة بغير حق مع علمه بذلك أو تغيير الحقيقة بأي حال من الاحوال، ويقصد بالعلامة التجارية كل وسيلة ظاهرة تستخدم لتمييز منتجات مشروع عن منتجات مشروعات اخرى.

٤. جميع الاعمال التي تؤدي الى خلق لبس أو خلط باية طريقة كانت مع الاسماء التجارية للمنافسين أو منتجاتهم أو نشاطهم الصناعي أو التجاري.

المادة (٦)

تخضع جميع البضائع المستوردة لاثبات المنشأ، ويحظر ادخالها الى الدولة اذا كانت تحمل علامة أو بياناً زائفاً أو مضللاً للمنشأ أو المصدر سواء كانت هذه العلامات أو البيانات على البضاعة عينها أو على اغلفتها أو على احزمتها.

ويقصد بمنشأ البضاعة في تطبيق احكام هذه اللائحة بلد انتاجها، كما يقصد بمصدر البضاعة البلد الذي استوردت منه مباشرة.

المادة (٧)

يحظر ادخال البضائع المستوردة التي لا تتوفر فيها الشروط المنصوص عليها في قوانين وانظمة حماية المنشأ والملكية الصناعية، ويجوز لوزير الاقتصاد والتجارة رفع هذا الحظر في كل حالة على حدة بناءً على تقرير اللجنة المشار اليها في المادة (٤٤) من هذه اللائحة.

الفصل الثاني
تنظيم استيراد المواد الخاضعة لاحكام القانون

المادة (٨)

لا يجوز استيراد اي شئ من اغذية الانسان أو الحيوان أو العقاقير الطبية أو الحاصلات الزراعية أو المنتجات الطبيعية أو اية مواد اخرى تكون مغشوشة أو فاسدة. ويحظر

ادخال تلك البضائع الى الدولة، وعلى المستورد اعادة تصديرها الى مصدرها خلال اسبوع من تاريخ اخطاره بذلك اذا كانت من البضائع سريعة التلف، وخلال اسبوعين بالنسبة الى البضائع الاخرى، ويجوز عند الضرورة مد المهلة.

فاذا تأخر المستورد أو امتنع عن اعادة تصدير البضائع خلال المهلة المحددة اعدمت على نفقته سواء حضر المستورد أو لم يحضر. ولا يخل ذلك بحق دائرة الجمارك أو الموانئ المختصة في مطالبة المستورد بأجور التخزين والمناولة ومقابل الخدمات التي قدمت للبضاعة التي اعيد تصديرها أو تم اعدامها.

ويصدر قرار اعادة تصدير البضاعة أو مد المهلة أو اعدام البضاعة من وزير الاقتصاد والتجارة بناءً على اقتراح مدير دائرة الجمارك المختصة.

ويجوز لوزير الاقتصاد والتجارة بناءً على طلب صاحب الشأن وموافقة اللجنة المنصوص عليها في المادة (٤٤) من هذه اللائحة، ان يقرر دخول البضائع المغشوشة أو الفاسدة الى الدولة وذلك لاستعمالها في اي غرض اخر تكون صالحة له. ويحدد القرار شروط تداول هذه البضائع ومجال استعمالها وتداولها.

الفصل الثالث
الرقابة على المواد الغذائية

المادة (٩)

يجب ان تكون المادة الغذائية ذات قيمة غذائية وصالحة للاستهلاك الآدمي ومباحة شرعاً وقانوناً، كما يجب ان تتوفر فيها المواصفات والاشتراطات التي يصدر بها قرار من وزير الاقتصاد والتجارة بالاتفاق مع الوزارات والدوائر الحكومية المختصة.

ويقصد بكلمة الاغذية[9] وعبارة المادة الغذائية في تطبيق احكام القانون رقم (٤) لسنة ١٩٧٩ المشار اليه وهذه اللائحة كل ما يتناوله الانسان من مأكولات ومشروبات فيما عدا المستحضرات الطبية.

المادة (١٠)

يجب ان تكون الاضافات الغذائية غير ضارة بالصحة ومباحة شرعاً وقانوناً وان تتوفر فيها المواصفات والاشتراطات التي يصدر بها قرار من وزير الاقتصاد والتجارة بالاتفاق مع الوزارات والدوائر الحكومية المختصة.

ويقصد بالاضافات الغذائية في تطبيق أحكام هذه اللائحة كل مادة تضاف الى الاغذية بقصد تلوينها أو تحسين مذاقها ونكهتها أو حفظها أو تثبيت قوامها أو لاي غرض اخر

---

[9]. وردت هذه الكلمة في نص الجريدة الرسمية "الآغذاية" والأصح ان تكون "الأغذية" فاقتضى التنويه.

مسموح به من اغراض لتصنيع أو التحضير أو التعبئة، ولا تعتبر بذاتها مادة غذائية أو مكوناً طبيعياً لاي مادة غذائية.

المادة (١١)

لا يجوز تفريغ اية مواد غذائية مستوردة في موانئ الدولة البحرية أو الجوية كما لا يجوز الترخيص بعبورها مراكز الدخول البرية في الدولة الا بعد معاينتها والتصريح بذلك بمعرفة مفتشي المحاجر أو قسم الصحة المختص بالميناء أو مركز الدخول، ولهؤلاء الموظفين أن يطلبوا من الناقل أو من يمثله تقديم المستندات الآتية:

١. صورة طبق الاصل من قائمة شحن المواد الغذائية الواردة (المنافيست).

٢. صورة طبق الاصل من خارطة ترتيب البضاعة.

٣. اقرار بعدم وضع المواد الغذائية اثناء الرحلة مع مواد اخرى سامة أو مضرة بالصحة.

٤. اية مستندات اخرى تنص القوانين واللوائح المعمول بها على ضرورة تقديمها.

وفي جميع الاحوال يكون لهؤلاء الموظفين حق الاطلاع على اصول المستندات المقدمة اليهم.

المادة (١٢)

لا يجوز الافراج عن اية مواد غذائية واردة من الخارج الا بموجب تصريح بذلك من المحجر أو قسم الصحة المختص حسب الاحوال.

المادة (١٣)

على كل من يزاول استيراد أو تجارة المواد الغذائية مسك سجلات منتظمة تقيد فيها انواع المواد الغذائية الموجودة في حيازته وكمياتها وعبواتها واوزانها ومصدرها وتاريخ بدء الحيازة ومقدار المبيع منها وتاريخ البيع مع بيان اسم المشتري اذا كان تاجر جملة أو تجزئة.

المادة (١٤)

يجب ان تتوفر في المصانع والمخازن والمطابخ وبصفة عامة كل محل يقوم بصنع أو تجهيز أو اعداد أو بيع أو تخزين المواد الغذائية المواصفات والشروط الصحية والفنية التي تقررها دائرة البلدية المعنية بالاتفاق مع الوزارات والدوائر الحكومية المختصة، كما يجب على هذه المحال الالتزام بقواعد الصحة العامة في صنع أو اعداد أو تجهيز المادة الغذائية أو المواد والادوات والاواني المستعملة.

المادة (١٥)

لا يجوز بيع اية مواد غذائية أو عرضها للبيع أو حيازتها بقصد البيع اذا انتهت مدة صلاحيتها للاستهلاك، وعلى كل من يتعامل في صنع أو تجارة أو تخزين المواد الغذائية اخطار دائرة البلدية المختصة عن المواد الغذائية الموجودة في حوزته وانتهت مدة صلاحيتها للاستهلاك لاعدامها بمعرفتها.

المادة (١٦)

يحظر بيع اللحوم والدواجن المجمدة أو المبردة أو المصنعة أو عرضها للبيع أو حيازتها بقصد البيع ما لم تكن مذبوحة وفقاً لاحكام الشريعة الاسلامية.

المادة (١٧)

يحظر بيع اللحوم والدواجن والاسماك المجمدة أو المفرغة من الهواء أو عرضها للبيع بوصفها لحوماً أو دواجن أو اسماكاً طازجة، كما يحظر تسييحها.

ولا يجوز لمحال الجزارة بيع اللحوم المجمدة بغير ترخيص من دائرة البلدية المختصة.

المادة (١٨)

يجب ان تتوفر في وسائل نقل المواد الغذائية الشروط والمواصفات الصحية والفنية التي يصدر بها قرار من وزير الاقتصاد والتجارة بالاتفاق مع الوزارات والدوائر الحكومية المختصة.

ولا يجوز نقل اية مواد غذائية غير المواد المصرح بها في الترخيص الصادر لوسيلة النقل.

المادة (١٩)

يجب على كل من يعمل في صنع أو تجهيز أو بيع أو تداول أو تخزين أو نقل أو طهو المواد الغذائية ان يحصل على شهادة صحية من وزارة الصحة، ويجب تجديد هذه الشهادة في المواعيد المقررة.

ولا يجوز لصاحب العمل ان يسمح للعامل بمزاولة العمل في الاعمال المشار اليها في الفقرة السابقة الا بعد حصوله على تلك الشهادة، ويتعين عليه منع العامل من مزاولة عمله فور علمه باصابته بمرض من الامراض المعدية التي تحددها وزارة الصحة أو عند عدم تجديد الشهادة الصحية، كما يجب على صاحب العمل تزويد هؤلاء العمال بالزي الذي تقرره دائرة البلدية المختصة، ومنعهم من مزاولة اعمالهم ما لم يكونوا مرتدين هذا الزي.

المادة (٢٠)

على المحال والجهات المرخص لها بتجارة المواد الغذائية فرز لحوم الخنزير والمواد الغذائية التي تدخل فيها مادة الخنزير او المواد الكحولية وعزلها في موضع خاص، على ان يكتب عليه بخط واضح وظاهر عبارة " لحوم خنزير ومواد غذائية بها مادة الخنزير او مواد كحولية لغير المسلمين " حسب الاحوال.

الفصل الرابع
بطاقات المواد الغذائية

المادة (٢١)

لا يجوز ان توصف البضاعة او تعرض ببطاقة او ببيانات ايضاحية غير حقيقية او خادعة او مضللة او توحي بطريقة مباشرة او غير مباشرة بأنها مادة اخرى او تؤدي بأي شكل من الاشكال إلى انطباع خاطئ عن طبيعتها وخصائصها او الى الخلط بينها وبين غيرها من المنتجات.

ويقصد بالبطاقة في تطبيق احكام هذه اللائحة كل بيان او ايضاح او علامة او مادة وصفية مصورة او مكتوبة او مطلوبة او ملصقة او محفورة على عبوة مادة من المواد او تكون متصلة بها، كما يقصد بالبيانات الايضاحية البطاقات او اية مادة مكتوبة او مطبوعة او مرسومة تصاحب مادة من المواد أو لها علاقة بها.

المادة (٢٢)

يجب ان تكون البيانات المدونة ببطاقات المواد الغذائية المعبأة او المصاحبة لها ظاهرة وواضحة بحيث يسهل على المستهلك قراءتها في الظروف العادية للشراء والاستعمال ولا يجوز اخفاء هذه البيانات بأي شيء اخر مرسوم او مكتوب او مطبوع. ويتعين ان تكون البيانات مكتوبة بلون مغاير عن لون خلفيتها بطريقة جيدة وثابتة بحيث يصعب ازالتها او اجراء اي تغيير فيها وان تكون الحروف الهجائية المكتوب بها اسم المادة الغذائية ذات حجم معقول بـالمقارنة بالبيانات الاخرى الموضحة على البطاقة.

واذا كانت العبوة مغطاة بغلاف[10] خارجي فيجب ان يحمل هذا الغلاف جميع البيانات الضرورية وان لا يكون من شأنه حجب بطاقة العبوة او الحيلولة دون قراءة بياناتها في سهولة.

وينبغي في جميع الاحوال ان يكون اسم المادة الغذائية وحجمها الصافي ظاهرين في جزء البطاقة المعد للعرض على المستهلك وقت البيع.

---

[10]. وردت هذه الكلمة في نص 'الجريدة الرسمية "بعلاف" والأصح ان تكون "بغلاف" فاقتضى التنويه.

ويقصد بالمعبأ في تطبيق احكام هذه اللائحة كل ما تمت تعبئته مقدماً ليكون جاهزاً للبيع بالتجزئة في عبوات كما يقصد بالعبوة اي شكل او صورة تعبأ فيها المادة الغذائية للبيع كوحدة مستقلة سواء كانت تحتويها بأكملها او بجزء منها وتشمل اللفافات والمغلفات.

المادة (٢٣)

اذا كانت المادة الغذائية تحتوي على دهون او لحوم او انزيمات او دماء او جيلاتين او اية مشتقات حيوانية اخرى وجب ان يذكر في البطاقة اسماء وانواع الحيوانات التي استخرجت منها المواد المذكورة. واذا كانت المادة الغذائية تحتوي على اية مواد كحولية وجب ان تتضمن البطاقة بياناً بذلك.

المادة (٢٤)

اذا كانت المادة الغذائية معدة لاغراض خاصة او كانت توصف بأنها تحتوي على فيتامينات او معادن او غيرها وجب ان يذكر في البطاقة البيانات الايضاحية والمعلومات الضرورية التي تدل على مطابقة المادة الغذائية لما وصفت به و ملاءمتها للغرض المعدة له.

وبالنسبة للمواد الغذائية التي تعالج بالاشعاع المؤين ينبغي ان يذكر ذلك في بطاقات عبواتها.

المادة (٢٥)

يجب ان يكون اسم المادة الغذائية محدد لطبيعتها الحقيقة وان يكون خاصاً بها لا بغيرها، واذا ما حددت احدى المواصفات القياسية المعتمدة اسماً او اسماء للمادة الغذائية وجب استعمال واحد منها على الاقل، والا فيستعمل الاسم الشائع او المعتاد ان وجد فاذا لم يوجد امكن استعمال اسم وصفي مناسب.

ويجوز استعمال اسم مبتكر للمادة الغذائية بشرط ان لا يكون مضللاً وان يكون مصحوباً باسم وصفي مناسب.

المادة (٢٦)

يجب ان يكتب على البطاقة قائمة بمكونات المادة الغذائية مرتبة ترتيباً تنازلياً حسب نسبة كل منها وذلك فيما عدا الحالات الاتية:

١. اذا كانت المادة الغذائية مجففة ومعدة للتجهيز باضافة الماء فيجوز ان ترتب المكونات ترتيباً تنازلياً وفقاً لنسبتها في المادة الغذائية المجهزة بعد اضافة الماء تحت عنوان " المكونات بعد التجهيز".

٢. اذا كانت المادة الغذائية معروفة التركيب ولا يؤدي عدم اعلان مكوناتها الى تضليل المستهلك بشرط ان تمكن البيانات الموضحة على بطاقة العبوة المستهلك من فهم طبيعة المادة الغذائية.

٣. اذا نصت احدى المواصفات القياسية المعتمدة على غير ذلك.

المادة (٢٧)

اذا احتوت احدى مكونات المادة الغذائية على عدة اجزاء وجب ان تتضمن قائمة المكونات اسماء هذه الاجزاء وذلك فيما عدا الاحوال التي يكون فيها هذا المكون مادة غذائية لم تنص مواصفاتها القياسية المعتمدة على ضرورة ذكر قائمة مكوناتها كاملة بالاجزاء.

المادة (٢٨)

فيما عدا الاحوال التي يكون فيها الماء جزءاً من احدى مكونات المادة الغذائية يجب ان يذكر الماء المضاف في قائمة المكونات اذا كان هذا التوضيح يؤدي الى فهم افضل لتركيب المنتج.

المادة (٢٩)

اذا كانت المادة الغذائية تحتوي على احدى المواد المضافة المسموح بها من مواد حافظة او مبيضة او ملونة او غيرها فيجب ان تتضمن قائمة المكونات بياناً عنها.

المادة (٣٠)

يجب ان توضح بطاقة المادة الغذائية التعليمات الخاصة بشروط التخزين والنقل وطريقة الاستعمال.

المادة (٣١)

يجب ان يكتب بيان صافي المحتويات بالوحدات المترية في عبارة خاصة به على بطاقة المادة الغذائية بحيث يكون واضحاً ومتميزاً وموازياً لقاعدة العبوة ، ويحدد صافي المحتويات حسب حالة كل مادة غذائية وفقاً لما يأتي:

١. بالحجم في حالة المواد الغذائية السائلة.

٢. بالوزن في حالة المواد الغذائية الصلبة فيما عدا المواد التي تباع بالعدد فيذكر العدد.

٣. بالوزن او بالحجم في حالة المواد الغذائية اللزجة وشبه الصلبة.

وفي الحالات التي تكون فيها [11] المادة الغذائية في وسط سائل يتم التخلص منه قبل الاستعمال يتعين ان يحدد في بيان صافي المحتويات الوزن الصافي للعبوة ووزن المادة المصفاة.

المادة (٣٢)

يجب ان يكون صافي محتويات العبوة معادلاً لوزن او حجم المادة الغذائية عند التجهيز وفقاً لحالتها على النحو الآتي:

١. بالنسبة الى المواد الغذائية المجمدة يحدد صافي الوزن او الحجم عند نقطة التجمد.

٢. بالنسبة الى المواد الغذائية المبردة يحدد صافي الوزن او الحجم عند درجة حرارة ٤ م.

٣. بالنسبة الى المواد الغذائية المحفوظة يحدد صافي الوزن او الحجم عند درجة حرارة ٢٠ م.

المادة (٣٣)

يجب ان يكتب اسم بلد منشأ المادة الغذائية واسم وعنوان صانعها او معبئها على بطاقة العبوة، ويجوز كتابة اسم المستورد او البائع على البطاقة وفقاً للشروط المنصوص عليها في المادة الثالثة من هذه اللائحة.

واذا كانت المادة الغذائية تتعرض لتجهيز يغير من طبيعتها الاساسية في بلد ثان، فيعتبر البلد الذي يتم فيه هذا التجهيز بلد المنشأ فيما يتعلق بالبطاقة والبيانات الايضاحية المصاحبة لها.

المادة (٣٤)

يجب ان توضح بطاقة المادة الغذائية تاريخ الانتاج او الصنع او التعبئة وتاريخ انتهاء الصلاحية للاستعمال وذلك بالنسبة للاغذية التي يصدر بها قرار من وزير الاقتصاد والتجارة.

المادة (٣٥)

يجب ان تكون اللغة العربية احدى اللغات المستعملة في بطاقات المواد الغذائية والبيانات المصاحبة لها، واذا استعملت لغة اخرى او اكثر بجانب اللغة العربية وجب ان تكون جميع البيانات باللغات الاخرى مطابقة للبيانات الواردة باللغة العربية.

---

[11] . وردت هذه الكلمة في نص الجريدة الرسمية "فيا" والأصح ان تكون "فيها" فاقتضى التنويه.

المادة (٣٦)

لا يجوز بعد مضي شهرين من تاريخ العمل باحكام هذه اللائحة استيراد او انتاج او تداول او بيع اية مواد غذائية معبأة ما لم تكن بطاقاتها مستوفية للشروط المنصوص عليها في هذه اللائحة.

الفصل الخامس
الضبط – العينات – التحقيق

المادة (٣٧)

على دوائر الجمارك في الامارات كل في دائرة اختصاصها معاينة البضائع المستوردة قبل الافراج عنها للتأكد من عدم مخالفتها لاحكام القانون رقم (٤) لسنة ١٩٧٩ المشار اليه او احكام هذه اللائحة، وعليها في حالة وجود مخالفة، ضبط البضاعة وعدم الافراج عنها اذا كانت المخالفة مما يؤدي الى منع دخولها الى الدولة.

وتثبت المخالفة في محضر، يحال مع الوثائق المتعلقة بالبضاعة الى مدير دائرة الجمارك وذلك في حالة ما اذا رفض المستورد اعادة تصدير البضاعة المخالفة الى مصدرها في الميعاد المنصوص عليه في المادة الثامنة من هذه اللائحة.

المادة (٣٨)[12]

على مفتشي دوائر الجمارك في الموانئ ومراكز الدخول البرية والجوية معاينة المواد المستوردة كلياً أو جزئياً قبل الترخيص بالافراج عنها، وعليهم في حالة الاشتباه بوجود مخالفة لاحكام القانون رقم (٤) لسنة ١٩٧٩م المشار إليه أو أحكام اللائحة أخذ عينات من البضاعة لتحليلها وتحرير المحضر اللازم في هذا الشأن وإبلاغ دائرة الجمارك المختصة للتحفظ على البضاعة وعدم الإفراج عنها.

وفي حالة ثبوت المخالفة يحال مع المحضر مع الوثائق المتعلقة بالبضاعة إلى مدير دائرة الجمارك المختص وذلك في حالة ما إذا رفض المستورد إعادة تصدير البضاعة المخالفة إلى مصدرها في الميعاد المنصوص عليه في المادة الثامنة من اللائحة وإبلاغ إدارة الرقابة التجارية بالوزارة بالاجراءات التي تم اتخاذها بهذا الشأن.

---

[12]. تم استبدال نص المادة (٣٨) من القرار الوزاري رقم (٢٦) لسنة ١٩٨٤م بهذا النص بموجب القرار الوزاري رقم (١٢٦) لسنة ٢٠٠٣م المعدل للقرار رقم (٢٦) لسنة ١٩٨٤.

المادة (٣٩)¹³

يقوم باثبات الجرائم التي تقع بالمخالفة لأحكام قانون قمع الغش والتدليس في المعاملات التجارية ولائحته التنفيذية مفتشون يمثلون الجهات التالية:

- وزارة الاقتصاد والتجارة.
- وزارة الزراعة والثروة الحيوانية والسمكية.
- وزارة المالية والصناعة – إدارة الملكية الصناعية.
- وزارة الإعلام – المصنفات الفكرية وحقوق المؤلف.
- وزارة الصحة.
- اقسام الصحة والرقابة الغذائية في البلديات فيما يتعلق بالمواد الغذائية.
- هيئة المواصفات والمقاييس.
- جهات الترخيص التجاري لدى السلطات المحلية المختصة.

ويكون لهؤلاء المفتشين كل في دائرة اختصاصه صفة الضبطية القضائية، ولهم في سبيل ضبط ما يقع من مخالفات لأحكام القانون والقرارات الوزارية المنفذة له ان يدخلوا جميع المحال والأماكن المعروضة أو المودعة فيها البضائع الخاضعة لأحكام القانون وأخذ العينات اللازمة للتحليل.

ويتولى هؤلاء المفتشون تحرير محضر ضبط البضاعة وأخذ العينات وفقاً للاجراءات المنصوص عليها في اللائحة التنفيذية للقانون وإحالة المحضر ومرفقاته إلى إدارة الرقبة التجارية بالوزارة للنظر في عرضه على اللجنة الوطنية لمكافحة الغش التجاري المشكلة بموجب القرار الوزاري رقم (٢٩٥) لسنة ٢٠٠٢م وتعديلاته لاتخاذ القرار اللازم بشأنه.

المادة (٤٠)

تؤخذ العينات حسب نوع البضاعة بطريقة عشوائية بحضور صاحب المحل او البضاعة او من يمثله وتخلط جيداً ثم تقسم الى ثلاث عينات توضع كل منها داخل حرز يختم بالشمع الاحمر وتعلق به بطاقة تتضمن البيانات الآتية:

١. تاريخ اخذ العينة.

٢. نوع العينة ومقدارها.

٣. اسم صاحب البضاعة التي اخذت منها العينة وعنوانه.

---

¹³. تم استبدال نص المادة (٣٩) من القرار الوزاري رقم (٢٦) لسنة ١٩٨٤م بهذا النص بموجب القرار الوزاري رقم (١٢٦) لسنة ٢٠٠٣م المعدل للقرار رقم (٢٦) لسنة ١٩٨٤.

٤. اسم الموظف الذي اخذ العينة ووظيفته.

وتسلم احدى العينات لصاحب الشأن وتحفظ العينة الثانية لدى الجهة التي اخذت العينات وترسل العينة الثالثة للتحليل.

المادة (٤١)

يحرر محضر لاثبات اخذ العينات، ويجب ان يشتمل المحضر بالاضافة الى البيانات المنصوص عليها في المادة السابقة ما يأتي:

١. تاريخ وساعة تحرير المحضر بالارقام والحروف.

٢. عنوان المحل المأخوذة منه العينات.

٣. عدد العينات ومقدار كل عينة.

٤. مقدار البضاعة التي اخذت منها العينات وقيمتها بالتقريب.

٥. ظروف اخذ العينات مع بيان العلامات التجارية واسم المادة التي اخذت منها وجميع البيانات الاخرى التي تفيد في تحديد العينات والمادة التي اخذت منها.

المادة (٤٢)

تعزل البضاعة المضبوطة ويؤشر عليها وتوضع لدى صاحبها وتحت مسؤوليته ويحرر بذلك محضر يشتمل على البيانات الآتية:

١. مكان وتاريخ وساعة تحرير محضر الضبط بالارقام والحروف.

٢. اسم محرر محضر الضبط ولقبه ووظيفته وتوقيعه.

٣. اسماء الموظفين القائمين بعملية الضبط والقابهم ووظائفهم وتوقيعاتهم.

٤. اسم صاحب البضاعة المضبوطة وصفته ومهنته وعنوانه.

٥. البضائع المضبوطة وانواعها وكمياتها وقيمتها التقريبية.

٦. البضائع الناجية من الضبط على ما أمكن معرفته او الاستدلال عليه.

٧. اقوال صاحب البضاعة او من يمثله وتوقيعه، وفي حالة امتناعه يثبت[14] ذلك في المحضر.

٨. جميع الوقائع الاخرى المفيدة واثبات[15] حضور المخالفين عند جرد البضاعة او امتناعهم عن ذلك.

٩. تاريخ وساعة الانتهاء من تحرير المحضر.

المادة (٤٣)

يجب اخطار صاحب البضاعة بنتيجة التحليل فاذا أظهر التحليل عدم صلاحية المواد المضبوطة وتبين لمدير الجهة التي ضبطت البضاعة في دائرة اختصاصها ان صاحب البضاعة حسن النية ووافق على اعدام البضاعة على نفقته حفظ الموضوع وتخطر وزارة الاقتصاد والتجارة بالقرار الصادر في هذا الشأن.

وفي جميع الاحوال الاخرى تحال الاوراق بعد استيفاء التحقيق وورود نتيجة التحليل الى النيابة العامة لتحريك الدعوى العمومية ضد صاحب البضاعة.

المادة (٤٤)

تشكل بقرار من وزير الاقتصاد والتجارة، لجنة برئاسة وكيل وزارة الاقتصاد والتجارة وعضوية ممثل عن كل من وزارة الاقتصاد والتجارة ووزارة الصحة ووزارة الزراعة والثروة السمكية يختار كل منهم الوزير المختص، وممثل عن الامانة العامة للبلديات يختاره الامين العام وممثل عن مجلس الجمارك يختاره رئيس المجلس، وممثل عن اتحاد غرف التجارة والصناعة يختاره الامين العام، وينضم الى عضوية اللجنة ممثل عن كل من دائرة الجمارك ودائرة البلدية التي ضبطت المخالفة في نطاق اختصاصهما يختاره رئيس الدائرة وممثل عن غرفة التجارة والصناعة المعنية يختاره رئيس الغرفة.

وتخصص هذه اللجنة بالتحقيق فيما يحال اليها من وزير الاقتصاد والتجارة والدوائر الحكومية المختصة، من مخالفات لاحكام القانون الاتحادي رقم (٤) لسنة ١٩٧٩ المشار اليه وهذه اللائحة.

وعلى اللجنة الانتهاء من التحقيق خلال خمسة عشر يوماً من احالة الموضوع اليها وتقديم تقريرها الى وزير الاقتصاد والتجارة ليتخذ ما يراه مناسباً في هذا الشأن.

---

[14]. وردت هذه الكلمة في نص الجريدة الرسمية "بثبت" والأصح ان تكون "يثبت" فاقتضى التنويه.
[15]. وردت هذه الكلمة في نص الجريدة الرسمية "اثباب" والأصح ان تكون "اثبات" فاقتضى التنويه.

المادة (٤٥)

ينشر هذا القرار في الجريدة الرسمية ويعمل به من تاريخ نشره.

سيف علي الجروان
وزير الاقتصاد والتجارة

صدر في أبو ظبي
بتاريخ: ١٤ رمضان ١٤٠٤هـ.
الموافق: ١٤ يونيو ١٩٨٤م.

قرار وزاري رقم (٤١٨) لسنة ٢٠٠٧م
في شأن اعتماد العلامة التجارية (Organic، عضوي)

وزير البيئة والمياه،

بعد الاطلاع على القانون الاتحادي رقم (١) لسنة ١٩٧٢م بشأن اختصاصات الوزارات وصلاحيات الوزراء والقوانين المعدلة له،

وعلى مرسوم بقانون اتحادي رقم (١) لسنة اسنة ٢٠٠٦م بتعديل بعض احكام القانون الاتحادي رقم (١) لسنة ١٩٧٢م بشأن اختصاصات الوزارات وصلاحيات الوزراء،

وعلى قرار مجلس الوزراء رقم (٥) لسنة ٢٠٠٦م في شأن تخويلنا ببعض المهام الوزارية،

وعلى القرار الوزاري رقم (١٠٠) لسنة ٢٠٠٤م بشأن انشاء وحدات تابعة لادارة الابحاث والارشاد الزراعي،

ونظراً لأهمية تطوير الزراعة العضوية في الدولة ومتابعة المنتجات العضوية خلال عمليات الانتاج والتسويق، وللحد من عمليات الغش والتدليس،

وبناءً على موافقة وزارة الاقتصاد بتسجيل علامة تجارية باسم وزارة البيئة والمياه خاصة بالمنتجات العضوية للدولة والتي تم تسجيلها تحت رقم (٨٢٢١٤) بتاريخ ٢٠٠٧/٦/١٣م، رقم الفئة (٤٢)،

وبناءً على مقتضيات المصلحة العامة،

تقرر ما يلي:

المادة (١)

تعتمد العلامة التجارية (Organic، عضوي) المسجلة في وزارة الاقتصاد تحت رقم (٨٢٢١٤) بتاريخ ٢٠٠٧/٦/١٣م، رقم الفئة (٤٢)، والخاصة بالمنتجات الزراعية

العضوية. وتعد هذه العلامة ملكاً لوزارة البيئة والمياه بدولة الامارات العربية المتحدة، وهي كما في الشكل التالي:

[صورة العلامة]

المادة (٢)

شروط استخدام العلامة التجارية:

١. لا يجوز استخدام العلامة التجارية إلا بموافقة وزارة البيئة والمياه، على ان يقوم مستخدمها بالتعاقد معها قبل البدء في استخدامها وفق الشروط والفترة المحددة له.

٢. تستخدم العلامة التجارية على المنتجات العضوية التي تم التفتيش والتصديق عليها واعتمادها من قبل وزارة البيئة والمياه.

٣. يجب على المستخدم لاصلي للعلامة التجارية إعلام وزارة البيئة والمياه عن كافة مستخدمي العلامة الفرعيين، ويكون هو مسؤولاً عن أي خطأ قد ينجم عن سوء الاستخدام لهذه العلامة.

٤. يمنع استخدام العلامة التجارية مع علامات اخرى مماثلة إلا بعد موافقة وزارة البيئة والمياه.

٥. يجوز وضع علامة "عضوي" مع علامة أخرى تخص الشركة المنتجة.

٦. يمنع استخدام العلامة كعلامة تجارية لغير الاسباب التي صدرت من أجلها.

٧. عند وضع العلامة التجارية على منتج غير معلب يجب الاشارة إلى أن المنتج مصدق أو معتمد من قبل وزارة البيئة والمياه.

٨. يمنع منعاً باتاً تغيير لون العلامة أو حجمها عند طباعتها على المنتج إلا بموافقة مسبقة من وزارة البيئة والمياه.

المادة (٣)

يعمل بهذا القرار اعتباراً من تاريخ صدوره، وعلى كل من يعنيهم الأمر عمل ما يلزم لتنفيذه، وينشر في الجريدة الرسمية.

الدكتور / محمد سعيد الكندي
وزير البيئة والمياه

صدر في: ١٨ شوال ١٤٢٨هــ.
الموافق: ٢٠٠٧/١٠/٢٩م.

قانون اتحادي رقم (٤٠) لسنة ١٩٩٢م
في شأن حماية المصنفات الفكرية وحقوق المؤلف

نحن زايد بن سلطان آل نهيان، رئيس دولة الإمارات العربية المتحدة،

بعد الإطلاع على الدستور المؤقت،

وعلى القانون الاتحادي رقم (١) لسنة ١٩٧٢م في شأن اختصاصات الوزارات وصلاحيات الوزراء والقوانين المعدلة له،

وعلى القانون الاتحادي رقم (١٥) لسنة ١٩٨٠م في شأن المطبوعات والنشر والقوانين المعدلة له،

وبناءً على ما عرضه وزير الإعلام والثقافة، وموافقة مجلس الوزراء، وتصديق المجلس الأعلى للاتحاد،

اصدرنا القانون الآتي:

المادة (١)

تعريفات

في تطبيق أحكام هذا القانون يقصد بالكلمات التالية التعريفات الموضحة أمام كل منها ما لم يدل سياق النص على غير ذلك:

الوزارة:	وزارة الإعلام والثقافة.
الوزير:	وزير الإعلام والثقافة.
المصنف:	أي عمل أدبي أو علمي أو فني مبتكر.
المؤلف:	أي شخص نشر المصنف منسوباً إليه سواء بذكر اسمه على المصنف أو بأية طريقة من الطرق المتبعة في نسبة المصنفات لمؤلفيها إلا إذا قام الدليل على عكس ذلك.
النشر:	نقل المصنف بطريق مباشر أو غير مباشر إلى الجمهور سواء بنقل المصنف ذاته أو استخراج نسخ أو صور منه أو من أي من أجزائه يمكن قراءتها أو سماعها أو رؤيتها أو أداؤها.

الاستنساخ: هو انتاج نسخة أو أكثر من أحد المصنفات الأدبية أو الفنية أو العلمية بأية صورة بما في ذلك التسجيلات المسموعة أو المرئية.

الفولكلور: المصنفات الأدبية أو الفنية أو العلمية التي تبتكرها الفئات الشعبية في الدولة تعبيراً عن هويتها الثقافية والتي تنتقل من جيل إلى جيل وتشكل أحد العناصر الأساسية في تراثها.

الباب الأول
نطاق الحماية

المادة (٢)

١. يتمتع بالحماية المقررة في هذا القانون مؤلفو المصنفات الفكرية المبتكرة في الآداب والفنون والعلوم أياً كانت قيمة هذه المصنفات أو نوعيتها أو الغرض من تأليفها أو طريقة التعبير عنها.

٢. وتشمل الحماية المصنفات الفكرية الآتية:

أ) الكتب والكتيبات وغيرها من المواد المكتوبة.

ب) المصنفات التي تلقى شفاهة كالمحاضرات والخطب والمواعظ.

ج) المؤلفات المسرحية والمسرحيات الموسيقية.

د) المصنفات الموسيقية سواء كانت مصحوبة بكلمات أو لم تكن.

هـ) مصنفات تصميم الحركات الإيقاعية والتمثيل الإيمائي.

و) أعمال التصوير الفوتوغرافي.

ز) المصنفات السينمائية والتليفزيونية والإذاعية والأعمال الإبتكارية السمعية والبصرية وبرامج الحاسوب.

ح) أعمال الفنون التطبيقية سواء كانت حرفية أو صناعية.

ط) أعمال الرسم والتصوير بالخطوط والألوان والعمارة والنحت والفنون الزخرفية والحفر والتصميمات والمخططات والمجسمات الجغرافية والطبوغرافية.

ي) الموسوعات والمنوعات والمختارات التي تشكل من حيث انتقاء مادتها وترتيبها وتحريرها أعمالاً فكرية إبداعية.

٣. كما تشمل الحماية بوجه عام المصنفات التي يكون مظهر التعبير عنها الكتابة أو الصوت أو الرسم أو التصوير أو الحركة.

المادة (٣)

تسري أحكام هذا القانون على ما يأتي:

١. مصنفات مواطني دولة الإمارات العربية المتحدة التي تنشر داخل البلاد او خارجها.

٢. مصنفات غير مواطني دولة الإمارات العربية المتحدة التي تنشر داخل دولة الإمارات العربية المتحدة لأول مرة.

٣. مصنفات مواطني أية دولة أجنبية تعامل مصنفات مواطني دولة الإمارات العربية المتحدة بالمثل.

المادة (٤)

تودع المصنفات لدى الجهة المختصة في الوزارة وفقاً لما ينص عليه هذا القانون، وتعتبر سجلات الإيداع بالوزارة مرجعاً لبيانات حقوق المؤلف.

ولا يترتب على عدم الإيداع الإخلال بحقوق المؤلف التي يقررها القانون.

الباب الثاني
أحكام الحماية

المادة (٥)

يتمتع بالحماية من قام بإذن من المؤلف الأصلي بترجمة المصنف إلى لغة أخرى وكذلك من قام بتلخيصه أو تحويره أو تعديله أو شرحه أو غير ذلك من الأوجه التي تظهر المصنف بشكل جديد ولا يخل ذلك بالحماية المقررة لمؤلفي المصنفات الأصلية.

وتنتهي حماية حق المؤلف وحق من ترجم مصنفه إلى لغة أجنبية أخرى في ترجمة ذلك المصنف إلى اللغة العربية إذا لم يباشر المؤلف أو المترجم هذا الحق بنفسه أو بوساطة غيره في مدى ثلاث سنوات من تاريخ أول نشر للمصنف الأصلي أو المترجم.

المادة (٦)

لا تشمل الحماية المقررة في هذا القانون الأمور الآتية:

١. القوانين والأحكام القضائية وقرارات الهيئات الإدارية والاتفاقيات الدولية وسائر الوثائق الرسمية وكذلك الترجمات الرسمية لها.

ومع ذلك تتمتع المجموعات سالفة الذكر بالحماية إذا كانت متميزة بسبب يرجع إلى الابتكار أو الترتيب أو أي مجهود شخصي آخر يستحق الحماية.

٢. الأنباء المنشورة أو امذاعة أو المبلغة علناً.

المادة (٧)

١. للمؤلف وحده الحق في أن ينسب إليه مصنفه وأن يذكر اسمه على جميع النسخ المنتجة منه كلما طرح هذا المصنف على الجمهور، إلا إذا ورد ذكر المصنف عرضاً في ثنايا تقديم إذاعي أو تلفزيوني للأحداث الجارية.

وهذا الحق غير قابل للتصرف أو التقادم.

٢. وللمؤلف وحده الحق في استغلال مصنفه بشرط ألا يكون قد تنازل عنه للغير.

٣. لا يجوز استغلال أي مصنف فكري عن طريق نقله للجمهور بدولة الإمارات العربية المتحدة إلا بإذن كتابي موثق من المؤلف.

المادة (٨)

لا يصرح بنشر أو عرض أو تداول أي مصنف أياً كان نوعه دون استيفاء الشروط الآتية:

١. أن يرفق مع المصنف شهادة من المنشأ تبين اسم المؤلف او من تم التنازل إليه عن حق الاستغلال.

٢. أن يرفق مع المصنف تصريح من المورد أو مالكه بالعرض أو التداول موضحاً فيه المنطقة الجغرافية والمكانية التي صرح بالعرض أو التداول في نطاقها.

٣. أن يرفق مع المصنف شهادة من المورد تفيد دفع حقوق النشر سواء كان بالأداء العلني او عن طريق عمل نماذج من المصنف أو نسخه للتوزيع.

الباب الثالث
حقوق المؤلف

المادة (٩)

للمؤلف وحده الحق في تقرير نشر مصنفه وفي تعيين طريقة النشر ويكون له وحده الحق في استغلال مصنفه بالطرق التي يحددها لهذا الاستغلال.

ولا يجوز لأحد غيره مباشرة هذا الحق دون إذن كتابي موثق منه أو ممن ينوب عنه من المخولين بذلك أو من يخلفه في حالة وفاته.

المادة (١٠)

يتضمن حق المؤلف في الاستغلال ما يأتي:

١. نقل المصنف للجمهور بأية صورة من الصور وخاصة النشر والتلاوة العلنية أو التوزيع الموسيقي أو التمثيل المسرحي أو العرض العلني أو الإذاعة أو الصوت أو الصور أو العرض.

٢. نقل المصنف إلى الجمهور بطريقة غير مباشرة ويتم ذلك بصفة خاصة عن طريق الطباعة أو الرسم أو الحفر أو التصوير الفوتوغرافي أو الصب في قوالب أو بأية طريقة أخرى من طرق الفنون التخطيطية أو المجسمة أو عن طريق النشر الفوتوغرافي او السينمائي.

المادة (١١)

للمؤلف وحده ادخال ما يرى من التعديل أو التحوير على مصنفه وله حق ترجمته إلى لغة أخرى ولا يجوز لغيره أن يباشر شيئاً من ذلك أو أن يباشر صورة أخرى من الصور المنصوص عليها في المادة (٥) إلا بإذن كتابي موثق منه.

المادة (١٢)

يجوز لورثة المؤلف ممارسة حق ترجمة المصنف.

المادة (١٣)

للمؤلف الحق في دفع أي اعتداء على حقوقه وله أن يمنع أي حذف أو إضافة أو تغيير في مصنفه، على أنه إذا حصل الحذف أو الإضافة أو التغيير في ترجمة المصنف فلا يكون للمؤلف الحق في منعه إلا إذا أغفل المترجم الإشارة إلى مواطن الحذف أو التغيير او ترتب على ذلك مساس بسمعة المؤلف ومكانته الفنية.

الباب الرابع
حرية استعمال المصنفات المحمية

المادة (١٤)

تعتبر الاستعمالات التالية للمصنفات المحمية مشروعة ولو لم تقترن بموافقة المؤلف:

١. الاستعانة بالمصنف للاستعمال الشخصي الخاص دون سواه بوساطة الاستساخ او الترجمة أو الاقتباس أو التوزيع الموسيقي أو التمثيل أو الاستماع الإذاعي أو المشاهدة التليفزيونية او التصوير بأي شكل آخر.

٢. الاستعانة بالمصنف على سبيل الايضاح في التعليم بوساطة المطبوعات أو البرامج والتسجيلات والإذاعية أو التليفزيونية أو الأفلام السينمائية لأهداف تربوية أو تثقيفية أو دينية أو للتدريب المهني وفي الحدود التي يقتضيها تحقيق هذا الهدف بشرط أن لا يكون الاستعمال بقصد تحقيق ربح مادي وأن يذكر المصدر واسم المؤلف.

٣. الاستشهاد بفقرات من المصنف في مصنف آخر بهدف الإيضاح أو الشرح أو النقد وفي حدود العرف المتبع وبالقدر الذي يبرره هذا الهدف على أن يذكر المصدر اسم المؤلف وينطبق ذلك أيضاً على الفقرات المنقولة من المقالات الصحفية والدوريات التي تظهر على شكل خلاصات صحفية.

المادة (١٥)

١. يجوز بدون إذن المؤلف استساخ المقالات الإخبارية السياسية أو الاقتصادية أو الاجتماعية أو الثقافية أو الدينية التي تعالج موضوعات الساعة أو نشرها من قبل الصحف أو الدوريات وكذلك أيضاً المصنفات الإذاعية ذات الطابع المماثل بشرط ذكر المصدر.

٢. ويجوز استساخ أي مصنف يمكن مشاهدته أو سماعه خلال عرض اخباري عن الأحداث الجارية أو نشرد بوساطة التصوير الفوتوغرافي أو التليفزيوني أو وسائل الإعلام الجماهيرية الأخرى بشرط أن يكون ذلك في حدود الهدف الإعلامي المراد تحقيقه ومع الإشارة إلى اسم المؤلف.

المادة (١٦)

١. يجوز للمكتبات العامة ولمراكز التوثيق غير التجارية والمعاهد التعليمية والمؤسسات العلمية والثقافية بدون إذن المؤلف استساخ المصنفات المحمية بالتصوير الفوتوغرافي او ما شابهه بشرط أن يكون ذلك الاستساخ وعدد النسخ مقصوراً على احتياجات أنشطتها وألا يضر بالاستغلال المادي للمصنف ولا يتسبب في الأضرار بالمصالح المشروعة للمؤلف.

٢. ويجوز للهيئات الإذاعية أن تعد لبرامجها وبوسائلها الخاصة تسجيلاً غير دائم لأي مصنف يرخص لها بأن تذيعه ويجب إتلاف جميع النسخ خلال مدة لا تجاوز سنة ميلادية اعتباراً من تاريخ صنعها وللمؤلف حق تمديد هذه المدة ويستثنى من هذا الحق التسجيلات ذات الصفة الوثائقية وبحدود نسخة واحدة.

المادة (١٧)

يجوز للصحافة وغيرها من وسائل الإعلام ان تنشر بدون إذن المؤلف الخطب والمحاضرات وكذلك المرافعات التي تلقى أثناء نظر المنازعات القضائية وغير ذلك من المصنفات المشابهة المعروضة علناً على الجمهور بشرط ذكر اسم المؤلف بوضوح وله وحده حق نشر هذه المصنفات في مطبوع واحد او بأية طريقة يراها.

الباب الخامس
احكام المصنف بعد وفاة المؤلف

المادة (١٨)

يكون لورثة المؤلف بعد وفاته الحق في مباشرة حقوق الاستغلال المالي للمصنف والمنصوص عليها في المادة (٧) من هذا القانون.

المادة (١٩)

إذا مات المؤلف قبل أن يقرر نشر مصنفه انتقل هذا الحق إلى من يخلفونه ولهؤلاء وحدهم مباشرة حقوق المؤلف على أنه إذا كان المؤلف قد أوصى بمنع النشر أو بتعيين موعد له وجب تنفيذ ما أوصى به.

المادة (٢٠)

١. تسري حقوق المؤلف مدى حياته ولمدة خمس وعشرين سنة ميلادية بعد وفاته.

٢. وتكون مدة سريان حقوق المؤلف خمس وعشرين سنة ميلادية من تاريخ النشر بالنسبة للمصنفات الآتية:

أ) أفلام السينما وأعمال الفنون التطبيقية
ب) المصنفات التي ينجزها الأشخاص الإعتباريون.
ج) المصنفات التي تنشر باسم مستعار أو دون ذكر اسم المؤلف حتى يكشف عن شخصيته.
د) المصنفات التي تنشر لأول مرة بعد وفاة مؤلفها.

٣. وتكون مدة سريان حق المؤلف على المصنفات الفوتوغرافية عشر سنوات ميلادية من تاريخ النشر.

٤. وتحسب مدة حماية حقوق المؤلف بالنسبة للمصنفات المشتركة من تاريخ وفاة آخر من بقي حياً من مؤلفيها.

٥. وإذا كان المصنف مكوناً من عدة أجزاء نشرت منفصلة وعلى فترات فيعتبر كل جزء مصنفاً مستقلاً بالنسبة لحساب مدة الحماية.

المادة (٢١)

تخضع للحماية المصنفات التي ينشرها الورثة لأول مرة بعد وفاة المؤلف ويكون لهم حق استغلالها مالياً.

المادة (٢٢)

إذا تقاعس ورثة المؤلف عن نشر مصنفه ورأى الوزير أن الصالح العام يقتضي نشر المصنف فله أن يطلب كتابة من الورثة نشره فإذا انقضت ستة أشهر من تاريخ هذا الطلب ولم يباشروا النشر فللوزير مباشرة الطبع وحق نشره. ويعوض الورثة في هذه الحالة تعويضاً عادلاً.

الباب السادس
الاشتراك في المصنفات

المادة (٢٣)

إذا اشترك عدة أشخاص في تأليف مصنف بحيث لا يمكن فصل نصيب كل منهم في العمل المشترك اعتبر الجميع ملاكاً للمصنف بالتساوي فيما بينهم إلا إذا اتفقوا على خلاف ذلك. ولا يجوز لأحد الشركاء مباشرة الحقوق المترتبة على حق المؤلف إلا باتفاقهم جميعاً وإذا وقع خلاف بينهم يكون الفصل فيه من اختصاص القضاء ولكل المشتركين في التأليف الحق في رفع الدعاوى عند وقوع أي اعتداء على حق المؤلف كما ينتقل ذلك الحق إلى ورثة أي منهم.

المادة (٢٤)

المصنف الذي تضعه جماعة من المؤلفين أو يضعه مؤلف واحد بتوجيه شخص طبيعي أو معنوي يتكفل بنشره تحت إدارته وباسمه يكون للشخص الطبيعي أو المعنوي الذي

وجه ابتكار هذا المصنف[16] وحده الحق في مباشرة حقوق المؤلف المالية إلا إذا نص العقد بين الطرفين على خلاف ذلك أو اشترط شروطاً محددة أما الحق الأدبي في نسبة المصنف فيبقى لمؤلفي أو لمؤلف هذا المصنف.

المادة (٢٥)

في حالة الاشتراك في تأليف مصنفات الموسيقى الغنائية يكون لمؤلف اللحن والموسيقى وحده الحق في الترخيص بالأداء العلني للمصنف كله أو تنفيذه أو نشره أو عمل نسخ منه مع عدم الإخلال بحق مؤلف الشطر الأدبي، ويسري ذلك الحكم في شأن المصنفات التي تنفذ بحركات مصحوبة بالموسيقى وفي الاستعراضات المصحوبة بموسيقى وفي جميع المصنفات المشابهة.

كما يكون لمؤلف الشطر الأدبي الحق في نشر الشطر الخاص به وحده على أنه لا يجوز له التصرف في هذا الشطر ليكون أساساً لمصنف آخر مماثل مالم يكن هناك اتفاق على خلاف ذلك.

المادة (٢٦)

يعتبر شريكاً في تأليف المصنف المسرحي أو السينمائي أو المصنف المعد للاذاعة أو التليفزيون كل من:

١. مؤلف السيناريو أو صاحب الفكرة المكتوبة للبرنامج الإذاعي أو التليفزيوني أو السينمائي أو المسرحي.

٢. مؤلف الحوار.

٣. من قام بتحرير المصنف الأدبي الموجود بشكل يجعله ملائماً للفن السينمائي أو التليفزيوني أو الإذاعي.

٤. واضع الموسيقى إذا قام بوضعها خصيصاً للمصنف السينمائي أو الإذاعي أو التليفزيوني أو المسرحي.

٥. المخرج إذا بسط رقابة فعلية وقام بعمل ايجابي من الناحية الفكرية لتحقيق المصنف بأشكاله السابقة.

واذا كان المصنف المعد للاذاعة اللاسلكية أو التليفزيون أو السينما أو المسرح مقتبساً أو مستخرجاً من مصنف آخر سابق عليه يعتبر مؤلف هذا المصنف السابق مشتركاً في المصنف الجديد ويشترط ذكر اسمه بالاشارة الى الاقتباس أو الاستخراج صراحة.

---

[16]. وردت هذه الكلمة في نص الجريدة الرسمية "الصنف" والأصح ان تكون "المصنف" فاقتضى التنويه.

المادة (٢٧)

إذا امتنع أحد المشتركين في تأليف مصنف سينمائي أو مسرحي أو مصنف معد للإذاعة أو التليفزيون عن القيام بإتمام الأعمال التي تخصه فلا يترتب على ذلك منع باقي المشتركين من استعمال الجزء الذي أنجزه وذلك مع عدم الإخلال بما للممتنع من حقوق مترتبة على اشتراكه في التأليف إذا كان الامتناع راجعاً إلى أسباب مقبولة حالت دون قيامه بإتمام العمل أما إذا كان الامتناع راجعاً إلى ارادته المنفردة دون وجود أسباب تبرر ذلك فيحرم من أية حقوق تترتب له نظير الجزء الذي أنجزه.

المادة (٢٨)

إذا قام مؤلف أدبي ومؤلف سيناريو ومؤلف حوار ومخرج ومؤلف موسيقي مجتمعين كل في مجال اختصاصه بإيداع عمل سينمائي أو مسرحي أو إذاعي أو تليفزيوني، فليس من حق أحد منهم منع انتاج أو عرض هذا العمل، مع عدم الإخلال بحقوق المعارض الأدبية والمالية، كما يحق لمؤلف الشطر الأدبي ومؤلف الشطر الموسيقي أن ينشر مصنفه بطريقة أخرى غير السينما أو المسرح أو الإذاعة أو التليفزيون ما لم يتفق على غير ذلك.

المادة (٢٩)

يعتبر منتجاً للمصنف المسرحي أو السينمائي أو الإذاعي أو التليفزيوني الشخص الذي يتولى تنفيذ الشريط ويتحمل مسؤولية هذا التنفيذ ويضع في متناول مؤلفي المصنف الوسائل المادية والمالية لكفيلة بانتاجه وتحقيق إخراجه.

ويعتبر المنتج دائماً ناشراً للمصنف وتكون له جميع حقوق الناشر على الشريط وعلى نسخه ويكون المنتج طوال مدة الاستغلال للشريط نائباً عن مؤلفي المصنف المسرحي أو السينمائي أو الإذاعي أو التليفزيوني وعن خلفهم في الاتفاق على عرض الشريط واستغلاله دون الإخلال بحقوق مؤلفي المصنفات الأدبية أو الموسيقية بنشر أعمالهم بطريقة اخرى ما لم يكن هناك اتفاق على خلاف ذلك.

الباب السابع
أحكام عامة

المادة (٣٠)

للوزارة الحق في إذاعة المصنفات العامة، كالندوات العامة والمحاضرات والخطب والأمسيات الشعرية، والأنشطة الثقافية والأدبية والدينية والمهرجانات الفنية العامة التي تعرض أو تؤدى في المسارح أو في أي مكان عام آخر، وعلى المسؤولين عن هذه الأمكنة تمكين هيئات الوزارة وتسهيل مهمتها وتذليل اية صعوبات أمام الإذاعة والتليفزيون بشرط إذاعة اسم المؤلف وعنوان المصنف.

المادة (٣١)

١. يعتبر الفولكلور الوطني لمجتمع الإمارات العربية المتحدة ملكاً عاماً للدولة.

٢. وتعمل الدولة ممثلة في الوزارة على حماية الفولكلور الوطني بكل السبل والوسائل القانونية وتمارس صلاحيات المؤلف بالنسبة للمصنفات الفولكلورية في مواجهة التشويه أو التحوير أو الاستغلال التجاري.

المادة (٣٢)

للمؤلف ان ينقل أي حق من حقوقه المالية التي يرتبها له مصنفه وفق أحكام هذا القانون إلى شخص أو أشخاص آخرين ويشترط لاتمام ذلك أن يكون نقل الحق مكتوباً وأن يحدد صراحة كل حق على حده يكون محلاً للتصرف، مع بيان مدة ذلك التصرف أو النقل وكيفيته وكميته والغرض منه ومكانه، ويمتنع على المؤلف اتيان أي تصرف من شأنه إعاقة المتصرف إليه في استعمال الحق المتصرف فيه.

المادة (٣٣)

تضع الوزارة نظاماً خاصاً لإيداع المصنفات المحمية بهذا القانون وما يطرأ عليها من تصرفات كما تنظم ما يلزم ذلك من نماذج وسجلات خاصة بالإيداع.

المادة (٣٤)

لأصحاب المصنفات الفكرية ومؤلفيها أن يتقدموا إلى الوزارة بطلب قيد مصنفاتهم على أن يرفق مع طلب القيد البيانات الآتية:

١. اسم المؤلف أو المؤلفين بالنسبة للمصنفات المشتركة.

٢. موضوع المصنف.

٣. عدد عشر نسخ من المصنف.

٤. بيان شامل بمواصفات المصنف.

٥. إقرار مكتوب من المؤلف أو المؤلفين بملكيتهم للمصنف وفقاً لأحكام هذا القانون.

٦. إقرار من المؤلف أو المؤلفين يحدد الطريقة التي يختارونها لنشر المصنف.

المادة (٣٥)

تعطي الوزارة لصاحب و أصحاب المصنف شهادة تتضمن تاريخ قيد المصنف وموضوعه ونوعه واسم صاحب المصنف أو أصحابه.

المادة (٣٦)

يشترط في المصنف المقدم للإيداع أن يكون مجازاً من إدارة الرقابة بالوزارة أو أن يكون من المصنفات التي يجيزها قانون المطبوعات والنشر.

المادة (٣٧)

للمؤلف وحده إذا طرأت أسباب جوهرية أن يطلب من المحكمة المختصة الحكم بسحب مصنفه من التداول أو بادخال تعديلات جوهرية عليه برغم تصرفه في حقوق الاستغلال المالي ويلزم المؤلف في هذه الحالة أن يعوض مقدماً من آلت إليه حقوق الاستغلال المالي تعويضاً عادلاً تحدته المحكمة.

الباب الثامن
في العقوبات

المادة (٣٨)

يعاقب بالحبس وبالغرامة التي لا تقل عن (٥٠٠٠٠) خمسين ألف درهم أو باحدى العقوبتين من قام بنشر مصنف غير مملوك له دون الحصول على إذن كتابي من مؤلف المصنف أو ورثته أو من يمثله ويعاقب بذات العقوبة من يدعي على خلاف الحقيقة أنه مالك مصنف من المصنفات.

المادة (٣٩)

يعاقب الناشر الذي يتولى نشر مصنف من المصنفات بالحبس وبالغرامة التي لا تقل عن (١٠٠٠٠) عشرة آلاف درهم او باحدى العقوبتين إذا عدل عند النشر في حقيقة المصنف وطبيعته وموضوعه وعنوانه مخالفاً بذلك تعليمات مؤلف المصنف ورغبته.

المادة (٤٠)

لا يجوز للناشر إعادة نشر المصنف إلا بعد الحصول على موافقة المؤلف وبالقدر المتفق عليه وفي حالة مخالفة الناشر ذلك يعاقب بالعقوبة المنصوص عليها في المادة (٣٩) من هذا القانون.

المادة (٤١)

لا يجوز لغير المحلات أو الاشخاص المرخص لهم بالدولة نشر أي مصنف من المصنفات أو نسخه أو طبعه ويعاقب من يخالف ذلك بالحبس مدة لا تزيد على ستة أشهر وبالغرامة التي لا تزيد على (١٠٠٠٠) عشرة آلاف درهم أو باحدى العقوبتين.

المادة (٤٢)

لا يجوز لأي من المحلات التي تتولى توزيع أو بيع أو نسخ نماذج المصنفات أن تقوم بعملية البيع أو النسخ إلا بموافقة كتابية من المؤلف مالك المصنف او من يخوله ويعاقب بالحبس وبالغرامة التي لا تقل عن (٥٠٠٠٠) خمسين ألف درهم أو بإحدى العقوبتين صاحب المحل الذي يخالف ذلك.

المادة (٤٣)

في جميع الأحوال المبينة في هذا الباب يتعين الحكم بمصادرة نسخ المصنفات موضوع الجريمة، كما يجوز للمحكمة أن تحكم بإغلاق المحل.

المادة (٤٤)

تطبق احكام العقوبات المقررة في هذا الباب على المصنفات المترجمة إذا قام الناشر أو الموزع المرخص له بإعادة نشر أو توزيع المصنف المترجم بمخالفة الاتفاق المحرر بينه وبين المؤلف.

الباب التاسع
أحكام ختامية

المادة (٤٥)

على جميع المحلات المرخص لها بنسخ او توزيع أو بيع المصنفات والمرخص لها بذلك في الدولة أن تحتفظ بالوثائق الكتابية التي تخول لها ذلك من صاحب المصنف أو السلطات المعنية الأخرى سواء كان المصنف من داخل الدولة أو من خارجها على أن يحدد بالنسبة للمصنفات المعدة خارج الدولة بيان يوضح مصدر هذه المصنفات والإذن أو الاتفاق الذي يخول له القيام بالنسخ أو التوزيع أو البيع وبشرط خضوعه المسبق للرقابة من قبل الوزراة.

المادة (٤٦)

١. يصدر وزير العدل بـاتفاق مع وزير الإعلام والثقافة وبعد التشاور مع السلطة المختصة في الإمارة المعنية قراراً بتحديد الموظفين الذين يكون لهم صفة مأموري الضبط القضائي في تنفيذ أحكام هذا القانون.

٢. ويكون لهؤلاء الموظفين الحق في دخول المحلات التي تقوم بنشر المصنفات وتوزيعها ونسخها وانتاجها في البلاد كما يحق لهم ضبط ما يقع من مخالفات لأحكام هذا القانون ولهم في سبيل ذلك ضبط المواد والنسخ والوسائل التي استخدمت في ارتكاب الجرائم المنصوص عليها في هذا القانون وعليهم الاستعانة برجال الأمن والشرطة إذا اقتضت الأحوال ذلك.

المادة (٤٧)

يصدر الوزير القرارات لمنفذة لهذا القانون.

المادة (٤٨)

يلغى كل حكم يخالف أحكام هذا القانون.

المادة (٤٩)

ينشر هذا القانون في الجريدة الرسمية، ويعمل به ستة أشهر من تاريخ نشره   .

زايد بن سلطان آل نهيان
رئيس دولة الإمارات العربية المتحدة

صدر عنا بقصر الرئاسة في أبو ظبي
بتاريخ: ١ ربيع الثاني ١٤١٣هـ.
الموافق: ٢٨ سبتمبر ١٩٩٢م.

قانون اتحادي رقم ٧ لسنة ٢٠٠٢م
في شأن حقوق المؤلف والحقوق المجاورة

نحن زايد بن سلطان آل نهيان، رئيس دولة الإمارات العربية المتحدة،

بعد الاطلاع على الدستور،

وعلى القانون الاتحادي رقم (١) لسنة ١٩٧٢ بشأن اختصاصات الوزارات وصلاحيات الوزراء والقوانين المعدلة له،

وعلى القانون الاتحادي رقم (١٥) لسنة ١٩٨٠ في شأن المطبوعات والنشر،

وعلى القانون الاتحادي رقم (٤٠) لسنة ١٩٩٢ في شأن حماية المصنفات الفكرية وحقوق المؤلف،

وبناءً على ما عرضه وزير الاعلام والثقافة، وموافقة مجلس الوزراء، وتصديق المجلس الاعلى للاتحاد،

أصدرنا القانون الآتي:

التعريفات

المادة (١)

في تطبيق أحكام هذا القانون يقصد بالكلمات والعبارات التالية المعاني الموضحة قرين كل منها ما لم يقض سياق النص بغير ذلك:

الدولة:	دولة الامارات العربية المتحدة.
الوزارة:	وزارة الإعلام والثقافة.
الوزير:	وزير الإعلام والثقافة.
المصنف:	كل تأليف مبتكر في مجال الآداب، أو الفنون، أو العلوم، أياً كان نوعه أو طريقة التعبير عنه، أو أهميته أو الغرض منه.

المؤلف:	الشخص الذي يبتكر المصنف، ويُعد مؤلفاً للمصنف من يذكر اسمه عليه، أو يُنسب إليه عند نشره باعتباره مؤلفاً له، ما لم يقم الدليل على غير ذلك.
	كما يُعتبر مؤلفاً للمصنف من ينشره بدون اسم أو بأسم مستعار أو بأية طريقة أخرى بشرط ألا يقوم شك في معرفة حقيقة شخصية المؤلف، فإذا قام الشك أعتبر ناشر أو منتج المصنف، سواء أكان شخصاً طبيعياً أم اعتبارياً، نائباً عن المؤلف في مباشرة حقوقه إلى أن يتم التعرف على حقيقة شخصية المؤلف.
الابتكار:	الطابع الإبداعي الذي يُسبغ على المصنف الأصالة والتميز.
أصحاب الحقوق المجاورة:	فنانو الأداء، ومنتجو التسجيلات الصوتية، وهيئات الإذاعة، المعرفون في هذا القانون.
فنانو الأداء:	الممثلون، والمغنون، والموسيقيون، والراقصون، وغيرهم من الاشخاص الذين يلقون أو ينشدون أو يعزفون أو يؤدون بأية صورة، في مصنفات أدبية أو فنية أو غير ذلك، محمية طبقاً لأحكام هذا القانون أو داخلة في إطار الملك العام.
منتج التسجيل الصوتي:	الشخص الطبيعي أو الإعتباري الذي يسجل لأول مرة أصواتاً لأحد فناني الأداء، أو غير ذلك من الأصوات.
هيئة الإذاعة:	أية جهة تقوم بالبث الإذاعي اللاسلكي السمعي أو البصري، أو السمعي البصري.
الإذاعة:	القيام بالبث السمعي أو البصري، أو السمعي البصري، للمصنف أو للأداء أو للتسجيل الصوتي أو للبرنامج وتسجيله، وذلك إلى الجمهور، وبطريقة لاسلكية. ويُعد كذلك البث عبر التوابع أو الأقمار الصناعية.
النشر:	إتاحة المصنف أو التسجيل الصوتي، أو البرنامج الإذاعي، أو أي أداء، للجمهور، وأياً ما تكون وسيلة ذلك.
الأداء العلني:	هو الأداء الذي يترتب عليه اتصال الجمهور بالمصنف اتصالاً مباشراً كالتمثيل للمصنفات المسرحية، أو التقديم أو الأداء للمصنفات الفنية، أو العرض للمصنفات السمعية البصرية، والعزف للمصنفات الموسيقية والتلاوة للمصنفات الأدبية، ويستوي في ذلك أن يكون الأداء حياً أو مسجلا.
التوصيل العلني:	البث السلكي أو اللاسلكي لمصنف، أو لأداء تسجيل صوتي، أو لبرنامج إذاعي بحيث يمكن التلقي عن طريق البث وحده غير أفراد العائلة والاصدقاء المقربين، في أي مكان مغاير للمكان الذي يبدأ منه البث، وبغض النظر عن الزمان أو لمكان الذي يتم فيه التلقي أو طريقته.
النسخ:	عمل نسخة أو أكثر من مصنف، أو تسجيل صوتي، أو برنامج إذاعي، أو أي أداء، في أي شكل أو

صورة، بما في ذلك التحميل أو التخزين الإلكتروني الدائم أو الوقتي، وأياً ما تكون الطريقة أو الأداة المستخدمة في النسخ.

التسجيل الصوتي: أي تثبيت يخاطب السمع لمجموعة من الأصوات المؤدية لأداء معين بغض النظر عن طريقة التثبيت، أو الدعامة المستخدمة. ويشمل التسجيل الصوتي عملية تثبيت الأصوات مع الصورة لإعداد مصنف سمعي بصري، ما لم يُتفق على غير ذلك

منتج المصنف السمعي البصري: الشخص الطبيعي أو الإعتباري الذي يوفر الإمكانات اللازمة لإنجاز المصنف السمعي البصري، ويضطلع بمسؤولية هذا الإنجاز.

المصنف الجماعي: المصنف الذي تضعه جماعة من المؤلفين بتوجيه شخص طبيعي أو إعتباري، يتكفل بنشره باسمه وتحت إدارته. ويندمج عمل المؤلفين فيه في الهدف العام الذي قصد إليه هذا الشخص، بحيث يستحيل فصل عمل كل مؤلف وتمييزه على حدة.

المصنف المشترك: المصنف الذي يساهم في وضعه عدة أشخاص سواء أمكن فصل نصيب كل منهم فيه أو لم يمكن، والذي لا يندرج ضمن المصنفات الجماعية.

المصنف المشتق: المصنف الذي يستمد اصله من مصنف سابق الوجود كالترجمات. ويعد كذلك مجموعات المصنفات الأدبية والفنية ومجموعات التعبير الفلكلوري ما دامت مبتكرة من حيث ترتيب أواختيار محتوياتها

الفلكلور الوطني: كل تعبير من المأثورات الشعبية الشفوية أو الموسيقية أو الحركية أو الملموسة في عناصر متميزة تعكس التراث التقليدي الفني الذي نشأ أو استمر في الدولة، والذي لا يمكن نسبته إلى مؤلف معلوم.

الملك العام: جميع المصنفات المستبعدة من الحماية بداية، أو التي تنقضي مدة حماية حقوقها المالية.

الفصل الأول
نطاق الحماية

المادة (٢)

يتمتع بالحماية المقررة في هذا القانون مؤلفو المصنفات وأصحاب الحقوق المجاورة، إذا وقع الاعتداء على حقوقهم داخل الدولة، وبوجه خاص المصنفات التالية:

١. الكتب والكتيبات والمقالات وغيرها من المصنفات المكتوبة.

٢. برامج الحاسب وتطبيقاتها، وقواعد البيانات، وما يماثلها من مصنفات تحدد بقرار من الوزير.

٣. المحاضرات والخطب والمواعظ والمصنفات الاخرى التي لها طبيعة مماثلة.

٤. المصنفات التمثيلية والمصنفات التمثيلية الموسيقية والتمثيل الصامت.

٥. المصنفات الموسيقية المصحوبة أو غير المصحوبة بكلمات.

٦. المصنفات السمعية أوالبصرية أو السمعية البصرية.

٧. مصنفات العمارة والرسوم والمخططات الهندسية.

٨. مصنفات الرسم بالخطوط أو بالألوان، والنحت، والنقش، والطباعة على الحجر، وعلى الأقمشة، وعلى الحشب، وعلى المعادن وأية مصنفات مماثلة في مجال الفنون الجميلة.

٩. المصنفات الفوتوغرافية وما يماثلها.

١٠. مصنفات الفن التطبيقي والتشكيلي.

١١. الصور التوضيحية، والخرائط الجغرافية، والرسوم التخطيطية، والمصنفات ثلاثية الأبعاد المتعلقة بالجغرافيا أو الطبوغرافيا أو التصميمات المعمارية وغيرها.

١٢. المصنفات المشتقة، دون الإخلال بالحماية المقررة للمصنفات التي اشتقت منها.

وتشمل الحماية عنوان المصنف إذا كان مبتكراً. كما تشمل الفكرة المبتكرة المكتوبة للبرنامج الإذاعي.

المادة (٣)

لا تشمل الحماية الأفكار والإجراءات وأساليب العمل والمفاهيم الرياضية والمبادئ والحقائق المجردة لكنها تطبق على التعبير المبتكر عن أي منها، كذلك لا تشمل الحماية ما يلي:

١. الوثائق الرسمية أياً كانت لغتها الأصلية، أو اللغة المنقولة إليها، مثل نصوص القوانين واللوائح والقرارات والاتفاقيات الدولية والاحكام القضائية، وأحكام المحكمين والقرارات الصادرة من اللجان الإدارية ذات الاختصاص القضائي.

٢. الأنباء وأخبار الحوادث والوقائع الجارية والتي تكون مجرد أخبار إعلامية.

٣. المصنفات التي آلت إلى الملك العام.

ومع ذلك تتمتع مجموعات ما ورد في البنود (١، ٢، ٣) من هذه المادة بالحماية إذا تميز جمعها أو ترتيبها أو أي مجهود فيها بالإبتكار.

المادة (٤)

تضع الوزارة نظاماً لإيداع أو تسجيل حقوق المصنفات أو ما يطرأ عليها من تصرفات لدى الجهة المختصة بها وفقاً لما تقرره اللائحة التنفيذية لهذا القانون.

وتعتبر سجلات الإيداع أو تسجيل الحقوق بالوزارة مرجعاً لبيانات المصنف.

ولا يترتب على عدم إيداع المصنف أو تسجيل حقوقه أو ما يطرأ عليه من تصرفات إخلال بأي وجه من أوجه الحماية أو الحقوق التي يقررها هذا القانون.

الفصل الثاني
حقوق المؤلف

المادة (٥)

يتمتع المؤلف وخلفه العام بحقوق أدبية غير قابلة للتقادم أو التنازل عن المصنف وتشمل هذه الحقوق ما يلي:

١. الحق في تقرير نشر المصنف لأول مرة.

٢. الحق في نسبة المصنف إليه.

٣. الحق في الاعتراض على أي تعديل للمصنف إذا كان في التعديل تشويه أو تحريف للمصنف أو إضرار بمكانة المؤلف.

٤. الحق في سحب مصنفه من التداول، إذا طرأت أسباب جدية تبرر ذلك. ويباشر هذا الحق عن طريق المحكمة المختصة، مع إلزامه بأن يدفع تعويضاً عادلاً مُقدماً إلى من آلت إليه حقوق الاستغلال المالي وذلك في الأجل الذي تحدده المحكمة وقبل تنفيذ الحكم بالسحب، وإلا زال كل أثر للحكم.

المادة (٦)

لا يعد التعديل في مجال الترجمة إعتداءً إلا إذا اغفل المترجم الإشارة إلى مواطن الحذف أو التغيير أو أساء بعمله لمكانة المؤلف.

المادة (٧)

للمؤلف وحده وخلفه من بعده، أو صاحب حق المؤلف أن يرخص باستغلال المصنف، بأي وجه من الوجوه، وخاصة عن طريق النسخ بما في ذلك التحميل أو التخزين الإلكتروني، أو التمثيل بأية وسيلة، أو البث الإذاعي، أو إعادة البث الإذاعي، أو الأداء أو التوصيل العلني، أو التَرجمة، أو التحوير، أو التعديل، أو التأجير، أو الإعارة، أو النشر بأي طريقة من الطرق بما في ذلك إتاحته عبر أجهزة الحاسب أو شبكات المعلومات أو شبكات الاتصال وغيرها من الوسائل.

المادة (٨)

لا ينطبق حق التأجير على برامج الحاسب إذا لم يكن البرنامج ذاته هو المحل الاساسي للتأجير. كما لا ينطبق على المصنفات السمعية البصرية إذا لم يكن من شأنه المساس بالاستغلال العادي لها.

المادة (٩)

للمؤلف أو خلفه أن ينقل إلى الغير، سواءً أكان شخصاً طبيعياً أم اعتبارياً، كل أو بعض حقوقه المالية المبينة في هذا القانون. ويشترط لانعقاد التصرف أن يكون مكتوباً ومحدداً فيه الحق محل التصرف، مع بيان الغرض منه، ومدة الاستغلال ومكانه، ويكون المؤلف مالكًا لكل ما لم يتنازل عنه صراحة من حقوق.

ومع عدم الإخلال بحقوق امؤلف الأدبية المنصوص عليها في هذا القانون لا يجوز للمؤلف القيام بأي عمل من شأنه تعطيل استغلال الحق محل التصرف.

المادة (١٠)

للمؤلف أو خلفه أن يتقاضى المقابل النقدي أو العيني نظير نقله حق أو أكثر من حقوق الاستغلال المالي للمصنف إلى الغير على أساس مشاركة نسبية في الإيراد الناتج من الاستغلال. كما يجوز له التعاقد على اساس مبلغ جزافي، او الجمع بين الأساسين.

المادة (١١)

إذا تبين أن الاتفاق المشار إليه في المادة (١٠) من هذا القانون مجحف بحق المؤلف أو لأي من اصحاب الحقوق المجاورة، أو أصبح كذلك لظروف طرأت بعد التعاقد، فيجوز للمؤلف أو خلفه أو من يخلفهما أن يلجأ إلى المحكمة المختصة بطلب إعادة النظر في قيمة المقابل المتفق عليه.

المادة (١٢)

مع عدم الإخلال بأحكام المادة (٩) من هذا القانون، يخضع نقل الحقوق المالية فيما يتعلق بمصنفات برامج الحاسب وتطبيقاته أو قواعد البيانات لترخيص التعاقد الوارد أو الملصق على البرنامج سواء ظهر على الدعامة الحاملة للبرنامج أو ظهر عند تحميل أو تخزين البرنامج في شاشة الحاسب، ويكون مشتري البرنامج أو مستخدمه ملزماً بالشروط الواردة في ذلك الترخيص.

المادة (١٣)

لا يترتب على تصرف المؤلف بأي صورة كانت في النسخة الأصلية من مصنفه نقل أي من حقوقه المالية عليه، ما لم يتفق على غير ذلك.

ومع ذلك لا يجوز – بغير اتفاق مسبق – إلزام من انتقلت إليه ملكية هذه النسخة بأن يمكن المؤلف من نسخها أو نقلها أو عرضها.

المادة (١٤)

يجوز الحجز على الحقوق المالية للمؤلفين على مصنفاتهم المنشورة. ولا يجوز الحجز على المصنفات التي يموت صاحبها قبل نشرها ما لم يثبت بصورة قاطعة أنه استهدف نشرها قبل وفاته.

المادة (١٥)

يقع باطلاً بطلاناً مطلقاً كل تصرف للمؤلف في مجموع انتاجه الفكري المستقبلي أو في أكثر من خمس مصنفات مستقبلية.

الفصل الثالث
نطاق حماية أصحاب الحقوق المجاورة

المادة (١٦)

يتمتع فنانو الأداء وخلفهم العام بحق أدبي لا يقبل التنازل أو التقادم، يخولهم ما يلي:

١. الحق في نسبة الأداء إليهم سواء كان الأداء حياً أو مسجلاً.

٢. الحق في منع أي تغيير، أو تحريف، أو تشويه أو تعديل في أدائهم من شأنه الإضرار بمكانتهم.

وتباشر الوزارة هذا الحق الأدبي بعد انقضاء مدة حماية الحقوق المالية المنصوص عليها في هذا القانون بهدف المحافظة على أدائهم بالصورة التي أبدع عليها.

المادة (١٧)

يتمتع فنانو الأداء وحدهم بالحقوق المالية التالية:

١. الحق في بث أدائهم غير المثبت ونقله إلى الجمهور.

٢. الحق في تثبيت أدائهم على تسجيل صوتي.

٣. الحق في نسخ أدائهم المثبت في تسجيل صوتي.

ويعد استغلالاً محظوراً على الغير تسجيل هذا الأداء الحي على دعامة أو تأجيرها بهدف الحصول على عائد تجاري مباشر أو غير مباشر أو بثها أو إتاحتها بأية وسيلة كانت دون موافقة صاحب الحق

وينطبق حكم هذه المادة على تثبيت أداء فناني الأداء لأدائهم ضمن مصنف سمعي بصري ما لم يُتفق على غير ذلك.

المادة (١٨)

يتمتع منتجو التسجيلات الصوتية وحدهم بالحقوق المالية الآتية:

١. الحق في منع أي استغلال لتسجيلاتهم بأية طريقة من الطرق دون ترخيص منهم، ويعد استغلالاً محظوراً على الغير نسخها أو تأجيرها أو البث الإذاعي أو إعادته لها أو إتاحتها عبر اجهزة الحاسب أو غيرها من الوسائل.

٢. الحق في نشر تسجيلاتهم بوسائل سلكية أو لاسلكية أو عبر أجهزة الحاسب أو غيرها من الوسائل.

المادة (١٩)

تتمتع هيئة الإذاعة وحدها بالحقوق المالية الآتية:

١. الحق في منح الترخيص باستغلال تسجيلاتها وبرامجها الإذاعية.

٢. الحق في منع أي توصيل لبرامجها أو تسجيلاتها إلى الجمهور بغير ترخيص منها. ويعد بوجه خاص محظوراً على الغير تسجيل هذه البرامج أو عمل نسخ منها أو استنساخ تسجيلاتها أو تأجيرها أو إعادة بثها إذاعياً أو نقلها إلى الجمهور بأية وسيلة كانت.

الفصل الرابع
مدة الحماية، والترخيص باستخدام المصنفات

المادة (٢٠)

١. تحمى الحقوق المالية للمؤلف المنصوص عليها في هذا القانون مدة حياته وخمسين سنة تبدأ من أول السنة الميلادية التالية لسنة وفاته.

٢. تحمى الحقوق المالية لمؤلفي المصنفات المشتركة مدة حياتهم جميعاً وخمسين سنة تبدأ من أول السنة الميلادية التالية لسنة وفاة آخر من بقي حياً منهم.

٣. تحمى الحقوق المالية لمؤلفي المصنفات الجماعية – باستثناء مؤلفي مصنفات الفن التطبيقي– مدة خمسين سنة تبدأ من أول السنة الميلادية التالية للسنة التي تنشر فيها لأول مرة. وذلك إذا كان المؤلف شخصاً إعتبارياً، أما إذا كان المؤلف بها شخصاً طبيعياً فيكون حساب المدة طبقاً للقاعدة المنصوص عليها في البندين (١، ٢) من هذه المادة.

وتنقضي الحقوق المالية على المصنفات التي تنشر لأول مرة بعد وفاة مؤلفها بمضي خمسين سنة تبدأ من أول السنة الميلادية التالية للسنة التي يتم نشرها فيها لأول مرة.

٤. تحمى الحقوق المالية على المصنفات التي تنشر بدون اسم مؤلفها أو باسم مستعار لمدة خمسين سنة تبدأ من أول السنة الميلادية التالية للسنة التي يتم فيها لأول مرة نشرها، فإذا كان مؤلفها معروفاً ومحدداً أو كشف مؤلفها عن شخصيته فتحسب مدة الحماية طبقاً للقاعدة المنصوص عليها في البند (١) من هذه المادة.

٥. تنقضي الحقوق المالية لمؤلفي مصنفات الفن التطبيقي بانقضاء خمس وعشرين سنة تبدأ من أول السنة الميلادية التالية لسنة نشرها لأول مرة.

٦. في الأحوال التي تحسب فيها مدة الحماية من تاريخ النشر لأول مرة، يتخذ تاريخ أول نشر أساساً لحساب المدة، بغض النظر عن إعادة النشر إلا إذا أدخل المؤلف على مصنفه عند الإعادة تعديلات جوهرية بحيث يمكن اعتباره مصنفاً جديداً.

فإذا كان المصنف يتكون من عدة اجزاء او مجلدات نشرت منفصلة وعلى فترات فيعتبر كل جزء أو مجلد مصنفاً مستقلاً عند حساب مدة الحماية.

٧. تحمى الحقوق المالية لفناني الأداء لمدة خمسين سنة تحسب من أول السنة الميلادية التالية للسنة التي تم فيها الأداء. فإذا كان الأداء مثبتاً في تسجيل صوتي فتحسب المدة اعتباراً من نهاية السنة التي تم فيها التثبيت.

٨. تحمى الحقوق المالية لمنتجي التسجيلات وذلك لمدة خمسين سنة ميلادية تحسب من أول السنة الميلادية التالية للسنة التي تم فيها نشر التسجيل، أو للسنة التي ثبت فيها التسجيل إذا لم يكن قد نشر.

٩. تحمى الحقوق لهيئات البث الإذاعي لمدة عشرين سنة تحسب من أول السنة الميلادية التالية للسنة التي تم فيها أول بث لهذه البرامج.

المادة (٢١)

يجوز لكل شخص أن يطلب من الوزارة منحه ترخيصاً إجبارياً بالنسخ أو الترجمة أو بهما معاً لأي مصنف محمي طبقاً لأحكام هذا القانون وذلك بعد مضي ثلاث سنوات من تاريخ نشر المصنف في حالة الترخيص بالترجمة ويكون إصدار الترخيص بقرار مسبب يحدد فيه النطاق الزمني والمكاني لاستغلاله، والمقابل العادل المستحق للمؤلف، على ان يقتصر الهدف دائماً من إصدار هذا الترخيص على الوفاء باحتياجات التعليم بكل أنواعه ومستوياته أو باحتياجات المكتبات العامة أو دور الحفظ، وذلك كله طبقاً لما تحدده اللائحة التنفيذية لهذا القانون من أحوال وضوابط وشروط لإصدار الترخيص، وعلى النحو الذي يضمن عدم إلحاق الضرر غير المبرر بالمصالح المشروعة للمؤلف أو خلفه أو المساس بالاستغلال العادي للمصنف.

ويصدر بتحديد الرسوم المطبقة في هذا الشأن قرار من مجلس الوزراء.

المادة (٢٢)

مع عدم الإخلال بحقوق المؤلف الأدبية المنصوص عليها في هذا القانون، ليس للمؤلف بعد نشر مصنفه أن يمنع الغير من القيام بأي عمل من الأعمال التالية:

١. عمل نسخة وحيدة من المصنف، وذلك لاستعمال الناسخ الشخصي المحض غير الربحي أو المهني. ويستثنى من ذلك مصنفات الفنون الجميلة أو التطبيقية إلا إذا وضعت في مكان عام، وبموافقة صاحب الحق أو خلفه. كما تستثنى مصنفات العمارة، إلا طبقاً لما ورد في البند (٧) من هذه المادة، وتستثنى برامج الحاسب وتطبيقاتها وقواعد البيانات إلا طبقاً لما هو مبين بالبند (٢) من هذه المادة.

٢. عمل نسخة وحيدة من برامج الحاسب أو تطبيقاته أو قواعد البيانات بمعرفة حائزه الشرعي وله وحده للاقتباس منه، على أن يتم ذلك في حدود الغرض المرخص به، أو بغرض الحفظ، أو الإحلال عند فقد النسخة الاصلية، أو تلفها، أو عدم صلاحيتها للاستخدام، وبشرط إتلاف النسخة الاحتياطية أو المقتبسة وإن كانت محملة أو مخزنة في جهاز الحاسب بمجرد زوال سند حيازته للنسخة الاصلية.

٣. النسخ من مصنفات محمية وذلك للاستعمال في اجراءات قضائية، أو ما في حكمها، في حدود ما تقتضيه هذه الاجراءات، مع ذكر المصدر واسم المؤلف.

٤. تصوير نسخة وحيدة من المصنف بمعرفة دار للوثائق او المحفوظات أو مكتبات الإطلاع أو مراكز التوثيق والتي لا تستهدف اي منها الربح سواءً أكان بصورة مباشرة أم غير مباشرة، وذلك كله في إحدى الحالتين الآتيتين:

أ) أن يكون النسخ بهدف المحافظة على النسخة الاصلية، او لتحل هذه النسخة محل نسخة فقدت، أو تلفت، أو أصبحت غير صالحة للاستخدام او استحال الحصول على بديل لها بشروط معقولة.

ب) ان يكون الغرض من النسخ تلبية طلب شخص طبيعي لاستخدامها في دراسة أو بحث، على ان يتم ذلك لمرة واحدة أو على فترات متفاوتة، وذلك كله إذا تعذر الحصول على ترخيص بالنسخ طبقاً لأحكام هذا القانون.

٥. الاستشهاد بفقرات قصيرة، أو اقتباسات، او تحليلات في حدود المألوف للمصنف، بقصد النقد او المناقشة، أو الإعلام، مع ذكر المصدر واسم المؤلف.

٦. أداء المصنف في اجتماعات داخل اطار العائلة او بواسطة الطلاب داخل المنشأة التعليمية على ألا يتم ذلك بمقابل مباشر أو غير مباشر.

٧. عرض مصنفات الفنون الجميلة، أو التطبيقية، أو التشكيلية، أو المعمارية في برامج إذاعية إذا كانت هذه المصنفات قائمة بصورة دائمة في الاماكن العامة.

٨. نسخ أجزاء قصيرة من المصنف في صورة مكتوبة أو مسجلة تسجيلاً سمعياً أو سمعياً بصرياً لأهداف تربوية تثقيفية، أو دينية، او للتدريب المهني، على أن يكون النسخ في حدود معقولة ولا يتجاوز الغرض منه. وأن يتم ذكر اسم المؤلف، وعنوان المصنف كلما كان ذلك ممكناً، وعلى ألا تكون الجهة الناسخة تهدف إلى الربح سواء أكان بصورة مباشرة أم غير مباشرة، وبشرط عدم إمكان الحصول على رخصة بالنسخ طبقاً لأحكام هذا القانون.

المادة (٢٣)

مع عدم الإخلال بحقوق المؤلف الأدبية طبقاً لاحكام هذا القانون، ليس للمؤلف أن يمنع النسخ عن طريق الصحف، أو الدوريات، أو هيئات الإذاعة، في الحدود التي يبررها الغرض المستهدف، من نشر أي مما يلي:

١. مقتطفات من مصنفاته التي اتيحت للجمهور بصورة مشروعة، وينطبق ذلك على نقل مقتطفات من مصنفات مشاهدة أو مسموعة أثناء أحداث جارية أو إذاعتها أو نقلها إلى الجمهور بأي وسيلة اخرى.

٢. المقالات المنشورة المتعلقة بالمناقشات في الموضوعات التي تشغل الرأي العام في وقت معين، ما دام لم يرد عند النشر ما يفيد حظر ذلك.

ويتعين في كل الاحوال المنصوص عليها في البندين (١، ٢) من هذا المادة الإشارة إلى المصدر الذي نقلت عنه، وإلى اسم المؤلف.

٣. الخطب والمحاضرات والأحاديث التي تلقى في الجلسات العلنية للمجالس النيابية والقضائية، والاجتماعات العامة، ما دامت هذه الخطب والمحاضرات والأحاديث موجهة إلى العامة، وتنسخ في إطار نقل الاخبار الجارية.

ويظل للمؤلف وحده، أو خلفه، الحق في جمع أي من هذه المصنفات في مجموعات تنسب إليه.

المادة (٢٤)

تطبق القيود الواردة على الحقوق المالية للمؤلف، المنصوص عليها في هذا القانون على أصحاب الحقوق المجاورة.

الفصل الخامس
أحكام خاصة ببعض المصنفات

المادة (٢٥)

إذا اشترك عدة اشخاص في تأليف مصنف بحيث لا يمكن فصل نصيب أي منهم عن الأخر اعتبر جميع الشركاء مؤلفين للمصنف بالتساوي فيما بينهم، ما لم يتفق كتابة على غير ذلك، وفي هذه الحالة لا يجوز لأحدهم الانفراد بمباشرة حقوق المؤلف إلا باتفاق مكتوب مسبق بينهم.

فإذا كان اشتراك كل من المؤلفين يندرج تحت نوع مختلف من الفن داخل ذات المصنف، كان لكل منهم الحق في استغلال الجزء الذي ساهم به على حدة، بشرط ألا يضر ذلك باستغلال المصنف بالنسبة للباقين ما لم يتفق كتابة على غير ذلك.

ولكل منهم الحق في رفع الدعاوى عند وقوع اعتداء على أي حق من حقوق المؤلف المحمية بهذا القانون.

وإذا توفي أحد المؤلفين الشركاء دون خلف عام، يؤول نصيبه إلى باقي الشركاء أو خلفهم من بعدهم، ما لم يتفق كتابة على غير ذلك.

المادة (٢٦)

يكون للشخص الطبيعي أو الاعتباري الذي وجه بابتكار المصنف الجماعي ان يباشر وحده حقوق المؤلف الأدبية والمالية عليه ما لم يكن هنالك اتفاق بخلاف ذلك.

المادة (٢٧)

١. يعتبر مؤلفاً شريكاً في المصنف السمعي البصري أو السمعي أو البصري:

أ) مؤلف السيناريو.
ب) من يقوم بتحوير مصنفاً أدبياً موجود بشكل يجعله ملائماً للأسلوب السمعي البصري.
ج) مؤلف الحوار.

د) واضع الموسيقى إذا قام بوضعها خصيصاً للمصنف.

هـ) المخرج إذا باشر رقابة فعلية في انجاز المصنف.

وإذا كان المصنف مستنبطاً أو مستخرجاً من مصنف آخر سابق عليه يعتبر مؤلف هذا المصنف السابق شريكاً في المصنف الجديد.

٢. لمؤلف الشطر الأدبي أو الشطر الموسيقي الحق في نشر ما يخصه بطريقة أخرى غير الطريقة المنشور بها المصنف المشترك ما لم يتفق كتابة على غير ذلك.

٣. إذا امتنع أحد الشركاء في تأليف مصنف سمعي بصري أو سمعي أو بصري عن اتمام الجزء الخاص به، فلا يترتب على ذلك منع باقي الشركاء من استغلال الجزء الذي أنجزه، وذلك مع عدم الإخلال بما للممتنع من حقوق مترتبة على اشتراكه في التأليف.

٤. يكون المنتج طول مدة استغلال المصنف السمعي البصري أو السمعي أو البصري المتفق عليه نائباً عن مؤلفي هذا المصنف، وعن خلفهم في الاتفاق على استغلاله دون الإخلال بحقوق مؤلفي المصنفات الأدبية، أو الموسيقية المقتبسة، أو المحورة، كل ذلك ما لم يتفق كتابة على غير ذلك.

ويعتبر المنتج ناشراً لهذا المصنف، وتكون له حقوق الناشر عليه وعلى نسخه في حدود أغراض الاستغلال المالي.

المادة (٢٨)

يعتبر مؤلف المصنف الذي لا يحمل اسم المؤلف أو الذي يحمل إسماً مستعاراً مفوضاً للناشر في مباشرة الحقوق المنصوص عليها في هذا القانون، ما لم يعين المؤلف وكيلاً آخر أو يعلن شخصيته ويثبت صفته أو ينتفي الشك في حقيقة شخصيته.

المادة (٢٩)

لا يجوز الحجز على المباني ولا يقضى بإتلافها أو بتغيير معالمها أو مصادرتها بقصد المحافظة على حقوق المؤلف المعماري الذي تكون تصميماته أو رسومه أو مخططاته الهندسية قد أستعملت بوجه غير مشروع، على أن لا يخل ذلك بحقه في التعويض العادل.

الفصل السادس
الإدارة الجماعية لحقوق المؤلف والحقوق المجاورة

المادة (٣٠)

يجوز لأصحاب حقوق المؤلف والحقوق المجاورة، أن يتنازلوا عن حقوقهم المالية إلى جمعيات مهنية متخصصة لإدارتها، أو أن يوكلوا جهات اخرى في مباشرة هذه الحقوق.

وتعتبر العقود التي تبرم بهذا الشأن عن طريق هذه الجمعيات أو الجهات عقوداً مدنية.

المادة (٣١)

تلتزم الجمعيات أو الجهات المنصوص عليها بالمادة (٣٠) من هذا القانون بعدم إجراء أي تفرقة بين طالبي التعاقد معها على استغلال المصنفات المعهود إليها إدارتها.

ولا يُعتبر من قبيل التفرقة قيام الجمعية أو الجهة بمنح تراخيص استغلال مقابل مالي مخفض في الحالتين التاليتين على أن يكون قرارها مسبباً:

١. استغلال المصنفات في حفلات عامة بواسطة أداء حي لفناني الأداء.

٢. استغلال المصنفات في إطار أنشطة تعليمية أو تثقيفية لا تدر عائداً مباشراً أو غير مباشر.

المادة (٣٢)

لا يجوز للجمعيات أو الجهات التي تتولى إدارة حقوق المؤلف والحقوق المجاورة ممارسة نشاطها إلا بترخيص سنوي من الوزارة، وللوزارة أن تضع في اللائحة التنفيذية أية قواعد تنظم عمل مثل هذه الجمعيات والجهات، وإدخال التعديل اللازم على قواعد ونظم تراخيصها ومباشرتها لعملها.

ويصدر بتحديد الرسوم المقررة على منح الترخيص قرار من مجلس الوزراء.

المادة (٣٣)

تلتزم الجمعيات وغيرها من الجهات التي تتولى إدارة حقوق المؤلف والحقوق المجاورة بمسك سجلات بأسماء أعضائهم وصفاتهم والأعمال التي تعاقدوا بشأنها، موضحاً بها نوعية العمل والمدة والمبلغ المتفق عليه، وعليهم إبلاغ الوزارة بذلك كلما يحدث تغيير في تلك السجلات، وعلى الجمعيات وتلك الجهات التقيد بالقرارات الإدارية الصادرة من الوزارة. ويجوز للوزارة سحب الترخيص في حالة عدم إلتزام تلك الجمعيات أو الجهات بأحكام القانون واللوائح ولقرارات الإدارية المنفذة له.

الفصل السابع
الإجراءات التحفظية والعقوبات

المادة (٣٤)

لرئيس المحكمة الابتدائية بناءً على طلب المؤلف أو من يخلفه، وبمقتضى أمر يصدر على عريضة أن يأمر بالاجراءات التالية بالنسبة لكل مصنف نشر أو عرض بدون إذن كتابي من المؤلف أو ممن يخلفه:

١. إجراء وصف تفصيلي للمصنف.

٢. وقف نشر المصنف أو عرضه أو صناعته.

٣. توقيع الحجز على المصنف الأصلي أو نسخه (كتباً كانت أو صوراً أو رسومات أو أداءات أو فوتوغرافيات أو تسجيلات صوتية أو برامج إذاعية أو غير ذلك). وكذلك على المواد التي تستعمل في إعادة نشر هذا المصنف أو استخراج نسخ منه بشرط أن تكون تلك المواد غير صالحة إلا لإعادة نشر المصنف.

٤. إثبات الأداء العلني بالنسبة لإيقاع أو تمثيل أو إلقاء مصنف بين الجمهور، ومنع استمرار العرض القائم أو حظره مستقبلاً.

٥. حصر الإيراد الناتج من النشر أو العرض بمعرفة خبير يندب لذلك إن اقتضى الحال، وتوقيع الحجز على هذا الإيراد في جميع الأحوال.

٦. إثبات واقعة الإعتداء على أي من الحقوق المحمية طبقاً لأحكام هذا القانون.

ولرئيس المحكمة الابتدائية في جميع الأحوال أن يأمر بندب خبير لمعاونة المحضر المكلف بالتنفيذ، وأن يفرض على الطالب إيداع كفالة مناسبة.

ويجب أن يرفع الطالب أصل النزاع إلى المحكمة المختصة خلال الخمسة عشر يوماً التالية لصدور الأمر، فإذا لم يرفع في هذا الميعاد زال كل أثر له.

المادة (٣٥)

يجوز لمن صدر ضده الامر أن يتظلم منه أمام رئيس المحكمة الذي أصدره خلال العشرين يوماً التالية لتاريخ صدوره، وفي هذه الحالة يكون لرئيس المحكمة تأييد الأمر أو إلغاءه كلياً أو جزئياً أو تعيين حارس مهمته إعادة نشر المصنف محل النزاع أو استغلاله أو عرض أو صناعة أو استخراج نسخ منه، ويودع الايراد الناتج خزانة المحكمة حتى يفصل في أصل النزاع.

المادة (٣٦)

يجوز للسلطات الجمركية من تلقاء نفسها أو بناءً على طلب المؤلف أو صاحب الحق أو من يخلفهما أن تأمر بقرار مسبب بعدم الإفراج الجمركي – لمدة أقصاها عشرون يوماً

ـ عن أي مواد مقلدة بالمخالفة لأحكام هذا القانون. وتحدد اللائحة التنفيذية الشروط والضوابط والاجراءات الخاصة بطلب عدم الإفراج، وما يجب إرفاقه به من مستندات وقيمة ما قد يلزم الطالب بإيداعه من كفالة مالية مناسبة لضمان جدية الطلب، ويبت في الطلب خلال ثلاثة أيام من تاريخ تقديمه مستوفياً ويخطر الطالب بالقرار فور صدوره.

وفي كل الأحوال لا يجوز للسلطات الجمركية منع أصحاب الشأن من معاينة المواد المأمور بعدم الافراج الجمركي عنها وفقاً للضوابط التي تحددها اللائحة التنفيذية.

المادة (٣٧)

مع عدم الإخلال بأية عقوبة أشد واردة في أي قانون آخر، يعاقب بالحبس مدة لا تقل عن شهرين وبالغرامة التي لا تقل عن عشرة آلاف درهم ولا تزيد على خمسين ألف درهم، أو بإحدى هاتين العقوبتين، كل من قام بغير إذن كتابي من المؤلف أو صاحب الحق المجاور أو خلفهما بأي من الأفعال الآتية:

١. الإعتداء على حق من الحقوق الأدبية أو المالية للمؤلف أو صاحب الحق المجاور المنصوص عليها في هذا القانون بما في ذلك وضع أي مصنف أو أداء أو تسجيل صوتي أو برنامج إذاعي مما تشمله الحماية المقررة في هذا القانون في متناول الجمهور سواءً عبر أجهزة الحاسب أو شبكات الإنترنت أو شبكات المعلومات أو شبكات الإتصالات أو غيرها من الطرق أو الوسائل الأخرى.

٢. البيع أو التأجير أو الطرح للتداول، بأية صورة من الصور لمصنف أو تسجيل صوتي أو برنامج إذاعي محمي طبقاً لأحكام هذا القانون.

وتتعدد العقوبة المنصوص عليها في هذه المادة بتعدد المصنفات أو الأداءات أو البرامج أو التسجيلات محل الجريمة.

ويعاقب بالحبس مدة لا تقل عن ستة أشهر وبغرامة لا تقل عن خمسين ألف درهم في حالة إرتكاب الجريمة مرة أخرى.

المادة (٣٨)

مع عدم الإخلال بأية عقوبة أشد واردة في أي قانون آخر، يعاقب بالحبس لمدة لا تقل عن ثلاثة أشهر وبالغرامة التي لا تقل عن خمسين ألف درهم ولا تزيد على خمسمائة ألف درهم من ارتكب أي من الأفعال الآتية:

١. التصنيع أو الاستيراد دون وجه حق بغرض البيع أو التأجير أو التداول لأي مصنف أو نسخ مقلدة أو لأية اجهزة أو وسائل أو أدوات مصممة أو مُعدة خصيصاً للتحايل على الحماية أو التقنية التي يستخدمها المؤلف أو صاحب الحق المجاور لبث أو طرح للتداول أو لتنظيم أو إدارة هذه الحقوق أو المحافظة على جودة نقاء معينة للنسخ.

٢. التعطيل أو التعييب دون وجه حق لأي حماية تقنية أو معلومات إلكترونية تستهدف تنظيم وإدارة الحقوق المقررة في هذا القانون.

٣. تحميل أو تخزين الحاسب بأية نسخة من برامج الحاسب أو تطبيقاته أو قواعد البيانات دون ترخيص من المؤلف أو صاحب الحق أو خلفهما.

ويعاقب بالحبس مدة لا تقل عن تسعة أشهر وبغرامة لا تقل عن مائتي ألف درهم في حالة إرتكاب الجريمة مرة أخرى.

المادة (٣٩)

استثناءً من حكم المادة (٣٧) من هذا القانون، يعاقب كل شخص استخدم برنامجاً للحاسب أو تطبيقاته أو قواعد البيانات دون ترخيص مسبق من المؤلف أو من يخلفه بالغرامة التي لا تقل عن عشرة آلاف درهم ولا تزيد على ثلاثين ألف درهم، لكل برنامج أو تطبيق أو قاعدة بيانات.

ويعاقب بغرامة لا تقل عن ثلاثين ألف درهم في حالة ارتكاب الجريمة مرة أخرى.

ويجوز للمحكمة إذا ارتكبت الجريمة باسم أو لحساب شخص اعتباري أو منشأة تجارية، أو مهنية أن تقضي بالغلق لمدة لا تجاوز ثلاثة أشهر.

المادة (٤٠)

مع عدم الإخلال بالعقوبات المقررة في المواد (٣٧) و(٣٨) و(٣٩) من هذا القانون تقضي المحكمة بمصادرة النسخ المقلدة محل الجريمة أو المتحصلة منها وإتلافها، كما تقضي بمصادرة المعدات والأدوات المستخدمة في ارتكابها والتي لا تصلح إلا لهذا الغرض، وإغلاق المنشأة التي ارتكبت فيها جريمة التقليد بما لا يجاوز ستة أشهر وبنشر ملخص الحكم الصادر بالإدانة في جريدة يومية أو أكثر على نفقة المحكوم عليه.

المادة (٤١)

مع عدم الإخلال بما ورد في هذا القانون من عقوبات، يعاقب بالحبس الذي لا يزيد على ستة أشهر والغرامة أو بإحدى هاتين العقوبتين كل من يخالف أي حكم آخر من أحكام هذا القانون أو اللوائح أو الأوامر الصادرة تنفيذاً له.

الفصل الثامن
أحكام عامة وختامية

المادة (٤٢)

تباشر الوزارة على أي مصنف في حالة عدم وجود وارث أو موصى له حقوق المؤلف الأدبية والمالية. وتستمر الوزارة في مباشرة الحقوق الأدبية المنصوص عليها في هذا القانون بهدف المحافظة على المصنف وذلك بعد انقضاء مدة حماية الحقوق المالية المقررة للمصنف.

المادة (٤٣)

لا يحق لمن قام بعمل صورة لأخر، بأي طريقة كانت، ان يحتفظ أو يعرض أو ينشر أو يوزع أصلها أو نسخاً منها دون إذن الشخص الذي قام بتصويره مالم يتفق على خلاف ذلك، ما لم يكن نشر الصورة قد تم بمناسبة حوادث وقعت علناً، أو كانت تتعلق بأشخاص ذوي صفة رسمية أو عامة أو يتمتعون بشهرة، أو كان النشر قد سمحت به السلطات العامة خدمة للصالح العام، وبشرط ألا يترتب على عرض الصورة أو تداولها مساس بمكانة الشخص الذي تمثله.

ويجوز للشخص الذي تمثله الصورة أن يأذن بنشرها في الصحف، وغيرها من وسائل النشر، ولو لم يسمح بذلك المصور، ما لم يتفق على غير ذلك.

المادة (٤٤)

في مجال تنازع القوانين، تُطبق أحكام هذا القانون على المصنفات والأداءات والتسجيلات الصوتية والبرامج الإذاعية الخاصة بالأجانب، وذلك بشرط المعاملة بالمثل ومع عدم الإخلال بأحكام الاتفاقيات الدولية النافذة في الدولة.

المادة (٤٥)

يصدر وزير العدل والشؤون الإسلامية والأوقاف بالاتفاق مع وزير الإعلام والثقافة قراراً بتحديد الموظفين الذين يكون لهم صفة مأموري الضبط القضائي في تنفيذ أحكام هذا القانون.

المادة (٤٦)

يصدر بتحديد الرسوم التي تستوفى عن الإجراءات التي تتم بموجب أحكام هذا القانون قرار من مجلس الوزراء.

المادة (٤٧)

يصدر الوزير اللائحة والقرارات اللازمة لتنفيذ أحكام هذا القانون.

المادة (٤٨)

يلغى القانون الاتحادي رقم (٤٠) لسنة ١٩٩٢م المشار إليه وكل حكم آخر يخالف أحكام هذا القانون.

المادة (٤٩)

وتظل اللوائح والقرارات المعمول بها نافذة فيما لا يتعارض مع أحكام هذا القانون لحين العمل باللائحة والقرارات الصادرة تنفيذاً له.

المادة (٥٠)

ينشر هذا القانون في الجريدة الرسمية، ويعمل به من تاريخ نشره.

زايد بن سلطان آل نهيان
رئيس دولة الإمارات العربية المتحدة

صدر عنا في قصر الرئاسة بأبو ظبي
بتاريخ: ٢٠ ربيع الآخر ١٤٢٣هـ.
الموافق: ١ يوليو ٢٠٠٢م.

قانون اتحادي رقم (٣٢) لسنة ٢٠٠٦م
بتعديل القانون الاتحادي رقم (٧) لسنة ٢٠٠٢م
في شأن حقوق المؤلف والحقوق المجاورة

نحن خليفة بن زايد آل نهيان، رئيس دولة الامارات العربية المتحدة،

بعد الاطلاع على الدستور،

وعلى القانون الاتحادي رقم (١) لسنة ١٩٧٢ بشأن اختصاصات الوزارات وصلاحيات الوزراء والقوانين المعدلة له،

وعلى القانون الاتحادي رقم (١٥) لسنة ١٩٨٠ في شأن المطبوعات والنشر،

وعلى القانون الاتحادي رقم (٧) لسنة ٢٠٠٢ في شأن حقوق المؤلف والحقوق المجاورة،

وبناءً على ما عرضته وزيرة الاقتصاد، وموافقة مجلس الوزراء، وتصديق المجلس الأعلى للاتحاد،

اصدرنا القانون الآتي:

المادة (١)

تستبدل عبارة "وزارة الاقتصاد" وعبارة "وزير الاقتصاد" بعبارتي "وزارة الاعلام والثقافة" و"وزير الاعلام والثقافة" اينما وردتا في القانون الاتحادي رقم (٧) لسنة ٢٠٠٢ المشار إليه.

المـادة (٢)

ينشر هذا القانون في الجريدة الرسمية، ويعمل به اعتباراً من تاريخ نشره.

خليفة بن زايد آل نهيان
رئيس دولة الامارات العربية المتحدة

صدر عنا في قصر الرئاسة بأبو ظبي:
بتاريخ ٩ رمضان ١٤٢٧هـ
الموافق: ١ اكتوبر ٢٠٠٦م.

قرار وزاري رقم (٤١١) لسنة ١٩٩٣م
بشأن الرقابة على المصنفات المحمية
طبقاً لاحكام القانون الاتحادي رقم (٤٠) لسنة ١٩٩٢م
في شأن حماية المصنفات الفكرية وحقوق المؤلف

وزير الاعلام والثقافة،

بعد الاطلاع على القانون الاتحادي رقم (١) لسنة ١٩٧٢م بشأن اختصاصات الوزارات وصلاحيات الوزراء والقوانين المعدلة له،

وعلى القانون الاتحادي رقم (١٥) لسنة ١٩٨٠م في شأن المطبوعات والنشر والقوانين المعدلة له،

وعلى القانون الاتحادي رقم (٤٠) لسنة ١٩٩٢م في شأن حماية المصنفات الفكرية وحقوق المؤلف،

وعلى قرار مجلس الوزراء رقم (١٢) لسنة ١٩٧٥م في شأن نظام وزارة الاعلام والثقافة،

وعلى القرار الوزاري رقم (٤١٢) لسنة ١٩٩٣م في شأن نظام ايداع المصنفات المحمية وما يطرأ من تصرفات،

قرر :

الباب الأول
احكام عامة

المادة (١)

في تطبيق احكام هذا القرار يكون للكلمات والعبارات التالية المعاني الموضحة قرين كل منها مالم يدل سياق النص على غير ذلك:

الدولة:	دولة الامارات العربية المتحدة.
الوزارة:	وزارة الاعلام والثقافة.
الوزير:	وزير الاعلام والثقافة.
الادارة:	ادارة الرقابة بالوزارة.
القانون:	القانون الاتحادي رقم (٤٠) لسنة ١٩٩٢م في شأن حماية المصنفات الفكرية وحقوق المؤلف.
المصنف:	كل مصنف فكري يتمتع بالحماية المقررة في القانون.
المؤلف:	المؤلف او المؤلفون بالنسبة للمصنفات المشتركة.

المادة (٢)

تسري أحكام هذا القرار على المصنفات المحمية بالقانون.

المادة (٣)

تختص الادارة بتنفيذ احكام هذا القرار.

الباب الثاني
اجازة المصنفات بغرض ايداعها.

المادة (٤)

لصاحب المصنف أو مؤلفه أو الوكيل الرسمي لأيهما بالدولة ان يطلب من الادارة اعطاءه شهادة تتضمن اجازة المصنف أو أنه مجاز طبقاً لقانون المطبوعات والنشر رقم (١٥) لسنة ١٩٨٠م المشار اليه، وذلك بغرض قيده في سجلات الايداع المنشأة طبقاً لأحكام القانون وقرار وزير الاعلام والثقافة رقم (٤١٢) لسنة ١٩٩٣م الخاص بنظام[17] ايداع المصنفات المحمية وما يطرأ عليها من تصرفات.

---

[17]. وردت هذه الكلمة في نص الجريدة الرسمية "بنظا" والأصح ان تكون "بنظام" فاقتضى التنويه.

ولا يجوز ان يتضمن الطلب أكثر من مصنف واحد.

المادة (٥)

لا يقبل طلب الحصول على الشهادة المشار اليها في المادة (٤) من هذا القرار الا من أصحاب الحقوق الادبية او المالية في المصنف او من الوكيل الرسمي لأي منهم بالدولة وهم:

١. المؤلف.

٢. ورثة المؤلف أو خلفاؤه بعد وفاته.

٣. المتنازل له عن استغلال المصنف من المؤلف أو من ورثته أو خلفائه بعد وفاته.

٤. الشخص الطبيعي أو المعنوي الذي أنجز المصنف وفقاً لنص المادة (٢٤) من القانون.

٥. المنتج للمصنف المسرحي أو السينمائي أو الاذاعي أو التلفزيوني الذي يتولى تنفيذ الشريط ويتحمل مسؤولية هذا التنفيذ ويضع في متناول مؤلفي المصنف الوسائل المادية والمالية الكفيلة بانتاجه وتحقيق اخراجه وفقاً لنص المادة (٢٩) من القانون.

المادة (٦)

يجب أن يشتمل طلب الشهادة المشار اليها في المادتين (٤) و(٥) من هذا القرار البيانات الآتية:

١. اسم الطالب وجنسيته وصفته.

٢. محل اقامة الطالب أو مركزه الرئيسي ومحله المختار في الدولة أن كان محل اقامته أو مركزه الرئيسي خارج الدولة.

٣. موضوع المصنف ونوعه واسمه إن وجد.

المادة (٧)

يرفق بالطلب ما يأتي:

١. المستند الدال على صفة الطالب ان كان غير المؤلف او اذا كان الطلب مقدما بواسطة وكيل.

٢. نسختان من المصنف الذي يمكن استخراج نسخ منه عن طريق الطبع أو أية وسيلة أخرى مشابهة اذا لم يكن قد سبق ايداع نسخ منه لدى الادارة طبقاً لقانون المطبوعات والنشر رقم (١٥) لسنة ١٩٨٠م المشار اليه.

المادة (٨)

تفحص الادارة الطلب للتحقق مما يأتي:

١. أن الطلب مستوف للشروط المنصوص عليها في المواد (٥) و(٦) و(٧) من هذا القرار.

٢. ان المصنف مجاز أو سبقت اجازته من الادارة أو لايوجد ما يمنع من اجازته وذلك طبقاً لأحكام قانون المطبوعات والنشر رقم (١٥) لسنة ١٩٨٠م المشار اليه.

المادة (٩)

اذا تبين للادارة من فحص الطلب انه مستوف للشروط المشار اليها في المادة (٨) من هذا القرار، تعطي الطالب شهادة تتضمن اجازة المصنف او انه مجاز طبقاً لأحكام قانون المطبوعات والنشر رقم (١٥) لسنة ١٩٨٠م المشار اليه بغرض تقديمها لادارة الثقافة بالوزارة مع طلب ايداع المصنف، على ان تكون هذه الشهادة مرفقاً بها نسخة من المصنف مختومة بخاتم الادارة.

الباب الثالث
التصريح بنشر أو عرض أو تداول المصنفات

المادة (١٠)

مع عدم الاخلال بأحكام قانون المطبوعات والنشر رقم (١٥) لسنة ١٩٨٠م المشار اليه والقرارات الصادرة تنفيذا له، يشترط للتصريح بنشر أو عرض أو تداول اي مصنف، أن يرفق به ما يأتي:

١. شهادة من المنشأ تبين اسم المؤلف أو من تم التنازل له عن حق الاستغلال.

٢. تصريح من المورد او مالك المصنف بالعرض او التداول موضحاً فيه المنطقة الجغرافية والمكانية التي صرح بالعرض او التداول في نطاقها.

٣. شهادة من المورد تفيد دفع حقوق النشر سواء كان بالأداء العلني أو عن طريق عمل نماذج من المصنف أو نسخه للتوزيع.

ويجب أن تكون هذه المستندات مصدقاً عليها حسب الاصول، ومصحوبة بترجمة الى اللغة العربية اذا كانت محررة بلغة اخرى.

المادة (١١)

مع مراعاة أحكام المادة (١٠) من هذا القرار يشترط للتصريح بطبع أو نشر أو عرض أو تداول أي مصنف فولكلوري ما يأتي:

١ . ان يقدم الطالب شهادة من ادارة الثقافة بالوزارة تفيد ان المصنف لا يتضمن تشويهاً او تحويراً للفلوكلور الوطني.

٢ . الا يكون الطبع أو النشر أو العرض أو التداول بغرض الاستغلال التجاري ما لم يقدم الطالب شهادة من ادارة الثقافة بالوزارة تفيد قيد المصنف في سجلات الايداع النوعي لديها.

الباب الرابع
الوثائق الواجب على المحلات الاحتفاظ بها.

المادة (١٢)

على كل محل من المحلات المرخص لها بنسخ أو توزيع أو بيع المصنفات في الدولة الاحتفاظ بالمستندات الآتية:

١ . الكتاب الصادر من الوزارة بالموافقة على مزاولة المحل للنشاط.

٢ . الترخيص الصادر للمحل من بلدية الامارة التي يمارس فيها النشاط.

٣ . اذن أو اتفاق مكتوب ومصدق عليه حسب الاصول صادر من أي من أصحاب الحق في استغلال المصنف المشار إليهم في المادة (٥) من هذا القرار تخول المحل حق نسخ أو توزيع أو بيع كل مصنف من المصنفات على حسب الاحوال سواء كان المصنف من داخل الدولة أو خارجها.

٤ . اجازة الادارة لكل مصنف من المصنفات الواجب اجازتها طبقاً لاحكام قانون المطبوعات والنشر رقم (١٥) لسنة ١٩٨٠م المشار اليه والقرارات الصادرة تنفيذا له.

٥ . بيان معتمد من الادارة يحدد المصنفات المعدة خارج الدولة ويوضح مصدر كل منها والاذن أو الاتفاق الذي يخول المحل القيام بالنسخ أو التوزيع أو البيع.

٦ . أية وثائق اخرى يجب الاحتفاظ بها طبقاً لاحكام قانون المطبوعات والنشر رقم (١٥) لسنة ١٩٨٠م المشار اليه والقرارات الصادرة تنفيذا له.

المادة (١٣)

على كل محل من المحلات المشار اليها في المادة (١٢) من هذا القرار ان يقدم الى الادارة خلال اسبوعين من تاريخ العمل باحكام هذا القرار، قائمة من أصل وصورة موقعاً عليها من صاحب المحل والمدير المسؤول تشتمل على جميع المصنفات الموجودة لدى المحل والتي لا تتوافر بشأنها الوثائق المشار اليها في البندين (٣) و(٥) من المادة (١٢) من هذا القرار ويجب أن يرفق بهذه القائمة البيانات الآتية بالنسبة لكل مصنف:

١. أسم المصنف ونوعه.

٢. مصدر المصنف سواء كان من داخل الدولة أو خارجها.

٣. عدد نسخ المصنف الموجودة بالمحل بما فيها النسخة الأصلية.

٤. ما سبق اجازته من تلك المصنفات من الادارة وتاريخ الاجازة.

وتختم كل صفحة من اصل وصورة هذه القائمة بخاتم الادارة التي تحتفظ بالاصل وتعيد الصورة الى مقدمها.

المادة (١٤)

تمنح المحلات المشار اليها في هذا الباب مهلة سنة من تاريخ العمل بهذا القرار للتخلص من جميع المصنفات الواردة بالقائمة المشار اليها في المادة (١٣) منه.

المادة (١٥)

ينشر هذا القرار في الجريدة الرسمية ويعمل به من تاريخ نشره.

خلفان محمد الرومي
وزير الاعلام و الثقافة

صدر بتاريخ: ١٤١٤/٣/١٥هـ.
الموافق: ١٩٩٣/٩/١م.

قرار وزاري رقم (٤١٢) لسنة ١٩٩٣م
بشأن نظام ايداع المصنفات المحمية وما يطرأ عليها من تصرفات

وزير الاعلام والثقافة،

بعد الاطلاع على القانون الاتحادي رقم (١) لسنة ١٩٧٢م بشأن اختصاصات الوزارات وصلاحيات الوزراء والقوانين المعدلة له،

وعلى القانون الاتحادي رقم (١٥) لسنة ١٩٨٠م في شأن المطبوعات والنشر،

وعلى القانون الاتحادي رقم (٤٠) لسنة ١٩٩٢م في شأن حماية المصنفات الفكرية وحقوق المؤلف،

وعلى قرار مجلس الوزراء رقم (١٢) لسنة ١٩٧٥م في شأن نظام وزارة الاعلام والثقافة،

قرر،

الباب الاول
احكام عامة

المادة (١)

في تطبيق احكام هذا القرار يكون للكلمات والعبارات التالية المعاني الموضحة قرين كل منها مالم يدل سياق النص على غير ذلك:

الدولة:	دولة الامارات العربية المتحدة.
الـــوزارة:	وزارة الاعلام والثقافة.
الـــوزير:	وزير الاعلام والثقافة.
الادارة:	ادارة الثقافة بالوزارة.
القـــسم:	قسم الايداع والملكية الفكرية بالادارة.

القانون: القانون الاتحادي رقم (٤٠) لسنة ١٩٩٢م في شأن حماية المصنفات الفكرية وحقوق المؤلف.

المصنف: كل مصنف فكري يتمتع بالحماية المقررة في القانون.

المصنف المشتق: المصنف الذي يظهر مصنفاً سابقاً بشكل جديد سواء بترجمته الى لغة اخرى أو بتلخيصه أو تحويره أو تعديله أو شرحه أو بأية طريقة اخرى وفقاً للمادة (٥) من القانون.

المؤلف: المؤلف أو المؤلفون بالنسبة للمصنفات المشتركة.

المادة (٢)

تسري أحكام هذا القرار على المصنفات المحمية بالقانون.

المادة (٣)

تختص الادارة بتنفيذ أحكام هذا القرار.

الباب الثاني
ايداع المصنفات

الفصل الاول
تقديم طلبات الايداع

المادة (٤)

يقدم طلب قيد المصنف في سجل الايداع الى القسم من صاحب المصنف أو مؤلفه أو الوكيل الرسمي لايهما بالدولة على النموذج رقم (١) المرفق بهذا القرار ولا يجوز أن يتضمن الطلب أكثر من مصنف واحد.

المادة (٥)

يجب ان يشتمل طلب القيد على البيانات الآتية:

١. اسم الطالب وجنسيته ومحل اقامته أو مركزه الرئيسي خارج الدولة.

٢. اسم وعنوان الوكيل بالدولة ورقم وتاريخ ومصدر الوكالة اذا قدم الطلب بواسطة وكيل.

٣. اسم المؤلف وجنسيته ومحل اقامته أو مركزه الرئيسي.

٤. موضوع المصنف ونوعه واسمه ان وجد.

٥. الطريقة التي اختارها المؤلف أو خلفاؤه – في حالة وفاته – لنشر المصنف.

المادة (٦)

يرفق بطلب القيد المستندات الآتية:

١. بيان شامل بمواصفات المصنف.

٢. المستند الدال على صفة الطالب اذا كان غير المؤلف، أو اذا كان الطلب مقدماً بواسطة وكيل.

٣. اقرار مكتوب من المؤلف أو من خلفائه – في حالة وفاته – بملكيته أو ملكيتهم للمصنف.

٤. اقرار مكتوب من المؤلف أو من خلفائه – في حالة وفاته – يتضمن تحديد الطريقة التي اختارها أو أوصى بها المؤلف لنشر المصنف أو الطريقة التي يختارونها لنشره اذا لم يكن المؤلف قد أوصى بشيء يتعلق بنشر المصنف.

٥. تنازل مكتوب من المؤلف أو من خلفائه – في حالة وفاته – عن حقه أو حقهم في استغلال المصنف وفقاً لاحكام المادتين (٣/٧) و(٣٢) من القانون اذا كان الطلب مقدما من المتنازل اليه عن هذا الحق.

٦. اذن مكتوب من مؤلف المصنف الاصلي أو من خلفائه – في حالة وفاته – اذا كان المصنف موضوع الطلب مشتقاً من المصنف الاصلي بأية طريقة من طرق الاشتقاق التي تظهره بشكل جديد طبقاً لأحكام المادة (٥) من القانون.

٧. العقد المبرم بين مؤلف المصنف وبين الشخص الطبيعي أو المعنوي الذي تم وضع المصنف بناءً على توجيهه، وتكفل بنشره تحت ادارته وباسمه وفقاً لاحكام المادة (٢٤) من القانون اذا كان الطلب مقدما من هذا الشخص.

٨. شهادة من ادارة الرقابة بالوزارة تتضمن اجازتها للمصنف أو انه مجاز طبقاً لقانون المطبوعات والنشر.

٩. عدد نسختين من المصنف الذي يمكن استخراج عدة نسخ منه عن طريق الطبع أو اية وسيلة اخرى مشابهة.

المادة (٧)

يجب ان تكون المستندات المشار اليها في البنود (٢) و(٣) و(٤) و(٥) و(٦) و(٧) من المادة (٦) من هذا القرار مصدقاً عليها حسب الاصول، وان تكون هي والمستند المشار اليه في الفقرة (١) من المادة المشار اليها مصحوبة بترجمة الى اللغة العربية اذا كانت محررة بلغة أخرى.

المادة (٨)

١. يتعين لاستلام الطلب أن يكون مشتملاً على ما يلزم من بيانات – حسب الاحوال – طبقاً للمادة (٥) من هذا القرار، وأن يكون مرفقاً به المستندات المشار اليها في البنود (١) و(٨) و(٩) من المادة (٦) من هذا القرار، أما المستندات الاخرى فيجوز في حالة عدم ارفاقها بالطلب أن يقدم الطالب تعهداً كتابياً – على النموذج رقم (٢) المرفق بهذا القرار – بتقديم ما يلزم تقديمه منها على حسب الاحوال خلال ستين يوماً من تاريخ تقديم الطلب.

٢. اذا لم يقدم الطالب المستندات التي تعهد بتقديمها خلال المدة المحددة بالفقرة (١) من هذه المادة اعتبر طلبه كأن لم يكن الاّ اذا تقدم قبل نهايتها بطلب منحه مهلة أخرى بناءً على مبررات جدية يقبلها مدير الادارة الذي له في هذه الحالة منح الطالب مهلة أخرى نهائية يتعين عليه خلالها تقديم المستندات والا اعتبر متنازلاً عن طلبه.

المادة (٩)

تعطى الطلبات أرقاماً متتابعة سنوياً حسب تاريخ تقديمها، ويؤشر على الطلب بالرقم المتتابع له وتاريخ تقديمه، ويختم الطلب ومرفقاته بخاتم القسم، ويسلم للطالب ايصال على النموذج رقم (٣) المرفق بهذا القرار يتضمن الرقم المتتابع للطلب وتاريخ تقديمه وبيان المستندات المرفقة به.

المادة (١٠)

يعد القسم سجلاً لطلبات القيد تدون فيه البيانات الآتية:

١. الرقم المتتابع للطلب.

٢. تاريخ تقديم الطلب.

٣. جميع البيانات الواردة بالطلب والمشار اليها في المادة (٥) من هذا القرار.

٤. قرار الادارة في الطلب وتاريخه.

٥. تاريخ اخطار الطالب بالقرار في حالة رفض الطلب.

٦ تاريخ ورقم قيد المصنف في السجل النوعي للايداع، وتاريخ تسليم شهادة القيد للطالب في حالة قبول الطلب.

المادة (١١)

يعد القسم ملفاً لكل مصنف طلب قيده يودع به الطلب والمستندات وجميع ما يتعلق به من أوراق وقرارات ويدون على ظاهره الرقم المتتابع للطلب وتاريخ تقديمه واسم الطالب وصفته واسم المؤلف وموضوع المصنف ونوعه.

المادة (١٢)

يعد القسم فهرس بطاقات هجدياً وفقاً لأسماء الطالبين طبقاً للنموذج رقم (٤) المرفق بهذا القرار ويدون به البيانات المشار اليها في المادة (١١) من هذا القرار، وقرار الادارة في الطلب.

الفصل الثاني
فحص طلبات الايداع

المادة (١٣)

تفحص الادارة طلبات القيد في سجلات الايداع في ضوء البيانات الواردة بها والمستندات الواجب تقديمها طبقاً لنصوص المواد (٦) و(٧) و(٨) من هذا القرار بعد تقديمها كاملة.

وللادارة في سبيل فحص الطلب الاستعانة بمن ترى ضرورة الاستعانة به من المختصين داخل الدولة أو خارجها بأجر أو بدون أجر على حسب الاحوال ووفقاً للقواعد المقررة لذلك.

المادة (١٤)

يجوز للادارة ان تكلف الطالب بتقديم أية مستندات أو بيانات اخرى تراها ضرورية للتحقق من توفر الشروط اللازمة لقبول الطلب، وذلك بموجب اخطار كتابي توجهه له وتحدد له فيه مدة لتقديمها، فاذا لم يتقدم بما طلب منه خلال تلك المدة اعتبر طلبه كأن لم يكن الا اذا تقدم قبل نهايتها بطلب منحه مهلة بناءً على مبررات جدية يقبلها مدير الادارة الذي له في هذه الحالة منح الطالب مهلة اخرى نهائية يتعين عليه خلالها تقديم تلك المستندات أو البيانات والاّ عتبر متنازلاً عن طلبه.

المادة (١٥)

يجب على الادارة التحقق مما يأتي:

١. ان المصنف لم يسبق قيده في سجلات الايداع النوعية.

٢. ان المصنف يندرج تحت احدى الفئات المنصوص عليها في المادة (٣) من القانون وهي:

أ) أن يكون المصنف لمؤلف من مواطني دولة الامارات العربية المتحدة سواء كان نشره داخل الدولة أو خارجها.

ب) أن يكون المصنف لمؤلف من مواطني دولة اجنبية وينشر داخل دولة الامارات العربية المتحدة لأول مرة.

ج) أن يكون المصنف لمؤلف من مواطني دولة اجنبية وينشر فيها بشرط أن يحمي قانونها مصنفات مواطني دولة الامارات العربية المتحدة التي تنشر داخل دولة الامارات العربية المتحدة.

٣. ان المصنف من المصنفات التي تتمتع بالحماية طبقاً لاحكام المادتين (٢) و(٥) من القانون.

٤. أن المصنف ليس من المصنفات التي لا تتمتع بالحماية طبقاً لأحكام المادة (٦) من القانون.

٥. ان المصنف ليس من المصنفات الفلوكلورية التي لا تعدو أن تكون مجموعات مختارة من الفولكور الوطني لا تتميز لاي سبب يرجع الى الابتكار أو الترتيب أو أي مجهود شخصي آخر يستحق الحماية أو التي يتضمن تشويهاً أو تحويراً لمصنفات فولكلورية سابقة.

٦. الا يكون قد انقضى خمس وعشرون سنة ميلادية من تاريخ أول نشر للمصنف اذا كان من المصنفات الآتية:

أ) افلام السينما وأعمال الفنون التطبيقية.

ب) المصنفات التي ينجزها الاشخاص الاعتباريون.

ج) المصنفات التي تنشر لأول مرة بعد وفاة مؤلفها.

د) المصنفات التي تنشر باسم مستعار أو دون ذكر اسم المؤلف ما لم يكن المؤلف قد كشف عن شخصيته قبل انقضاء تلك المدة.

٧. الا يكون قد انقضى عشر سنوات ميلادية من تاريخ النشر اذا كان المصنف من المصنفات الفوتوغرافية.

٨. الا يكون قد انقضى خمس وعشرون سنة ميلادية من تاريخ وفاة المؤلف أو وفاة آخر من بقي حياً من مؤلفي المصنف المشترك، اذا كان المصنف قد نشر في حياة مؤلفه أو احد مؤلفيه، ولم يكن من المصنفات المشار اليها في البنود (٦) و(٧) و(٨) من هذه المادة.

٩. أن يكون مقدم الطلب من أصحاب الحقوق الادبية أو المالية في المصنف وهم:

أ) المؤلف.

ب) ورثة المؤلف أو خلفاؤه بعد وفاته.

ج) المتنازل له عن استغلال المصنف من المؤلف أو من ورثته أو خلفائه بعد وفاته.

د) الشخص الطبيعي أو المعنوي الذي انجز المصنف وفقاً لنص المادة (٢٤) من القانون.

هـ) المنتج للمصنف المسرحي أو السينمائي أو الاذاعي أو التلفزيوني الذي يتولى تنفيذ الشريط ويتحمل مسئولية هذا التنفيذ ويضع في متناول مؤلفي المصنف الوسائل المادية والمالية الكفيلة بانتاجه وتحقيق اخراجه وفقاً لنص المادة (٢٩) من القانون.

١٠. أن الوكيل الذي قدم الطلب نيابة عن صاحب الحق في الطلب له صفة في تقديمه بموجب وكالة مصدقاً عليها حسب الاصول.

الفصل الثالث
البت في طلبات الايداع

المادة (١٦)

اذا تبين من فحص الطلب انه لا تتوفر فيه الشروط المنصوص عليها في القانون وهذا القرار تصدر الادارة قراراً مسبباً برفض الطلب و تخطر الطالب بهذا القرار بكتاب مسجل.

واذا كان سبب هذا القرار انقضاء مدة الحماية المشار اليها في المادة (٢٠) من القانون والبنود (٦) و(٧) و(٨) و(٩) من المادة (١٥) من هذا القرار فانه لا يخل بأي حق ادبي للمؤلف غير قابل للتقادم وفقاً لاحكام القانون.

المادة (١٧)

اذا تبين من فحص الطلب أنه تتوفر فيه الشروط المنصوص عليها في القانون وهذا القرار تصدر الادارة قراراً بقبوله.

المادة (١٨)

١. يصدر قرار رفض أو قبول الطلب من مدير الادارة بعد اطلاعه على تقرير الفحص وذلك خلال مدة اقصاها ستون يوماً من تاريخ استكمال مستندات وبيانات الطلب وفقاً لاحكام المواد (٥) و(٦) و(٧) و(٨) و(١٤) من هذا القرار.

٢. كما يصدر من مدير الادارة قرار اعتبار الطلب كأن لم يكن أو اعتبار مقدمه متنازلاً عنه اعمالاً لحكم المادتين (٨) و(١٤) من هذا القرار.

٣. يجوز لمن يصدر قرار باعتبار طلبه كأن لم يكن أو اعتباره متنازلاً عنه ان يتقدم الى القسم في أي وقت بطلب جديد، ويتعين لاستلام هذا الطلب منه ان يكون مستوفياً لجميع المستندات والبيانات الواجب استكمالها طبقاً لاحكام هذا القرار بما فيها المستندات والبيانات التي تكون قد طلبتها منه الادارة وكان عدم استكماله لها سبباً في صدور القرار باعتبار طلبه السابق كأن لم يكن او اعتباره متنازلاً عنه.

الفصل الرابع
قيد المصنفات في سجلات الايداع

المادة (١٩)

يقيد كل مصنف صدر قرار بقبول طلب قيده في سجل الايداع النوعي ويعطى مقدم الطلب شهادة بقيد المصنف وذلك وفق احكام المواد (٢٠) و(٢١) و(٢٢) و(٢٣) من هذا القرار.

المادة (٢٠)

يعد القسم سجلات ايداع نوعية تقيد فيها المصنفات المقبول قيدها حسب نوعها وفقاً للتقسيم الذي يراه مناسباً لانواع المصنفات.

وتعطى السجلات ارقاماً مسلسلة، ويدون على ظاهر كل منها رقمه المسلسل، ونوع المصنفات التي تقيد به، ويتم قيد المصنفات كل في السجل النوعي الخاص به بأرقام متتابعة.

المادة (٢١)

يجب أن يشتمل كل سجل من سجلات الايداع النوعية على البيانات الآتية:

١. رقم وتاريخ قيد المصنف.

٢. رقم طلب القيد وتاريخ تقديمه.

٣. رقم وتاريخ قرار مدير الادارة بقبول طلب القيد.

٤. موضوع المصنف ونوعه واسمه ان وجد.

٥. اسم المؤلف وجنسيته وعنوانه.

٦. اسم مقدم الطلب وجنسيته وصفته وعنوانه ان كان غير المؤلف.

٧. الطريقة التي اختارها المؤلف أو خلفاؤه – في حالة وفاته – لنشر المصنف وتاريخ ومكان أول نشر.

٨. رقم وتاريخ شهادة ادارة الرقابة بالوزارة باجازة المصنف.

٩. عدد النسخ المودعة من المصنف.

١٠. تاريخ صدور شهادة قيد المصنف ورقم وتاريخ ايصال استلام الطالب لها.

١١. مدة الحماية المقررة للمصنف وفق احكام القانون.

المادة (٢٢)

تصدر الادارة شهادة بقيد المصنف على النموذج رقم (٥) المرفق بهذا القرار وتشتمل على البيانات الآتية:

١. رقم وتاريخ قرار مدير الادارة بقبول طلب القيد.

٢. تاريخ ورقم قيد المصنف في سجل الايداع النوعي.

٣. موضوع المصنف ونوعه واسمه ان وجد واسم مؤلفه.

٤. اسم صاحب أو اصحاب المصنف.

٥. اسم مستلم الشهادة وصفته.

المادة (٢٣)

تصدر شهادة قيد المصنف من أصل وصورة يسلم الأصل الى مقدم طلب القيد بموجب ايصال استلام على النموذج رقم (٦) المرفق بهذا القرار وتودع صورة الشهادة وصورة ايصال الاستلام ملف المصنف.

الباب الثالث
ايداع التصرفات

المادة (٢٤)

يقدم طلب قيد أي تصرف يطرأ على مصنف مقيد بسجل ايداع المصنفات الى القسم من المتصرف أو المتصرف اليه أو من خلفاء أيهما بحسب الاحوال أو من قبل الوكيل الرسمي بالدولة لأي منهم على النموذج رقم (٧) المرفق بهذا القرار.

المادة (٢٥)

يجب ان يشتمل طلب القيد على البيانات الآتية:

١. اسم الطالب وجنسيته وصفته ومحل اقامته أو مركزه الرئيسي، ومحله المختار في الدولة اذا كان محل اقامته أو مركزه الرئيسي خارج الدولة.

٢. اسم وعنوان الوكيل بالدولة ورقم وتاريخ ومصدر الوكالة اذا قدم الطلب بواسطة وكيل.

٣. موضوع المصنف الذي يطرأ عليه التصرف ونوعه ورقم وتاريخ قيده في السجل النوعي.

٤. تاريخ التصرف المطلوب قيده ونوعه، والحق أو الحقوق التي يشملها.

المادة (٢٦)

يجب ان يرفق بطلب القيد المستندات الآتية:

١. سند التصرف مكتوباً ومصدقاً عليه حسب الاصول ومصحوباً بترجمة الى اللغة العربية اذا كان محرراً بلغة أخرى ومحدداً به صراحة كل حق من الحقوق المالية محل التصرف على حدة ومدة ذلك التصرف وكيفيته وكميته والغرض منه ومكانه.

٢. المستند الدال على صفة الطالب اذا كان غير المؤلف، أو كان الطلب مقدماً بواسطة وكيل.

المادة (٢٧)

تعطى الطلبات ارقاماً متتابعة سنوياً حسب تاريخ تقديمها، ويؤشر على الطلب بالرقم المتتابع له وتاريخ تقديمه، ويختم الطلب بخاتم الادارة ويسلم للطالب ايصال على

النموذج رقم (٨) المرفق بهذا القرار يتضمن الرقم المتتابع للطلب وتاريخ تقديمه والمستندات المرفقه به.

المادة (٢٨)

يعد القسم سجلاً لطلبات قيد التصرفات تدون فيه البيانات الآتية:

١. الرقم المتتابع للطلب وتاريخ تقديمه.

٢. جميع البيانات الواردة بالطلب والمشار اليها في المادة (٢٥) من هذا القرار.

٣. قرار الادارة في الطلب وتاريخه.

٤. تاريخ اخطار الطالب بالقرار في حالة رفض الطلب.

٥. تاريخ ورقم قيد التصرف في سجل ايداع التصرفات في حالة قبول الطلب.

المادة (٢٩)

يودع طلب قيد التصرف وكل ما يتعلق به من اوراق وقرارات في ملف المصنف الوارد عليه التصرف.

المادة (٣٠)

تفحص الادارة طلب قيد التصرف للتحقق مما يأتي:

١. ان المصنف الوارد عليه التصرف مقيد في احدى سجلات الايداع النوعية.

٢. ان التصرف موضوع الطلب لا يتعارض مع تصرف سبق قيده في سجل ايداع التصرفات المشار اليه في المادة (٣٢) من هذا القرار.

٣. ان الطلب مستوف لجميع الشروط الواردة في المادتين (٢٥) و(٢٦) من هذا القرار.

المادة (٣١)

اذا تبين من فحص الطلب انه لا تتوفر فيه الشروط المشار اليها في المواد (٢٥) و(٢٦) و(٣٠) من هذا القرار تصدر الادارة قراراً مسبباً برفض الطلب وتخطر الطالب بهذا القرار بكتاب مسجل أما اذا تبين لها توفر تلك الشروط في الطلب تصدر قراراً بقبوله، ويصدر القرار في الحالتين من مدير الادارة بعد اطلاعه على تقرير الفحص.

المادة (٣٢)

يعد القسم سجلاً لايداع التصرفات، تقيد فيه التصرفات المقبول قيدها، ويجب ان يشتمل هذا السجل على البيانات الآتية:

١. رقم طلب القيد وتاريخ تقديمه.

٢. اسم المتصرف وجنسيته وصفته وعنوانه.

٣. اسم المتصرف اليه وجنسيته وصفته وعنوانه.

٤. تاريخ التصرف ومدته.

٥. بيان كل حق من الحقوق المالية محل التصرف على حدة ومدة التصرف فيه، وكيفيته وكميته والغرض منه ومكانه.

٦. رقم وتاريخ قرار مدير الادارة بقبول طلب القيد.

٧. موضوع المصنف الوارد عليه التصرف ونوعه واسمه ان وجد.

٨. رقم وتاريخ قيد المصنف في السجل النوعي.

المادة (٣٣)

يؤشر بكل تصرف يقيد في السجل المشار اليه في المادة (٣٢) من هذا القرار قرين بيانات المصنف الوارد عليه التصرف، في سجل الايداع النوعي المقيد به ذلك المصنف.

الباب الرابع
احكام ختامية

المادة (٣٤)

على الادارة ان تحتفظ لديها في القسم بنسخة على الاقل من نسخ المصنفات التي تقدم لها طبقاً للمادة (٦) من هذا القرار، ولها ان توزع باقي هذه النسخ على المكتبات العامة وغيرها من الجهات التي تختارها.

المادة (٣٥)

يؤشر في سجلات الايداع النوعية أو فيها وفي سجل ايداع التصرفات بحسب الاحوال بكل حكم نهائي واجب التنفيذ يقتضي تنفيذه الغاء أو تعديل أي بيان من البيانات المقيدة في كل أو بعض تلك السجلات، وذلك اذا صدر حكم في مواجهة الوزارة او قدم لها ذوو الشأن صورة رسمية من الحكم وتودع صورة الحكم ملف المصنف.

المادة (٣٦)

يجوز لكل ذي شأن الاطلاع على أي سجل من السجلات المشار اليها في هذا القرار بحضور الموظف المسؤول بالقسم، والحصول على شهادة بما يتضمنه من البيانات بشأن أي مصنف أو أي تصرف مقيد فيها.

المادة (٣٧)

للقسم بموافقة مدير الادارة اعداد سجلات اضافية علاوة على السجلات المشار اليها في هذا القرار وفقًا لما يراه لازمًا لحسن سير العمل.

المادة (٣٨)

يجوز لكل ذي شأن ان يطلب من القسم تصحيح أي خطأ مادي يقع في أي سجل من السجلات المشار اليها في هذا القرار.

المادة (٣٩)

ينشر هذا القرار في الجريدة الرسمية ويعمل به من تاريخ نشره.

خلفان محمد الرومي
وزير الاعلام والثقافة

صدر بتاريخ: ١٤٠٤/٣/١٥هـ.
الموافق: ١٩٩٣/٩/١م.

دولة الامارات العربية المتحدة
وزارة الاعلام والثقافة
إدارة الثقافة

نموذج رقم ١ طلب قيد مصنف في سجل الايداع

للاستعمال الرسمي فقط	يلتمس الطالب قيد المصنف موضوع
رقم الطلب: —————————	الطلب في سجل الايداع النوعي ومنحه
تاريخ تقديمه: —————————	شهادة بقيده وفقاً للبيانات الآتية:
—————————————	

١ – بيانات خاصة بالطالب:

أ – اسم الطالب وجنسيته وصفته: ————————————
————————————————————————

ب – محل إقامة الطالب أو مركزه الرئيسي داخل الدولة: ————————
————————————————————————

جـ – المحل المختار للطالب في الدولة إذا كان محل إقامته أو مركزه الرئيسي
خارج الدولة: ————————————————————
————————————————————————

د – رقم الهاتف: ———— رقم الفاكس: ———— رقم التلكس: ————

٢ – بيانات خاصة بالمؤلف:
أ – اسم المؤلف وجنسيته: ————————————————
————————————————————————

ب – محل اقامته أو مركزه الرئيسي داخل الدولة أوخارجها ————————
————————————————————————

٣- بيانات خاصة بالوكيل إذا كان الطلب مقدماً بواسطة وكيل:

أ – اسم الوكيل وعنوانه داخل الدولة: ---------------------------

----

ب – رقم الوكالة --------- تاريخها --------- مصدرها ---------

ج – رقم الهاتف -------- رقم الفاكس -------- رقم التلكس ---------

يرفق بطلب القيد المستندات الآتية:

١.بيان شامل بمواصفات المصنف.

٢. المستند الدال على صفة الطالب إذا كان غير المؤلف، او اذا كان الطلب مقدماً بواسطة وكيل.

٣. اقرار مكتوب من المؤلف او من خلفائه حال وفاته بملكيته او ملكيتهم للمصنف.

٤. اقرار مكتوب من المؤلف او من خلفائه حال وفاته يتضمن تحديد الطريقة التي اختارها او اوصى بها المؤلف لنشر المصنف او الطريقة التي يختارونها لنشره اذا لم يكن المؤلف قد اوصى بشيء يتعلق بنشر المصنف.

٥. تنازل مكتوب من المؤلف او من خلفائه حال وفاته عن حقه او حقهم في استغلال المصنف وفقاً لأحكام المادتين (٣/٧) و(٣٢) من القانون إذا كان الطلب مقدماً من المتنازل إليه عن هذا الحق.

٦. اذن مكتوب من مؤلف المصنف الاصلي او من خلفائه حال وفاته إذا كان المصنف موضوع الطلب مشتقاً من المصنف الأصلي بأي طريقة من طرق الاشتقاق التي تظهره بشكل جديد طبقاً لأحكام المادة (٥) من القانون.

٧. العقد المبرم بين مؤلف المصنف وبين الشخص الطبيعي أو المعنوي الذي تم وضع المصنف بناءً على توجيهه، وتكفل بنشره تحت ادارته وباسمه وفقاً لأحكام المادة (٢٤) من القانون إذا كان الطلب مقدماً من هذا الشخص.

٨. شهادة من ادارة الرقابة بالوزارة تتضمن اجازتها للمصنف أو أنه مجاز طبقاً لقانون المطبوعات والنشر.

٩. عدد عشر نسخ من المصنف الذي يمكن استخراج عدة نسخ منه عن طريق الطبع أو أية وسيلة اخرى مشابهة.

١٠. تعهد كتابي على النموذج رقم (٢) بتقديم اللازم من المستندات من (٢ - ٧) عدا المرفق منها.

ملحوظة:

١. يجب ان تكون المستندات من (١-٧) مصحوبة بترجمة إلى اللغة العربية بمعرفة

مترجم معتمد إذا كانت محررة بلغة اجنبية.

٢. يجب ان تكون المستندات من (٢-٧) مصدق عليها حسب الاصول.

---

٤ – بيانات خاصة بالمصنف:

أ – اسم المصنف إن وجد ——————————————

ب– موضوع المصنف ونوعه:

———————————————————————
———————————————————————
———————————————————————
———————————————————————

ج – الطريقة التي اختارها المؤلف او خلفاؤه – حال وفاته – لنشر المصنف

———————————————————————

الوكيل	الطالب

ه[18]– التوقيع: —————— ——————————

التاريخ: ——————————————

ملحوظة: إذا تعددت اسماء الطالبين أو المؤلفين تذكر بيانات الباقين في ورقة تابعة ترفق بهذا النموذج

---

[18]. ورد الترقيم في الجريدة الرسمية (٧) والاصح أن يكون (٥) فاقتضى التنويه.

دولة الامارات العربية المتحدة
وزارة الاعلام والثقافة
إدارة الثقافة

نموذج رقم ٢
تعهد بتقديم مستندات متعلقة بطلب ايداع مصنف

رقم الطلب:
تاريخ تقديم الطلب:
اسم الطالب:
اسم الوكيل :

اتعهد انا الموقع أدناه : ————————————————

بصفتي : ——————————————————————

بأن اقدم لإدارة الثقافة المستندات المبينة ادناه خلال ستين يوماً من تاريخ تقديم الطلب:

(١) ——————————————————————

(٢) ——————————————————————

(٣) ——————————————————————

(٤) ——————————————————————

(٥) ——————————————————————

(٦) ——————————————————————

تحريراً في :   /   /

التوقيع

————————————————

دولة الامارات العربية المتحدة
وزارة الاعلام والثقافة
إدارة الثقافة

نموذج رقم ٣
ايصال استلام طلب قيد مصنف ومرفقاته

رقم الطلب:
تاريخ تقديم الطلب:
اسم الطلب وجنسيته وصفته:

بيان المستندات المقدمة مع الطلب:

١. بيان شامل بمواصفات المصنف.

٢. المستند الدال على صفة الطالب إذا كان غير المؤلف، او كان الطلب مقدماً بواسطة وكيل.

٣. اقرار مكتوب من المؤلف او من خلفائه حال وفاته بملكيته او ملكيتهم للمصنف.

٤. اقرار مكتوب من المؤلف او من خلفائه حال وفاته يتضمن الطريقة التي اختارها او اوصى بها المؤلف لنشر المصنف او الطريقة التي يختارونها لنشره اذا لم يكن المؤلف قد اوصى بشيء يتعلق بنشر المصنف

٥. تنازل مكتوب من المؤلف او من خلفائه حال وفاته عن حقه او حقهم في استغلال المصنف وفقاً لأحكام المادتين (٣/٧) و(٣٢) من القانون إذا كان الطلب مقدماً من المتنازل إليه عن هذا الحق.

٦. اذن مكتوب من مؤلف المصنف الاصلي او من خلفائه حال وفاته إذا كان المصنف موضوع الطلب مشتقاً من المصنف الأصلي بأي طريقة من طرق الاشتقاق التي تظهره بشكل جديد طبقاً لأحكام المادة (٥) من القانون.

٧. العقد المبرم بين مؤلف المصنف وبين الشخص الطبيعي أو المعنوي الذي تم وضع المصنف بناءً على توجيهه، وتكفل بنشره تحت ادارته وباسمه وفقاً لأحكام المادة (٢٤) من القانون إذا كان الطلب مقدماً من هذا الشخص.

٨. شهادة من ادارة الرقابة بالوزارة تتضمن اجازتها للمصنف أو أنه مجاز طبقاً لقانون المطبوعات والنشر.

٩. عدد عشر نسخ من المصنف الذي يمكن استخراج عدة نسخ منه عن طريق الطبع أو أية وسيلة اخرى مشابهة.

١٠. تعهد كتابي على النموذج رقم (٢) بتقديم اللازم من المستندات من (٢ الى ٧) عدا المرفق منها مع الطلب.

الختم الرسمي   مجموع المستندات المستلمة

المستلم: —————————————

الاسم: —————————————

التوقيع: —————————————

ملاحظة: يؤشر بعلامة √ امام المستندات المستلمة

نموذج رقم ٤

دولة الامارات العربية المتحدة
وزارة الاعلام والثقافة
إدارة الثقافة

بطاقة الفهرس الأبجدي لطلب قيد مصنف

١– اسم الطالب وصفته: ––––––––––––––––––––––––––––––
––

٢– الرقم المتتابع للطلب: –––––––––––––––––––––––––––––––

٣– تاريخ تقديم الطلب: ––––––––––––––––––––––––––––––––

٤– اسم المؤلف: –––––––––––––––––––––––––––––––––
––

٥– موضوع المصنف ونوعه: ––––––––––––––––––––––––––––
––
––

٦– قرار الإدارة: –––––––––––––––––––––––––––––––––––

تاريخ قرار الإدارة: –––––––––––––––––––––––––––––––––

دولة الامارات العربية المتحدة
وزارة الاعلام والثقافة
إدارة الثقافة

نموذج رقم ٥
شهادة بقيد مصنف في سجل الإيداع النوعي

تشهد إدارة الثقافة بأن المصنف موضوع هذه الشهادة قد تم قيده بسجل الإيداع
النوعي رقم (-----) الخاص _____ وذلك وفق البيانات الآتية:

١. تاريخ قيد المصنف في سجل الأيداع النوعي ----------------------

٢. رقم القيد -----------------------------------

٣. موضوع المصنف ------------------------------

----

٤. نوع المصنف -----------------------------------

٥. اسم المصنف -----------------------------------

٦. اسم مؤلف المصنف أومؤلفيه --------------------------
----

٧. اسم صاحب المصنف أو أصحابه ------------------------

وقد سلمت الشهادة إلى السيد -----------------------------

بصفته:

مؤلف المصنف [   ]   وريثه أو خلفه [   ]

صاحب المصنف [   ]   وريثه أو خلفه [   ]   وكيل [   ]

وذلك دون أدنى مسؤولية على الإدارة.

تحريراً في / /

————————————————

مدير الإدارة

دولة الامارات العربية المتحدة
وزارة الاعلام والثقافة
إدارة الثقافة

نموذج رقم ٦
ايصال استلام شهادة قيد مصنف مودع

استلمت أنا الموقع أدناه: ———————————————————————

بصفتي: ———————————————————————

شهادة قيد المصنف المودع بسجل الايداع النوعي رقم (——————————)

والمقيد بتاريخ   / /   برقم: ——————————

تحريراً في   / /

اسم المستلم وصفته ——————————

التوقيع ——————————

دولة الامارات العربية المتحدة
وزارة الاعلام والثقافة
إدارة الثقافة

نموذج رقم ٧
طلب قيد تصرف وارد على مصنف مودع

يلتمس الطالب قبول قيد التصرف موضوع الطلب بسجل ايداع التصرفات الواردة على مصنفات مودعة وذلك وفقاً للبيانات الآتية:	**للاستعمال الرسمي فقط** رقم الطلب: ------------ تاريخ تقديمه: ------------

١ – بيانات خاصة بالطالب:

أ – اسم الطالب وجنسيته وصفته: ------------------------

ب – محل إقامة الطالب أو مركزه الرئيسي داخل الدولة: ---------------
----

جـ – المحل المختار للطالب في الدولة إذا كان محل إقامته أو مركزه الرئيسي خارج الدولة:

د – رقم الهاتف: -------------- رقم الفاكس: -------------- رقم التلكس: ------

٢ – بيانات خاصة بالمصنف المودع:

أ – اسم المصنف إن وجد: --------------------------------

ب – نوع المصنف وموضوعه ———— ——————————————

——————————————————————————————

——————————————————————————————

جــ – رقم وتاريخ قيد المصنف بسجل الإيداع النوعي: ——————————

٣ – بيانات خاصة بالوكيل إذا كان الطلب مقدماً بواسطة وكيل:

أ – اسم الوكيل وعنوانه داخل الدولة: ——————————————

——————————————————————————————

ب – رقم الوكالة ———— تاريخها ———— مصدرها ————

ج – رقم الهاتف ———— رقم التلكس ———— رقم الفاكس ————

يرفق بطلب القيد المستندات الآتية:

١. سند التصرف مكتوباً ومصدقاً عليه حسب الاصول ومصحوباً بترجمة إلى اللغة العربية إذا كان محرراً بلغة اخرى، ومحدداً به صراحة كل حق من الحقوق المالية محل التصرف على حدة ومدة ذلك التصرف وكيفيته وكميته والغرض منه ومكانه.

٢. المستند الدال على صفة الطالب إذا كان غير المؤلف، أو كان الطلب مقدماً بواسطة وكيل.

٤ – بيانات خاصة بالتصرف موضوع الطلب:

أ. نوع التصرف المطلوب قيده ——————————————————

ب. تاريخ السند المكتوب المثبت للتصرف المطلوب قيده وتاريخ التصديق عليه ———

ج. ماهية الحق أو الحقوق التي يشملها التصرف تفصيلاً ————————

——————————————————————————————

——————————————————————————————

<table>
<tr><td>□</td><td>□</td></tr>
<tr><td>الوكيل</td><td>الطالب</td></tr>
</table>

ه – **التوقيع**: ———————— ————————————————

التاريخ: ———————— ————————————————

ملحوظة: إذا تعددت اسماء الطالبين تذكر بيانات الباقين في ورقة تابعة ترفق بهذا النموذج.

دولة الامارات العربية المتحدة
وزارة الاعلام والثقافة
إدارة الثقافة

نموذج رقم (٨)
ايصال استلام طلب قيد تصرف

الرقم المتتابع للطلب: —————————————————————

تاريخ تقديم الطلب: —————————————————————

اسم الطالب وجنسيته وصفته: ———————————————————

١– سند التصرف المؤرخ في / / —————————— ☐

٢– المستند الدال على صفة الطالب إذا كان غير المؤلف، أو كان الطلب مقدماً
بواسطة وكيل ———————————————— ☐

تحريراً في / /

_____

التوقيع

قرار وزير الاعلام والثقافة رقم (١٣١) لسنة ٢٠٠٤م
بشأن تسجيل المصنفات

وزير الاعلام والثقافة،

بعد الاطلاع على القانون الاتحادي رقم (١) لسنة ١٩٧٢ بشأن اختصاصات الوزارات وصلاحيات الوزراء، والقوانين المعدلة له،

وعلى القانون الاتحادي رقم (٧) لسنة ٢٠٠٢ في شأن حقوق المؤلف والحقوق المجاورة، وبناءً على ما عرضه وكيل الوزارة،

قرر:

المادة (١)

تعريفات

في تطبيق أحكام هذا القرار يكون للكلمات والعبارات التالية المعاني المبينة قرين كل منها ما لم يقض سياق النص بغير ذلك:

الدولة:	دولة الامارات العربية المتحدة.
الوزارة:	وزارة الاعلام والثقافة.
الوزير:	وزير الاعلام والثقافة.
القانون:	القانون الاتحادي رقم (٧) لسنة ٢٠٠٢ في شأن حقوق المؤلف والحقوق المجاورة.
المكتب:	مكتب المصنفات الفكرية.
السجل:	السجل الذي تقيد فيه بيانات المصنف بما في ذلك الحقوق أو التصرفات الواردة عليه.

المادة (٢)

ينشأ في المكتب سجل تقيّد فيه بيانات المصنفات، ويتم بموجبها الحصول على شهادة تسجيل المصنف.

المادة (٣)

يجوز للمؤلف أو لأي من أصحاب الحقوق المجاورة أو لأي من خلفائهم أن يتقدم بطلب تسجيل المصنف وفقاً لأحكام هذا القرار.

المادة (٤)

أولاً: يجب أن يشتمل طلب التسجيل على البيانات الآتية:

١. عنوان المصنف ونوعه ووصفه ولغته.

٢. اسم مقدم الطلب وجنسيته وصفته وعنوانه، ونسخة من سند الوكالة.

٣. اسم المؤلف، والاسم المستعار واسم الشهرة (إن وجدا)، وجنسيته وعنوانه، وتاريخ الوفاة (إن وجد).

٤. اسم الجهة التي وجهت بالعمل (إن وجدت)، وعنوانها والمستند الذي يثبت العلاقة بينها وبين المؤلف.

٥. اسم الناشر وعنوانه وتاريخ ومكان اول نشر، والرقم الدولي (إن وجد).

٦. اسم المتصرف إليه، وجنسيته، وعنوانه، ونوع التصرف ومدته ونطاقه الجغرافي، وبيان الحقوق المالية التي اكتسبها من التنازل والمستند الذي يثبت وقوع التصرف من المؤلف أو صاحب الحق.

ثانياً: يجب أن يرفق بطلب التسجيل ما يأتي:

١. صورة من جواز سفر أو هوية كل من مقدم طلب التسجيل والمؤلف والمتصرف إليه.

٢. نسختان من المصنف، أو صورتان فوتوغرافيتان منه مقاس ٢٠×٢٠ سم وفقاً لطبيعة المصنف.

المادة (٥)

لا يجوز أن يتضمن طلب التسجيل تدوين أكثر من مصنف، ويراعى في ذلك طبيعة المصنفات.

المادة (٦)

يمنح مقدم الطلب رقماً تسلسلياً وفقاً لتاريخ تقديمه، كما يمنح ايصال استلام تذكر فيه المرفقات المقدمة مع الطلب.

المادة (٧)

يقوم المكتب بدراسة الطلب والتحقق من الآتي:

١. عدم تسجيل المصنف في وقت سابق.

٢. ان المصنف ليس من المصنفات التي لا تتمتع بالحماية طبقاً لأحكام المادة (٣) من القانون.

٣. أن المصنف ليس من المصنفات الفلكلورية التي تتضمن تشويهاً أو تحريفاً أو تتطلب تصريحاً من الجهات المختصة بالدولة.

٤. استيفاء البيانات والمستندات الواردة بالمادة (٤) من هذا القرار.

٥. أن المصنف قد أصبح في شكله النهائي وليس مجرد مسودة أو عمل تحضيري لإعداده.

المادة (٨)

يجوز للمكتب أن يتسلم الطلبات عن طريق البريد الالكتروني متى سمح نظام العمل بذلك، ويحدد المكتب أية متطلبات إضافية للاحتفاظ بالسجلات الإلكترونية وكذلك أية اجراءات اخرى تتصل بذلك بعد تسلم المصنف وتسديد الرسوم المقررة.

المادة (٩)

يجوز للمكتب أن يكلف مقدم الطلب بتقديم أية مستندات أو بيانات اخرى يراها ضرورية للتحقق من توافر الشروط اللازمة لقبول طلبه وذلك بموجب إخطار كتابي يوجه إليه.

المادة (١٠)

إذا لم يستوف مقدم الطلب المستندات أو البيانات المطلوبة منه خلال مدة ستين يوماً من تاريخ إخطاره يُعتبر الطلب مرفوضاً.

المادة (١١)

يجوز للمكتب في سبيل فحص طلبات التسجيل الاستعانة بمن يرى من المختصين داخل الدولة أو خارجها، ويعتبر الرأي المقدم من المختص استشارياً للمكتب.

المادة (١٢)

يصدر المكتب قراراً مسبباً برفض الطلب إذا تبين أن المصنف لا تتوافر فيه الشروط المنصوص عليها في القانون أو أن الطلب مخالف لأحكام هذا القرار، ويخطر مقدم الطلب بذلك.

المادة (١٣)

يجوز لمن صدر قرار برفض طلبه أو اعتبار طلبه مرفوضاً أن يتقدم إلى المكتب في أي وقت لاحق بطلب جديد بعد استيفاء المستندات والبيانات التي كانت سبباً في صدور قرار الرفض.

المادة (١٤)

لا يعد التأشير في السجل أو إصدار الشهادة بتسجيل المصنف تصريحاً للاستغلال أو للتداول أو لعرض المصنف، وعلى صاحب العلاقة مراجعة الجهة المختصة بالوزارة لإجازة المصنف من الناحية الموضوعية.

المادة (١٥)

يجوز لكل ذي شأن أن يطلب من المكتب تصحيح أي خطأ مادي يقع في بيانات السجل.

المادة (١٦)

لا يجوز شطب البيانات الواردة في السجل أو تسجيلها لشخص أخر إلا بناءً على حكم قضائي نهائي واجب التنفيذ.

المادة (١٧)

يجوز للمكتب إجراء اللازم لتنظيم السجل وفقاً لما يراه مناسباً لسير العمل و بما لا يتعارض مع احكام هذا القرار.

المادة (١٨)

يلغى كل حكم يخالف احكام هذا القرار.

المادة (١٩)

ينشر هذا القرار في الجريدة الرسمية ويعمل به من تاريخ نشره.

عبد الله بن زايد آل نهيان
وزير الاعلام والثقافة

صدر بتاريخ ١٤٢٥/٢/١هـ
الموافق: ٢٠٠٤/٣/٢٢م.

قرار وزير الاعلام والثقافة رقم (١٣٢) لسنة ٢٠٠٤م
في شأن سجل مستوردي وموزعي المصنفات

وزير الاعلام والثقافة،

بعد الاطلاع على القانون الاتحادي رقم (١) لسنة ١٩٧٢ بشأن اختصاصات الوزارات
وصلاحيات الوزراء، والقوانين المعدلة له،

وعلى القانون الاتحادي رقم (٧) لسنة ٢٠٠٢ في شأن حقوق المؤلف والحقوق
المجاورة، وبناءً على ما عرضه وكيل الوزارة،

قرر:

المادة (١)

تعريفات

في تطبيق أحكام هذا القرار يكون للكلمات والعبارات التالية المعاني المبينة قرين كل
منها ما لم يقض سياق النص بغير ذلك:

الدولة:	دولة الامارات العربية المتحدة.
الوزارة:	وزارة الاعلام والثقافة.
الوزير:	وزير الاعلام والثقافة.
القانون:	القانون الاتحادي رقم (٧) لسنة ٢٠٠٢ في شأن حقوق المؤلف والحقوق المجاورة.
المكتب:	مكتب المصنفات الفكرية.
السجل:	سجل مستوردي وموزعي المصنفات.

المادة (٢)

ينشأ في المكتب سجل يسمى سجل مستوردي وموزعي المصنفات، تقيد فيه اسماء المستوردين والموزعين وسند حقوقهم في استيراد أو توزيع المصنفات في الدولة، وبيانات عن انشطتهم والجهات التي خولتهم استيراد أو توزيع المصنفات على النحو المبين في السجل.

المادة (٣)

لا يجوز لأي شخص طبيعي أو اعتباري ممارسة نشاط يتعلق بالمصنفات بما في ذلك الاستيراد أو التوزيع أو البيع أو التأجير أو الإعارة ما لم يكن مقيداً في السجل وحاصلاً على ترخيص من الجهة المختصة بالوزارة.

المادة (٤)

يقدم طلب القيد في السجل إلى المكتب من المستورد أو الموزع أو الوكيل القانوني لأي منهما على النموذج المعد لذلك.

المادة (٥)

أولاً: يشتمل السجل على البيانات والمستندات الآتية:

١. اسم طالب القيد وجنسيته وصفته ومحل اقامته وعنوانه واسم المخول بالتوقيع عنه.

٢. اسم الشخص الطبيعي أو الاعتباري المطلوب قيده وجنسيته وعنوانه ونشاطه.

٣. المستندات الواجب توافرها مع الطلب على ان تقدم مرة واحدة خلال السنة وتكون سارية المفعول وهي نسخة طبق الاصل مما يأتي:

أ) ترخيص ممارسة النشاط الصادر عن الجهة المختصة في الوزارة.
ب) شهادة غرفة التجارة والصناعة بالإمارة التي يقع فيها مركز نشاط الشخص الاعتباري.
ج) ترخيص البلدية أو دائرة التنمية الاقتصادية أو أية جهة مختصة بالإمارة التي يقع فيها مركز نشاط الشخص الاعتباري.

ثانياً: يشتمل طلب قيد حقوق استيراد أو توزيع المصنفات في السجل على البيانات

والمستندات الآتية:

١. عنوان المصنف ونوعه ولغته.

٢. اسم الجهة المنتجة وعنوانها ومكان الانتاج.

٣. المستند الذي يثبت العلاقة القانونية التي تجيز الاستيراد أو التوزيع موضحاً به الآتي:

أ) المنطقة الجغرافية المتفق عليها لتوزيع المصنف.

ب) المدة الزمنية للاستغلال المالي للمصنف.

ج) وسيلة الاستغلال المالي للمصنف.

د) مكان وتاريخ توقيع المستند المشار إليه.

هـ) التوثيق الرسمي للمستند وفقاً للأصول القانونية المتبعة.

٤. ترجمة قانونية للمستند إلى اللغة العربية إذا كان محرراً بلغة اجنبية.

المادة (٦)

يمنح الشخص رقماً رمزياً تعريفياً من قبل المكتب يتم تقديمه إذا طلب هذا الشخص تسجيل حقوقه في استيراد أو توزيع المصنف أو بهما معاً، كما يمنح رقماً لكل معاملة يقدمها وفقاً للمادة (٥) من هذا القرار، وعليه الاشارة إلى هذا الرقم كلما تقدم بطلب تسجيل حقوقه في الاستيراد أو التوزيع أو بهما معاً لمصنفات لها علاقة بالمعاملة المعنية.

المادة (٧)

تمنح طلبات تسجيل حقوق الاستيراد أو التوزيع أو كليهما معاً للمصنف أرقاماً مسلسلة، ويتم تسليم مقدم الطلب ايصالاً يشتمل على البيانات الآتية:

١. الرقم الرمزي.

٢. رقم المعاملة.

٣. التاريخ والوقت.

٤. بيانات المستندات المرفقة بالطلب.

المادة (٨)

في حالة قبول المكتب لطلب غير مستوف للبيانات أو المستندات يخطر صاحب الشأن بذلك مع بيان المطلوب توضيحه أو إرفاقه من بيانات أو أوراق أو مستندات، وعليه تقديمها خلال ستين يوماً من تاريخ الإخطار وإلا اعتبر لاغياً. كما يجوز للمكتب عدم قبول تسجيل أية طلبات لاحقة له خلال مدة الستين يوماً.

المادة (٩)

للمكتب أن يكلف مقدم الطلب بتقديم ما يراه مناسباً من بيانات أو وثائق أو توضيحات تدعم الطلب والوثائق المرفقة، كما يجوز للمكتب مخاطبة أية جهة للتحقق من سلامة الوثائق أو البيانات المقدمة.

المادة (١٠)

يجب على المكتب رفض الطلب إذا كان مخالفاً لأحكام القانون أو هذا القرار. ويخطر صاحب الشأن بذلك.

المادة (١١)

في حالة قبول الطلب يتم تسجيل أنواع الحقوق الممنوحة ومدتها وعدد المصنفات وأسمائها ولغتها والنطاق الجغرافي لاستغلالها.

ويخطر المكتب الجهة المختصة في الوزارة بقيد هذه الحقوق للجهة التي قامت بتقديم الطلب، كما يخطر الطالب بقرار المكتب بقبول طلبه، وعليه أن يتقدم إلى الجهة المختصة بالوزارة لإجازة الطلب من الناحية الموضوعية.

المادة (١٢)

لا يجوز للمرخص له باستيراد أو توزيع المصنفات المدونة في السجل استغلالها مالياً أو توزيعها أو طرحها للتداول إلا بعد حصوله على إذن الجهة المختصة بالوزارة.

المادة (١٣)

يجوز للجهة المختصة في الوزارة بقرار مسبب أن تسحب الترخيص بطرح المصنف للتداول.

المادة (١٤)

يجوز أن يتضمن القيد في السجل اسم اكثر من مورد أو موزع لذات المصنف إذا توافرت في الطالب مسوغات هذا القيد.

المادة (١٥)

على الاشخاص المقيدة اسماؤهم في السجل إخطار المكتب بكل تعديل أو تغيير يطرأ على بيانات السجل أو المستندات المرفقة خلال عشرين يوماً من تاريخ التعديل أو التغيير، ويكون الإخطار بموجب كتاب يقدم من صاحب العلاقة. ويقوم المكتب بالتأشير في السجل بأية تعديلات أو تغييرات مطلوبة.

المادة (١٦)

يلتزم الحاصلون على ترخيص باستيراد أو توزيع المصنفات بالاحتفاظ في مكان مباشرة النشاط بالمستندات والتراخيص الآتية:

١. الترخيص الصادر من الجهة المختصة بالوزارة بمزاولة نشاط استيراد أو توزيع أو استغلال المصنفات.

٢. الترخيص الصادر من بلدية الإمارة أو الجهة المختصة فيها بمزاولة النشاط.

٣. سند العلاقة المكتوب والمصدق حسب الأصول الصادر من أي من أصحاب الحق في استغلال المصنف والذي يخول الجهة حق استيراد أو استغلال أو توزيع أو بيع المصنف، وما يفيد تسجيل ذلك الحق لدى المكتب.

٤. إذن تداول الجهة المختصة بالوزارة لتداول المصنف.

وعلى اصحاب الشأن تقديم هذه المستندات للاشخاص المخولين بالتفتيش عند الطلب.

المادة (١٧)

يقوم المكتب بإعداد السجل، وله إجراء التغييرات اللازمة به وفقاً لما يراه مناسباً لسير العمل.

المادة (١٨)

١. للمؤلف أو صاحب الحق أو من يخلفهما أن يقدم طلباً بعدم الافراج الجمركي المؤقت للسلطات الجمركية قبل خروج المصنفات الفكرية من النطاق الجمركي وعلى السلطات الجمركية ان تبت في الطلب خلال ثلاثة ايام من تقديمه مستوفياً ويخطر صاحب الطلب بالقرار فور صدوره.

٢. يجوز للسلطات الجمركية من تلقاء نفسها عدم الافراج الجمركي المؤقت في حالة الشك في صحة أي من المستندات المقدمة إليها.

٣. في جميع الحالات يتعين أن يكون قرار السلطات الجمركية بعدم الافراج المؤقت مسبباً ولمدة اقصاها عشرون يوماً.

٤. يرفق مقدم الطلب بطلبه المستندات التي تثبت حقه في مضمون الطلب مصدقة حسب الاصول.

وعلى السلطات الجمركية التأكد من صحة المستندات المشار إليها بالتعاون مع الوزارة.

٥. يقدم الطالب كفالة مالية أو ضمان مصرفي مشروط بقيمة (٢٥%) من قيمة المواد الواردة في الطلب ويكون للسلطات الجمركية حق تجديده أو تسييله بمجرد طلبها ذلك.

ولا يلزم الطالب بتقديم هذه الكفالة إلا في حالة عدم توفر أدلة تؤيد طلبه.

٦. لا يرد الضمان للطالب إذا قضي بإلغاء قرار عدم الافراج الجمركي من محكمة مختصة أو قدم المستورد أو المصدر مستندات رسمية دالة على عدم صحة الطلب.

٧. تلتزم السلطات الجمركية بتمكين الطالب من الحضور – إن شاء – لدى معاينة المواد الواردة في الطلب، على أن يصدر الإذن بالحضور محدداً فيه اسم وصفة المأذون بحضوره ويكون صالحاً لمرة واحدة فقط.

المادة (١٩)

على كل من يباشر نشاط استيراد أو توزيع المصنفات في الدولة وقت صدور هذا القرار أن يوفق أوضاعه طبقاً لأحكامه خلال ستة اشهر من تاريخ العمل به.

المادة (٢٠)

يلغى كل حكم يخالف أو يتعارض مع أحكام هذا القرار.

المادة (٢١)

ينشر هذا القرار في الجريدة الرسمية ويعمل به من تاريخ نشره.

عبد الله بن زايد آل نهيان
وزير الاعلام والثقافة

صدر بتاريخ ١٤٢٥/٢/١هـ
الموافق: ٢٠٠٤/٣/٢٢م.

قرار وزير الاعلام والثقافة رقم (١٣٣) لسنة ٢٠٠٤م
بشأن الإدارة الجماعية لحقوق المؤلف والحقوق المجاورة

وزير الاعلام والثقافة،

بعد الاطلاع على القانون الاتحادي رقم (١) لسنة ١٩٧٢ بشأن اختصاصات الوزارات وصلاحيات الوزراء، والقوانين المعدلة له،

وعلى القانون الاتحادي رقم (٧) لسنة ٢٠٠٢ في شأن حقوق المؤلف والحقوق المجاورة، وبناءً على ما عرضه وكيل الوزارة،

قرر:

المادة (١)

تعريفات

في تطبيق أحكام هذا القرار يكون للكلمات والعبارات التالية المعاني المبينة قرين كل منها ما لم يقض سياق النص بغير ذلك:

الدولة:	دولة الامارات العربية المتحدة.
الوزارة:	وزارة الاعلام والثقافة.
الوزير:	وزير الاعلام والثقافة.
القانون:	القانون الاتحادي رقم (٧) لسنة ٢٠٠٢ في شأن حقوق المؤلف والحقوق المجاورة.
المكتب:	مكتب المصنفات الفكرية.
ترخيص الإدارة الجماعية:	الموافقة الصادرة من الوزارة على قيام جمعيات أو غيرها من الجهات المتخصصة بإدارة ومباشرة أعمال حقوق المؤلف والحقوق المجاورة.

المادة (٢)

تلتزم الجمعيات وغيرها من الجهات التي ترغب في تولي الإدارة الجماعية لحقوق المؤلف والحقوق المجاورة بالحصول على ترخيص من الوزارة قبل ممارسة هذا النشاط.

المادة (٣)

على الجمعيات وغيرها من الجهات المتقدمة بطلب ترخيص الإدارة الجماعية الحصول قبل تقديمه على الموافقة اللازمة من الجهات المعنية في الدولة وفقاً للأوضاع المقررة في هذا الشأن.

المادة (٤)

يشترط للحصول على ترخيص الإدارة الجماعية تقديم المستندات والبيانات الآتية:

١. نسخة من النظام الأساسي لطالب الترخيص وعقده التأسيسي.

٢. نسخة من المؤهل الدراسي وصورة جواز سفر أو هوية المدير المسؤول لطالب الترخيص.

٣. بيان بنسبة العمالة المواطنة في الجهة طالبة الترخيص.

٤. ترخيص من البلد الأصلي يثبت ممارسة نشاط طالب الترخيص في ميدان الإدارة الجماعية، إذا كان طالب الترخيص فرعاً معتمداً لشخص اعتباري مقره خارج الدولة.

٥. بيان بعدد المؤلفين وأصحاب الحقوق المجاورة الذين تعاقدوا مع الشخص الاعتباري مقدم الطلب إن وجدوا.

٦. نسخة من العقد المبرم بين الشخص الاعتباري والمتعاقدين معه من المؤلفين وأصحاب الحقوق المجاورة إن وجدوا.

المادة (٥)

يلتزم الشخص الاعتباري الصادر له الترخيص بما يأتي:

١. إعداد السجلات اللازمة التي تحتوي على أسماء الأشخاص وصفاتهم وعناوينهم وبياناتهم ومصنفاتهم والأعمال التي تعاقدوا بشأنها ومدة التعاقد وقيمته، مع ابلاغ الوزارة بأي تغيير يطرأ على بيانات هذه السجلات.

٢. الاحتفاظ بسند الاتفاق المبرم بينه وبين مستغلي الحقوق المالية والمحدد به نفقات التحصيل المالي المتفق عليها.

٣. اتخاذ جميع الاجراءات الإدارية والقانونية لحماية حقوق المتعاقدين.

٤. إعداد الحسابات الختامية وتوزيع الأرباح على المتعاقدين مرة على الأقل خلال السنة.

٥. السماح للمتعاقدين بالإطلاع على الحسابات الختامية وطريقة توزيع الارباح متى أرادوا ذلك.

٦. القيام بإعداد تقارير دورية لأصحاب الحقوق مبيناً بها الجهات التي استخدمت أعمالهم والمبالغ التي تم تحصيلها.

٧. تقديم المعلومات والوثائق الواردة بهذا القرار إلى الوزارة كلما طلب منه ذلك.

المادة (٦)

يلتزم طالب الترخيص بعد توافر شروط الترخيص في شأنه، بسداد الرسوم المقررة لممارسة النشاط لدى الجهة المختصة بالوزارة، ويجدد سنوياً بعد دفع الرسوم المقررة.

المادة (٧)

يجوز للوزارة إلغاء الترخيص بعد صدوره في حالة عدم التزام المرخص له بأحكام القانون أو القرارات المنفذة له.

المادة (٨)

لا يجوز للمرخص له أن يرفض إدارة حقوق المؤلفين أو أصحاب الحقوق المجاورة دون سبب يبرر ذلك.

المادة (٩)

ينشر هذا القرار في الجريدة الرسمية ويعمل به من تاريخ نشره.

عبد الله بن زايد آل نهيان
وزير الاعلام الثقافة

صدر بتاريخ: ١٤٢٥/٢/١هـ
الموافق/ ٢٠٠٤/٣/٢٢م.

قرار وزير الاعلام والثقافة رقم (١٣٤) لسنة ٢٠٠٤م
بشأن التراخيص الإجبارية بنسخ أو ترجمة المصنفات

وزير الاعلام والثقافة،

بعد الاطلاع على القانون الاتحادي رقم (١) لسنة ١٩٧٢ بشأن اختصاصات الوزارات وصلاحيات الوزراء، والقوانين المعدلة له،

وعلى القانون الاتحادي رقم (٧) لسنة ٢٠٠٢ في شأن حقوق المؤلف والحقوق المجاورة، وبناءً على ما عرضه وكيل الوزارة،

قرر:

المادة (١)

تعريفات

في تطبيق أحكام هذا القرار يكون للكلمات والعبارات التالية المعاني المبينة قرين كل منها ما لم يقض سياق النص بغير ذلك:

الدولة:	دولة الامارات العربية المتحدة.
الوزارة:	وزارة الاعلام والثقافة.
الوزير:	وزير الاعلام والثقافة.
القانون:	القانون الاتحادي رقم (٧) لسنة ٢٠٠٢ في شأن حقوق المؤلف والحقوق المجاورة.
المكتب:	مكتب المصنفات الفكرية.
الترخيص:	الترخيص الإجباري الذي يمنح طبقاً للقانون.

المادة (٢)

يجوز لكل شخص أن يتقدم إلى المكتب بطلب الحصول على ترخيص بالنسخ أو الترجمة أو بكليهما لمصنف محمي بالقانون، وذلك للوفاء باحتياجات التعليم بجميع

أنواعه ومستوياته، أو باحتياجات المكتبات العامة أو دور الحفظ، ووفقاً للشروط الواردة في هذا القرار.

المادة (٣)

١. على طالب الترخيص لنسخ أو الترجمة أن يقدم ما يثبت أنه طلب من المؤلف أو صاحب الحق التصريح له بنسخ المصنف أو ترجمته ونشر الطبعة المنسوخة أو المترجمة فرفض طلبه أو أنه تعذر التوصل للمؤلف أو صاحب الحق في استغلال المصنف.

٢. إذا لم يتمكن طالب الترخيص من التوصل للمؤلف أو صاحب الحق في استغلال المصنف فعليه أن يخاطب الناشر الذي ظهر اسمه على المصنف وتقديم ما يثبت اتخاذه الاجراءات المنصوص عليها في الفقرة السابقة.

المادة (٤)

مع عدم الاخلال بأحكام المـادة (٣) من هذا القرار، يشترط لاصدار الترخيص بنسخ المصنف ما يأتي:

١. أن تنقضي خمس سنوات من تاريخ أول نشر للمصنف وألا تكون نسخة المصنف المرخصة من المؤلف أو صاحب الحق في استغلال المصنف متوافرة في اسواق الدولة، أو لا تلبي احتياجات التعليم أو المكتبات العامة أو دور الحفظ بثمن مقارب للثمن المعتاد في الدولة بالنسبة لمصنفات مماثلة، ويستثنى من ذلك الحالتان الآتيتان:

أ) أن يحتوي على موضوعات تتعلق بالعلوم الرياضية أو الطبيعية أو التقنية فيجوز أن تكون المدة ثلاث سنوات من تاريخ أول نشر للمصنف.
ب) إذا كان المصنف يحتوي على موضوعات تتعلق بعالم الخيال كالروايات والمؤلفات الشعرية والمسرحية والموسيقية وكتب الفن فيشترط أن تمضي فترة سبع سنوات من تاريخ أول نشر له.

٢. أن تنقضي على تاريخ أوْل اتصال بالمؤلف أو صاحب الحق في استغلال المصنف ثلاثة أشهر لاحقة على مدتي الخمس سنوات والسبع سنوات المشار إليهما في هذه المادة أو تنقضي ستة أشهر لاحقة على انتهاء الثلاث سنوات المبينة بالمادة ذاتها.

المادة (٥)

مع عدم الاخلال بأحكام المادة (٣) من هذا القرار، يشترط لإصدار الترخيص بالترجمة ما يأتي:

١. ان تمضي ثلاث سنوات من تاريخ أول نشر للمصنف دون توفر نسخة منه مترجمة إلى اللغة العربية أو إلى لغة عامة التداول في الدولة تلبي احتياجات التعليم أو المكتبات العامة أو دور الحفظ، أو إذا كانت النسخة المترجمة قد نفدت في الدولة بعد تلك المدة.

٢. أن تمضي ستة أشهر من تاريخ أول اتصال بالمؤلف أو صاحب الحق في استغلال المصنف لاحقة على انتهاء الثلاث سنوات الواردة بالبند (١) من هذه المادة وعلى حائز الترخيص بالترجمة الألتزام بأحكام المادة (٤) من هذا القرار إذا كان المصنف يحتوي على صور توضيحية.

المادة (٦)

لا يجوز منح الترخيص في أي من الحالتين الآتيتين:

١. إذا تم سحب المصنف من التداول بناءً على طلب المؤلف أو صاحب الحق في استغلال الحقوق المالية.

٢. إذا قام المؤلف أو صاحب الحق في استغلال الحقوق المالية بطرح المصنف للتداول خلال المدة الإضافية المنصوص عليها في المادتين (٢/٤) و(٢/٥) من هذا القرار تلبية لاحتياجات التعليم أو المكتبات العامة أو دور الحفظ بثمن مقارب للثمن المعتاد في الدولة بالنسبة لمصنفات مماثلة.

المادة (٧)

على حائز الترخيص الالتزام بما يلي:

١. ان يذكر اسم المؤلف على الطبعة المترجمة أو المنسوخة مع وضع عنوان المصنف كما ورد في لغته الأصلية.

٢. ان يضمن النقل الأمين للطبعة المعنية وذلك بنسخ أو ترجمة المصنف بصورة صحيحة.

٣. ان يقوم بالتأشير على كل طبعة منسوخة أو مترجمة بأنها صالحة للتداول داخل الدولة فقط، مع ذكر أن الطبعة صدرت بناءً على ترخيص اجباري.

٤. أن يستخدم الترخيص بهدف الوفاء باحتياجات التعليم أو المكتبات العامة أو دور الحفظ.

٥. أن يؤدي مقابلاً مالياً عادلاً للمؤلف أو صاحب الحق في استغلال المصنف يتم تحديده في القرار الصادر بمنح الترخيص، بالاسترشاد بالمعايير الدولية المعمول بها في هذا المجال.

٦. أن يقدم للمكتب قبل تسلم الترخيص ما يثبت أن المقابل المالي المشار إليه في البند السابق قابل للتحويل بعملة البلد الذي صدر فيه المصنف الأصلي، وأنه قد تم تسليمه للمؤلف أو صاحب الحق فيه.

٧. عدم تصدير المصنف المرخص إلى خارج الدولة.

المادة (٨)

يكون الترخيص بالنسخ أو الترجمة صادراً باسم الطالب، ولا يجوز التنازل عنه للغير.

المادة (٩)

تنتهي صلاحية الترخيص بالنسخ أو الترجمة إذا قام المؤلف أو صاحب الحق في استغلال المصنف بتوفيره منسوخاً أو مترجماً بثمن مقارب لثمن المصنفات المماثلة في الدولة.

ويتم تداول الطبعة التي صدر لها ترخيص بالنسخ أو الترجمة حتى نفادها.

المادة (١٠)

يجوز للمكتب أن يقوم بالاتصال بالمنظمات الدولية العاملة في مجال حقوق المؤلف والحقوق المجاورة لمعرفة طرق الاتصال بالمؤلف أو صاحب الحق، أو تقدير المكافأة العادلة أو التحقق من وصولها إلى المؤلف أو صاحب الحق.

المادة (١١)

ينشر هذا القرار في الجريدة الرسمية ويعمل به من تاريخ نشره.

عبد الله بن زايد آل نهيان
وزير الاعلام والثقافة

صدر بتاريخ: ١٤٢٥/٢/١هـ
الموافق: ٢٠٠٤/٣/٢٢م.

قرار وزاري رقم (۲۸۸) لسنة ٢٠٠٤م
في شأن الرسوم المتعلقة بحقوق المؤلف والحقوق المجاورة

وزير الاعلام والثقافة،

يعد الاطلاع على القانون الاتحادي رقم (١) لسنة ١٩٧٢م بشأن اختصاصات الوزارات وصلاحيات الوزراء والقوانين المعدلة له،

وعلى القانون الاتحادي رقم (۷) لسنة ٢٠٠٢م في شأن حقوق المؤلف والحقوق المجاورة،

وعلى قرار مجلس الوزراء رقم (١٤) لسنة ١٩٩٩م في شأن رسوم التراخيص الإعلامية ذات الطابع التجاري التي تصدرها وزارة الأعلام والثقافة،

وبعد التنسيق مع وزارة المالية والصناعة،

قرر:

المادة (١)

تحدد رسوم تراخيص المصنفات وشهاداتها التي تصدرها وزارة الإعلام والثقافة على النحو التالي:

بدل فاقد	التجديد السنوي	الرسم المقرر	نوع الترخيص	م
١٠٠	٥٠٠٠	١٠٠٠٠	ترخيص (الإدارة الجماعية)	١-
٥٠	–	١٠٠	ترخيص ترجمة مصنف	٢-
٥٠	–	١٠٠	ترخيص نسخ مصنف	٣-

١٠٠	–	٢٠٠	ترخيص ترجمة ونسخ مصنف	٤–
١٥	–	٣٠	إصدار شهادة تسجيل مصنف	٥–
١٥	–	٣٠	إصدار شهادة تصرف في مصنف	٦–

المادة (٢)

يتم تحصيل الرسم في حالة الموافقة على الطلب.

المادة (٣)

ينشر هذا القرار في الجريدة الرسمية، ويعمل به اعتباراً من تاريخ نشره.

عبد الله بن زايد آل نهيان
وزير الاعلام والثقافة

صدر بتاريخ: ٩ جمادى الآخرة ١٤٢٥هـ
الموافق: ٢٠٠٤/٧/٢٦م.

APPENDIX
B28

دولة الامارات العربية المتحدة
دائرة جمارك دبي
United Arab Emirates
Department of Dubai Customs

مكتب المدير العام
Director General Office
التاريخ: ٢٠٠٦/٩/٦

سياسة جمركية

رمز السياسة: DCP 11

اسم السياسة: قيد العلامات التجارية للاغراض الجمركية

تفاصيل السياسة

المادة (١)

لأغراض دعم ومساندة وتسهيل أعمال المكافحة الجمركية وحماية حقوق الملكية الفكرية ولتسهيل قيام وحدة ادارية مختصة بإخطار مالك العلامة التجارية في حالة إيقاف أو حجز أو مصادرة أو إتلاف أية شحنات تتعلق بعلامته التجارية المسجلة وأي تعدي عليها، يقوم قسم حقوق الملكية الفكرية بقيد العلامات التجارية والمسجلة لدى الجهة المختصة.

المادة (٢)

ينشأ لدى القسم سجل يسمى "سجل قيد العلامات التجارية" وذلك لغرض إدخال وأرشفة البيانات والمعلومات والمستندات المتعلقة بالعلامات التجارية الصادرة من الجهة المختصة والمقدمة من قبل مالك العلامة التجارية أو وكيلها القانوني.

المادة (٣)

يتم قيد العلامات التجارية نظير رسوم ادارية قدرها مائتي درهم "٢٠٠ درهم" مقابل كل فئة عن كل علامة تجارية وذلك حسب التصنيف الدولي للفئات، يقوم بتحصيلها قسم حماية حقوق الملكية الفكرية وذلك مقابل الخدمات والحماية التي يقدمها القسم إلى مالكي العلامات التجارية.

المادة (٤)

يتم تحصيل هذه الرسوم الادارية عند استلام المستندات واستكمال طلبات القيد والشروط لفتح ملف باسم صاحب العلاقة، ولا تسترد هذه الرسوم حتى لو تم رفض طلب القيد.

المادة (٥)

يقوم قسم حقوق الملكية الفكرية بالبدء في اجراءاته العملية بشأن المكافحة الجمركية في مجال حماية حقوق الملكية الفكرية بعد استلام ودراسة الشكوى والبلاغ المقدم من صاحب العلاقة، ومتابعة قضية التعدي على العلامة التجارية مقابل رسم وقدره ألفين درهم (٢٠٠٠ درهم)، يضاف إليها مبلغ وقدره خمسة آلاف درهماً (٥٠٠٠ درهم) كتأمين لضمان وتغطية نفقات التفتيش والنقل والمتابعة المتوقعة تسترد في حال صحة الشكوى ولا تسترد في حال بيان عدم صحتها.

المادة (٦)

يتحمل صاحب العلاقة رسوماً إضافية في حالة الشكوى المستعجلة قدرها خمسمائة درهم (٥٠٠ درهم) كما يتحمل رسوماً إضافية قدرها ألف درهم (١٠٠٠ درهم) في حال صادفت الشكوى يوم عطلة أو الإجازات الرسمية أو إجازة نهاية الاسبوع.

المادة (٧)

في حال عدم ثبوت صحة شكواه وخلو الشحنة من أي بضائع مخالفة، يتحمل صاحب العلاقة جميع المصاريف والرسوم المترتبة على إيقاف الشحنة موضوع الشكوى والرسوم المفروضة على إيقاف أو تأخير وسائل النقل الحاملة لها، ورسوم التخزين والأرضية والمناولة والنقل أو أية مصاريف أو رسوم أخرى تترتب بناءً على شكواه، على أن يقدم صاحب العلاقة إقرار تعهد مكتوب بهذا عند تقديم الشكوى والبلاغ.

المادة (٨)

يتحمل صاحب العلاقة رسوم الفحص الفني بواسطة المختبر في حال تطلب إثبات التعدي على العلامة أو تقليدها فحصاً فنياً متخصصاً.

المادة (٩)

يتحمل المشكو ضده "صاحب الشحنة المخالفة أو الناقل" مصاريف النقل والإتلاف في حال ثبوت مخالفة البضائع المضبوطة وبعد صدور قراراً بالمصادرة والإتلاف.

المادة (١٠)

يعمل بهذه السياسة الجمركية اعتباراً من الأول من اكتوبر ٢٠٠٦.

أحمد بطي أحمد

Index